*To my
grandchildren
Michele and
Giorgio*

*To my son
Gerardo for his
affectionate
assistance during
the preparation
of this book*

1st edition:
April 2002
2nd edition:
March 2005
3rd edition:
July 2018

ISBN 978-88-492-3500-5

Michele Spera

**Graphic Design
between Creativity and Science**

Gangemi Editore

Michele Spera
Graphic Design
between Creativity
and Science

Graphic Design and
Video Layout
Michele Spera

Translation by
Paul David Blackmore
pdb srls

This book was
composed in Frutiger
on a Mac

16 pages on 100 g
Arcoprint
592 pages on 115 g
matt coated paper
Cover on 350 g
matt coated paper

Printer:
Gangemi Editore
Rome - Italy

Layout:
38 sextodecimi with
stitched paperback
binding
Laminated matt cover

Table of Contents

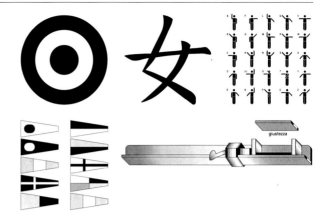

5

7

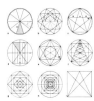

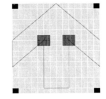

9

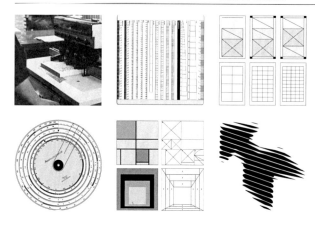

Domenico De Masi
Hay for One Hundred Horses

With ironic disappointment, in the delightful collection entitled *Palchetti Romani*, Alberto Savinio notes: "While Alexander the Great was crossing Persia, one night he observed tall flames rising from the ground. He did not understand at the time that one day those flames would help a man named Deterding earn millions".

How much human genius, more precious than oil, has been lost in the South because the Alexander the Greats, indigenous peoples or travellers, were unable to understand the signs of talent in time? How many young people, thwarted by endemic unemployment, have continued to wander hopelessly through the one hundred praetorian squares of Southern Italy, stunned by those rare examples who have escaped from this hell without devils?

"Alle cinque della sera	*"At five in the evening*
nella piazza di Matera	*in the square in Matera*
da una millecento nera	*Giovannino Russo arrived*
scende Giovannino Russo	*in a black [Fiat] eleven-hundred*
del "Corriere della Sera".	*he worked for the Corriere della Sera.*
Mamma mia che carriera!"	*Oh my, what a career!"*

Ennio Flaiano taunted, as if he were unaware, as a native of Pescara, how many dramas remained sealed forever inside and behind the rare number of successful young émigrés.

Michele Spera is one of them: mortally wounded like La Capria, he has lived his extraordinary career not as if it were some prize earned at great labour, but instead as some undeserved gift, not his own doing but that of who knows what saint in heaven; a bashfully accepted gift, to be set aside, not in his name but in the name of so many friends who were left behind along the way, in Lucania or elsewhere.

As Carlo Levi psychologically abandoned industrial Turin to become a farmer, Leonardo Sinisgalli and Michele Spera attempted to psychologically abandon Lucania to become European artists. They attempted, without ever succeeding (and, what is more, without wishing to succeed) because the acquired mastery of culture inferred by industrial machinism would never have managed to cancel their original imprinting, the call of their own private Ithaca in Basilicata, as much a point of departure as a point of return.

What Sinisgalli found in his unsurpassed journals – *Civiltà delle Macchine* and *La botte e il violino* – Spera found in his equally unsurpassed brands, posters, photographs and graphic designs: sirens, Laestrygonians and

Cyclopes encountered during travels far from Ithaca, competing with the twelve memories of Argos and Penelope who remained in Ithaca.

I first encountered Michele Spera's graphic designs as a very young man, while working at Francesco Compagna's review *Nord e Sud*, an experience that allowed us, in Achille Lauro's Naples, to read and write in harmony with the rest of Europe. Everything at this publication referred to Mario Pannunzio, to Ugo La Malfa, to Adriano Olivetti and to the laic-technocratic certainty of progress based on the rationality of labour and the perfection of a possible enlightened democracy.

It was a place where one came into contact with the best people, reviews and books and, with them, the perfect images of Michele Spera. Together with the graphic design of Olivetti under the guidance of Adriano and Gian Lupo Osti's Italsider, he established a chasm between their work and that of all other groups, political parties and entrepreneurs.

An émigré, like the majority of young intellectuals my age, initially to Milan and later to Rome, for many years I had the good fortune to walk out of my home and be welcomed, on bright mornings, by the posters of Michele Spera. From the walls of the city they imposed a pause of composed clarity and conscious strength upon urban chaos.

One day I finally met Michele Spera in person. I had either commissioned him to develop or plagiarized his brands for a host of companies, reviews and businesses I created. We worked together on more than one occasion, developing slogans or designing posters.

I worked with many other graphic designers, but with Michele it was always possible in 30 minutes to imagine what others took two weeks to present. These lightning-quick ideas were followed, for Michele, by a meditated, highly attentive and almost surgical period of development, which ended only when the result was considered perfect.

Many young people, born after the advent of the computer, have difficulty imagining that some of Michele Spera's designs were created when the only way to draw was by hand. In reality, computer graphics, which Michele has now mastered, and which are connatural to his style, allowed him not only to work faster but also to be more precise.

If a computer were nature, in Michele's case we could say that nature imitates art. We need only look at some of his drawings for the "*Voce repubblicana*" campaign (1973), or the logo used by IBI for its international conventions (1978), or the Unioncamere logo (1984).

Rural society is characterised by the fact that the centre of its system is occupied by agricultural production. Industrial society, which replaced it, is instead characterised by the fact that its epicentre is occupied by mass produced material goods (automobiles, refrigerators, etc.). Post-industrial society, which in turn replaced its industrial predecessor, is characterised by an epicentre occupied by the production of intangible goods: information, symbols, aesthetics and values.

The first and most important sociologist to study post-industrial society was Daniel Bell, a professor at Harvard University.

He claimed it was not possible to arrive at a post-industrial society without having first passed through an industrial society. Unlike him, I believe this leap to be possible in some cases: for individuals as much as for specific organisations and, even, for entire nations.

Michele Spera is evidence that I may be on the right track. Born in Lucania, a rural native of Basilicata to the core, he has always refuted industrial culture and its structures of collective labour, choral and efficient organisation, vast technological apparatuses, frenetic travel and Taylorist procedures. In 1977, for example, Spera was invited to Milan by Renzo Zorzi to fill the role of art director at Olivetti, the Holy of Holies for designers around the globe. For four days Michele wandered like some foreigner through the ant farm of offices, telephones and urgency, without being provided even a drawing table, or any hope of free invention.

On the fifth day, our Robinson Crusoe of the graphic arts returned to Rome, to his workshop, the workshop of a chronic craftsman, where he could create, in protected solitude, respecting his own biorhythms.

Impermeable to industrial culture, the graphic designs of Michele Spera are as post-industrial as they come: computerised prior to the existence of the computer, complex prior to the theorisation of the epistemology of complexity.

Also coherent with this leap from the rural to the post-industrial without an industrial intermezzo is the very content of this book: the iconographic portion catapults us ahead, surprising us with its futuristic vibrations, for its being so far ahead with respect to coeval Italian graphic design; the written part, instead, takes us back, to the familialism of Southern Italy theorised precisely in Lucania by Edward G. Banfield, to the dense rustic *gemeinshaft* of relatives, friends, countrysides, the memories of a community "impoverished by a misery with no culture and no pride".

Michele is picky, even notarial, in the evocation of this community that expands from Potenza to Rome to the Versilia, though always comprised of ties that are more affectionate than professional, rich with names, of large and small clients, though in all cases familiar, of places and episodes. It is almost as if he wishes to bring together in his book all of the people and shadows encountered during the course of his life: as if there was no time to lose, as if there was an urgency for a plenary meeting during which attendees could draw final conclusions.

13

Long life to Michele, who had enough hay for one hundred horses: the one hundred unbridled horses of his inexhaustible, disciplined and surprising creativity.

But what is creativity? What nurtures it? Freud stated that it was a sublimation of sensuality. Jung held that it was a human instinct not possessed by animals. Greenacre and Schachtel tell us that it is a love story with the world, a game for entering into contact with it. Hillman says it is used by man to draw soul into the world. Arieti calls it a magic synthesis.

Michele Spera has all the traits of a purebred creative: he possesses and intellectual curiosity that flirts with exasperation, dominated by a highly acute desire for novelty. He has a range of talents, and cares little for the opinions of others. He is an independent thinker and spontaneous, vital and incredibly tenacious in his relationships.

If he wished, if he loved surrounding himself with the legends that Kris and Kurz see in the relations between the artist and his public, he could exhibit his surprising technical skills, the furore that Spadolini saw in his eyes, the tempestuous relations with some of his colleagues and some of his clients: indifferently ranging from vast multinational corporations to the countless, almost tribal mass of small factories and shops selling cookies, books and underclothes. It is said that the great Polish contemporary painters spend one week a month drowned in alcohol, one week to rid themselves of the hangover, one week to create and one week desiring another drink, and so on for the rest of their lives. Michele has no need for drink or other psychological prostheses; all he requires is the inspiring presence of Rosalba, the infinite source of his imagination and the highly sophisticated concreteness of his techniques.

Every creation by Michele Spera is the sum of a playful approach and exhausting labour. His formal composure, his sign speaks of content so taught as to be nervous, even neurotic. His imagination is nurtured by an ultra-modern vision of aesthetics and a continuous memory of the past: the earth, friends, masters, patrons.

Looming large among them is Ugo La Malfa, who sensed not only Spera's grandeur but also the importance of a highly original approach to political communication such as that proposed by Michele.

Those who recall the exasperating repetitiveness of posters by the Communists, Socialists and Christian Democrats, or those who remember the crassness of those of the Italian Social Movement, will also recall, by contrast, the great graphic revolution introduced by the Italian Republican Party: sharp colours, heavy signs, a balance between the one and the other, intelligent slogans, a nonchalant familiarity with an elevated level of culture without fear of losing contact with its voters.

Such a refined client, the direct heir to Adriano Olivetti, would already be admirable if it were tied to a business; but it was instead a political party. Looking back, it seems like a miracle. A laic miracle arising out of the fortunate encounter between a young artist from the deep South, his pockets filled with the dream of a renewed aesthetic, and a mature politician from the deep South, with a dream of renewing the country.

Creativity unfolds when it has the necessary tools, when the artist is open to diverse and even contrasting cultural stimuli, when he is not the object of discrimination, when his emphasis falls on the future, when he interacts with important people, when he is gratified not only materially for his work, when he is in a position of dialogue with the culture that surrounds him and even his client. A proper mixture of dissatisfaction and exaltation is the indispensable formula for producing brilliant ideas and bringing them to the public's attention.

14   The quality of the result derives in part from stimuli external to the artist, and which the artist introjects as heteropoietic experience. Lucania, political militancy, a circle of brilliant people are, for Michele Spera, the three great creativogenic inputs.

On the other hand, perhaps more important, the result derives from the inner and autopoietic maturity of the artist himself, from his personal anxieties and elaborations, from incubation and explosion which transform existential materials into original ideas.

For Michele Spera these continuous workings become signs and verbal and figurative intuitions that tend to innovate the panorama before our eyes, considered the indispensable context of political and civil innovation.

As an essential condition for remaining creative, Spera demands complete freedom of movement and expression, a constant osmosis between work and life. He refuses any hierarchical subordination and any organisational cage, an absolute indisposition toward controlling others or being controlled by others.

Under these conditions, graphics and design become less and less applied arts and more and more pure art: this makes Michele Spera immune to any corporate seduction; it makes him the most post-industrial, the most technical and the most human of our great graphic artists, with his heart in Potenza and his brain in Seattle.

Domenico De Masi
Professor Emeritus of Sociology of Labour
Sapienza Università di Roma

Author's Note

I never intended to use this material, collected from lessons taught during the Graduate Course in Industrial Design offered by the First Faculty of Architecture at the Sapienza Università di Roma[1], to create a graphic design manual. This is an undertaking that would normally require an entirely different approach, a different sentiment and investigations of a much more speculative and organic nature. I simply wished to assemble the results of an educational experiment, retracing my days of study and teaching. The order is based less on the geometric structure of the material presented, and more on the exploration of topics triggered by the progressive analysis of the work produced by students over the course of a year.

The graphic examples are not inspired by complicated "collections" or illustrious examples, nonetheless mentioned in the bibliography. Collected from my "projects", it could be said that they provided the educational pretext for the structure of my lessons and considerations.

To a certain degree, these notes, these kernels of mine, complete a book I published in 1996: *194 storie di un segno* (194 Stories About a Sign).

The approach to this labour, the design pursued, was exactly inverse to that which, generally, sees an author intent on "formalising" his work.

In fact, while *194 storie di un segno* collects the emotions linked to the profession of graphic design, grouped together in periods and events, this book retraces the disciplinary and highly personal structures underlying my codes and my geometries.

In general, I begin my lessons by assigning students a visual design study, correlated with experiences that become a collage of acquired elements. They may take the form of a proposal for a grid or format, the discovery of the codes of a brand or a geometric figure, the construction of a letter of the alphabet or simply the elaboration of a project designed on the computer or by hand. This initial encounter helps me enter into the world of each of my students, into their way of intending the profession of graphic design, their speculative preferences and specific interests. My aim is to understand the tools they adopt, whether pictorial or electronic, manual or automated, and whether they possess a design methodology. The results are always extremely interesting.

What emerges from this initial contact is a desire to learn not only about aesthetics and form, but also about the science of this profession. Students have an urgency to experiment, a desire to learn how to create what they wish to express. Through this approach to teaching I have been

1) This book, printed in a first edition in 2002, under the title Michele Spera La progettazione grafica tra creatività e scienza, preface by Tonino Paris, 400 pages, Gangemi Editore, Rome, 2000, was very well received; when copies of the first edition ran out, Gangemi asked me for a second edition in 2005, printed in 4 colours.
The current edition, printed in Italian and English in 2018 is thus a third edition, with updated and expanded content.

2) Michele Spera, Centonovantaquattro storie di un segno, preface by Domenico De Masi, 500 pages, Edizioni Socrates, Rome, 1996.

able to observe how the first few projects, into which students pour all of their impulsive creativity, gradually give way to a powerful need for rationality and codification, for science penetrated by problems of perception. After initial flights of fantasy they manage to perceive the worlds of order and chaos in a context bound to the objective nature of communication.

It also becomes clear that each student has a final objective in mind. My role is to help them understand how to proceed, to find the point of synthesis in their ideas, to make them a reality in the objective realm of communication and, more than anything else, to graft their work onto a rational structure, as close as possible to that of an exact science.

There is only one postulate, almost a categorical imperative to be respected, and which has guided our shared work: the emotions produced by aesthetics can only be a product of logic, of articulated, assiduous and in-depth research.

It is clear how a course structured in this manner does not intend to create graphic designers who are artists, but instead graphic designers who have assimilated the techniques, methodologies, history and science of this profession; substantially, the intention is to focus on the development of this specialisation as a fundamental moment in the correct structuring of a freer and higher moment of flight, when it becomes possible to overturn everything one has learned. The point at which the role of the teacher ceases to be important.

The students, who seem to have appreciated my tiptoeing approach, studied topics that, despite the many rules acquired, remain open to further investigation as part of the endless search for definitive and universal codes.

What is more, during countless reviews in my studio I established a relationship that moved far beyond the time spent in the classroom. This relationship was almost comitial, and without a doubt productive and fruitful. Students were able to express themselves to their fullest potential, with the enthusiasm of invention and intuition, but above all with a passion for research and for the exploration of an ancient science: all guarantees of an ability to "govern" the profession of graphic design.

I would like to thank my students for their attention to what I was able to transmit to them and what I knew how to teach them, and for that which, through maieutics, I was able to learn from them. It is my hope that these lessons will offer other young people, whom I did not have the pleasure of teaching in a classroom, information and know-how of use to their future careers, but also a passion for such an extraordinary profession.

The Author

Notes
The book can be read on various levels, almost establishing a sort of interdisciplinary navigation through the text.

The Notes:
Generally additional texts, often small specifications on broader themes, in other cases curiosities related to the themes explored.

The Workbook:
A guide to work developed by students to augment the lessons. The book intentionally avoids mentioning the themes of the various studies carried out during the lessons, also to offer, to those interested in this trip through the world of graphics, to freely choose from different themes.

The Bibliography:
Other than canonical references, listed at the end of the book, it was also considered useful to list a more detailed bibliography in the margins of individual pages, with the intent of involving students in the exploration of specific topics.

16

Note

This graphics manual, which uses many of the author's projects as examples, together with the work of Gerardo Spera, with whom the author collaborated for many years, privileges those considered most correct. Some, considered too innovative, were originally discarded. More space has been given to alternative drawings, to certain details that were initially an appendix, preparatory sketches or research tied to much larger projects, which are now an integral part of this book. (Editor's Note)

1.

A Container for Projects and Research

The Booklets from the Graduate Course in Industrial Design

Students at the DUDI - Department of Technological Innovation in Architecture, are asked to layout their research and projects in a small booklet that can be easily printed and assembled without the services of a printer or graphic artist. Each step in this process is managed directly by students.

1. The booklets measure 105x148.5 millimetres. They are realised by dividing an A4 page into four parts.
The resulting grid is composed of three equal modules, each 35 mm wide by 42.5 mm in height. The resulting space occupied corresponds with half a square.
With a margin of 10 mm at the top, and left and right edges, the grid frames a space of 85 mm in width by 127.5 mm in height
At the bottom, a 1 mm gap separates a small grid for the page number.

When laying out a page using a computer, input the coordinates for the X and Y axes to obtain a practical and immediate layout.
I suggest working with a file based on the dimensions of a single page, to be successively transferred into a general layout grid using the exact coordinates and correct position based on the layout of the signatures.

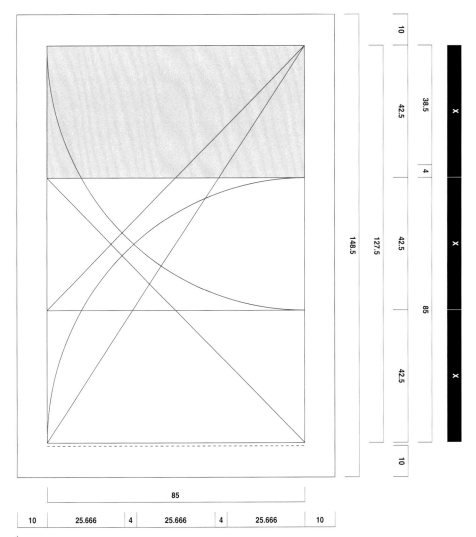

1.

The "Graphics 2" and "Industrial Design for Visual Communication" courses, taught by Giorgio Bucciarelli, operate in synergy with the precise aim not only of teaching students design techniques, but also testing concrete applications and producing a real final product.

Some research projects with successive applications in the field of design are motivated by the investigation of issues explored by Mario Morcellini in the "Visual Perception" course.
Themes include: models and theories of communication; the evolution of writing and *gestalttheorie*; the function of the visual sign in the realisation of images and pictograms; colour and gesturality from perception to symbolism; brand and corporate image; labelling, packaging and signage: paths of recognition; hyper-media devices for artistic and industrial production.

Annual themes also explore more specifically "graphic" issues, through general and detailed investigations, whose contents are presented on the pages of this book.

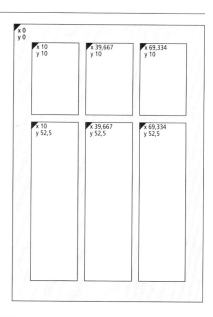

18

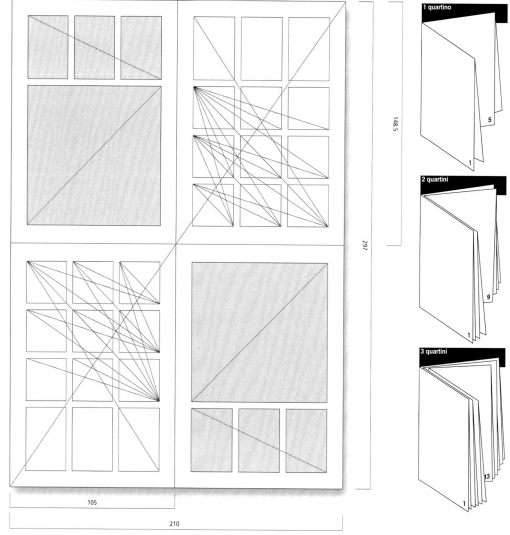

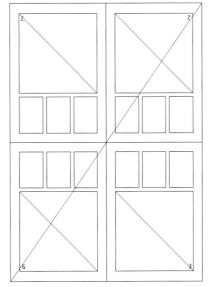

The layout of the booklets produces a structure that makes it possible to print four pages in recto and four in verso. Folding the sheet two times along the diagonal, we obtain an octavo which will constitute the first signature.

The final booklet is obtained by overlapping the various signatures inside one another, held together by a staple.

The adjacent illustration and the following pages simulate the location of the pages and their orientation on an A4 leaf of paper.

Below is a project by Alessandro Biondi.

19

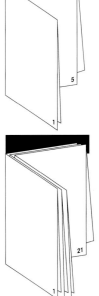

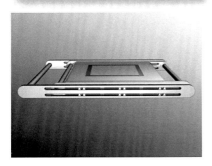

di rappresentare.
e quindi dall'esigenza
a due con un lato in comune,
idealmente collegati a due
in cui i punti principali sono
Esso nasce su un triangolo,
del lavoro.
del marchio dei Consulenti
e la logica costruttiva
matrice progettuale, l'origine
propongono di descrivere la
Queste prime tre tavole si
espressione compiuta.
che ha ispirato una
progettuale, ad un concetto
alla rivelazione di un intento
Una forma geometrica,

Progettazione
di un disegno strutturale

Il percorso dell'ideazione

organizzata.
geometrica una struttura
impalcatura che sostituisca
uno scheletro, una
possano creare un'armatura,
eccezionali di sostegno che
traccia, aggiunga elementi
che ripercorra il modello
geometrico, ne conserva la
di un disegno strutturale
si articola sulla progettazione

triangolazione fra Consulente.
di rappresentare la
e quindi dall'esigenza
a due con un lato in comune,
idealmente collegati a due
in cui i punti principali sono
Esso nasce su un triangolo,
del lavoro.
del marchio dei Consulenti
e la logica costruttiva
matrice progettuale, l'origine
propongono di descrivere la
Queste prime tre tavole si
espressione compiuta.
che ha ispirato una
progettuale, ad un concetto
alla rivelazione di un intento
Una forma geometrica,

Progettazione
di un disegno strutturale
che ripercorra il modello
geometrico

Il percorso dell'ideazione
si articola sulla progettazione
di un disegno strutturale
che ripercorra il modello
geometrico, ne conserva la
traccia, aggiunga elementi
eccezionali di sostegno che
possano creare un'armatura,
uno scheletro, una
impalcatura che sostituisca
alla semplice figura
geometrica una struttura
organizzata.

dei concetti e dei moduli.
innovativi, l'ordinamento
di questi elementi grafici
logico è la classificazione
Il punto d'arrivo di processo

triangolazione fra Consulente.
di rappresentare la
e quindi dall'esigenza
a due con un lato in comune,
idealmente collegati a due
in cui i punti principali sono
Esso nasce su un triangolo,
del lavoro.
del marchio dei Consulenti
e la logica costruttiva
matrice progettuale, l'origine
propongono di descrivere la
Queste prime tre tavole si
espressione compiuta.
che ha ispirato una
progettuale, ad un concetto
alla rivelazione di un intento
Una forma geometrica,

Progettazione
di un disegno strutturale
che ripercorra il modello
geometrico

Progettazione di un disegno strutturale che ripercorra il modello geometrico

Una forma geometrica, alla rivelazione di un intento progettuale, ad un concetto che ha ispirato una espressione compiuta. Queste prime tre tavole si propongono di descrivere la matrice progettuale, l'origine e la logica costruttiva del marchio dei Consulenti del lavoro. Esso nasce su un triangolo, in cui i punti principali sono idealmente collegati a due a due con un lato in comune, e quindi dall'esigenza di rappresentare la triangolazione fra Consulente.

Il percorso dell'ideazione si articola sulla progettazione di un disegno strutturale che ripercorra il modello geometrico, ne conserva la traccia, aggiunga elementi eccezionali di sostegno che possano creare un'armatura, uno scheletro, una impalcatura che sostituisca alla semplice figura geometrica una struttura organizzata. Il punto d'arrivo di processo logico è la classificazione di questi elementi grafici innovativi, l'ordinamento dei concetti e dei moduli.

Progettazione di un disegno strutturale che ripercorra il modello geometrico

Esso nasce su un triangolo, in cui i punti principali sono idealmente collegati a due a due con un lato in comune, e quindi dall'esigenza di rappresentare la triangolazione fra Consulente. società a lavoro. Una forma geometrica, alla rivelazione di un intento progettuale, ad un concetto che ha ispirato una espressione compiuta.

Il punto d'arrivo di processo logico è la classificazione di questi elementi grafici innovativi, l'ordinamento dei concetti e dei moduli, un programma.

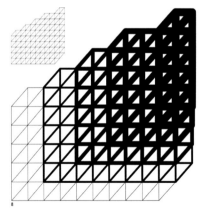

compiendo.
In queste pagine esaminiamo la possibilità di intervenire sullo spazio fra lettere ricorrendo a quei comandi del computer e le illustrazioni ci mostrano il risultato di queste prove. Siamo quindi in grado di dare gli accostamenti che vogliamo, ma rimane un quesito da risolvere: quanto spazio assegnare ad una lettera in relazione a quella che le sta accanto.
Nella figura 2 osserviamo che nell'acronimo «dpx» gli spazi ottenuti fra le lettere non rispondono ad una lettura armonica e soprattutto che alcune lettere, nell'accostamento fra alcune lettere, nel nostro caso fra la lettera «p» e la lettera «x», il risultato non è soddisfacente.
Più avviciniamo le lettere, più scopriamo disarmonie. Diventa quindi necessario operare sui singoli accostamenti e trovare una metodologia che ci aiuti in questa ricerca.

I caratteri tipografici in metallo sono fusi sul loro supporto in modo da offrire una distanza, la più giusta possibile, fra un parallelepipedo e l'altro. Non a caso il parallelepipedo è infatti chiamato avvicinamento. Ovviamente questa distanza non può che essere una media fra le esigenze di accostamento giacché ogni lettera deve poter essere accostata a tutte le altre che compongono l'alfabeto.
Quando i vecchi compositori si applicavano a una riga di testo in corpi rilevanti compensavano disarmonie non risolvibili con i caratteri di piombo (per esempio l'accostamento «T» e «A») ricorrendo a piccoli spazi inseriti fra le altre lettere che componevano la parola. Ottenevano un testo assai spaziato, ma armonico. Il loro occhio era esercitato a cercare un risultato coerente nella loro composizione, possedevano una scienza empirica che li guidava in questa operazione.
Oggi con la composizione elettronica questi problemi sono risolvibili: possiamo infatti stringere, allargare e accostare le lettere a nostro piacimento.
Ma proprio l'avvento di queste nuove straordinarie possibilità ci obbliga a prendere coscienza e a capire come ottenere un testo il più possibile perfetto, ossia la giusta spaziatura di un carattere. Nessuno dei vari sistemi di spaziatura disegnati da grafici può essere considerato definitivo, ma piuttosto straordinari contributi alla scientificizzazione del nostro mestiere. Essi fanno parte di quella storia della grafica che si sta ancora

compiendo.
In queste pagine esaminiamo la possibilità di intervenire sullo spazio fra lettere ricorrendo a quei comandi del computer e le illustrazioni ci mostrano il risultato di queste prove. Siamo quindi in grado di dare gli accostamenti che vogliamo, ma rimane un quesito da risolvere: quanto spazio assegnare ad una lettera in relazione a quella che le sta accanto.
Nella figura 2 osserviamo che nell'acronimo «dpx» gli spazi ottenuti fra le lettere non rispondono ad una lettura armonica e soprattutto che alcune lettere, nell'accostamento fra alcune lettere, nel nostro caso fra la lettera «p» e la lettera «x», il risultato non è soddisfacente.
Più avviciniamo le lettere, più scopriamo disarmonie. Diventa quindi necessario operare sui singoli accostamenti e trovare una metodologia che ci aiuti in questa ricerca.

Questa area risulterà uguale a mm2 470.32.
Lo spazio tra la H e la C dovrà quindi essere uguale a questa area meno l'area che fa parte della lettera C. Procederemo via via con identiche misurazioni che serviranno soprattutto a fornirci di un occhio addestrato alla valutazione di un corretto accostamento e a guidarci nello stabilire la metodologia per assegnare una certa quantità di spazio fra una lettera e l'altra.

L'accostamento che richiederà più spazio è quello fra due H, ovvero fra due caratteri con aste dritte che quindi non hanno un loro proprio spazio naturale.
Ci accorgeremo anche che in altri casi, per esempio nell'accostamento tra AT o tra AY, occorrerà, per mantenere uniforme lo spazio tra lettere, uno spazio negativo, quindi un valore uguale a −3 unità, −2, −1, ecc.

Gli spazi base in un codice possono essere riassunti in tre tipologie: fra due lettere dritte (HH), accostando le quali avremo un'area uguale a zero; fra una lettera con asta dritta e una lettera curva (HC), dove l'area fra le lettere è misurabile; fra due lettere curve (OO), dove l'area è la maggiore possibile al di là dei casi limite come LA, TV, YY, ecc.

I contrografismi

Area di misurazione

Book and Portfolio

Layout and Format

Students are asked to assemble the projects, research and objects created during lessons in the form of a book. One chapter of the book must deal specifically with the results of their internship, a three month experience with a company or business. The design of the book is one of the themes explored during the year. The format, layout and design of the grid and the general appearance of the book must consider diverse needs related to the themes of the courses.

As the book must be produced by students using means at their immediate disposal, the choice was made to adopt an A3 format, measuring 297x420 mm. This format serves to create a square measuring 297x297 mm, with a 15 mm margin along the binding edge for the holes required by the binding rings.

1. The pages features 4 holes with a diameter of 5 mm, at 80 mm on centre.
The distance between the holes and the binding edge is 10 mm, measured from their centre; the distance between the holes and the upper and lower margins is 28.5 mm. This system of holes makes it possible to add new pages to the book as they are produced.

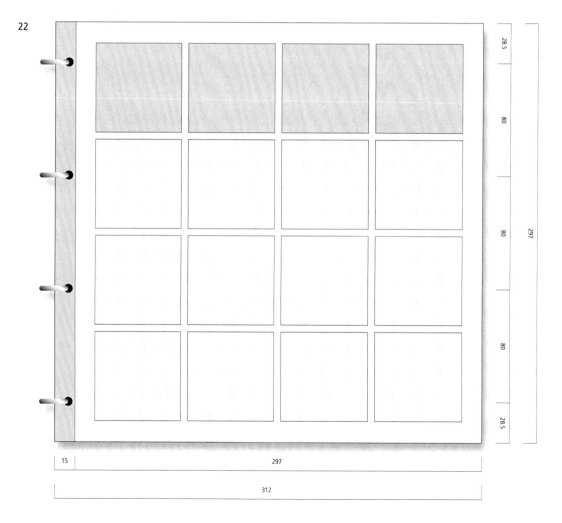

1.

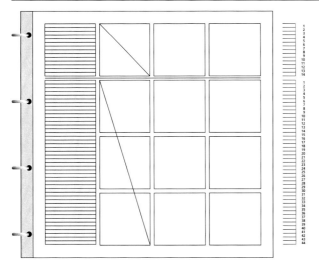

2. The grid is obtained by providing a uniform margin of 15 mm along the binding and outer edge and at the top and bottom. Useful format measures 267x267 mm. Dividing the cage into 4 parts and assigning a distance of 5 mm between the modules, we obtain 9 equal modules measuring 63x63 mm.

The first three modules at the top are assigned the function of hosting text; the remaining modules are for images.

A 0.3 point horizontal line divides the two zones. The typeface (the example shown here uses Times bold and regular), identifies the priority of information in relation to the general layout. One module hosts 14 lines of 12 point text with an equal 12 point leading; introductory texts can also be placed in the area reserved for images; in this case, the space of three vertical modules can contain 44 lines.

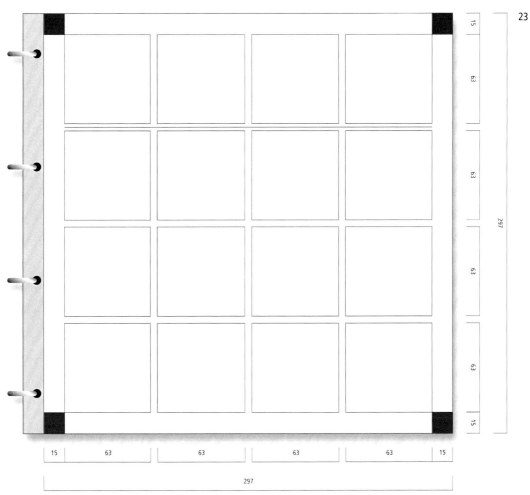

Texts are positioned inside the first 4 cages at the top. The premise, preface and introductory texts can be laid out in the space normally occupied by images.

In the example, the texts are composed in 12 point Times regular and bold, with a 12 point leading and flush left alignment.

The width of the columns of text is equal to 63 mm; the quantity of lines contained in one module is equal to 14 lines of 12 point text.

A separator, indicated here in black, divides the various sections. With an additional width of 15 mm, for a total of 327 mm, these pages project beyond the edges of the other pages, similar to an index card.

24

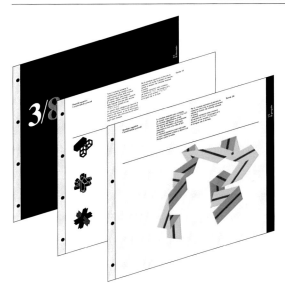

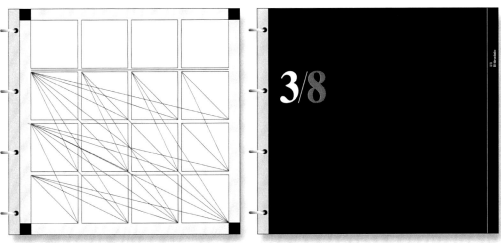

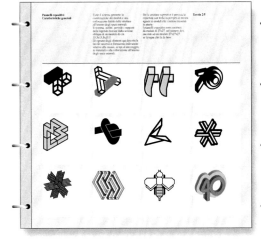

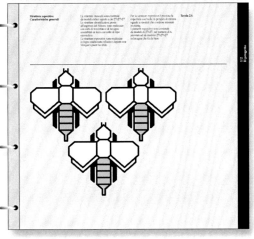

A Format for Research and Projects

A Book Made From an A4 Page

Students are asked to collect the projects, research and objects developed during their studies in a book. The format, layout, grid and general appearance must consider that the book is to be produced by students using means at their immediate disposal (formats compatible with common printers). The format is an A4 page, measuring 210x297 mm. From this dimension a 15 mm margin is to be subtracted along the binding edge for the binding rings. The internal grid corresponds with a golden section.

Each page features four 5 mm diameter holes at 80 mm on centre. The distance between the holes and the binding edge is 10 mm, from the centre of the holes; the distance between the holes and the top and bottom edges is 28.5 mm. This system of holes makes it possible to add new pages to the book as they are produced.

26

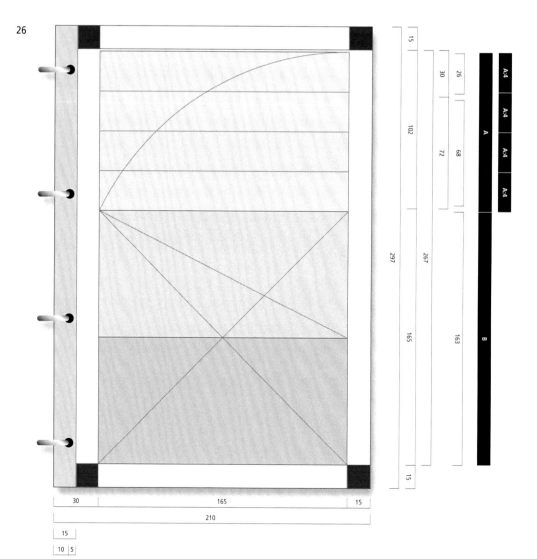

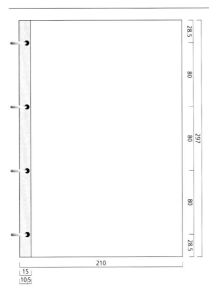

The grid is obtained by providing a uniform margin of 15 mm along the binding and outer edge and at the top and bottom, with a correction deriving from the golden section.

The useful area can be seen in the illustrations. Dividing the cage into 3 parts and assigning a distance between the modules of 5 mm, we obtain 6 primary modules for graphics.

The first 6 modules at the top are for text; the lower module is for images.

The two zones are divided by two horizontal lines, the first 0.3 points and the second 0.5 points.

The silhouette can be used as a constant dimensional element that, beyond progressively expressed measurements, provides an immediate relationship, which is also visual, for all of the graphic content.

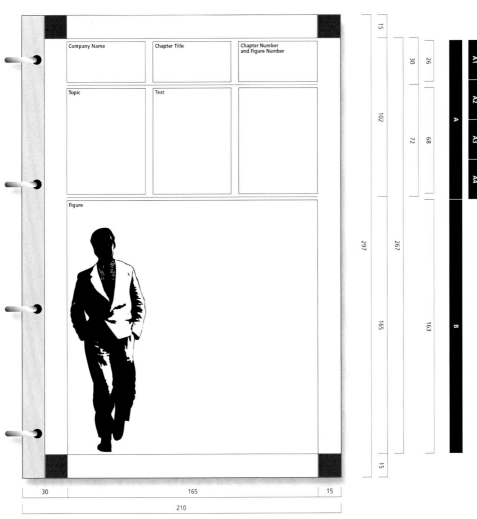

Trastevere
Arredo urbano

Indagine sulla vita
del quartiere

Tavola 2/8

Strutture identificative
Strutture espositive
Pannelli espositivi
Caratteristiche generali

La strutture museali
sono costituite da moduli cubici
di misura fissa di cm 27x27x27.
Le strutture identificative, poste
all'ingresso del Museo, sono
realizzate con cubi di travertino
e di lavagna assemblati in loco con
colle di tipo epossidico.
Le strutture espositive sono
realizzate in legno multistrato rifinito
e dipinto con Morgan's paint
lavabile. Anche queste sono
assemblate in loco in base alle
~~esigenze di spazio e al materiali~~
da esporre. Per le strutture
espositive è prevista la copertura
con teche in perspex di misura
uguale ai moduli che contiene
misurati in pianta.

I pannelli espositivi sono costituiti
da moduli di 27x27, nei numero di 6,
ancorati ad un modulo 27x27x27
in lavagna che fa da base.
Tutto il sistema permette la
combinazione dei moduli e una
collocazione duttile delle strutture
all'interno degli spazi museali.
Il sistema, inoltre, prevede i supporti
delle legende ricavate dalla sezione
obliqua di un modulo
di cm 13,5x13,5x13,5.
Di ognuno degli elementi qui
descritti le tavole successive
forniscono indicazioni relative alle
misure, ai tipi di ancoraggio,
ai materiali e alla collocazione
all'interno degli spazi museali.

The typeface style identifies the priority of information in relation to the general context. Bold text is used for key information, regular text for the main body and italics for notes and captions.

The first three horizontal modules can host a maximum of 7 lines per module. This space is used for primary information (general theme, theme of the page and page number). The second three modules contain the text that decodifies the iconographic content. Each of the three modules contains 19 lines of 10 point text with a 10 point leading.

Introductory texts can also be located in the area reserved for images; in this case, the height of each of the three vertical modules can contain 46 lines of 10/10 text. The chart shows the formats of the template and the various grids; all measurements are in millimetres; the quantity of text that each page can contain; the position and use of each space.

Separators, shown here in black card, can be used to divide various sections or chapters. Projecting 15 mm beyond the edge of the pages like index cards, they are a total of 225 mm in width. Separators can be personalised in relation to the theme of each chapter with photographs, drawings and progressive reference numbers.

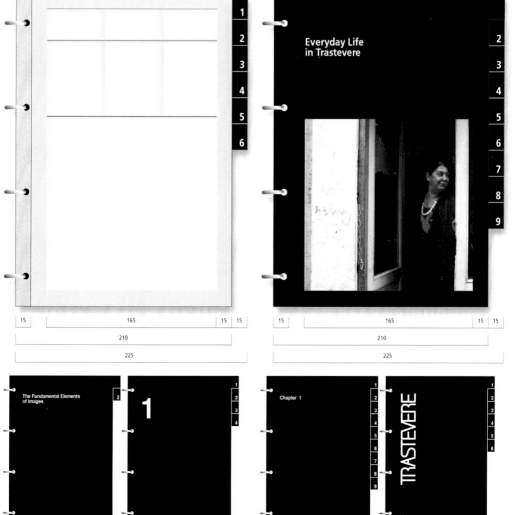

The Print Layout

9 Pages on a 70x100 Folio

When the pre-selected format for the book is an A4 (210x297 mm) it can be printed on a 70x100 mm folio. Unlike a classical book, which requires assembly in octavi, sextodecimi or other number of pages, requiring the folding of a leaf printed in recto and verso, the pages of this book, printed on one side only, require only the cutting and gathering of the pages. They are laid out side by side and without a double cut.

The pages feature a 15 mm margin. When a page is to contain an image larger than the assigned space it will have to be doubled: in this case the left page of 210x297 mm, with binding holes, is coupled with the right page, with a folded crease.

If an image to be reproduced requires even larger space, for example a photographic survey of a street, it may occupy up to three pages that, in this case, requires more than one fold. A crease will be indispensable to the construction of this page. The facing page shows the general layout of a triple-size page with two folds.

2.

3.

Pinza

700

| 210 | 210 | 210 |
| 210 | 195 | 195 |

297 297 297 1000

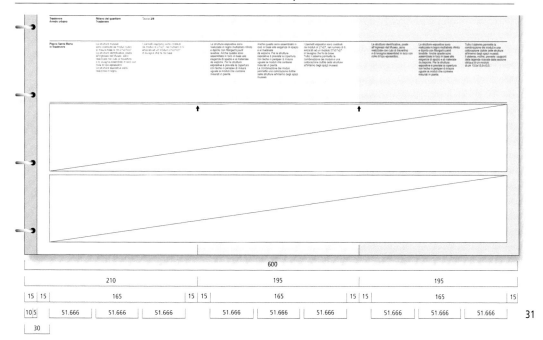

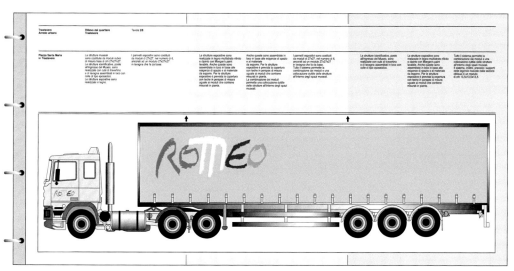

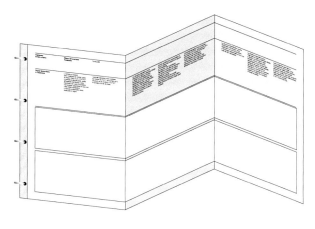

2.
Codes of Communication

Chinese Characters

1. The passage from pictograms to ideograms allows for more in-depth communication; in fact, ideograms make it possible to communicate an abstract concept, something impossible with pictograms. For a closer look at Chinese characters, I suggest Edoardo Fazzioli's book *Caratteri cinesi*, listed in the bibliography.

1.

Writing is a way to communicate thoughts, events and ideas to others.

It is a conventional system of graphic signs made to correspond with the sounds and words of a language.

Before man could draw any graphic sign, the simplest form of writing was entrusted to a certain arrangement of objects, bunches of branches, canes and cords that, opportunely selected and laid out, expressed and communicated something. The embryo of writing is found in the first images depicted, carved or painted in lieu of symbolic objects. This means of expression is known as pictography or pictorial mnemonics. Pictography represents objects in thier entirety or only a detail. If the object is very well known it may be represented only in part (i.e. the head, horns, a footprint, etc.). In this latter case we can refer to this means of expression as pictographic symbolism. To signify the word "combat", primitive man would trace out two opposing arrows; for the word "morning" he would draw the sun; to indicate a desert island, the Eskimos drew a circle and, if the island was inhabited, a point was added inside it (figs. 2 & 3).

In the oldest writings (i.e. hieroglyphics and cuneiform) the graphic unit was the word, defined by one or more of the following elements:
a) an ideographic symbol that used drawings, gradually more stylised over time, to express the word to be communicated;
b) one or more phonetic complements hinting at the "phonetic aspect" of the word; c) a "determinative" indicating the conceptual category of the word. The development of phonetic elements gradually led to "syllabic" writing, which used a small quantity of signs and, finally, "alphabetic" writing (Greek and Latin), with as many signs as the distinctive sounds of a language.

China was immune to this evolution in writing and to this day Chinese writing is composed of thousands of signs corresponding with an equal number of words.

It is useful here to briefly mention the elements of Chinese writing.

This form of writing, in fact, offers a graphic artist the joy of an immersion in a universe of signs of rare beauty and harmony.

We could state, with the awareness of culture today, that any Chinese "character" is a brand, a logo, a sign that inherently contains all of the brevity derived from centuries of constant application. While many civilisations have modified their specific cultural baggage over the centuries, the characteristics of Chinese civilisation have remained almost unaltered to the present day.

The history of Chinese writing can be identified to a certain degree with the history of Chinese painting; indeed, we are dealing with a form of writing steeped in art.

In a bronze from the 16th-11th century BC, we can already admire the drawing of one of the first writing instruments, a sort of fountain pen, fitted with a sort of leather straw through with the ink passed; an instrument that produced a rigid and rather irregular sign. Only in 220 BC, with the invention of the brush by a general from the Qin Dynasty, did this writing acquire a softer and more sinuous sign.

The traditional leather pen was substituted by a tuft of soft animal hairs. This different instrument, associated with a support for writing like paper, permitted the hands of talented calligraphers to evolve graphic signs into the typical traits of Chinese writing.

This was the moment of the birth of the art of Chinese calligraphy, comprised of an intelligent and refined use of four elements: the pen, paper, ink and a stone (a sort of inkwell).

In broad strokes, the evolution of Chinese characters can be subdivided into four chronological phases: the primitive period, from 8000 to 3000 BC, during which man expressed himself with pictograms, drawings reproducing the reality surrounding him.

The Archaic Period, from 3000 to 1600 BC, which includes the pre-Dynastic period and the Xià Dynasty, marking the passage from pictograms to ideograms, and the command of the possibility to express abstract concepts. The Historic Period, which began with the Shang Dynasty and ended with the fall of the Eastern Han (220); a lengthy period during which writing evolved and was refined. Finally, the Contemporary Period, which began in 1949 with the foundation of the People's Republic of China, witness to a series of interventions involving writing, above all owing to the need for exemplification to raise the nation's literacy rate.

Speaking of Chinese writing, it must be immediately clarified that it is an extremely difficult type of writing, whose in-depth understanding requires more than one lifetime. Furthermore, ancient Chinese scribes often filled spaces with incorrect or even invented characters, provoking no shortage of difficulties for modern philologists. To resolve these inconveniences, the Emperor Qin ordered his Prime Minister Li Si to compile an official catalogue of characters, to be employed in official documents and literature; this marked the birth of the first Chinese dictionary, the Sancang, with 3,300 characters.

Three centuries later, in 121, the scholar Xu Shen composed the first researched lexicon in 15 volumes, in practical terms an update to and enrichment of Li Si's dictionary. There were now 10,516 terms, ordered under 540 radicals.

The last Imperial Dynasty, the Qing (1644-1911), 1,600 years later, saw another updated version of the dictionary, by the Emperor Kang Xi, with a staggering 40,000 characters, ordered under 214 radicals.

In 1976 the Xinhua Zi Dian, the dictionary of the new China was published; a total of 227 radicals for a modern and ordered publication.

Bibliography
Edoardo Fazzioli,
Caratteri cinesi,
dal disegno all'idea,
214 caratteri per
comprendere la Cina,
Arnoldo Mondadori
Editore, Milano 1986.

Notes
I include six examples of Chinese radicals. They are positioned as suggested by Edoardo Fazzioli, in a grid subdivided into nine squares to emphasise the perfect equilibrium of the proportions.

2.

3.

4.
Man
5.
Father
6.
Woman
7.
Son
8.
Family
9.
Scholar

10.
Water
"While in the character for fire the flame rises upward, in that for water the flow is downward: the pictogram depicts the eddies produced by water.
In addition to the central current, the character also represents the drips and lateral sprays" [...]
From *Caratteri cinesi*, by Edoardo Fazzioli.

The Families
1a. Rén (man)
1b. Zhong (centre)
1c. Shan (mountain)

Indicators
2a. San (three)
2b. Shàng (climb up)
2c. Xià (climb down)

Ideograms
3a. Rì (sun)
3b. Yuè (moon)
3c. Mìng (luminosity)

Phonograms
4a. Ta (him)
4b. Ta (her)
4c. Song (pine tree)

Deflectives
5a. Lao (elderly)
5b. Kao (exam)
5c. Wang (to capture)

Borrowed Words
6a. Wan (ten thousand)
from scorpion
6b. Xi (West)
from bird in a nest
6c. Lai (to come)
from cereals

However, the official and most scientifically correct classification would remain that of Kang Xi.
The radicals are the root of all Chinese writing and make it possible to find a character in the dictionary.
The first step is to find the radical that composes the character; this makes it possible to identify the list of all of its related composites.

One fascinating characteristic of Chinese writing is that any character can be written in very different ways. A good calligrapher must be familiar with six fundamental styles, the six classical styles. These calligraphic styles were born over the centuries, through individual, personal and very often genial contributions from a different calligraphers.

Notes   33
*Hieroglyphics are the ideographic writing used by the Ancient Egyptians. They were deciphered in 1822 by J. F. Champollion.
Cuneiform writing was invented by the Sumerians and later used by the Assyrians-Babylonians and other peoples of Asia Minor.
It consists of ideographic or syllabic characters with the form of a wedge engraved in clay or stone. When the drawing or sign suggests the sound of the name, the graphic symbol becomes a phonogram. This latter, in it diverse forms (verbal, syllabic or alphabetic) gave birth to the alphabet we know today.
Mexican hand written documents make it possible to capture the passage from the pictographic to the hieroglyphic phase, when figures no longer signify the objects represented, but become phonetic symbols that express or allow for the expression of the sound of names.*

10.

4.

7.

1a.   1b.   1c.

2a.   2b.   2c.

3a.   3b.   3c.

4a.   4b.   4c.

5.

8.

5a.   5b.   5c.

6.

9.

6a.   6b.   6c.

Morse Code

An Alphabet of Dashes and Dots

Morse Code
Unable to transmit the letters of the alphabet, Morse imagined his own code made from a combination of dashes and dots.
The transmission of electrical impulses, translated into lines and points, occurs by pushing a button: a light tap produces a dot and a longer touch a dash.
Special procedures mark the beginning and end of a transmission.

How is an invitation to start a conservation sent? Line, dot, line.
How is the end of a transmission signalled? Point, dot, point line, dot, line.
How does one communicate the beginning of a transmission? Line, dot, line, dot, line.

34   Samuel Finley Breese Morse was born in Charleston, Massachusetts in 1791. After witnessing a number of experiences with electricity first hand during his travels, he created the first electric telegraph in 1835. In 1844 he successfully sent the first telegram from Washington to Baltimore.
His device worked in this manner: electrical current from a battery passed through an electromagnet that moved a pen on a piece of paper. The paper was wound on a bobbin and, as the pen wrote, the bobbin unrolled the paper.
It was not yet possible for the machine to write the letters of the alphabet, so Morse created his own alphabet from a combination of dashes and dots.
The transmission of electrical signals, which the machine translated into dashes and dots, occurred by tapping a button: a soft tap produced a dot, while a longer contact produced a dash. When the button was not pushed, the rear part of the machine established an electrical contact that connected the device to the intended receiver of the message.

A	dot, dash
B	dash, dot, dot, dot
C	dash, dot, dash, dot
D	dash, dot, dot
E	point
F	dot, dot, dash, dot
G	dash, dash, dot
H	dot, dot, dot, dot
I	dot, dot
J	dot, dash, dash, dash
K	dash, dot, dash
L	dot, dash, dot, dot
M	dash, dash
N	dash, point
O	dash, dash, dash
P	dot, dash, dash, dot
Q	dash, dash, dot, dash
R	dot, dash, dot
S	dot, dot, dot
T	dash
U	dot, dot, dash
V	dot, dot, dot, dash
W	dot, dash, dash
X	dash, dot, dot, dash
Y	dash, dot, dash, dash
Z	dash, dash, dot, point
0	dash, dash, dash, dash, dash
1	dot, dash, dash, dash, dash
2	dot, dot, dash, dash, dash
3	dot, dot, dot, dash, dash
4	dot, dot, dot, dot, dash
5	dot, dot, dot, dot, dot
6	dash, dot, dot, dot, dot
7	dash, dash, dot, dot, dot
8	dash, dash, dash, dot, dot
9	dash, dash, dash, dash, dot

1. In addition to being sent with a special electrical device, messages in Morse Code can also be sent using flags, lamps, or other devices that emit short or long bursts of light or using a continuous low source of light.
In particular emergencies this makes it possible to communicate using a lantern that can be obscured by any type of screening element.

SOS

Save Our Souls:
Dot, dot, dot,
dash, dash, dash,
dot, dot, dot

An SOS is a universally recognised distress call. The abbreviation is derived from the English *Save Our Souls*. It is said to have been used for the first time by the telegraph operator aboard the Titanic, as the ship was about to do down. The extreme simplicity of this call has made it universal: it is composed by tapping out three dots, three dashes and a further three dots.

Flashing light signals are sent using blinders that alternately show or hide a light beam. The call uses the international Morse Code system, whose symbols represent letters and numbers as a combination of dots and dashes. The transmitter repeats the distress call until an answer is received.

A ●▬	P ●▬▬●	4 ●●●●▬
B ▬●●●	Q ▬▬●▬	5 ●●●●●
C ▬●▬●	R ●▬●	6 ▬●●●●
D ▬●●	S ●●●	7 ▬▬●●●
E ●	T ▬	8 ▬▬▬●●
F ●●▬●	U ●●▬	9 ▬▬▬▬●
G ▬▬●	V ●●●▬	
H ●●●●	W ●▬▬	
I ●●	X ▬●●▬	
J ●▬▬▬	Y ▬●▬▬	
K ▬●▬	Z ▬▬●●	
L ●▬●●	0 ▬▬▬▬▬	
M ▬▬	1 ●▬▬▬▬	
N ▬●	2 ●●▬▬▬	
O ▬▬▬	3 ●●●▬▬	

1.

Braille

The Letters and Numbers of this International Alphabet

1. Braille
Braille is a tactile writing system used by people who are visually impaired. It is traditionally written with embossed paper. Braille users can read computer screens and other electronic supports thanks to refreshable braille displays. They can write braille with the original slate and stylus or type it on a braille writer, such as a portable braille notetaker or computer that prints with a braille embosser. Braille is named after its creator, Louis Braille, a Frenchman who lost his sight as a result of a childhood accident. In 1824, at the age of fifteen, he developed a code for the French alphabet as an improvement on night writing. He published his system, which subsequently included musical notation, in 1829.[1][2] The second revision, published in 1837, was the first small binary form of writing developed in the modern era. These characters have rectangular blocks called cells that have tiny bumps called raised dots. The number and arrangement of these dots distinguish one character from another. Since the various braille alphabets originated as transcription codes for printed writing, the mappings (sets of character designations) vary from language to language, and even within one; in English Braille there are three levels of encoding: Grade 1 – a letter-by-letter transcription used for basic literacy; Grade 2 – an addition of abbreviations and contractions; and Grade 3 – various non-standardized personal stenography.

Wikipedia, the free encyclopedia
16 December 2017

To the right:
2. Braillewriter

36

1.

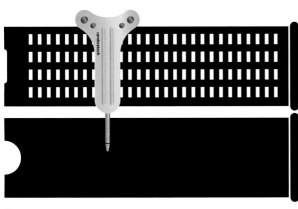

Louis Braille was born in France in 1809. Blind since childhood, he invented the alphabet that takes his name. It consists of a tactile system of writing that uses raised dots. Blinded in an accident, Braille was a musician and organist. While teaching music at the same institute where he had studied as a blind student, he raised the question of how to overcome his disability. In 1829 he created a system of writing based on raised dots, later perfected by the French physicist Léon Foucault.

1

37

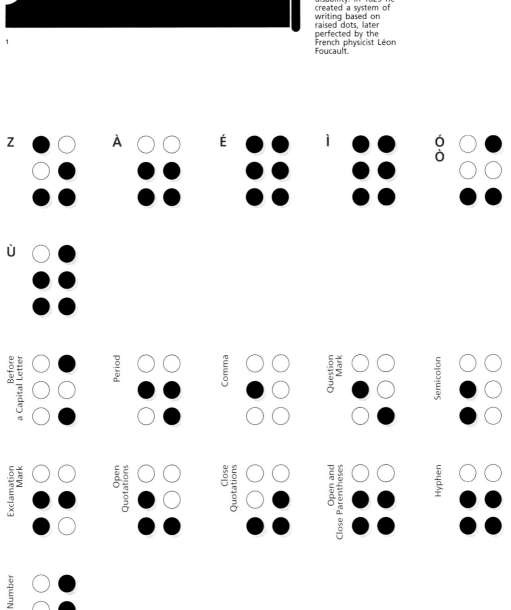

Two Flag Hand Signals

The Semaphore.
A System of Alphabetic
Signalling Based on the
Movement of a Pair of
Flags Held by a Signalman

The semaphore alphabet is a faster and less demanding form of signalling than Morse Code. It is transmitted almost exclusively using two flags. The disadvantages of the semaphore alphabet are a maximum distance, which must not exceed 200 or 300 meters, beyond which the signals are no longer visible, and the fact that the symbols are harder to learn than Morse Code. This is because the letters are formed by positioning the arms at different angles. Flags must not overlapped, otherwise the message could be misunderstood. The positions of the semaphore alphabet resemble those of the hands of a watch: the movements (a total of 8) move from right to left.

Unlike Morse Code, numbers are communicated like letters. This is done using the letters from A to I, with K representing 0. A conventional sign marks the beginning of the transmission of numbers (the letter J).

38

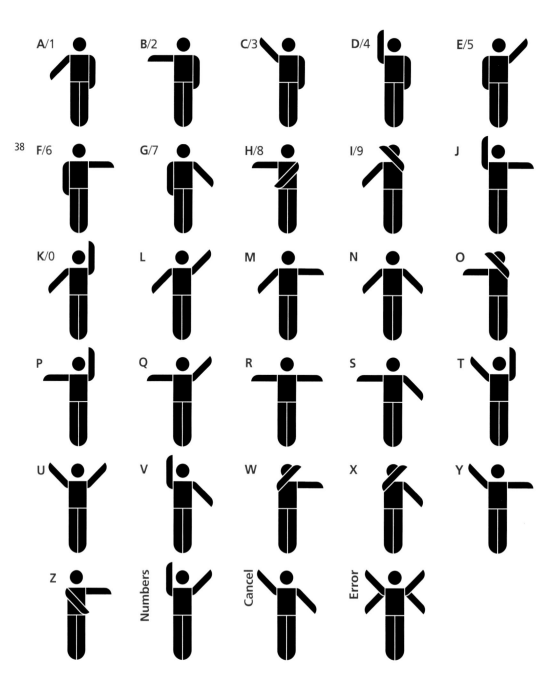

A/1 B/2 C/3 D/4 E/5

F/6 G/7 H/8 I/9 J

39

K/0 L M N O

P Q R S T

U V W X Y

Z Numbers Cancel Error

The International Code of Signals

Signal Flags

The International Code of Signals is composed of:
a) single letter signals for the most immediate communications (D Keep clear of me; I am manoeuvring with difficulty)
b) two letter signals for other communications (AC I am abandoning my vessel)
c) three letter signals for medical signals (it is possible to say: I have stomach pains; the doctor can respond: take an aspirin)
d) position signals (to indicate latitude and longitude in an analogous mann er to the old system). The signal flags of the International Code of

Signals consist of 26 alphabet flags, 10 numerical pennants, 3 repeater flags and answering pennant. To signal a ship, a group of flags is hoisted representing the name of the ship to whom the signal is addressed. If no name is hoisted, the signal is intended for all ships within signal range. The intended receiver of the signal hoists the answering pennant to half mast as soon as they observe the raising of the signal flags. They then raise the pennant to full mast as soon as they have understood the meaning of the group of flags at each hoisting.

The answering pennant is raised to half mast as soon as the transmitting ship lowers the raised flags, and it must be raised again when the next signal is understood, and so on, until the signal is terminated. To indicate the end of a signal, the transmitting vessel raises only the answering signal, after the final set of signal flags. The code provides all regulations for indicating that a signal has not been understood, to render a signal negative or cancel it and to repeat a letter using special repeater flags.

40

	Letter	Phonetic Name	Morse	Meaning
	A	Alfa	· —	I have a diver down. Keep well clear at slow speed
	B	Bravo	— · · ·	I am taking in or discharging or carrying dangerous goods. *Originally used by the Royal Navy specifically for military explosives*
	C	Charlie	— · — —	Affirmative
	D	Delta	— · ·	Keep clear of me. I am manoeuvring with difficulty
	E	Echo	·	I am altering my course to starboard
	F	Foxtrot	· · — ·	I am disabled. Communicate with me
	G	Golf	— — ·	I require a pilot. *By fishing vessels near fishing grounds:* I am hauling nets

	Letter	Phonetic Name	Morse	Meaning
	H	Hotel	. . . .	I have a pilot on board
	I	India	. .	I am altering my course to port
	J	Juliet	. — — —	I am on fire and have dangerous cargo on board: keep well clear of me. *Or*: I am leaking dangerous cargo
	K	Kilo	— . —	I wish to communicate with you
	L	Lima	. — . .	*In harbour*: The ship is quarantined. *At sea*: You should stop your vessel instantly
	M	Mike	— —	My vessel is stopped and making no way through the water
	N	November	— .	Negative
	O	Oscar	— — —	Man overboard
	P	Papa	. — — .	All persons should report on board as the vessel is about to proceed to sea
	Q	Quebec	— — . —	My vessel is healthy and I request free pratique
	R	Romeo	. — .	No ICS meaning as a single flag
	S	Sierra	. . .	I am operating astern propulsion

41

	Letter	Phonetic Name	Morse	Meaning
	T	Tango	—	Keep clear of me. I am engaged in pair trawling
	U	Uniform	· · —	You are running into danger
	V	Victor	· · · —	I require assistance
	W	Whiskey	· — —	I require medical assistance
	X	Xray	— · · —	Stop carrying out your intentions and watch for my signals
	Y	Yankee	— · — —	I am dragging my anchor
	Z	Zulu	— — · ·	I require a tug

42

Principal Two Letter Signals

AC	I am abandoning my vessel	QD	I am approaching
AN	I need a doctor	QT	I am travelling backwards
BR	I need a helicopter	QQ	I am asking for a sanitary inspection
CB	I need help	QU	Anchoring is forbidden
DV	I am drifting	QX	I am seeking permission to drop anchor
EF	The SOS/Mayday is Cancelled		
FA	I am asking for my position	RU	Keep your distance
GW	Man Overboard	SO	Stop immediately
JL	You risk running aground	UM	The port is closed to traffic
LO	I am not in the correct location	UP	I am seeking permission to enter port I have an emergency
NC	I am in trouble and asking for help		
PD	Your navigation lights are not visible	YU	I am communicating with your station
PP	Stay Back	ZL	Your signal was not understood

Number Flags

Morse Code and Repeater Flags

The special signage flag separates the main part of a message from the part of a number and indicates that the response to a message or a message just received was understood.
The International Code of Signals:
a) immediate one letter signals for immediate communications (D Keep clear of me; I am manoeuvring with difficulty)

b) two letter signals for other communications (AC I am abandoning my vessel)
c) three letter signals for communicating with medical teams (it is possible to say: I have stomach pains; the doctor may respond: take an aspirin)
d) position signals (for indicating latitude and longitude in a manner analogous to the old system).

The symbols are comprised of the 26 alphabet flags of, 10 numerical flags and 3 repeater flags.

	Number	Phonetic Name	Morse		Repeater Flags
	0	Nadazero	— — — — —		
	1	Unaone	• — — — —		
	2	Bissotwo	• • — — —		
	3	Terrathree	• • • — —		
	4	Kartefour	• • • • —		
	5	Pantafive	• • • • •		
	6	Soxisix	— • • • •		
	7	Setteseven	— — • • •		
	8	Oktoeight	— — — • •		
	9	Novenine	— — — — •		
		Intelligenza	— .		

43

3.
The Harmony of Ratios

The Golden Section

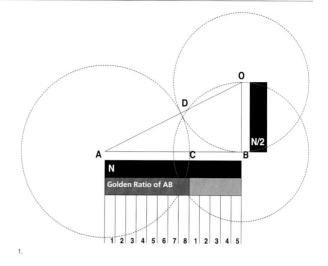

1.

44 "Harmony is expressed in numbers. Whether in pictorial or architectural space, or in the realm of music, many have tried to express harmony in the language of numbers. In Classical thought the beautiful was said to be lodged in a wonderful number called the golden number, represented by the Greek letter φ, $\varphi = (1 + \sqrt{5})/2$, one of two roots of the equation $x^2 - x - 1 = 0$, ordinarily used in its decimal value of 1.618.

The golden number turns up everywhere, from the architecture of the Egyptian pyramids and Greek temples to compositions by Raphael, Leonardo da Vinci, Poussin, Cézanne, and Le Corbusier."

When laying out a book, a page, anything printed, this ratio is of great importance. The elements of a page are, on the one hand, its surface, in other words, the format of the paper; on the other hand, the texts, illustrations and white spaces. Ensuring the harmony of a page requires rules and creativity, in a word, the application of the binomial emotion-rationale. A correct template is that with a structure of rhythmic measures that provides for the harmonious coexistence between variations and inequalities.

Every page, every drawing, every image we employ will have its own ratios. These ratios are established between white and black, between figure and ground, between two or more images of different sizes, yet everything must relate back to a proportion. Working in two dimensions, the ratio is configured between base and height.

The golden section is that part of a line that represents the proportional average between the entire segment and the remaining part. We will now look at its construction.

Given a line AB of length N (in our example N = 4 cm), from point B we draw a line BO, perpendicular to AB and with a length equal to half of N (N/2, in our case = 2 cm). Joining points O and A we obtain a diagonal of a scalene triangle. From point O we draw a circle with a radius of BO. It intersection with the diagonal AO marks point D. Line AD defines the radius of a second circle whose centre is point A, and whose intersection with line AB marks point C. AC provides us with the golden section. The existing ratio is expressed by the proportion: AB:AC=AC:CB.

In numerical terms, this ratio corresponds with the fixed value of 1.618 (in theory 1.618122977).

Line AC will be equal to 2.472187886 cm and CB to 1.527812114 cm.

To identify the golden ratio of our line AB, all we need to do is divide the length of this line by the fixed value. Indeed, dividing AB (4 cm) by the fixed value 1.618 (in theory 1.618122977), we obtain the value 2.4721 (in theory 2.472000001 cm). In even simpler terms, if we wish to construct a page using the rule of the golden section, we need only adopt the ratio of 5:8 (in theory 5:8.090614885).

We will now look at another example. If we need to construct a book, and if we assign our page a base of 21 cm, by multiplying 21x1.618, we obtain the value 33.978, the height of a page constructed according to the golden ratio, using the fixed value.

We can also adopt the ratio of 5:8. In this case: 5:8.09=21:x, 8.09x21÷5=33.978.

Notes
Golden rectangle: the sides of the rectangle are a line, and its golden section (ratio 1:1.618).
Golden section: part of a line that is the proportional average between the entire length of the line and the remaining part.
Jay Hambige studied a geometric-mathematical theory known as "dynamic symmetry" based on a rule that allows for the harmonious subdivision of a space constructed using the golden proportion into other spaces of decreasing size similar to the first. This foresees a ratio in which the long side of a rectangle is equal to 3/5 of its minor side.

Bibliography
▼Denis Guedj
Numbers: The Universal Language
Harry N. Abrams

1. 2. The golden ratio. The illustration to the right shows the golden ratio 5:8.
3. The *Iri News* designed using the golden ratio 5:8.

4. Photograph: Leonardo Sinisgalli, mathematician and poet, with the author; to the left, the poet Vito Riviello.

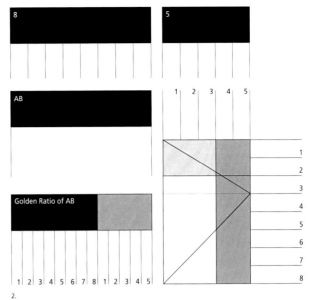

2.

45

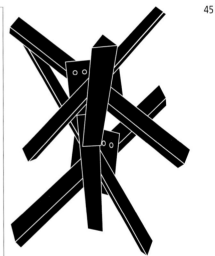

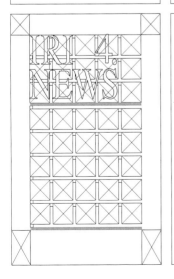

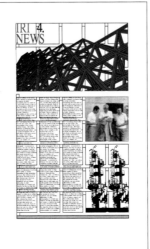

4.

3.

1. The golden rectangle can also be identified in the drawing of a square by dividing it into two parts and tracing the diagonal of one of the two parts; transferring the diagonal onto the vertical we obtain the height of the golden rectangle.

2. The double square provides the proportion for "Japanese tatami mats", which form the bases for asymmetrical design in Japan.
This system is used in Japanese architecture and measures roughly 91x183 cm.
It consists of a double square that divides the area of a floor into a certain proportion, with a vast variety of asymmetrical options in Japanese houses.

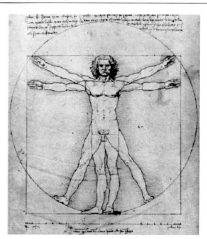

In *L'Uomo*, Leonardo da Vinci studied the proportions of the golden section based on the dictates of *De architectura* by Vitruvius, which obey the golden ratios. Leonardo established that human proportions are perfect when the navel divides the body in accordance with the golden section.

In *De Architectura* Vitruvius writes:"in the human body the central point is naturally the navel. For if a man be placed flat on his back, with his hands and feet extended, and a pair of compasses centred at his navel, the fingers and toes of his two hands and feet will touch the circumference of a circle described therefrom".

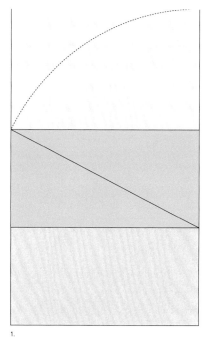

1.

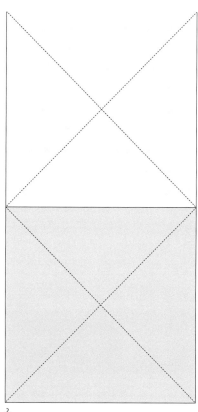

2.

Notes
Leonardo da Vinci sought to accompany human anatomy with an anatomy of machines and the Earth; this research can be considered the fil rouge of his scientific work.

The Harmony of Forms

The Secret of the Architects of the Past

1. 10. The ratios inside a decagon. The studies of Ernst Moessel, vast and proven by calculations, have demonstrated that the majority of classical buildings can be broken down into ratios based on the golden section.

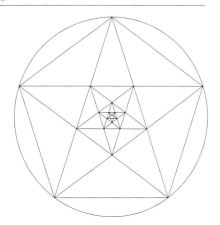

Based on the golden proportions, the smallest line m is related to the largest M as the latter to the sum of the two:
m:M=M:(m+M).

2. The line m of the regular decagon inscribed within a circle with a radius M is equal to its golden section.

3. The decagon produces a geometric series based on a golden ratio.

4. The pentagon or pentagram (the Seal of Solomon) has affinities with the golden section.

5. The Pythagorean triangle obtained in a rectangle inscribed in a circle has vast applications.

6. The construction of equilateral triangles inscribed in a circle whose intersection produces a hexagon.

7. The triangle of A. Drach. It was successfully applied by its creator to details and instruments.

8. 9. The dimensional ratios of the octagon according to the research of L.R. Spitzenpeil can be found in a series of ancient monuments. In these figures the starting point is the diagonal triangle whose highet is equal to the diagonal of the square constructed on half the base.

10. The isosceles triangle, in which the base and height correspond with the sides of a square, was successfully used by Knauh, the architect of Cologne Cathedral to determine dimensional ratios.

47

1.

2.

3.

4.

5.

6.

7.

8.

9.

10.

The Human Body as the Measure of All Things

From Menfi to Le Corbusier

1. The proportions of the human body according to A. Zeising who, during the past century, studied human proportions more than any other. He analysed the ratios between its parts and comparisons with the golden section.
The oldest canon on the ratios of the human body was found in a tomb near Menfi (approx. 3000 BC). Other canons to have survived include that of Ptolemy, the Greeks and Romans, and that of Polycletus, for many years considered a fixed regulation.

We are familiar with the applications of the golden section by Leon Battista Alberti, Leonardo da Vinci, Michelangelo and Durer.
The latter fixed the subdivisions using the following fractions:
1/2 h = the bust from the groin upward;
1/4 h = distance from the malleolus to the keen and from the chin to the navel;
1/6 h = length of the foot;
1/8 h = distance from the top of the head to the chin; etc., with subdivisions arriving at 1/400 of body height.

2. Le Corbusier developed the *Modulor* to be applied in architecture, though it was rapidly adopted in other fields of research, including graphic design, also by Le Corbusier himself in his book *Le Modulor*.
His 44 divisions of the space of a rectangle were part of a study designed to establish the distances, positions and options for laying out his book.

48

1.

Note
For more on the canons of measurement and the application of the golden section I suggest consulting the manual by Ernst Neufert, Architect's Data, *the source of a selection of images on this page.*

2.

3. Leonardo da Vinci's drawing establishes the proportions of the human body within a square and a circle. No one had ever amassed such an imposing collection of studies, observations and explanations in which it is possible to recognise the knowledge of an era.

4. An example of the application of the rule of the golden section to the structure defining the composition of the *Descent from the Cross* by Roger van der Weyden.

5. The module by Le Corbusier. Le Corbusier developed the *Modulor* in the wake of the historic tradition of Vitruvius, borrowed by Leonardo da Vinci for his Vitruvian Man, in the work of Leon Battista Alberti and other attempts to identify geometric and mathematical proportions related to the human body and to use this knowledge to improve both the aesthetics and functionality of architecture. The system is based on human measurements, the double unit, the Fibonacci sequence and the golden section. Le Corbusier described it as a "range of harmonious measurements to suit the human scale, universally applicable to architecture and to mechanical things". Le Corbusier published *Le Modulor* in 1948, followed by *Modulor 2* in 1955. He used the scale of the *Modulor* to design numerous buildings, including Notre-Dame du Haute and others at Chandigarh, in the construction of the first *Unité d'Habitation* in Marseille, where a version of the *Modulor* was cast into the concrete pier beside the entrance.

The graphic illustration of the *Modulor* depicts a stylised human figure with one arm raised above his head. The figure is accompanied by two vertical yardsticks: a red series based on the height of the solar plexus (108 cm in the original version, 1.13 m in the revised version), divided into segments based on Pi; a blue series based on the entire height of the figure, doubled with respect to the solar plexus (216 cm in the original, and 2.26 in the revised version) and divided into similar segments. A spiral, developed graphically between the red and blue series, appears to mimic the volume of the human figure.

49

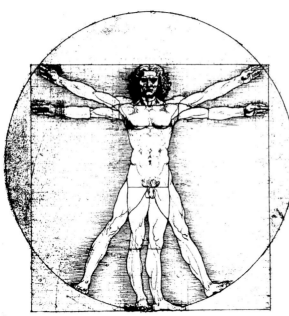

3.

5

4

4. 5. The paintings of Mondrian are filled with elementary and complex geometric forms.
In this painting
a) is a square;
b) is a double square;
c) is a rectangle based on the ratios of the golden section. The Dutch artist Piet Mondrian, a member of the abstract art movement, found the journal *De Stijl*.
He conceived form as plane, line and colour.

6. 7. In the painting by Josef Albers, an exponent of American Pop Art, entitled *Far off, 1958*, geometrically reconstructed here, it is possible to observe a construction based on the ratio 1/2/3.

8. 9. We must be careful not to confuse the golden section with the UNI formats.
While the golden section is based on the ratio 1:1.618, the UNI formats are based on the ratio 1: 2.
The square root of 2 of the rectangle is derived from the extension of the root along the arc of its diagonal.
This is the base of the standardised formats of the UNI regulations.

The examples clearly show the difference between the two proportions and the ratios of the two systems: in other words, a ratio of 5:8 (5:8.09) for the golden section (9); and 5:7 (5:7.06) for the UNI formats (8), where A0 (a rectangle with an area of 1 m2, where one side x=0.841 m and the other side y=1.189 m. This is the base of the A series that is obtained by halving the base format to create the formats A1, A2, A3, etc.) which is equal to 841x1189 mm.

50

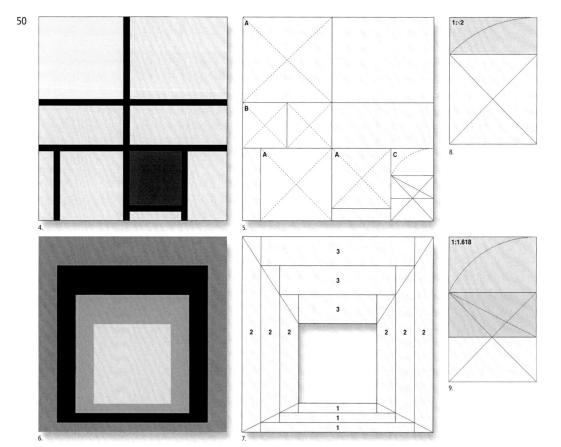

4.

5.

6.

7.

8.

9.

De Divina Proportione

The Treatise of Fra' Luca Pacioli on the Application of the Golden Section

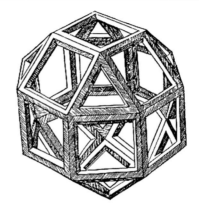

The stellated dodecahedron is a Kepler-Poinsot polyhedron: this means it is "regular" but not convex. Its 12 faces are stellated polygons that intersect at multiple points. Like all regular polyhedrons, all faces of the stellated dodecahedron are regular and identical, all of the corners of the same length and with the same type of cusp at each vertex.

1

1.
Rhombicuboctahedron
One of the 60
Illustrations
by Leonardo da Vinci
for the *De Divina Proportione*.

2. 3. Reconstruction of the stellated dodecahedron.

De Divina Proportione
Luca Pacioli had three copies of his treatise drawn up by diverse amanuensis; two copies have survived, one conserved at the Biblioteca Ambrosiana in Milan and the second at the Bibliothèque Publique et Universitaire in Geneva, Switzerland. Pacioli gifted the first copy with a dedication to Ludovico Sforza, (the one conserved in Switzerland), the second was given to Galeazzo Sanseverino (that in Milan), while the third, now lost, was instead offered to Pier Soderini, Gonfaloniere of Florence.
De divina proportione was printed in Venice in 1509 by Paganino Paganini (A. Paganius Paganinus characteribus elegantissimis accuratissime imprimebat).
Pacioli worked on the *Divina Proportione* from 1496 to the end of 1497; in the printed version, at the end of the first part, that most closely connected with the golden section, the friar dates the moment when he terminated his work:
Finis adi decembre in Milano nel nostro almo convento MCCCCXCVII (December 1497).

In his work, Pacioli returns to many previous works, including the well known *De prospectiva pingendi* by Piero della Francesca. For Pacioli, divine proportion was applied to all of the arts and it was necessary that all men of intelligence possessed a copy of the work that would offer them delight and new knowledge. The printed version of 1509 is composed of three clearly distinct parts. The first, of 71 chapters on the ratio of the golden section and its applications in the various arts; the second, of 20 chapters, is instead a treatise on architecture that refers to the theories of Vitruvius; the third part is in reality an Italian translation of the *Libellus de quinque corporibus regularibus* by Piero della Francesca on the five regular solids. This led Vasari to accuse the Tuscan friar of plagarism. The three parts conclude with two sections of illustrations, the first with the capital letters of the alphabet, designed using a ruler and compass by Luca Pacioli himself, with the second featuring the 60 drawings of Leonardo.
[translated from the Italian]
Wikipedia, L'enciclopedia libera, 20 September 2015

2

3

Notes
De Divina Proportione *is of particular importance, above all because it testifies, with its 60 drawings by da Vinci, to the mutual exchange of experiences between Luca Pacioli and da Vinci, during the prolific period of the century at the court of Ludovico Sforza, known as "Il Moro". Three manual copies were made of the* De Divina Proportione, *completed in 1498. The first is conserved at the Civic Library in Geneva, the second at the Biblioteca Ambrosiana in Milan while the third has been lost.*

Dodecahedron
*In geometry, a dodecahedron is any polyhedron with twelve flat faces. The most familiar dodecahedron is the regular dodecahedron, which is a Platonic solid. There are also three regular star dodecahedra, which are constructed as stellations of the convex form. All of these have icosahedral symmetry, order 120.
Wikipedia, the free encyclopedia, 16 December 2017*

1. The diagram below includes eight rectangles constructed using the golden section in a series positioned to create a logarithmic spiral. This construction inspired Le Corbusier's design of the plan for a famous museum.

The early twentieth century saw a great and renewed interest in the ratio defined by the golden section. In 1920 Jay Hambidge published a very interesting book on this issue entitled *Elements of Dynamic Symmetry*. The author makes ample reference to the precedents of Plato and Vitruvius.

Two millenia after Vitruvius wrote *De Architettura*, another architect, Le Corbusier, published *Le Modulor*, in which he theorised a clear system of proportions and visual identification applied to architecture.

How to design an alphabet. A quick note to be further explored.

1. The first letters to be studied and studied with dedicated attention are the "n" and the "o".
2. The "o" is the base for all round letters.
3. The letter "n" is the base for all letters with vertical lines.
4. The "r" is an "n" that has been cut;
5. the "e" is inscribed within the "o".
6. now study the letters "l", "e" and "a".
7. now study the letters "p" and "s".

8. The "n" is the base for the letters "hlmu".
9. The "o" is also the base for "cg".
The letters "ab" are used for the union of the straight part of the "n" with the cure of the "o". The letters "a=n" reflected with the curve of the "o". The letter "b" is created from the "a" reflected with an extension of the vertical line. And so on. Enjoy.

52

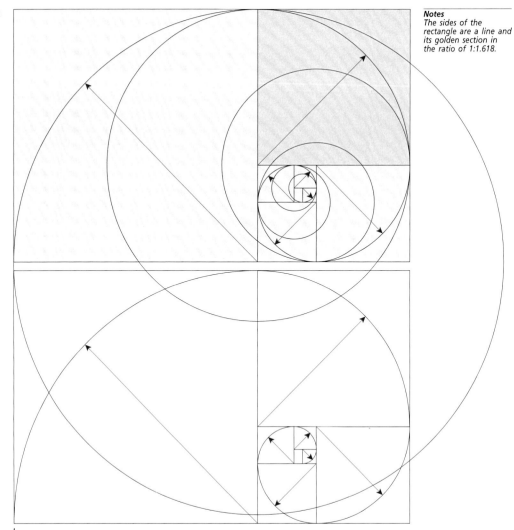

Notes
The sides of the rectangle are a line and its golden section in the ratio of 1:1.618.

2. 3. The letter G, one of the letters of the alphabet designed by Fra' Luca Pacioli. In the preface to his book, Pacioli expressly thanks Leonardo da Vinci and Piero della Francesca for their assistance in drawing the letters. This alphabet was used to print the *De Divina Proportione*, completed in 1497 and published twelve years later in Venice.

It also contains the principles for drawing the letters and a disquisition on how the divine proportion is the principle of the beauty of all things.
He reduced the ratio between the thickness of the vertical lines and their height to 1/9.
This alphabet, what is more beautiful, is one of the most important examples of the application of the golden section to the design of typographic letters.

2.

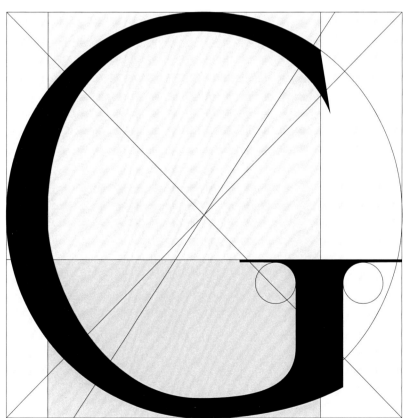

3.

53

Notes
*The ratio of the letters designed by Fra' Luca Pacioli is 1/9, a value measured between the thickness of the vertical lines and their height. Roman inscriptions from the Augustan period featured a ratio of 1/10.
Damiano de Moille, a calligrapher who lived between 1457 and 1500, established the ratio of 1/12.
What can be found in all studies of the forms of the characters is the intention to avoid at all costs an arbitrary design and to link the construction of the letters to mathematical proportions that guarantee a harmony of forms.*

The Harmony of Forms

A Recurring Symbol in Architectural Decoration

The flower of life is a geometric figure of multiple overlapping circles in a symmetrical hexagon. The resulting figure is similar to a flower. Each circle sits along the circumference of six circles with the same diameter.

It is common to architectural decoration the world over, and to the Italic area since the 8th c. BC. It spread from the Middle Ages, to the present day, with examples in: Assyria, at the Palace of Ashurbanipal; Egypt at the Temple of Abydos and near Mount Sinai; in Israel, Masada; China, The Forbidden City; Japan; India, Harimandir Sahib, Hampi, Ajanta; Bulgaria, in the city of Preslav and the ruins of Kabyle; Turkey; Spain; Austria; Morocco;

Lebanon; Peru and Mexico. In Italy it can be found in the art from the 7th century BC: the Etruscan urn at Civitella Paganico; the shield of the Etruscan warrior Aule Feluske at Vetulonia, in the halo of San Romualdo, the Hermitage of Camaldoli in the Parco Nazionale delle Foreste Casentinesi, the ceiling of the Hypogeal Grotto at Piagge; the funereal monuments of the Pre-Roman necropoli in the province of Foggia, in Medieval decorations across the centre of Carpino, in the fourteenth century church of St. Domenic at Lucera, the architraves of buildings in the historic centre of Forio, in the mosaic floors of a *domus romana* at San Benedetto dei Marsi, in the abbey of San

Clemente at Casauria, on the facade of the church of San Tommaso at Varano, on the ambon of the church of Saints Cesidio and Rufino at Trasacco, on the external archlet of the basilica of San Pelino at Corfinio, on a church facade at Galdo degli Alburni, in the basilica of San Clemente a Roma, in the crypt of the Church of San Fermo Minore at Verona, in diverse capitals of the Pieve of Saints Cornelio and Cipriano at Codiponte in Lunigiana, in the crypt of the Cathedral of Lodi, the Cathedral of St Peter of Sorres at Borutta, in the Church of the Consolation of Cleto.

54

In symbology each of the various parts of this figure correspond with a day of Creation.

1

2

1.
The Flower of Life at Erbanno.
Erbanno is a hamlet of Darfo Boario Terme, at the feet of Monte Altissimo.
2.
Faggiano Museum.
The "Flower of Life" on the upper floor of the building, realised in a splendid window by Maria Colamonaco di Artiffany
from Altamura.

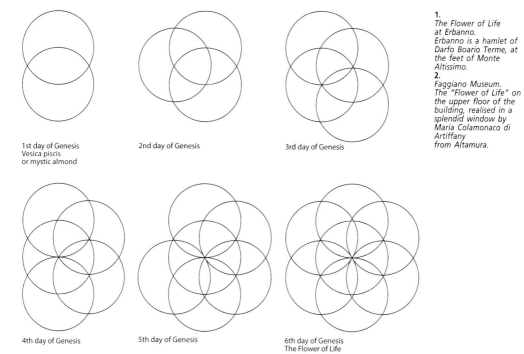

1st day of Genesis
Vesica piscis
or mystic almond

2nd day of Genesis

3rd day of Genesis

4th day of Genesis

5th day of Genesis

6th day of Genesis
The Flower of Life

Even Ambiguity is Born of Geometry

The Drawings of Escher

Escher created his images by combining reversible figures in the same composition on flat surfaces and using the technique of triangular, square and hexagonal mosaics.
The regular subdivisions of some of his studies are obtained simply by dividing the surfaces progressively by half to the limits of their legibility.

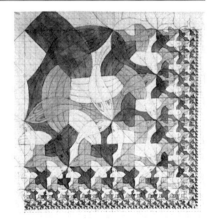

2.

56

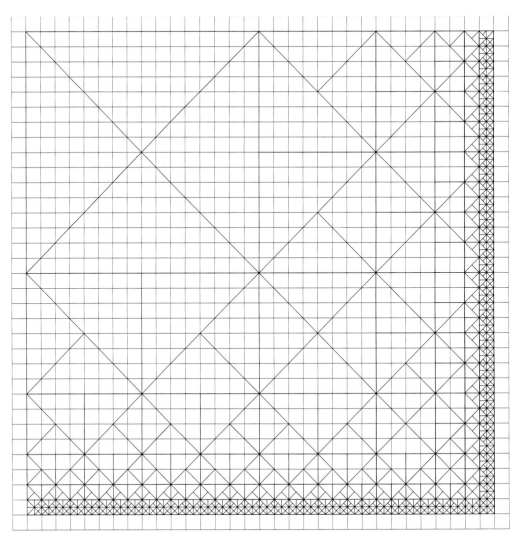

1.

Escher's structure for the xylography *The Limit of the Square*. The study begins with an isosceles triangle ABC. Two other isosceles triangles are constructed along BC, to create DBE and DCE. Repeating these figures produces triangles 3, 4, 5, etc. The square EFCD, the largest of the structure, is repeated with a ratio of 1/2, 1/4, 1/8, 1/16, 1/64 and so on.
This is the space in which Escher created his composition.

To the right are the five regular solids recognised by Greek mathematicians. Three are defined by equilateral triangles: the tetrahedron (four regular faces); the octahedron (eight regular faces); the icosahedron (twenty regular faces); the cube, made of four squares (six regular faces); the dodecahedron, made of regular pentameters (twelve regular faces). Escher sculpted some of these regular solids in wood and other materials.

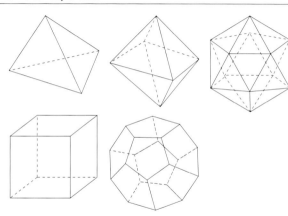

Bibliography
Bruno Ernst
The Magic Mirror of
M.C. Escher
Ballantine Books, New York, 1976.

57

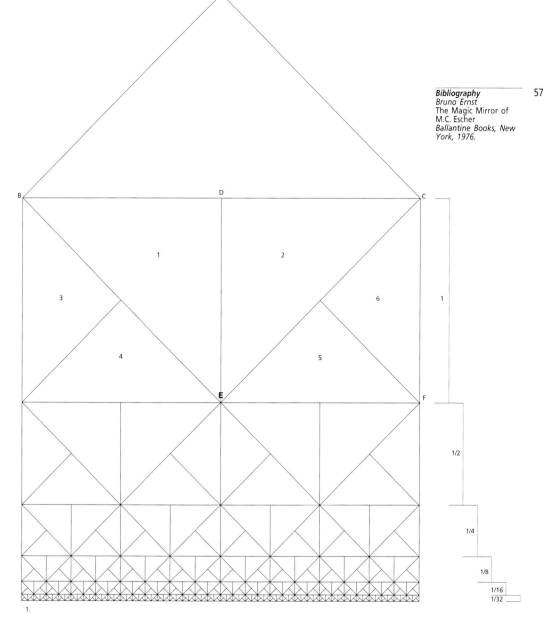

1.

4. Typesetting

From Handwriting to Composed Text

Digital composition makes it possible to modify type size and leading, up to decimal point values.

We can narrow or expand the space between letters. This allows us to "fix" pages whose content must enter into pre-established spaces without reducing or adding text.

These systems are very helpful for laying out a page; however, we must be careful not to exaggerate: we must not ruin the harmony of the typeface. A very simple system for calculating the number of characters, in a given typeface and point size, occupied by a text composed with other criteria involves the search for the coefficient (or fixed number) that exist

between the length of a line of the original text and the measure of the alignment selected.

The coefficient is calculated by dividing the number of characters of an original row by the number of characters of a (justified) row of the selected typeface. For example: original = 64 characters; selected justified = 41 characters in Helvetica 14. The equation 64:41=1.56 signifies that for each row of the original text we obtain a composition of 1.56 rows.

For example: 33 rows x 1.56 = 51.48 rows. Some typeface catalogues contain the coefficients - increased or decreased - relative to each typeface and in relation to point size.

However, these coefficients can also be found automatically for fonts we generally use. But how?

The coefficient is based on the calculation of how many characters enter into the space of 1 millimetre.

The table below shows how 14 point Helvetica Light occupies 41 characters in the space of 100 millimeters. It follows that 41:100=0.41.

This is the number of characters in 1 millimetre, and the fixed number for this typeface and size, which is independent of the alignment we may choose to adopt in our project.

58 Today's electronic devices allow graphic artists to digitally compose most of the texts they are asked to lay out. Texts are generally provided as typed pages or on a disk.

In any case, it is necessary to make a few rapid calculations to understand the space required by the text when it has been laid out using a selected typeface and point size, in order to establish the thickness of a book and, as a consequence, develop a cost estimate based on a realistic number of pages.

To calculate the space required we count the number of characters of the typed version: a character is a letter, a comma, as well as the space between words.

In general, a typed document is composed of 30 rows of 60 characters per row, for a total of approximately 1,800 characters. Multiplying this number of characters by the number of pages, let's say 50, gives us 1,800x50=90,000 characters.

Now, having chosen the typeface, point size and alignment we wish to apply to our layout, we can compose a test page and count the number of characters, for example 2,400. Now all we need to do is divide the total characters of the original document (90,000) by the total characters of the test page (2,400), to obtain the number of pages of the book that, in this specific case, is approximately 37 (90,000÷2,400=37.5).

Normally, a typed document is not aligned and may contain very irregular rows: in this case it is best to establish an average number of characters per row.

For long texts, it is best to seek professional assistance; in this case it is worthwhile reviewing the text to ensure it contains all indications relative not only to its alignment, but also the type size, tabs, titles, captions, regular and italic, bold and upper case characters.

Another operation to be carried out involves a check of best practices in spelling and editing.

This responsibility may be assumed by the author of the text or, for a publisher, by an editing expert. It is still best to check yourself: everything indicated before a text is typed up will be in its correct place in the end.

When texts are provided on a disk, it is a good idea to decide beforehand how they will be provided: whether it can be transcoded using your software, whether your software recognises it and whether it is compatible with the operating system and language of your computer. In some cases it is sufficient that the original is "saved" in a certain way so that it can be transcoded.

Forget asking for tables and formulas: you will lose more time trying to fix them than to lay them out from scratch.

When you transfer your file - not only composed but also with the pages meticulously laid out - it is best to include on the same disk for the printer a copy of the typeface you have selected: the advance of computers has multiplied the number of typefaces, their names, styles and families.

Make sure that the spacing code used by your computer and its setting for the lay out are the same as those used by the service that will produce the print files: this will avoid the risk of pages that are cut off or unexpected page breaks.

Note
Draft prints for a client should provide sufficient margins around the text: this allows for clear indications of corrections to be made. Don't use a pencil or mark corrections directly in the text. Never cancel the wrong word: if it is to be substituted with another word, the graphic artist has to be able to find it to change it.

Often it is necessary to correlate the measurements of a typed document with its publishing layout or with the dimensions of the metric decimal system or the system of inches.
1 inch (")
=6 rows of Pica
=72 pica points
1 inch
=25.4 mm
1 pica row
=1/6"
=4.23 mm
1 row of Cicero
=4.5127 mm
1 Didot point
=0.376065 mm
1 Pica point
=1/72"=0.3527 mm

Fonts	Helv regular	Helv bold	Times Roman	Times bold	Garamond light	Garamond bold	Lubalin book	Optima light
24	0.24	0.22	0.25	0.24	0.24	0.22	0.22	0.24
20	0.28	0.26	0.30	0.28	0.28	0.26	0.25	0.28
18	0.31	0.29	0.33	0.31	0.32	0.28	0.27	0.31
16	0.36	0.32	0.38	0.36	0.37	0.32	0.32	0.37
14	0.41	0.38	0.43	0.41	0.41	0.38	0.37	0.40
13	0.44	0.40	0.47	0.44	0.45	0.40	0.40	0.43
12	0.48	0.43	0.50	0.48	0.49	0.43	0.43	0.47
11	0.52	0.49	0.54	0.52	0.52	0.47	0.47	0.52
10	0.57	0.52	0.60	0.57	0.57	0.51	0.51	0.57
9	0.64	0.67	0.67	0.64	0.65	0.57	0.56	0.64
8	0.72	0.66	0.76	0.71	0.72	0.65	0.64	0.72
7	0.91	0.75	0.86	0.81	0.81	0.74	0.73	0.81
6	0.96	0.86	1,00	0.95	0.95	0.86	0.84	0.95
5	1.15	1,04	1.21	1.15	1.15	1,03	1.02	1.15
4	1.44	1.27	1.51	1.43	1.44	1.29	1.25	1.44

Using the method illustrated in the table below it is possible to calculate the coefficient of any character, with the certainty that the space required is exact, because it is derived from characters you are accustomed to using. The table to the left contains a number of codes developed for programmes running on Macintosh computers.

| mm | 10 | 20 | 30 | 40 | 50 | 60 | 70 | 80 | 90 | 100 |

mm

Abcdefghijklmnopqrstuvxywz — Size 24 — Coefficient 0.24

AbcdefghijklmnopqrstuvxywzAbcde — Size 20 — Coefficient 0.28

AbcdefghijklmnopqrstuvxywzAbcdefgh — Size 18 — Coefficient 0.31

AbcdefghijklmnopqrstuvxywzAbcdefghijklm — Size 16 — Coefficient 0.36

AbcdefghijklmnopqrstuvxywzAbcdefghijklmnopqrs — Size 14 — Coefficient 0.41

AbcdefghijklmnopqrstuvxywzAbcdefghijklmnopqrstuv — Size 13 — Coefficient 0.44

AbcdefghijklmnopqrstuvxywzAbcdefghijklmnopqrstuvxywz — Size 12 — Coefficient 0.48

AbcdefghijklmnopqrstuvxywzAbcdefghijklmnopqrstuvxywzAbcd — Size 11 — Coefficient 0.62

AbcdefghijklmnopqrstuvxywzAbcdefghijklmnopqrstuvxywzAbcdefghijk — Size 10 — Coefficient 0.67

AbcdefghijklmnopqrstuvxywzAbcdefghijklmnopqrstuvxywzAbcdefghijklmnopq — Size 9 — Coefficient 0.64

AbcdefghijklmnopqrstuvxywzAbcdefghijklmnopqrstuvxywzAbcdefghijklmnopqrstuvxywz — Size 8 — Coefficient 0.72

AbcdefghijklmnopqrstuvxywzAbcdefghijklmnopqrstuvxywzAbcdefghijklmnopqrstuvxywzAbcdefghijk — Size 7 — Coefficient 0.91

AbcdefghijklmnopqrstuvxywzAbcdefghijklmnopqrstuvxywzAbcdefghijklmnopqrstuvxywzAbcdefghijklmnopqrstuvxyw — Size 6 — Coefficient 0.96

AbcdefghijklmnopqrstuvxywzAbcdefghijklmnopqrstuvxywzAbcdefghijklmnopqrstuvxywzAbcdefghijklmnopqrstuvxywzAbcdefghijklmnopqrstu — Size 5 — Coefficient 1.15

AbcdefghijklmnopqrstuvxywzAbcdefghijklmnopqrstuvxywzAbcdefghijklmnopqrstuvxywzAbcdefghijklmnopqrstuvxywzAbcdefghijklmnopqrstuvxywzAbcdefghijklmnopqrstuvxyw — Size 4 — Coefficient 1.44

The Frequency
of Letters

Calculating Percentages

The greater or lesser frequency of some letters with respect to others may determine the calculation of the space required by a text.
In the text to the left of the page, used as an example for our study, we counted the total number of characters (1,335), the number of capital letters (13), the number of each letter of the alphabet and their frequency.
The number of total characters was used to calculate the percentage of their frequency that, from a total number of characters equal to 100% for the entire text, ranges from 0.3745% for the letter "q".

So, our count of the quantity of letters that fits into the space of 1 mm must consider that a line of text includes various letters based on the percentage of their frequency.

The table beside these values, very different and expressed as numbers, no longer refers to the alphabet, but to our specific text.

60   The city of Bath, situated in the south-east of England, is a "unique" and unrepeatable example of urban planning, where the fortune of being located in an enchanting corner of Britain, coupled with the presence of renowned thermal waters, was happily combined with the entrepreneurial spirit of acute architects and audacious builders, who, thanks to a series of fortunate circumstances, spent more than a century creating a true gallery of masterpieces from scratch.

Unfortunately, this illustrious creation did not survive the devastation of the War, and the successive period of neglect, and the twentieth century, and more precisely recent decades, the city and its neighbourhoods that had so strongly influenced Dickens' descriptions of English society in his literary masterpieces, were decimated by a policy of construction marked by bad taste and scarce culture; and their conservation (the only contemporary example) became an issue combined with the conservation of the natural environment.

The history of Bath is that of an ancient Roman thermal bath city which remained such until sixteenth century, with the typical urban structure of a medieval city, known until this time solely for this characteristic, and confused among the many English cities producing wool,.

But it is also the story of John [...]

Frequency		%
characters =	1335	100
capitals =	13	0.9629
e =	124	9.2883
i =	123	9.2134
a =	121	9.0636
t =	85	6.3670
o =	77	5.7677
l =	73	5.4681
n =	73	5.4681
r =	68	5.0936
c =	60	4.4943
s =	57	4.2696
u =	49	3.6704
d =	43	3.2209
p =	17	1.2734
h =	12	0.8988
b =	10	0.7490
f =	8	0.5992
q =	5	0.3745
total =	1018	76.2546
spaces =	317	23.7453
Total characters	1335	100

Workbook
Using any original text, calculate the number of characters and translate it into the typeface and point size and alignment of your project. Calculate the characters, rows of text and pages.

mm	10	20	30	40	50	60	70	80	90	100

mm

Abcdefghijklmnopqrstuvxy — Size 24 — Coefficient 0.22

Abcdefghijklmnopqrstuvxywz Ab — Size 20 — Coefficient 0.26

Abcdefghijklmnopqrstuvxywz Abcde — Size 18 — Coefficient 0.29

Abcdefghijklmnopqrstuvxywz Abcdefghi — Size 16 — Coefficient 0.32

Abcdefghijklmnopqrstuvxywz Abcdefghijklmn — Size 14 — Coefficient 0.38

Abcdefghijklmnopqrstuvxywz Abcdefghijklmnopq — Size 13 — Coefficient 0.40

Abcdefghijklmnopqrstuvxywz Abcdefghijklmnopqrstu — Size 12 — Coefficient 0.43

61

mm	10	20	30	40	50	60	70	80	90	100

mm

The city of Bath, situated in — Size 24 — Coefficient 0.285

The city of Bath, situated in the s — Size 20 — Coefficient 0.345

The city of Bath, situated in the sou — Size 18 — Coefficient 0.38

The city of Bath, situated in the south-ea — Size 16 — Coefficient 0.415

The city of Bath, situated in the south-east of I — Size 14 — Coefficient 0.49

The city of Bath, situated in the south-east of Eng — Size 13 — Coefficient 0.525

The city of Bath, situated in the south-east of England, — Size 12 — Coefficient 0.585

The city of Bath, situated in the south-east of England, is a " — Size 11 — Coefficient 0.630

The city of Bath, situated in the south-east of England, is a "uniqu — Size 10 — Coefficient 0.700

The city of Bath, situated in the south-east of England, is a "unique" and — Size 9 — Coefficient 0.765

The city of Bath, situated in the south-east of England, is a "unique" and unrepeat — Size 8 — Coefficient 0.860

The city of Bath, situated in the south-east of England, is a "unique" and unrepeatable examp — Size 7 — Coefficient 0.975

The city of Bath, situated in the south-east of England, is a "unique" and unrepeatable example of ur the fortu — Size 6 — Coefficient 1.165

The city of Bath, situated in the south-east of England, is a "unique" and unrepeatable example of urban planning, where the fortun — Size 5 — Coefficient 1.395

The city of Bath, situated in the south-east of England, is a "unique" and unrepeatable example of urban planning, where the fortune of being located in an enchant — Size 4 — Coefficient 1.715

A Typewritten Document

Dedicated Codes

1. It is more and more common for texts to be shared on a disk (now rapidly disappearing), already composed and presumably, given that they were typed up by an editor, corrected and error-free, with all of the italics and bold texts in the right place. However, beware of transcoding.
Every system has its own language that must be compatible with that used by your personal computer.

2. In proportional typing the width of each character is based on multiples of an elementary unit and corresponds to 0.705 mm (1/36"). Wide characters measure 4 elementary units, or 2.82 mm (1/9"); intermediates 3 units, or 2.117 mm (1/12"); narrow 2 units, 1.41 mm (1/18").

62 Typing is based on systems of measurement that do not exactly correspond with typography (Didot and Pica), or with the metric decimal system, but generally with measurements in inches.
The dimensions and sizes offered by typewriters vary from unit to unit.
The measurements, based on the space occupied by a glyph (its point size), may be in:
Microns, equal to 1.337 mm (1/19 inch, or 19 characters per inch);
Elite, equal to 2.117 mm (1/12 inch, or 12 characters per inch);
Pica (not to be confused with the homonymous typographic system), equal to 2.54 mm (1/10 inch, or 10 characters per inch);
Giant, equal to 5.08 mm (1/5 inch, or 5 characters per inch).
The most common pass is Pica, equal to 1/10 inch, or 2.54 mm; the most common leading is 5 mm, or 1/6 inch, equivalent to 4.23 mm; the possible combinations between points and leading are:
a) point=1/10 inch, leading 5 mm;
b) point=1/10 inch, leading 4.23 mm.

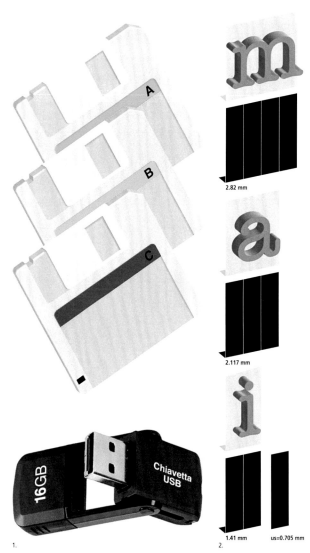

A

B

C

16GB

Chiavetta USB

2.82 mm

2.117 mm

1.41 mm   us=0.705 mm

1.

2.

The table below contains the scale of the principal typefaces used by typewriters. The sub-multiples of an inch indicate the quantity of characters in an inch.

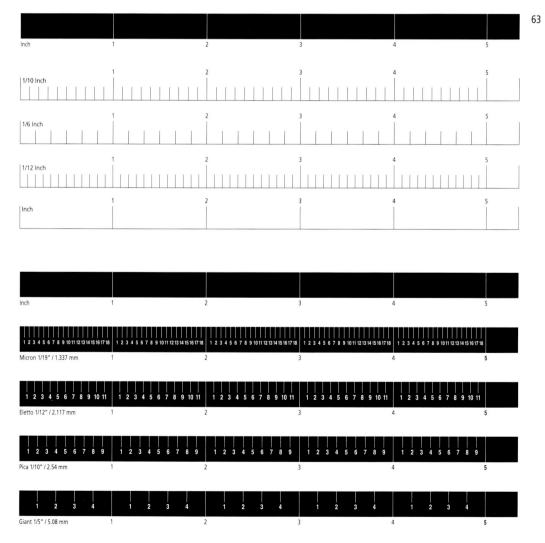

Inch

1/10 Inch

1/6 Inch

1/12 Inch

Inch

Inch

Micron 1/19" / 1.337 mm

Eletto 1/12" / 2.117 mm

Pica 1/10" / 2.54 mm

Giant 1/5" / 5.08 mm

A Typewritten Document

The Editor's Template

1. 2. When texts are prepared on a typewriter, it is necessary to be familiar with the type of machine the editor will use, and thus the system and point adopted.
It is opportune, above all for reviews or journals, with rhythmic cadence, to lay out an A4 page with a template whose margin shows the number of horizontal characters and above all the vertical rows.

In the example on these pages, the 21x29.7 mm format features a 3 cm margin at the binding edge and 2 cm at the outer edge, top and bottom, with a resulting 16x25.4 template.
Imagining that the typewriter has a point of 1/10 inch and a leading of 1/6 inch, we have 63 characters for row, and a total of 60 rows, or 3,780 characters. If the text is to be typed up with a double leading, the multiplication is 63 characters by 30 rows, or a total of 1,890 characters.

3. The facing page features a reproduction of a template that summarises the indications, in centimetres and inches, necessary to lay out the page an editor will use for his texts.
This table and its data is intended as an example for the reconstruction of the template by students; however, it is obvious that the final template will be much simpler and feature only the indication of the rows in the left margin, while the header can be personalised with the name of the review, and a space for the page number, date, etc.

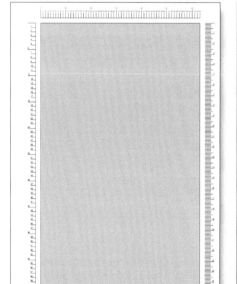

1 2 3 4 5 6 7 8 9 10 11 12 13 14 15 16 17 18 19 20 21

1.

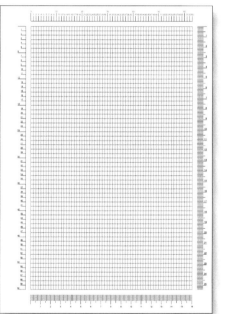

1 2 3 4 5 6 7 8 9 10 11 12 13 14 15 16 17 18 19 20 21

2.

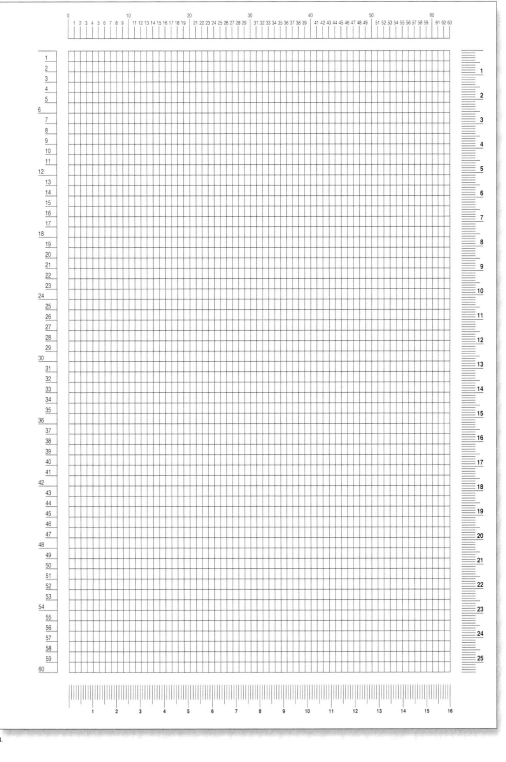

65

1. 6. A journal article is almost always assigned a largely organised space.
The amount of space is assigned by the page editor in the draft and the "flatplan".
The flatplan is a reduced reproduction of all pages of the journal. It serves to develop the first hypothesis of the layout based on a complete visual arrangement of the pages. The flatplan indicates the space allocated to an article by the editor.

7. The editor of a journal generally writes texts based on a precise number of characters, and a predetermined length.
For this reason, the editor uses pages prepared and printed by the graphic artist, featuring the template and space allocated for each text, and, in the margins, the number of rows.
This number will coincide with the type of typewriter used by the journal's editing team.

Writing on this sheet, the editor maintains a constant understanding of the length of the "piece" he is writing.
On the other hand, the graphic artist who lays out the journal can calculate the space required for a text long before it is completed and thus organise the draft page layout.
In the examples on these pages we imagined a typewriter that uses the pica system, with a 1/10 inch point and a leading of 1/6 inch.

The typed document generally adopts a double leading, thus equal to 1/3 inch.
This system, now largely surpassed by the advent of the computer, which can automatically calculate the number of characters, is indispensable to current practice, above all for articles whose length may vary based on the need to ensure content.

66

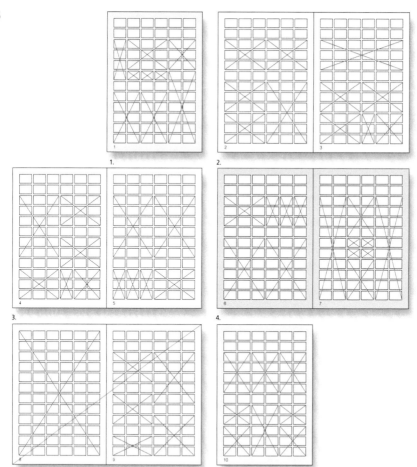

1.

2.

3.

4.

5.

6.

Journal	Date	Article Title	Page n.

1	
2	
3	
4	
5	
6	
7	
8	
9	
10	
11	
12	
13	
14	
15	
16	
17	
18	
19	
20	
21	
22	
23	
24	
25	
26	
27	
28	
29	
30	

67

7.

Draft Corrections

Conventional Copy Editing Marks and Correction Symbols

Drafts are corrected using conventional signs that refer to letters, to words, to incorrect phrases. They are placed in the margins, together with the correction to be made.
The signs made to a letter or an incorrect word are known as "copy editing marks". They indicate the point where a correction is to be made and are placed beside the corresponding row.

"Correction symbols" can be indicated beside the marks or exist on their own, when their meaning is evident. In Italy these largely universal symbols were codified by the UNI 5041 regulation.

68

Mark	Meaning
⅄	Insert one or more letters or entire words
⅄③	Inserted attached text (i.e. 3)
◠	Join and eliminate space
✕	Eliminate one or more letters or words
⊗	Eliminate and join (in the body of a word)
⚹	Add a space
‖‖	Space a word
⋀⋀⋀	Expand the space between words
⊢⊣	Add equal space between two words
⊥⊤	Add equal space between two lines of text, two paragraphs or two periods
○@	Wrong letter or other character (letter inside the circle)
(|)	Tighten space between letters, words, periods
)|(	Widen space between letters, words, periods
⊃⊂	Tighten lines of text
⊃⊂	Distance lines of text
⁓	Raise and align
⁓	Lower and align
=	Align horizontally
‖	Align vertically
ϑ	Start new paragraph and straighten
⌇	Eliminate a tab
⌇	Add a tab

Note
Even the ancients needed to correct their texts.
To cancel writing on a papyrus they used a sponge, while parchment was scraped with a razor.
Cancellations were indicated on manuscripts above or below the letters to be erased (*litterae expunctae*), hence the term "expunge", also used today in copy editing.

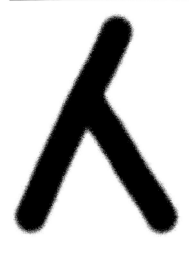

		Character	Sign	Annotation	
					69
[ ]	Centre horizontally	Lowercase		(lc)	
	Centre vertically	Uppercase	≡≡≡	(U)	
	Reset text to push out a line	Lowercase with first letter in uppercase		(U/lc)	
	Reset text to pull in a line				
	Place after				
	Start a new line	Small caps	≡≡	(sc)	
	Start a new paragraph	Small caps with first letter in uppercase	≡≡	(U/sc)	
	Join to previous row				
	Invert letters or words in a row of text	Italics	——	(it)	
	More one or more rows of text	Regular		(reg)	
	Superscript	Light		(li)	
	Subscript	Bold		(bo)	
(?)	Check	Heavy	~~~	(H)	
(live)	Keep original text, despite corrections	Extra bold		(Ebo)	
		Uppercase italics	≡≡≡		
		Uppercase bold italics	≡≡≡		

Draft Corrections

A Text to be Corrected

In general, the first version of a text is an "off-press proof", in other words without page layout parameters. This text is used to make the first corrections, while the second corrections, known as "press proof" are made directly on the layout.

1. In the fragment of text on this page the corrections to be made have been indicated in the margins using conventional marks.

2. In the text on the facing page, the corrections have been made. It is possible to note how an attentive editor has added a number of words (in red) to correct two paragraph interruptions that were too short.

70

The city of Bath, situated in the south-east of England, is a "unique" and unrepeatable example of urban planning, where the fortune of being located in an enchanting corner of Britain, coupled with the presence of renowned thermal waters, was happily combined with the entrepreneurial spirit of acute architects and audacious builders, who, thanks to a series of fortunate circumstances, spent more than a century creating a true gallery of masterpieces from scratch. Unfortunately, this illustrious creation did not survive the devastation of the War, and the successive period of neglect, and the twentieth century, and more precisely recent decades, the city and its neighbourhoods that had so strongly influenced Dickens' descriptions of English society in his literary masterpieces, were decimated by a policy of construction marked by bad taste and scarce culture; and their conservation (the only contemporary example) became an issue combined with the conservation of the natural environment.

The history of Bath is that of an ancient Roman thermal bath city which remained such until sixteenth century, with the typical urban structure of a medieval city, known until this time solely for this characteristic, and confused among the many English cities producing wool.

But it is also the story of John Wood, the architect brilliant who imagined the city's transformation during the reign of George I and began its implementation; also of John Wood the second, who gave the city its best examples of architecture, which led in turn to the most characteristic neighbourhoods of England's cities, from Exeter to Edinburgh, to London itself. Finally, to generations of architects who successively continued its construction, in some cases making structural modifications to the rigorous projects by the first John Wood.

Note
Typing errors made by the typist are generally referred to as "misprints", while changes inside a text made by the copy editor or the author are referred to as "author's corrections". When composing a page, the copy editor and author must remember to compensate eventual additional or suppressed words in order to limit the need to reset lengthy sections of text. It is a good idea for those making edits to use a marker or ballpoint pen, and never a pencil. Corrections are best made in a different colour than the text to be corrected. Avoid inserting corrections between rows of text. For more corrections to the same row, it is necessary to vary the copy editing marks. Always clearly indicate the character to be used.

1.

Draft Corrections

The Correct Text

3. The same text was corrected here using the method shown in the figure that, while not using conventional and canonical copy editing marks is, in my opinion, clear and immediate.
I recommend, above all with this method, using a red ballpoint pen that covers the original text, without making it illegible.

The city of Bath, situated in the south-east of England, is a "unique" and unrepeatable example of urban planning, where the fortune of being located in an enchanting corner of Britain, coupled with the presence of renowned thermal waters, was happily combined with the entrepreneurial spirit of acute architects and audacious builders, who, thanks to a series of fortunate circumstances, spent more than a century creating a true gallery of masterpieces from scratch.

Unfortunately, this illustrious creation did not survive the devastation of the War, and the successive period of neglect, and the twentieth century, and more precisely recent decades, the city and its neighbourhoods that had so strongly influenced Dickens' descriptions of English society in his literary masterpieces, were decimated by a policy of construction marked by bad taste and scarce culture; and their conservation (the only contemporary example) became an issue combined with the conservation of the natural environment.

The history of Bath is that of an ancient Roman thermal bath city which remained such until sixteenth century, with the typical urban structure of a medieval city, known until this time solely for this characteristic, and confused among the many English cities producing wool.

But it is also the story of John Wood, the brilliant architect who imagined the city's transformation during the reign of George I and began its implementation; also of John Wood the second, who gave the city its best examples of architecture, which led in turn to the most characteristic neighbourhoods of England's cities, from Exeter to Edinburgh, to London itself. Finally, to generations of architects who successively continued its construction, in some cases making structural modifications to the rigorous projects by the first John Wood.

3.

2.

5.
The Rules of Editing

The Rules of Grammar Every Graphic Artist Should Know

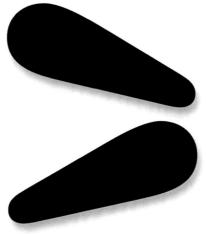

Left:
a grave and an acute
accent in the
Garamond typeface.

72 The word *editing* is derived from the verb *to edit*, "to curate and manage the printing and publication of a text". Editing thus summarises all of the work required to "prepare and organise a text". Large publishers and important journals use a small manual containing the rules to be adopted when editing a text. It contains regulations for the appropriate use of italics, when to begin words with a capital letter, punctuation, foreign expressions, abbreviations, the use of upper and lower case, italics and small caps, accents, acronyms, how to present a dialogue, how to deal with asides, what typeface to use for titles; in short, all of the regulations to be adopted when laying out and reviewing a text, before it goes to print.
Some of these rules contemplate different solutions, for example the adoption of Italian *caporali* (or *sergenti)* in lieu of English quotation marks.
Typesetting was once the responsibility of the typesetter, who worked by hand; then came the linotypist who set the letters he was given into linotype; more recently it is the phototypesetter. Today, thanks to the computer, a graphic designer sets most of the texts before laying them out. Hence, an attentive graphic designer should be familiar with the rules of typographic tradition.
This means being familiar with the signs indicating how a text is to be set: italics for everything underlined in the original with one line; small caps for everything that is underlined twice; upper case for everything that is underlined three times. A word underlined with dots requires more space between letters; a straight line and a dotted line means spaced italics, while four lines means upper case italics, etc.

A graphic designer must also bear in mind the difference between an acute and a grave accent, between upper and lower quotation marks and, in short, be familiar with all the principal rules of editing that are nothing more than a proper knowledge of the language in which he or she is working.
The rules established by each publisher for its publications are often different and, in some cases, even contain contrasting indications.
A graphic designer must make choices: for a "given" client, it is necessary to adopt a general criterion, a unique standard of punctuation that is uniform across all publications, above all when they are part of the same series.
To provide students with knowledge that should already be part of their cultural baggage from previous studies, we used various texts, what is more listed in the bibliography, as well as the norms codified by Unification Organisms.
Above all, I refer to the text on grammar by Luca Serianni, written in collaboration with Alberto Castelvecchi, *Italiano, grammatica, sintassi, dubbi,* published by Garzanti. This text is also very useful for more specific studies.

For more on editing, I suggest:
http://www.webalice.it/claudiusdubitatius/Trivium/Editing.htm

1. The English Alphabet
The English alphabet is a Latin alphabet consisting of 26 letters. The table below lists the letters and their relative pronunciation, respectively in Italian and English.

Aa	"a"	"ei"
Bb	"bi"	"bi"
Cc	"ci"	"si"
Dd	"di"	"di"
Ee	"e"	"i"
Ff	"effe"	"ef"
Gg	"gi"	"gi"
Hh	"acca"	"eich"
Ii	"i"	"ai"
Jj	"i lungo"	"gei"
Kk	"cappa"	"kei"
Ll	"elle"	"el"
Mm	"emme"	"em"
Nn	"enne"	"en"
Oo	"o"	"ou"
Pp	"pi"	"pi"
Qq	"qu"	"chiu"
Rr	"erre"	"ar"
Ss	"esse"	"es"
Tt	"ti"	"ti"
Uu	"u"	"iu"
Vv	"vu"/"vi"	"vi"
Ww	"vu o vi doppio"	"dabliu"
Xx	"ics"	"ex"
Yy	"ipsilon", "i greco"	"uai"
Zz	"zeta"	"zed"

Current practice permits the use of a graphic symbol between quotation marks or in italics, or the name of the letter:
"Lubalin is written with a capital "l", "Lubalin is written with a capital "l", "Lubalin is written with a capital "*el*".

The division in syllables of a justified text responds to the rules listed under point 6 (see Division in syllables).
A graphic artist setting a text on a computer with automatic syllabic division must take care to select the option relative to the language adopted. It must also be remembered that this option can be very imprecise.

This is why the editor of a publication must accurately control the division of words that change lines and eventually correct divisions and small graphic dissonances that are inevitable when using editing software.
Remember, it is good practice not to begin a new line with a vowel, in order to avoid altering the meaning of the text and to respect best practices in typography.

1./4. Pages from the "Ravello Festival 2004" program in Italian and English.
The Italian text was edited by Paola Maritati and the English version by Stefano Valanzuolo.

1.

2.

3.

4.

73

Notes
English syllabification (or American-English) follows very different rules from its Italian counterpart.
Again, it is not possible to blindly trust software. An editor must control syllabic divisions with particularly minute care and, above all, be familiar with the respective language.

Diphthongs

A diphthong (sliding vowel) is a phonetic group formed of a semi-constant combined with a vowel in the same syllable: high [haɪ] or cow [kaʊ], in which [aɪ] and [aʊ] represent diphthongs. A diphthong is rising when the accent falls on the second element ([ja] in yard); falling when the accent falls on the first element ([aɪ] in eye). The Italian language also contains mobile diphthongs, such as the *uò* and *iè*, which are reduced to o and e when the accent shifts to another syllable (*muòvo*).

Acronyms

In Italian it is common to write acronyms capitalising only the first letter; however, when written entirely in capitals or repeated many times in a text, this can be highly anti-aesthetic. Similarly, it is best to shun the formula that places a period after each letter of an acronym. A quick look at Italian publications indifferently offers (Pri), (PRI), (P.R.I.), or the specified form (P.R.I., *Partito Repubblicano Italiano*, Italian Republican Party). There is no doubt that acronyms that can be treated as a single word require no punctuation (i.e. DOC wines).

I prefer the simplest form (Pri, Ansa, Fiat, Agip, BBC, Censis, etc.).

Abbreviations

There are many abbreviations of words
a) for contractions (Dr);
b) for a compendium (a.s.a.p., for as soon as possible);
c) for a sequence (ps. for postscript).
Other abbreviations are:
Rt Hon. (with a space);
BC, before Christ
AD, after Christ (without a space);
art., for article
arts., per articles
vol., for volume
vols., per volumes.

74

2. Punctuation

Punctuation consists of a group of signs used to insert pauses in a written text.
The signs are: the period (.), the comma (,), the colon (:), the semi-colon (;), the exclamation mark (!), the question mark (?), the ellipsis.
There are also punctuation marks between quotations marks (" ", " ", ' '), the hyphen (-, –), rounded brackets ( ), square brackets [ ], the slash (/) and the asterisk (*).
Other signs include curly brackets { } used in mathematics, angle brackets or chevrons (< >) used in philology, and other signs with much more specific uses.

2.1. The Period

It is placed at the end of a sentence or a phrase to indicate a prolonged pause.
When a phrase concludes with an abbreviation that requires an abbreviation point, the point is omitted ("etc." and not "etc..").
When an argument has been concluded, and a new one is introduced, a new paragraph should be started.
This is normally marked by an *indent*, a space at the beginning of a paragraph with a distance from the left margin that may vary depending upon the layout of the text.
Some graphic designers, such as Massimo Vignelli, prefer not to use the indent, but to leave a blank line.
The period can be placed in acronyms (S.R., Sinistra Repubblicana), though it is better to write SR; a period is not use when referring to the provinces

indicated on Italian automobile licences (RM) or the provinces themselves (PD).
A period is often used when an acronym refers to a plural (vv.).

2.2. The Comma

It indicates a short pause. It is used: in lists (buy paper, pencils, ink); between a subject and predicate (Giacomo creates, Aldo follows); to divide a secondary proposition from a principal proposition (graphics is a combination of invention, creativity and science); to separate an aside (counting pages, while listening to music, may be distracting); in temporal constructs (the typographer, after hearing the request, decided to back out).

2.3. The Colon

It introduces an explanation (the typographer, after hearing the request, decided to back out: he did not have enough time).
It also introduces a list: to be able to print I require many things: paper, ink, film).

2.4. The Semi-Colon

Indication of an intermediate pause, shorter than a period, and longer than a comma.
It is used for complex lists, to separate propositions, in lieu of the comma to avoid misunderstandings. As proof of the contribution made by typography to the definition of language, Luca Serianni reminds us that the semi-colon was invented by Aldo Manuzio, who used it for the first time in an edition of Petrarch printed in Venice in 1501.

2.5. The Question and the Exclamation Mark

They serve, respectively, at the end of a sentence, to indicate a question or an exclamation.
They are often used in combination (?!) or repeated (???).
Their acceptance by linguistics belongs to another field; there is no doubt however that they are the source of perplexity in graphic terms.

2.6. The Ellipsis

An indication of a pause in a dialogue (I really don't have the time..., I don't believe I can find the time...). Set between two square brackets [...] they also indicate an interruption in a citation. The ellipsis is always composed of three periods.

2.7. Quotation Marks

They serve to frame a direct discourse or a citation. They can be either single (' ') or double (" "). The Italian language includes a third option: guillemets (« »), known by Italian typographers as *sergeants* or *corporals* for their similarity to chevrons indicating military rank. They are not used in the English language.
The use of single or double quotation marks depends on typographic traditions. Both are used for nested citations.
For example: "He said: "I do not have enough time to print the book", as he walked away from us".
In similar cases, it is also possible to opt for single quotes: "He said: 'I don't have enough time to print the book', as he walked away from us".
Or: "He said: 'I don't have

enough time to print the book', as he walked away from us".
Single quotes can also be used to emphasise a single expression.

2.8. Hyphens

The hyphen can be short (-) or long (–).
The short hyphen is neither preceded nor followed by a space. The long hyphen requires a space before and after.
The short hyphen (-) serves:
a) to indicate a new line, equivalent to the hand written (=).
b) To reinforce a link between two composites (pre-industrial).
c) To separate two numbers (17-18 October).
d) To indicate a relation between two names (graphic designer-printer).
e) In couples of adjectives, (evident graphic-editorial connotations).
f) With some prefixes (anti-graphic); though the term anticommunist is the accredited form.
The long hyphen (–) serves:
a) To introduce a direct discourse, and in this case it is only required at the start of a phrase.
b) To introduce an aside, in which case it is placed at the beginning and end.

2.9. Rounded and Square Brackets

Rounded brackets serve:
a) To contain an aside, or an clarification.
b) To include a phrase with another grammatic structure: The typographer (if that is what we could call him) rested...
c) In lieu of long dashes in an aside.
d) In a list, as in this case, after a letter or a number.

Square brackets serve:
a) To introduce a parenthesis inside another parenthesis (the typographer [if that is what we could call him] rested...).
b) To indicate, separated by three periods [...] an interruption in a citation.

It must be remembered that the question mark and the exclamation mark are placed before the closure of a parenthesis, while other punctuation marks come after. "This typographer is the most talented (and this is what we prefer).".

2.10. The Slash

It is used:
a) To mark a division, for example, the separation between the verses of a poem presented in a text without returns (in this case with a space before an after the slash).
b) To indicate an alternation (and/or).

1. When two texts in different languages share the same page, the same type size should be used for both languages.

2. In summaries or quotations, the two texts have the same graphic appearance, though in different colours.

3. 4. This poem, presented in its original language, German, is reproduced as it was written by the poet; the Italian translation is instead justified and provided with hyphens to indicate the start of a new line.

1.

2.

Notes 75
Pages from the journal Abitare la Terra, directed by Paolo Portoghesi, format 290x465 cm, Gangemi editore. Italian editor Stefania Tuzi and Lucia Galli; English translations and editing by Erika Young. The photograph of the window was taken by Paolo Portoghesi.

3.

4.

Verses
Whe they are incorporated in a text they are to be set in italics between quotation marks ('...') or ("...").
Verses can be separated by a slash, preceded and followed by a space:
To everything and nothing / you are impervious / and frivolous / you touch the soul / of some present destiny / and keep silent / about some solicitous idea / happily concealed / from shadow to shadow / you move / like some lapping wave / between gulf and sea.

Numbers
The universal system of numbers is based on the decimal, comprised of ten numbers (0, 1, 2, 3, 4, 5, 6, 7, 8, 9) known as Arabic numerals.
Roman numerals (additive numbers) consist of 7 symbols (I, V, X, L, C, D, M).
In current writing (with the exception of accounting texts or tables) numbers are written in letters (one million, not 1,000,000).
When centuries are indicated using Roman numerals (V century BC) do not use an exponent, which instead accompanies Arabic numerals (24th).

Symbols
These conventional signs are used to express abbreviations of a mathematical entity, something physically large, a chemical element, etc.
Units of measurement are to be written in numeric values, without a period (10 mm, 10 cm or 10 kg);
When a unit of measurement is not accompanied by a numerical value, it is written in full (take measurements in millimeters, in centimeters, and weigh objects in kilograms or tonnes).

The Apostrophe
The apostrophe is a punctuation mark, and sometimes a diacritical mark, in languages that use the Latin alphabet and some other alphabets.
It is used for several purposes in English: marking the omission of one or more letters (contraction of do not to don't); marking possessive case (as in the bird's nest, or in one month's time); marking plurals of individual characters (mind your p's and q's, three a's, four i's, and two u's, Oakland A's).

The apostrophe can also be used to indicate the elision of the first two numbers of a year ('96 or '97).
The apostrophe is also used to indicate a duration in minutes (9', for 9 minutes).

76 **3. Diacritical Marks**
Some English language terms have letters with diacritical marks. Most are loanwords from French, with others coming from Spanish, Portuguese, German, or other languages.
Though limited, the following diacritical marks in English may be encountered, particularly for marking in poetry:
the acute accent (née) and grave accent; the circumflex (entrepôt), borrowed from French; the diaeresis (Zoë), the umlaut (über), altering Germanic vowels; the cedilla (soupçon), in French and in Portuguese softening c, indicating 's-' not 'k-' pronunciation
the tilde (Señor).

When representing European personal names, anthroponyms, place names and toponyms, the following are often encountered:
the caron (as in Karel Čapek). In most fonts the caron looks like an apostrophe sitting inside the Slovak capital L, as " ", but in fact is only another form of caron.
The Polish crossed Ł and nasal ogonek (as in Lech Wałęsa).
The Croatian and Serbian crossed (as inFranjo Tuđ? man or Zoran Đinđić), halfway between D and Dj; the Maltese crossed (as in the al- town prefix, al Far Industrial Estate), a hard H;the Swedish overring Å (as in the Åland Islands), the å vowel sound; the Romanian (as in Chisinău), the voiceless postalveolar fricative
For a more complete list see diacritical marks.

We may come across ligatures, such as the Latin and Anglo-Saxon Æ (minuscule: æ), and German eszett (ß; final -ß, often - ss even in German and always in Swiss-German).

Accents, sometimes combined with italics, are often applied to foreign terms not commonly used in or that are not fully assimilated into English: for example, *vis-à-vis*, *pièce de résistance* and *crème brûlée*.

4. Division in Syllables
Graphic designers will often use software that divides syllables. As this operation can sometimes be imprecise, I have listed a few recommendations for typography.
The division, indicated in handwriting with the symbol (=), is marked in typography by a short hyphen (-).
a) Separate prefixes and suffixes from root words (pre-view, work-ing, re-do, end-less, out-ing).

b) When two (or more) consonants are next to each other divide between the 1st and 2nd consonants (buf-fet, des-sert, ob-ject, ber-ry, pil-grim).
c) Never split 2 consonants that make only 1 sound when pronounced together and aren't the same letter (i.e., 'ff', th, sh, ph, th, ch, wh).
d) When a consonant is surrounded by vowels and the vowel has a long sound (like the 'i' in line) divide before the consonant (ba-by, re-sult, i-vy, fro-zen, Cu-pid).
e) When the vowel has a short sound (like the 'i' in mill) divide after the consonant (met-al, riv-er, mod-el, val-ue, rav-age).
f) When the word ends in 'ckle' divide right before the 'le' (tack-le, freck-le, tick-le, buck-le).
g) When the word ends with 'le' (not 'ckle') and the letter before the 'le' a consonant divide 1 letter before the 'le' (ap-ple, rum-ble, fa-ble, ta-ble).
h) Finally, when the letter before the 'le' a vowel, no division is to be made (ale, scale, sale, file, tile).

Notes
▼*Luca Serianni, Alberto Castelvecchi,* Italiano, *Grarzanti, Milano 1997.*
▼*Melina Insolera,* Italiano, grammatica, *Zanichelli, Bologna 1991.*
▼*Giorgio Fioravanti,* Il manuale del grafico, *Zanichelli, Bologna 1987.*
▼*A. Bandinelli, G. Lussu, R. Iacobelli,* Farsi un libro, *Biblioteca del Vascello Stampa Alternativa, Roma 1990.*

The exclamation point in Times (left) and Optima (right).

Regarding the use of symbols, I am reminded of a warning from the *Grande dizionario Garzanti della lingua italiana*: "The dictionary uses the following symbols [...] bold sanserif for headwords [...] in other cases the secondary forms are in light sanserif [...] regular text for descriptions, italics for examples [...] square brakcets for references to illustrations [...].

Small caps are often used for sections of text that should be emphasised and where a run of uppercase capital letters would appear jarring to the reader and for the names of quoted authors [...] square brackets for references from the headword of prefixes or suffixes to inserts outside the text.

5. Capitals

Capitals are used primarily:
a) to begin a sentence;
b) after a full stop;
c) after a question or an exclamation mark;
d) for the names of people (Hermann Zapf), geographic names (America, Dolomites), for common names used as titles (the Constitution), for street names (Via Gregorio VII), organisations and institutions (Monetary Fund), for holidays (Easter, Christmas);
e) at the beginning of a direct discourse, preceded by quotations or long dashes: I was wondering: "When do you plan to edit?". He answered: "Tomorrow".
Or: "He asked me: – When do you plan to edit?";
f) in titles (*The Divine Comedy*, *La Repubblica*);
g) when mentioning foreign titles when it is correct to maintain the original capitals (David Coffin, The Villa in the Life of Renaissance Rome; Tilman Falk, Studien zur Topographie und Geschichte der Villa Giulia in Rom);
h) for reverential references (I believe in the Lord);
i) for terms that may generate confusion (State, Country, The West);
l) when referring to a specific body and not a generic institution (The City of Rome).

6. Regular, Italics, Bold, Bold Italics and Small Caps

Depending on the text to be laid out, a graphic artist will select a typeface and the rules for its use. When the base text is in regular typeface, italics are used:
a) for words to be highlighted;
b) for foreign terms not commonly used;
c) for the titles or articles, books and works in general;
d) for Latin or foreign phrases that are not quotations (*mare magnum, in extremis, sub iudice*);
e) in all cases when it is necessary to differentiate a text, for example, in a preface.
Bold will be used for titles and running headlines (it is best not to use it to emphasise an excerpt).
Bold italics will be used for subtitles, and so on.
There are no specific rules for the use of small caps: for example they are used in some cases to list the names of authors in a bibliography or in similar cases.
The Serianni glossary of grammar warns: "In this glossary italics are reserved for forms (words, locutions, etc.) of the Italian language; bold small caps indicate grammatical categories and terms".
It should be remembered that the use of one typeface family is a guarantee of a dignified graphic result.

7. Foreign words

Commonly used foreign words are to be composed in the same typeface as the rest of the text.
The same is true for the names of entities, companies, institutes, locations and people (Lancaster University, Utrecht, Bristol-Myers).
Less common foreign words are to be presented in italics when the main text is regular, and in regular typeface when the main text is in italics.
In these cases it is a good idea to provide a translation in round brackets and to use the foreign term as it is written in its original language.

8. Units of Measurement

In 1960 the International System of Units (SI) was officially adopted and its use is recommended by the CIPM (International Committee for Weights and Measures).
The system is based on the adoption of seven fundamental quantities (length, mass, time, electric current, thermodynamic temperature, amount of substance and luminous intensity) and the symbols assigned to the seven corresponding units:

m   metre
kg   kilogram
s   second
K   kelvin
A   ampere
cd   candela
mol mole

They are written after the value, and without a period:
km for kilometre
m for meter,
cm for centimetre
mm for millimetre
cd for candela,
A for ampere,
W for watt,
mg for milligram
cg for centigram
g for gram
hg for hectogram
kg for kilogram
q for quintal (uncommon)
t for tonne
s for second
m for minute
h for hour.

Workbook:
Study the editing rules adopted by a collection of diverse publications. Compare more or less important publications. Circle eventual errors and list corrections in the margins.
If possible, try to find a copy of the rules used by qualified publishers.

77

The Rules of Editing Used by Journals

A Rapid Guide

In addition to the general rules of editing described above, the following section, in the most concise manner, and in alphabetical order, looks at the principal rules for correctly composing a text.

The rules are a compendium of those found in the handbooks distributed to journalists at leading national newspapers, including *Il Sole-24 Ore*, *Panorama* magazine and other journals. Recomendations include: "Scientific names: use scientific names only when absolutely indispensable".

Students are reminded that the rules established by each publisher for its publications often vary and may even include contrasting indications. When forced to choose between different solutions, it is best to adopt a single unified criteria for all publications that belong to the same series.

78

Abbreviations
Avoid abbreviations where possible.
Article 3 of the Law, architect Lamberto Rossi (not arch.).
The following abbreviations are admissible: TV, ed, TN.
Define abbreviations the first time they are mentioned in the abstract, text; also the first time they are mentioned in a table or figure.
Write don't, can't... in full, i.e. do not, cannot

Accents
The vowel e has a grave accent in the following cases: when using foreign words (canapè, narghilè, etc.); in proper names
Use original accents in foreign words.
Use it is and not it's, does not rather than doesn't.

Articles
English has two articles: the and a/an. The (definite article) is used to refer to specific or particular nouns; a/an (indefinite article) is used to modify non-specific or non-particular nouns. We call the the definite article and a/an the indefinite article.

Italics
Italics are used:
1) for legal phrases and terminology and the scientific "Latin" names of animals and plants (*habeas corpus*);
2) in notes in parentheses followed by the indica ed and TN (in regular text);
3) in quotations and normative texts, when foreseen.

Decades
They are to be written in numbers (the 1970s, and not the '70s).

Direct Discourse
Always begin with a capital when followed by a colon and preceded by quotation marks (The typographer: "I set the texts in bold").
Start with a capital when the quoted text is part of a discourse (A text that is not "composed" in bold); or when there are no quotation marks after the colon (The typographer: I set the texts in bold).

Signatures
For journals with two articles written by the same journalist, the more important is to be signed, the other initialled. In this case there are to be no spaces between the letters (example: A.D., B.Da).

Interviews
Questions are to be set in bold, and answers in regular text.
Do not use Q and A, or quotation marks or hyphens; leave a full line between the question and the answer.

Capitals
Capitalize all words in headings including hyphenated words (e.g. Anti-Antagonist), except conjunctions (and, or, but, nor, yet, so, for), articles (a, an, the), and all prepositions (including those of five letters or more) (in, to, of, at, by, up, for, off, on, against, between, among, under). First and last words in the title are always capitalized.
Proper names, those indicating "personalities" and "uniqueness" are to be written in capital letters: the Parliament, when speaking of that in Rome. The same for Government, State, Town, etc. Al-

ways write "Ministry of Foreign Affairs".
The cardinal points are written with capitals when they refer to geopolitical realities (the South), but not when they indicate a direction (southward).
In general, the following capitalization rules apply across in title case:
a) capitalize the first word in the title
b) capitalize the last word in the title
c) capitalize the important words in the title
Some words are generally not capitalized when using title case. These include short words and conjunctions: articles (a, an, the); coordinating conjunctions (and, but, for); short \(less than 5 letters); Prepositions (at, by, from).
The other major form of title capitalization is sentence case, which simply means capitalizing the first letter of a sentence and nothing else as opposed to capitalizing almost every first letter in title case.
Street names should be capitalised (Broadway Avenue).
Always write: USA, Iraq, ANCD; President of the United States (and, in the case of a unique reference, the President); International Monetary Fund, Chamber of Commerce, The White House; Town, Province, Region (administrative entities), town as a geographic reference; Country (for State); Civil Code, Limited Company, etc.
Capitalize words such as Group, Section, Method, etc. if followed by a number, e.g. "In Group 4, five patients..."
The measurement mL: the L is always a capital.

First and Last Names
The first time an article mentions a person, even well known, always include the first name (President of the United States, Barack Obama).

Composite Names
Vice President and not vice-president.

Scientific Names
Use scientific names only when indispensable.

Foreign Names
Use commonly accepted names (Gheddafi, Gorbaciov).
Rome and not Roma.

Numbers
Up to the number ten they are written in letters, with the exception of dates and times (before 8 a.m. on the 4th of February, five hours later).
Letters are used for one hundred, one thousand, one million and one billion.
For numbers after four decimal places, use a comma separator (3,420, 23,840).
Numbers that are part of names are written in Roman numerals (Victor Emanuel II).
Letters are always used for numbers indicating a date and hour (the 7:30 p.m. bus, the 3 March). Letters are used for numbers at the beginning of a sentence.
Numbers 1 to 9 are written in full, except if part of a measurement (6–8 mL) or in the experimental/materials/methods section.
Numbers at the beginning of a sentence should be written in full, i.e. 152 mL must be written as: One hundred and fifty two milliliters.

Notes
It may occur that while laying out a work for a client, you receive a telephone call with a small correction.
You should have the words spelled out (the separate pronunciation of each letter making up a word), or the spelling of the word; this will help avoid unfortunate errors in the printed version.
The table to the upper right lists the "telephone alphabet", or how to pronounce each single letter in Italian, British and American English.

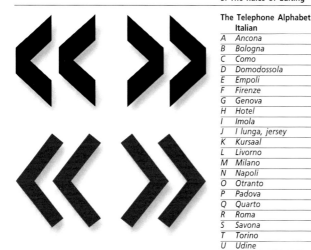

The Telephone Alphabet

	Italian	British English	American English
A	Ancona	Andrew	Abel
B	Bologna	Benjamin	Baker
C	Como	Charlie	Charlie
D	Domodossola	David	Dog
E	Empoli	Edward	Easy
F	Firenze	Frederick	Fox
G	Genova	George	George
H	Hotel	Harry	How
I	Imola	Isaac	Item
J	I lunga, jersey	Jack	Jig
K	Kursaal	King	King
L	Livorno	Lucy	Love
M	Milano	Mary	Mike
N	Napoli	Nellie	Nan
O	Otranto	Oliver	Oboe
P	Padova	Peter	Peter
Q	Quarto	Queenie	Queen
R	Roma	Robert	Roger
S	Savona	Sugar	Sugar
T	Torino	Tommy	Tare
U	Udine	Uncle	Uncle
V	Venezia	Victor	Victor
W	Washington	William	William
X	Ics, xeres	Xmas	X
Y	York, yacht	Yellow	Yoke
Z	Zara	Zebra	Zebra

Ordinals
They are written in numbers or letters following the rules for numbers. Example: the third sextodecimo, the second signature, the 5th octavo The 'th' in 19th or 20th should NOT be written in superscript.

Dates
Dates are written out in the full, April 20, 2004 (or 20 April, 2004) rather than 20.4.04.
Write 1990s rather than with an apostrophe (1990's) or just 90s.

Foreign Words
Over the centuries the English language has assimilated words and phrases from a variety of other languages. They are often printed in italics (*a cappella*, *agent provacateur*).

Percentages
Always use a number followed (without a space) by the percent sign (2%). One exception: when a percentage value ends a sentence, the percentage is written in letters (2 per cent).

Proclitics
Some monosyllables and Latin terms are written as proclitics with respect to the word that follows them, without a hyphen (ex minister, ex aequo, ex libris, per capita, pro loco). Others require a hyphen (off-limits).

Punctuation
For phrases set in quotations use a hyphen (a long hyphen preceded and followed by a space) to separate the indication of the speaker. For example: "Yesterday – Begliomini stated – I purchased a new set of typefaces...".

A colon is followed by lowercase letters, unless the text contains a quoted phrase (Begliomini: can I use the "*mulinello*" to print ..."; Begliomini: "Can I print on the "*mulinel-lo*"...").

Centuries
Always use letters (twelfth century).

Following Line or Page
Leave a space between the period at the end of p. and the number of the page (p. 3).

Acronyms
Acronyms are to written like names, without periods (NATO, UN).
The first time an acronym appears in a text it should be explained.

Titles
Never separate a concept and, most importantly, an adjective from a noun on two separate lines.

Hyphen
For phrases set in quotations use a long hyphen preceded and followed by a space to separate the indication of the speaker. *Example:* "Yesterday – the linotypist stated – I uploaded a new set of typefaces...".
Use a long hyphen in all cases, except when uniting two words. In this case, use a short hyphen without spaces (socio-economic).

Quotation Marks
Use double quotation marks to set off a direct (word-for-word) quotation ("I hope you will be here," he said). Always capitalize the first word in a complete quotation, even midsentence (John said, "The case is far from over, and we will win."). Do not capitalize quoted material that continues a sentence (Albert said that the case was "far from over" and that "we will win."). Use commas to introduce or interrupt direct quotations (He said, "I don't care."; "Why," I asked, "don't you care?"). Periods and commas ALWAYS go inside quotation marks. (The sign said, "Walk.") Quotation marks are used for chapter titles in a book, individual episodes of a TV series, songs from a Broadway show or a music album, titles of articles or essays in print or online and shorter works such as short stories and poems (Richard Burton performed the song "Camelot" in the 1960 Broadway musical Camelot). Use single quotation marks for quotations within quotations (Dave said: "In a town outside Rome, I saw 'Tourists go home' written on a wall. But then someone told me, 'Ignore what you saw.'"
Single quotation marks are valid only within a quotation.

Guillemets
They are used in the Italian language for direct discourses and verbatim citations of words or phrases.

Source English
American English or UK English are fine so long as there is consistency.

Websites
All websites need to be referenced as does unpublished data or personal communications.

And and But
A sentence should not start with But or And (use however or find alternatives).

Units
There is a space after a number and before °C and units such as µL, h, min, days, but NOT before % or ° (angle).

Bibliography
▼*How to write for* Il Sole-24 Ore
▼*When writing for* Panorama

Authorities in Language

The *Accademia della Crusca*

VOCABOLARIO
DEGLI
ACCADEMICI
DELLA
CRUSCA
EDIZIONE SECONDA VENETA
ACCRESCIUTA DI MOLTE VOCI
Raccolte dagli Autori approvati dalla stessa Accademia.
VOLUME QUINTO.

IN VENEZIA, MDCCLXIII.
APPRESSO FRANCESCO PITTERI
CON LICENZA DE'SUPERIORI, E PRIVILEGIO.

1

1. *Vocabolario degli Accademici della Crusca,* Venice, 1763.

80   The *Accademia della Crusca* provides users with a Linguistic Advice service for all those looking for grammatical and lexical information and clarification, explanation of linguistic facts, origin and history of words. A staff composed of linguists examines the asked queries (about twenty per day on average), and answers to the most asked ones. The answers published on the website are structured in a way to retrace the history of the linguistic facts, motivate and document their evolution.
The Linguistic Advice also deals with issues of general importance with the aim of stimulating reflection on the features of contemporary Italian. According to this perspective, the answers aim at providing not only the solutions to the queries, but also a critical orientation for facing problems and phenomena that involve both the linguistic and the cultural evolution. This activity, started more than ten years ago, has led to the creation of an archive of hundreds of answers, steadily increasing at the rate of one every week.
In the last ten years, the Linguistic Advice has received tens of thousands of queries and most of them have been answered with personal advices to the person concerned. The periodical "La Crusca per voi" is still another important channel of dialogue with the public, in which answers by linguists and academicians are published.

In this section, it is possible to consult the answers to the questions through the list or through the searching tool in the archive. If you do not find the answer you were looking for, you can ask directly to the Accademia.The activity of Linguistic Advice is not a recent innovation. For a look back at the past read the history of Linguistic Advice.

From the website:
http://www.accademiadellacrusca.it/en/italian-language/language-consulting

Notes
The Accademia della Crusca *is an Italian institution comprised of experts in linguistics and the philology of the Italian language. It is one of the most prestigious linguistic institutions in Italy and the world.*

Created in Florence by Leonardo Salviati as an informal group of friends (the "brigata dei crusconi") dedicated, in opposition to the pedantry of the Accademia Fiorentina, to playful discourse (the "cruscate"), the Academy was officialy constituted on the 25th March 1585, two years after the period during which its members began to imagine a possible organisation based on a statute (gathering on the 25th January 1583).

"In the world of publishing, the term editing refers to the editorial revision of a manuscript (this is the term used, even when dealing with a document written on the computer) with a view to its publication, typically in the form of a book.

All the same, in recent years editing is no longer synonymous with "editorial revision" – an operation (we could say) that requires a love for books and good culture – but tends increasingly more often to be identified with a part of it, the more bureaucratic and impoverished application of the rules of editorial standardisation. It is perhaps for this reason that in Anglo-Saxon nations editing is something serious, or at least a little more serious than it is here in Italy, because they use the term "editing" and it is clear that this signifies "editorial revision" (clear in the term itself, from the Latin *edere*, corresponding with the Greek *ekdidónai*: these terms signify "to publish", or also "prepare to be published"), while in Italy we say "editing" with the pretext however of interpreting this term at our convenience [...]".

"Paraphrasing [Luciano] Bianciardi we can say that the ideal editor in a decaying editorial context "marks out a zone, chooses a sector and makes it important". This sector is that of regulations of editorial standardisation. In reality, in publishing houses it occurs that editors have been deprive of some of the essential functions of editorial revision (analysis of content, linguistic control, etc.) or they have found it opportune to excuse themselves of this responsibility. Thus all of their "professionalism" is displayed in the editorial kitchen. If an external collaborator lets slip some euphonic "d" where sacred rules expressly prohibit it (for example "*ad esso*", rather than "*a esso*"), the editor, with unquestionable judgment, is out and out horrified. What is so serious is that this horror is not simulated, but authentic: otherwise, without this horror, what would he be doing in the first place in the publishing industry? [...]".

"The structuring of issues becomes a serious affair for the editor who is a true editor, above all when a book contains information that could conveniently be placed in a table, or when the tables provided by the authors could be arranged differently, or even converted into graphics.

The expert editor decides with full knowledge of the facts what is to be done, and personally develops the text in the form of tables or graphics, instead of leaving this job to the internal graphic designer or to the external graphic design practice, only to say "I like it" or "I don't like it" and to move the images back and forth. It is a question of content, as the technologies are available to everyone, all we need to know is how to use them, and a good editor never holds back.

Many books containing figures and tables already appear shoddy at first glance, above all when they belong to a series that does not generally include illustrations and tables, hence there is no familiarity in dealing with such insignificant problems. Despite the progress in digital typesetting and layout, correct solutions to the presentation of content and balanced graphics are still very rare, all too rare in relation to the state-of-the-art. This is due, other than to malpractice, also to carelessness, and in certain cases to the total absence of any analysis of the content of a book during the phase of editorial revision [...]".

This very important text, which I suggest reading, is from:
Retorica minimalista: l'editing dei libri, n.d.
http://www.webalice.it/claudiusdubitatius/Trivium/Editing.htm

Notes

Any graphic designer must be familiar with the English language. In fact, the English language is most open to new words with foreign origins. This is due both to its vast use as a lingua franca, and in virtue of the mixed Latin-Germanic origins of so many of its root words and, probably, thanks also to the extreme poverty of definitions and typical elongations that recognisably characterise its nouns.

Diffusion
In reality, the English language has become the lingua franca par excellence. It is the most studied language in the world, not to mention the most important in the workplace and an essential instrument for communication. It is estimated that there are more than 400 million native English speakers, and 300 million who speak it along with their national or native language.

81

Scientific Reviews

International Conventions

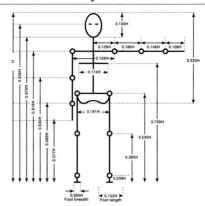

The table contains the coefficients to be multiplied by the length of parts of the body in order to identify the position of the respective centres of gravity (from Winter 1, modified).

82

Typologies of Articles

Didactic:
a succint treatment of fundamental concepts. By the editorial board or a guest author.

Clinical Kinesiology:
description of pathological motor behaviour and review of related literature. Structured in paragraphs at the discretion of the author.

Classical Themes:
updates on general themes concerning the rationale of rehabilitation interventions. Structured in paragraphs at the discretion of the author.

Current Events:
review of recent literature on specific themes with the aim of presenting the state of the art and a critical analysis of knowledge. Structured in paragraphs at the discretion of the author.

Original Article:
experimental study focused on determining the effects of a particular rehabilitation treatment, therapeutic exercise, etc. Mandatory structure in sections; introduction, materials and methods, results, discussion.

Clinical Case Study:
description of the treatment of a clinical case study of particular interest.
Mandatory structure in sections; introduction, materials and methods, results, discussion.

Technical Note:
short though detailed description of particular measures, modifications

and equipment, innovations and ideas that the author wishes to bring to the attention of his/her colleagues. Structured at the discretion of the author.

Letters to the Editor:
critical observations supported by information and/or a bibliography of scientific articles published in the review or other publications and presented in a concise format.

Editorial:
comment on current issues in rehabilitation. By the editorial board or a guest author.

Preparation of a Text

Articles are to be typed on A4 pages (210x297 mm), double spaced and with margins of at least 2.5 cm. Number all pages beginning from the title page. Submit two copies of the final text.

Text Structure:

Title page:
a) title of the text;
b) initials and last name of each author;
c) name and address of the institution where each author works;
d) complete address and telephone number of the author selected to manage all communications;
e) eventual acknowledgements.

Text page (subdivision in sections):
Introduction:
concise description of the nature and objective of the work and current state of knowledge;
Materials and methods:
detailed illustration of the characteristics of the subjects examined, the equipment utilised, the protocol adopted.
Results:
presented clearly and concisely, without comments;
Discussion:
explain the results, comparing them with eventual other results obtained by other authors, emphasising their clinical relevance and applications; critical analysis; advancement of hypotheses or criticisms.

Bibliography:
Bibliographic references, indicated in the text using progressive Arab numerals, in parentheses, must

be listed in progressive order (1., 2., etc.). Only material quoted in the text is to be included in the bibliography, to be drawn up based on international standards.
Examples:
– Review Article: Last name and initial of the authors, separated by a comma (list all authors up to a maximum of three, for more than three use et al.) - period - title of the article - period - name of the review (abbreviations as per the Index Medicus) - year of publication - semicolon - volume number - colon - first page number - hyphen - last page number - period.
Example:
Johnson RJ. Anterior cruciate ligament injury rehabilitation in athletes: biomechanical considerations. Am J Sports Med 1996; 22:54-64.

– Book and monograph. Last name and initial of the authors - period - title of the work - period - edition number - period - place of publication - colon- publisher - comma - year of publication - colon - first page consulted - hyphen - last page consulted - period.
Example:
Chaffin DB, Anderson GBJ. Occupational biomechanics. 1st edition. New York: John Wiley & Sons, 1984:355-368.
– Chapter in a book of contributions.
Example:
Pedotti A, Frigo C, Santambrogio GC. Sistemi di acquisizione di grandezze cinematiche e dinamiche. In: Leo T, Rizzolati G eds. Bioingegneria della riabilitazione. Bologna: Patron, 1987:80-106.

Notes
Scientific reviews are often filled with mathematic symbols that are to be correctly written.
For example, the multiplication sign cannot be typed with a small x: it is necessary to use special alphabets for this type of character.
Below is a text developed for the scientific review Scienza Riabilitativa indicating the rules to be respected by contributing authors.

Mathematical Symbols

+	plus, positive
−	less, negative
±	more or less
×	multiply
:	divide
=	equal to
≠	not equal to, different tha
≡	identical to, equivalent to
~	similar to
≈	approximately
÷	equal to
>	greater than
<	lesser than
≥	greater than or equal to
≤	lesser than or equal to
%	percent
‰	per-mille
∞	infinity
°	degree
′	minute
″	second
‖	parallel to
⊥	perpendicular to
<	angle
∟	90° angle
△	triangle
∩	arc

Notes
A brand is a company's signature. As such it is generally used in publications and literature by a company, just like a signature and to accompany a wide range of communications. In any case, it is not possible to exclude its application as an illustration that occupies the majority of a cover, as in the example shown here to the left.

– Conference Precedings. Example: Cristiani E. Il trattamento fisiochinesiterapico post-operatorio in un caso di sindrome del tunnel carpale. In: Atti del VI Congresso nazionale della AITM. Riccione, 14 September 1994:16-25.

Illustrations:
each of the two copies of the text must be complete with illustrations.
Tables must be numbered progressively with Roman numerals and referenced in the text, typed with double spacing on separate pages and with a header.
Figures must be numbered progressively using Arab numerals and referenced in the text. The back of each figure should feature its referenc number, the name of the first author and an arrow indicating the direction in which it is to be printed. Captions, opportunely numbered, should be typed in succession on a separate page.
Sketches to be finalised are not accepted.
Photographs must be clear and printed on glossy paer in b&w, maximum size 18.6 (w) x 22.2 (h) cm.

Style:
use a simple and concise language, avoiding long sentences and unfamiliar technical terms.
Limit the use of abbreviations and acronyms: when necessary, an abbreviation should be followed by the corresponding term in parentheses the first time it is mentioned.
Foreign words, to be written in italics, are to be used only when a corresponding term does not exist in the language of the text.

Texts prepared on a Personal Computer:
texts may be prepared on a PC or Macintosh.
If possible the following programs are preferred: Word for Windows version 2.0, Word for Macintosh version 5.0.
Disks must be labelled with: Author's Name, Title of the text, word processor used, including the version number.

BIBLIOGRAPHY
1. Berchuck M, Andriacchi TP, Bach BR et al. Gait adaptations by patients who have a deficient anterior cruciate ligament. J Bone Joint Surg 1990; 72: 871-7
2. Noyes FR, Schipplein OD, Andriacchi TP et al. The anterior cruciate ligament-deficient knee with varus alignment. Am J Sports Med 1992; 20:707-16
3. De Vita P, Hortobagyi T, Barrier J, et al. Gait adaptations before and after anterior cruciate ligament reconstruction surgery. Med Sci Sports Exerc1997; 29:853-9
4. Larson R. The knee – physiological joint. J Bone Joint Surg 1983; 65:143-4
5. Czerniecki JM, Lippert F, Obrud JE. A biomechanical evaluation of tibiofemoral rotation in anterior cruciate ligament knees during walking and running. Am J Sports Med 1988; 16:327
6. Pope MH, Stankewich CJ, Beynnon BD et al. Effect of knee musculature on anterior cruciate ligament strain in vivo. J Elect Kinesiol 1991; 3:191-8
7. Boccardi S, Lissoni A. Cinesiologia III. I edizione. Roma: Società Editrice Universo,1984:621
8. De Vita P, Torry M, Glover KL et al. A functional knee brace alters joint torque and power pattern during walking and running. J Biomechanics 1996;29:583-88
9. Cawley PW, France P, Paulos LE. The current state of functional knee bracing research. A review of the literature. Am J Sports Med 1991; 19:226-33
10. Cook FF, Tibone JE, Redfern FC. A dynamic analysis of a functional brace for anterior cruciate ligament insufficiency. Am J Sports Med 1989; 17:519-24
11. Sinkjaer T, Arendt-Nielsen L. Knee stability and muscle coordination in patients with anterior cruciate ligament injuries. J Electromyo Kines 1991;1:209-17
12. Limbird TJ, Shiavi R, Frazer M et al.

BIBLIOGRAPHY
1. Berchuck M, Andriacchi TP, Bach BR et al. Gait adaptations by patients who have a deficient anterior cruciate ligament. J Bone Joint Surg 1990; 72: 871-7
2. Noyes FR, Schipplein OD, Andriacchi TP et al. The anterior cruciate ligament-deficient knee with varus alignment. Am J Sports Med 1992; 20:707-16
3. De Vita P, Hortobagyi T, Barrier J, et al. Gait adaptations before and after anterior cruciate ligament reconstruction surgery. Med Sci Sports Exerc1997; 29:853-9
4. Larson R. The knee – physiological joint. J Bone Joint Surg 1983; 65:143-4
5. Czerniecki JM, Lippert F, Obrud JE. A biomechanical evaluation of tibiofemoral rotation in anterior cruciate ligament knees during walking and running. Am J Sports Med 1988; 16:327
6. Pope MH, Stankewich CJ, Beynnon BD et al. Effect of knee musculature on anterior cruciate ligament strain in vivo. J Elect Kinesiol 1991; 3:191-8
7. Boccardi S, Lissoni A. Cinesiologia III. I edizione. Roma: Società Editrice Universo,1984:621

Notes
*The review Scienza Riabilitativa publishes scientific articles related to rehabilitation and human movement. The submission of a text is based on the premise that it has not been published elsewhere and that, should it be accepted, it will not be published successively by others, either in whole or in part.
All iconographic material must be original; illustrations from other publications must be authorised in writing by the editor.
Authors implicitly accept that texts will be evaluated anonymously by the editor and the editorial board.
Acceptance is subject to a review process that includes the indication of eventual corrections, both in style and content, the suggestion and/or submission of additional bibliographic material, the evaluation of the relevance and appropriateness of the study to the review.
All authors will receive a reply.
Texts that are not accepted will be returned, complete with all original material, to the author.*

6.
Typing

The Generation of a Glyph

1. Glyphs are constructed on a grid and composed of numerous pixels: the greater the number of pixels, the more perfect the resolution of the glyph.
The definition of a glyph thus depends on the quantity of pixels used to design it.
In some of these examples, the curves of the glyphs are illegible: the number of pixels is so low that it is impossible to visualise the glyph with sufficient detail.

2. The quality of the resolution of a glyph is not only the result of the quality of its original design, but also of the quantity of pixels used to view it. This example clearly illustrates how as the number of pixels increases the glyph becomes sharper and more legible.

84   Digital electronics, combined with the high resolution offered by cathode ray video terminals, completely revolutionised traditional typography. The computer has practically substituted its mechanical predecessor and there are now no limits on the layout of a text, its size or the possibilities to modify it. Furthermore, the definition of a text on film offers an exceptional quality. A computer system is composed of hardware, software and firmware. Hardware is the physical structure of the computer and its components; software is the combination of program data used to manage a computer; firmware is a micro-program inserted in the hardware. The brain of the computer is the CPU, the central processing unit. All of those components that do not belong to the CPU are referred to as peripherals. Central memory is referred to as RAM (Random Access Memory). The CPU consists of three independent components: the arithmetic logic unit (ALU), central memory and the control unit. This is what controls all of the functions and generates the setting of typefaces in a digital environment. The computer digitalises the characters on a grid, within which it recognises the design of each glyph based on a certain number of points, each with its own X and Y coordinates. The instructions for finding each point are sent to the CRT (Cathode Ray Tube), which visually represents the character on the video monitor. The resolution of digital glyphs is very important. The higher its value, the more faithful the visualisation of the glyph. As each glyph is constructed on a grid, curved lines are made from a series of small squares that follow the curve. The smaller the squares, the more precise the curve appears. Hence, the quality of a glyph is not only a result of the perfection of its design, but also of its digital resolution.

Notes
Today we have arrived at the definition of characters based on no less than 8,000 lines per square. This permits the faithful reproduction of even the most complex characters originally designed with sophisticated constructions and intertwining curves.

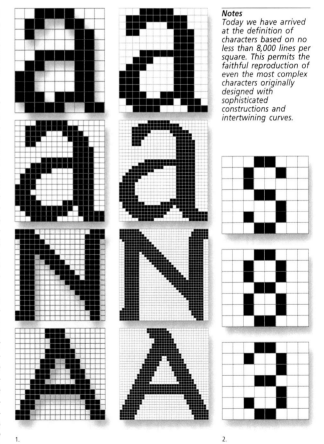

1.

2.

2. The alphabet represented here is used for dot-matrix printers.
It is constructed on a grid of 45 squares (5x9), within which the glyphs are drawn in upper and lower case. A grid of such a low density offers very modest possibilities to represent the letter.

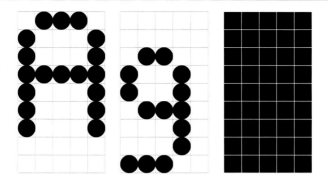

Workbook
Choose a letter and draw it on a grid based on a module of given dimensions. Draw the same letter on a grid with the same module reduced by half. Repeat this exercise until you obtain the design of a letter with the least approximation possible with respect to the original.

3.

Points memorised by the computer are united by lines or curves known as splines. The letter is thus recognised based on a structure that a computer can modify to create endless variations.

86

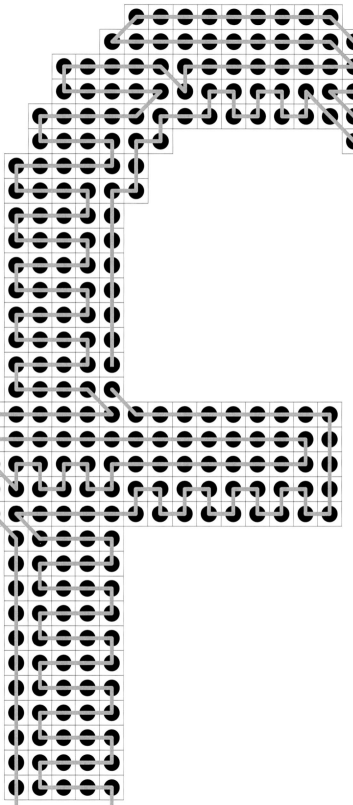

1.

1. 2. In photocomposition, a glyph is visualised by the projection of a negative matrix crossed by a source of light.
In CTR or laser ray composition (used by a computer) it is the light source, opportunely programmed,
that designs the character.

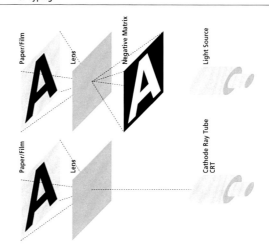

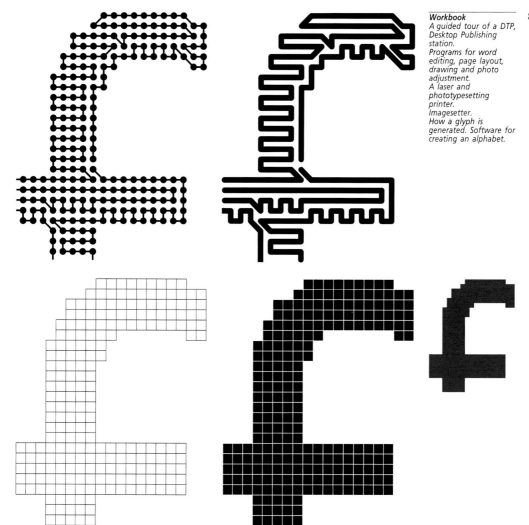

2.

Typing Special Glyphs

Tables for Finding Them Quickly

1. Examples of special glyphs requiring combinations of keys. To the rights is the so-called "triple"for Mac: by simultaneously holding down these three keys it is possible to easily access a number of rapid commands.

88

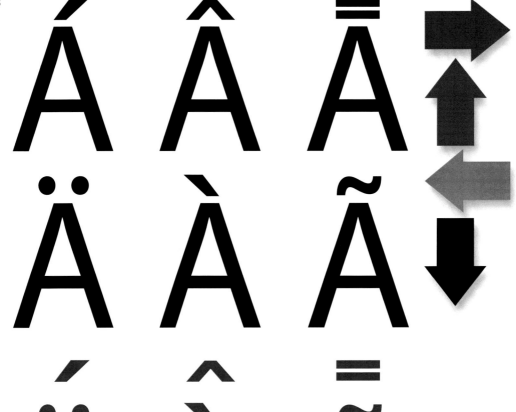

1.

2.

Multiple keys are also required to access current punctuation marks. The example to the right shows the so-called *caporali* obtained by holding down: option + 1 for the opening of a quotation and caps + option + 1 for its closing.

The è with an acute accent (third conjugation of the Italian verb *essere*) and the é with the grave accent (for example, in the French language) requires a familiarity with the rules of grammar.

A graphic designer can print out a personalised list of characters with corresponding typefaces. "Suitcases" can be loaded to use "The Type Book" software, programmed by Jim Levis, to print out sample pages of typeface families in different point sizes. The program also provides all indications relative to the key combinations for special characters.

In the example to the right, the correct apostrophe is that on the left, which requires the use of two keys, as opposed to that to the right which requires only one key.

The example of the two apostrophes presented below demonstrates just how indispensable it is to be familiar with the rules of grammar to ensure a correctly typed text. A graphic designer who lays out a text (the computer has made this normal, above all for short texts) must be familiar with the rules of editing and typesetting.

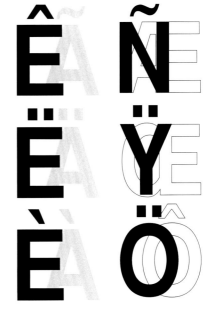

3.

7.
The Legibility of Text

A Fifth of a Second
between One Letter and
the Next
Linguistic Structure
and Typographic Structure

A comma in Optima
and Peignot.

90 The first studies of text legibility date back to the early nineteenth century.
Anison tested the response to the reading of two texts, gradually moved away from the reader, one composed in Didot and the other in Garamond. The text in Garamond was deemed more legible, though this is certainly because at the time almost all books were published in this typeface. Not by chance, Stanley Morison suggested that the typographer use the same typefaces used by daily newspapers, in other words, those the reader was most accustomed to seeing.
In 1843, the notary Leclerc published a curious little book entitled *How to Reduce Printing Costs*, in which he focused on five points: more than reading, the reader intuits; half of a vowel is sufficient for it to be fully intuited; if a vowel is missing from a text it can be intuited; the majority of readers read only the upper portion of a line of text; the upper part of the lines is sufficient for a reading of the entire text. This theory was confirmed by Tinker and Paterson, two American psychologists, whose studies showed that lower case letters are 13% more legible than upper case characters. In 1905 Emile Javal, an opthalmologist, completed the first scientific study of reading processes. Thanks to the advanced laboratories at the Sorbonne, by connecting a microphone to the eyelid, he managed to apply sound to the movement of the eyes. The result of this research demonstrates that a reader reads approximately 10 letters at a time, pauses, and then moves on to the next reading. Studies using more advanced techniques have confirmed that a focused stare lasts for an average of 1/3 to 1/4 of a second, the pause for 1/40 of a second, and that the reader fixes on a section comprised of an average of 5 to 15 letters.

In her book *Il carattere in tipografia, omaggio a Bodoni*, Marina Di Bernardo writes: "Legibility is tied to optics and the habit of reading one typeface with respect to another.
It was possible to observe how the eye stops approximately three times on a line of text and almost always at the same point. This, obviously, does not always coincide with the basic syntactic elements of a sentence, yet our mind is able to rapidly assemble every detail to arrive at the sense of a discourse.
In other words, reading is not purely analytical, as it may seem, but occurs through a process of synthesis [...].
The length of a printed line must always be referred to the mechanism of human reading. As the eye rests for one fifth of a second between one stare and the next, the possibility that it groups together a series of letters, taking them in at a single glance, is strictly related to precisely this length. If this length is excessive, it tends to make it difficult to begin reading the start of a new line while, on the contrary, when it is too short, it causes the inconvenience of increasing optical fixation, diminishing overall perception.
A sufficiently tested rule considers the optimum length of a line of text, including spaces, to be one and a half to two times a lower case alphabet".

Bibliography
Marina Di Bernardo,
Il carattere in tipografia,
omaggio a G.B. Bodoni,
Sintesi grafica, 1989.
Pierre Duplan, Roger
Jauneau, Progetto
grafico e
impaginazione,
Tecniche nuove, 1987

Notes
*Obviously there are
many exceptions to
these considerations.
The ratios between the
factors listed can serve
to privilege a more
emotional vision, or an
aesthetic order, or be
conditioned by the fact
that one is designing
the pages of a manual
rather than a novel. To
the same degree, the
size of a typeface has
different parameters
depending on whether
a book is being laid
out for a children's
book publisher or, as in
the case of a dictionary
or scientific text, for a
specific audience. Or,
whether an advertising
text wholly ignores the
rules of typography
and optics. The book
you are reading
certainly does not
respond to the best
criteria of legibility; the
particular nature of the
issues examined, the
need to present as
many examples as
possible, variegated
texts and diverse levels
of reading obliged an
aesthetic approach.
Narrow columns, a
flush left alignment
and a minuscule
typeface could never be
justified in a
continuous text that,
instead, would require
maximum legibility.*

"Legibility. The degree to which a text, a page or a character can be easily read. In graphic terms, there are no rules for establishing the degree of legibility with certainty; however, it is considered that glyphs with serifs are easier to read than those without, and for this reason they tend to more widely used in the publishing sector. Furthermore, legibility depends on how a character is set; for example, a text composed with a justification that is either too long or too short is less legible than one with a medium level of justification, where medium is intended as containing between 7 to 10 words".
Giorgio Fioravanti, *Il dizionario del grafico*, Zanichelli 1993.

The legibility of a text is conditioned by various factors.
a) Its design:
by the general layout, format, page layout, number of columns and arrangement of the template;
b) its typesetting:
by the typeface and its form, type size, leading, kerning and tracking, by the quantity of characters in a single line of text;
c) its printing:
by the quality of the printer
(as well as the correct pressure of the cylinders and the correct ink);
d) its materials:
the type of paper on which the text is printed and, obviously, its colour;
e) its general structure:
by the relationship between the issues explored and the graphic choices listed above.
In any case it is necessary to identify a proper relationship of contrast: between black and white, between figure and ground, between positive and negative (where black, the positive and the solid are the texts and images), elements that establish a dialectic in the architecture of a page.

A few suggestions are always helpful.
If you are designing a book, the type size must be commensurate with the space to be filled; privilege a typeface with serifs for an edition that contemplates a continuous layout; separate lines of text with a leading that is slightly taller than the type size; ensure that margins are appropriate to the type of book being designed (in general, the larger they are the more important the book); avoid overly white paper: it can make reading tiresome, so opt for ivory tones.

Garamond will look very different depending on the type of paper it is printed on: on glossy paper it is very thin and not very legible, on book paper, the ink can penetrate the fibres and thicken the characters, giving it the proper weight and an optimum degree of legibility; even different effects are obtained from characters printed on paper that is smooth, calendered, satin finish, laid, etc.
As far as possible, within the same project avoid the use of different typefaces: a typeface family offers a range from normal to italics, from bold to extra bold, from upper case to all caps, from light to extra light, sufficient to differentiate various levels of information.
Reading a text means providing a graphic rhythm that moves hand in hand with its content.
Designing a book means correlating these two requirements, identifying the correct equilibrium between them, a proportion that exalts neither the one nor the other. Unlike the use of typefaces in advertising, the text of a book requires composure, uniformity, an understated and sober formal expression, a graphic harmony that increases or decreases, while always being obtained using a constant and rhythmic guide. In short, a "symphonic division of space", to use the definition of dynamic symmetry.
The theme of legibility and the pleasure of a text can be supported by much more scientific information. I will limit myself here to what has been said, and suggest a visit to a bookstore to explore all that can be found there.

Notes
Don't let yourself be influenced by a client who asks for different typefaces on the same page: a good publication can highlight different texts using the same typeface, modifying only its size, strength, presentation in normal or bold or italics, etc.

Workbook
Analyse the proportions between type size and alignment, between formats and margins, between figure and ground in various books. Record your observations of this investigation.

91

Alignment and Type Size

Width in Proportion to Height

Settings of text with very different space requirements and results.
The choice of the typeface to be used in a publication is the first creative act made by the designer. The typeface, with its design, weight, size and style defines the initial "image" of the project.
Choices involve diverse typefaces depending on the type of printing. The impact of a text is strongly influenced by these choices.

It is impossible to suggest what typeface to use for a particular project, though if it is for a book the most opportune choice is the classical Garamond, while a promotional brochure may look better in Helvetica, and so on.
In any case, it must be remembered that the legibility of a typeface changes in relation to its alignment and size. The narrower the alignment, the smaller the typeface; books tend to have a greater leading, while a promotional brochure can use a leading equal to the height of the typeface.

A title can be composed with a lower kerning value, and so on. Even the type of setting will vary from project to project; starting a new paragraph with an indent is a rule that should not be ignored in a book designed to be read quickly, to the same degree that advertising texts can substitute the indent with a line of space.

92 Line length measures the width of a line of text.
A line length of 18 means that the horizontal setting of a line of text is equal to 18 Didot lines.
In fact, the line length is normally indicated in typesetting lines the size of the typeface in points.
However, while type size remains anchored to typographic measurements, the advent of the computer makes it simpler to indicate line lengths using the metric decimal system, what is more in harmony with paper formats, photography formats, etc.
When composing a text we can easily indicate the line length in millimetres and the type size in typographic points (the examples in this book almost always use both measurements to allow for the establishment of a visual relationship between the two systems).
When defining these measurements it is important to identify a harmonic proportion between line length and type size in order to obtain the proper legibility of the text: a small line length should not host a large type size and vice versa.

The city of Bath, situated in the southeast of England, is a "unique" and unrepeatable example of urban planning, where the fortune of being located in an enchanting corner of Britain, coupled with the presence of renowned thermal waters, was happily combined with the entrepreneurial spirit of acute architects and audacious builders, who, thanks to a series of fortunate circumstances, spent more than a century creating...

1.

The city of Bath, situated in the southeast of England, is a "unique" and unrepeatable example of urban planning, where the fortune of being located in an enchanting corner of Britain, coupled with the presence of renowned thermal waters, was happily combined with the entrepreneurial spirit of acute architects and audacious builders, who, thanks to a series of fortunate circumstances, spent more than a century creating a true gallery of masterpieces from scratch. Unfortunately, this illustrious creation did not survive the devastation of the War, and the successive period of neglect, and the twentieth century...

2.

1. Text composed in 10 point Garamond bold with a 10.5 point leading aligned at 52 mm.

2. Text composed in 10 point Garamond bold with a 12 point leading aligned at 52 mm.

3. Text composed in 10 point Garamond bold with a 10.5 point leading aligned at 80 mm.

4. Text composed in 10 point Garamond bold with a 12 point leading aligned at 80 mm.

5. Text composed in 7 point Garamond bold with a 7 point leading aligned at 24 mm.

6. Text composed in 7 point Garamond bold with an 8 point leading aligned at 24 mm.

7. 8. 9. Three types of setting a non-justified text composed in 6 point text with 6 point leading and an alignment of 24 mm. Text alignment can be: flush left and ragged right; flush right and ragged left; centred or justified.

10. In typesetting alignment is established by the compositor who lays the composing stick atop a copper wire of the desired size and alignment to assign the space inside which the letters are set.

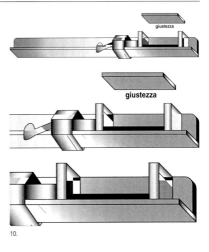

10.

The city of Bath, situated in the south-east of England, is a "unique" and unrepeatable example of urban planning, where the fortune of being located in an enchanting corner of Britain, coupled with the presence of renowned thermal waters, was happily combined with the entrepreneurial spirit of acute architects and audacious builders, who, thanks to a series of fortunate circumstances, spent more than a century creating a true gallery of masterpieces from scratch. Unfortunately, this illustrious creation did not survive the devastation of the War, and the successive period of neglect, and the twentieth century, and more precisely recent decades...

3.

The city of Bath, situated in the south-east of England, is a "unique" and unrepeatable example of urban planning, where the fortune of being located in an enchanting corner of Britain, coupled with the presence of renowned thermal waters, was happily combined with the entrepreneurial spirit of acute architects and audacious builders, who, thanks to a series of fortunate circumstances, spent more than a century creating a true gallery of masterpieces from scratch. Unfortunately, this illustrious creation did not survive the devastation of the War, and the successive period of neglect, and the twentieth century, and more precisely recent decades, the city and its neighbourhoods that had so strongly influenced Dickens' descriptions of English society in his literary masterpieces, were decimated by a policy of construction marked by bad taste and scarce culture; and their conservation (the only contemporary example) became an issue...

4.

The city of Bath, situated in the south-east of England, is a "unique" and unrepeatable example of urban planning, where the fortune of being located in an enchanting corner of Britain, coupled with the presence of renowned thermal waters, was happily combined with the entrepreneurial spirit of acute architects and audacious builders, who, thanks to a series of...

5.

The city of Bath, situated in the south-east of England, is a "unique" and unrepeatable example of urban planning, where the fortune of being located in an enchanting corner of Britain, coupled with the presence of renowned thermal waters, was happily combined with the entrepreneurial spirit of acute architects and audacious builders, who, thanks to a series of fortunate circumstances, spent more than a century creating a true gallery of masterpieces from scratch. Unfortunately, this illustrious creation did not survive the devastation...

6.

Workbook
Compose any text in various typefaces and sizes and with various line spacings, relating the sizes with line lengths considered sufficient for proper reading. In the margins list the measurements in millimetres and lines.

93

The city of Bath, England, is a unique and unrepeatable example of urban planning, where the fortune of being located in an enchanting corner of Britain coupled with the presence of renowned thermal waters, was happily combined with the entrepreneurial spirit of acute architects and audacious

7.

The city of Bath, England, is a unique and unrepeatable example of urban planning, where the fortune of being located in an enchanting corner of Britain coupled with the presence of renowned thermal waters, was happily combined with the entrepreneurial spirit of acute architects and audacious

8.

The city of Bath, England, is a unique and unrepeatable example of urban planning, where the fortune of being located in an enchanting corner of Britain coupled with the presence of renowned thermal waters, was happily combined with the entrepreneurial spirit of acute architects and audacious

9.

Text Setting

Legibility in Relation to Type Size

1. Text composed in 10 point Times Roman with a 10 point leading aligned at 52 mm. Approx. 40 characters per line. Total 1131 characters. First line indent: 5 mm.

2. Text composed in 8 point Times Roman with an 8 point leading aligned at 24 mm. Approx. 23 characters per line. Total 835 characters. First line indent: 4 mm.

3. Text composed in 7 point Times Roman with a 7 point leading aligned at 24 mm. Approx. 26 characters per line. Total 1092 characters. First line indent: 3 mm.

4. Text composed in 10 point Times Roman with a 10 point leading, aligned at 52 mm. Approx. 35 characters per line. Total 1008 characters. No first line indent.

5. Text composed in 8 point Times Roman with an 8 point leading, aligned at 24 mm. No first line indent. Approx. 20 characters per line. Total 761 characters.

6. Text composed in 7 point Times Roman with a 7 point leading, aligned at 24 mm. No first line indent. Approx. 23 characters per line. Total 961 characters.

94

1131 characters. The city of Bath, situated in the south-east of England, is a "unique" and unrepeatable example of urban planning, where the fortune of being located in an enchanting corner of Britain, coupled with the presence of renowned thermal waters, was happily combined with the entrepreneurial spirit of acute architects and audacious builders, who, thanks to a series of fortunate circumstances, spent more than a century creating a true gallery of masterpieces from scratch.

Unfortunately, this illustrious creation did not survive the devastation of the War, and the successive period of neglect, and the twentieth century, and more precisely recent decades, the city and its neighbourhoods that had so strongly influenced Dickens' descriptions of English society in his literary masterpieces, were decimated by a policy of construction marked by bad taste and scarce culture; and their conservation (the only contemporary example) became an issue combined with the conservation of the natural environment.

The history of Bath is that of an ancient Roman thermal bath city which remained such until sixteenth century...

835 characters.
The city of Bath, situated in the south-east of England, is a "unique" and unrepeatable example of urban planning, where the fortune of being located in an enchanting corner of Britain, coupled with the presence of renowned thermal waters, was happily combined with the entrepreneurial spirit of acute architects and audacious builders, who, thanks to a series of fortunate circumstances, spent more than a century creating a true gallery of masterpieces from scratch.

Unfortunately, this illustrious creation did not survive the devastation of the War, and the successive period of neglect, and the twentieth century, and more precisely recent decades, the city and its neighbourhoods that had so strongly influenced Dickens' descriptions of English society in his literary masterpieces, were decimated by a policy...

1092 characters.
The city of Bath, situated in the south-east of England, is a "unique" and unrepeatable example of urban planning, where the fortune of being located in an enchanting corner of Britain, coupled with the presence of renowned thermal waters, was happily combined with the entrepreneurial spirit of acute architects and audacious builders, who, thanks to a series of fortunate circumstances, spent more than a century creating a true gallery of masterpieces from scratch.

Unfortunately, this illustrious creation did not survive the devastation of the War, and the successive period of neglect, and the twentieth century, and more precisely recent decades, the city and its neighbourhoods that had so strongly influenced Dickens' descriptions of English society in his literary masterpieces, were decimated by a policy of construction marked by bad taste and scarce culture; and their conservation (the only contemporary example) became an issue combined with the conservation of the natural environment.

The history of Bath is that of an ancient Roman thermal bath city which...

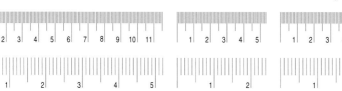

1.

2.

3.

Studies confirm
that lower case
letters are 13%
more legible than
upper case letter

S T U D I E S
C O N F I R M
TH AT   L OWER
CA SE LET TERS
ARE 13% MORE

Covering the lower part of a line of text clearly demonstrates how lower case letters are more legible than the same text in upper case letters.
The studies of Tinker and Paterson, two American psychologists, confirm that lower case letters are 13% more legible than upper case letters.

1008 characters. The city of Bath, situated in the south-east of England, is a "unique" and unrepeatable example of urban planning, where the fortune of being located in an enchanting corner of Britain, coupled with the presence of renowned thermal waters, was happily combined with the entrepreneurial spirit of acute architects and audacious builders, who, thanks to a series of fortunate circumstances, spent more than a century creating a true gallery of masterpieces from scratch. Unfortunately, this illustrious creation did not survive the devastation of the War, and the successive period of neglect, and the twentieth century, and more precisely recent decades, the city and its neighbourhoods that had so strongly influenced Dickens' descriptions of English society in his literary masterpieces, were decimated by a policy of construction marked by bad taste and scarce culture; and their conservation (the only contemporary example) became an issue combined with the conservation of the natural...

761 characters.
The city of Bath, situated in the south-east of England, is a "unique" and unrepeatable example of urban planning, where the fortune of being located in an enchanting corner of Britain, coupled with the presence of renowned thermal waters, was happily combined with the entrepreneurial spirit of acute architects and audacious builders, who, thanks to a series of fortunate circumstances, spent more than a century creating a true gallery of masterpieces from scratch. Unfortunately, this illustrious creation did not survive the devastation of the War, and the successive period of neglect, and the twentieth century, and more precisely recent decades, the city and its neighbourhoods that had so strongly influenced Dickens' descriptions of...

961 characters.
The city of Bath, situated in the south-east of England, is a "unique" and unrepeatable example of urban planning, where the fortune of being located in an enchanting corner of Britain, coupled with the presence of renowned thermal waters, was happily combined with the entrepreneurial spirit of acute architects and audacious builders, who, thanks to a series of fortunate circumstances, spent more than a century creating a true gallery of masterpieces from scratch. Unfortunately, this illustrious creation did not survive the devastation of the War, and the successive period of neglect, and the twentieth century, and more precisely recent decades, the city and its neighbourhoods that had so strongly influenced Dickens' descriptions of English society in his literary masterpieces, were decimated by a policy of construction marked by bad taste and scarce culture; and their conservation (the only contemporary example) became an issue...

Notes
In his book Confessions of an Advertising Man, *David Ogilvy describes a number of rules he applies.*
They are provided here for students, though it must be remembered that Ogilvy refers above all to advertising texts.
A title is read 5 times more than the text; composite titles of 6/12 words are more effective than short ones; captions are read after people read the content of an article; subtitles and headers increase the legibility of a text and urge readers to continue reading; short paragraphs are read more than long ones. Other suggestions: 40 keystrokes per line for a magazine; 26 for a daily newspaper; don't use type sizes smaller than 9; use glyphs with serifs because they are more legible; a space between paragraphs increases the percentage of reading by 12%.

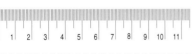

4.

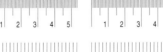

5.

6.

Phototypesetting

Typeface Manipulation

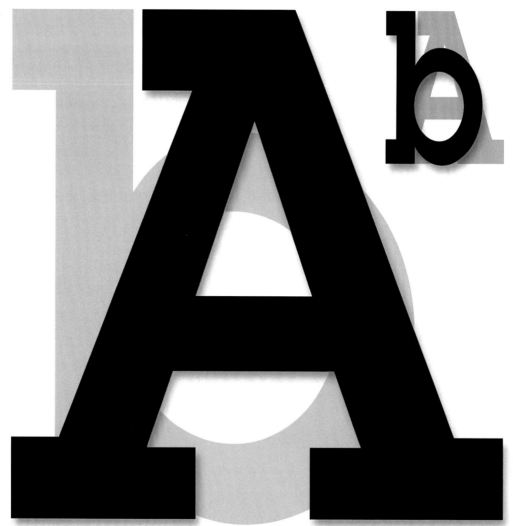

1.

Beginning in the early 1980s, thanks to systems that made it possible to rapidly obtain a text on paper or film, photocomposition revolutionised the processes of traditional typography.
A few years later, electronic desktop publishing (DTP) made it possible to simultaneously layout texts and images with a level typeface manipulation once unimaginable: classical Bodoni could be expanded, tightened, deformed and subjected to any imaginable variation or combination of glyphs.

There were many advantages for graphic artists, though with dangerous results that affected legibility.
All of the codes of harmony so accurately studied by the designers of this typeface went out the window. New codes were invented through creative processes, some highly questionable. Different approaches to leading, kerning and tracking became an exercise to be confronted by any graphic artist.

2. The composition below, constructed from four groups of the same letters (dpx) for each row, shows the visual results of the application of the horizontal scale to the Helvetica regular typeface.
Red indicates those groups whose original height and width were not varied in any way. The margin contains the relative kerning values (horizontal scale).
The logo to the right is an example of how a typeface (Avant Garde extra light) can be modified and adapted to create an axonometric representation.

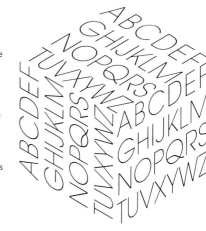

dpxdpxdpxdpx	scale 360, 330, 300, 270
dpxdpxdpxdpx	scale 290, 270, 250, 230
dpxdpxdpxdpx	scale 230, 210, 190, 170
dpxdpxdpxdpx	scale 190, 170, 150, 130
dpxdpxdpxdpx	scale 160, 140, 120, 100
dpxdpxdpxdpx	scale 120, 110, 100, 90
dpxdpxdpxdpx	scale 100, 90, 80, 70
dpxdpxdpxdpx	scale 85, 75, 65, 55
dpxdpxdpxdpx	scale 68, 62, 56, 50

2.

Phototypesetting

Text as Image and Communication

1. 2. In the two tables of the left column, the typeface is shown in its original design, without any tightening or expansion.
The other columns contain the values of progressively more accentuated alterations.

The table helps demonstrate the progressive loss in the legibility of this typeface; it also suggests how a typeface can become a drawing, an image, even an emotion, thanks to the use of new technologies.

98

| 100% | 75% | 50% | 25% | 10% | 100% | 125% | 150% | 175% |

1.

3. Studies of typeface legibility suggested the image for this 1979 poster commemorating the death of Ugo La Malfa (see the chapter on Political Graphics).

4. The assembly of the letter "N", borrowed from figure 2, creates a texture.

99

3.

Ugo La Malfa

Ugo La Malfa
16.5.1903
15.4.1979

4.

100%   75%   50%   25%   10%   100%   125%   150%   175%

2.

"Noise"

The Limits of Legibility of a Sign

The "stronger" a sign, the greater its incisiveness and impact. But to what point we can "dilate" it, pushing its visual impact, is an issue that must be explored case by case in relation to the typology of the sign itself.

The design method explored here is triggered by an analysis of a sign rendered with a constant thickness or, as we will see later on, "noise".

1./5. Figure 1 shows a polygonal (the name of this sign) in what appears to be its optimum thickness: that which, at the strongest level, leaves its movements legible. Figures 2 and 4 trace the construction of this sign, in other words the steps in its creation. Figure 3, similar to a puzzle (what will appear?, when different zones are blacked out), traces a diagram with 35 progressive dilatations (though we could go much further, in a sort of graphic delirium) and imagine an equal number of dilatations of the sign. Figure 5 shows how the overlapping of elements of different thicknesses, alternating in white or in black, produces a myriad of expressive possibilities and graphic dynamics.

Workbook
Starting with an existing sign, create a succession of thicknesses with a constant dilatation. Fill it in and compare the results testing legibility and reduction.

100

1.

2.

101

3.

4.

5.

102

Workbook
Starting with an existing sign, create a succession of thicknesses with a constant dilatation. Fill it in and compare the results testing legibility and reduction.

Workbook   103
*Starting with an
existing sign, create
a succession of
thicknesses with a
constant dilatation.
Fill it in and compare
the results testing
legibility and reduction.*

"Disturbance"

The Limits of Legibility of a Typeface

A typeface read under poor light, or at a great distance, or out of focus, produces "noise", a visual "fog" that hinders its perception.
A typeface is considered out of focus when it has blurred edges and lacks sharpness; as reading conditions become more critical, this sense of being out of focus increases, leading to problems of legibility.

This test is a useful experiment when designing a typeface. It establishes a code for leading, kerning and tracking. It can also help select a typeface for a book, for a sign read by the public, or for any communication subject to variable reading conditions.

1. 2. The alphabets in the tables are, in order, in Helvetica, Optima, Lubalin and Times, composed using the automatic spacing assigned by a computer program.
A "disturbance" was then added, equivalent to a shift out of focus of approximately 1/7 of the type size (5 points to size 36).
The results show us how each typeface responds to "noise".

104

Workbook
Add "noise" to various typefaces, surrounding them progressively with "disturbances". We can discover which typefaces best "resist" the disturbance provoked by the dilation of its original design. We should consider this research when selecting the lettering for a sign whose type size and above all legibility in relation to the distance from which it is to be read play a determinant role.

1.

3. The upper case letter A, reproduced from the top left, in Avant Garde, Futura, Garamond, Helvetica, Lubalin, Geneva, Optima, Peignot and Times. Disturbance is calculated as a progressive increase in thickness of 1/5 of the type size.
It is interesting to note the different behaviour of the letters and the point of non-legibility demonstrated by the graphic dilations.

ABCDEFGHIJKLM
NOPQRSTUVXYWZ
abcdefghijklm
nopqrstuvxywz
0123456789

ABCDEFGHIJKLM
NOPQRSTUVXYWZ
abcdefghijklm
nopqrstuvxywz
0123456789

ABCDEFGHIJKLM
NOPQRSTUVXYWZ
abcdefghijklm
nopqrstuvxywz
0123456789

ABCDEFGHIJKLM
NOPQRSTUVXYWZ
abcdefghijklm
nopqrstuvxywz
0123456789

2.

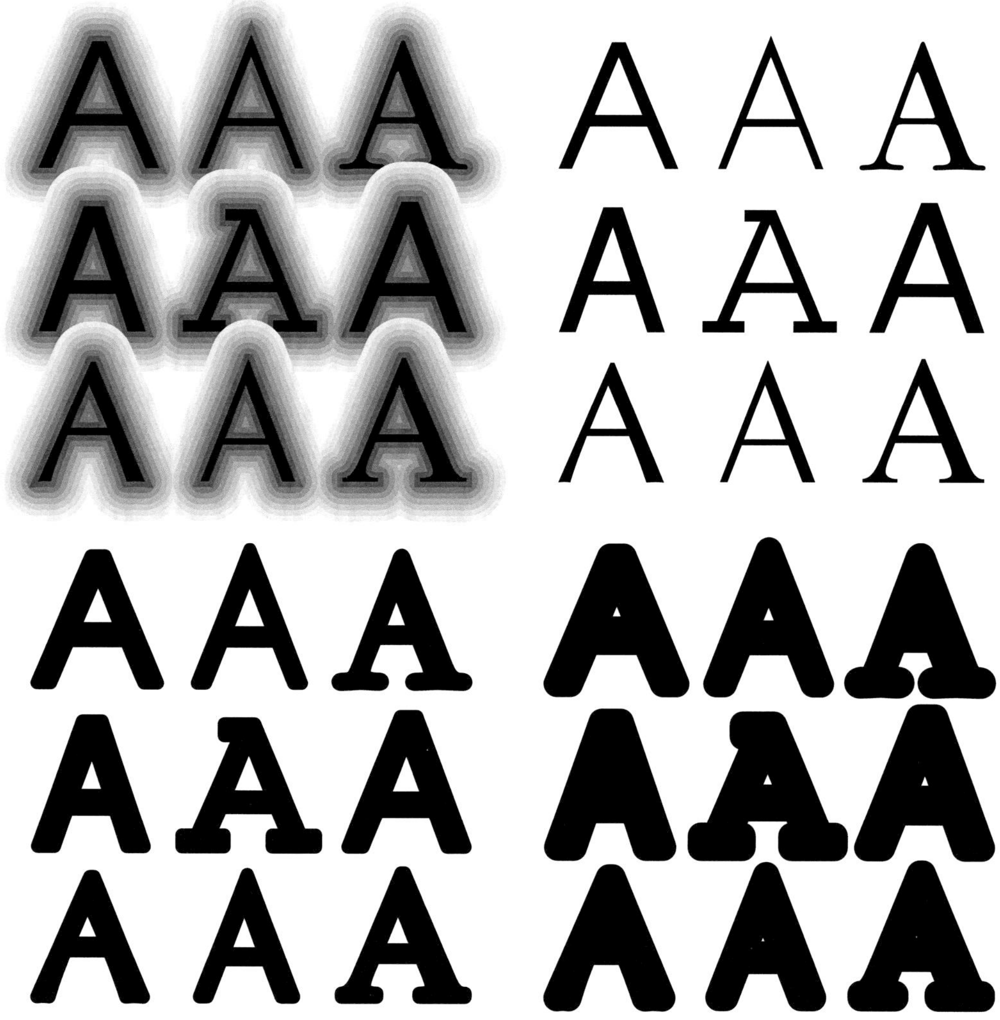

105

3.

8.

Typography

The Origins of Printing

1.

106 It is impossible to speak about typography without briefly looking back at its origins. Prior to Gutenberg's development of moveable type, the only known method of printing multiple copies of an image or text was xylographics, or woodcut (from the Greek *xúlon*, wood and *gràphein*, to write). The woodcut technique uses different sized burins to carve a subject into a wooden block by removing the area around it so that it remains in relief (the technique is known as relief engraving, as opposed to metal engraving, in chalcography, *acquaforte*, *acquatinta* and drypoint, obtained instead using a reverse process known as intaglio).

After applying ink to the raised surface, the block is placed on a piece of paper to create a print either pressing by hand or using a press.

The technique of xylographics was used initially to print fabrics and reproduce drawings; later, it was used more frequently for texts, including small booklets of pages that were stitched together. Each printed page required a carving of each and every letter, with no possibility to make corrections or reuse what had already been engraved.

Gutenberg's invention was based on an absolutely different principle: the assembly of loose type as needed, to compose a text and reuse the letters afterward. The loose type created by Gutenberg initially consisted of small pieces of engraved wood marked at one end by the figure of a glyph; Gutenberg himself later managed to obtain metal engravings of the letters. It was his historic partner Joachim Fust, together with Pietro Schöffer, who later perfected the punches required to hammer out the relative matrixes used to obtain parallelepipeds with raised glyphs, all perfectly identical.

The matrix could then be used to forge thousands of examples of the same glyph by pouring a lead alloy, an operation carried out by hand.

The matrix was set in a form that served to contain the molten alloy. The form was made of two easy to separate pieces and it was necessary to wait for the alloy to cool before removing the letters.

The adoption of moveable type gave the printed page a uniform appearance unknown until this moment.

Notes
Xylographics reached its apex with Dürer, and was later enriched by chiaroscuro effects by Campagnola and Ugo of Capri.
Wood has now been substituted by linoleum.

Bibliography
▼*Bruno Blasselle*
Il libro dal papiro a Gutenberg
Universale
Electa/Gallimard

Johannes Gutenberg

The 42-Line Bible

1. The city of Mainz in a historic woodcut print.

2. Selected pages from the *42-Line Bible*, the first book to be produced in identical multiple copies.

3. The page layout grid used for the *42-Line Bible*, in a reconstruction that emphasises the harmony of every part the page.

Johannes Gutenberg was born in Mainz in 1400. Regarding his time in Strasbourg we know that in 1439 he was involved in a trial: a certain Andres Dritzehen had lent him some money in exchange for information about a mysterious art that employed a press and small pieces of metal, an art referred to by one of the witnesses as *dem Trucken*, undoubtedly tied to some form of printing.

The first examples of typographic art appear in Mainz between 1445 and 1450. They include a small fragment of a German poem on the Universal Judgment (*Sibyllenbuch*), composed using the same letters found in fragments of the Latin grammar of Donatus and the successive *Catholicon*, printed in 1460.

Gutenberg returned to Mainz in 1449, where he partnered with Joachim Fust, who provided the necessary funding. Together they created the first real book: *The 42-Line Bible*, most likely printed in 1455. The book, named for the number of lines per page, is also known as the *Mazarin Bible*. Printed in two columns in folio format, it is a true masterpiece of typography. With it, the newly born art of typography produced, in its first attempt, a work that was already perfect, and has yet to be surpassed.

The investments required to create the book were significant, and the copies sold were not sufficient to cover expenses. Gutenberg and Fust argued, separated and each went his own way.

Fust later partnered with Schöffer and together, in 1457, they produced the first book bearing the name of a printer, and some thirty other volumes.

2.

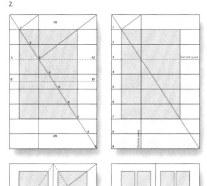

3.

Notes
The colophon is an indication that is generally found at the end of a book. It contains the name of the printer and the year of the edition. In manuscripts, it often contains the name of the amanuense and other news about the work. The first colophon in the history of typography appeared in the Mainz Psalter. It reads: "This volume of the Psalms, adorned with a magnificence of capital letters and clearly divided by rubrics, has been fashioned by a mechanical process of printing and producing letters, without use of a pen, and it was laboriously completed, for God's Holiness, by Joachim Fust, citizen of Mainz, and Peter Schoeffer of Gernsheim, on Assumption Eve in the year of Our Lord, 1457".

The Spread of Printing Works Across Europe

From 1445 to 1500

Following the printing of the first book, this new art spread across Europe at surprising speed. In only twenty years, a market of almost unlimited potential was established, with countless requests arriving from universities and religious institutions. The new technique invented by Gutenberg was destined to profoundly mark the spread of culture and ideas.

108

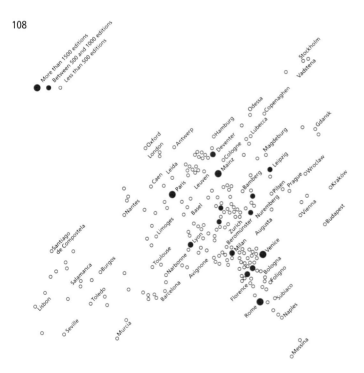

Workbook
Take a guided tour of a printing works that still works with lead letters.
Learn about the terms type case, glyph, type size, em, en, thick, mezzano, filetti, setting stick, vantaggio, forme. From setting to printing.

Universities
in Europe

From 1450 to 1650

Printing works almost
always developed near
universities, which
provided the most
requests for printed
material.

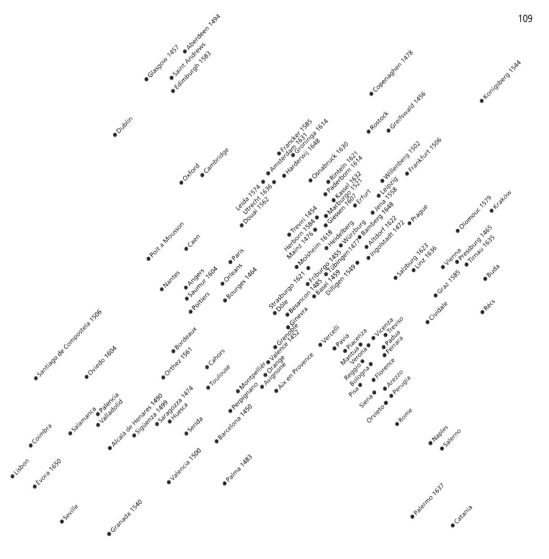

A Visit to a Historic Printing Works

The Relics of An Ancient Tradition

1. The entrance to a historic printing works in Rome. In the foreground is the *"proto"*, the manager and coordinator of each phase of work.

110

1.

Piles of forms bound with string, desks covered by lead sheets piled one atop the other, black ink and lampblack everywhere, the unmistakable smell of petroleum mixed with the exhaust from the fusion of a linotype, the ordered rhythmic movement of typesetters returning type to their cases, pulling on the handle of a setting stick or tightening a form or inking and pressing the first draft:

this is the image of the printing works of graphic designers of the past.
It has its own fascination, and its own rhythm.
It also had its own names, a precise nomenclature and ways of doing things, steeped in ancient traditions.

2. The alloy used to cast type was composed of variable percentages of lead, antimony and tin.
Lead was used for its malleability and ease of fusion; antimony for its hardness; tin served to create an alloy resistant to oxidation.
The percentages of these elements varied based on the size of the type. The table to the right lists some of these values.

	Pb Lead %	Sb Antimony %	Sn Tin %
Weak alloy Line spacing and margins	80	19	1
Ordinary alloy Large type	75	21	4
Hard alloy Medium sized type	69	24	7
Very hard alloy Small type	54	29	17

Centuries after Gutenberg's invention, the process of producing letters has remained substantially the same. New techniques and advanced electronic processes have sped up the production of a process that has remained largely unchanged.
Systems of production have passed through various stages and been gradually perfected: from the system of hammering letters with a stamp, no longer in use, to a galvanic bath, to engraving with a lathe-pantograph, to the invention, in 1840 in New York by David Bruce and the Danish Brandt, of a foundry machine.
Over time the Parisian Foucher, the German Kustermann, the American Supra and England's Wicks Rotary Typecaster perfected the fabrication of type to the point that it was possible to produce 12,000 pieces an hour.
Following the introduction of cold typesetting using computers and digital systems, old world typography has been relegated to the realm of industrial archaeology: marking the dawn of a new era of typography.
Despite all of this, traditional typography conserves its fascination, an unmatched quality of printed letters and, above all, its own educational function that is retraced here, albeit very briefly.

111

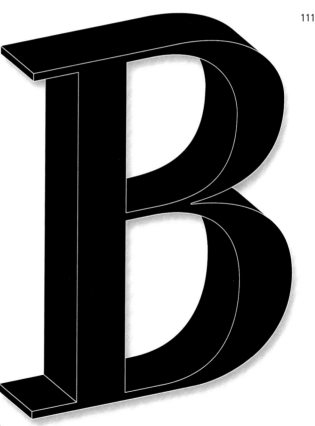

2.

Moveable Type

A Parallelepiped with Many Names

1. The nomenclature of a piece of type: shoulder, height, face, body, groove, nick, foot, kerning.

2. Various types of nicks. The nick is a notch on the front or rear of a sort. It varies in depth and thickness. The arrangement of the nicks helps the typesetter recognise the type and ensure that all pieces are aligned in the same direction.

In typography, dimensions are expressed in rows and points using a duodecimal system. One row is equal to twelve points, half a row to 6 points, and each point is equal to 0.376065 millimetres.

112 Moveable type consists of parallelepipeds known as sorts cast in lead, antimony and tin, and topped by a reversed glyph.
Each part of the parallelepiped has its own specific name and function.
Each moveable type letter is composed of the following elements:
Face. The relief of the upper part of the letter or symbol. The depth of the face is the height of the relief of the letter. The dimension of the face establishes the width of the character; the thickness of the print, in other words the intensity and blackness of the letter, is known as type strength.
Shoulder. Upper or lower part of the sort, not occupied by the face. Depending on how the glyph is constructed, the shoulder establishes the distance between rows. In type setting there are glyphs with very pronounced ascenders and descenders and thus with large shoulders; they cannot be set close together more than the size of the shoulder, automatically creating the leading.
Height. The distance between the foot and the surface of the face. This distance coincides with that of the printing machine and varies from country to country.
Body or Point Size. The distance between the front and back of the body (face + shoulder). The body or point size is the measure of the height of the letter and is expressed in points. Technically, the body should be measured from the extremities of an ascender and descender, however, this measurement must be accompanied by that of the shoulder, which can vary widely depending on the design of the letter.
Foot. The base of the block supporting the letter.

Kerning. The distance between the extreme left and right edge of each glyph. It determines the distance between glyphs. Kerning is subordinated to the way in which the sort has been cast. In type setting, the kerning between a capital A and a capital T is an example of a critical combination: it is compromised by the space of the sort that creates a visually unattractive "approach".
Nick. A notch in the front or back of the body at diverse distances from the foot. The nick helps the typesetter recognise the sorts by touch and to place them in the composing stick in the proper direction.
Groove. A notch that serves for the most part to lighten the sort and save on casting material.

Notes
During the second half of the 1800s a new machine was introduced, known as the linotype. It allowed type to be set by tapping on a keyboard; each tap corresponds with a matrix dropped from a warehouse, making it possible to set an entire row, which was then fused into a single block.

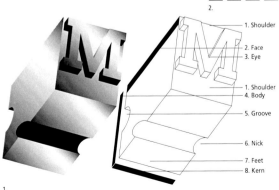

2.

1. Shoulder
2. Face
3. Eye
1. Shoulder
4. Body
5. Groove
6. Nick
7. Feet
8. Kern

1.

Type-height varies from country to country. Manufacturers and type foundries produce sorts that are taller than the maximum size on order so that they can reduce them to the required height. The following table lists some of the most common type-heights. It should be remembered that a regulation establishes a unified type-height of 23.576 mm.

American Height	22.875 mm
English Height	23.317 mm
French Height	23.566 mm
Fournier Height	23.620 mm
Prague Height	23.869 mm
Piedmont Height	24.024 mm
Italian Height	24.809 mm
German Height	25.560 mm
Russian Height	27.091 mm

4. A sort is a metal parallelepiped engraved with a raised and reversed letter or other glyph.
Inked and pressed onto a sheet of paper, the glyph can be read in the proper direction. The total height of a letter, including the foot, is 63 typography points.

5. The sum of typography lines set by hand, with margins, white spaces, *filleti*, etc., are known as a forms.
Forms are tightened using a letterpress. This tool serves to tighten the composition that, at this point, is ready to be inserted in the press.

To compose a line of text, sorts are aligned by hand in a horizontal row using a composing or setting stick; this operation is known as alignment when the letters are all of the same size and *paragonaggio* when the letters have a different face. Kerning is the act of placing letters beside one another. It varies from letter to letter based on how they have been cast.
The typesetter can insert spacers between letters to create a harmonic line of text, considering the critical combinations of the letters A and T, Y and A, and so on. Letters are then tightened into a fixed width, which defines a row of text or the width of a row. A page is created by adding rows to one another. They are then tightened in a frame known as a form. The printing machine then inks the raised letters and prints them on a sheet of paper. Sorts are now pieces of industrial archaeology.
Even the most modest computer contains entire families of typefaces and allows them to be manipulated, kerned, compressed or expanded at will.
The basic rules that required one to deal with line spacing and kerning without the possibility to make visual corrections have changed radically. In some cases they have become simpler, thanks to the computer, and in others more complex precisely because it is now possible to assemble letters at a speed once unimaginable (differentiated spacing is a perfect example). Even if you never use a sort, it is without a doubt useful to know about them: a leap back into an unknown world, before it becomes impossible to even visit a printing works.

4.

6.

Notes 113
When Johannes Gutenberg invented moveable type in 1446, he revolutionised the system of printing. Peter Schöffer, who once worked with Gutenberg, engraved the punches used to hammer out the matrixes that served to create the sorts with their raised glyphs.

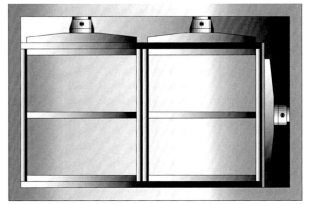

5.

1. The printing works. In manual typesetting, the typesetter retrieves the sorts from a *type case* to compose a line of text aligned in a *composing* or *setting stick*.

Sorts are always stored in the same dedicated trays in type cases so they can be easily found and recognised. Every type case is divided into two parts: one, known as the lower case, for lower case letters and spacers; the other (the upper case) for upper case letters and less frequently used letters. The cases resemble shallow drawers. A single cabinet usually contains about twenty. Each case contains an alphabet and for each alphabet either regular, italic or bold letters.

2. Typeset compositions with or without spaces. Blank spaces, which are lower approximately 10 points lower than a letter (53 instead of 63 points), are not printed. They are known as *spacers* are used to separate letters; *line spacers* are used to separate rows; when necessary, *margining* is used to frame a text.
3. Margining.
Spacing is obtained by inserting spacers between letters or rows of text: the quad is the base measurement of these spaces. It is equivalent to the letter strength, such that a quad with a body of 10 is 10 points wide, measured against the strength and width.

4. Line spacers serve to distance rows of text. Spaces have the following names:
Finissimo=1 point;
Fino=1 and a half points;
1/2 EN=6 points;
Grosso (thick)=4 pt;
EN=6 points;
EM=12 points;
Double EM=24 points;
Triple EM=36 points.

2.

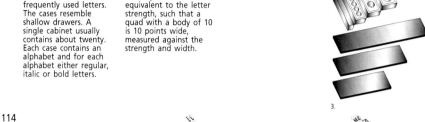

3.

114

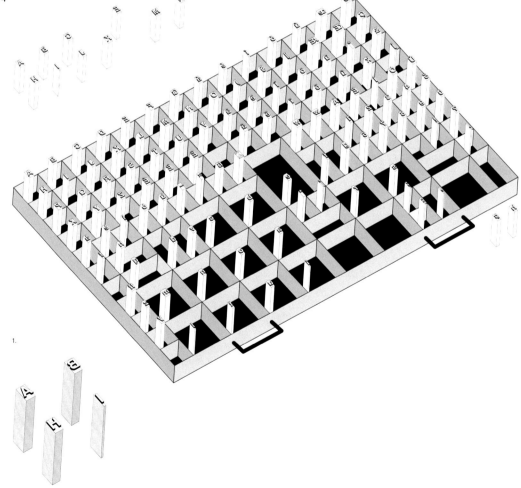

1.

	1 point
	3 points
	6 points
	12 points
	24 points
	36 points

4.

5. Line spacers serve to distance rows of text. Spaces have the following names:
Finissimo=1 point;
Fino=1 and a half points;
1/2 EN=6 points;
Grosso (thick)=4 pt;
EN=6 points;
EM=12 points;
Double EM=24 points;
Triple EM=36 points.

6. The composing stick is used by the typesetter to collect and align the sorts extracted from the type case to a predefined column width.
To create this width, the typesetter lays a *filetto* of the desired length on the composing stick and tightens the handle: this is the space in which the sorts will be aligned.

7. The *vantaggio* is the tool used by the typesetter to lay the rows that have been composed in the composing stick and, in so doing, to create a page and the type *forme*. Large compositions require the use of a *balestra* in lieu of the *vantaggio*.

8. The type case containing the sorts. Their arrangement depends on the frequency of use. As shown in the illustration, less frequently used sorts are found at the back of the case.
Type cases vary depending on the arrangement of the sorts inside them.

9. 10. Pneumatic mail systems were commonly used to move articles as quickly as possible from the editorial offices to the typography.
Below, a copy editor controls the first copies of a newspaper that have just come off the rotary printing press.

11. In this ancient engraving, a typesetter closes a typography *forme*.

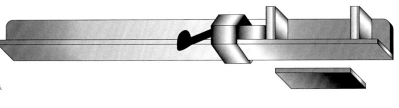

6.

Notes 115
Once a page has been laid out, it is placed in a forme *together with the other pages that together form, for example, a* quartino, *in the order corresponding with the page numbers.*
To regulate this structure, it is necessary to understand the size of the paper on which the material is to be printed.

7.

A	B	C	D	E	F	G	á	é	í	ó	ú	œ	æ
H	I	JK	L	M	N	O	)	§	*]	Æ	Œ	Ç	ç
P	Q	R	S	T	U	V	â	ê	î	ô	û	✳	&
X	Y	Z	É	Ê	Ë		ä	ë	ï	ö	ü	k	j

à	è	ì	ò	ù	–	«	f	ff		e	w	W	À	È	Ì	Ò	Ù
fi	h	b	v	c		d				f	g	1	2	3	4	5	
fl	q											6	7	8	9	0	
fi	m	n	o	a					'	.	r		s	spazi fini	!	?	
z										p				spazi mezzani		.	
y	l	t	u	i					spazi forti	quadratini		;	,	quadrati			
x										:							

8.

9.

10.

11.

Images from a Printing Works Prior to the Digital Age

1. A composing stick. The text, composed in reverse, prints the letters in the correct direction when placed in the printing machine.

2. A letter with a body of 6 points in the hands of a typesetter. Prior to the advent of the linotype, even a page of very small type was composed entirely by hand.

3. The typesetting shelf with its properly arranged margins set to the correct dimensions and the column width. The margins are parallelepipeds cast in an alloy that are set into the composition of the text to create white spaces that are not printed and to set the various margins around the pages.

116

1.

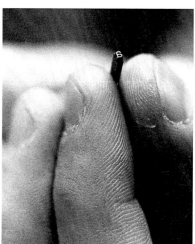

2.

3.

4.

4. A spatula used to ink the rolls of a galley proof.

5. A type case subdivided into various slots.

6. A key for a chase. This tools serves to tighten the letters, margins, clichés and any other elements placed in the chase.

7. A chase in which the various elements of the print matrix have been tightened.

8. Type cases from a historic printing works in an image from the 1960s.

9. Linotypists at work in a historic printing works in San Carlo al Corso, Rome. It was here that the texts of *La Voce repubblicana* were composed in the early 1960s. The linotype composes and melds single rows of text.

9.

117

5.

6.

7.

8.

9.
Typefaces

A General Classification

The common English word font derives from the medieval French word *"fonte"*, "(something that has been) fused"(from the Latin *fundere*). It refers to the moveable type produced for typography, obtained by pouring molten metal into a mould containing the matrix of a single glyph.
A typeface consists of a series of glyphs (images) belonging to a family with a particular style or design.
A font generally contains a variable number of symbols, known as glyphs, comprised of letters, numbers and punctuation.

Typefaces may also contain ideograms and symbols, such as mathematical symbols, musical notes, geographic signs, icons, designs and much more.
In the broadest terms, the design of a font can be defined as a series of rules (for example, of style, image or impression) that a designer can use to create each individual glyph.
This definition also permits the addition of new glyphs for existing typefaces, for example the introduction of the Euro symbol.

Ammon the many criteria for classifying typefaces used during the twentieth century, that of Francois Thibaudeau (1924) was adopted for its clarity of structure and simple terms. It is commonly used by type foundries and printing works to subdivide glyphs in type cases.
Thibaudeau determined the style of Latin characters based on the visual form of their serifs and identified 4 main groups: sans serif, rectangular serifs, triangular and modelled serifs, thin serifs.

118 Understanding the form of glyphs is the first step in the study of a typeface, or better yet, of typography. As typography is the art of using mechanical means to multiply writing, its principal function should be that of reproducing alphabets based on the forms in use in different nations.
Typefaces can be considered the most important of the graphic elements commonly referred to as "iterative", that is, those components of a printed work that are normally reutilised. Already in the past, there was a need to compile samples of glyphs. Over time, there was a need to stylistically combine various groups to establish universally valid criteria.
An initial basic classification, given by form, size and proportion, was followed by the classifications Roman, Italics and Chancery. These criteria are now wholly insufficient, most likely due to the existence of a vast variety of styles linked to the introduction of industrial processes to manufacture glyphs, which subjected them to increasingly more numerous elaborations.
The attempt to develop an exhaustive classification was complicated by the infinite variety of typefaces. Numerous designers and typesetters, and even specific commissions to scholars, have proposed various systems over the past decades.

When designing an alphabet, it assumes different "forms" and "styles" based on the variations made to the two fundamental elements that make up a glyph: the strokes and the serifs. The stylistic classification introduced by Francois Thibaudeau considers 4 fundamental families of characters:
1. Antique or sans-serif or linear
2. Egyptian
3. Antique Roman
4. Modern Roman

A successive classification is based on series. The same style can produce a series of glyphs differentiated by inclination, tone, etc.
There are 6 fundamental denominations:
1. Upper case, small caps, lower case, when referring to their orthographic use.
2. Regular and italics, when referring to the uprightness or inclination of a character.
3. Ultra light, light, normal, medium, bold, extra bold, to describe the thickness of the strokes.
4. Extra condensed, condensed, normal, medium, wide, extra wide, depending on the face of the glyph.
5. Simple, ornate (dashed, dotted, shadowed) to describe the particular ornamentation that can be applied.
6. Positive or negative, based on the reversal of type during printing.

Note
The classification of typefaces has yet to be fully completed. That developed in 1921 by Francois Thibaudeau considers two primary elements consisting of the strokes and serifs. The classification of Maximilien Vox, from 1954, inspired above all by the history of a typeface, expanded Thibaudeau's classification to 9 families.
In 1962, ATypl, the Association Typographique Internationale, drew up its own classification of 11 families.
In 1964 Erman Zapf and Willy Mengel developed the DIN 16518 regulation, which retraces that of ATypl, and adds references relative to each family.
The classification of Aldo Novarese includes 10 distinct families, differentiated by the form of their serifs. The classification of Marcel Jacno reduces the families to 4, each identified by their alignments and decorative elements.
The Alessandrini classification (Codice 80) expands on its predecessors by specifying historic, stylistics and aesthetic influences.

Thibaudeau	Vox	Codice 80
Sans-Serif	Sans-Serif	Linear
Egyptian / English Egyptian	Egyptian / English Egyptian	Egyptian
Modern Roman	Bodoni	Modern Roman, Transitional
Antique Roman	Venetian / Garalde / Transitional	Elzevir
Triangular Serif		Deltapod, Transitional
Hellenics	Lapidaries	Engraved
Script	Script	Script Calligraphy
	Manual	Onciati
Gothic	Gothic	Gothic
	Other Forms	Others / Non-Latin / Mechanical / Fantasies / Hybrids

An initial classification of typefaces is based on the presence or absence of serifs: this gives us two principal groups characterised by glyphs with or without (sans) serifs.
A more in-depth classification derives from the strength of the strokes and the design of the serifs. Gothic typefaces, script and fantasy characters are considered sub-families. The Chancery family, not represented here, is commonly used for typewriters.
Further distinctions are made within each family.

The Egyptian family (whose name derives from their good fortune during the Napoleonic campaigns) is subdivided into 4 typologies:
a. Classical Egyptian: characters with serifs of a thickness equal to that of the strokes and a radiused fillet, also known as Classical Egyptian.
b. With serifs of the same thickness as the strokes and a 90° fillet.
c. With serifs whose ends feature an oblique connection.
d. Italics, with serifs of a greater width than the strokes and a 90° fillet.

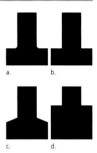

119

	Family 1	Linear, Sans-Serif, Etruscan, Grotesque	Uniform strokes	No serifs
	Family 2	Egyptian	Uniform strokes	90° serifs with a thickness equal to or greater than the strokes
	Family 3	Ancient Romans or Elzevir	Thin and thick strokes with accentuated contrasts. Oblique strokes to round glyphs	Triangular serifs with curved connections to strokes
	Family 4	Modern Romans	Thin and thick strokes with heavily accentuated contrasts. The axis of round glyphs is vertical	Horizontal serifs whose thickness is almost always equal to the thin strokes
	Family 5	Gothic or Medieval Imitation of handwriting used in Codexes		
	Family 6	Script or English Imitation of handwriting	Strokes featuring strong contrasts. Imitation of broad pen strokes	
	Family 7	Fantasy Elaborate and often decorative glyphs		

A Graphic Line of Text

The Relationship between Upper Case, Lower Case and Numbers

1. *Ascender line:* an imaginary line marking the maximum height of the body; *intermediate line:* a line that establishes the height of the body; *base line:* a line below the foot of each upper case letter; *descender line:* the point on which descender letters rest; *height* or *face:* distance between the intermediate line and the base line, generally measured using the lower case letter x.

Ascender: upper part of the stroke of the letter d; *descender:* lower part of the stroke of the letter p. The d is the first letter of the alphabet with an ascender, the p the first letter of the paradigmatic descenders and the x permits the most correct measurements. Note the projection of the curved letters.

2. Letters wlth a circular and triangular scheme are optically corrected and project beyond the ascender and descender lines.

120

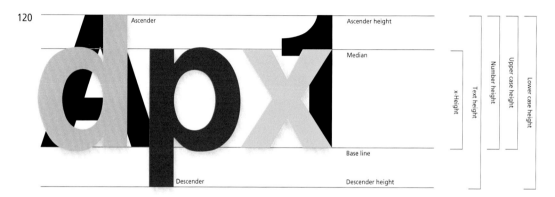

1.

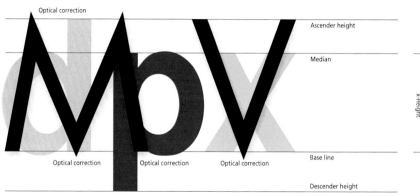

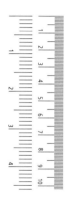

2.

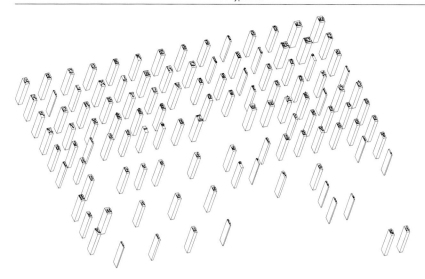

Body Upper Case Height		Minimum Line Spacing without initial letters		Minimum Line Spacing with initial letters		Type Size 1/48 of an EM
		Normal Descender Strokes	Large Descender Strokes	Normal Descender Strokes	Large Descender Strokes	
Didot Points	mm	mm	mm	mm	mm	mm
5	1.32	2	2	2.25	2.5	0.0390
6	1.59	2.25	2.5	2.5	2.75	0.0468
7	1.85	2.75	3	3	3.5	0.0546
8	2.12	3	3.25	3.5	3.75	0.0625
9	2.38	3.5	3.75	4	4.25	0.0703
10	2.65	3.75	4	4.25	4.75	0.0781
11	2.91	4.25	4.5	4.75	5.25	0.0859
12	3.18	4.5	4.75	5.25	5.75	0.0937
13	3.44	5	5.25	5.75	6.25	0.1015
14	3.71	5.25	5.75	6	6.5	0.1033
15	3.97	5.75	6.25	6.5	7	0.1171
16	4.24	6	6.5	7	7.5	0.1250
17	4.5	6.5	7	7.5	8	0.1328
18	4.77	6.75	7.25	7.75	8.5	0.1406
19	5.03	7.25	7.75	8.25	9	0.1484
20	5.3	7.5	8.25	8.75	9.5	0.1562
21	5.56	8	8.5	9	10	0.1640
22	5.83	8.25	9	9.5	10.25	0.1718
23	6.09	8.75	9.5	10	10.75	0.1796
24	6.36	9	9.75	10.25	11.25	0.1875
25	6.62	9.5	10.25	10.75	11.75	0.1953
26	6.89	9.75	10.5	11.25	12.25	0.2031
27	7.15	10.25	11	11.75	12.75	0.2100
28	7.42	10.5	11.5	12.25	13.25	0.2187
29	7.68	11	12	12.5	13.75	0.2265
30	7.95	11.25	12.25	13	14.25	0.2343
31	8.21	11.75	12.75	13.5	14.5	0.2421
32	8.48	12	13	13.75	15	0.25
33	8.74	12.5	13.5	14.25	15.5	0.2578
34	9.01	12.75	14	14.75	16	0.2656
35	9.27	13.25	14.25	15.25	16.5	0.2734
36	9.54	13.5	14.5	15.5	17	0.2812

Notes
The tables to the left, from a type foundry catalogue, refer to measures relative to hot type. These measurements guarantee the harmony of the composition and the proper spacing for the selected typeface.

The Parts
of a Glyph

Adopting the UNI Standards

The vast bibliography on typefaces includes often contrasting definitions.

The *Ente italiano di unificazione* has produced a number of studies (UNI 9874) with the intention of regulating and standardising a nomenclature that remains very confusing and contradictory. We will not delve too deeply into this issue here, limiting the discussion to a few indications that in general terms respect the definitions that appear most correct.

Recognising a typeface signifies understanding its components. A glyph is composed of:
straight lines
ascender strokes
descender strokes
transversal strokes
curve lines
and a series of additional parts known as:
tails
arms
barbs
posts
ties
shoulders
vertexes
terminals
or serifs.

The strokes can be straight, curved, mixed, etc. Straight strokes are vertical and can be either ascenders, descenders or medians. Transversal strokes are those that unite vertical strokes.
Curved strokes can be open as in the letter C, or closed as in the letter O.
A tail is the hanging stroke of particular glyphs.

122

Vertical Strokes

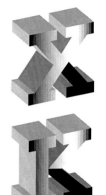

Lower Strokes

Cross Bars

Cross Bars

XKK
DQR

Tail

DPX ABCEFGHIJKL
MNOQRSTUVWYZ
dpx abcefghijkl
mnoqrstuvwyz

Arms

DPX ABCEFGHIJKL
MNOQRSTUVWYZ
dpx abcefghijkl
mnoqrstuvwyz

Loops

DPX ABCEFGHIJKL
MNOQRSTUVWYZ
dpx abcefghijkl
mnoqrstuvwyz

Typeface Styles

Many Series Make Up a Family

1. 2. Each family of type can be comprised of diverse series. Faces can be regular, italic (inclined from left to right) or atypical italic (inclined from right to left). The strength of the face can be extra light, light, regular, bold, extra bold, heavy, etc.

The strength of type varies widely from one typeface to another, as shown in the comparison between Helvetica and Futura. The proportion of a typeface can be normal, condensed, extra condensed, wide or extra wide.

124

Helvetica extra light

ABCDEFGHIJK
LMNOPQRSTUV
XYWZ
abcdefghijklmno
pqrstuvxywz
1234567890

Helvetica extra light italic

ABCDEFGHIJK
LMNOPQRSTUV
XYWZ
abcdefghijklmno
pqrstuvxywz
1234567890

Helvetica heavy

ABCDEFGHIJ
KLMNOPQRST
UVXYWZ
abcdefghijklmn
opqrstuvxywz
1234567890

Helvetica regular

ABCDEFGHIJK
LMNOPQRSTUV
XYWZ
abcdefghijklmno
pqrstuvxywz
1234567890

Helvetica medium italic

ABCDEFGHIJK
LMNOPQRSTUV
XYWZ
abcdefghijklmno
pqrstuvxywz
1234567890

Helvetica heavy oblique

ABCDEFGHIJ
KLMNOPQRST
UVXYWZ
abcdefghijklmn
opqrstuvxywz
1234567890

Helvetica bold

ABCDEFGHIJK
LMNOPQRSTUV
XYWZ
abcdefghijklmno
pqrstuvxywz
1234567890

Helvetica bold italic

ABCDEFGHIJK
LMNOPQRSTUV
XYWZ
abcdefghijklmno
pqrstuvxywz
1234567890

Condensed typefaces are designed beforehand: this means they respect the original design of a typeface and its proportions.

Digital typesetting makes it possible to condense a typeface at will, both in its width and height.
We must be careful: this process, which is mathematical and not analytical, deforms the typeface and damages the harmony created by its designer.
It can happen that we come across texts that have been rendered illegible by the improper use of this tool.

125

Futura light

ABCDEFGHIJK
LMNOPQRSTUV
XYWZ
abcdefghijklmno
pqrstuvxywz
1234567890

Futura light italic

ABCDEFGHIJK
LMNOPQRSTUV
XYWZ
abcdefghijklmno
pqrstuvxywz
1234567890

Futura heavy

ABCDEFGHIJK
LMNOPQRSTUV
XYWZ
abcdefghijklmno
pqrstuvxywz
1234567890

Futura book

ABCDEFGHIJK
LMNOPQRSTUV
XYWZ
abcdefghijklmno
pqrstuvxywz
1234567890

Futura book italic

ABCDEFGHIJK
LMNOPQRSTUV
XYWZ
abcdefghijklmno
pqrstuvxywz
1234567890

Futura heavy oblique

ABCDEFGHIJK
LMNOPQRSTUV
XYWZ
abcdefghijklmno
pqrstuvxywz
1234567890

Futura bold

ABCDEFGHIJK
LMNOPQRSTUV
XYWZ
abcdefghijklmno
pqrstuvxywz
1234567890

Futura bold italic

ABCDEFGHIJK
LMNOPQRSTUV
XYWZ
abcdefghijklmno
pqrstuvxywz
1234567890

The Design of a Typeface

The Matrixes for Constructing Type

Approaching the design of a typeface signifies recognising its characteristics and form and thus opting for the choice of one typeface or another in an informed manner.
The principal and most traditional schemes for designing a typeface are the grid and the decimal.
In general, these schemes constitute the base for the construction of upper and lower case letters; however, in some cases a different geometry is more suitable to the definition of upper and lower case letters and numbers.

1. 2. Grid scheme and decimal division for the construction of the Garaldus typeface, as it was proposed, for educational purposes, in an illustration from the Enciclopedia della stampa published by the Politecnico di Torino.

Bibliography
▼*Antonio and Ivana Tubaro Lettering Studi e ricerche Idea Books*
□*Luigi Astori Disegno geometrico dei caratteri Enciclopedia della stampa Politecnico di Torino*

126

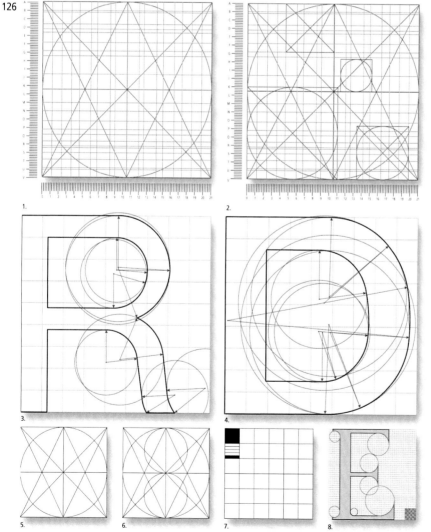

1.

2.

3.

4.

5.

6.

7.

8.

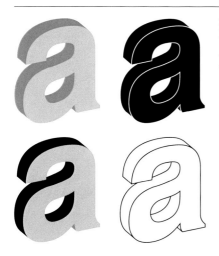

3. 4. Construction of the letters R and D from the word *Dreher* in an image designed for Dreher Beer distributed by Unimark.

5. 9. Antonio and Ivana Tubaro in the book *Lettering, studi e ricerche*, show the construction of the grids of the Bodoni typeface with the proportions of the strokes in the upper left and the geometric grid for the construction of the Romain du Roi alphabet designed in 1702, inspired by the forms of Roman letters.

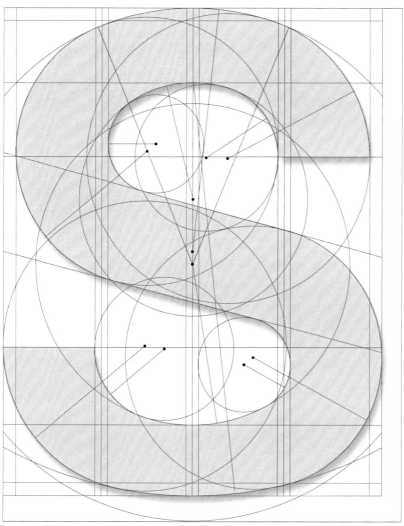

Workbook
Imagine the choice and application of letters from different typeface families and drawings in relation to various types of printed documents.
Typefaces, in their various forms, inherently possess the characteristics to become the visualisations of a communication project.

Understanding and historic study of typeface design.
Individual notes and further investigations.
Recovery of design techniques.
Development of typeface construction charts and grids.

10.
Spacing

The Ancient EM is
Still a Reference for
Measurements

128 Typefaces were initially produced by small workshops, each with its own measurements and systems deriving from the processes of fabrication adopted by these artisans. There was no rule establishing identical measurements for all type foundries. The issue of identifying a unique measure, and thus a compatibility of printing processes, was first approached by Moxon in his *Mechanik exercise* from 1683, in which he advanced the first proposal for unified measurements. He was followed by Fourier, who proposed a system based on a unit of measurement known as the "point": he imagined a scale of 144 points divided into 12 lines, each further subdivided into 24 parts, measuring 6 points.

In 1770 François Ambrois Didot assigned the point with a dimension corresponding to one 864th of the *pied du roi*, the official measurement used in France at the time.

From this moment the measurement of typefaces (typometry) has remained unchanged, and has been adopted almost everywhere in Europe.

The system is based on the row and the point: the point measures 0.376065 mm; the row (also known as the Cicero, from the typeface adopted in 1468 to print the works of this Roman orator) is equal to 12 points, or 4.51278 mm.

There are other systems of measurement: that adopted in Anglo-American countries and based on the Pica (pronounced pàica) equivalent to one 72nd of an inch (25.4 mm) or 4.216416 mm, in turn subdivided into 12 points, each measuring 0.351368 mm.

A fundamental element of typeface is the EM: a parallelepiped with a square base with the same body as the typeface it belongs to and which defines the base, in all systems, of the measure of spaces, and thus also the entire system and the codes for the spacing of a typeface.

Leading, the gaps between two letters or two words, is generally equal to one third of the dimension of the body (thick); multiples and sub-multiples of the EM, where the height of the body remains equal and the width varies, are used to assign additional spaces between letters.

In phototypesetting and word processing programs, which originated in America, and thus based on the Pica, leading still refers to the EM.

This unit of measurement, despite being empirical because it varies from typeface to typeface, refers to the size of the parallelepiped occupied by the largest character that, in general, is the letter W.

The width of the square containing the letter of reference, the upper case W, is divided into 18 units; consequentially, all of the other letters are measured as fractions of the number 18: the *i* is 5/18, the *p* 10/18, the *t* 6/18, the *O* 16/18 and so on.

There are also other systems of spacing, for example the "set", which is based on the inch, where the unit of measure is equal to one 18th of a Pica point.

In the codes of differentiated spacing produced by graphic designers, the system for identifying the unit of measure, used to define th quantity of space between two letters, consists in dividing the height of an upper case letter by a certain dimension, which is nothing other than the simulation of the size of an EM.

This will be examined in more detail on the following pages.

Notes
The measure of the typographic Didot, established by UNI regulations and measured at 20 degrees centigrade, is equal to 0.376065 mm.
The typographer Fournier was responsible for the first measurement in points. He is also the designer of different typefaces, restoring a certain form of writing in use in 1490. It should be said that rather than improving it, he damaged it, creating something midway between a vertical and an italic alphabet. It was known as "bastard" writing, a name that is still applied to certain ambiguous characters.

1. The subdivision of an EM into a certain number of sub-multiples defines the base of the system for identifying a unit of measurement to be linked to the entire kerning code of a typeface.
Phototypesetting, like word processing, uses the division of an EM (from the American system) into 18 parts, each of which constitutes the unit of measurement.

This makes it possible to justify lines of text by inserting rhythmic spaces between letters. In typesetting, which uses metal sorts, spaces between letters are obtained by inserting spacers corresponding with sub-multiples of an EM (in general a thick, which is one third the size of an EM).
Other thinner spacers, up to one point, are used to arrive at the requested justification.

2. In traditional typesetting, as we have seen, an EM is the same as the specified type size.
Half of an EM, known as an EN, is the same as half the specified type size; a third of an EM is known as a thick and corresponds with a standard spacer; a fourth of an EM is known as a middle; one fifth of an EM is a thin; one sixth a hair.
A space known as a *finissimo* is equal to 1 point.

It is worth being familiar with these terms: they derive from the American system developed in Pica; the same system we now find on a computer screen.

The term EM will appear when we want to reduce or expand the space between two glyphs (in Illustrator it is possible to assign the space between letters with dimensions in thousandths of an EM).

24 point EM   24 point EM divided into 18 units   36 point EM   36 point EM divided into 18 units   72 point EM   72 point EM divided into 18 units

18 units   18 units   9 units   12 units   5   16 units

1.

1 EM   1/2 EM   1/3 EM   1/4 EM   1/5 EM

EM
Em quads

EN
En quads
o two to the em

Thick
Three to the em
spaces

Middle
Four to the em
spaces

Thin
Five to the em
spaces

2.

Kerning

A World to be Discovered

1.

1. In typesetting, even when using an alphabet cast without margins with respect to the parallelepiped of the sort (possible, though rare), the coupling between an "A" and a "T", or an "A" and a "V", is critical.
The glyphs in red hypothesise the most correct kerning, where the spacing between letters is managed in thousandths of an EM.

130 Metal sorts are cast to their support designed to create a gap, as correct as possible, between letters. Not by chance, a sort is also known as a kern.
Obviously, this distance cannot be other than an average between the requirements of placing letters beside one another, as each letter must be placed beside all other letters in the alphabet.
When historic typesetters worked with a row of text in raised letters, they compensated eventual disharmonies between lead sorts (for example, between a "T" and an "A") using small spacers inserted between the letters making up a word.
In this manner, they achieved a highly spaced, though harmonic text. Their eye was accustomed to seeking a coherent result for the entire composition, guided by an empirical science.
Today, electronic typesetting makes it easy to resolve these issues: they allow us to condense, stretch and combine letters at will. However, precisely the advent of this extraordinary possibility obliges us to study and understand how to obtain a text that is as perfect as possible, in other words, the correct kerning.
None of the various spacing systems designed by graphic artists can be considered definitive, but instead extraordinary contributions to the scientific advancement of our profession. They are part of that history of graphic design that continues to unfold.
On the following pages we will take a look at the possibility to work with the space between letters, using the commands offered by the computer. The illustrations serve to demonstrate the various results of these tests.
We are able to adjust the space between letters as we wish, yet one question remains to be answered: how much space to assign to a letter in relation to that beside it.
In figure 2 we can observe how in the acronym "dpx" the spaces obtained between the letters does not respond to a harmonic reading. Above all we can note that the combination of some letters, in our case the letter "p" and the letter "x", the results are not satisfactory.
The closer the letters, the greater the disharmonies we can observe.
This makes it necessary to introduce individual adjustments and identify a methodology that assists us in this study.

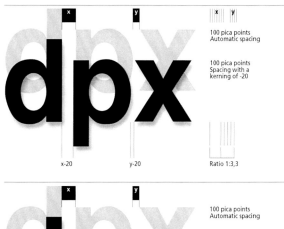

100 pica points
Automatic spacing

100 pica points
Spacing with a kerning of -20

Ratio 1:3,3

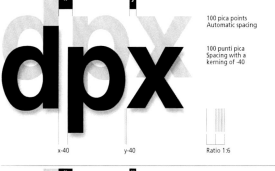

100 pica points
Automatic spacing

100 punti pica
Spacing with a kerning of -40

Ratio 1:6

100 pica points
Automatic spacing

100 pica points
Spacing with a kerning of -20 (dp)
kerning of -60 (px)

Ratio 10:1

2.

2. The image shows the result of automatic kerning in the first two examples, and a more carefully considered third version. Also shown are the ratios of kerning provided by computer software.

3./5. We can narrow the space occupied by a glyph using the *kerning* command, or the that occupied by an entire row of text, using the *tracking* command. The image shows the result we can obtain using the *tracking* command, where the automatic spacing accounted for by the program is visualised as an outline, and the tracking attempts in solid black.

The acronym "dpx" is shown in a series of attempts with different tracking values:

a +120 units
b +80 units
c +40 units
d original
e −40 units
f −80 units
g −120 units

Reducing the space between glyphs in a uniform manner does not produce a balanced final product.

6. Digital glyphs allow for corrections to kerning and tracking resulting from the rigidity of a computer program. It is possible to differentiate the spacing between letters by seeking a more harmonic kerning. The example shows the acronym "dpx", which has been given a spacing by modifying the kerning.

If we apply the spacing of our hypothetical code to these letters and link these dimensions to those provided by the Illustrator software, we can find the distances in the values listed in the table. This is a comparison that shows how the system becomes progressively more complex as the standard unit becomes smaller.

3.

4.

5.

6.

	a	dpx
	b	dnx
	c	dox
	d	dux
	e	dax
	f	dex
	g	dix

7.

	a	dpx
	b	dnx
	c	dox
	d	dux
	e	dax
	f	dex
	g	dix

Notes
*We have tried a tracking exercise based on scientific measurements, making numerous calculations; we have learned to mnemonically consider a measurement and a dimension; we can now trust our eyes, our perception, basing our work on acquired skills of observation.
In this way we enhance our logical structure with the necessary optical corrections, many already present in any alphabet.*

Workbook
Find the code for the kerning and tracking of a digital typeface used by a program selected at will. Compose a table with the values of this code expressed in units: note any evident disharmonies.

Letter	Kerning	Letter	Kerning	Letter		Unit	Unit
d	−48	p	−75	x	=	+3	−1
d	−54	n	−50	x	=	+3	+1
d	−50	o	−80	x	=	+2	−1
d	−54	u	−55	x	=	+3	+1
d	−42	a	−20	x	=	+2	+1
d	−34	e	−72	x	=	+2	−1
d	−56	i	−60	x	=	+3	+1

Non-Image Areas

Areas of Measurement

1. When we read a line of text, we read the glyphs of which it is composed; at the same time, without being aware, we also read the white spaces that exist between and around them.

These areas are known as "non-image areas". They are the unprinted areas in a *forme*. They are the "negative" of any glyph, the counterform, the "zones" that make it possible for us to read a text.

It is the correct measure of these white areas that makes it possible to read, with more or less effort, and which confer an overall harmony on a composition.

2. However, the white spaces are also the spaces that live between letters and words.

In a typeface, the space between words is defined by the thick, which is one third of an EM; in phototypesetting, where the EM is divided into 18 parts, it corresponds with 6 units, once again a third of an EM.

Between one letter and the next the spaces are fractions of these fixed measurements.

In both systems, this becomes a code. Though it is not perfect.

In the world of typography, during the process of casting, a typeface designer allows for a certain space before and after each letter, seeking an "average" value for combining any letter with any other.

While this code may function in running text and at the small to medium size, in large type (generally from 24 points upward) it begins to reveal a number of disturbing disharmonies.

132

1.

Defining the quantity of non-image areas helps us evaluate the amount of space that should exist between glyphs. In fact, in theory, the area between the glyphs, whatever its quantity, should be harmonic. The successive step is to modify the spaces by making optical corrections.

3. If we take the letters A, B and C and inscribe them within a space that contains them, we can measure four areas:
a) the area inside which the letter is inscribed;
b) the area of the letter;
c) the area inside each letter;
d) the area that remains at the sides of each letter.
The ratio between these areas, in other words between solids and voids, and the evaluation of these ratios, determines the space between letters.

4. As perfect examples of non-image areas, we are showing the logos designed by Pino Tovaglia for Nava, and by Gerardo Spera for Format 41.12

5. The spaces created by the combination of various letters. They are considered areas and as such can be measured.

4

3.

a

b

c

d

Spacing between AA   Spacing between BA

5

1. If we place the letters beside one another, to the point that their edges touch, we can measure the area between one letter and the next. In so doing, we note that while between the two H's the area is equal to 0, between the V and the Y, or between the H and the C, there exists a measurable area.

We begin with the principle that the space between all the letters of an alphabet must be equal. The largest space is that between the V and the Y, beyond extreme examples, and we can consider this area as the base measure for all other combinations.

This area is equal to 470.32 mm². The space between the H and the C must thus be equal to this area, less the area belonging to the letter C itself. We then proceed with identical measurements that serve, above all, to train our eye to evaluate a correct degree of kerning and to guide us in establishing the methodology for assigning a certain quantity of space between one letter and another.

The combination that requires the most space is that between two H's, in other words between two letters with upright strokes, and thus without their own natural space. We can also note how, in other cases, for example when combining AT or AY, it is necessary to maintain a uniform space between the letters, a negative space, with a value of -3 units, -2, -1, etc.

The basic spaces of the code can be summarised in three typologies: between two letters with upright strokes (HH), with an area equal to 0; between a letter with an upright stroke and a curved letter (HC), where the area between the letters can be measured; between two curved letters (OO), with the largest possible area, beyond such extreme examples as LA, TV, YY, etc.

134

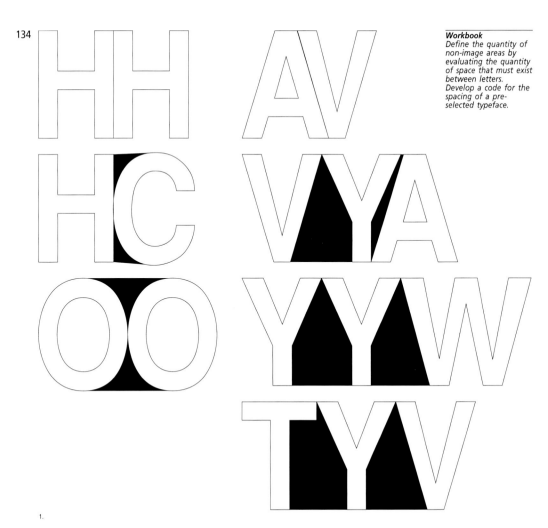

1.

Workbook
Define the quantity of non-image areas by evaluating the quantity of space that must exist between letters. Develop a code for the spacing of a pre-selected typeface.

2. To identify a spacing code, we must first identify a unit of measurement that is a constant ratio with the body of the typeface to which it is applied. This means it should be found within the typeface itself. Following the standards applied so far, we can find this value by dividing the width of the letter W into 40 parts.

This means that the standard units will be equal to 1/40 the width of the letter W. As a base we select the area between the T and the Y (470.32 mm²) and compare it to the area that contains the letter W (1263.57 mm²) already divided into 40 parts. We then establish the ratio of 1263.57:40=470.32:x. The result is the area between T and Y in standard units.

This value is equal to 15 standard units. This is the value to be assigned between two H's; between the H and the C we assign the same area that exists between the two H's, less the area of 98 mm², which is already part of the letter C. This calculation gives us 3 standard units, that we must subtract from the 15 base units, which gives us a total space of 12 su.

The space between two O's will thus be equal to 9 su, and so on. Finally, if we subtract the internal space of the H and divide by 2 (because half the value belongs to the first letter and the other half to that which follows it), after the necessary calculations we find that the space between the two H's is equal to 6 standard units. We can now apply these calculations to differentiated spacing and proceed with the measurement of all possible combinations between AA, AB, AC, AD, etc., and then BA, BB, BC, BD, and so on.

135

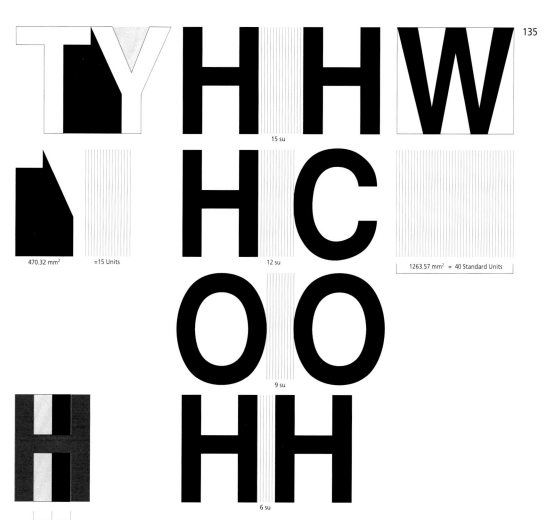

470.32 mm² =15 Units

15 su

12 su

9 su

6 su

1263.57 mm² = 40 Standard Units

2.

Student Theses

Acquiring Instinctive Perception

Students chose to develop their final projects on the theme of differentiated spacing. Each student performed a series of studies and area calculations for a specific typeface. Each thesis concluded with the proposal for a differentiated spacing code.
The objective of this approach was to provide students with the tools of optical perception and an almost instinctive evaluation of the quantity of space necessary between glyphs.

1. A selection of drawings by Francesco Tozzi.
The area calculations deal with the area of the left and right margins of the Monaco typeface at 72 point, expressed in square millimetres and, in the table, the areas necessary for the combination of different glyphs.

The bright yellow space indicates the reading of the letters CG and EG. The spaces obtained were translated into standard units by dividing the maximum area by the height in millimetres of the 72 point typeface.
In this case, the standard unit is equivalent to 0.5 mm.

136

External areas in mm²
Monaco 72 point

	Left Area	Right Area
A	98	98
B	0	43.5
C	65	219
D	0	43.5
E	0	171
F	0	207
G	65	171
I	109	109
J	218	11
K	0	141
L	0	228
O	43.5	43.5
P	0	141
Q	43.5	43.5
R	0	98
S	130	120
T	163	163
U	11	11
V	98	98
W	33	33
X	98	98
Y	141	141
Z	120	120

Internal areas in mm²
Monaco 72 point

A	91.5
B	105.5
D	156
H	200
K	112
M	200
N	170
O	179
P	76
Q	179
R	125
U	200
V	115
W	134
X	90

	AR VX	BD OQ	CJ	EG	HM N	I	KP Y	SZ	T	U	W
AVX	196	141	317	269	98	207	239	218	261	109	131
BDEFHK LMNPR	98	43	219	171		109	141	120	163	11	33
CG	165	108	284	236	65	174	206	185	228	76	98
I	207	152	328	280	109	218	250	229	272	120	142
J	316	261	437	389	218	327	359	338	381	229	251
OQ	141	87	262	215	43	152	184	163	206	54	76
S	228	174	349	302	130	239	271	250	293	141	163
T	261	206	382	334	163	272	304	283	326	174	196
U	109	54	230	182	11	120	152	131	174	22	44
W	131	76	252	204	33	142	174	153	196	44	66
Y	239	184	360	312	141	250	282	261	305	152	174
Z	218	163	339	191	120	229	261	240	283	131	153

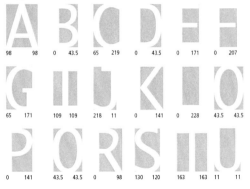

A		B		C		D		E		F	
98	98	0	43.5	65	219	0	43.5	0	171	0	207

G		I		J		K		O	
65	171	109	109	218	11	0	141	0	228

P		Q		R		S		U	
0	141	43.5	43.5	0	98	130	120	163	163	11	11

1.

2. 3. In their joint thesis, Simona Cecchini, Maria Paola Foggetti, Massimiliano Nicastro and Natalia Pinti inserted an in-depth analysis of particular typologies of specific cases. Their exploration was based on the SanSerif typeface.

LA

LA/ Oblique lines: in letters such as the A, V and W etc., the lines tend to lead the eye toward the space above. This generates the illusion that between two adjacent letters the area is greater than that calculated mathematically.

JB

JB/ Convex parts: as per the oblique lines, the curves lead the eye toward the surrounding space, creating the illusion of an area that appears larger than it actually is.

BB

BB/ Symmetrical areas with respect to a horizontal axis: letters like the B do not present particular problems. In fact, the eye is not drawn above or below the axis, and the axes are almost identical.

CC

CC/ The letter C features a very large open area. This free space has a strong impact on our optical perception. The very form of the C induces the eye to see an accessible space, a well defined inlet that creates problems in combinations with other letters.
Nonetheless, the eye sees a closed space, with an area that eludes us into believing it is smaller than it is actually is (interrupted areas). With respect to the calculations made, the letters should slightly distanced (by approx. 1 unit).

EE

EE/ The letter E does not present any particular problems. Like the B, it is symmetrical along a horizontal axis. Placed beside other letters, it requires an extra 1/2 of a unit because the internal area "reverberates" between the surfaces and its impact is lessened.

FF

FF/ The letter F, like the letter P, has an irregular free area, narrow at the top, and wider below. The eye perceives a greater area, identified by a hypothetical trapezoid and it moves below the space occupied by the geometry of the letter. This effect is caused by the lack of a lower margin, sought by the eye to balance the upper edge.

PP

PP/ The SansSerif typeface features a P with an elongated form. The upper projection creates two spaces, though the eye sees only the second one.

XY

XY/ The form of these "perfect" letters is enclosed in the space in which they are inscribed, keeping them from flowing outside of it. The space appears to increase in the central zone.

SS

SS/ The movements of the eye along the letter S are facilitated by the regular movement of the curves. It is possible to identify two open spaces that, gently, embrace the reading of the glyph.
Two areas area generated: that outside the S and that inside the open inlet.

Notes 137
The material developed by the students was of such a specific and broad scope that it merits a dedicated publication, as a relevant contribution to the study of differentiated spacing explored by so few graphic designers.
All of the students concluded their research with a proposed code; some hypothesised a signage project that applied the codes to the selected typeface.
Furtherore, all of the material produced was presented on paper and grids backed by studies and very interesting proposals.

How to Develop a Differentiated Spacing Code

The Unit of Measurement

First and foremost, we come across the unit of measurement known as the *standard unit*, whose size is determined in relationship to the body. The standard unit, in the examples illustrated, was identified by dividing the width of the upper case letter W by 40; with another system, dividing the height of the upper case letter A or the leg of the lower case letter b by 32, we obtain a similar standard.

The division into 32 parts is measured using the proper letters, without optical corrections.
The division is made from the ascender line to the base of a letter without curves.
In the example, it is clear how the letter O, in Helvetica bold, has an evidently greater height than the letters A or N.
Avoid taking measurements using letters that, like the f, can create interferences because of the curves in the terminal part.

Why is it important to identify a standard unit of measurement?
This is because it will always be proportionate to the typeface used, regardless of its type size.
The unit may also vary based on the needs of representation (for example, the need for greater spacing in a text broadcast on a television screen, where the resolution is lower than an element of wayfinding signage, which offers a perfect reproduction of letters), however, its ratio with the character to which it is applied, regardless of the type size, remains in all cases constant.

138

Width W : 40 = 1 Standard Unit

Height A : 32 = 1 Standard Unit

Height A : 32 = 1 Standard Unit

Kerning measurements are identified beginning with the vertical line passing through the extreme left and right points of each letter.
The table contains examples of vertical lines for the letters A and b.

The vertical lines to the left, before the zero line, have a growing positive value (+1, +2, +3, etc.).
The vertical lines to the right, before the zero line, have a decreasing negative value (–1, –2, –3, etc.).
The vertical lines to the right, after the zero line, have a growing positive value (+1, +2, +3, etc.).

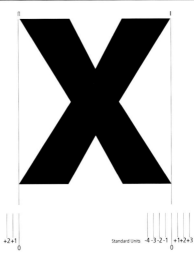

The letters of the alphabet, numbers and punctuation marks are combined using a differentiated spacing code.
It can be noted how the extreme upper ends of the lower case letter x do not coincide with the vertical line.
The reference points are to be taken at the extreme lower points of the letter.

139

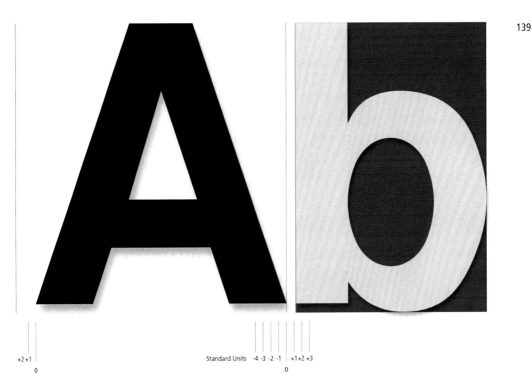

+2 +1
0

Standard Units   -4 -3 -2 -1   +1 +2 +3
0

+2 +1
0

Standard Units   -4 -3 -2 -1   +1 +2 +3
0

Kerning Letters

Optical Corrections to Mathematical Structures

1. The measurements for assigning spaces between two letters are taken from the vertical line passing through the extreme left and right points of each letter.
This gives us positive spaces, such as those of the combination Ab, or negative spaces, as in the combination Af.
In the example, 2 standard units have been assigned between the A and the b; between the A and the f the distance is -1 standard unit.

Having established the standard unit, all other measurements referred to the spacing of the letters of an institutional typeface will be expressed in s.u. (standard units).

140

+2
Standard Units

-1
Standard Unit

+3
Standard Units

−3
Standard Units

1.

When to Tighten the Space between Rows

2. The leading between the rows of text in a composition corresponds with 3 standard units. The units are measured from the bottom end of the descender line of a glyph and the top end of the ascender line.
In the example, the points coincide with the lower extremity of the letter p and the upper extremity of the letter A.

The space to be assigned between an A and a B or between a B and a C varies according to the typeface.
While it is possible to provide a methodology for constructing a code of differentiated spacing, it would be an arduous task to provide codes for all typefaces.
In a single typeface, the kerning between medium and bold already varies; there is an enormous variation between a sans-serif typeface and a typeface with accentuated serifs; even typefaces that at first glance appear similar prove to be completely different when the time comes to apply differentiated spacing.

If we multiply these problems by the myriad of typefaces in existence, we are forced to come to grips with the fact that each of them, when we must construct a code, has its own inherent problems, also in relation to the use we intend to make of it.
It must also be remembered that the smaller the standard unit, the more difficult it is to assign the correct spacing between glyphs; the larger the unit of measurement, the more approximate the spacing code.

3 su

3 Standard Units

Height A : 32 = 1 Standard Units

Height A : 32 = 1 Standard Units

2.

When to Bring Words Closer Together

1. The distance required between one word and the next is measured by dividing the height of the letter A, equal to 32 standard units, by 2.
The resulting 16 standard units are to be augmented by the addition of as many standard units as the number foreseen for the combination between the final letter of the first word and the first letter of the following word.

In the example shown in the table, the first word ends with a t; the second word begins with a p.
This means that we will add 2 units (the space of the combination between the t and the p) to the 16 su, for a total of 18 su.

To the side: the structure of the study to determine the space between letters.
A very useful suggestion for students involved in the construction of a differentiated spacing code, is that of setting the *move* command in the graphic software being used so that it perfectly coincides with the standard unit.
This will make it possible to condense or expand individual letter spacing, and to proceed with a series of legibility tests, simply by pushing a button.

142

| Standard Units | 0 | +1 | +2 | −1 |

| Standard Units | 0 | +2 |

x+2=18 su
18 su

16 su

Height A: 32 = 1 unit a standard

x=16 su

x=16 su

Applying the Code

The maximum units are 6, and they are applied to combinations such as HH, MN, etc.
The units are reduced in a logical sequence ordered by the combinations Hh, Ho, Oo, to negative values, as in the cases of Af, Tx, etc.
Some combinations remain very distant from the indications provided by area measurements, confirming the complexity of a code when it has very small values.

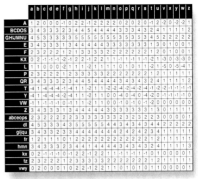

	a	b	c	d	e	f	g	h	i	j	k	l	m	n	o	p	q	r	s	t	u	v	w	x	y	z
A	1	2	0	0	0	-1	0	2	2	2	-1	2	2	2	2	2	0	2	0	2	0	-1	2	-2	0	-2
BCDOS	3	4	3	3	2	3	4	4	5	4	4	4	3	3	3	4	3	2	4	1	1	1	1			
GHIJMNU	4	5	3	3	3	3	5	5	5	5	5	5	5	3	5	3	5	3	4	5	2	2	2	2		
E	3	4	3	3	1	3	4	4	4	4	3	3	3	3	3	3	1	3	0	1	0	0	1			
F	2	3	2	2	2	1	2	1	3	3	3	3	2	2	2	2	2	2	1	2	0	1	0	0	1	
KX	0	2	-1	-1	-1	-2	-1	2	2	-1	2	2	1	1	-1	-1	1	-1	1	-2	1	-3	0	-3	3	0
L	1	1	0	0	0	-2	1	1	1	-2	1	1	1	1	1	0	1	0	1	1	-2	1	-5	0	-5	4
P	2	3	2	2	2	1	2	3	3	3	3	3	2	2	2	2	2	2	1	2	1	1	1	1		
QR	3	4	3	3	3	2	3	4	4	5	4	4	4	3	4	3	4	3	2	4	1	1	1	1	2	
T	-4	1	-4	-4	-4	-4	1	1	-2	1	1	-2	-2	-4	-2	-4	-2	-4	-1	-2	-2	-1	-1	-1	-1	
Y	-4	1	-4	-4	-4	-2	-4	1	1	-2	1	1	0	0	-4	0	-4	0	-4	-2	0	-1	-1	-1	-1	0
VW	-1	1	-1	-1	-1	0	-1	1	1	1	1	-2	1	1	0	1	0	-1	0	-1	-2	0	0	0	0	0
Z	3	4	3	3	3	1	3	4	4	4	4	3	3	3	3	3	3	3	1	3	0	1	1	1	1	
abceops	2	3	2	2	2	2	2	3	3	3	3	3	3	3	2	3	2	3	2	2	3	0	0	0	0	1
dl	4	5	3	3	3	4	3	5	5	5	5	5	4	4	3	4	3	4	3	4	4	2	2	2	2	
gijqu	3	4	3	3	2	3	3	4	4	4	4	4	4	2	4	2	4	2	3	4	1	1	1	1		
fr	1	2	1	1	1	0	1	2	2	2	2	2	2	2	2	2	2	1	2	1	1	1	1	1		
hmn	3	4	3	3	3	2	3	4	4	1	4	4	4	4	3	4	3	4	2	4	1	1	1	1		
kx	0	2	-1	-1	-1	-2	-1	2	2	-1	2	2	1	1	-1	-1	1	-1	-1	-2	-1	1	0	0	0	1
tz	2	3	2	2	2	1	2	3	3	3	3	3	2	2	2	2	2	2	1	2	1	1	1	1		
vwy	0	2	0	0	0	1	0	2	2	-1	2	2	1	1	0	1	0	1	0	1	1	0	0	0	0	1

	1	2	3	4	5	6	7	8	9	0
1	2	2	3	2	3	3	1	3	3	3
2	1	2	2	1	2	2	0	2	2	2
3	0	1	0	1	2	2	0	2	2	2
4	-1	1	1	1	1	2	-2	2	2	2
5	0	1	1	1	1	2	0	2	2	2
6	0	1	2	1	1	2	0	2	2	2
7	1	0	0	-4	-2	0	1	0	0	0
8	0	1	2	1	1	2	0	2	2	2
9	0	1	2	1	1	2	0	2	2	2
0	0	1	2	1	1	2	0	2	2	2

143

Verifying the Results

1. The application of the differentiated spacing code to a sign on the facade of the Banca Mediterranea building.
The ratios are derived from the specific study included in the Bank's corporate image manual.

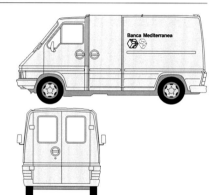

144

Banca MYa 74

3   3   3   2   3+16   1   -4   -4

Mediterranea

3   2   5 2   2   3   2   1   3   3   2

Uffici Sportelli

3   1   3 3   3   4+16   3   2   3   2   2   3   5   5

Direzione MN

4   4   1   1   3 3   3   3   5

Parcheggio

2   3   1   3   2   2   3   3 3

1.

2. When designing a coordinated image manual, especially in those cases that require the use of large text, for example the sign of a bank or wayfinding signage, the code becomes indispensable in providing not only an alphabet, but also the spaces to be inserted between letters, words and rows of text.

A successful coordinated image package must include this study based on the use of an institutional typeface.
The following pages present a differentiated spacing code for the Helvetica typeface. The tables define the spaces between letters. The code was approached by students in exercises focused on its application to lettering for signage, signboards, trade fair stands and their projects.

The standard unit was identified by dividing the W into 40 units. On the following pages, the two tables present the differentiated spacing codes.

	A	B	C	D	E	F	G	H	I	J	K	L	M	N	O	P	Q	R	S	T	U	V	W	X	Y	Z	1	2	3	4	5	6	7	8	9	0
A	2	2	-2	2	2	2	-2	2	2	1	2	2	2	2	-2	2	-2	2	0	-6	0	-7	-6	2	-8	2	-1	2	0	0	0	-1	2	1	0	-1
B	0	3	2	3	3	3	2	3	3	1	3	3	3	3	2	3	2	3	2	0	2	0	0	-1	-1	1	1	1	2	2	2	2	0	2	1	2
C	-1	2	2	2	2	2	2	2	2	0	2	2	2	2	2	2	2	2	2	0	2	-1	-1	-2	-1	0	2	2	2	2	1	2	1	2	2	2
D	-2	2	2	2	2	2	2	2	2	-1	2	2	2	2	2	2	2	2	2	-1	2	-1	-1	-3	-2	0	1	2	2	2	2	2	0	2	2	2
E	2	3	2	3	3	3	2	3	3	3	3	3	3	3	2	3	2	3	2	3	2	2	1	3	1	3	1	2	2	2	2	2	2	2	2	2
F	-3	3	2	3	3	3	2	3	3	3	3	3	3	3	2	3	2	3	1	2	3	2	2	1	2	3	2	3	3	2	2	2	2	2	2	2
G	2	3	2	3	3	3	2	3	3	3	3	3	3	3	2	3	2	3	2	1	3	0	0	2	0	3	2	3	3	2	2	2	2	2	2	2
H	2	3	2	3	3	3	2	3	3	3	3	3	3	3	2	3	2	3	2	2	3	2	2	2	2	2	2	2	2	2	2	2	2	2	2	2
I	2	3	2	3	3	3	2	3	3	3	3	3	3	3	2	3	2	3	2	2	3	2	2	2	2	2	2	2	2	2	2	2	2	2	2	2
J	0	3	2	3	3	3	2	3	3	1	3	3	3	3	2	3	2	3	2	2	3	2	2	1	2	2	2	2	2	2	2	2	2	2	2	2
K	2	2	-3	2	2	2	-3	2	2	2	2	2	2	2	-3	2	-3	2	-1	1	1	1	1	2	1	2	-1	2	-1	-1	0	-2	1	-1	-1	-2
L	2	2	-1	2	2	2	-1	2	2	2	2	2	2	2	-1	2	-1	2	1	-6	1	-6	-5	2	-7	2	-1	2	1	-2	2	0	0	2	-1	0
M	2	3	2	3	3	3	2	3	3	3	3	3	3	3	2	3	2	3	2	2	3	2	2	2	2	2	2	2	2	2	2	2	2	2	2	2
N	2	3	2	3	3	3	2	3	3	3	3	3	3	3	2	3	2	3	2	2	3	2	2	2	2	2	2	2	2	2	2	2	2	2	2	2
O	-1	2	2	2	2	2	2	2	2	0	2	2	2	2	2	2	2	2	2	0	2	-1	-1	-2	-2	0	1	2	2	2	1	2	0	2	2	2
P	-4	2	2	2	2	2	2	2	-4	2	2	2	2	2	2	2	2	2	1	2	1	1	-1	0	1	2	2	2	-1	1	2	1	2	2	1	1
Q	-1	2	2	2	2	2	2	2	2	0	2	2	2	2	2	2	2	2	2	0	2	-1	-1	-2	-2	0	1	2	2	2	1	3	0	2	2	2
R	2	2	1	2	2	2	1	2	2	0	2	2	2	2	1	2	1	2	2	1	3	1	1	1	2	0	2	2	2	2	2	2	2	2	2	2
S	0	2	2	2	2	2	2	2	2	2	2	2	2	2	2	2	2	2	0	2	0	0	1	0	1	2	2	2	2	2	2	1	2	2	2	2
T	-6	2	-1	2	2	2	-1	2	2	-3	2	2	2	2	-1	2	-1	2	1	3	3	2	2	2	3	2	1	1	-5	1	0	3	1	0	0	0
U	0	3	2	3	3	3	3	3	3	1	3	3	3	3	2	3	2	3	2	2	3	2	2	1	2	2	2	2	2	2	2	2	2	2	2	2
V	-7	2	-2	2	2	2	-2	2	2	-4	2	2	2	2	-2	2	-2	2	0	2	2	2	2	2	2	1	0	1	-4	-1	-1	2	0	0	1	1
W	-5	2	-1	2	2	2	-1	2	2	-3	2	2	2	2	-1	2	-1	2	0	2	2	2	2	2	2	1	1	1	-3	0	0	2	0	0	0	0
X	2	2	2	2	2	2	-2	2	2	2	2	2	2	2	-2	2	-2	2	1	1	1	1	1	2	1	1	-1	2	0	-2	0	-1	1	0	-1	-1
Y	-7	2	-2	2	2	2	-2	2	2	-4	2	2	2	2	-2	2	-2	2	-1	2	2	2	2	2	2	2	0	0	-6	-1	-2	2	-1	-1	-2	-2
Z	2	2	1	2	2	2	1	2	2	3	2	2	2	2	1	2	1	2	3	3	3	2	2	2	1	3	1	2	2	-3	2	1	2	1	1	1

	A	B	C	D	E	F	G	H	I	J	K	L	M	N	O	P	Q	R	S	T	U	V	W	X	Y	Z	1	2	3	4	5	6	7	8	9	0
1	2	3	2	3	3	3	2	3	3	3	3	3	3	3	2	3	2	3	2	2	3	2	2	2	2	2	2	2	2	2	2	2	2	2	2	2
2	2	3	1	3	3	3	1	3	3	3	3	3	3	3	1	3	1	3	2	1	2	0	0	2	0	3	1	3	2	-1	2	1	1	1	2	1
3	0	2	2	2	2	2	2	2	2	1	2	2	2	2	2	2	2	2	0	2	0	0	-1	-1	1	1	2	2	2	2	2	1	2	2	2	2
4	0	3	2	3	3	3	2	3	3	0	3	3	3	3	2	3	2	3	2	-2	3	-2	-2	-1	-2	1	0	1	2	3	2	2	1	2	2	2
5	0	2	2	2	2	2	2	2	2	1	2	2	2	2	2	2	2	2	0	2	0	0	-1	0	1	1	2	3	2	2	2	1	2	2	2	2
6	0	2	2	2	2	2	2	2	2	2	2	2	2	2	2	2	2	2	0	2	0	0	-1	-1	2	1	2	2	2	2	2	1	2	2	2	2
7	-6	2	0	2	2	2	0	2	2	3	2	2	2	2	0	2	0	2	1	3	3	2	2	1	2	2	2	-3	0	0	3	1	1	1	1	1
8	0	2	1	2	2	2	1	2	2	2	2	2	2	2	1	2	1	2	1	2	1	2	0	0	-1	-1	1	1	1	2	2	2	2	1	2	2
9	-1	2	2	2	2	2	2	2	2	0	2	2	2	2	2	2	2	2	2	0	2	-1	-1	-2	-1	0	1	2	2	2	2	2	1	2	2	2
0	-1	2	2	2	2	2	2	2	2	0	2	2	2	2	2	2	2	2	2	0	2	-1	-1	-2	-1	0	1	2	2	2	2	2	1	2	2	2

	A	B	C	D	E	F	G	H	I	J	K	L	M	N	O	P	Q	R	S	T	U	V	W	X	Y	Z	1	2	3	4	5	6	7	8	9	0
a	2	3	2	3	3	3	2	3	3	2	3	3	3	3	2	3	2	3	2	-6	3	-2	-2	-2	-4	2	3	3	2	2	2	0	2	2	2	2
b	-1	2	2	2	2	2	2	2	2	0	2	2	2	2	2	2	2	2	2	-6	2	-3	-3	-2	-5	0	-1	1	2	2	2	2	-3	2	2	2
c	-1	2	2	2	2	2	2	2	2	0	2	2	2	2	2	2	2	2	2	-6	2	-3	-3	-2	-5	0	-1	1	2	2	2	2	-3	2	2	2
d	2	3	2	3	3	3	3	3	3	3	3	3	3	3	2	3	2	3	2	2	3	2	2	2	2	2	2	2	2	2	2	2	2	2	2	2
e	2	3	2	3	3	3	2	3	3	2	3	3	3	3	2	3	2	3	2	-6	2	-3	-3	-2	-5	0	-1	1	2	2	2	2	-3	2	2	2
f	-3	3	1	3	3	3	1	3	3	-2	3	3	3	3	1	3	1	3	2	3	3	2	2	1	2	3	2	3	3	2	2	-2	2	2	2	2
g	2	3	2	3	3	3	2	3	3	3	3	3	3	3	2	3	2	3	2	-4	3	-2	-1	2	-2	3	0	3	2	3	3	2	2	0	2	2
h	2	3	2	3	3	3	2	3	3	3	3	3	3	3	2	3	2	3	2	-6	3	-2	-1	2	-4	3	0	3	2	3	3	2	2	0	2	2
i	2	3	2	3	3	3	2	3	3	3	3	3	3	3	2	3	2	3	2	2	3	2	2	2	2	2	2	3	3	3	2	3	3	2	2	2
j	2	3	2	3	3	3	2	3	3	2	3	3	3	3	2	3	2	3	2	2	3	2	2	2	2	2	2	3	3	3	2	3	3	2	2	2
k	2	2	0	2	2	2	0	2	2	2	2	2	2	2	0	2	0	2	1	-2	2	0	0	-2	2	2	2	1	-1	0	0	0	1	1	1	1
l	2	3	2	3	3	3	2	3	3	3	3	3	3	3	2	3	2	3	2	2	3	2	2	2	2	3	3	3	2	3	3	2	2	3	2	2
m	2	3	2	3	3	3	2	3	3	3	3	3	3	3	2	3	2	3	2	-6	3	-2	-1	2	-4	3	0	3	2	3	3	2	2	0	2	2
n	2	3	2	3	3	3	2	3	3	3	3	3	3	3	2	3	2	3	2	-6	3	-2	-1	2	-4	3	0	3	2	3	3	2	2	0	2	2
o	-1	2	2	2	2	2	2	2	2	0	2	2	2	2	2	2	2	2	2	-6	2	-3	-3	-2	-5	0	-1	1	2	2	2	2	-3	2	2	2
p	-1	2	2	2	2	2	2	2	2	0	2	2	2	2	2	2	2	2	2	-6	2	-3	-3	-2	-5	0	-1	1	2	2	2	2	-3	2	2	2
q	2	3	2	3	3	3	2	3	3	3	3	3	3	3	2	3	2	3	2	-4	3	-2	-1	2	-2	3	0	3	2	3	3	2	2	0	2	2
r	-3	2	2	2	2	2	2	2	2	-4	2	2	2	2	2	2	2	2	2	-3	2	-1	-1	-3	-3	-2	1	2	1	1	1	1	2	-2	1	2
s	0	2	2	2	2	2	2	2	2	2	2	2	2	2	2	2	2	2	1	-6	2	-2	-2	-1	-4	1	0	2	2	2	2	2	-2	2	2	2
t	2	3	2	3	3	3	2	3	3	3	3	3	3	3	2	3	2	3	2	1	3	1	1	2	-1	3	3	3	2	-1	2	2	1	2	2	2
u	2	3	2	3	3	3	2	3	3	3	3	3	3	3	2	3	2	3	2	-4	3	-2	-1	2	-2	3	0	3	2	3	3	2	2	0	2	2
v	-1	2	1	2	2	2	1	2	2	-3	2	2	2	2	1	2	1	2	2	-3	2	0	0	-2	-1	0	2	2	2	-1	0	1	-4	1	1	1
w	-4	2	1	2	2	2	1	2	2	-3	2	2	2	2	1	2	1	2	2	-3	2	0	0	-2	-1	0	2	2	2	-1	0	1	-4	1	1	1
x	2	2	0	2	2	2	0	2	2	1	2	2	2	2	0	2	0	2	1	-4	2	-1	-1	-2	-2	2	1	2	1	-2	-1	0	0	1	0	0
y	2	3	1	3	3	3	1	3	3	2	3	3	3	3	1	3	1	3	2	-4	3	-1	-1	2	-2	3	2	3	2	-1	2	1	0	2	1	1
z	2	3	1	3	3	3	1	3	3	3	3	3	3	3	1	3	1	3	2	-4	3	-1	-1	2	-2	3	3	2	-1	2	1	2	0	2	1	1

	A	B	C	D	E	F	G	H	I	J	K	L	M	N	O	P	Q	R	S	T	U	V	W	X	Y	Z	1	2	3	4	5	6	7	8	9	0
. ,	2	3	0	3	3	3	0	3	3	2	3	3	3	3	0	3	0	3	2	-4	3	-5	-5	2	-5	3	1	3	2	1	1	1	2	2	1	1
: ;	2	3	2	3	3	3	2	3	3	2	3	3	3	3	2	3	2	3	2	2	3	2	2	2	2	3	3	3	2	3	3	2	3	2	2	2
!	2	3	2	3	3	3	2	3	3	2	3	3	3	3	2	3	2	3	2	2	3	2	2	2	2	3	3	3	2	3	3	2	3	2	2	2
?	-4	2	2	2	2	2	2	2	2	-2	2	2	2	2	2	2	2	2	1	2	0	0	-1	-1	1	1	2	2	2	-2	-1	1	2	1	1	1
(	0	0	-3	0	0	0	-3	0	0	0	0	0	0	0	-3	0	-3	0	-2	0	0	0	0	0	0	0	2	2	2	-2	-1	1	2	1	1	1
)	-1	2	2	2	2	2	2	2	2	0	2	2	2	2	2	2	2	2	1	2	0	0	-1	-1	0	2	2	2	2	1	2	2	2	1	2	2
&	2	2	2	2	2	2	2	2	2	2	2	2	2	2	2	2	2	1	-5	2	-3	-3	2	-5	2	0	2	1	1	1	1	2	0	1	1	1

	a	b	c	d	e	f	g	h	i	j	k	l	m	n	o	p	q	r	s	t	u	v	w	x	y	z	.	,	:	;	–	!	?	(	)	&
A	1	2	0	0	0	0	0	2	2	-2	2	2	2	2	2	2	0	2	0	-2	1	-4	-4	2	-3	2	2	2	2	2	2	2	-4	-1	-2	0
B	2	2	2	2	2	0	2	2	2	2	2	2	2	2	2	2	2	2	2	1	2	1	1	0	1	1	2	2	2	2	2	2	1	2	-3	2
C	1	2	2	2	2	2	2	2	2	2	2	2	2	2	2	2	2	2	2	2	2	2	2	1	1	1	2	2	2	2	2	2	2	2	-3	2
D	2	2	2	2	2	2	2	2	2	3	2	2	2	2	2	2	2	2	2	1	2	1	1	1	1	1	3	3	3	3	2	3	2	2	-4	2
E	2	3	2	2	2	2	2	3	3	-1	3	3	3	3	2	3	2	3	2	3	3	1	1	2	2	3	3	3	3	3	3	3	1	2	-1	2
F	1	3	1	1	1	1	1	3	3	3	3	3	2	2	1	2	1	2	1	2	2	1	1	0	1	1	3	3	3	3	3	3	2	2	0	0
G	2	3	2	2	2	2	2	3	3	-1	3	3	3	3	2	3	2	3	2	2	3	2	2	2	2	3	3	3	3	3	3	3	2	2	-1	2
H	2	3	2	2	2	2	2	3	3	3	3	3	3	3	2	3	2	2	2	2	3	2	2	2	2	2	3	3	3	3	3	3	2	3	-1	2
I	2	3	2	2	2	2	2	3	3	3	3	3	3	3	2	3	2	3	2	2	3	2	2	2	2	2	3	3	3	3	3	3	2	2	-1	2
J	2	3	2	2	2	2	2	3	3	3	3	3	3	3	2	3	2	3	2	2	3	2	2	2	2	2	3	3	3	3	3	3	2	2	0	2
K	0	2	-2	-2	-2	0	0	2	2	-1	2	2	2	2	-2	2	-2	2	-1	-2	2	-4	-4	3	-1	3	2	2	2	2	-2	2	-2	-2	0	0
L	2	2	0	0	0	0	1	2	2	1	2	2	2	2	0	2	0	2	1	-1	2	-3	-3	3	-2	3	2	2	2	2	-1	2	-4	0	-1	1
M	2	3	2	2	2	2	2	3	3	3	3	3	3	3	2	3	2	2	2	2	3	2	2	2	2	2	3	3	3	3	3	3	2	3	-1	2
N	2	3	2	2	2	2	2	3	3	3	3	3	3	3	2	3	2	3	2	2	3	2	2	2	2	2	3	3	3	3	3	3	2	2	-1	2
O	1	2	2	2	2	2	2	2	2	-2	2	2	2	2	2	2	2	2	2	1	2	1	1	1	1	1	3	3	3	3	2	3	2	2	-4	2
P	2	2	1	1	1	2	1	2	2	-2	2	2	2	2	1	2	1	2	2	2	2	2	1	2	2	1	-3	-3	2	2	1	2	2	2	-2	-1
Q	-1	2	2	2	2	2	2	2	2	2	2	2	2	2	2	2	2	2	2	1	2	1	1	1	1	1	2	2	2	2	2	3	1	2	-4	1
R	2	2	1	1	1	2	2	2	2	2	2	2	2	2	1	2	1	2	1	2	2	2	2	2	2	2	2	2	2	2	2	2	2	2	-3	2
S	2	2	2	2	2	2	2	2	2	2	2	2	2	2	2	2	2	2	2	1	2	1	1	1	1	1	1	2	2	2	2	2	1	2	2	2
T	-5	2	-5	-5	-5	0	-5	2	3	2	2	2	1	1	-5	1	-5	1	-4	1	1	-3	-3	-4	-3	-3	0	0	0	0	0	1	0	0	0	-1
U	2	3	2	2	2	2	2	3	3	3	3	3	3	3	2	3	2	3	2	2	3	2	2	2	2	2	3	3	3	3	3	3	2	2	-1	2
V	-2	2	-3	-3	-3	0	-3	2	2	2	2	2	1	1	-3	1	-3	1	-2	0	1	0	0	0	0	0	-1	-1	-1	-1	-2	2	0	-1	0	-2
W	-2	2	-2	-2	-2	0	-2	2	2	-3	2	2	1	1	-2	1	-2	1	-1	0	1	1	1	0	1	-1	-1	-1	0	0	-1	2	1	0	0	-2
X	0	2	-1	-1	-1	0	-1	2	2	2	2	2	2	2	-1	2	-1	2	-1	-2	2	-3	-3	2	-3	2	2	2	2	2	-2	2	-2	-1	0	0
Y	-4	2	-4	-4	-4	-1	-4	2	2	2	2	2	-1	-1	-4	-1	-4	-1	-3	-1	-1	0	0	-1	-1	-2	-3	-3	-3	-3	-4	2	0	-1	0	-3
Z	2	2	1	1	1	1	1	2	2	2	2	2	3	3	1	3	1	2	1	0	3	1	1	2	0	3	3	3	3	3	-2	3	1	1	0	1

	a	b	c	d	e	f	g	h	i	j	k	l	m	n	o	p	q	r	s	t	u	v	w	x	y	z	.	,	:	;	–	!	?	(	)	&
1	2	3	2	2	2	2	2	3	3	3	3	3	3	3	2	3	2	3	2	2	3	2	2	2	2	2	3	3	3	3	3	3	2	2	0	2
2	2	3	2	2	2	2	2	3	3	3	3	3	3	3	2	3	2	3	2	1	3	1	1	2	1	3	3	3	3	3	2	3	2	2	-2	2
3	2	2	2	2	2	1	2	2	2	1	2	2	2	2	2	2	2	2	2	1	2	1	1	1	1	1	2	2	2	2	2	2	1	2	2	2
4	2	3	2	2	2	1	2	3	3	3	3	3	3	3	2	3	2	3	2	0	3	-1	-1	-1	-1	0	2	2	2	2	2	2	-2	2	-3	2
5	2	2	2	2	2	1	2	2	2	2	2	2	2	2	2	2	2	2	2	0	2	0	0	0	0	2	2	2	2	2	2	2	0	2	-1	2
6	2	2	2	2	2	1	2	2	2	2	2	2	2	2	2	2	2	2	2	2	2	2	2	2	2	2	1	2	2	2	2	2	1	2	-2	2
7	-2	2	-2	-2	-2	1	-2	2	2	2	2	2	1	1	-2	1	-2	1	-1	1	1	2	2	1	1	0	-2	-2	-2	-2	-2	3	-1	0	0	-1
8	2	2	2	2	2	1	2	2	2	2	2	2	2	2	2	2	2	2	2	1	2	1	1	1	1	1	2	2	2	2	2	2	1	2	-2	2
9	1	2	2	2	2	2	2	2	2	0	2	2	2	2	2	2	2	2	2	0	2	-1	-1	-2	-1	0	1	2	2	2	2	2	1	2	2	2
0	-1	2	2	2	2	2	2	2	2	2	2	2	2	2	2	2	2	2	2	2	2	2	1	2	1	2	2	2	2	2	2	2	1	-3	2	2

	a	b	c	d	e	f	g	h	i	j	k	l	m	n	o	p	q	r	s	t	u	v	w	x	y	z	.	,	:	;	–	!	?	(	)	&
a	2	3	2	2	2	2	2	3	3	-1	3	3	3	3	2	3	2	3	2	1	2	1	1	2	1	2	3	3	3	3	3	3	1	2	-1	2
b	2	2	2	2	2	1	2	2	2	2	2	2	2	2	2	2	2	2	2	0	2	0	0	-1	0	1	1	1	1	1	2	2	0	2	4	2
c	2	2	2	2	2	1	2	2	2	2	2	2	2	2	2	2	2	2	2	0	2	0	0	-1	0	1	1	1	1	1	2	2	0	2	4	2
d	2	3	2	3	2	2	2	3	3	3	3	3	3	3	2	3	2	3	2	2	3	2	2	2	2	2	3	3	3	3	3	3	2	3	0	2
e	2	2	2	2	2	1	2	2	2	2	2	2	2	2	2	2	2	2	2	0	2	0	0	-1	0	1	1	1	1	1	2	2	0	2	4	2
f	1	3	0	0	0	0	0	3	3	3	3	3	3	3	0	2	0	2	1	3	2	2	2	1	2	2	-1	-1	-1	-1	-2	3	2	2	-1	0
g	2	3	2	2	2	2	2	3	3	3	3	3	3	3	2	3	2	3	2	2	3	2	2	2	2	3	3	3	3	3	3	3	2	2	-1	2
h	2	3	2	2	2	2	2	3	3	3	3	3	3	3	2	3	2	3	2	1	3	1	1	2	1	3	3	3	3	3	3	3	1	2	0	2
i	2	3	2	2	2	3	2	3	3	3	3	3	3	3	2	3	2	3	2	2	3	2	2	2	2	3	3	3	3	3	3	3	2	3	0	1
j	2	3	2	2	2	3	2	3	3	3	3	3	3	3	2	3	2	3	2	2	3	2	2	2	2	3	3	3	3	3	3	3	2	3	0	2
k	0	2	-1	-1	-1	1	-1	2	2	2	2	2	2	2	-1	2	-1	2	-1	1	2	2	2	2	2	2	2	2	2	2	-2	2	2	0	0	2
l	2	3	2	2	2	2	2	3	3	3	3	3	3	3	2	3	2	3	2	2	3	2	2	2	2	3	3	3	3	3	3	3	2	3	0	2
m	2	3	2	2	2	2	2	3	3	3	3	3	3	3	2	3	2	3	2	1	3	1	1	2	1	2	3	3	3	3	3	3	1	2	0	1
n	2	3	2	2	2	2	2	3	3	3	3	3	3	3	2	3	2	3	2	1	3	1	1	2	1	2	3	3	3	3	3	3	1	2	0	1
o	2	2	2	2	2	1	2	2	2	2	2	2	2	2	2	2	2	2	2	0	2	0	0	-1	0	1	1	1	1	1	2	2	0	2	4	0
p	2	2	2	2	2	1	2	2	2	2	2	2	2	2	2	2	2	2	2	0	2	0	0	-1	0	1	1	1	1	1	2	2	0	2	4	0
q	2	3	2	2	2	2	2	3	3	3	3	3	3	3	2	3	2	3	2	2	3	2	2	2	2	3	3	3	3	3	3	3	2	2	2	2
r	1	2	1	1	1	2	1	2	2	-2	2	2	2	2	1	2	1	2	1	1	2	1	1	0	1	1	-3	-3	-3	-3	2	2	1	2	-4	1
s	2	2	2	2	2	1	2	2	2	2	2	2	2	2	2	2	2	2	2	1	2	0	0	0	0	1	1	1	1	1	2	2	0	2	3	0
t	2	3	0	0	0	3	0	3	3	1	3	3	3	3	0	3	0	3	1	3	3	2	2	2	2	3	3	3	3	3	3	3	2	2	0	2
u	2	3	2	2	2	2	2	2	3	3	3	3	3	3	2	3	2	3	2	2	3	2	2	2	2	3	3	3	3	3	3	3	2	2	-1	2
v	-1	2	-1	-1	-1	2	-1	2	2	2	2	2	2	2	-1	2	-1	2	0	2	2	2	2	2	2	1	-2	-2	-2	-2	2	2	2	1	-4	2
w	-1	2	-1	-1	-1	2	-1	2	2	2	2	2	2	2	-1	2	-1	2	0	2	2	2	2	2	2	1	-2	-2	-2	-2	2	2	2	1	-4	2
x	0	2	-2	-2	-2	1	-2	2	2	2	2	2	2	2	-2	2	-2	2	-1	2	2	1	1	2	1	2	2	2	2	2	2	2	1	0	-1	1
y	0	2	0	0	0	2	0	2	2	2	2	2	2	2	0	2	0	2	1	2	2	2	2	2	2	1	-2	-2	-2	-2	-2	2	2	1	-3	2
z	2	3	1	1	1	2	1	3	3	3	3	3	3	3	1	3	1	3	1	2	3	2	2	2	2	3	2	2	2	2	2	3	2	1	0	2

	a	b	c	d	e	f	g	h	i	j	k	l	m	n	o	p	q	r	s	t	u	v	w	x	y	z	.	,	:	;	–	!	?	(	)	&
. ,	1	3	2	2	2	1	2	3	3	-1	3	3	3	3	2	3	1	3	2	0	3	0	0	1	0	0	3	3	3	3	3	3	2	2	-4	2
:;	2	3	2	2	2	3	2	3	3	-1	3	3	3	3	2	3	2	3	2	3	3	2	2	2	2	3	3	3	3	3	3	3	2	2	2	2
!	3	3	2	2	2	3	2	3	3	1	3	3	3	3	2	3	2	3	2	3	3	2	2	2	2	3	2	2	2	2	3	3	2	2	-1	2
?	0	2	0	0	0	2	0	2	2	-2	2	2	2	2	0	2	0	2	1	2	2	2	2	2	2	1	2	2	2	2	0	2	2	1	3	1
(	2	0	-3	-3	-3	-2	-3	0	0	2	0	0	0	0	-3	0	-3	0	-3	-3	0	-4	-4	-1	-1	0	0	0	0	0	-3	0	-3	-4	3	-3
)	1	2	2	2	2	2	2	2	2	2	2	2	2	2	3	2	2	2	2	1	2	1	1	1	1	1	1	1	1	1	2	2	2	2	-4	2
&	1	2	2	2	2	0	2	2	2	1	2	2	2	2	2	2	2	2	1	1	2	-1	-1	2	0	2	2	2	2	2	2	2	-3	2	-1	1

11.
Measurements and Conversions

Systems of Measurement

1. Measurement is an operation by which we compare one dimension with another, assumed as units, and determining a ratio between the former and the latter.
The table, in addition to a decimal metric scale, also shows the heights in rows and points from the Didot and pica systems, a scale in inches and selected scales in fractions of inches, among those most commonly used.
Comparing the various systems of measurement and observing them one beside the other may be useful for visually grasping their scale.

The Decimal Metric System
is based on the number 10.
Deliberated in France in 1790 by the National Constituent Assembly, it became mandatory in 1801, and international in 1875.
Its unit of measurement is the metre, and its multiples and sub-multiples.
The Decimal Metric System gave us the current International System of Units (SI, from the French *Système international (d'unités)*).

The Didot System
Measurements are expressed in rows (Cicero) and points as part of a duodecimal system.
One row is equal to 12 points and half a row to 6 points. Each point is equal to 0.376065 mm.

Notes
*In 1790 Talleyrand presented a report to the National Constituent Assembly deploring the enormous variability in units of measurement across the country. He proposed the formation of a committee to develop a universal system. In 1791 a deliberation was made to adopt a unit of length equivalent to one forty-millionth part of the Earth's meridian. In 1795 the unit of measurement equivalent to one metre was adopted, followed by numerous multiples and sub-multiple.
The new sample metre corresponding with the correct measurement resulting from geodetic measurements was created using an X-shaped bar held at Sèvres, near Paris. Originally defined as one ten-millionth of the distance from the equator to the North Pole it is now defined as the distance travelled by light in a void in an interval of time measured as 1/299,792,458 s.*

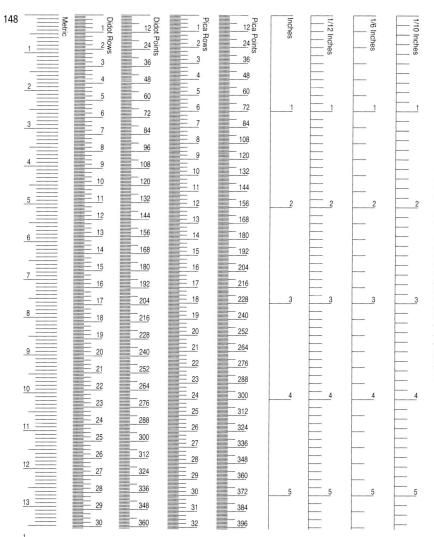

1.

The Anglo-American System
Measurements are expressed in rows (pica) and points using a duodecimal system. One row is equal to 12 points, half a row to 6 points, with one point equal to 0.3527 mm.

The Imperial System
This is the name of the current English system, codified in 1893 under the Board of Trade Regulations. It is also adopted in the United States of America, with minor variations. The fundamental unit is the measure of length known as the **yard**. In Great Britain it is equivalent to 0.9143992 metres, while the American yard measures 0.91440183 metres.

Units are derived from the **foot**, equal to 1/3 of a yard, or a 0.3048 metres (0.3047997); the **inch**, equal to 1/12 of a foot and 1/36 of a yard, or 2.54 cm; the **mile**, equal to 1/1000 of an inch; the **fathom**, which measures 2 yards; the **rod** or **perch**, equal to 5.5 yards; the **chain** or **100 links**, which measures 22 yards; the **chain**, equal to 66 yards; the **statute mile**, equal to 1,760 yards; the **league**, equivalent to 3 miles or 5,280 yards.

All of the measures of the Imperial System are kept by the Standards Department of the Board of Trade.

2. A typometer (reduced by 84.5%) showing the measurements of the Didot and pica systems; the measures of row spacing; common measurements in inches and fractions of inches; the spaces for measuring type size.

149

2.

How Many Points for Each Leading, and What Width for Each Point

1. The scales show the measures of the Didot system, from 8 to 36 points. The left column lists the progression in points; the right column lists the number of rows. For example, 34 rows of text composed in 11/11 point develop 374 points; 23 rows of text in 14/14 point develop 322 points. When the leading is greater than the type size, the measurements are taken of the corresponding leading.

For example, 34 rows of 11/12 point text develop 408 points. To the right is a comparison between the Didot typographic system and the decimal metric system.

2. On the facing page the scale shows columns in which the text is composed in various point sizes, from 8 to 36. Beside the text is the number of rows corresponding with the leading equal to the type size.

150

6/6 Type · 6/6 Rows	7/7 Type · 7/7 Rows	8/8 Type · 8/8 Rows	9/9 Type · 9/9 Rows	10/10 Type · 10/10 Rows	11/11 Type · 11/11 Rows	12/12 Type · 12/12 Rows	14/14 Type · 14/14 Rows	16/16 Type · 16/16 Rows	18/18 Type · 18/18 Rows	24/24 Type · 24/24 Rows	36/35 Type · 36/36 Rows
6 · 1	7 · 1	8 · 1	9 · 1	10 · 1	11 · 1	12 · 1	14 · 1	16 · 1	18 · 1	24 · 1	36 · 1
12 · 2	14 · 2	16 · 2	18 · 2	20 · 2	22 · 2	24 · 2	28 · 2	32 · 2	36 · 2	48 · 2	72 · 2
18 · 3	21 · 3	24 · 3	27 · 3	30 · 3	33 · 3	36 · 3	42 · 3	48 · 3	54 · 3	72 · 3	108 · 3
24 · 4	28 · 4	32 · 4	36 · 4	40 · 4	44 · 4	48 · 4	56 · 4	64 · 4	72 · 4	96 · 4	144 · 4
30 · 5	35 · 5	40 · 5	45 · 5	50 · 5	55 · 5	60 · 5	70 · 5	80 · 5	90 · 5	120 · 5	180 · 5
36 · 6	42 · 6	48 · 6	54 · 6	60 · 6	66 · 6	72 · 6	84 · 6	96 · 6	108 · 6	144 · 6	216 · 6
42 · 7	49 · 7	56 · 7	63 · 7	70 · 7	77 · 7	84 · 7	98 · 7	112 · 7	126 · 7	168 · 7	252 · 7
48 · 8	56 · 8	64 · 8	72 · 8	80 · 8	88 · 8	96 · 8	112 · 8	128 · 8	144 · 8	192 · 8	288 · 8
54 · 9	63 · 9	72 · 9	81 · 9	90 · 9	99 · 9	108 · 9	126 · 9	144 · 9	162 · 9	216 · 9	324 · 9
60 · 10	70 · 10	80 · 10	90 · 10	100 · 10	110 · 10	120 · 10	140 · 10	160 · 10	180 · 10	240 · 10	360 · 10
66 · 11	77 · 11	88 · 11	99 · 11	110 · 11	121 · 11	132 · 11	154 · 11	176 · 11	198 · 11	264 · 11	
72 · 12	84 · 12	96 · 12	108 · 12	120 · 12	132 · 12	144 · 12	168 · 12	192 · 12	216 · 12	288 · 12	
78 · 13	91 · 13	104 · 13	117 · 13	130 · 13	143 · 13	156 · 13	182 · 13	208 · 13	234 · 13	312 · 13	
84 · 14	98 · 14	112 · 14	126 · 14	140 · 14	154 · 14	168 · 14	196 · 14	224 · 14	252 · 14	336 · 14	
90 · 15	105 · 15	120 · 15	135 · 15	150 · 15	165 · 15	180 · 15	210 · 15	240 · 15	270 · 15	360 · 15	
96 · 16	112 · 16	128 · 16	144 · 16	160 · 16	176 · 16	192 · 16	224 · 16	256 · 16	288 · 16		
102 · 17	119 · 17	136 · 17	153 · 17	170 · 17	187 · 17	204 · 17	238 · 17	272 · 17	306 · 17		
108 · 18	126 · 18	144 · 18	162 · 18	180 · 18	198 · 18	216 · 18	252 · 18	288 · 18	324 · 18		
114 · 19	133 · 19	152 · 19	171 · 19	190 · 19	209 · 19	228 · 19	266 · 19	304 · 19	342 · 19		
120 · 20	140 · 20	160 · 20	180 · 20	200 · 20	220 · 20	240 · 20	280 · 20	320 · 20	360 · 20		
126 · 21	147 · 21	168 · 21	189 · 21	210 · 21	231 · 21	252 · 21	294 · 21	336 · 21			
132 · 22	154 · 22	176 · 22	198 · 22	220 · 22	242 · 22	264 · 22	308 · 22	352 · 22			
138 · 23	161 · 23	184 · 23	207 · 23	230 · 23	253 · 23	276 · 23	322 · 23				
144 · 24	168 · 24	192 · 24	216 · 24	240 · 24	264 · 24	288 · 24	336 · 24				
150 · 25	175 · 25	200 · 25	225 · 25	250 · 25	275 · 25	300 · 25	350 · 25				
156 · 26	182 · 26	208 · 26	234 · 26	260 · 26	286 · 26	312 · 26	364 · 26				
162 · 27	189 · 27	216 · 27	243 · 27	270 · 27	297 · 27	324 · 27					
168 · 28	196 · 28	224 · 28	252 · 28	280 · 28	308 · 28	336 · 28					
174 · 29	203 · 29	232 · 29	261 · 29	290 · 29	319 · 29	348 · 29					
180 · 30	210 · 30	240 · 30	270 · 30	300 · 30	330 · 30	360 · 30					
186 · 31	217 · 31	248 · 31	279 · 31	310 · 31	341 · 31						
192 · 32	224 · 32	256 · 32	288 · 32	320 · 32	352 · 32						
198 · 33	231 · 33	264 · 33	297 · 33	330 · 33	363 · 33						
204 · 34	238 · 34	272 · 34	306 · 34	340 · 34							
210 · 35	245 · 35	280 · 35	315 · 35	350 · 35							
216 · 36	252 · 36	288 · 36	324 · 36	360 · 36							
222 · 37	259 · 37	296 · 37	333 · 37								
228 · 38	266 · 38	304 · 38	342 · 38								
234 · 39	273 · 39	312 · 39	351 · 39								
240 · 40	280 · 40	320 · 40	360 · 40								
246 · 41	287 · 41	328 · 41									
252 · 42	294 · 42	336 · 42									
258 · 43	301 · 43	344 · 43									
264 · 44	308 · 44	352 · 44									
270 · 45	315 · 45	360 · 45									
276 · 46	322 · 46										
282 · 47	329 · 47										
288 · 48	336 · 48										
294 · 49	343 · 49										
300 · 50	350 · 50										
306 · 51	357 · 51										
312 · 52	364 · 52										
318 · 53											
324 · 54											
330 · 55											
336 · 56											
342 · 57											
348 · 58											
354 · 59											
360 · 60											

Cicero (Rows and Points) scale: 1–30.
Metric scale: 1–13.

	To transform	into	multiply by the values indicated below
0.3937	inches	centimetres	2.54
3.2808	feet	metres	0.3048
1.0933	yards	metres	0.9144
0.6214	statute miles	kilometres	1.6093
0.5396	nautical miles	kilometres	1.85315
0.1550	square inches	square centimetres	6.4516
10.7639	square feet	square metres	0.09290
1.1960	square yards	square metres	0.8361
0.3861	square miles	square kilometres	2.590
0.06102	cubic inches	cubic centimetres	16.3870
35.3148	cubic feet	cubic metres	0.02831
1.3080	cubic yards	cubic metres	0.7646
2.20462	pounds avoirdupois	kilogrammes	0.4536
0.03527	ounces avoirdupois	grammes	28.3495
15.3846	grains	grammes	0.064
0.01968	hundredweights	kilogrammes	50.80
0.984	(English) long tons	(metric) tons	1.016
0.220	imperial gallons	litres	4.546
0.9863	horsepower	chevaux-vapeurs	1.0139

151

2.

Converting between Systems

1. The Typometer. Historically realised in brass, they are now almost exclusively made from transparent plastic or acetate. This tool lists measurements in millimetres, Didot points, and in some cases pica. Their transparency facilitates the measurement of rows of text in relation to type size and leading.
Other measurements normally found on a typometer include various leading dimensions, in other words the space between rows of text.

2. 3. The typographic measures of *filetti* (horizontal lines) are expressed in points and printed in Didot and pica points.
The difference in width, imperceptible in thin lines, is accentuated as the size of the lines increases. in typography, the height of a line is the same as the typeface (63 Didot points or 0.918 inches).

4. American computers offer a choice of the measurement system that one wishes to use. In general there are three systems to choose from:
pica, inches and centimetres (or millimetres). The Didot system, used in Europe, is rarely available.
The following table contains conversion values for the dimensions of filetti.

152 In typography, measurements are expressed in rows and points, using a system that is not decimal based, but instead duodecimal. One row (cicero) is equal to 12 points, half a row to 6 points, where each point is equal to 0.376065 mm.
One row is equal to 4.51278 mm. These numbers refer to the Didot system, generally used in Italian print works, and introduced by the Frenchman F.A. Didot in 1870. Anglo-American countries tend to use the pica system, also duodecimal, and also introduced during the decade 1870/80, where one point is equivalent to 0.3527 millimetres. American computers do not consider the measurements of the Didot system, though they do offer a conversion table that makes it possible to work with the decimal of pica systems.
It is inevitable that during a lengthy career a graphic artist will be required to translate values expressed in one system into their equivalent in another system.
The following pages offer a series of conversion tables and instruction on how to apply them.
Spaces are calculated using a *typometer*, a ruler of typographic measurements. It lists row measurements in typographic Didot rows, and in some cases in pica, scales for calculating leading, useful for measuring the rows of a text, so long as it has been composed with a leading equal to the type size, and a ruler in centimetres
The length of a row of text is known in Italian as the *giustezza*. Once measured in typographic rows, with the advent of the personal computer, it can also be set in millimetres.

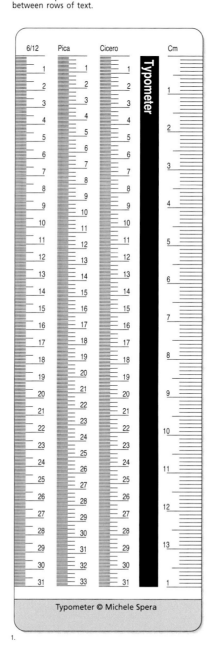

1.

Basic Measurements:

1 Didot point	= 0.376065 mm
1 pica point	= 0.3527 mm
1 inch	= 25.4 mm
1 foot	= 0.3048 m

Measurement is an operation by which we compare one dimension with another, assumed as units.
A conversion serves to determine a ratio between the former and the latter.

5. The table to the right lists a selection of fixed numbers that are useful for identifying conversion values between different systems of measurement. Instructions: if we wish to convert between measurements expressed in pica points, for example 68.239750 pica points, in Didot points, we must divide this number by the fixed number 1.0662461. This gives us a value of 64 Didot points.

If, instead, we wish to convert a measurement expressed in millimetres into Didot points, for example 24.06816 mm, we divide this number by the fixed number 0.376065 and obtain a value of 64. If, for example, we divide 22.5728 millimetres by 0.3527, we obtain a value of 64, that is, the number of corresponding pica points.

Systems of Measurement

Anglo-American System (pica)

1 pica pt	= 1/12 pica	= 0.3527 mm	= 1/72 inch
6 pica pts	= 1/2 pica	= 2.1162 mm	= 1/12 inch
12 pica pts	= 1 pica	= 4.2324 mm	= 1/6 inch
72 pica pts	= 6 pica	= 25.3944 mm	= 1 inch (0.996 inches)
1 pica pt		= 0.3527 mm	

Didot System (cicero)

12 Didot pts	= 1 cicero (row)	= 4.51278 mm
1 Didot pt	= 0.376065 mm	= 1.0662461 pica pts
6 Didot pts	= 2.256390 mm	= 6.3974771 pica pts
12 Didot pts	= 4.512780 mm	= 12.794954 pica pts
72 Didot pts	= 27.07668 mm	= 76.769726 pica pts
1 Didot mm	= 2.6591147 pts	= 2.8352707 pica pts

0.3 Cicero Points	0.3 Pica Points
1 points	1 points
2 points	2 points
4 points	4 points
6 points	6 points
8 points	8 points
10 points	10 points
12 points	12 points
16 points	16 points
20 points	20 points
24 points	24 points

2.   3.

Didot Points	equal to mm	Pica Points	equal to mm	Didot Points converted into Pica Points
1 point	0.376065	1 point	0.3527	1.0662461
2 points	0.75213	2 points	0.7054	2.1324922
4 points	1.50426	4 points	1.4108	4.2649844
6 points	2.25639	6 points	2.1162	6.3974766
8 points	3.00852	8 points	2.8216	8.5299688
10 points	3.76065	10 points	3.5270	10.662461
12 points	4.51278	12 points	4.2324	12.794953
16 points	6.01704	16 points	5.6432	17.059937
20 points	7.52130	20 points	7.0540	21.324922
24 points	9.02556	24 points	8.4648	25.589906
28 points	10.52982	28 points	9.8756	29.854890
32 points	12.03408	32 points	11.2864	34.119878
64 points	24.06816	64 points	22.5728	68.239756

4.

From	To	Fixed Number
pica point	cm	28.352707
pica point	mm	2.8352707
pica	mm	2.8352707
Didot	mm	2.6591147
pica point	Didot point	1.0662461
Didot point	pica point	0.9378697
Cicero	pica	0.9378697
mm	pica points	0.3527
mm	Didot points	0.376065
inches	mm	25.400050
mm	inches	2.5400050

5.

Conversion Table

Use the fixed numbers in the table to the left to convert from one system to another. To convert 64 pica points into the decimal metric system, for example millimetres, the conversion is 64/2.8352707 (fixed number) = 22.5728 mm. To convert 64 Didot points into millimetres, use the ratio 64/2.6591147 (fixed number) = 24.06816.
To convert 12 Didot points into pica points use the ratio 12/0.9378697 (fixed number) = 12.794954. In fact, 12 Didot points are equal to 4.51278 mm, exactly as 12.794954 pica points are equal to 4.51278 mm.
To convert 64 pica points into Didot points use the conversion rate 64/1.0662461 (fixed number) = 60.023666; in fact, 64 pica points = 22.5728 mm, and 60.023666 Didot points are also equal to 22.5728 mm.
To convert 1 cicero into pica, the formula is 1/0.9378697 (fixed number) = 1.0662461; in fact, 1 cicero = 4.51278 mm, exactly as 1.0662461 pica is equal to 4.51278 mm.
If we wish to convert a measurement expressed in millimetres into pica points, we divide the value by the fixed number 0.3527. If, instead, we wish to convert a measurement expressed in millimetres into Didot points, we divide the value by the fixed number 0.376065. In fact, the ratio 10.52982/0.376065 gives us the value of 28, the number of points expressed in the Didot system.

12.
Proportions

Systems of Proportional Enlargement and Reduction

When laying out photographs and images, a graphic designer is required to redimension originals to match the dimensions of the layout grid.
The geometric method for reducing an image, and understanding its new height, is based on the diagonal.
By laying out a diagonal on the original image, or the part to be printed, this line can be used to identify a constant proportion that serves to determine the new height of the image.

1. 2. The mathematical method is based on a very basic formula.
Image 1 has a 108 mm base and is 80 mm in height.
We want to reduce it to 52 mm in width.
We use the following formula:
$108 \div 80 = 52 \div x$;
$80 \times 52 = 4160$;
$4160 \div 108 = 38.518$.
This is the height of the newly formatted image.
Image 2 measures 108x52 mm.
When the base is reduced to 52 mm, the new height will be 25.037 mm.
Once again, we use the equation $108 \div 52 = 52 \div x$, where x is equal to 25.037 mm.

We use the following formula:
$70 \div 160 \times 100 = 43.75\%$ (percentage of reduction).
To find the height, all we need to do is multiply the percentage of reduction (43.75%) by the height of the original image, and divide the result by 100.
This is the formula:
$43.75\% \times 93 \div 100 = 40.6875$ mm (height of the new image).

154

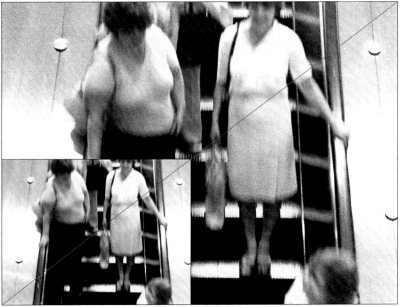

1.

2.

Beyond the measurements offered by calculations, we may also need to know the percentage of reduction, or enlargement, of an image.

3. Once again, we are assisted by a simple equation.
In the example offered in figure 3, the photograph is 136 mm wide x 80 mm in height.
If we reduce the width to 95.2 mm, the height will be equal to 56 mm.
Here is the formula: $136 \div 100 = 95.2 \div x$, where x is the percentage of reduction, in this case equal to 70%.

If we wish to use this number to calculate the new height, using an inverse process, we multiply the percentage of reduction (70%) by the original height (80 mm) and divide the result by 100÷ 70%x80÷100=56, where 56 is the new height of the image.

4. The original is equal to 136x52 mm.
We want to reduce it to 80 mm in width, obtaining a height of 30.588 mm.
In an even simpler fashion, we can obtain this reduction using a computer by dragging one corner of an image using the command *scale* (command, alt, caps lock) until we obtain the desired dimension.

155

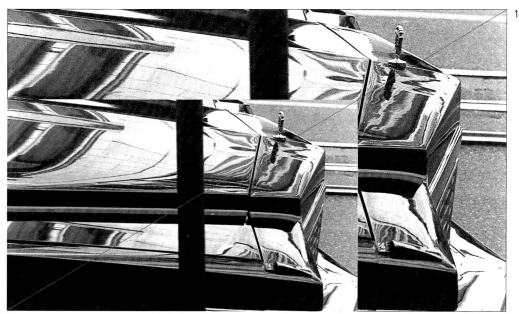

3.

4.

Finding Proportions

The Small Amount of Math any Graphic Designer Must Know

1. 2. The pages of this book, which measure 160 mm x 240 mm in height, have been reduced in the examples to two columns measuring 52 mm in width.
To find the new height, we use this simple formula:
$160 \div 52 = 52 \div x$,
$52 \times 52 \div 160 = 16.9$.
We can find the same proportion using a simpler system: if we divide 160 (the width of the original page) by 52 (the new width) we obtain the fixed number 3.076923.

This value, our *fixed number*, is the proportional coefficient of *conversion factor* between the two measurements.
If we divide the original width by the fixed number, we obtain
$160 \div 3.076923 = 52$.
Similarly, 240 (the original page height) divided by 14.201183 become 16.9.
The reduction of the page is equivalent to 32.5%.
Using the conversion factor, any element of a book - drawings, photographs and even type size - are proportionally linked to the new format.

3. 4. 5. In this case, our original dimensions of 160x240 are proportionally linked to the grid, which is 33.333 mm wide.
We divide 160 by 33.333 to obtain the fixed number 4.8.
Every element of the original page is to be divided by this number to transpose them to the new format.
The reduction in this case is equal to 20.833%.

156

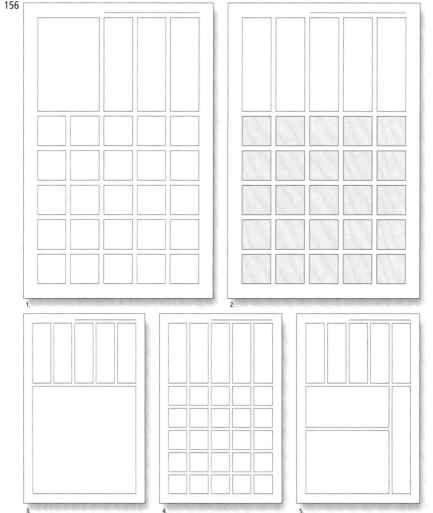

1.

2.

3.

4.

5.

Notes
"The method of the symphonic division of space", a term used to refer to dynamic symmetry, serves to construct a base for obtaining rhythmically distributed spaces.
According to a very ancient definition, rhythm is an 'order determined by time'. It serves, in turn, to avoid errors in measurements and the aesthetic qualities of an arrangement".
From the book Omaggio a Bodoni, by Marina Di Bernardo.

Workbook
As part of your project, dimension a series of images to match the measurements of your layout, establishing the ratios between measurements used a fixed number.
Identify the fixed number for each of the reductions.

6. The proportion between an 80 mm module and the second 52 mm module is equal to 80÷52=6÷x, where x=3.9.
Using a very simple equation we have obtained the required proportion.
Instead, by dividing the first measurement by the second, we obtain: 80÷52=1.5384615.
This number, which will be our *fixed number,* is the proportional coefficient or the *conversion factor* between the two values.

Using a very simple and extremely fast application we obtain all of the reductions in an indexical proportion. If we wish to reduce the height of the first module, which is equal to 6 mm in the same proportion, all we need to do is divide the number 6 by 1.5384615 to obtain the value of 3.9 mm, the height of the second module in proportion to the first.

7. 8. If the photograph to be reduced is 80 mm wide and 52 mm high, dividing these numbers by the fixed number 1.5384615 we immediately obtain the new width and the new height, respectively 52 and 33.8 mm.
The percentage of reduction will be: 100x52÷80 (original).
The resulting value of 65 is the reduction expressed as a percentage of 100.
The photograph, originally equivalent to 100%, will be reproduced at a scale of 65%, or using the dimensions provided by the calculation using the fixed number.

9. 10. The image of a cat, originally, 100%, has been reproduced in a second image, with a percentage of reduction equal to 76.470588%, rounded up to 76.5%.

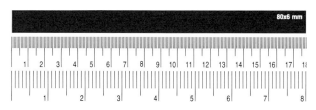

6.

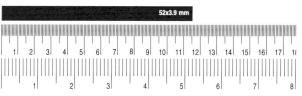

7.

9.

10.

8.

Notes
The equation A÷B=C÷X si always valid, though it forces us to make a calculation for every dimension we come across.
For constant reductions, the coefficient of reduction is also a constant; this makes its application immediate.

157

Calculating Percentages of Reduction

How to Obtain Them with Ease

1. 5. We have seen how an A4 page from this book, reduced to a width of 61 mm, is reduced by 29.04% and with a new width of 39 mm is reduced by 18.57%.

Yet, how do we obtain the reduction value as a percentage?

If the original was reduced on a computer, all that is required is to create an EPS (a sort of photograph of the page) to create an exact reproduction of the original image.

However, when using the *Save page in EPS format* command, the computer will ask you the proportion of the reduction (scale command).

At this point all of the formulas studied on the previous pages will prove very handy.

There is more: the percentage of reduction is equal to 29.047619 and we have obtained this value with from a proportion: 210 (original width) is to 100 (percentage of the original) as 61 is to x (where x is the percentage we are looking for)

$210 \div 100 = 61 \div x$.

Multiplying 100 by 61, and dividing the result by 210, gives us the value 29.047619.

This is the number required to obtain our proportional reduction. Using the same method we can obtain the value of 18.57% for the conversion to the three pages with a width of 39 mm;

$210 \div 39 = 5.3846153$
$100 \div 5.3846153 = 18.57$.

158

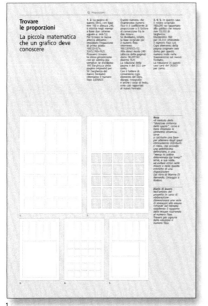

1.

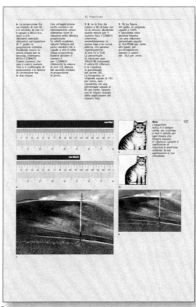

2.

Notes
The pages were reproduced in EPS using the proportions of 1:29 and 1:18.57. The same proportion was applied to the reduction of the images, texts, filetti, etc.
It is important to be observe a page designed in a certain format in its reduced version: this operation offers us a global vision and thus a synthesis of our work.

Workbook
As part of your project, dimension a series of images to match the measurements of your layout, establishing the ratios between measurements used a fixed number.
Identify the percentage of reduction for each of the reductions.

3.

4.

5.

Unusual Proportions

Same Height, Different Widths

1. 3. Computers also make it possible to modify proportions based on width and height.
In the images of the woman below we have modified the relations between proportions: maintaining the same height, figure 2 has the same proportions, while the width of figure 1 has been increased by 112%, while in figure 3 the width has been reduced by 87%.

4. 6. Similarly, and using the same identical percentages, we have modified the relationship between the width and height of a letter.
In this case we used the horizontal scale command in QuarkXPress.

Notes
Naturally, it is possible to exasperate the limits in proportions between width and height, in some cases obtaining pleasantly surprising results.

159

1.　　　　2.　　　　3.

4.　　　　5.　　　　6.

Finding Proportions

Resizing Images Using a Circular Slide Rule

1. The circular slide rule (wheel)

A very common method for identifying proportions and ratios involves the use of a proportional scale, offering graphic designers a similar tool to that employed by engineers and architects.

With this tool not only can we directly identify percentages of reduction and enlargement, but we can also make many other calculations.

The operations made possible by a slide rule are many, and they go far beyond the needs of a graphic designer.

A slide rule can be used for multiplications, divisions, exponents, square roots, logarithms and trigonometry, sine, cosine, the tangent and co-tangent of a given angle or the corresponding angle of trigonometric functions.

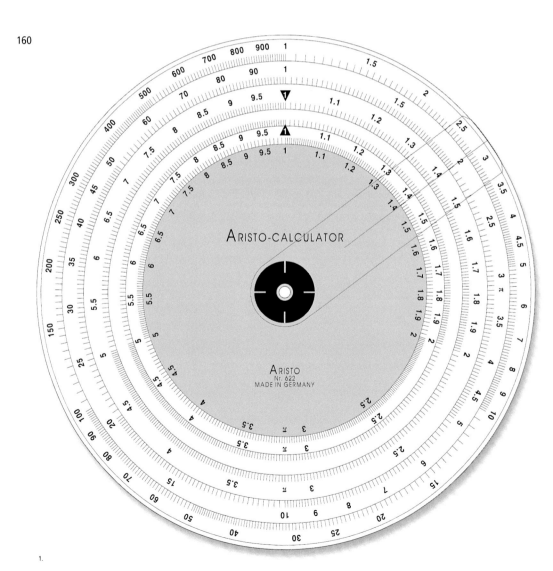

1.

The only disadvantage of a slide rule, very useful for day to day calculations given its ease of use and compact nature (it fits in your pocket), is that for very calculations using very small numbers, the results can be very approximate given the difficulty in clearly reading the lines. This occurs above all when using small linear slide rules. The scale of a slide rule can be rectilinear or circular. The latter are often much easier to read.

As the reading of a slide rule requires that we align the desired values on an outer and inner wheel, when both elements are very small, the human eye can only establish their correspondence with an approximation in the range of 0.02 mm; in these cases it is worth considering the use of a magnifying glass: this raises the level of precision to one hundredth of a millimetre. In any case, this limit has been overcome by the use of a simple pocket calculator.

2. The original measurement is 9x11 cm (wxh).
If we wish to increase the width to 12 cm, we align the number 9 on scale A with the number 11 on scale B. We align the cursor with the number 11 on scale A, where we can read the number 14.66, on scale B. This is the new dimension for the height.

3. Thus an original measuring 110x12 cm (wxh), modified to 16 cm in width will have a height of 1.745 cm;
4. an original measuring 12x15 cm (wxh), with a modified width of 11 cm, will have a new height of 13.75 cm;
5. an original measuring 18x15 cm (wxh) with a new width of 13 cm will have a modified height of 10.83 cm.

161

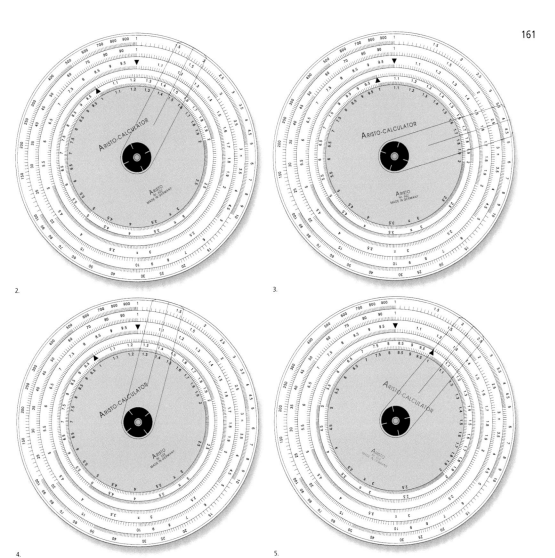

2.

3.

4.

5.

Finding Proportions

Resizing Images Using a Linear Slide Rule

1. A linear slide rule.
It has various scales, known as A, B, C, and so on, each of which serves specific calculations.
The scales are represented on one fixed and one sliding bar. The cursor, which slides along the rule, is used to mark the points of correspondence between the various scales.

2. Proportions
If we have a photograph that measures 7.5x4.3 cm (wxh), and wish to modify the base to 9 cm, we match the value of 7.5 on scale A with the value of 4.3 on scale B.
We align the cursor on the number 9 on scale A and read the value of 5.16 on scale B.
This is the dimension of the new height.

162

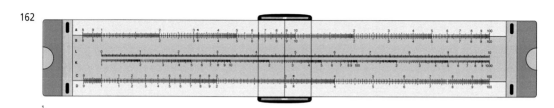

1.

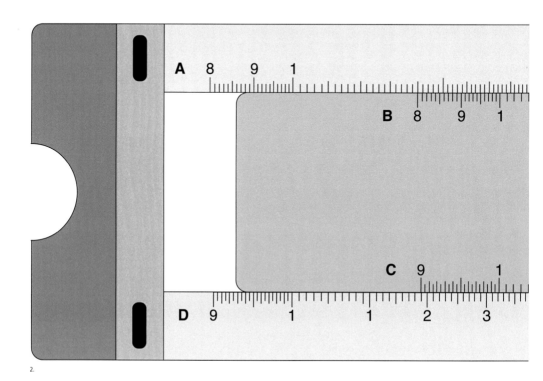

2.

3. Multiplication
We wish to obtain the result of the equation 16x22. The value of 16 is read on scale A, which is then aligned with the beginning of scale B, on the sliding part.
If we align the transparent cursor with scale B, in correspondence with the value 22, we find the result of 352, on scale A.

Naturally, as the slide rule is a tool used by professionals, the result of the operation is to be read with a sense of mathematical logic that presupposes a value of 352, and not 3.52 or 35.2.

4. Division
We wish to obtain the result of the equation 730÷40.
The dividend 730 is read on scale A; the divider, 40, read on scale B, is placed in correspondence with the beginning or end of scale B, depending on whether the slide rule protrudes from the right or the left.
The result, 18.25, is read in correspondence with the beginning of scale B.

5. An image designed for Agci, the General Association of Italian Cooperatives.
Find the proportion between the space occupied by text and the page format.

5.

163

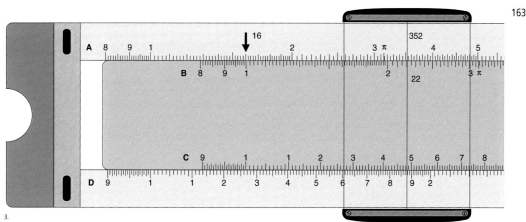

3.

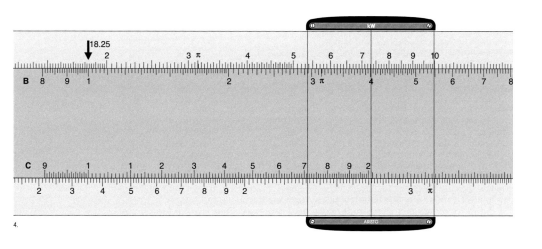

4.

13.
Paper

From the Earliest Examples to the Continuous Machine

Paper is made from different raw materials: fibrous materials; glues; fillers; colouring agents. Pulp generally consists of rags, cord, scrap, fabrics, wood, straw, various vegetals and recycled paper. Rags, which have always been a part of the process, are the most valuable element of pulp because they are made of fibres whose cellulose is resistant to oxidising agents and offer the greatest guarantee of durability over time.

Prior to the introduction of chemical agents pulp was obtained by through processes of pounding, selection, cutting, shredding, boiling, etc., and, in any case, without mechanical processes. The requirements of production, in recent times, led the paper industry to adopt various chemical processes, including alkaline treatments, and the use of such substances as soda caustic and lime.

164 Paper is prepared in sheets obtained through the pressing and filtering of specially treated celluloid fibres suspended in water. It consists of various elements: raw materials (linen rags, hemp, jute, cotton, cellulose, wood pulp, scrap paper and wastepaper; glues; colouring agents. Based on a weight per surface unit (equal to 1 square metre) the term paper refers to those products with a weight up to 150 g/m^2; the term card is used for 150 g/m^2 to 300 g/m^2; and cardboard above 300 g/m^2.

The invention of paper has been dated back to the Chinese. In *The Million* Marco Polo describes the paper banknotes circulating in the empire of Kubla Khan and how this support was constructed using sheets of gesso.

However, some time earlier in China, Ts'ai Lun, minister under Emperor Ho-ti, in 105, managed to fabricate paper using a pulp of bamboo canes, various wood fibres, hay from rice or tea. Left to macerate it was later pounded consistently with wood pestles in stone mortars to obtain a raw material used to create thin dry sheets.

Andrea Gasparinetti, the respected scholar of paper, has reconstructed the entire history of papermaking in three distinct periods: Arabic, Arabic-Italic, Fabrianese.

The art of papermaking was in fact introduced in Europe by the Arabs. They used primarily hemp or linen rags. While the form of the pages was equal to that invented by the Chinese, consisting of a dense grid to which the fibres were attached after being filtered with water, the system of sizing used a starch glue created from rice and grain. However, this procedure made the paper subject to deterioration, and offered favourable conditions for the development of microorganisms.

Papermaking was perfected in Italy by master craftsmen in the paper mills of Fabriano during the twelfth century. It seems certain that they learned their techniques of papermaking from Arab prisoners captured during one of the frequent assaults on Ancona and the Marche region, after the eleventh century in the upper Esino valley. However, it is a fact that the paper makers from Fabriano were responsible for the development and renewal of this art, which they perfected by introducing innovative techniques that would have a determinant influence on its durability over time, its pathogens and its quality.

Paper was once made exclusively by hand. The first industrial papermaking machine (the Fourdrinier machine) was invented in 1799 in the Didot paper mill in Essonnes, France.

Among the most important discoveries in the world of production, with lesser benefits to conservation, was the introduction of chemical agents (chlorine) used to bleach the rags that, until this moment, could only be made from white fabric.

It was once again the chemical industry that made it possible to obtain pulp using such fibrous materials as wood and other vegetal products. The use of chemical pulps, made possible using soda, bisulphate, aluminium sulphate, resins, etc., which also serve to macerate the pulp in lieu of mechanical shredding, reduced paper to a product with an almost unlimited lifespan.

Today, thankfully, paper mills are confronting this issue and adopting various new processes. The best produce almost exclusively ecological papers using selected raw materials, avoiding any chemical processes of bleaching or de-colouring.

Notes
The oldest document on paper is conserved in the Palermo State Archives. It comes from the chancellery of the Norman kings of Sicily and dates back to 1109.

There are different ways of making paper. Different pulps can be created to make different types of paper: rag pulp, cellulose, hay cellulose, wood pulp, scrap paper pulp, etc. Depending on their intended use, the various pulps are subject to different processes, such as refining, the binding of fibres, sizing, the addition of binding substances to keep ink from bleeding, colouring organic mineral substances. Sheets can be made by hand or industrially.

Hand fabrication is almost identical to the processes once used to produce small quantities of valuable paper, above all using rag pulp. Industrial papermaking uses a continuous machine that is either flat or round, producing either sheets or rolls of paper. More modern facilities tend to use round paper machines.

The Papermaking Process

1. Pulp made from wood, cellulose, scrap paper and water
2. Purification in a conical refiner
3. Tank
4. Continuous flat conveyor
5. Press
6. Flat machine
7. Drying section
8. Sizing section
9. Coil winder
10. Paper cylinder
11. Coil rewinder
12. Calender stack
13. Finishing room
14. Cylinder storage
15. Cutting and packing of reams
16. Packing

Paper is made in two main phases: the preparation of the pulp and the production of a roll of paper.

Pulp, once produced from rags, is now created from fibrous materials, such as wood pulp, cellulose, rags and reclaimed paper. Wood pulp is made from the wood of tall evergreen trees.

Cellulose is the principal component of the cellular walls of plants. Wood is 50% cellulose, while cotton is pure cellulose. Cellulose is prepared principally from wood pulp, that is, from trees stripped of their bark and shredded. The wood is then cooked using acidic or alkaline procedures. Pulp made from rags and reclaimed paper uses materials that are recycled during the process of papermaking.

These raw materials are reduced to pulp by hydrodynamic action, before being filtered and refined. The resulting fibrous suspension is dosed and mixed with diverse substances such as glues that give paper a surface that holds ink, and colouring agents that give paper a specific colour.

Stored in large tanks, the pulp is then gradually fed into the continuous machine (flat, round or mixed). It is here that the process of pressing takes place, followed by the drying of rolls of paper, either on a flat surface or large drums. Once dry, the rolls are smoothed and eventually sent to the calender section to improve the smoothness and gloss, before being wound on cylinders.

Special treatments are used to create high gloss and other finishes.

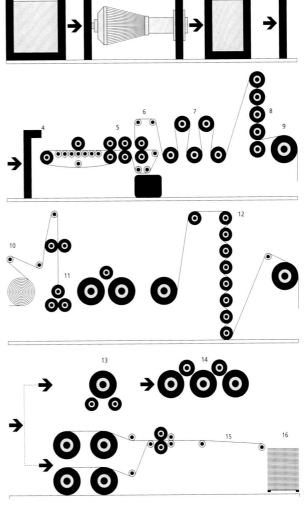

165

Papermaking

Raw Materials

166 The raw materials used in papermaking can be subdivided into four groups: fibrous materials, fillers, glues and colouring agents.

Fibrous Raw Materials

They are composed of rag cellulose or half pastes; cellulose or chemical pulp; mechanical wood pulp or wood pulp; reclaimed pulp and waste paper. Today, it is no longer possible to harness cellulose from rags owing to the impossibility of finding rags free of artificial fibres. The fabrication of securities and durable papers, in which cellulose is an important component, uses cotton vegetals, hemp and linen.

Cellulose is also obtained also from conifers, leafy trees, grasses and other annual plants (cord grass, alfalfa, cane, etc.). Celluloses made from wheat and rice straw are used for the most part to make thin papers (India paper, copy paper for typing, tissue papers for packaging citrus fruits). Cotton fibres, raw cotton, cotton balls and combed cotton (in other words, the by-products of the textile industry) are very resistant but also costly; they are used for securities and drawing papers.

Cotton linters are used in watermarked and filter papers. Hemp and linen fibres are optimum for use in the fabrication of cigarette papers, securities and handmade papers.

Fillers

These mineral substances are added to the suspension of fibrous materials. They give paper special characteristics: the level of whiteness, a greater opacity (cellulose alone is very transparent), an increased smoothness (mineral particles ensure a constant surface after the phase of calendering), a greater uniformity to the external characteristics of paper.

Glues

These materials make paper water resistant and give the surface the proper characteristics for holding ink. In general, glue is created by adding soap resins or colloidal suspensions of free resin, synthetic glues or synthetic resins; sizing by immersion of rolls of paper in solutions of animal gelatin is now limited to special papers. Particular cases that use synthetic resins (which ensure an elevated resistance to humidity) include banknotes used in tropical countries, as well as bags for liquids.

Colouring Agents

They are used to colour paper.
Natural pigments include ochre, terra di Siena, *terre d'ambra*, ferrous oxides, chromium yellow, Prussian blue.
Natural organic colours include redwood, madder, cochineal carmine, yellow woods, *grani di Persia*.
In general, natural colouring agents have weak colouring properties.
Artifical organic colouring agents (anilines) are most commonly used in papermaking. Other than colouring paper, they also ensure a broader range of colours, a greater resistance to atmospheric agents, ease of treatment and use.

Workbook
*Write to the most important paper manufacturer and request a visit from a representative.
Ask to be kept up to date on the latest processes and products.
Collect samples of different types of paper, divided by typology.*

The first table lists the raw materials used to make the principal types of paper; the second table lists the types of paper in relation to their weight, characteristics and most common uses.

The third table lists the qualities of cellulose used in quality papermaking, distinguished by the nature of their fibres and processes used in their production. The Miliani paper mills in Fabriano, Italy specify the denominations "sulphate, soda" etc., to indicate the type of chemical reagent used during the cooking of the vegetal matter to solubilize the encrusting substances that characterise the production of cellulose.

Bibliography
▼*Yearbook of the Associazione fra le Aziende Grafiche cartotecniche e Trasformatrici di Roma e Provincia, 1997 edition.*
▼*L'arte della carta a Fabriano, Comune di Fabriano, Cartiere Miliani Fabriano, Museo della carta e della filigrana Fabriano, 1991.*
▼*Giorgio Fioravanti, Grafica & Stampa, Zanichelli Editore, April 1997.*

167

Raw Materials	Paper Types
Hemp, linen, jute and cotton rags	Handmade, mould made, precious papers
Cellulose in chemical pulp (60÷80% wood)	Mould made and semi-precious papers
Wood pulp in mechanical pulp with cellulose	Medium or common papers
Scrap paper (offcuts from printed material)	Common paper
Grain or rice hay cellulose	Onion skins, typing overlays, tissue paper for fruit
Linters (the part wrapping cotton seeds)	Filigreed papers, filter papers, securities
Use of synthetic resins	Banknotes, bags for liquids
Canàpuli (residual material from scutching)	Cigarette paper, securities, handmade papers

Paper Type	Weight per m²	Characteristics	Use
India paper	From 10/12 to 45 g	Limited resistance	Air mail
Gloss coated paper	From 50 to 150 g	Limited resistance	Books, pamphlets, magazines
Coated paper	From 70 to 150 g	Glossy or opaque coated	All printed material
Coated paperboard	From 150 to 300 g	Glossy or opaque coated	All printed material
Offset paper	From 150 to 300 g	Smooth or rough (worked)	All printed material
Rotogravure paper	From 70 to 130 g	Smooth, soft and flexible	Magazines
Card and cardboard	From 150 to 500 g	Smooth, worked or coloured	Covers, packaging

Family	Wood Types	Process
Conifers or resinous trees	fir, larch	bisulphate process
	pine, cypress	sulphate process
Leafy or deciduous trees	poplar	bisulphate, sulphate, soda process
	beech, aspen, birch	bisulphate process
	chestnut	bisulphate, soda process
	eucalyptus	sulphate process
Grasses	wheat straw	caustic soda or sodium sulfide process
	rice straw	sodium sulfide process
Annuals	alfa, cord grass	soda and caustic soda process
	cane	bisulphate process
	cotton, balls, combed	bland alkaline treatment
	cotton linters, hemp, linen	soda process

Paper

Types, Weights and a Few Curiosities

1. Paper fibre always runs parallel to the direction the paper roll exits the continuous machine.
When the roll is cut into sheets, we can imagine in the formats 64x88 or 70x100, the fibres are parallel to the long side, in this case 88 or 100.
Printed sheets are also inserted in the printer with the long side parallel to the rollers: thus in the direction of the fibres.

Note how the fibres of the pages of a book are parallel to the spine.
Printing against the fibres does not generally create serious problems.
However, when printing labels for bottles, to be attached without problems, it is indispensable that the fibres are parallel to the bottom of the label.
This means it is necessary to position the labels with their bases on the long side of the sheet.

168   Paper is the support for our projects, it is the material that brings our ideas and our work to life.

Choosing a type of paper is always a very difficult moment, because it requires an in-depth evaluation of what we can obtain during printing.

If glossy paper brings out the brilliance of colours, the elegance of a printed text on laid paper ensures unparalleled pleasure to the eye but renders photographic images opaque.

However, it is simply a question of choice, entrusted to the graphic designer and his or her experience and talent.

There are substantially three types of paper, each with infinite variations owing to the type of pulp, fibre, smoothing, colour, manufacturer, etc.

They are:

Glossy and opaque coated papers.

They are recommended when photographs or images are to have a strong impact.

Mould made papers.

Indispensable for low-cost series, books and publications. Nonetheless, there are also very good mould made papers with good printing qualities.

Special papers.

These are special papers that can ensure extra-special printed materials. The beauty of these papers can be measured in specific samples, which manufacturers are currently focusing on, and which are spectacular on their own.

Ask your local paper supplier: they will be happy to present and leave samples, allowing you to choose the paper most suitable to the material to be printed.

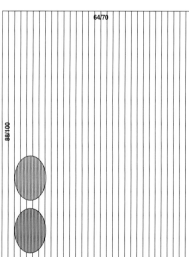

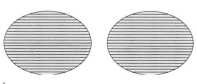

1.

Notes
Looking for personalised watermarked paper? The following section contains an extract from the StylPaper newsletter:
"Have you ever thought of your name, or that of your business or office printed in transparency on a marvellous sheet of letterhead?
A sign of recognition and distinction that clearly expresses your style, and makes it impossible to counterfeit your private or personal documents. All that is required is to hold them up to the light, and everyone will know who you are.
The novelty is that personalised watermarked paper is now affordable. Belmarque is available from a minimum of 1,000 A4 sheets, ready to be printed with your name or your company's logo. White or ivory, smooth or laid, Belmarque paper is available in a choice of four finishes. Available in 90 gr/m2 weight with coordinated envelopes".

Terminology

One would have to be Pico della Mirandola to remember all of the formats and their inventive and often occasional names.
This was a source of great confusion.
Many printers referred to the 70x100 poster as an *elephant*, a 100x140 as a *double elephant*, while a 70x100 is traditionally known as an *Italiano*, because it is a format manufactured only in Italy; however, the term *Italiano* is also used for the 19x24 format and *Italiana* for the 64x88.

There are infinite types of paper for specific and particular uses.
The first distinction is between handmade and machine-made papers.
The best papers are those fabricated above all with pulps made from rags and cellulose, the cheapest with wood pulps and other fibres and mixtures.
Glues are added to pulps to ensure they hold ink.
Glues are a mixture that fills the pores of paper to make it smooth and resistant.

Paper is smoothed in a machine by the pressure exerted by calenders.
Papers are subdivided into diverse classes, each of which has its own properties, weight per square metre, format, pulp characteristics, tensile strength and sizing.

2. Samples can be extraordinary, rich and above all very useful when choosing a type of paper or showing it to your client.
Manufacturers are very happy to send out samples, because they look for clients able to discern one type of paper from another.
Representatives can tell you about the type of pulp, the use of each specific type of paper, the results of printing based on each specific finish.

While today in Italy we use the UNI formats, which offer internationally unified regulations, for centuries Italian printers employed a rich and creative terminology to identify different formats.
The following is a list of only some of them, dimensioned in centimetres:

sestina, 18x22
quartina, 21x27
olandina, 25x39
quadrotta, 27x42
doppia quadrotta or *bastarda*, 44x56
rispetto or *officio*, 33x44
doppio rispetto, 45x68
quadruplo rispetto, 68x90
imperiale, 68x80
imperialino, 54x74
doppio imperialino, 74x108
royale, 48x66
realone, 50x70
doppio realone or *acquila*, 70x100
notarile or *processo*, 28x38
doppio notarile, 39x57
quadruplo notarile, 57x78
protocollo, 31x42
doppio protocollo, 43x64
quadruplo protocollo, 64x86
leona, 36x48
doppio leona or *stato*, 50x75
quadruplo leona, 75x100
elefante, 66x96, 73x100
italiana, 64x88
scolastica piccola, 78x108
scolastica grande, 88x112.

Photographic papers, now referred to by their format, also had onomatopoeic names:
minimo, 4.5x6; *visita*, 605x9; *margherita*, 8x10; *gabinetto*, 10x15; *cartolina*, 9x14; *boudoir*, 12x19; *salon*, 17x23; *album*, 21x27.

2.

Notes
If you are printing a book, for example a novel, never use coated paper: it is too white, too smooth to the touch, and too hard on the eyes.
A text printed on glossy coated paper is actually illegible in the long run.
There are specific papers for publishing, in general mould made that, in addition to being less costly, also feature a slight shadowing from the type of pulp, which makes them pleasant to the touch.

Workbook
Have a sample book made by a paper merchant, using a selection of different papers. Note how the thickness of a sample created from mould made papers is almost twice as thick as a sample made from coated paper of the same weight.

Some samples contain useful information about the type and quality of paper, suggestions for their best use and notes on their performance in printing.
This information assists the choice of which paper to use based on the type of work to be printed.

The descriptions that follow are only a few examples referred to different types of paper listed in the Fabriano catalogue.
For each type of paper Fabriano also lists the eventual askance of any chlorines or acids (Totally chlorine free, elementary chlorine free, acid free).

Murillo
A particular surface grain and extraordinary resistance of colours to sunlight are the primary characteristics of Murillo paper. This "acid free" paper is recommended for fine printed material.

Fabria
Made from pure cellulose, this "acid free" and 100% T.C.F. (total chlorine free) paper is highly ecological. The surface features a light grain created by a particular type of felt-marker.

Rusticus
This series of papers and cards, with a lightly marked surface, is particularly suitable to multi-coloured offset prints.

Gentile
Gentile features a felt-marked surface and a natural white colour: it is made from a fine paste of pure cellulose and 25% cotton. It is "acid free" and guarantees a long conservation period.

Palatina
Paper with a natural, ivory coloured surface. Ecological.

170

	Murillo	Fabria	Rusticus	Gentile
Editions	Recommended	Recommended	Recommended	Indicated
Special Editions	Indicated	Recommended	Recommended	Indicated
Monographs	Indicated	Recommended	Recommended	Indicated
Posters	Indicated	Recommended	Recommended	Indicated
Papermaking	Recommended	Recommended	Recommended	Indicated
Albums	Indicated	Indicated		Recommended
Binding	Recommended	Recommended	Recommended	Indicated
Brochures	Recommended	Recommended	Recommended	Indicated
Calendars	Recommended	Recommended	Recommended	Recommended
Inserts	Recommended	Recommended	Recommended	Indicated
Catalogues	Indicated	Recommended	Recommended	Indicated
Greeting Cards	Recommended	Indicated	Indicated	Recommended
Fly leaves	Indicated	Recommended	Recommended	Indicated
Dust jackets	Indicated	Recommended	Recommended	Indicated
Separators	Recommended	Recommended	Recommended	Indicated
Covers	Recommended	Recommended	Recommended	Indicated
Lists	Indicated	Indicated	Indicated	Indicated
Wedding invitations	Indicated	Indicated	Indicated	Recommended
Menus	Recommended	Indicated	Indicated	Recommended
Passe partout	Recommended	Indicated	Indicated	Indicated
Invitations	Indicated	Indicated	Indicated	Recommended
Correspondence		Recommended	Recommended	
Envelopes		Recommended	Recommended	
Frames	Recommended	Indicated	Indicated	Indicated
Four-Colour	Recommended	Recommended	Recommended	Recommended
Lithography	Indicated	Indicated	Indicated	Indicated
Silk Screens	Indicated	Indicated	Indicated	Indicated
Coloured backgrounds	Recommended	Indicated	Indicated	

	g/m2	Format	Kg/ream	Pack
Murillo	190	70x100	67.300	100
	260	70x100	91.800	100
	360	70x100	127	50
Fabria	100	72x101	36.360	250
	120	72x101	43.632	250
	160	72x101	58.176	125
	200	72x101	72.720	125
	240	72x101	87.264	125
	300	72x101	109.080	240
	360	72x101	130.900	50

	g/m2	Format	Kg/ream	Pack
Rusticus	95	72x101	34.950	250
	140	72x101	51.700	125
	200	72x101	73.500	125
	280	72x101	102.800	100
Gentile	160	70x100	56	125
	240	70x100	84	125
Ingres 90	90	70x100	31.900	250
Ingres 160	160	70x100	56.800	125
Ingres 160	160	50x70	28.400	125
Vergatone	130	70x100	46.300	125

	Palatina	Bioprima book	Offset finissimo	Fabriano Bristol
Editions	Recommended	Recommended	Recommended	Indicated
Special Editions	Indicated	Indicated	Indicated	
Monographs	Indicated	Indicated	Indicated	Indicated
Posters				Indicated
Papermaking	Indicated	Indicated	Indicated	Indicated
Albums			Indicated	Recommended
Binding	Indicated	Indicated		
Brochures	Indicated		Indicated	Indicated
Calendars	Indicated	Indicated		Indicated
Inserts	Indicated	Indicated		Indicated
Catalogues	Recommended	Recommended	Recommended	Indicated
Greeting Cards				Indicated
Fly leaves	Indicated			Indicated
Dust jackets	Indicated			
Separators				Indicated
Covers			Indicated	Indicated
Lists	Recommended	Indicated	Recommended	
Warehouse Charts			Indicated	
Accounting Charts			Indicated	
Warehouse Charts			Indicated	
Accounting Charts			Indicated	
Agendas	Recommended	Recommended	Indicated	
Forms			Recommended	
Four-Colour	Recommended	Indicated	Recommended	Indicated
Lithographs	Recommended	Indicated	Indicated	Indicated
Silk Screens				Indicated
Offset Printing	Recommended	Recommended	Recommended	Recommended

The Weight of Paper

Calculating the Weight of a Ream, a Sheet or a Book

Calculating the weight:
(64x88 cm paper,
weighing 140 grams
per square metre).
$64x88 = 0.5632$ m^2.
0.5632x140 per square
metre = 78.848 kg.
78.848÷2 = 39.424 per
ream of 500 sheets.
39.424÷500 = 78.848 g.
One sheet weighs
approximately
79 grams.

172 When you have printed a pamphlet, a brochure or a book, your client may ask you to load his or her car with 30 books or a thousand pamphlets.
The question will arise of how much this material weighs. Let's look at a few numbers.
An A4 format book printed on 140 gram per square metre 64x88 cm paper.
Multiplying 64x88 gives us a surface area in square meters of 0.5632.
Multiplying 0.5632x140 grams gives us 78.848 Kg.
This is the weight of 1000 sheets.
78.848÷1000 = 78 g, the weight of one sheet.
Given that a ream of paper contains 500 sheets, we divide 78.848 by 2 and obtain a weight of 39.424 kg, the weight of a ream.
To calculate the weight of one sheet, we divide 39.424 by 500 (the number of sheets in a ream), obtaining 78.848 grams. One sheet thus weighs approximately 79 grams.
Let's look at another example.
If we use is 70x100 cm paper with a weight of 140 grams per square metre, we have the formula $70x100 = 0.7$ m^2.
0.7x140=98 kg (1000 sheets).
98÷2=49 kg (weight of a 500-sheet ream).
49÷500=98 grams (weight of one 70x100 sheet).
We can imagine a three page pamphlet measuring 29.7 by 210 cm (100x210 cm when closed) printed in 5,000 copies on 140 gram paper.
The pamphlet will be created by placing the film copies of the pamphlet on 64x88 paper to create 8 recto pages and 8 verso pages. (This gives us a run of 650 passages per colour and 8 pamphlets per sheet). A sheet will weigh 79 grams, a pamphlet will weigh 9.875 grams and 5,000 pamphlets will weigh 49 kg.
The following page provides a very handy

ruler, now almost impossible to find, that serves to measure, with an optimum level of approximation, the weight of paper in the two most commonly used formats.
One side of a ruler contains the measurements relative to 70x100 cm paper, and the other side for 64x88 cm paper.
The ruler has a cursor and, at the top end, in the negative, the weight in grams per square metre of the paper whose weight has to be calculated.

In the first example,
with a format of 70x100
and a weight per square metre
of 240 grams,
weight of one sheet = 168 grams,
weight of 100 sheets = 16.800 kg
weight of 125 sheets = 21 kg
weight of 250 sheets = 42 kg
weight of 500 sheets = 84 kg

In the second example,
with a format of 64x88
and a weight per square metre
of 140 grams,
weight of one sheet = 78.8 grams,
weight of 100 sheets = 7.88 kg
weight of 125 sheets = 9.85 kg
weight of 250 sheets = 19.7 kg
weight of 500 sheets = 39.4 kg

In the third example,
with a format of 64x88
and a weight per square metre
of 340 grams,
weight of one sheet = 198 grams,
weight of 100 sheets = 19.8 kg
weight of 125 sheets = 23.9 kg
weight of 250 sheets = 47.85 kg
weight of 500 sheets = 95.7 kg.

Workbook
Calculate the weight of a book, brochure or pamphlet you are designing in relation to the various types of paper and their format. Update the table with the specifications relative to paper weight.
Try to construct your own ruler and cut it out to make it operable.

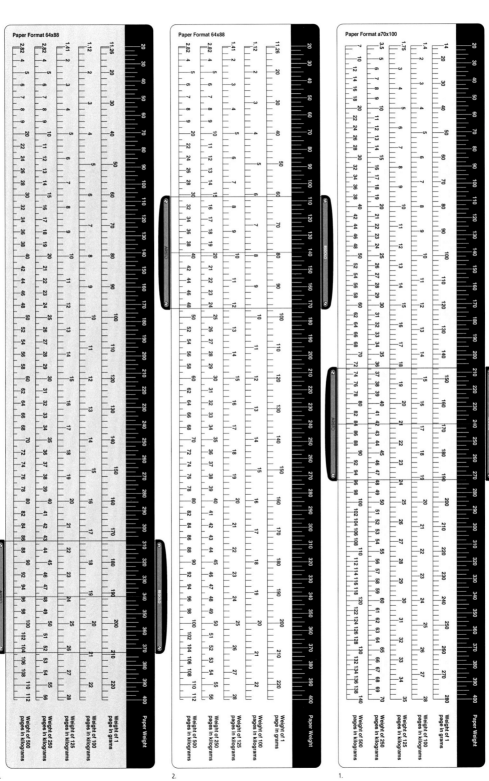

173

Paper Dimensions

DIN Regulations and UNI Formats

1. 5. The formats adopted by UNI were created by Dr. Walter Porstmann using a rectangular surface ($x \cdot y = 1$) of 1 m², with a ratio between sides of $x:y=1:\sqrt{2}$ which gives us the system:
$x:y=1:\sqrt{2}$, $x \cdot y=1$.
From the format A0 (a base rectangle of 1 m² with side $x = 0.841$ m and side $y = 1.189$ m gives us the A series, obtained by halfing the base A0 format to create the formats A1, A2, A3, etc.
The B and C series were created for items that contain the A series (envelopes, folders, registers) in relation to them.

Thus, a sheet of A4 letterhead (210x290 mm) will be contained in a C4 envelope (229x324 mm) that in turn can be contained in a B4 folder (250x353 mm).

174 The criteria that determines the use of UNI formats is based on compatibilities:
if a sheet of letterhead is to be contained in an envelope that in turn must fit into a folder, that in turn has to be stored in a cabinet that in turn has to fit into a room, which is part of a building, it is necessary that all of these dimensions correspond to precise ratios. With regards to our work, the UNI regulations provide indications about the formats to be selected, when and where this is possible, for our projects. The history of the unification of measurements is very long and complex.

The need for rules in the industrial world produced collective agreements and unified regulations that were not always adopted by everyone. Regulations included symbols, names, units of measurement, dimensions and materials.

With regards to paper formats, we will refer to Italian UNI regulations.

Approximately one and a half centuries ago, the physicist Lichtenberg observed that one sheet of paper with an area of 1 square metre, with a ratio between sides of 5:7, measuring 841x1189 mm, created a format whose multiples and submultiples conserved the same proportions, without wasting paper.

In 1884, a decree by the German chancellery established a number of formats: in 1922 the *Deutsche Industrie Normenausschuss* established a table of formats known as DIN, based on the relationship between the two sides of a sheet of paper (1:$\sqrt{2}$). These regulations were adopted for all official publications by the government of the Reich.

Today in Italy we can ask the *Istituto Italiano di Unificazione* to provide us a copy of the DIN Standards Manual.

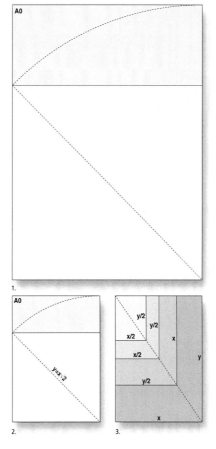

1.

2.

3.

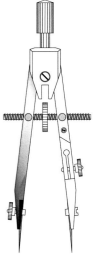

Notes
In simpler terms, we can state that a UNI A0 sheet is made from a rectangle with an area of 1 square metre, whose long side is equal to the diagonal of the root of the short side (see fig. 1) and where the ratio between the base and the height is 5:7 (5:7.068965517).
By halving the A0 format we obtain submultiples whose ratio between the long and short sides remains a constant proportion. UNI formats are not used for posters, newspapers, etc.

A Series		C Series		B Series	
A0	841 x 1189	C0	917 x 1297	B0	1000 x 1414
A1	594 x 841	C1	648 x 917	B1	707 x 1000
A2	420 x 594	C2	458 x 684	B2	500 x 707
A3	297 x 420	C3	324 x 458	B3	353 x 500
A4	210 x 297	C4	229 x 324	B4	250 x 353
A5	148 x 210	C5	162 x 229	B5	176 x 250
A6	105 x 148	C6	114 x 162	B6	125 x 176
A7	74 x 105	C7	81 x 114	B7	88 x 125
A8	52 x 74	C8	57 x 81	B8	62 x 88
A9	37 x 52	C9	40 x 57	B9	44 x 62
A10	26 x 37	C10	28 x 40	B10	31 x 44

Format	Code	mm
1÷2 length A4	1÷2 A4	105 x 297
1÷4 length A4	1÷4 A4	52 x 297
1÷8 length A7	1÷8 A7	9 x 105
1÷2 length C4	1÷2 C4	114 x 324
1÷3 width A4	1÷3 A4	99 x 210
1÷4 width A4	1÷4 A4	74 x 210
1÷8 width A4	1÷8 A4	13 x 74

Maximum differences +1.5 to –1.5

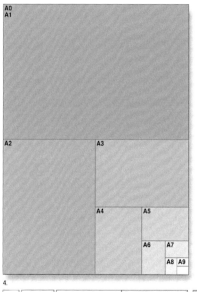

4.

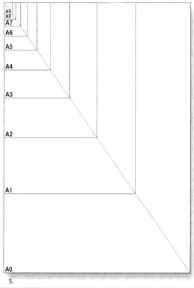

5.

175

Notes
The short side of the B series formats is the geometric average of the sides of the A series.
The largest is equal to the largest value multiplied by 2. The formats of the C series are geometric averages of the A and B series.
Oblong formats (rail tickets, special forms, etc.) are obtained by dividing the A, C and B series formats into 2, 4 or 8 parts and so on. In any case, we will find measurements from the UNI system.

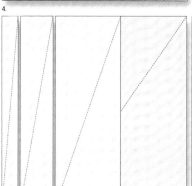

6.

Paper Dimensions

The Most Common Formats

1. A 70x100 sheet gives us two 50x70 or four 35x50 posters; eight 25x35 or sixteen 17.5x25 pages, and so on. Obviously, from these formats we must remove the space for the press and cutting, such that a useful format of 17.5x25 becomes 17x24, etc.

2. A 70x100 format for the printing of an octavo (sixteen pages, 8 verso and 8 recto) whose pages will measure 24x34 cm.

3. A 64x88 sheet gives us two 44x64 or four 22x32 or sixteen 16x22 pages, and so on. Obviously, from these formats we must remove the space for the press and cutting, such that a useful format of 22x32 may become 21x29.7, which gives us the UNI A4 format.

176 We have already taken a close look at a printing works and familiarised ourselves with type sizes and alignments; we have explored the form of type, made a few calculations and taken a few measurements.

The time has come to put these notions into practice and create a page.

In almost all cases the support for our creation will be a sheet of paper.

What are the measurements of commercially available paper?

Paper can be made to order, but only for large quantities. Large publishers are generally the only ones who can manage such an order. For our prints, we can use substantially two formats: 64x88 cm and 70x100 cm. Another readily available format is 100x140 cm, though it is used almost exclusively to print posters (the double elephant) and is available only in a monoglazed finish, in other words, it can be printed on only one side.

When designing a book, for example, we must decide on the format to be adopted. This will be the result of considerations of the type of book we wish to create, its target audience, the prestige and appearance it must have, the type of paper we plan to use and the format of the equipment it will be printed on.

Based on these technical considerations we can choose a format of paper that, opportunely folded in octavos, duodecimos, sextodecimos, etc., ensures the proper page size, without waste.

1.

2.

4. A 64x88 format for the printing of an octavo (sixteen pages, 8 verso and 8 recto) whose pages will measure 21x29.7 cm.
5. A 70x100 sheet for the printing of twelve pages in verso and recto, measuring 24x23 cm.

6. A 64x88 sheet for the printing of twelve pages in verso and recto, measuring 21x20.5 cm.
7. A 70x100 sheet for the printing of twelve pages in verso and recto, measuring 32x16 cm.

To the right: a table with the biblio-technical classification of book formats based solely on their height. A book "in sextodecimos" is one whose height varies from 175 to 200 millimetres.

Format	Height in mm
In folio	from 380 to 500
in quarto	from 280 to 380
in octavo	from 240 to 280
in duodecimo	from 200 to 240
in sextodecimo	from 175 to 200
in octodecimo	from 150 to 175
in vicesimo-quarto	from 125 to 150
in vicesimo-octavo	from 100 to 125
in trigesimo-secundo	from 75 to 100
in quadragesimo-octavo	less than 75

177

3.

4.

5.

6.

7.

14.
Layout and Binding

Folding Paper

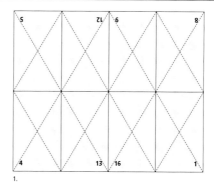

1./3. From this structure of 8 pages in recto and verso, folding the folio as shown in the illustration gives us the signature (also known as a gathering). The folio is folded to ensure that page 1 corresponds with the first page of the signature.

1.

178 Once we have selected the format, whatever it may be and preferably from the UNI formats, the layout of the pages must take into account how they will be printed to create, for example, a book.

The printer will arrange the pages to be printed on a flat sheet, with 8 pages in recto and verso, arranged to that, once the sheet is folded, the pages are in the correct numerical sequence.

The sheet will be folded once, twice and three times, and so on, to obtain a signature, in this case for a sextodecimo.

Obviously, the layout can be a quarto, octavo, sextodecimo, trigesimo-secundo, depending on the format of the book, the paper and the printing machine.

The various signatures are assembled and collated based on the selected structure.

This structure is known as *a incarto*, in other words, one octavo inside another, if the signatures are held together with a metal staple; *a raccolta* for *paperback* bindings. Paperback bindings can be *saddle stitched* or held together by glue applied at 300 degrees celsius, after the binding edge has been cut.

Paperback covers are glued to the binding edge; for bound books the cover is glued to the first and last pages of the book.

2.

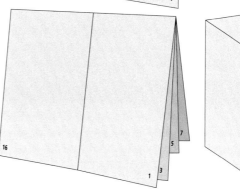

3.

Notes
When designing a book, remember that while it is possible to print 32 pages at one time, they must be laid out by splitting the folio, as they say, and assigning no more that sixteen pages to each signature.
This will give you signatures that are less bulky and without folds or malformations caused by swellings created by too many folds.
This is most common when using heavier papers. For paper weights greater than 150 g/m², sheets must first be folded and creased using a mechanical press.

4. The layout of sixteen leafs (sextodecimo) is obtained using 8 pages in recto and verso. The recto is the side containing page number 1 of the signature, and the verso the other side of the folio.
The pages are laid out to ensure the correct numerical sequence after the sheet has been folded.

5. Signature for a sextodecimo. When the folio printed with 8 pages in recto and verso is folded (figs. 1 and 2), this is how the 16 pages appear.
Various signatures stitched or glued to the spine give us the final book.
The cover is then glued to the spine and, as a final step, the book is trimmed using a special three-blade cutter to clean up the right margin (the cut edge), the top (header) and bottom (footer).

6. This type of signature is known as a *folio* (2 leaves, 4 pages, of which 2 recto and 2 verso). A quarto is a signature of 2 leaves and four pages; an octavo 4 leaves and 8 pages; a sextodecimo 8 sheets and 16 pages; a trigesimo-secundo 16 leaves and 32 pages. In the sextodecimo below, the only facing pages, which can be occupied by a photographic image spanning both pages, are the 8 and the 9. They are the only two that will remain perfectly aligned.

The Phases of Producing a Book

Printing
Squaring of the signatures
Folding

Saddle Stitch
Overlapping
Stitching
Trimming of 3 sides
Wrapping

Paperback
Gathering
Stitching or milling
Covering or gluing
Trimming of 3 sides
Wrapping

Paperboard binding
Gluing
(end paper - boards)
Gathering
Stitching or milling
Spine gluing
Trimming of margins
Colouring of trimmed edges
Rounding or false
Gauze
Endbands - paper
Exposed stitching
Pressing
Space
Dust Jacket
Packing

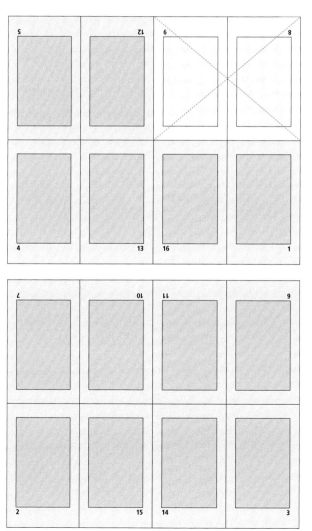

4.

5.

6.

179

Notes
A signature mark is the small progressive number (I, II, II, IV, etc.) placed at the bottom left for the first page of each leaf to be printed, and which was once found in every book.
When there are many signatures, this number is used by the book binder to fold and assemble the various signatures.
It serves to indicate the regular succession of the signatures.
The introduction of the signature is attributed to the typographer Johann Koelhoff the Elder, who used one for the first time in Cologne in 1472.
In ancient books, the signature used upper case letters, in alphabetical order: A, B, C, etc. When the first alphabet had been consumed, the order was re-started by adding the equivalent upside down letter to the first letter.

Folding Paper

Layouts and Signatures

1. 2. 3. The binder will arrange the printed leafs based on the format of the book, the paper and the printing machine. Folding a sample folio to create the final desired format, the binder will mark them with the progressive sequence of page numbers. Unfolding the folio, he or she will have an exact sample of the pages and the direction in which they are to be laid out. The pages will then be assembled based on this structure.

The structures reproduced on this page are only some of the many possible ones. Each structure has its own series of folds. They are known as a *cross* when the first fold is normal to the successive one; *parallel* if the direction of the fold is always the same. A prototype of the folded printed folio with signatures helps define the type of layout (a sextodecimo in octavos is more precise), the facing pages and the insertion of a supplementary quarto.

180

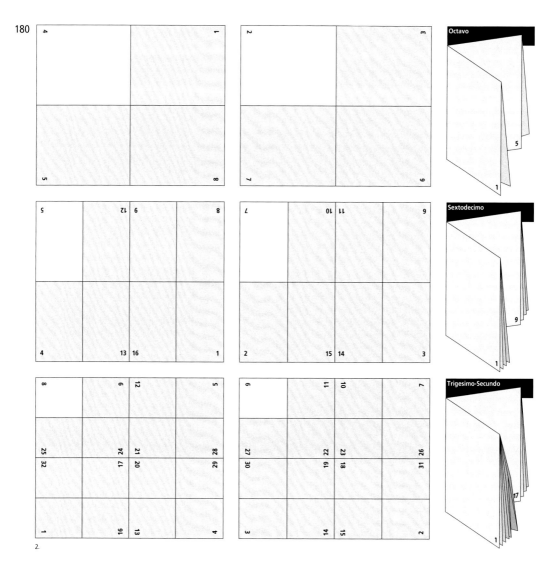

2.

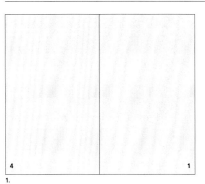

4		1

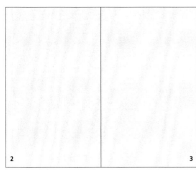

2		3

Quarto

3

1

1.

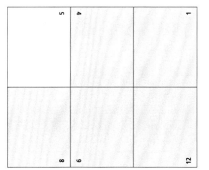

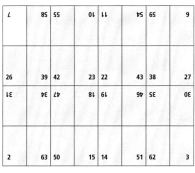

Sexagesimo-Quarto

Duodecimo

7

1

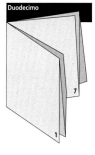

Vicesimo-Quarto

13

1

3.

Signatures

A Guideline

A table with the contents of the book, indicating the pages, the signatures and the type of paper to be used for each signature.
It also lists the facing pages, which can be used for images spanning two pages.
The table will also prove useful during the layout phase and provide indications to the printer about the layout and assembly of the book.

First signature: first pages (principles) in coated paper (1 and 2, blank pages; 3, end paper; 4, copyright; 5, frontispiece; 6, blank; 7, table of contents; 8, blank).
Second and third signatures: preface on Manuzio paper on 12 pages. From the fourth signature onward (body of the book) on matt coated paper. 30th and 31st signatures: Manuzio paper for the bibliography, etc.

32nd signature: coated, closing pages. Bold letters indicate the signature whose structure is illustrated on the facing page. Five colours are used for four-colour process printing plus a two-tone passage for photographs.

182

Pages	Sig. Marks	Layout	Type of Paper	Colours	Facing Pages
1/8	1° sig. mark	octavo	Coated paper	b/w	4/5
9/16	2° sig. mark	octavo	Manuzio paper	b/w	12/13
17/20	3° sig. mark	quarto	Manuzio paper	black/shaded	18/19
21/36	4° sig. mark	sextodecimo	Coated paper	Four-colour process	28/29
37/52	5° sig. mark	sextodecimo	Coated paper	Four-colour process	44/45
53/68	**6° sig. mark**	**sextodecimo**	**Coated paper**	**5 colours**	**60/61**
69/84	7° sig. mark	sextodecimo	Coated paper	5 colours	76/77
85/100	8° sig. mark	sextodecimo	Coated paper	Four-colour process	92/93
101/116	9° sig. mark	sextodecimo	Coated paper	Four-colour process	108/109
117/132	10° sig. mark	sextodecimo	Coated paper	Four-colour process	124/125
133/148	11° sig. mark	sextodecimo	Coated paper	Four-colour process	140/141
149/164	12° sig. mark	sextodecimo	Coated paper	Four-colour process	156/157
165/180	13° sig. mark	sextodecimo	Coated paper	Four-colour process	172/173
181/196	14° sig. mark	sextodecimo	Coated paper	Four-colour process	188/189
197/212	15° sig. mark	sextodecimo	Coated paper	Four-colour process	204/205
213/228	16° sig. mark	sextodecimo	Coated paper	Four-colour process	220/221
229/244	17° sig. mark	sextodecimo	Coated paper	Four-colour process	236/237
245/260	18° sig. mark	sextodecimo	Coated paper	Four-colour process	252/253
261/276	19° sig. mark	sextodecimo	Coated paper	Four-colour process	268/269
277/292	20° sig. mark	sextodecimo	Coated paper	Four-colour process	284/285
293/308	21° sig. mark	sextodecimo	Coated paper	Four-colour process	300/301
309/324	22° sig. mark	sextodecimo	Coated paper	Four-colour process	316/317
325/340	23° sig. mark	sextodecimo	Coated paper	Four-colour process	332/333
341/356	24° sig. mark	sextodecimo	Coated paper	Four-colour process	348/349
357/372	25° sig. mark	sextodecimo	Coated paper	Four-colour process	364/365
373/388	26° sig. mark	sextodecimo	Coated paper	Four-colour process	380/381
389/404	27° sig. mark	sextodecimo	Coated paper	Four-colour process	396/397
405/420	28° sig. mark	sextodecimo	Coated paper	Four-colour process	412/413
421/436	29° sig. mark	sextodecimo	Coated paper	Four-colour process	428/429
437/452	30° sig. mark	sextodecimo	Manuzio paper	Four-colour process	444/445
453/460	31° sig. mark	octavo	Manuzio paper	b/w	456/457
461/464	32° sig. mark	quarto	Coated paper		462/463

1. Structure of the 6th signature in sextodecimo, from page 53 to page 68, with eight verso (53, 56, 57, 60, 61, 64, 65, 68) and eight recto (54, 55, 58, 59, 62, 63, 66, 67). The only double page for uncut two-page images after folding is comprised of pages 60 and 61.

Book format 16x24 cm, machine with print format 50x70 cm.

2. Structure of the 6th and 7th signatures in trigesimo-secundo with a sextodecimo layout, from page 53 to page 84, with 17 pages in recto and verso. The leaf will be printed on the verso side and then returned to the printing machine, overturned, for the printing of the recto pages. During assembly, the leaf will be divided in two and folded.

Book format 16x24 cm, machine print format 70x100 cm.

183

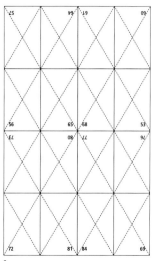

2.

1.

The Finished Book

Pleasing to the Eyes and the Hands

1. The book is finished, its pleasing appearance is a result of its graphic design, its layout but above all, its binding. The binding of a book represents the most elegant way to package it.
Sophisticated techniques can be used to create a truly precious object.

Binding serves to assemble a book by stitching the leafs together, finishing the spine with gauze and adding various precious finishes, such as the endband, a cord used to finish the ends of the stitching.
The cover, prepared separately, is a sheet of heavy card covered by paper, fabric or other materials.

It may have either a rounded or flat spine or a space at the edge of the spine; it is glued to the flaps, the first and last pages of the book.
The cover usually bears only the title, dry or heat pressed, while everything else that defines the image of the book is entrusted to the dust jacket with folded flaps.

184

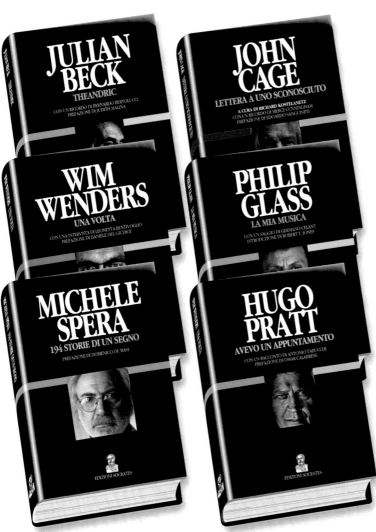

1.

Notes
When designing the cover for a book that is part of a series, the title is assigned a space that ensures we do not need to modify the type size when designing the covers of the other books in the same series.
It is good practice to forecast a maximum number of keystrokes and agree with the publisher on the maximum space for lines of text.
The books shown on these pages are part of the Galleria delle arti series published by Edizioni Socrates, curated by the author of this book.
The series used only the Garamond typeface, in all of its various forms.

2. The names of the parts of a book:
1. Dust Jacket
2. Flap
3. Cover
4. Sheet flyleaf
5. End paper
6. Frontispiece
7. Spine
8. Footband
9. Endband
10. Pastedown

Page 7 is known as the frontispiece.
It is occupied, in more or less different type sizes, though always in the same typeface, by the name of the author, the title of the book, its subtitle, the names of authors of prefaces and presentations, the publisher, etc.
Other pages are dedicated to the colophon, copyright, the year of publication, the number of editions and other information. Blank pages are generally positioned based on ancient traditions.

3. The image to the left shows two paperback books.
The pages were folded in duodecimos, the leafs assembled and stitched together. Finally, the cover was glued to the stitched spine of the assembled book.

Workbook
Design a book.
Page layout structure.
Format and paper.
Prepare the mock-up.
Divide the book into signatures, after establishing the format, type of paper and structures. Consider eventual inserts on special paper.
Samples of the signatures with page numbers.
Text: calculate the dimensions, choose the typeface, the type size, the leading and justification.
Layout the book.
Captions, other levels of text, notes and illustrations.
Cover, first and last pages.
Printing.
Layout, packaging.
Distribution.

Bibliography
▼*Bandinelli, Lussu, Iacobelli*
Farsi un libro
Stampa alternativa

Other Types of Binding

From Metal Staples to Spirals

1. 2. One very practical way of keeping pages together, useful for works in progress, is to simply punch them with four holes (using a commercially available hole punch, generally at 8 cm on centre) and insert them in a ring binder.
The inconvenience of this system is that is steals space from the margin on the punched side.
Imagine a work printed in A4 format;
in this case, we must increase the format by 26 mm (UNI A4 divided by 8) to create a space for the holes.

This notebook has been set up in the American style, in other words with the pages glued together at the head margin.
This type of assembly makes it possible to tear off the pages easily.
3. An *a incarto* layout (the signatures are placed one inside the other and held together by metal staples at the fold) is less costly.
The staples can be placed along the left edge of the page (in Italian slang *alla traditora*).
This system requires a cut along the spine and has the defect of not consenting the full opening of the pages.
This method is used above all to bind photocopies and loose sheets.

To the left are a few examples from a guide for financing small and medium sized companies published by Basica spa.
Ring binding, with a silkscreen printed black plastic cover.
Topics are fixed and issues variable and modifiable.
Topics are divided by coloured tabs.

186

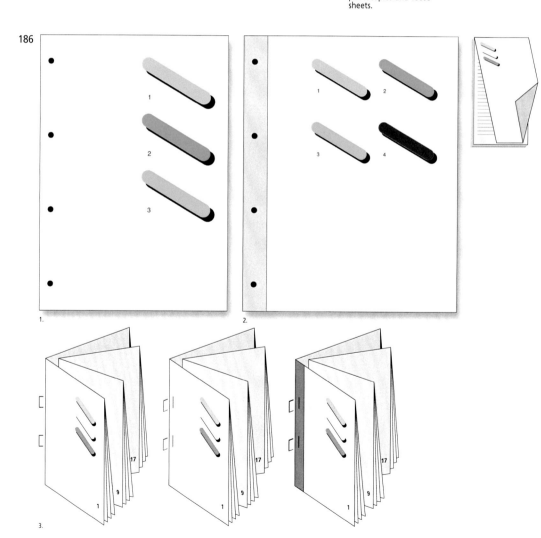

1.

2.

3.

4. A Project 2000.02 folder, with a closing and fixing flap, designed to host A4 format sheets. Commonly used for short reports, it features a transparent cover that shows the title of the report. It can be personalised with a silkscreened image at points that do not interfere whit the frontispiece of the document.

5. The application of a spiral makes it possible for small offices to bind together notable quantities of sheets. This system is widely used to bind manuals that are practical and easy to consult and permits the full opening of all pages. Various types are available, including models that allow for the removal of pages. Spirals come in different sizes to suit the thickness of printed material.

187

Notes
Die cutting is used for packing boxes, labels, etc.
The so-called half cut method is a technique by which paper is scored enough to remove it from its support without being cut.

Workbook
Guided tour of a book binding facility.
Printing and binding; economic issues of binding; the die cutter; half cutting; labels and labelling.

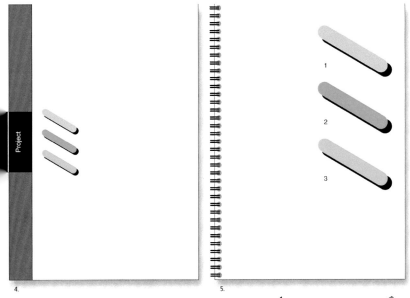

4.

5.

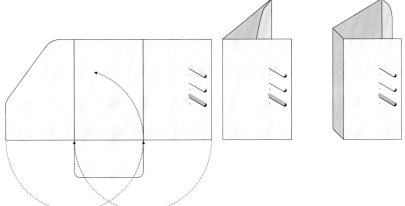

Ring Binding

A "Homemade" Book

1. 2. A paper punch. This type of machine can punch blocks of paper up to a certain thickness, generally creating 4 holes at 80 mm on centre.
Below are two of the most common types of ring bindings suitable for binding pages.
The second type of ring guarantees the alignment of the pages along the binding edge.

1.

2.

188

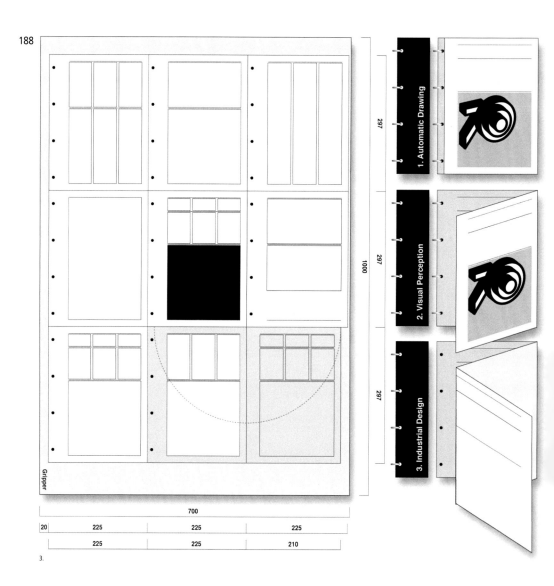

3.

3. Nine 22.5x29.7 cm pages can be printed on a 70x100 sheet of paper.
Unlike a book which has to be bound in octavos, sextodecimos, etc., and which requires the folding of the sheets, ring binding requires only cutting and gathering.
It is interesting to note how it is possible for this format to obtain up to three fold-out pages.

4. The punch shown to the right, available at a low cost, makes it possible to easily bind the pages of a manual, or any "homemade" project.

4.

5. Some examples of a book of coordinated images bound with rings planned during the original idea for the book.

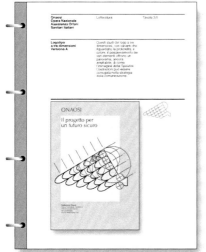

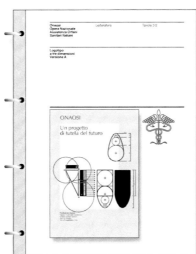

5.

Workbook   189
Collect your work in progress in a ring-bound book.
Establish the format based on the type of LaserWriter used and its printing dimensions (A4 or A3).
Organise your work using tabs.
Design a container, also using rings, that can host a CD-ROM.

A Custom Folder

A Snowboard Catalogue

1. The catalogue shown here was bound with a spiral.
The snowboard is the theme of this work by Valerio Di Cecco.
This sport is his passion, as he explains in the book, as well as the theme chosen for his exam.
Below are some images of the snowboard graphics designed by Valerio.

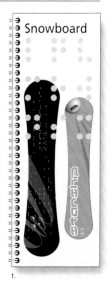

1.

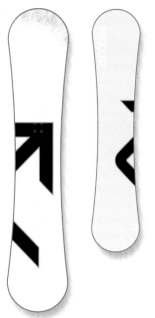

I have been fully immersed in the world of snowboards for approximately seven years.
Those with a passion for this sport share a common lifestyle, from music to clothing to language and a never-ending desire to spend entire days on the slopes. Here everyone creates his own interpretation of snowboarding, expressing a personal instinct and creativity.
My passion, and the choice to enrol in the graduate course in Industrial and Graphic Design and Visual Communication led me to search for a "road" that would allow me to reconcile passion and work.

The possibility to receive more or less immediate feedback on the improbability of pursuing a competitive career in this sport, and a passion for digital graphics, led me over the past three years to start designing snowboard graphics.
I use mixed techniques; inspiration comes from anything that interests me and draws my attention.
To create the drawings I start from the forms of the boards, based on the style for which they were created (freestyle, backcountry, wide).
I then adapt my sketches to these "forms" and drawings (outlines); this is followed by the phase

of colouring and the application of lettering, with is about identity and information.
As digital supports I use Rhinoceros and Autocad to create the matrixes, Adobe Photoshop, Adobe Illustrator and Macromedia Flash for the colours, texts and layouts.

Valerio Di Cecco

191

    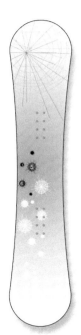 

15.
The Architecture of a Page
Searching for Codes

1. 2. Johannes Gutenberg was born in Mainz in 1400. After early experiences in printing, he partnered with J. Fust. Together they printed a number of essays on typography, followed by a Latin Bible set in two columns of 42 rows each: the so-called *42-Line Bible* or *Mainz Bible*.

Printed in Mainz in 1445, this Bible is considered a true masterpiece of printing: the first article produced by this art reached the maximum heights and an unparalleled perfection. Following Gutenberg's death in 1468, his type was initially acquired by Konrad Humery, and later by the Bechtermuncze brothers from Eltville, near Mainz. Gutenberg's first partner J. Fust, and his son-in-law P. Schoffer then took this invention to its fullest development.

Some precious relics of typography from this period include a fragment of a German poem on the Universal Judgement (*Sibyllenbuch*). The same typeface was probably used to compose the Latin grammar of Donatus and the 36-Line Latin Bible. This latter was without a doubt initiated by Gutenberg, though it was completed some time around 1460 by Pfister. Gutenberg can also be considered the creator of the *Catholicon*, a large book printed some time around 1460.

192 During a lecture in London in 1962, Hermann Zapf, an extraordinary designer of typefaces, including *Optima*, noted how the harmony of forms achieved by the early printers of the 1500s has yet to be surpassed.

The secret of these ancient prints, according to Zapf, does not depend on the quality of the techniques used at the time, what is more highly primitive, but is intrinsic to the works themselves; a secret that has long since been lost.

Vast studies were made of these works by Raúl Rosarivo, in Buenos Aires; he studied the rules used by ancient printers and the proportional ratios they adopted to search for the measures, reasons and codes concealed in their harmony.

These works and the techniques used to create them, are the collection of know-how we must consider when designing a page or a format, though without hindering the search for new approaches. When we start laying out a book or a magazine, we must design the page. Its dimensions may be derived from the UNI format or the paper size used in printing, for example that fabricated for publishing houses that generally use special equipment.

Whatever the size of our page, we must design a layout grid, identify the margins, establish repetitive modules and constants that guarantee the uniform appearance of the pages and the harmony between them and across their surfaces.

The examples shown here serve to suggest a methodology steeped in ancient tradition. As they say, while it may not be important to know all the words in a dictionary, it is important to know how to look for them.

1.

2.

Notes
It is interesting to note how the number 3, which possessed its own sacredness and evident symbolism, is the common denominator in the proportions adopted not only in Gutenberg's 42-Line Bible, but also in the 36-Line Bible from 1458, the 48-Line Bible from 1462 and the Catholicon printed in 1460 in Mainz.

3./7. Reconstruction of the grid of the *42-Line Bible*, as described by Raúl M. Rosarivo in his book *Divina proportio typographica*.
It is designed using the golden section, with a division of the resulting diagonal into nine parts. Point 3 is identified by a second diagonal, normal to the first, and by the resulting perpendicular line. The grid is identified by point 1 and the second diagonal. The space occupied by the text includes the space from point 1 to point 7. The horizontal line A/A2 identifies the golden ratio of the page. The margins are in a ratio of 2, 3, 4, 6. The ratio between the grid and the format is 1:1.5.

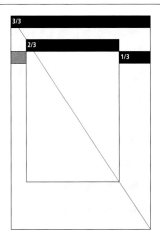

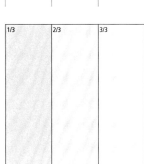

8. The page presents a ratio of 1/3 for the margins, and 2/3 for the space of the grid. The ratios 1/3 and 2/3 signify that the space of the grid is equal to 2/3 the format of the page and the total space of the margins is equal to 1/3 the format of the page.

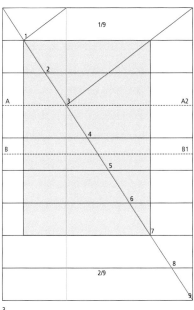

3.

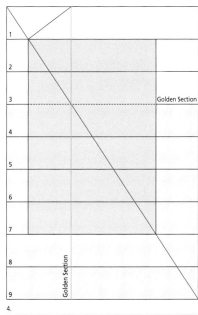

4.

Bibliography 193
▼*Raúl M. Rosarivo*
Divina proportio typographica
Richard Scherpe Verlag, Krefeld, 1961
▼*Hermann Zapf*
Dalla calligrafia alla fotocomposizione
Edizioni Valdonega Verona, 1991
▼*Pierre Duplan, Roger Jauneau*
Progetto grafico e impaginazione
Tecniche nuove, Milan, 1987

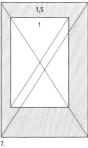

7.

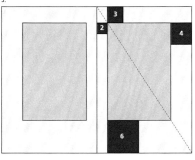

5.

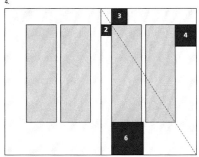

6.

Laying Out a Book

The Same Codes for Other Formats

1. 5. Studies of the adaptation of Gutenberg's grid to formats of the same height and different widths.
In the images, regardless of the format adopted, the grid maintains its own construction, despite modifications to the ratios with respect to the margins.

The ratio 1/3 and 2/3 between the paper format and the grid remains unchanged. The images are based on a hypothesis of formats with a fixed height and variable width that is gradually reduced.
From left to right, in proportion, the formats respond to the following dimensions (in cm): 13x21, 12x21, 10x21, 9x21 to a format that we have intentionally exasperated.

194

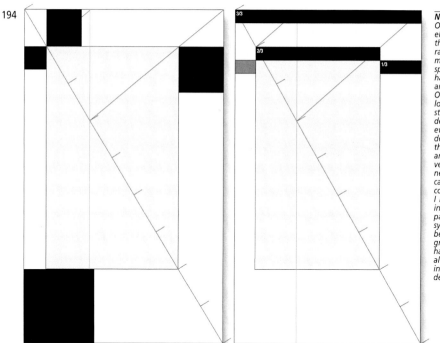

1.

2.

Notes
Organising graphic elements and ensuring they respond to a rational approach means designing the space into which to harmoniously insert text and images.
On these pages we look at the classical structures that have determined the evolution of graphic design, fully aware that the rigidity of these ancient layouts is not very suitable to the new and often more casual needs of communication.
I remain convinced that in the architecture of a page concepts of symmetry, the balance between figure and ground and the harmony of ratios must always be rigorously inspired by a logical design.

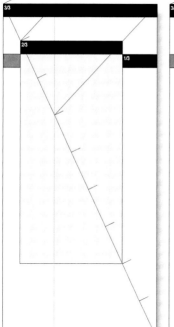
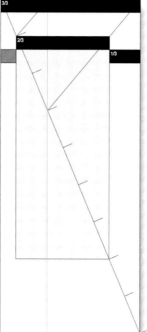
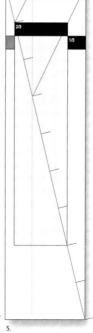

3. 4. 5.

Notes
How to unite the lessons of the past and the new needs of communication is the challenge entrusted to a graphic designer, who can now count on new technologies and new means of expression.

Workbook
Design the grid for a page of advertising using texts that respond to different percentages of reading area.
Note the codes and measures.

The Design
of a Page

A Grid Contained
in a Golden Section

This grid was constructed using the golden section. The diagonals identify the starting points for the grid, which coincide with the ratio 5:8. The grid designed on the page will always have margins with a ratio of 2, 3, 4, 6.

The ratio 2, 3, 4, 6 signifies that 2 is the inner margin, while the outer margin is 4; if the top margin is 3, than the footer will be 6. The outer margin is always twice the inner margin, and the top margin is always twice the bottom margin.

196

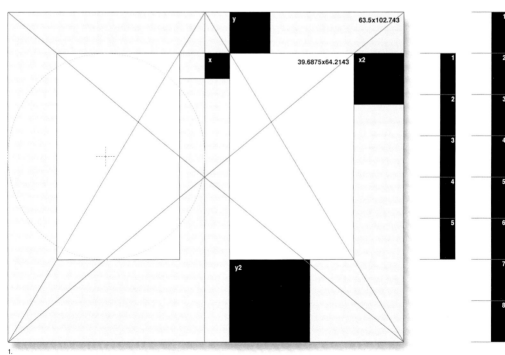

1.

1. 2. The example illustrated in figure 1 is based on a format with a 63.5 mm base.
The height is calculated using the rule of the golden section: multiplying 63.5x1.618 h=102.743.
The ratio of the golden section is 5:8 (more precisely (5:8.090614885).
The simple equation 5÷8.09=63.5÷x gives us h=102.743.

The format hypothesised in the figure is thus 63.5x102.743 mm; the internal grid once again corresponds with the golden section.
It has a base of 39.6875x1.618 mm, or 64.2143 mm.
The inner margin of 12.8428 mm corresponds with an outer margin of 25.6857 mm;
the lower margin is exactly twice the upper margin.
The examples tested show the modules resulting from the golden section 5:8 (theoretically 5:8.09) present on the page. This ratio exists both horizontally and vertically.

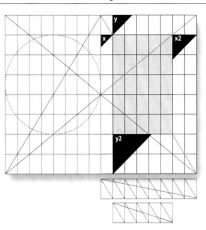

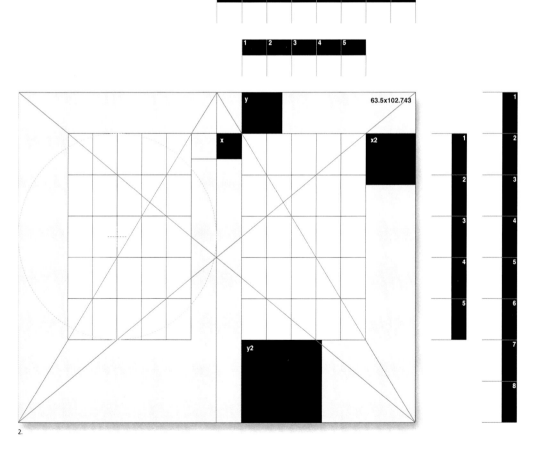

2.

The Design
of a Page

All Formats
and Their Diagonals

1. 3. Experiments with the construction of grids obtained using the system of diagonals.
Diagonals are laid out on two facing pages as shown in the image. The grid is the simple result of an alignment at the intersection of the diagonals.

If the grid respects the golden section, all of the ratios thus correspond with the canonical values 2, 4, 3, 6.
Line A, which intersects the meeting point between two diagonals (and continues to the lower left corner of the left page) identifies the grid that once again corresponds with the ratios 2, 4, 3, 6.

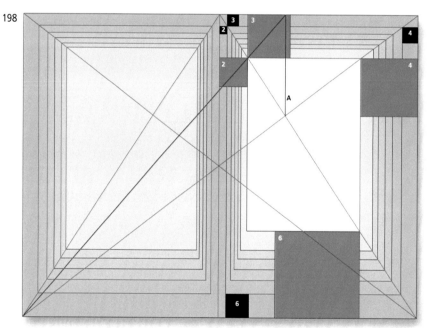

Notes
The construction of a grid using the system of diagonals assigns no fixed initial measurements to the margins or the grid itself. The initial measurement is taken along the diagonals and may vary according to the starting points and page layout requirements.
The system of two diagonals is not attached to any particular formats: it can be applied to any format so long as the proportions are maintained.

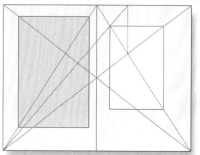

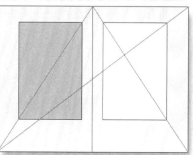

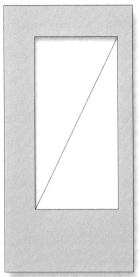

4./8. The system of diagonals can also be applied to a-typical formats to easily and immediately layout a grid. However, it will provide constant ratios only between the upper and lower, and inner and outer margins.

The outer margin will always be double the inner margin, and the upper margin will always be double the lower margin.
The two diagonals also identify a point of intersection that is considered the focal point of the grid; it may mark a very harmonious visual separation in the layout of the page.
We can note how the formats illustrated on these pages, not constructed using the golden section, do not maintain the ratio of 5:8.

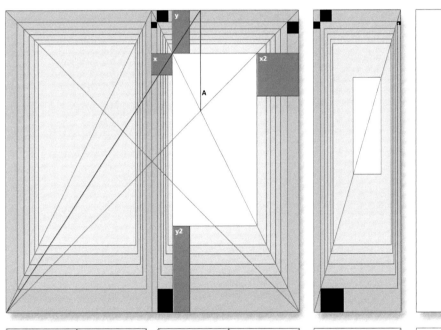

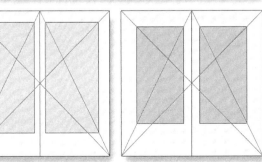

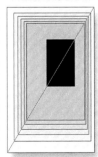

The Design of a Page

Grids Obtained Using Constant Ratios

1. The ratio of 1/3 and 2/3. This is obtained by dividing the base of the page by three, and assigning two parts to the grid for text and images, and one part to the margins.
After dividing this latter part once again by three, we assign two parts to the outer margin and the lower margin and one to the upper margin and the inner margin.

In the example illustrated, based on a format of 210x210 mm, we calculate 210÷3=70. The grid will be equal to 70x2=140.
The margins are obtained by dividing 70÷3=23.33 (margin module) and assigning one module to the upper and inner margin, and two modules to the lower and outer margins (23.33x2=46.66).

2. Ratio of 2/5 and 3/5. This is obtained by dividing the base of the page and assigning three parts to the grid for text and images, and two parts to the margins.
After dividing this latter part once more by five, we assign three parts to the outer margin and the lower margin and two to the upper margin and the inner margin.

Notes
*Subdivide the spaces of a page.
Find an inner proportion and a harmonious ratio between the page, the grid and the margins.*

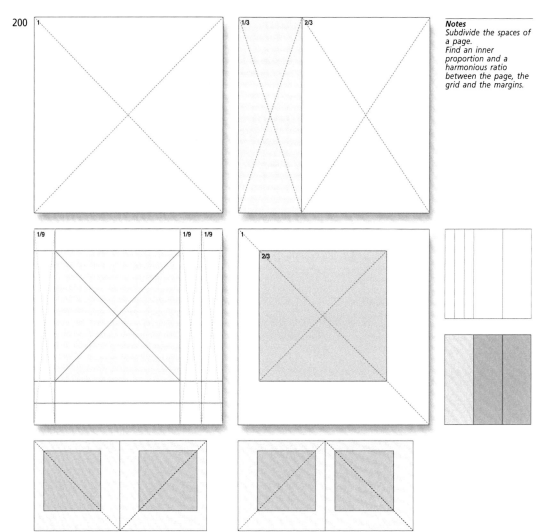

1.

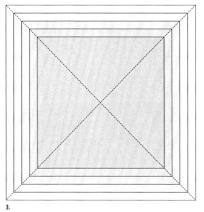

3.

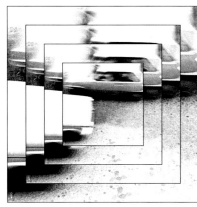

3. This grid contemplates equal margins around the entire page. The diagonals identify the position of the various formats on the page.

Notes
Ratio of 2/5 and 3/5.

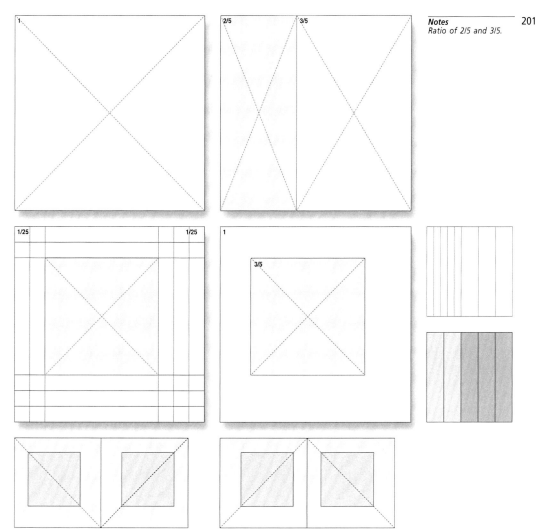

2.

1. Ratio of 1/5 and 4/5. This is obtained by dividing the base of the page by five, and assigning four parts to the grid for text and images, and one part to the margins.
After dividing this latter part once again by five, we assign three parts to the outer margin and the lower margin and two to the upper margin and the inner margin.

In the example illustrated, based on a format of 210x210 mm, we calculate 210÷5=42. The grid wil be equal to 42x4=168.
The margins are obtained by dividing 42÷5=8.4 (margin module) and assigning three modules (8.4x3=25.2) to the upper and inner margin, and two modules to the lower and outer margins (8.4x2=16.8).

202

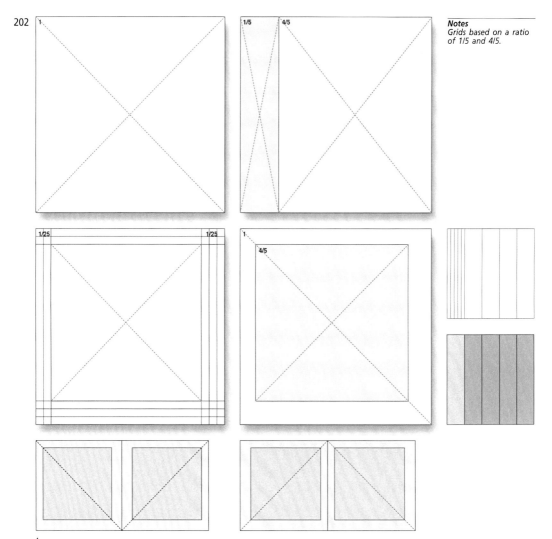

Notes
Grids based on a ratio of 1/5 and 4/5.

2. A grid based on the ratio of 1/5 and 4/5 was used to construct the page layout. The selected format is a square with constant dimensions in width and height. The texts and photographs can be placed in one or more modules, in one or more columns and in three or four columns.

203

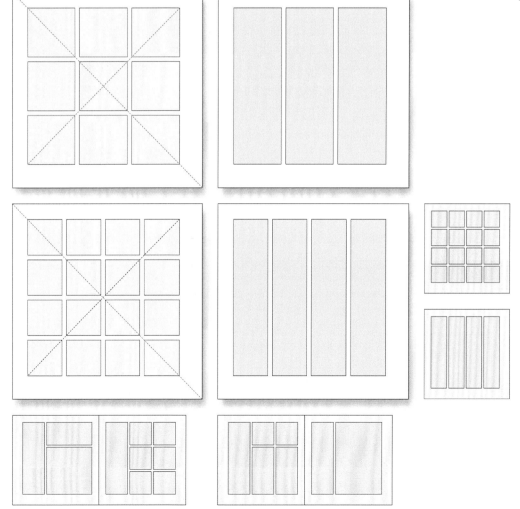

2.

The Design
of a Page

The Ratio of 2/3
and the Typographical
Divine Proportion of 1.5

A grid designed using diagonals in a constant ratio of 2/3.
The base of the page is 2/3 its height.
The margins are established using the classical ratio of 2, 3, 4, 6 derived from the diagonals.
Margins 2 and 6 occupy 1/3 the width of the page; margins 3 and 6 occupy 1/3 the height of the page.
The grid on the page occupies 2/3 of the width and height of the respective width and height of the page.
The diagonals identify the grid, the margins and a focal point which can be considered the harmonic visual centre of the page.

We can layout a diagram using the diagonals starting from the vertical line divided into 9 equidistant parts. We then ensure that diagonal 9 coincides with the upper left corner of the page, and that diagonal 0 coincides with the base of the page.
Diagonal 8 will identify the inner margin; diagonal 7 the visual centre of the page; diagonal 3 the outer margin; diagonal 2 will identify the lower margin.

The construction of the grid using the 2/3 method has a constant ratio of 1.5. This value was considered by Rosarivo to be the typographical divine proportion.
This ratio is integrated within the duodecimal scale of typographical values in which on typographic row is equal to 12 points.

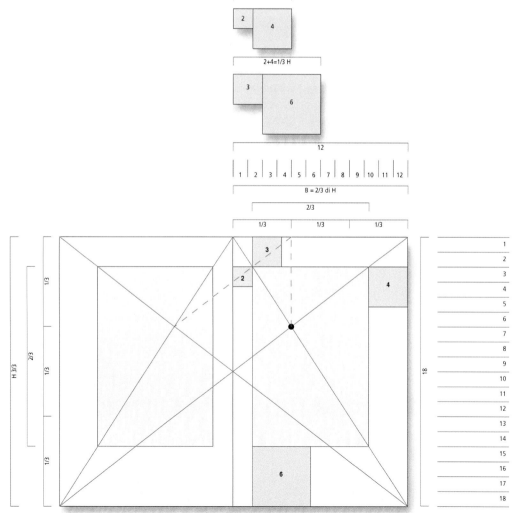

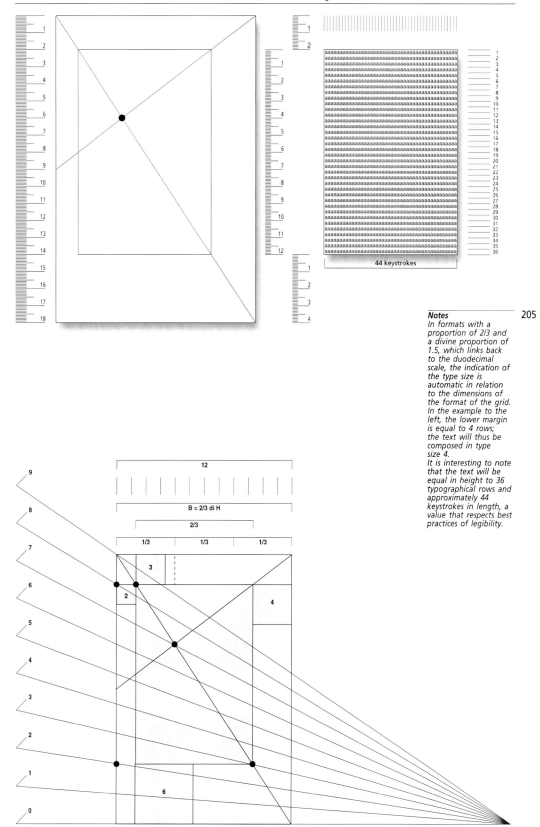

44 keystrokes

Notes

In formats with a proportion of 2/3 and a divine proportion of 1.5, which links back to the duodecimal scale, the indication of the type size is automatic in relation to the dimensions of the format of the grid. In the example to the left, the lower margin is equal to 4 rows; the text will thus be composed in type size 4.

It is interesting to note that the text will be equal in height to 36 typographical rows and approximately 44 keystrokes in length, a value that respects best practices of legibility.

B = 2/3 di H

2/3

1/3 1/3 1/3

The Design
of a Page

The Ratios
4/10, 5/10, 6/10, 7/10

We can test the rule of 4/10, 5/10, 6/10, 7/10 on a page with a format of 210x297 mm (reproduced here with a reduction of 34%). The width of the internal grid, and the justification, is 2/3 the width of the page. The alignment will be equal to 210÷3x2=140mm. From the width of the page we subtract the width of the grid, obtaining a value of 70 mm. Thus 210-140=70. 70 millimetres is the space to be assigned to the margins, to which we assign a value of 10/10.

It follows that 1/10 of the margin is equal to 70÷10=7. We can now apply the rule of 4/10, 5/10, 6/10, 7/10. This gives us: inner margin = 4/10 of the margin, = 4x7=28; upper margin = 5/10 of the margin, = 5x7=35; outer margin = 6/10 of the margin, = 6x7=42; lower margin = 7/10 of the margin, = 7x7=49.

206

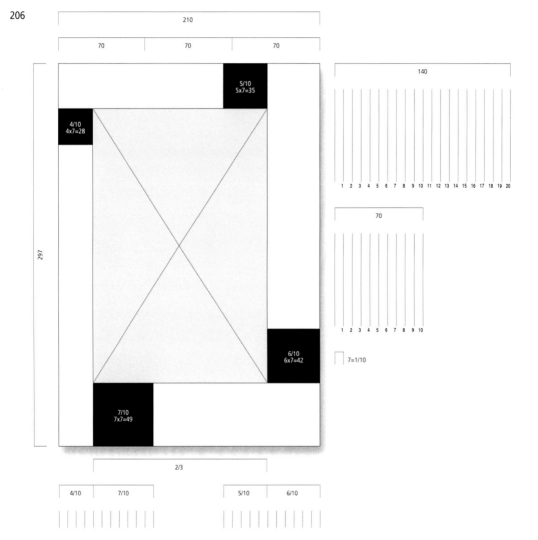

We assign the width of the grid, and thus the alignment, 3/4 of the width of the page. The alignment will thus be equal to 210÷4x3=157.5 mm. From the width of the page we subtract the width of the grid, obtaining the value of 52.5 mm. Thus 210-157.5=52.5. 52.5 millimetres is the space to be assigned to the margins, to which we assign a value of 10/10.

It follows that 1/10 of the margin is equal to 52.5÷10=5.25. We can now apply the rule of 4/10, 5/10, 6/10, 7/10. This gives us: inner margin = 4/10 of the margin, = 4x5.25=21; upper margin = 5/10 of the margin, = 5x5.25=26.25; outer margin = 6/10 of the margin, = 6x5.25=31.5; lower margin = 7/10 of the margin, = 7x5.25=36.75.

The page with the dimensions is reprinted here with a reduction of 34%. The image to the right is a cover to which we have assigned a width of the grid equal to 2/3 the width of the page.

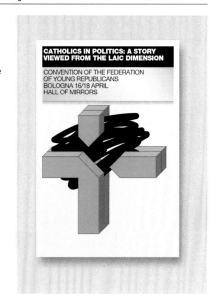

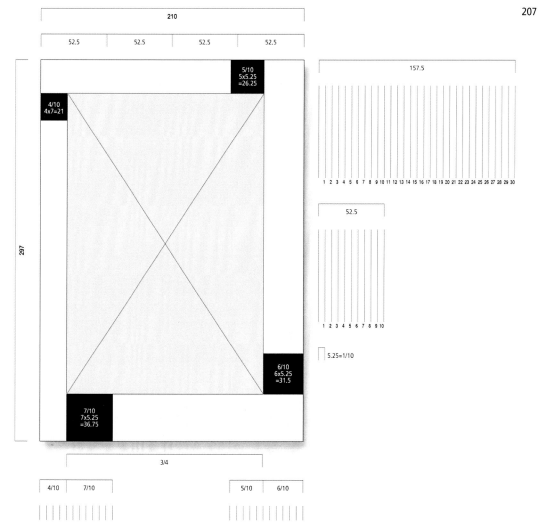

Laying Out a Page Based on Type Size

Grids Designed in Relation to Leading

Scientific reviews in general, and specifically those in English, shown here, are laid out according to graphic criteria that belong to the traditions of scientific literature. They must be translated into the architecture of a page with absolute uniformity and repetitive uniform rhythms. While during lessons it was suggested to forgo unjustified fantastical ideas and concentrate on the "rationale" of a layout, in this case we find all of the reasons for respecting this logic.

1./6. In examining this topic what emerges is that, beyond pre-established canons (perhaps the best example being the "rules for authors"), owing to a series of graphic requirements that respond to real needs, almost all scientific reviews are laid out in two adjacent columns. To maintain this structure, and at the same time to manage the density of text this creates, a grid based on five columns was studied. The first functions as "service space", the second and third for text/images, and the fourth and fifth a second space for text/images.

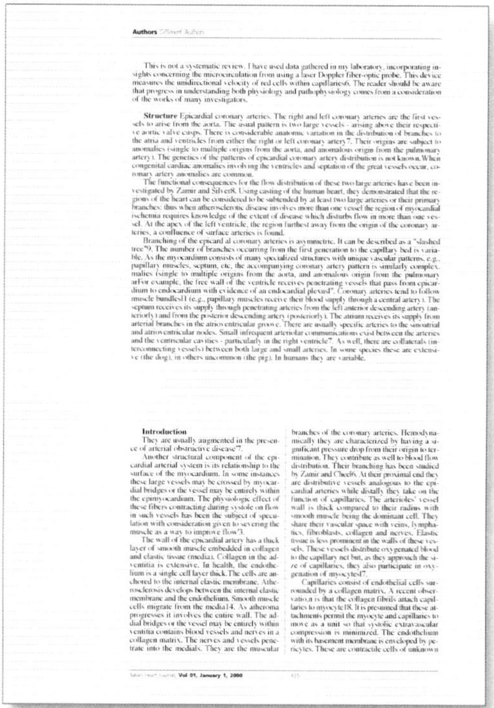

Inside this primary structure, whose codes can be modified case by case to fit other projects and meet different needs, we developed a complementary grid based on the type size selected for the entire review, in this case 10/10 Times. This second grid consists of horizontal lines that, beginning from a zero point, are consistently repeated based on a dimension corresponding to the leading of the text, in this case 10 points. If you use a Macintosh, your graphic editing software will feature a command "show baseline grid", to make things a lot easier.

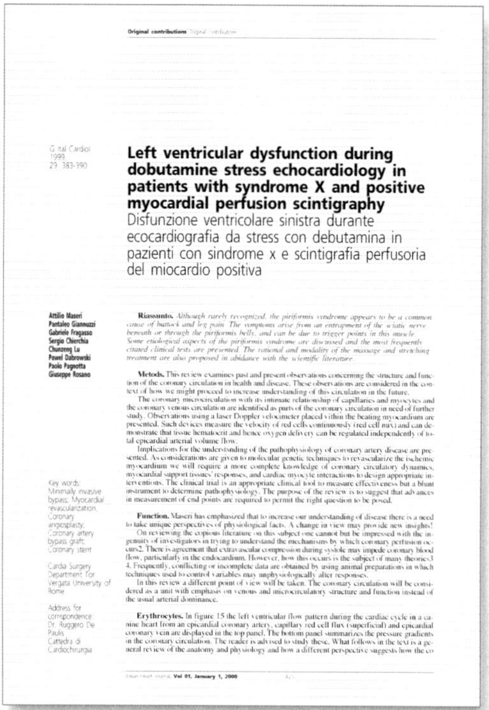

208

1.

Left ventricular dysfunction during dobutamine stress echocardiology in patients with syndrome X and positive myocardial perfusion scintigraphy

Disfunzione ventricolare sinistra durante ecocardiografia da stress con debutamina in pazienti con sindrome x e scintigrafia perfusoria del miocardio positiva

2.

Italian Heart Journal

Italian Heart Journal

8/33

Official Journal
of the Italian Federation
of Cardiology

As shown in the examples illustrated here, this supporting grid makes it easy to cleanly lay out all of the vertical alignments. When it is necessary to use a different type size, the logic of the layout suggests the use of multiples or submultiples of the base type size.
In this case, the titles are set in a type size twice that of the base size, in other words, 20 with a leading of 20. Also refer to the chapter entitled "Magazines and Periodicals".

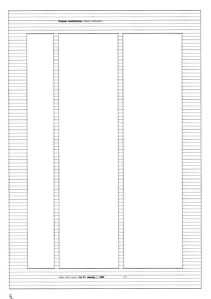

5.

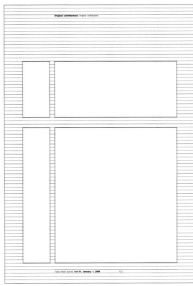

6.

3.

4.

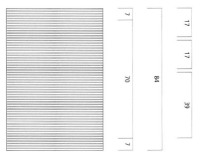

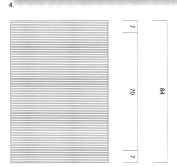

16.
Spaces
in Page Layouts

Calculating Spaces
Before Starting

Designing a magazine means designing its general layout.
Imagining the spaces for text offers a general vision of a project and allows the editor to seek articles of a pre-established length.
The images shown here suggest one way to approach a similar project.

1. The layout of this magazine, designed for an A4 format, is based on 8 modules per column.
The illustrations simulate the space occupied by text.
The texts are in Times 10/10; the number of keystrokes was calculated for each module and is shown in bold at the top of each column.

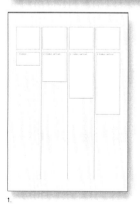

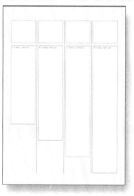

1.

Workbook
*As part of the design of your magazine, insert a chapter dedicated to a scientific concept of the "rationale" behind the choices made.
Pages with the calculation of the keystrokes and the space occupied by texts, with a simulation of the dimensions; propose space for titles and subtitles with measurements in points; typeface, type size and alignments..*

Modules	Keystrokes	Rows
1	173	6
2	394	14
3	602	21
4	826	29
5	1057	37
6	1279	45
7	1487	52
8	1720	60

2. Note the codes relative to the vertical and horizontal axes of each module and the main spaces for images.

As part of the design of a magazine, we can insert a drawing that highlights the characteristics of titles, typeface, type sizes, specifying the sizes for titles, subtitles, subheadings, etc.

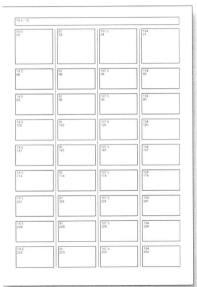

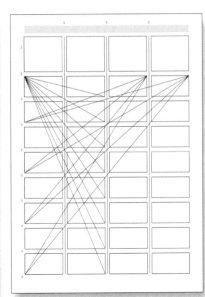

Frutiger light Italic

ABCDEFG
HIJKLMNO
PQRSTUVX
YWZ
abcdefghij
klmnopqrs
tuvxywz
0123456789

Frutiger Roman Italic

ABCDEFG
HIJKLMNO
PQRSTUVX
YWZ
abcdefghij
klmnopqr
stuvxywz
0123456789

Frutiger Bold Italic

ABCDEFG
HIJKLMNO
PQRSTUVX
YWZ
abcdefghij
klmnopqr
stuvxywz
0123456789

8.

Framing Spaces in Page Layouts

The Number of Possible Grids for the Same Format

Whatever the format selected, it is necessary to give the grid a "rationality".
We will now look at some possible solutions to this task, though it must be remembered that the grid to be selected is that which is most appropriate to the content of the publication.
We have chosen to use a pamphlet with a format of 11x22 cm, comprised of duodecimos on a 70x100 sheet of paper and destined to host a collection of logos.
The layout is born with a code, formed of two 11x11 cm squares.
The following section looks at some of the solutions proposed.

1. We can design a grid using the golden section.
With a base of 9 cm, we will have a height of 14.562 cm.
The remaining space is marked by a horizontal line at the top.
The margins in the examples on this page are constant.

2. This grid is composed of a 9x9 cm square module and a module of 9x55.62 cm calculated using the golden section.
The resulting module is doubled and placed at the top of the page with a total height of 9+55.62+55.62=120.24 cm.

3. We can now invert the grid created using the golden section: this will give us a small module at the top, a square module at the centre, and another small module at the bottom.

4. In the square central module we can create a grid of 9x9 modules.

5. A margin of 1 cm to the left and right, and 2 cm at the top and bottom, gives us two 9x9 cm squares.

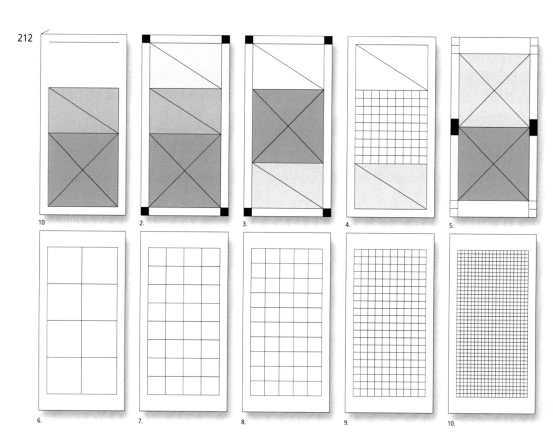

212

6./10. In the grid made from two 9x9 cm square modules we can construct a series of submodules.

11./13. We construct the grid using the system of division in nine parts (see the previous pages). This scheme can be adopted when we decide to use a symmetrical page layout.

14. Once again, we can subdivide the grid into two equal parts.

15. Or, we can create the grid from the subdivision suggested by the construction.

16./19. We can further subdivide the grid according to a ratio of 8:8. This permits a whole new series of modules.

20. Using the same format, it is possible to create square modules whose repetition and size depend only on what is to be laid out on each page.

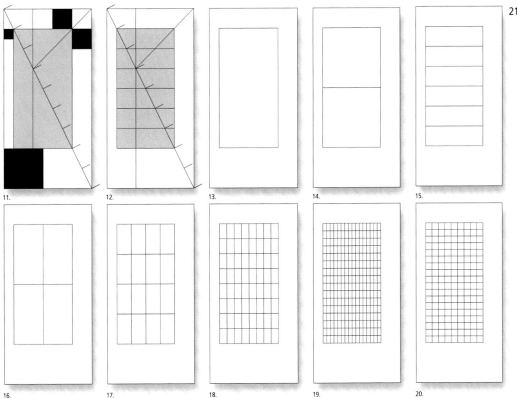

11.   12.   13.   14.   15.

16.   17.   18.   19.   20.

A Grid for an Information Brochure

Another Use for the Golden Section

The grid constructed using the golden section is also useful for laying out brochures, such as that reproduced here. In fact, the space to the left is used for the binding holes, or for other types of binding that require extra space along the binding edge. Once again, an image is placed in a square module at the bottom, while the upper part is filled with text, with a ratio of 5:8.

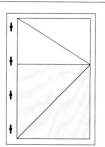
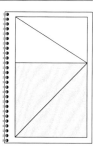

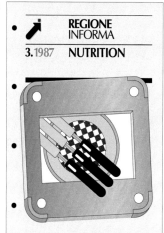

REGIONE
INFORMA
3.1987 **NUTRITION**

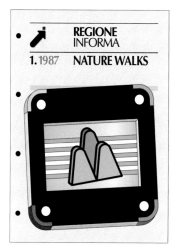

REGIONE
INFORMA
1.1987 **NATURE WALKS**

REGIONE
INFORMA
5.1987 **TRAINING COURSES**

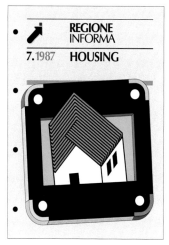

REGIONE
INFORMA
7.1987 **HOUSING**

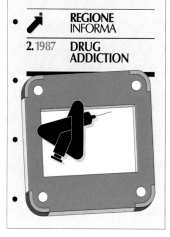

REGIONE
INFORMA
2.1987 **DRUG ADDICTION**

REGIONE
INFORMA
8.1987 **HOME**

A Grid
for Posters

Calculating a Cut
and Cut to Bleed Printing

1. On a sheet of paper measuring 33x70 cm (one third of 70x100) we can create a format of 32x67.
The background is a full bleed, with a double cut and a space in correspondence with the long cut edge.

215

Notes
These posters, with their curious alternation, were hung in newspaper stands throughout the Southern Italian city of Potenza, and in shops, hotels and public spaces.

A Grid
for Posters

The *Edizioni della Voce* Book Series

1./5. Using a 33x50 format (one quarter of 70x100) we can create a format that measures 32x50.
With a negligible waste of paper, we can inscribe a grid designed using the golden section.

As shown in the examples reproduced here, just some of the infinite possibilities, the identification of a "rationale" in the layout of the format also plays a determinant role in laying out the various parts of this poster.

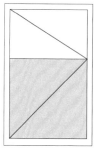

216

EDIZIONI DELLA VOCE / NOVITÀ 1973
NELLA COLLANA VENTESIMOSECOLO
ODDO BIASINI
SCUOLA SECONDARIA SUPERIORE
IPOTESI DI RIFORMA
PREFAZIONE DI GIOVANNI SPADOLINI

EDIZIONI DELLA VOCE / NOVITÀ 1976
NELLA COLLANA VENTESIMOSECOLO
GIOVANNI SPADOLINI
CULTURA E POLITICA
GOBETTI, ALBERTINI E ALTRI SAGGI

EDIZIONI DELLA VOCE / NOVITÀ 1981
NELLA COLLANA VENTESIMOSECOLO
GIOVANNI SPADOLINI
PER IL RISANAMENTO MORALE,
ISTITUZIONALE, ECONOMICO
DELLA REPUBBLICA

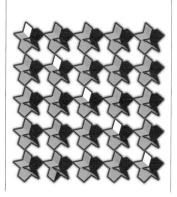

EDIZIONI DELLA VOCE / NOVITÀ 1971
NELLA COLLANA VENTESIMOSECOLO
LUCIANO TAS
CARTINA ROSSA DEL MEDIO ORIENTE
LA STORIA DELLO STATO DI ISRAELE
RACCONTATA DALL'UNITÀ / 1

Arranged on a 50x70 format, these posters were designed in 1970/1975 for piano concerts.
The drawings generate an abundance of languages, a means for sounding out all of the dissonances of a musical language.

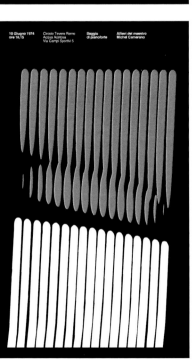

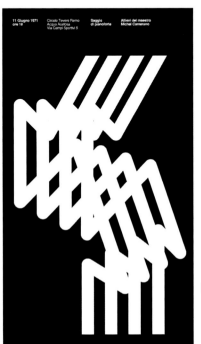

A Grid for
a Book of Poetry

Gutenberg's Grid

1./6. This book of poems was designed by students of the course in Publishing Graphics, curated by the Piofs in Potenza, financed by the ECC and the Basilicata Regional Government.
It was one of the topics developed over the course of the year.
The grid is inspired by that used for the *42-Line Bible*.

The choice to print the poems by dividing the lines with a slash, rather than respecting the start of new phrases, is based on the decision made by students to occupy the entire grid, and to emphasise its presence. Even the horizontal lines above and below are a result of the same formal choice: their position is intended as a constant presence, similar to a trace overlay on the structure of the grid.

218

1.

2.

3.

4.

5.

6.

Printed in November 1997 for Edizioni Casarsa by Arti Grafiche Fernando Begliomini in Rome.

The book of poems was designed, composed and laid out by: Gaia Bitetti, Antonio Bruno, Giuseppina Ciminelli, Carmela Franco, Carmela Genzano, Isabella Laurita, Vitina Lovallo, Carmela Nolé, Vita Pace, Vincenzo Piro, Marinella Santopietro, Emanuela Satriani, Daniela Sileo, Rocco Tricarico, Marilena Zaccagnino

*130 g Fabriano Vergatona paper, 300 g ivory Fabria cover, dustjacket: 120 g ivory Fabria.
Stitched paperback binding with dustjacket printed by Felici in Rome.*

The layout of the book was curated by students of the course in Publishing Graphics under the guidance of professors Michele and Gerardo Spera. The grid was inspired by that designed by Gutenburg for the 42-Line Bible and based on the golden section.

This was one of the graphic themes explored during the course, together with a real client who provided a brief and agreed to finance the printing of the book.

A Bi-Fold Pamphlet

Each student is to produce his or her own format and page layout criteria, considered most suitable to the material to be laid out. The project illustrated here consists of two leaves and re-proposes the classical division in which the first and second leaves each measure 100 cm in width by 210 cm in height.

This format responds to the criteria adopted for stationery and can be inserted in American format envelopes.

Below to the right are various symbols used in works printed by *Sinistra Repubblicana*.

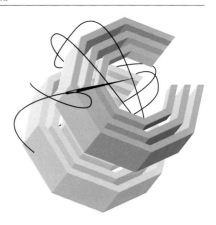

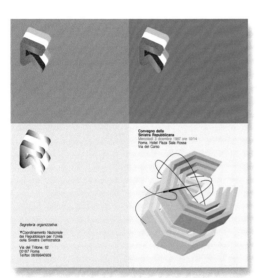

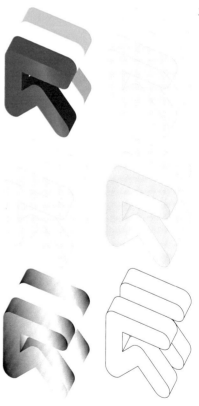

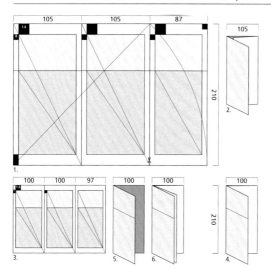

105	105	87

105

210

2.

The tri-fold pamphlet illustrated here consists of three leaves and re-proposes the classical division of the UNI format, where the first and second leaves measure 100x210 mm and the third 99x210 mm.

Pamphlets, like letterhead, do not feature uniform folds: the third leaf must be slightly shorter to ensure that, once folded, it fits into the first two.

Pay attention to the weight of the paper: to avoid paying extra postage, a pamphlet and its envelope should not weigh more than a total of 200 grams. For a three leaf pamphlet, it is possible to use paper up to a weight of 170 gr/m2. With 200 gram paper and a normal envelope, the total weight is approximately 21 grams.

1.

100	100	97

100	100

210

100

3.   5.   6.   4.

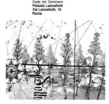

There appears to be a new and lively interest in the issue of Southern Italy. The Italian Prime Minister recently declared it to be a "new frontier" for the Government. The Ministries of the Treasury and Finance have began to systematically visit the Southern regions. Organisations of entrepreneurs and workers are making Southern Italy the centre of their attentions. Economic and political debate in the press has become more intense.

At the same time, the confines and substance of the question of Southern Italy have changed significantly. The arrival in Italy of the Euro, the expansion of the European Union into Eastern Europe, the vaster phenomena of economic globalisation impose a new policy, which must be clearly differentiated, also to make up for the inconveniences and degenerations that have made themselves manifest, from that adopted in the past. In fact, there are now new problems and others, already known, have grown into urgent matters. The character of infrastructural networks and their

suitability to a policy of development; the model of industrial districts; the type of incentive to be agreed upon; the tools of partnerships between various stakeholders in development and the spread of technologies and industrial culture; professional training; the creation of the most suitable conditions for attracting foreign investments; privatisations; the efficiency and efficacy of the administration of the entire institutional framework at all levels (Regional, Provincial, Municipal); the system of credit and financing necessary for development: these appear to be the key elements of a truly new

policy, directed toward inverting the continuing gap between growth in Northern and Southern Italy as well as the divarication between employment in the North and employment in the South. The Naples Convention has the ambitious objective of ordering the new terms of the question of Southern Italy and organically inserting it within national economic policy. If Southern Italy were to expand beyond the Alps – to repeat the ancient metaphor of a

great supporter of the South – or whether it precipitates definitively into the Mediterranean in a state of difficulty, remains the problem to be solved. With trust in the possibilities of Southern Italy and European Italy, the scholars, technicians and men of politics gathered in Naples aim to lay down the lines of an internally coherent commitment to which the country's ruling class and public opinion are called to respond.

221

A Pamphlet
with Seven Leaves

Using
Other Formats

A folded seven-leaf pamphlet.
Laid out on 64x88 cm, each leaf measures 85 mm in width, for a total width of 595 mm and a total height of 210 mm. This pamphlet was used during a workshop at the MACRO, Museo d'arte contemporanea di Roma, promoted by the Graduate Course in Industrial Design at the First Faculty of Architecture.

To the right of the image, in alphabetical order, are the names of the professors and students. The group consisted of graphic design professionals who worked with children from an elementary school in Rome to produce posters, gadgets and a film as part of shared design experience.

222

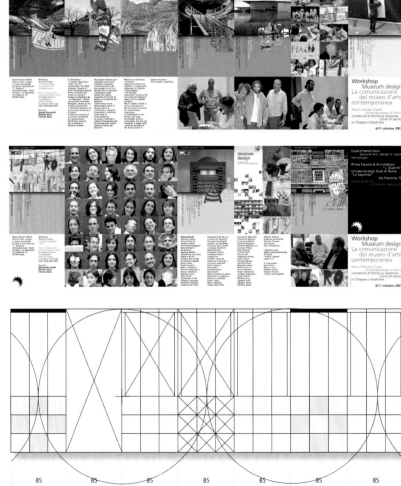

Notes
Adriano Amati
Ilaria Antonini
Jacopo Ardito
Flavia Aventaggiato
Alex Barbiero
Ilic Barocci
Daniela Bellini
Achille Bonito Oliva
Stefano Bruni
Giorgio Bucciarelli
Emanuele Cappelli
Ilaria Catini
David Cesaria
Marco Chialastri
Teresa Comanducci
Paola Coltellacci
Daniela Cono
Alex Conti
Gianpaolo Conti
Viviana Coporaso
Michele Costabile
Federica Dal Falco
Giuseppe D'Ambrosio
Lorenza De Agostini
Giacomo De Angelis
Damien De Besombes
Francesca De Cataldo
Leonardo Dominici
Danilo Eccher
Francesco Faccini
Francesca Faenzi
Filippo Fea
Amarilli Felizzola
Giannina Francalanci
Francesca Gabrielli
Pietro Gallucci
Alessandra Gianfranceschi
Itala Giretti
Maria Vincenza Guarini
Gabriella La Cappuccia
Gianluca Lambiase
Bruno Lanzi
Marco Maietta
Chiara Mancinelli
Donatella Marinelli
Giancarlo Martino

Francesca Marsili
Daniela Maggiori
Daniele Malantrucco
Lorenzo Palma
Ines Paolucci
Tonino Paris
Paola Polli
Valentina Pratesi
Marco Pucci
Giorgia Ranieri
Carlotta Rossi
Marianna Rossi
Roberta Sacco
Flavia Salvatori
Chiara Santarelli
Claudia Sebastiani
Arash Sharifi
Michele Sica
Agnese Sordi
Fabiano Spera
Michele Spera
Daniele Statera
Susanna Succhiarelli
Oliviero Toscani
Rita Vaccai
Ilaria Vitanostra

223

The children were students from class III B at the "Franco Cesana" elementary school in Rome.

Numbers

"Spaces" Intended as Fractions

In some publications, it may be necessary to create fractions, to accentuate sections, to establish clear separations between parts.
Separations are obtained by inserting a photograph in the background on the even numbered page and a number, indicating the section, on the odd numbered page.

224

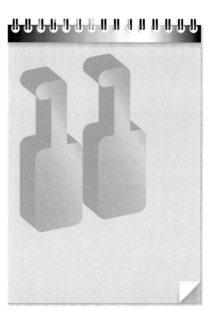

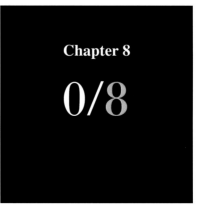

Notes
In these examples, a great deal of importance is given to numbers.
They are the first tool of communication and form.
In this publication the numbers are designed by the author, often with great importance inside the book itself.

Try to design the fractions of a book using the Bodoni typeface (above).
This is no accident, as Bodoni, in its Bauer and Old Face versions, was chosen as the institutional typeface for the entire publication.

A Convention at Santo Spirito in Sassia

The Sky and Mathematical Symbols

The Tenth Anniversary of the Industrial Design Course at the Sapienza Università di Roma

Two Spaces for Each Page

1. The layout of a vast quantity of material from different sources and in a wide variety of formats requires a very flexible grid. While it should not condition aspects of communication, it should conserve a recognisable rigour on every page. Considering the need to ensure the coexistence between images and texts, the structure subdivides the page into two main spaces: the first, above, for images and photographs, in turn subdivided into modules and submodules; the second, below, designed to contain texts and captions and various types of information. The evaluation of these spaces and their relationship was dictated by the material supplied, without ignoring the possibility, where necessary, to invade one field with the content of another.

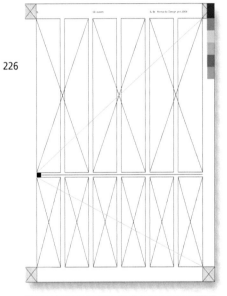

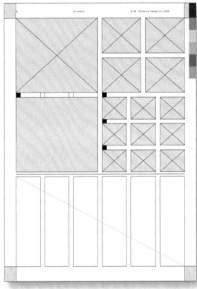

Notes
Design alla Sapienza was created to retrace the important moments in a rich panorama of design-related activities spanning ten years at the La Sapienza University of Rome. They included educational events such as the start of the Graduate Course in Industrial Design, an international master in Design and Management and a PhD in Industrial Design. Together they produced experiments in the form of the Factory LSD or such events as "Roma design più", moments of encounter, debates and communication, such as the "Disegno industriale" review.

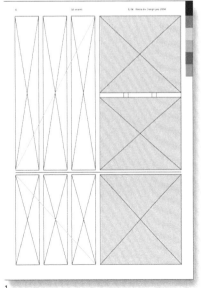

3.
Gli eventi

3/1
1994/2004
10 anni

1.

The field of design education now embraces an ample spectrum of thematic areas that depend on the increasingly more complex nature of the manufacturing sector: from product design to the design of product strategies; from the design of visual communications and multimedia to eco-design, design management and design direction.

In this constantly evolving scenario the commitments of the University cannot end with the construction of a traditional approach to education, but must also propose an innovative cultural policy that, other than institutional bodies, also involves those subjects who belong to the network that defines the world of industry today, and in which the designers of the future must find a place.

This conviction underpins the cultural approach that has characterised the ten year history of the Graduate Course in Industrial Design offered by the Sapienza Università di Roma, whose curriculum has always been accompanied by experimentation and research tied to new fields in which to apply design with the objective of offering young people the necessary tools for confronting and competing in the international world of design.

Notes 227
The publication has one peculiarity: the graphic design is by Alberto Lecaldano, Giovanni Lussu, Michele Spera, in other words, three people with very different languages and backgrounds, and with very personal theoretical and methodological approaches to their work. Three professionals and professors from our school, each assigned a chapter. They transformed what may have seemed incompatible into an extraordinarily rich final product.
Tonino Paris

2.

1. Four of the six section separators, printed on a full bleed black background from chapter 3.

2. The six sections of the third chapter are marked by a coloured tab that breaks the margins in the upper right corner.
To the side is the colour code applied to the publication.

228

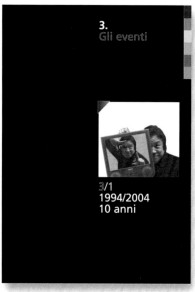

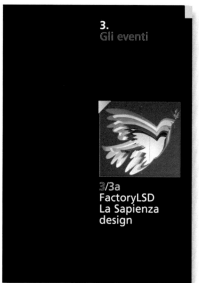

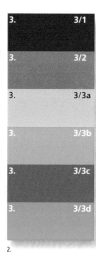

2.

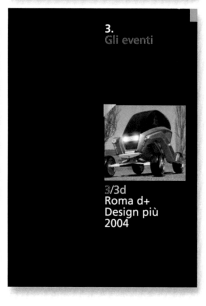

1.

To the left:
the texts are set on a background whose colour changes from section to section.

Notes   229
Tracce di memoria
L'esperienza di comunicazione
dei diritti umani
Rome, 15-20 September
Casa delle Culture
The project consisted of 140 drawings divided into nine chapters. It was also reproduced in a 64-page printed publication.
In the realm of corporate identity, design loses its habitual function of being a tool of description, auxiliary to a project, to assume the central role of coordinating a complete program of communication. A program that, in very concise terms, can be described as follows: how and using what tools to achieve a unity of meaning required by a product through the diversity of signs. The research that preceded the design phase developed around the texts and images of intellectuals who opposed the old Argentinian dictatorial regime. This was made possible thanks to the passionate collaboration of students in Michele Spera's Graphics course and Giorgio Buccarelli's Industrial Design for Visual Communications course, guided by Stefania Tuzi, chair of the course in History of the Decorative Arts.

1.
2.
3.
4.
5.
6.

1. Auditorium Parco della Musica
2. Atelier of Giovanni Zuccon
3. Galleria A.A.M. Architettura Arte Moderna
4. Art Hotel
5. Atelier of Massimiliano Fuksas
6. Atelier of Michele Spera

230

Notes
The images above are photographs from the book Design Roma, Guida ai luoghi di eccellenza.

The Guide selected and mapped the most significant "design presences" in the city of Rome.
It is the result of a research conducted by the Cdl in Rome, in collaboration with the review Disegno Industriale and presents all of those spaces in Rome "with an elevated content of design" - shops, museums, spaces of entertainment, restaurants, hotels, the ateliers of artists, architects, designers and stylists - where it is possible to acquire design products, observe new trends in design, enjoy the particular and refined quality of spaces and internal furnishings, appreciate expressions of excellence in fashion, art, design and craftsmanship.

1. Henry Fonda posing with a Speedgraphic in Rome, 03/07/1955
2. Fiat 600 Multipla in St. Peter's Square Rome, 14/01/1956
3. Interior of the Necchi sewing machine factory: 14/06/1958
4. The actors Edmund Purdom and Genevieve Page on a Vespa in Rome, 20/04/1957
5. Presentation of the Fiat 500 D to Italian Prime Minister Adone Zoli in Rome, 01/07/1957
6. Anna Magnani photographed inside an Alfa Romeo Giulietta Spider in Via XX Settembre Rome, 30/05/1958

231

Notes
The exhibition "Il Design nei documenti dell'Istituto Luce" offered a selection of films and newsreels on design and fashion conserved in the Archives of the Istituto Luce. This exploration of the world of the Made in Italy gathered together historic images from important events, such as the Saloni dell'Auto in Turin, fashion shows, the Saloni del Mobile in Milan, which helped make Italian creativity famous the world over. A look at the past and the history of Italian industry to better understand the origins and developments of the Made in Italy brand.

Grids for an Agenda

2003/2004: A "Soft" Book in a Pocket-Sized Format

1. A 95x165 mm format agenda. It consists of various chapters with information about graduate courses in Industrial Design and diverse sections related to services. A colour code, which breaks the margin to the left and right of each page, identifies the sections (see the following page).

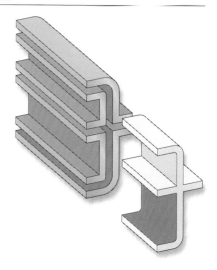

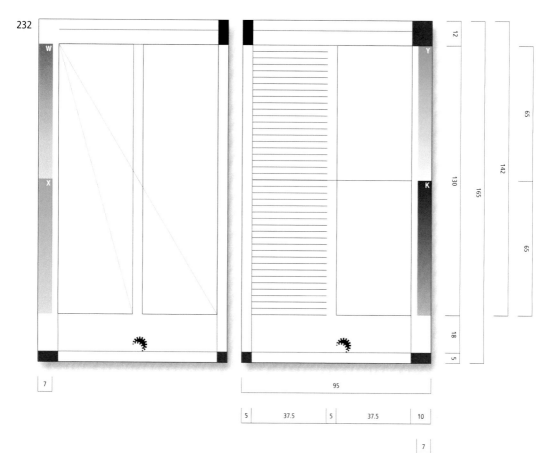

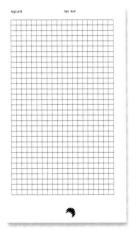

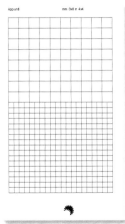

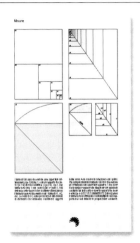

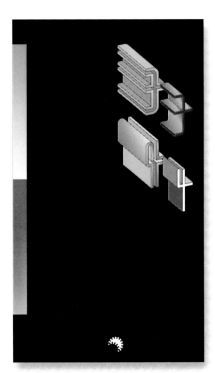

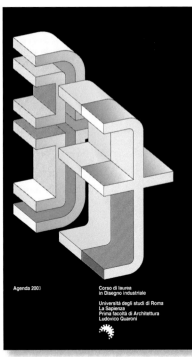

Notes 233
*Returning to the page
with the calendars we
can clearly see two
numbers:
the 3 and the 4.
Studied partially for the
agenda illustrated here,
these numbers were
redesigned a year later,
integrated and used to
generate a sort of
lexicon, a complete
lettering system from
zero to nine.*

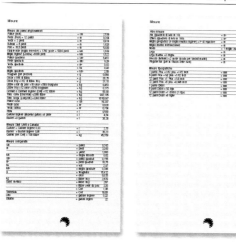

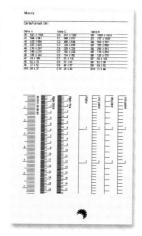

1. Pages of information: UNI formats, typographic measurements, measurements used in Anglo-Saxon countries and a comparison of measurements; area codes and postal codes; telephone alphabets (spelling) in Italian and British and American English; dates to be remembered; zodiac signs; notes, contacts.

234

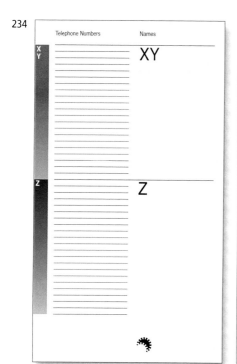

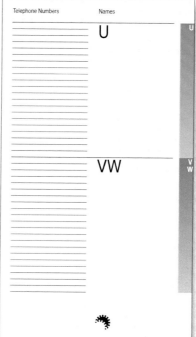

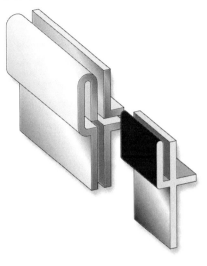

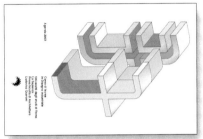

Telephone Numbers	Names	
Aries	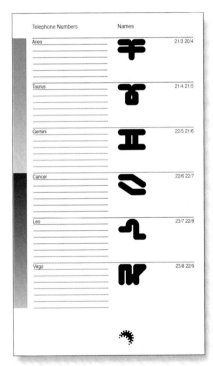	21/3 20/4
Taurus		21/4 21/5
Gemini		22/5 21/6
Cancer		22/6 22/7
Leo		23/7 22/8
Virgo		23/8 22/9

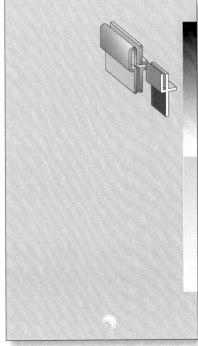

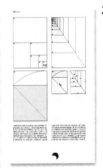

17.
Magazines and Periodicals

Sistan the ISTAT Magazine:
A Fixed Central Space

1. To begin the discussion of how to conceive of the structure for a magazine, we will examine that designed for ISTAT. It was selected for the particular qualities of its graphic structure, which involves the division of the page into three parts. Titles, summaries, etc. are placed in a central module.

A uniform margin of 20 mm on all four sides was applied to a format of 210x297 mm. The resulting space, which measures 170x257 mm, was divided into three equal parts measuring 82.333 mm in height. The modules are separated by a constant space of 5 mm. Tracing the diagonal of the lower square along the vertical we obtain the height of the cut along the upper margin of the page. The further subdivision of the grid into three parts generates the measure of a column, which is equal to 53.333 mm in width.

Dividing the primary module of 53.333 mm in height by 82.333 mm in height by half generates a secondary module of 53.333x38.666 mm. This grid can now be used to layout texts and images.

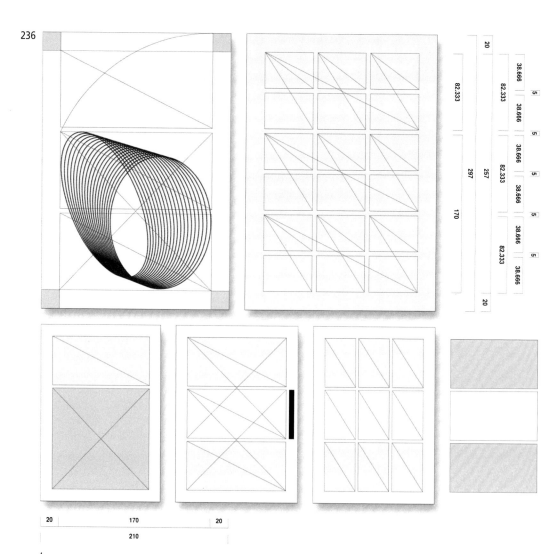

1.

2. The grid shown here is a reworking of another grid used a few years earlier. Here the central space has been reduced and the areas occupied respond to a criteria of page layout dictated by the rows of text counted in the margin.

The two pages present the studies of the grid for the magazine. The first, on the facing page, is from 1982; the second, on this page, is a reworking of the first project made a few years later. As the images show, the central module was reduced to create more room for texts and images.

237

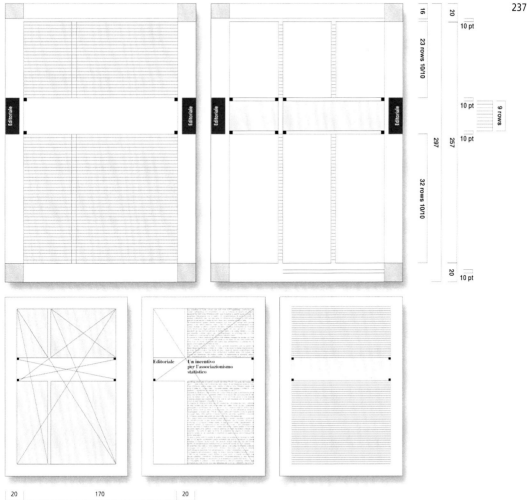

2.

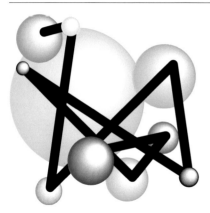

1. For *Il Giornale del Sistan* we developed an insert for internal use by ISTAT.
These pages list the location and addresses of different Ministries, Regional Governments and other organisms linked to ISTAT.

238

Workbook
Using pre-established formats of paper, design the relative grids and define their geometric logic. Remember that the formats 64x88 and 70x100 do not respect either ISO formats or the golden section.

1.

2. An illustration and its page layout. The right side of the drawing has been lightened to facilitate the reading of the overlapping texts.

3. *Sistan* stands for *"Sistema Statistico Nazionale"* (National Statistics System). This highly "graphic" drawing played a very important role in the illustration of the magazine.

3.

239

2.

1. The left column is almost never occupied by text, with only a few rare exceptions. Titles, authors, summaries and subheadings occupy the central module in a structure based on two or three columns.
The text is based on a constant value of 2/3 of the entire width. The central space is also dedicated to images that can obviously occupy adjacent modules.

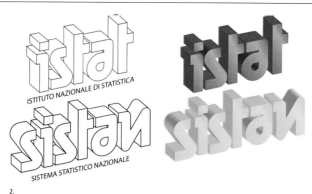

ISTITUTO NAZIONALE DI STATISTICA

SISTEMA STATISTICO NAZIONALE

2.

2. Studies of the ISTAT and Sistan logo used in the *Giornale del Sistan*.

Notes
The drawing that reproduces the symbols of the magazine, printed on some pages in cyan at 20%, serves as a background to the texts: it occupies the full width of the two upper modules.

Il programma statistico comunitario 2003-2007

Gilles Decand

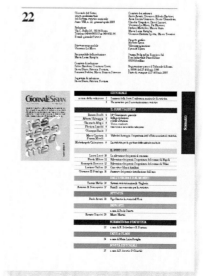

1.

This page shows the
drawings developed by
the author and by
Fabiano Spera to
illustrate articles on
statistics about families.

241

1. A selection of covers designed over the years. In general, they illustrate topics related to statistics, first and foremost numbers, the basic element of everything communicated by ISTAT.

The drawing of a disabled person in a wheelchair, not by accident, shows the figure from behind: a means of emphasising this challenging condition, and an often solitary existence. This drawing by Fabiano Spera is a sanguine on paper.

On the facing page: above is an elaboration of the same numbers created for *Sistan* for the 2016 *Festival delle Generazioni*; below is the review published by the CNEN at the Casaccia Nuclear Research Centre from 1969.

242

Articoli di: Manlio Calzaroni / Valerio Terra Abrami / Ennio Fortunato / David Lazzari / Roberto Tomei / Franco S. Corea / Sabina Del Corso / Renato Guarini / Patrizia Grossi / Alfonso Feleppa / Efisio Espa / Carlo Mochi Sismondi / Andrea Mancini / Gian Paolo Oneto / Algirdas Semeta / Lia Coniglio / Fabio Losa

www.sistan.it

Articoli di: Renato Profili / Alberto Valmaggia / Giancarlo Allegri / Floriana Ippoliti / Giuseppe Basile / Mario Casciato / Franca Minelli / Michelangelo Calcopietro / Laura Leoni / Nicola Milone / Rosangela Dominici / Luciano Gallino / Giovanni B. Pittaluga / Tamás Mellár / Antoine Simonpietri / Paolo Arvati / Renato Guarini

25

www.sistan.it

Articoli di: Renato Profili / Alberto Valmaggia / Giancarlo Allegri / Floriana Ippoliti / Giuseppe Basile / Mario Casciato / Franca Minelli / Michelangelo Calcopietro / Laura Leoni / Nicola Milone / Rosangela Dominici / Luciano Gallino / Giovanni B. Pittaluga / Tamás Mellár / Antoine Simonpietri / Paolo Arvati / Renato Guarini

26

www.sistan.it

Articoli di: Renato Profili / Alberto Valmaggia / Giancarlo Allegri / Floriana Ippoliti / Giuseppe Basile / Mario Casciato / Franca Minelli / Michelangelo Calcopietro / Laura Leoni / Nicola Milone / Rosangela Dominici / Luciano Gallino / Giovanni B. Pittaluga / Tamás Mellár / Antoine Simonpietri / Paolo Arvati / Renato Guarini

27

www.sistan.it

1.

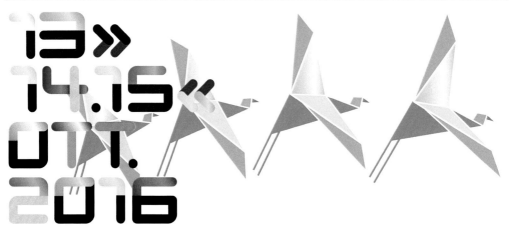

IL CENTRO
STUDI NUCLEARI
DELLA CASACCIA
COMITATO NAZIONALE
ENERGIA NUCLEARE
CNEN

Notiziario

Rivista mensile del Cnen

È il puntuale informatore per gli studiosi,
i ricercatori e gli operatori economici
che vogliono essere aggiornati
sulle realizzazioni nel settore nucleare
in Italia e all'estero.
A chi sottoscrive un abbonamento
verrà inviato in omaggio un volume
a propria scelta tra quelli riportati a fianco

**Pubblicazioni
scientifiche
edite dal CNEN
nel 1968/69**

Serie Trattati

Piero Caldirola
e Roberto Fiocchi
**Separazione
isotopica
dell'uranio**
pagine 448

Maurizio Cumo
**Aspetti
fondamentali
dell'ebollizione**
pagine 380

**Serie
documentazioni**

**Norme di protezione
contro le radiazioni
relative ad orologi
radioluminescenti**
pagine 50

**La ricerca
scientifica in Italia**
Volume terzo
della collana
«Ricerca scientifica
e sviluppoeconomico»
pagine 806

**Il regime giuridico
dell'impiego
pacifico dell'energia
nucleare**
pagine 224

**Direttive e
raccomandazioni
della CEEA
in materia
di protezione
sanitaria contro
le radiazioni
ionizzanti**
pagine 68

Serie Simposi

**I processi soi-gel
per la produzione
di combustibili
ceramici**
Atti del Simposio
nucleare di Torino
2/3 ottobre 1967
pagine 440

**Problemi
della separazione
isotopica dell'uranio**
Atti del Simposio
nucleare di Torino
1/2 ottobre 1968
pagine 288

**Atti del XII
Congresso
Nucleare di Roma**
pagine 352

**Atti del XIII
Congresso
Nucleare di Roma**
pagine 384

**Applicazioni
dell'energia
nucleare
in agricoltura**
Atti del Simposio
nucleare di Palermo
30 maggio 1967
pagine 155

**Giornata
dell'energia
nucleare 1968**
pagine 376

**Serie
divulgativa**

**Programmi
e attività del CNEN**
pagine 152

**Rapporto di attività
del CNEN 1965/67**
pagine 164
e tavole
fuori testo

Notiziario

Rivista mensile del Cnen

È il puntuale informatore
per gli studiosi, i ricercatori
e gli operatori economici
che vogliono essere aggiornati
sulle realizzazioni nel settore
nucleare in Italia e all'estero

A chi sottoscrive
un abbonamento
verrà inviato in omaggio
un volume a propria scelta
tra quelli riportati a fianco

1/1969

IL CENTRO
STUDI NUCLEARI
DELLA CASACCIA
COMITATO NAZIONALE
ENERGIA NUCLEARE
CNEN

Smoking

A Magazine for Smokers: A Variety of Typologies in a Rigorous Structure

The editor who commissions the design of a magazine will undoubtedly ask for lively and attractive pages that invite people to read it. This is the brief that will surely be developed, and this is why almost every magazine features pages full of fixed and floating blocks of text, frames, bleeds and countless doodles and paraphernalia provided precisely to respond to this request. Almost always to the detriment of a rational page layout.

The project for *Smoking* magazine, published by Fit, the *Federazione Italiana Tabaccai* (Italian Federation of Tobacconists), illustrated on these pages, is by Gerardo Spera, who is also the art director. The project offers a vast range of design solutions, without ever betraying the logical and rational structure underlying the entire project, and managing to give each page a varied, attractive and pleasing, though always rigorous appearance.

1. 2. Format 230x300 mm. The base module measures 24x36 mm, the same as a reflex negative, also useful for trimming photographs to its multiples. The grid, composed of 40 modules, intentionally accentuates the horizontality of the page. Additional modules above and below contain various types of information. The last column to the right is a "service" space.

244

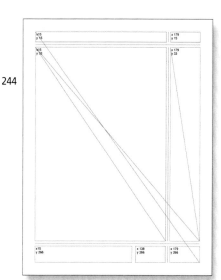
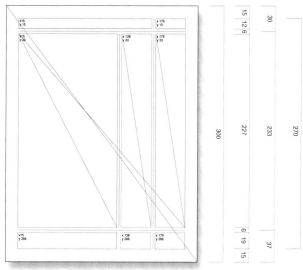
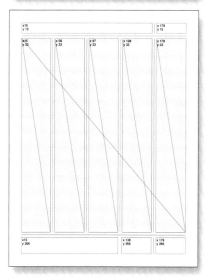
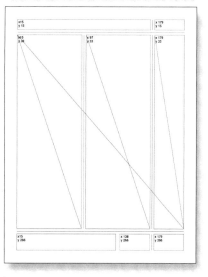

1.

3. An immense cigar, wrapped by a band bearing the *Smoking* magazine header, in white letters on a red background, was used to advertise this magazine for smokers.

3.

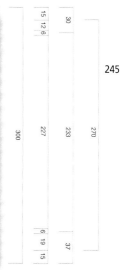

245

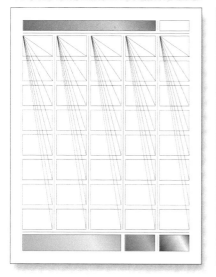

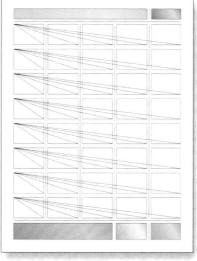

2.

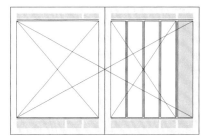
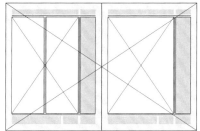

A constant "work in progress". Images, drawings and articles are overlapped each month to give form to the pages of the magazine.

246

Notes
We do not know whether love is blind, whether dedication must be total. We do know that our love for the pipe and the cigar keeps us faithful.
We also know, however, that this love brings an inherent mystique, and the fussiness of ritual: how we light it, how we conserve it, the respect for a pipe, the way we cradle a cigar... all topics explored in this issue and which we will continue to explore.
That said, we would like to defend ourselves against the lost and stunned gaze of those in love.
So, thanks also to our colleague who agreed to pose for the cover, we will try to remember that irony and self-mockery are splendid systems for defending oneself against a misplaced seriousness.
Smoking must not be an obsession, but a pleasure.
A pleasure that is renewed each time, and which remains clean, fresh and tasteful.
Any reference to the portrait is in no way casual.
(From the Editorial of issue number one).

Various pages from
Smoking.
To the left is a drawing
of a crocodile used to
illustrate an article
considered well
represented by this
animal.

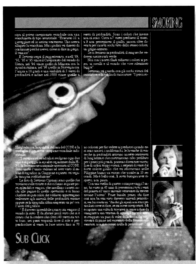

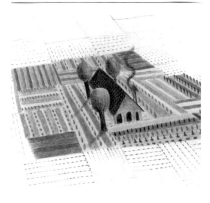

Pages with drawings, photographs and collages of different images.

248

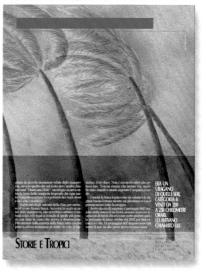

The *Italian Heart Journal*

Official Journal of the Italian Federation of Cardiology

If you are asked to design a scientific review, we suggest you read an article such as "Come dovrebbe essere una rivista scientifica" (What a Scientific Review Should Be Like) published on the Bats Blog, https://blogbats.wordpress.com/2011/06/30/come-dovrebbe-essere-una-rivista-scientifica/

[...]"The system of accepting articles to be published, the so-called "peer review" system, is based on the review of an article by a certain number of experts in a given field, before it can be published by a journal or review."

Giuseppe Lipari, associate professor at the Sant'Anna high school in Pisa published a post on his personal blog, *The land of algorithms*, containing some ideas about what a scientific review should be in light of technological changes and the recent and necessary tranformations of publishing policies by editors and publishers.

Italian Heart Journal

Official Journal of the Italian Federation of Cardiology

8/33

Abitare la Terra

The New Alliance between Man and His Environment

The pages of the magazine *Abitare la Terra*, directed by Paolo Portoghesi, expand, compress and come together across an unusually large format. The grid studied by Michele Spera is based on a structure of nine columns. This structure responds to criteria of creative flexibility and agility, within a structure created by Spera while thinking of Luca Pacioli, the mathematician of the *De divina Proportione*, illustrated by Leonardo Da Vinci.
The golden section, highlighted here in light blue, guarantees the harmony of the ratios. It permeates every page and every graphic element.
Mario Pisani

The construction of a magazine is – like a work of architecture – a symbol and paradigm of man's ability to express his own ideas, and see his dreams become reality.
This conviction is reinforced each time I have the occasion to work with Michele Spera, for a short or long period of time, on the layout and editing of our quarterly publication.
In the quiet and measured space in which Michele welcomes me, in the intense dialogue between the eyes and the screen, the hands and the keyboard, I am an active witness to the tranquility and awareness of someone who, with a multiple

and often babelian universe of authors and proposals, figures and colours, manages time and again to compose a magazine that is both coherent and surprising. It is never the mere mechanices of dimensions and proportions that construct a page, but always also the profound participation in the intrinsic value of images and words.
With the simple and amorous intelligence expressed by an able craftsman in modelling, with a smile, the stuff of which dreams are made.
Andrea Pesce Delfino

250

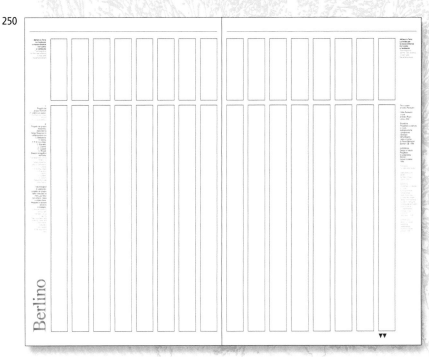

Berlino

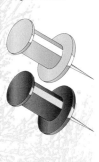

Notes
Abitare la terra, formato 290x465 cm, quarterly, printed on uncoated paper, Gangemi Editore

The encounter with Michele Spera was very positive for the story of *Abitare la Terra*. Our man, who boasts an education and a vision that tend toward abstraction and, in some ways, an opposition to a figurative vision of graphics, by debating and welcoming various proposals and then successfully incorporating them, has instead demonstrated that be believes in a model able to reconcile a vision steeped in abstract graphics. A model that pursues geometric elegance and a figurative legacy accepting of the symbol, of overlapping of images and other material. Thus our encounter was a happy one, because what could have been a conflict of taste was instead resolved through the comprehension of the needs of each actor. In this sense, I believe that also through what is a clear tendency to modify and absorb experiences, we arrived at a strong harmony. *Abitare la Terra* is a continuous and uninterrupted work in progress and never proposed a crystallised object.

Magazines are no longer obliged to accept graphics like a straitjacket, but on the contrary must develop their own image through research. They must foster experimentation and a desire for continuous reinvention that is never crystallised in one formula.
Paolo Portoghesi

251

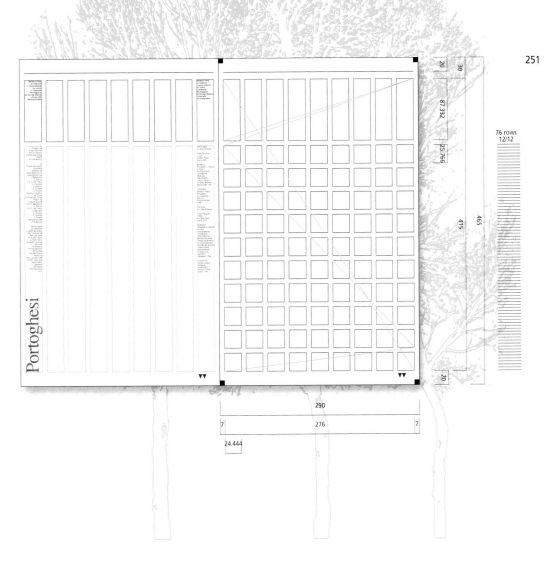

Many of the photographs were provided by Paolo Portoghesi, who proved to be an excellent photographer. They almost always accompanied a traditional page dedicated to a poet.

252

Prisciani

Wellcome Wing
Science Museum, Londra

Recensioni

Hans Ibelings
Supermodernismo
L'architettura nell'età
della globalizzazione
a cura di
Michele Costanzo,
Clanvitelecchi Editore,
Roma 2001,
pp. 90, Euro 12,40

Hans Ibelings
Supermodernism
Architecture in the age
of globalization
edited by
Michele Costanzo,
Clanvitelecchi Editore,
Roma 2001,
pp. 90, Euro 12,40

Fritjof Capra
La scienza della vita.
Le connessioni
nascoste fra natura e
gli esseri viventi
Rizzoli, Milano 2002,
pp. 388, Euro 19,50

Fritjof Capra
The science of life.
Hidden links between
nature and living
beings
Rizzoli, Milano 2002,
pp. 388, Euro 19,50

Peter Tompkins
La magia
degli obelischi
Marco Tropea Editore,
Milano 2001, pp. 480,
Euro 35,12

Peter Tompkins
The Magic of Obelisks
Milan 2001, pp. 480,
Euro 35,12

Autori vari
Arquitectura y
Transhumanismo
Nuevo monográfico di
Arquitectonics.
Mind, Land & Society
Universitat Politècnica
de Catalunya,
Barcelona 2001,
pp. 112, Euro 8,65

Various authors
Architecture and
Transhumanism
Monographic issue of
Arquitectonics.
Mind, Land & Society
Universitat Politècnica
de Catalunya,
Barcelona 2001,
pp. 112, Euro 8,65

I H L' E L T I T

254

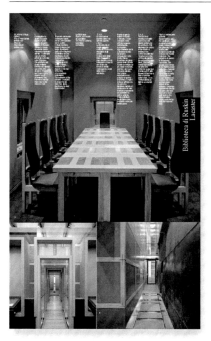

From the cover:

"Il mondo dell'architettura, dopo il tuffo nell'irrazionalismo che ha caratterizzato la fine del Novecento e i primi anni del terzo millennio, sta tornando a riflettere sulle sue responsabilità nel rapporto conflittuale che si è formato tra il nostro pianeta e la civiltà tecnologica. Se vuoi seguire il dibattito su questo argomento acquista il decimo numero di "Abitare la terra", la rivista che si batte per una nuova alleanza tra l'uomo e il suo ambiente. Following its dive into irrationalism at the end of the 20th century and the early years of the third millenium, the world of architecture is again starting to debate its responsibility in the growing conflict between our earth and technology. If you are interested in this debate, buy the tenth issue of "Abitare la Terra", the magazine fighting for a new alliance between man and the environment".

255

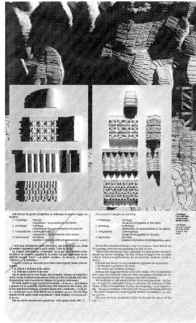

Abitare la Terra

LA RIVISTA PER LA NUOVA ALLEANZA TRA L'UOMO E L'AMBIENTE
THE MAGAZINE FOR THE NEW ALLIANCE OF MAN WITH THE ENVIRONMENT
DIRETTA DA / CHIEF EDITOR PAOLO PORTOGHESI

Il mondo dell'architettura, dopo il tuffo nell'irrazionalismo che ha caratterizzato la fine del Novecento e i primi anni del terzo millennio, sta tornando a riflettere sulle sue responsabilità nel rapporto conflittuale che si è formato tra il nostro pianeta e la civiltà tecnologica. Se vuoi seguire il dibattito su questo argomento acquista il settimo numero di "Abitare la terra", la rivista che si batte per una nuova alleanza tra l'uomo e il suo ambiente. Following its dive into irrationalism at the end of the 20th century and the early years of the third millennium, the world of architecture is again starting to debate its responsibility in the growing conflict between our earth and technology. If you are interested in this debate, buy the seventh issue of "Abitare la Terra", the magazine fighting for a new alliance between man and the environment.

IN QUESTO NUMERO: 2. PAOLO PORTOGHESI EDITORIALE / 4. STEFANIA TUZI STORIA DEI PROGETTI PER IL PONTE DI MESSINA HISTORY OF THE PROJECTS FOR THE MESSINA BRIDGE / 9. ALBERTO CASSANDRA IL PROGETTO THE PROJECT / 12. ALBERTO CASSANDRA L'IMPATTO AMBIENTALE THE IMPACT ON THE ENVIRONMENT / 14. GIUSEPPE ZAMBERLETTI IL PONTE SULLO STRETTO DI MESSINA STRAITS THE BRIDGE ON THE STRAIT OF MESSINA / 16. AMARO LAMBERTI PONTE SULLO STRETTO, IL FANTASMA DELL'OPERA THE BRIDGE OVER THE STRAIT CONSTRUCTION / 16. GUGLIELMO BILANCIONI I PONTI DI GIANFRANCO DE MICHELI BRIDGES BY GIANFRANCO DE MICHELI / 20. ADRIANA LABELLA L'ARCHITETTURA SOSTENIBILE DI GILLES PERRAUDIN SUSTAINABLE ARCHITECTURE BY GILLES PERRAUDIN / 24. MARIO PISANI L'ARTE DEL MUTARE THE ART OF BUILDING / 28. CLAUDIO LUGLI LA CITTÀ DEL XXI SECOLO THE 21ST CENTURY CITY / 30. LUIGI MAZZELLA VIAGGIO A BERLINO JOURNEY TO BERLIN / 34. BARBARA FIORE UN ARTE FEMMINILE IN SUDAFRICA A FEMALE ART IN SOUTH AFRICA / 38. LUIGI GIAZZOLA L'AGO NEL GIARDINO DELL'EDEN THE NEEDLE IN THE GARDEN OF EDEN / 42. CARLO BASSI FERRARA, LA CITTÀ IDEALE DI FRISCIANI FERRARA, FRISCIANI'S IDEAL CITY / 46. RECENSIONI REVIEWS

DIFFUSION IN USA AND CANADA: ACORN ALLIANCE DISTRIBUTION, INC

Abitare la Terra

LA RIVISTA PER LA NUOVA ALLEANZA TRA L'UOMO E L'AMBIENTE
THE MAGAZINE FOR THE NEW ALLIANCE OF MAN WITH THE ENVIRONMENT
DIRETTA DA / CHIEF EDITOR PAOLO PORTOGHESI

Il mondo dell'architettura, dopo il tuffo nell'irrazionalismo che ha caratterizzato la fine del Novecento e i primi anni del terzo millennio, sta tornando a riflettere sulle sue responsabilità nel rapporto conflittuale che si è formato tra il nostro pianeta e la civiltà tecnologica. Se vuoi seguire il dibattito su questo argomento acquista l'ottavo numero di "Abitare la terra", la rivista che si batte per una nuova alleanza tra l'uomo e il suo ambiente. Following its dive into irrationalism at the end of the 20th century and the early years of the third millennium, the world of architecture is again starting to debate its responsibility in the growing conflict between our earth and technology. If you are interested in this debate, buy the eighth issue of "Abitare la Terra", the magazine fighting for a new alliance between man and the environment.

IN QUESTO NUMERO: 2. PAOLO PORTOGHESI EDITORIALE EDITORIAL / 4. ROCCO FAMILIARI CINQUE DEDICHE FIVE DEDICATIONS / 6. MARIO PISANI CHIELI GESTO STORICHE A POTSDAM THE HEIDGESTISCHE IN POTSDAM / 12. PAOLO PORTOGHESI UN NUOVO RACCONTO DI PIERO DEROSSI A NEW STORY OF PIERO DEROSSI / 16. BENEDETTO MARZULLO ARCHITETTO SENZA ARCHITETTURA? ARCHITECT WITHOUT ARCHITECTURE? / 22. RENATO RIZZI SINDONE DI PIETRA THE SHROUD OF STONE / 28. CARLA BAROZZI PAROLE DI SABBIA RECORDS OF A MOSTRA FOTOGRAFICA WORDS OF SAND MEMORIES OF A PHOTOGRAPHIC EXHIBITION / 30. ENRICO SICIGNANO ARCHITETTURE IN AFRICA ARCHITECTURES IN AFRICA / 34. LIVIO MARTINI L'INCASTELLAMENTO UN MODO NUOVO DI CONCEPIRE LO SPAZIO FORTIFICATION A NEW WAY OF DESIGNING SPACE / 36. PIPPO GIACOBINO L'INCASTELLAMENTO MEDIOEVALE DELLA VALLE DEL TREIA MEDIEVAL FORTIFICATION IN THE TREIA VALLEY / 39. VALERIA GUACANELLI CASE RURALI MEMORIA DELL'AMBIENTE NATURALE RURAL BUILDINGS MEMORIES OF THE NATURAL ENVIRONMENT / 42. PAOLO PORTOGHESI PIAZZA SPROVIERI PIAZZA SPROVIERI / 46. RECENSIONI REVIEWS

256

Abitare la Terra

LA RIVISTA PER LA NUOVA ALLEANZA TRA L'UOMO E L'AMBIENTE
THE MAGAZINE FOR THE NEW ALLIANCE OF MAN WITH THE ENVIRONMENT
DIRETTA DA / CHIEF EDITOR PAOLO PORTOGHESI

Il mondo dell'architettura, dopo il tuffo nell'irrazionalismo che ha caratterizzato la fine del Novecento e i primi anni del terzo millennio, sta tornando a riflettere sulle sue responsabilità nel rapporto conflittuale che si è formato tra il nostro pianeta e la civiltà tecnologica. Se vuoi seguire il dibattito su questo argomento acquista il nono numero di "Abitare la terra", la rivista che si batte per una nuova alleanza tra l'uomo e il suo ambiente. Following its dive into irrationalism at the end of the 20th century and the early years of the third millennium, the world of architecture is again starting to debate its responsibility in the growing conflict between our earth and technology. If you are interested in this debate, buy the seventh issue of "Abitare la Terra", the magazine fighting for a new alliance between man and the environment.

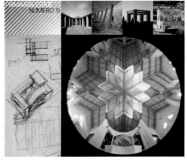

IN QUESTO NUMERO: 2. PAOLO PORTOGHESI EDITORIALE: DISEGNI INEDITI DI TERRAGNI EDITORIAL / 8. REINER MARIA RILKE: QUASI OGNI COSA... QUASI OGNI COSA / 10. FABIO CAPANNI: PAOLO ZERMANI, LA MISURA IMMAGINATA THE IMAGINARY MEASUREMENT / 14. LEONE SPITA: SHOEI YOH, IL GIOCO DELLA NATURA SHOEI YOH THE ENJOYMENT OF NATURE / 20. MARIO PISANI LA NUOVA CHIESA A TERNI DI PAOLO PORTOGHESI THE NEW CHURCH IN TERNI BY PAOLO PORTOGHESI / 28. GIANNI PETTENA L'ARTE DELL'ARCHITETTO THE ART OF ARCHITECTS / 32. GAETANO FUSCO: LA FORMA DELL'OMBRA THE FORM OF SHADOW / 38. ALESSANDRA SCARANO: MEDITERRANEO, IDENTITÀ CULTURALI E ANTICHI SEGNI PER UN NUOVO LINGUAGGIO DELL'ARCHITETTURA MEDITERRANEO CULTURAL IDENTITY AND OLD SYMBOLS FOR A NEW ARCHITECTURAL STYLE / 44. MARCO CATUCCI: LE CASE DI ROBINSON ROBINSON'S HOUSES / 46. RECENSIONI REVIEWS

Abitare la Terra

LA RIVISTA PER LA NUOVA ALLEANZA TRA L'UOMO E L'AMBIENTE
THE MAGAZINE FOR THE NEW ALLIANCE OF MAN WITH THE ENVIRONMENT
DIRETTA DA / CHIEF EDITOR PAOLO PORTOGHESI

Il mondo dell'architettura, dopo il tuffo nell'irrazionalismo che ha caratterizzato la fine del Novecento e i primi anni del terzo millennio, sta tornando a riflettere sulle sue responsabilità nel rapporto conflittuale che si è formato tra il nostro pianeta e la civiltà tecnologica. Se vuoi seguire il dibattito su questo argomento acquista il decimo numero di "Abitare la terra", la rivista che si batte per una nuova alleanza tra l'uomo e il suo ambiente. Following its dive into irrationalism at the end of the 20th century and the early years of the third millennium, the world of architecture is again starting to debate its responsibility in the growing conflict between our earth and technology. If you are interested in this debate, buy the tenth issue of "Abitare la Terra", the magazine fighting for a new alliance between man and the environment.

IN QUESTO NUMERO: 2. PAOLO PORTOGHESI EDITORIALE: IL REALISMO DI RIDOLFI RIDOLFI'S REALISM / 4. GEORG TRAKL SERA D'INVERNO WINTER EVENING / 6. PIERO GALLINA: IRAQ, UNA TERRA SENZA CANTO IRAQ A LAND WITHOUT SONG / 12. PAOLO PORTOGHESI MARIO BOTTA CAPPELLA DI AZZANO A SERANZZOL TOUR DE MERON TEATRO ALLA SCALA / 18. MARIO PISANI SHISEIDO NEW GINZA BUILDING SHISEIDO NEW GINZA BUILDING / 24. MARIANO RANISI LA NUOVA AEROSTAZIONE DI VERONA THE NEW AIRPORT / 28. LEONE SPITA: WING-SHED WING-SHED / 32. FILIPPO RELLI LA REINVENZIONE DEL LUOGO E PAESAGGIO DEL GIARDINO BOTANICO DI BARCELLONA / 36. ALBERTO CASSANDRA IL RESTAURO DELLA FONTANA DEL GIANICOLO / 40. STEFANO BORSI IL MERAVIGLIOSO PALAZZO DI MADONNA INTELLIGENZA / 44. LUIGI MAZZELLA SPLEDORE E CASTIGO GIUSTO NELL'ERA DELLA GLOBALIZZAZIONE / 46. RECENSIONI REVIEWS

Abitare la Terra

LA RIVISTA PER LA NUOVA ALLEANZA TRA L'UOMO E L'AMBIENTE
THE MAGAZINE FOR THE NEW ALLIANCE OF MAN WITH THE ENVIRONMENT
DIRETTA DA / CHIEF EDITOR PAOLO PORTOGHESI

Il mondo dell'architettura, dopo il tutto nell'ornamentalismo che ha caratterizzato la fine del Novecento e i primi anni del terzo millennio, sta tornando a riflettere sulle sue responsabilità nel rapporto conflittuale che si è formato tra il nostro pianeta e la civiltà tecnologica. Se vuoi seguire il dibattito su questo argomento acquista il sesto numero di "Abitare la terra". la rivista che si batte per una nuova alleanza tra l'uomo e il suo ambiente. Following its dive into irrationalism at the end of the 20th century and the early years of the third millennium, the world of architecture is again starting to debate its responsibilities in the growing conflict between our earth and technology. If you are interested in this debate, buy the sixth issue of "Abitare la Terra", the magazine fighting for a new alliance between man and the environment.

IN QUESTO NUMERO: 2. PAOLO PORTOGHESI EDITORIALE / 4. WILLIAM BUTLER YEATS L'ISOLA DEL LAGO DI INNISFREE THE LAKE ISLE OF INNISFREE / 6. LEONE SPITA KUROKAWA MAESTRO DEL GRIGIO KUROKAWA MASTER OF GREY / 16. ALESSANDRO CAPRABIANCA CINEMA E ARCHITETTURA ESPRESSIONISTA CINEMA AND EXPRESSIONIST ARCHITECTURE / 22. RICCARDO MARIA PULSELLI E ENZO TEZZI DEPOSITO ORGANIZZATO DI ARTE CONTEMPORANEA A SIENA A WAREHOUSE FOR CONTEMPORARY ART IN SIENA / 26. PETRA BERNITSA MACCORMAC, LO SPIRITO DELLA MEMORIA MACCORMAC, THE SPIRIT OF MEMORY / 34. MARISA TABARRINI UN INEDITO PIANO URBANISTICO PER ROMA BAROCCA AN UNPUBLISHED PLAN FOR BAROQUE ROME / 38. MARIANO RANISI SAMYN & PARTNERS, UNA TECNOLOGIA 'DOLCE' TRA ARCHITETTURA E NATURA SAMYN & PARTNERS, 'SOFT' TECHNOLOGY BETWEEN ARCHITECTURE AND NATURE / 44. MARIO PISANI IL MODO DI ESPORRE DI FRANCO PURINI FRANCO PURINI'S EXHIBITION METHOD

Abitare la Terra

LA RIVISTA PER LA NUOVA ALLEANZA TRA L'UOMO E L'AMBIENTE
THE MAGAZINE FOR THE NEW ALLIANCE OF MAN WITH THE ENVIRONMENT
DIRETTA DA / CHIEF EDITOR PAOLO PORTOGHESI

Il mondo dell'architettura, dopo il tutto nell'ornamentalismo che ha caratterizzato la fine del Novecento e i primi anni del terzo millennio, sta tornando a riflettere sulle sue responsabilità nel rapporto conflittuale che si è formato tra il nostro pianeta e la civiltà tecnologica. Se vuoi seguire il dibattito su questo argomento acquista il sesto numero di "Abitare la terra". la rivista che si batte per una nuova alleanza tra l'uomo e il suo ambiente. Following its dive into irrationalism at the end of the 20th century and the early years of the third millennium, the world of architecture is again starting to debate its responsibilities in the growing conflict between our earth and technology. If you are interested in this debate, buy the sixth issue of "Abitare la Terra", the magazine fighting for a new alliance between man and the environment.

IN QUESTO NUMERO: 2. PAOLO PORTOGHESI EDITORIALE / 4. WILLIAM BUTLER YEATS L'ISOLA DEL LAGO DI INNISFREE THE LAKE ISLE OF INNISFREE / 6. LEONE SPITA KUROKAWA MAESTRO DEL GRIGIO KUROKAWA MASTER OF GREY / 16. ALESSANDRO CAPRABIANCA CINEMA E ARCHITETTURA ESPRESSIONISTA CINEMA AND EXPRESSIONIST ARCHITECTURE / 22. RICCARDO MARIA PULSELLI E ENZO TEZZI DEPOSITO ORGANIZZATO DI ARTE CONTEMPORANEA A SIENA A WAREHOUSE FOR CONTEMPORARY ART IN SIENA / 26. PETRA BERNITSA MACCORMAC, LO SPIRITO DELLA MEMORIA MACCORMAC, THE SPIRIT OF MEMORY / 34. MARISA TABARRINI UN INEDITO PIANO URBANISTICO PER ROMA BAROCCA AN UNPUBLISHED PLAN FOR BAROQUE ROME / 38. MARIANO RANISI SAMYN & PARTNERS, UNA TECNOLOGIA 'DOLCE' TRA ARCHITETTURA E NATURA SAMYN & PARTNERS, 'SOFT' TECHNOLOGY BETWEEN ARCHITECTURE AND NATURE / 44. MARIO PISANI IL MODO DI ESPORRE DI FRANCO PURINI FRANCO PURINI'S EXHIBITION METHOD

Abitare la Terra

LA RIVISTA PER LA NUOVA ALLEANZA TRA L'UOMO E L'AMBIENTE
THE MAGAZINE FOR THE NEW ALLIANCE OF MAN WITH THE ENVIRONMENT
DIRETTA DA / CHIEF EDITOR PAOLO PORTOGHESI

Il mondo dell'architettura, dopo il tutto nell'ornamentalismo che ha caratterizzato la fine del Novecento e i primi anni del terzo millennio, sta tornando a riflettere sulle sue responsabilità nel rapporto conflittuale che si è formato tra il nostro pianeta e la civiltà tecnologica. Se vuoi seguire il dibattito su questo argomento acquista il quinto numero di "Abitare la terra", la rivista che si batte per una nuova alleanza tra l'uomo e il suo ambiente. Following its dive into irrationalism at the end of the 20th century and the early years of the third millennium, the world of architecture is again starting to debate its responsibilities in the growing conflict between our earth and technology. If you are interested in this debate, buy the fifth issue of "Abitare la Terra", the magazine fighting for a new alliance between man and the environment.

IN QUESTO NUMERO: 2. PAOLO PORTOGHESI EDITORIALE / 4. RENATO RIZZI IL DRAMMA DELLA FORMA THE DRAMA OF FORM / 6. CORRADO CALABRO' L'ULTIMA LUNA DI GIUGNO THE LAST JUNE MOON / 8. CLAUDIO LUIGI PER UNA MAPPA DEL CINEMA AUSTRALIANO A MAP OF AUSTRALIAN CINEMA / 14. CECILIA BARTOLI UN TESORO RITROVATO A RETRIEVED TREASURE / 16. VITTORIO SANT'AMBOGIA TRENTANNI DI DUE ARCHITETTURE DI MARIO BOTTA COMMENTATE DA PAOLO PORTOGHESI TWO ARCHITECTURES BY MARIO BOTTA / 26. IL TEATRO POLITEAMA A CATANZARO DI PAOLO PORTOGHESI COMMENTATO DA FRANCO PURINI THE THEATRE POLITEAMA IN CATANZARO BY PAOLO PORTOGHESI / 38. MARIO PISANI ABITARE POETICAMENTE DWELLING POETICALLY / 40. STEFANO BORSI LA SALA DELLE ASSE, TRA GIARDINO FINTO E POLITICA VERA THE SALA DELLE ASSE, BETWEEN FALSE GARDENS AND REAL POLITICS / 44. ANDREA PESCE DELFINO ENERGIA NEL TERRITORIO ENERGY IN THE LAND

Abitare la Terra

LA RIVISTA PER LA NUOVA ALLEANZA TRA L'UOMO E L'AMBIENTE
THE MAGAZINE FOR THE NEW ALLIANCE OF MAN WITH THE ENVIRONMENT
DIRETTA DA / CHIEF EDITOR PAOLO PORTOGHESI

Il mondo dell'architettura, dopo il tutto nell'ornamentalismo che ha caratterizzato la fine del Novecento e i primi anni del terzo millennio, sta tornando a riflettere sulle sue responsabilità nel rapporto conflittuale che si è formato tra il nostro pianeta e la civiltà tecnologica. Se vuoi seguire il dibattito su questo argomento acquista il sesto numero di "Abitare la terra", la rivista che si batte per una nuova alleanza tra l'uomo e il suo ambiente. Following its dive into irrationalism at the end of the 20th century and the early years of the third millennium, the world of architecture is again starting to debate its responsibilities in the growing conflict between our earth and technology. If you are interested in this debate, buy the sixth issue of "Abitare la Terra", the magazine fighting for a new alliance between man and the environment.

IN QUESTO NUMERO: 2. PAOLO PORTOGHESI EDITORIALE / 4. MARCO BIRAGHI CARNET D'IRAQ THE IRAQ ALBUM / 10. WILLIAM WORDSWORTH POESIA POEM / 12. PIETRO GALLINA IL CANTO DEL CIELO E DELLA TERRA THE SONG OF HEAVEN AND HEARTH / 16. MARIO PISANI LA NUOVA BASILICA DI SAN FRANCESCO DI PAOLA THE NEW BASILICA OF SAN FRANCESCO DI PAOLA A PROJECT OF SANDRO BENEDETTI / 20. BENEDETTO GRAVAGNUOLO L'UFFICIO POSTALE DI MORCONE THE POST OFFICE IN MORCONE PROJECT OF SANDRO RAFFONE / 22. MARCO SPESSO PIENZA GEOMETRIA DELLA NATURA PIENZA GEOMETRY OF NATURE / 28. ITALO TOMASSONI IL FONDAMENTO DELL'ARTIFICIO THE PRINCIPLE OF ARTIFICE / 30. LEONE SPITA CANCELLARE L'ARCHITETTURA ERASING ARCHITECTURE PROJECTS OF KENGO KUMA / 40. M. POPOLONIA CITTA' DI OSAKA POPOLONIA OSAKA PROJECT OF USCHIDA-FINDLAY / 44. GUGLIELMO BILANCIONI I DISEGNI DI FRANZ PRATI DRAWINGS BY FRANZ PRATI

Territorio

A Magazine in Lucania

Commissioned by Vito D'Elia, a young Lucanian entrepreneur, this magazine, published since 1974, has survived economic hardships and perhaps even a certain provincial hostility for some years.

Design work included page layouts, graphic design, cover designs and often the photographs.
It can happen that one brings a curious love to certain works, and this almost always occurs when we are left free to invent and create.

258

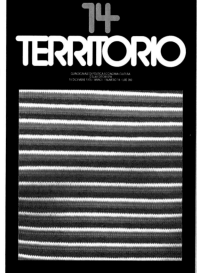

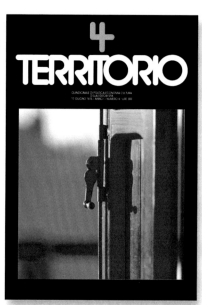

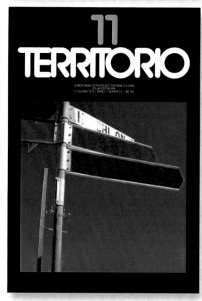

Sinistra Oggi

A Fornightly Political Review

With the creation of this new publication, left-wing Republicans pursue two objectives. Contibruting, first and foremost, to the creation of a solid network of connections between those, linked with or close to Eder in the past, who believe that the ideal and political legacy of this area must today be directed toward a precise destination. The consolidation, in other words, of bipolarism and the birth of a broader unified Italian left, animated by Europeanism and modern reformism. With these aims in mind, the decision was made to create the "Coordinamento Nazionale dei Repubblicani" and Sinistra Oggi. They testify to the actions of the many, in Parliament and local institutions, who labour to give this left-wing Republican structure concrete contents. They are ambitious proposals, above all when compared to the poverty of the means at our disposal. But they are also coherent with the desire to participate, with clarity, in political debate during this complex and at the same time decisive phase in Italian life. This conviction will help us confront this new commitment with the necessary vigour. Antonio Duva

259

7.

5.

6.

Sinistra Oggi

260

A brochure for the ICI, the Institute for Foreign Trade. This Exporter Guide is from the 1960s.

18.
Illustrations

The Importance of Drawings in Publications

A drawing can help embellish a page. It can help make a magazine more attractive, and better and more freshly express the content of an article.
Using the work of an illustrator, in those cases when a photograph may seem banal, obvious and tired, is fundamental.

There is no questioning the beauty of a good photograph. However, aside from the difficulties in finding the right photograph, a drawing brings an added value through the interpretation of a person or event, often summarising concepts that are otherwise difficult to express. The illustrations on these pages, like many others in this book, are the work of Fabiano Spera.

1. 3. Pages from *Smoking* magazine, the first with an article dedicated to the mythical Humphrey Bogart and his ever-present cigarette.

262

1.

2.

3.

1.

2.

3.

4.

1. 4. Pages from
Smoking.
Four variations on the
theme of the
telephone.

263

Notes
*This page traces the
evolution of a drawing
based on a very evident
theme. The four
proposals show an
escalation in
communication, where
the concept becomes
increasingly more
dramatic and evident.
Yet, upon closer
inspection, the most
communicative
drawing, that which
best expresses the
concept, is the first
one, in which the
figure's hand is
concealed. Here the
hand may hide some
misdeed and the
reading of the image is
entrusted, with
discretion, to the
reader's imagination. It
intends rather than
manifests; it merely
suggests.
It should come as no
surprise that the editor
selected this image.*

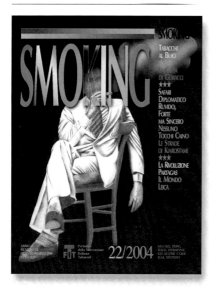

A cover illustration is a work of analysis and synthesis. It must be rooted in the main theme of the issue and clearly communicate its message, opinion and central idea through an image.
The upper text well expresses this concept.

...This time, for the cover we have chosen a drawing by Fabiano Spera: a man with his head between the letters of the word Smoking. To some, he will be the object of hostile thoughts, perhaps for his own good, ignoring his own well being. Yet this has nothing to do with him; he has learned to live also with this strange and petulant way of thinking about the issue of health. The darkness that surrounds him is not that of some clandestine act, but instead a space of calm and reflection, a reflection on the fact that in the darkness, the heaviest and darkest, it is possible to do many things, but not to smoke. Regarding the cover, we, who watched the magazine grow, are amazed to look at the collection of issues published so far. This is the twenty-second issue and, while it is not up to us to judge our work, it is significant that the wager made some time ago has proven a winner: dedicating a magazine to a love for the taste and joys of a good smoke. We worked as amateurs, with few means, with the passion of volunteers and without the coldness of mercenaries. To look at it today, the work completed thus far, compared to other similar experiences around the world, we believe perhaps we could have done better, but what we have done is not so bad. Davide Giacalone, presentation of issue number 22, February 2004.

On these pages: the cover of issue n. 22 and some of the people who animated the magazine.

264

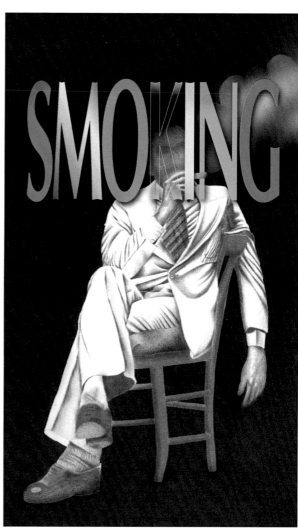

266

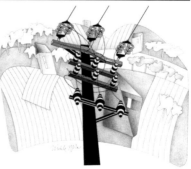

Michele Spera and Alessandro Cecchi Paone, *I luoghi del perduto*, Florence, 2014, Cisl/FNP
In a series of 40 drawings, Michele Spera interprets the irreversible and dramatic modifications of the landscape, and the painful neglect of the environment in Italy.
It is an intense work designed to raise awareness about the heritage of landscapes marred by wind farms, solar farms, horrendous constructions, widespread daily illegal activity and hydrogeological disasters that devastate sites charged with poignant beauty.
A synonym for the precarious state of our towns and villages are the shoring, the reinforcements and supports beneath homes, as if protecting them against the looming threat of some maritime leviathan that swallows and destroys everything. The drawings juxtapose landscapes of soft hills and fairytale villages, in tenuous pastel colour,s against unsettling and delirious visions of a destructive reality, collapsing homes, jungles of steel and *cheval de frise*, dark panels with no sun, barriers that keep out all hopes. This alternation of images reveals Michele's recognisable graphic style, in which a strong geometry is intelligently and measuredly integrated in an ordered structure and a sense of wonder offers us a vision of the world.

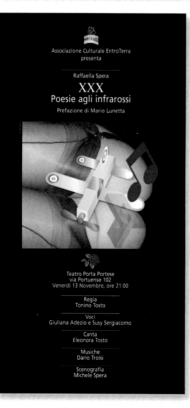

Notes
Posters for the
presentation
of the book by
Raffaella Spera,
XXX Poesie agli
infrarossi,
Casarsa Editore

A Book and
An Exhibition

*Emigranti di poppa,
emigranti di prua*

Welcome to *Emigranti di poppa, emigranti di prua*, a new book in which the unmistakable signs of Michele Spera and the texts by his sister Raffaella overlap drawings by their grandchildren Giorgio and Michele Jr, to offer us a joint reflection on the most dramatic and inescapable topic of our time.

A double welcome, because in this pleasing and unsettling book, the co-presence of generations represents a passing of the torch from a mature and recognised graphic designer and an author to their artistic heirs, making their debut.

Two masters who, skilled by years of experience, desublimate the theme of emigration by rendering it aesthetic; two heirs who, rendered sincere by infancy, offer a tragic reading of this theme without any mediations or solutions. And we know that what is "tragic" is such because it is necessary and yet impossible. Today, seven hundred million people, equivalent to 10% of the world's population, wish to emigrate from their homeland. Many wish to come above all to Europe. This need is in part created by the centrifugal force exercised by misery, unemployment, dictatorships, wars, and in part by the centripetal force

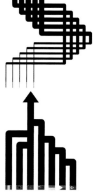

Notes   269
Michele Spera
Raffaella Spera
*Emigranti di poppa,
emigranti di prua*
Preface by
Domenico De Masi
Gangemi Editore
Testimonials by:
Rosario Altieri /
Massimo Barra / Enzo
Bianco / Alessandro
Cecchi Paone /
Arianna De Biasi /
Domenico De Masi /
Stefano Folli / Fabrizio
Gatti / Mario Lunetta /
Giuseppe Marchetti
Tricamo / Riccardo
Noury / Antonio
Scurati

exercised by the wellbeing of rich nations, including ours, rendered so evident and attractive by mass media.
Of the 196 nations of the international chessboard, Italy has the eighth highest Gross National Product.
On average each Italian earns approximately 36,000 dollars, compared to the 7,000 earned in China and 1,500 in India.
The entire Planet is crisscrossed by endless flows of populations moving from central to coastal regions, from mountainous areas to flatlands, from war-torn nations to those at peace, from poor to opulent countries.

And we, whether we like to admit it or not, are a wealthy country in a very wealthy continent.
Yet emigration occurs not only when there is an awareness of one's poverty and the material and intellectual wealth of others.
People also flee when violence becomes intolerable, or when technological progress expels masses of manual labour from job markets, or when nations such as ours, with an aging population, attract a younger workforce from younger nations [...].
Domenico De Masi

270

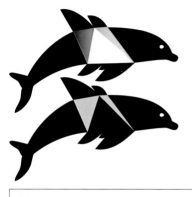

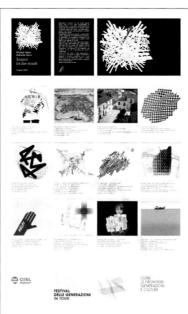

Notes
Organise an exhibition of your term work. Establish the dimensions and sequence of materials. Contact a printer to discuss the resolution of the files for digital printing. Study the supports and their layout in the exhibition space.

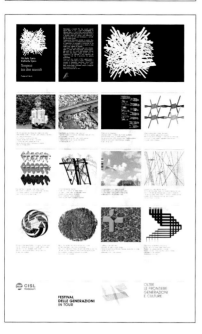
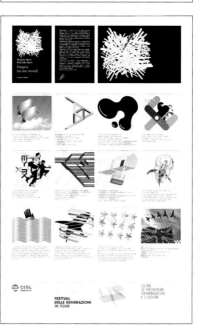

19.
Calendars

2002 Calendar
A Succession of Numbers, Animated by Time

In this calendar numbers overlap one another in succession from month to month to create a new image, similar to an animation. To reinforce the identity of the month, the corresponding number is added to the same number, reduced by 50% and using a different colour.

Notes
Designed for a typographer, Fernando Begliomini, beyond its inventive graphics this series of calendars stands out for the quality of the printing. Precisely because it was produced by the client, the obsessive attention by Begliomini during the phase of printing makes for an extraordinary example of technical perfection.

Notes
The study of the design
of the numbers for the
2002 calendar. The
construction of a grid
consisting of 60 circles,
6 horizontal and 10
vertical.
The grid was used to
test diverse solutions
for each number.

These pages show
experiments with the
sequence of movement
of the numbers.
The first runs from the
number 1 to the
number 12; the second
from 12 to 1.
The second sequence
was selected.

274

Notes
*From the work in
progress shown here,
the most captivating
page is December,
where the succession of
numbers is completed,
giving the calendar a
unique look.*

GEPI calendar about Southern Italy.
It marries the faces of farmers with images of technological equipment.

275

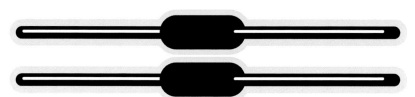

2003 Calendar

The Entropy of Objects

The Stubbornness of Invention

The house in Piazza dell'Orologio, located exactly below the tower designed by Borromini, was furnished entirely with items made from long and thin strips of wood, assembled with the stubbornness of invention.
The table, the bed, the wardrobe that functioned as a screen, chairs cobbled together from an infinite number of small pieces of wood cut according to logarithmic dimensions, glued together, fastened with screws and jointed.
These were our perfect pieces of furniture. Improbable sculptures to be inhabited and experienced.
These artefacts were created in natural wood, though a few lozenge-shaped pieces and a few inserts were painted in bright colours like the light signals of a Morse code alphabet.
This was the season of poetry, of invention. The carpenter's shop was transformed over time into a workshop of images.

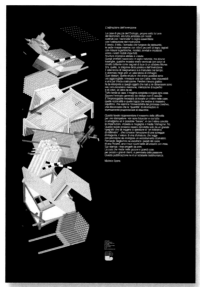

Notes
This calendar, as better explained in the text, uses technical drawings of objects made from wood and graphically assembled in a series of overlapping images.

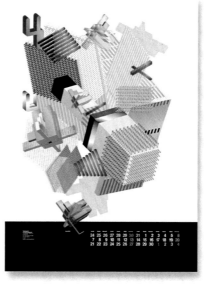

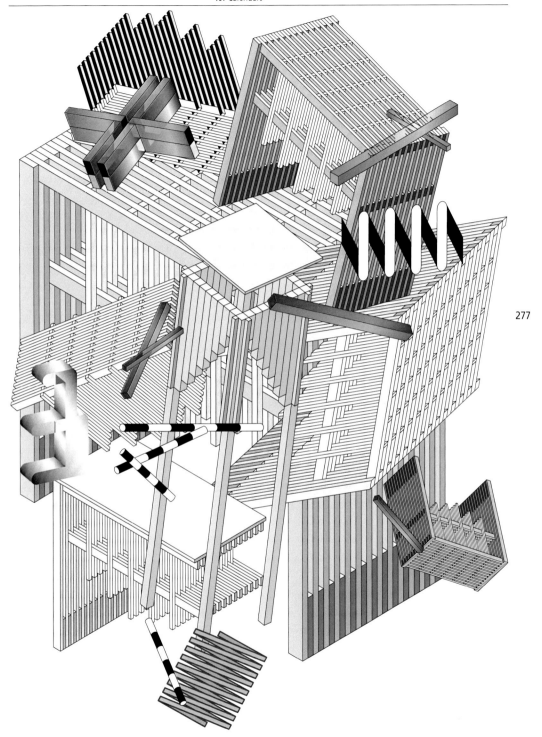

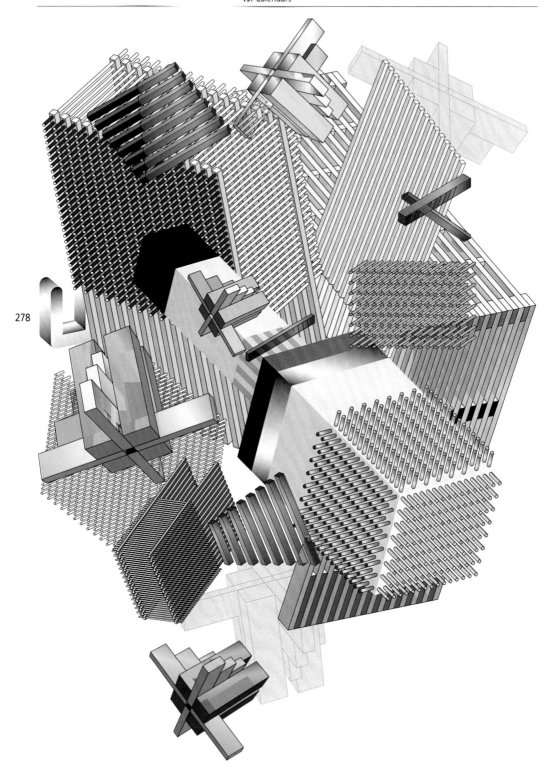

Those drawings, those structures that were once possible are now knotted together, woven into one another, impossible to use for even the most timid of constructions. Because the work of the graphic designer is to be an interpreter of objects that, born in three dimensions, are now visual communication, the interaction of surfaces and colours, something other than what they were.

Everything tends toward chaos, the magma absorbs and swallows everything. Yet the entropy generated by the drawings is not casual.

There is a pressing need to find an order in objects, the rationale and the logic that evolves into the most correct equilibrium, which expresses the irreversibility of the creative process, which refuses to accept that the "quantity" of information is inversely proportional to a lack of order.

These drawings present the maximum challenges faced by a printer: they are not colour transparencies in which everything is amalgamated and where is possible to "cheat", or where a halftone corrects eventual imperfections and errors or mediates an image. No. These drawings can only be printed by a very talented printer with an ability to see "a thousandth of a millimetre", who is familiar with the emotion generated by a sliver of magenta, the value of a fade, who reads colour combinations with the precision of a watchmaker.

Fernando Begliomini knows how to listen to the heartbeats of a Roland or, better yet, his heart beats at the same rhythm. He has been printing my projects for years. The attention he pays to small and large details, to small and large clients, is infused with passion.

This publication is a striking example.

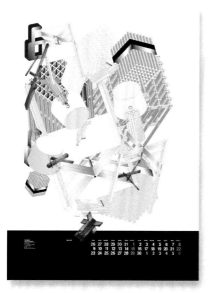

Notes
The drawings of the objects reproduced in this calendar are taken from studies for furniture items designed by the author in the 1970s. Some, protected by copyright, were later manufactured.

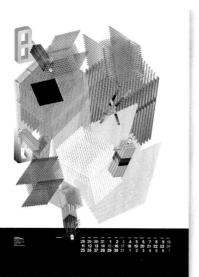

2004 Calendar

Numbers Treated Like Three-Dimensional Objects

1. The cover of this calendar and the pages for the months of January, March and April. To the side is the text that accompanied the calendar.

2. The numbers designed for the calendar in thier primary form. Translated into three dimensions, each can be broken down and reassembled, like a puzzle.

The numbers succeed one another in a line. Each time a new one is added, the number becomes larger, in a succession stretching to infinity. The numbers are placed in order, or better yet, they constitute the archetype of order. As far as I know, we will never find a "final number", but only a first one. The numbers have two faces: the ordinal and the cardinal. The first orders, the second measures.

The ordinals indicate the order in which the numbers are arranged (first, second, third), the cardinals indicate the quantities (1, 2, 3, etc.). The numbers are divided by categories. The units: one, two, three, four, up to zero; the sets of ten: ten, twenty, etc.; followed by hundreds, thousands millions, billions and trillions. The values are special signs that can represent all numbers. They are the Arab numerals from 0 to 9.

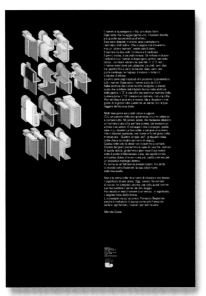

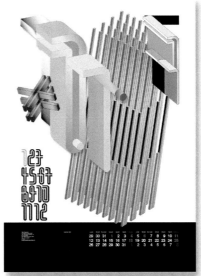

Notes
Returning to the page with the agenda of the Graduate Course in Industrial Design, we find two numbers, the 3 and the 4. Partially studied for this specific project, these numbers were used again and redesigned one year later in a more complete manner, generating a specific lexicon, a complete set, from zero to nine.

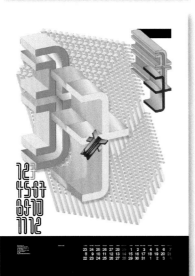

1.

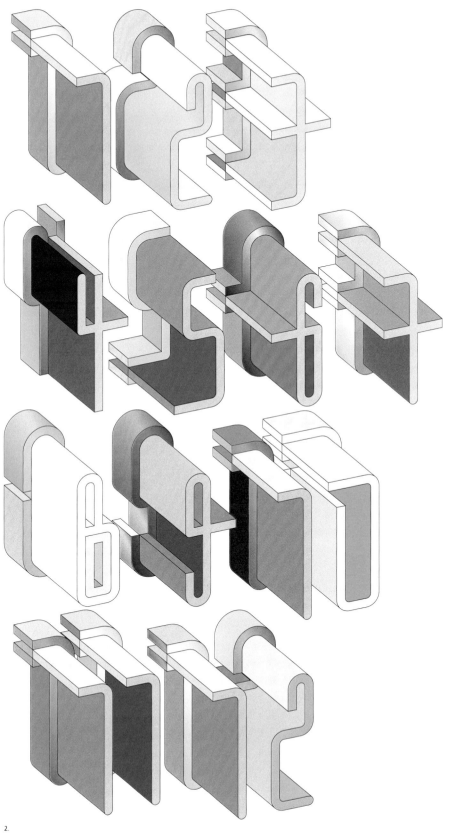

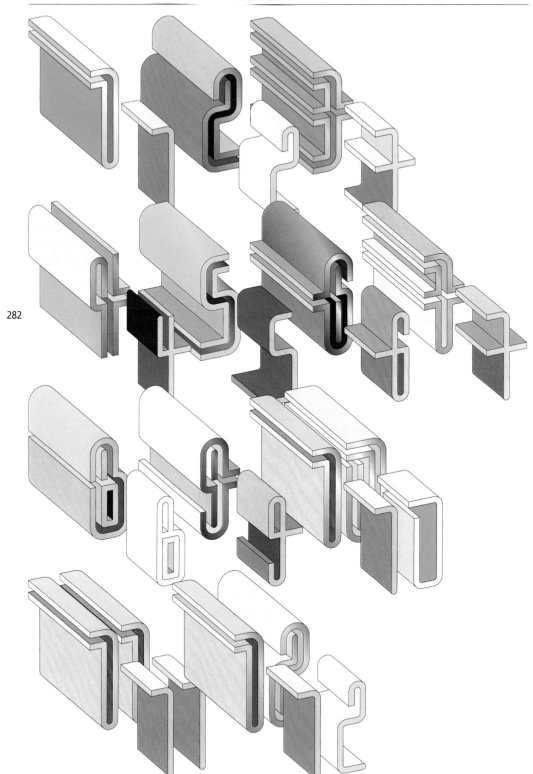

282

When writing, numbers have the same role as the letters of the alphabet in the writing of words. The "3" is a figure but also a number in the series. The "13" is instead a number, and not a figure.

This may seem anonymous and annoying. But if I go back over my days of childhood, all of this has some meaning, and contains a story.

I spent many dark and gloomy days. There was a time in my childhood when I had to count everything. At the time, I believed it was enough to whisper a number or a figure to create a poem, to evoke some beloved or a friend. I even managed to taint my companions. That night we stayed up late, seeking a number that spoke to us of something, similar to a game of blind man's bluff.

"Four, five, six!", we yelled into the clear night of our youth. That night the only thing we were unable to count were the stars.

Excited by this game, we looked for Luca's house among the street numbers, yelling his name at the top of our lungs beneath Montereale. Luca, with his black hair and gentle smile, who was no longer with us, departed undoubtedly toward some dark future.

It was as if I had been struck by a thunderbolt, though I felt, and I remember it as though it were yesterday, his gentle hand on my shoulders.

It was not the first time I sought to understand the significance of this event. Today, grey with age, I drew these numbers once again to avoid losing the sense of my travels. In them I sought the sounds of the past, a meaning, perhaps the secret of harmony.

I now consign them to a friend, Fernando Begliomini, so that he will multiply them and print them as only Fernando knows how: he has all the right "numbers" to bring them to life.

283

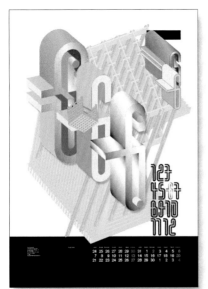

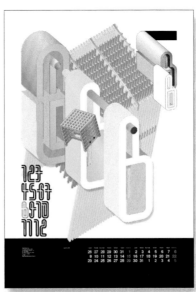

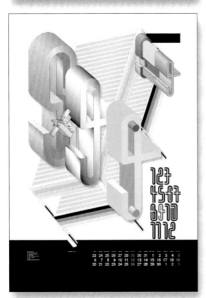

2005 Calendar

Numbers Amalgamated in Textures

1. A stylised page, printed in various colours, chromatically intersects, overlaps and merges with the numbers of each month, provoking other chromatic experiences and painterly effects. The theme of this calendar is illustrated in the text found on the following pages.

2. The number of the month is repeated five times in the foreground and five times in the background, until it grows so small as to become illegible. At each repetition the number is reduced by 50%, and given a different colour.

Notes
Like the others, this calendar is also constructed using a progression of numbers, though this time they are overlapped and reduced each time by 50%.

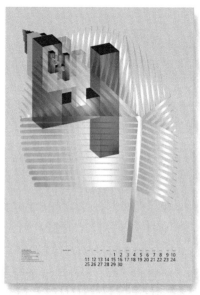

1.

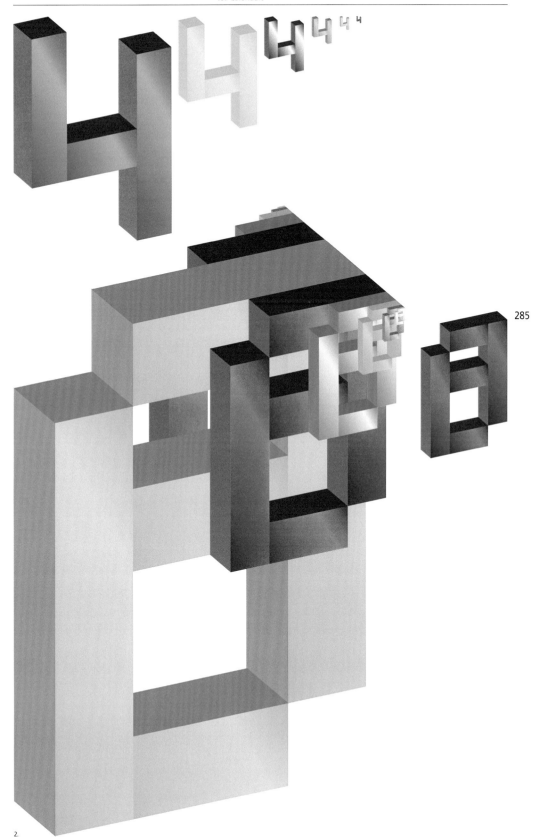

2.

Calendars are made of numbers, unavoidable signs of the passing of time. But other numbers, tragic ones, mark the conditions of our planet.

The world's population is growing exponentially: in 1950 we were 2.5 billion, in 2050 we will be almost 9 billion.

The average life expectancy is 67 years, a number that drops to 53 in Africa and rises to 88 in Japan.

Twenty percent of the world's population lives in developed nations that consume 53% of the world's energy, eat 44% of the world's meat and possess 80% of the vehicles on the Planet.

A North American consumes 590 litres of water per day, an Italian 320. In China this number is 88 and in Africa 12.

One out of every seven people on the Planet is undernourished; one out of six does not have access to potable water; one out of five does not attend school and is unable to read and write; 19% of children work.

Twenty-four percent of all mammals, 12% of birds and 30% of all fish are threatened by extinction. Fifty percent of the world's mangrove forests have disappeared. Rain forests are reduced by 15 million hectares per year, in other words, twice the area of Ireland.

It was while flipping through pages and pages of these numbers that from one of them a note, a sign fell out: a colourful leaf, which accompanies the seasons, a sign of a possible vindication, a message of the urgency for sustainable development.

In my youth I spent a great deal of time in smoky print shops. Entering into those subterranean spaces was like dropping down into a mine. You were supposed to wear "smock", similar to that used by my father in the early 1900s when he rode on coal powered trains.

It was like reliving the world of *The Citadel* or *The Stars Look Down* by A.J. Cronin.

286

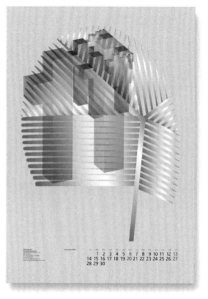

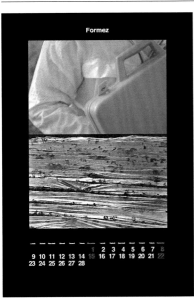

A calendar for Formez, the *Formazione per il Mezzogiorno* (Training for Southern Italy). It marries Southern Italian landscapes with colour photographs of technological devices.

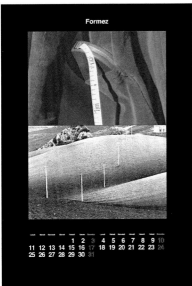

287

Calendars for a Women's Lingerie Shop and a Calendar for Callegari & Ghigi

A promotional calendar for a women's lingerie shop.
A photographic reportage and a text by Alberto Bevilacqua.

On the facing page is the calendar for Callegari & Ghigi.

289

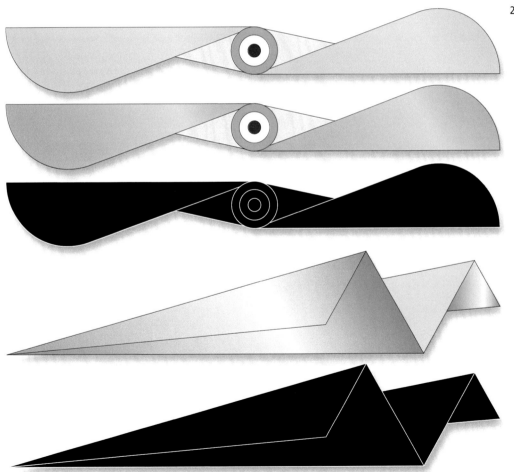

2006 Calendar

Numbers Amalgamated in Textures

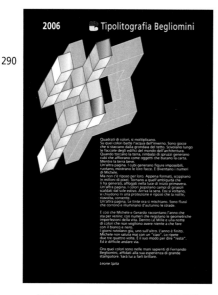

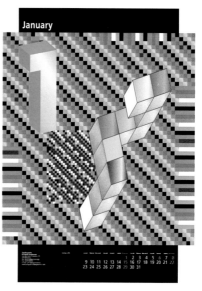

Notes
This calendar was created using all the various styles of the Avant Garde typeface. Elaborated in three dimensions, it accompanies the pages of each month.

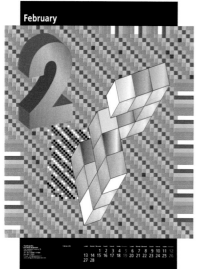

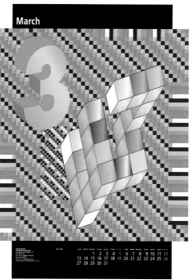

A multiplication of coloured squares. Colours beaten by the waters of the winter. Drops that fall from gutters. That move along the elevations of buildings in the world of architecture. When they touch the ground, splashes create cubes that flower into objects that break the surface of the page. While the earth drinks. Another page. The cubes generate impossible figures, they rotate, to show their faces.

And they become Michele's numbers. Yet there is no rest for them. As soon as they form, they explode into a million pixels. They return to the ambiguity that generated them, drowned in the light of early spring. Another page. The colours populate fields of sunflowers warmed by the summer sun. Evening falls. They turn, they close to protect themselves and rest, actions consented by the coming of the night.

Another page. Here the colours blend together. They are flows that run and illuminate the streets in autumn. This is how Michele and Gerardo recount th year to come: with numbers that regulate the geometric imperfections of life. In the midst of the Thousand and One Nights of colours that wish to have nothing to do with the world of black and white. The days slip away, one after the other.

The year is over. Michele never says goodbye with a simple "ciao". He repeats it two, three or four times. It is his way of saying "stay". It is difficult to leave. These colours are now in the skilled hands of Fernando Begliomini, entrusted to his experience as a great printer. He will bring them to life.
Leone Spita

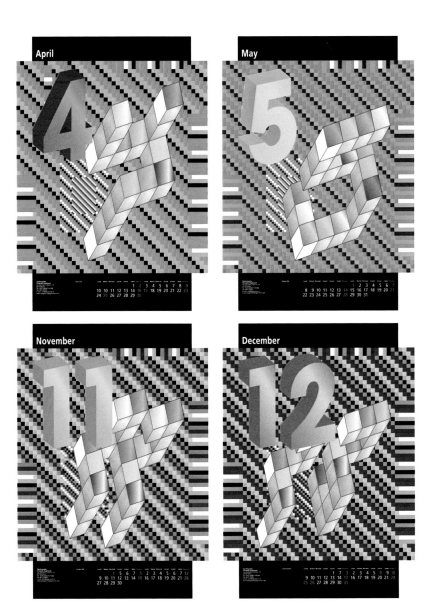

2007 Calendar

Graphics
and Illustration

It used to be said that life is like a waltz. Perhaps because no other dance is as intense, fast and rhythmic as the waltz, with its whirlwind turns.
Just like life.
For a moment there is a harmonious rhythm and then, suddenly, everything stops and we remain suspended for an instant, before the rhythm returns and we turn and turn in a room of endless dimensions.
Precisely like the space of life, which alternates moments of magical harmony with a whirling turbine of events.

Over years and years we sew, we build and reap in a seesaw of measured and calculated steps. And now that plans have been well made we can justly demand the proper respect for our good name.
Even more worthy, in this enthusiastic and fantastic ascension, is the insertion of one's children with the precision and tenacity of those familiar with the rhythm, the music to be followed, the proper notes.
In a world that appears constantly on the brink of catastrophe there are those, like Fernando

Begliomini, who counted the fertile years of his labours and recognise that forty years have not passed in vain.
There is no doubt he is old and tired, but the experience acquired becomes the skills of a master for new arrivals, and the faces around us soften and motivate so much fatigue.
Forty years become a new beginning for a new generation. And the saga continues and the dances begin again.
Rosalba Galli

Notes
This calendar combines a powerful graphic of background textures with playful images of dancing figures.
The drawings are the work of Fabiano Spera.

0123456789 0

June 2007

October 2007

November 2007

December 2007

Notes 293
*Above is the study of
the numbers designed
to match the gestures
and freshness of the
drawings by Fabiano
Spera.*

2008 Calendar

Three Dimensions, Pictograms and Striped Numbers

Art is beauty, wonder, synthesis and system. Michele Spera is an artist. A great artist, who each year gifts his friends with the wonder of beauty in the form of a calendar that is both synthesis and system. Spera has chosen this apparently simple, daily and domestic instrument to induce us to follow him through a 365-day long seminar in which the lessons are entrusted to images. The monographic theme is selected year by year based on the unavoidable attraction of crucial issues.

Order and chaos, the face of numbers, the urgency of sustainability and the waltz of life are the *leitmotif* of these calendars-seminars with which, in recent years, Michele has attempted to educate us about awareness and happiness.

For 2008 he decided to ask us to meditate month by month, day by day, on the fecund and cruel universe of communication, with all of its armament of atoms and bits, celluloids and pixels, connections and gaps, ethers and cables, planets and universes. And, as a key to understanding, he presents us with colours and symbols, metaphors and images.

Keats stated that a work of art is a joy created for eternity. Even this 2008 calendar is a work of art that will last more than 365 days. At the end of the year, in fact, no one will have the courage to throw away a similar masterpiece of geometric emotion.

However art, other than being beauty and wonder, is also synthesis and system. Behind every great artist is the fantasy of the inspiring muse and the seductive critic, but there is also the concreteness of the farsighted patron and the entrepreneurial gallery owner. In our case, there is the intelligence of a great printer – Fernando Begliomini – who each year confirms Spera's graphic art through the art of typography. Without the one, the other could not come to life, the word could not be made flesh, and fantasy could not become reality. Herman Melville put the following words of pride in the mouth of the main character in *Moby Dick*: "I like to take in hand none but clean, virgin, fair-and-square mathematical jobs, something that regularly begins at the beginning, and is at the middle when midway, and comes to an end at the conclusion". The same could be said by Spera of Begliomini. And by me of both.

Domenico De Masi

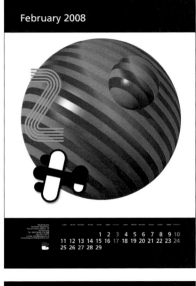

1234567 8910 1112

May 2008

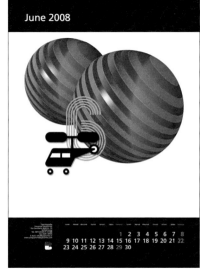

June 2008

Notes
*Above is the study of the numbers for the 2008 calendar.
They are designed in stripes to avoid excessive interference with the graphics beneath them.*

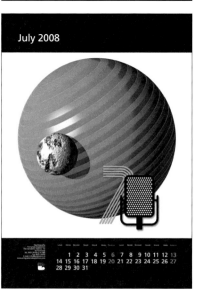

July 2008

August 2008

2012 Calendar

Never

Never

"I love soft verbs, / rich with different shades. / Ambiguous, chameleonic, / windows on airy landscapes. / I love them for the intolerances of misuse / of others. / Intransigent, penalising, / the verbs of definitions".
Speaking of words in this manner, through her poems the poet Barbara De Luca enriches this calendar with even more precious emotions.

But the same could be said of the words: as soft as clouds and warmth, or hard like a blade and ice.
The same could be said of lines: as free and sensual as the curve, or as hard and inflexible as a straight line. There are times for transversal sentiments, blurred and accommodating; there are times for sharp, clear and intransigent sentiments.
Michele and Gerardo made a good choice when they selected the word NEVER for this 2012 calendar: it leaves no room for choice nor offers any shortcuts.

It is not a time of half measures when the number of the elderly surpasses the number of children; when technology forces us to reformulate our categories of space and time each day; when economics replaces politics and finance replaces the economics; when the confines between beautiful and ugly are blurred, like those between good and bad, true and false, living and dead. The time has come to say NEVER.

Notes
The 2012 calendar features drawings by Michele and Fabiano Spera.
The calendar uses the Didot typeface.

Never waste, never alienate, never war, never excesses, never acts of self harm. To express this intransigence, Michele and Gerardo have once again opted for beauty adding this new calendar to those of the past to create an amorous and irrenunciable garland. Yet they could not draw each year on the vertexes of their clean and surprising style without the ancient art of the litho printing of Fernando Begliomini: skilled hands, ready to create stunning ideas.

The word NEVER well suits the exclamation mark, and their calendar, with the drawings of Michele and Fabiano Spera, is filled to the brim with exclamation marks. To which I add another one, after the word *thank you*!

Domenico De Masi

ABCD EFGHILMN WXY

Never kill again!

PINO CHET

298

January 2012

Tipolitografia
Fernando Begliomini
Via Gerolamo Adorno, 55
00154 Roma
Tel. 06/5126444.5141488
Fax 06/5139959

2   3
9 10
16 17 1
23 24 25
30 31

Notes
Design the page of a calendar to be printed in a very large format using silhouettes that exalt its visual impact.

Calendar AGCI

2014, Women's Coordination Group of the AGCI, the General Association of Italian Cooperatives

The 2014 calendar for the *Coordinamento Donne* of the AGCI and the *Alleanza delle Cooperative Italiane.* To the right is the phrase by Giuseppe Mazzini dedicated to women used on the cover.

"I consider women to be better than men. I consider you more given to pity and less calculating by nature: when you are so, it is our fault, it is the fault of the education you are given and the way in which society is organised around you, an organisation that depends entirely on us men."
Giuseppe Mazzini
29 June 1837

Notes
Pick a theme for a new year and construct a calendar in a 140x210 mm format.
12 pages + a cover.
Black metal spiral binding.

I CONSIDER WOMEN TO BE BETTER THAN MEN. I CONSIDER YOU MORE GIVEN TO PITY AND LESS CALCULATING BY NATURE: WHEN YOU ARE SO, IT IS OUR FAULT, IT IS THE FAULT OF THE EDUCATION YOU ARE GIVEN AND THE WAY IN WHICH SOCIETY IS ORGANISED AROUND YOU, AN ORGANISATION THAT DEPENDS ENTIRELY ON US MEN.
Giuseppe Mazzini
29 JUNE 1837

Calendar GEPI

1976 With a Zero Budget

A calendar designed for GEPI, *Gestione e partecipazioni statali* in 1976, with the intention to reduce business costs. With a zero budget GEPI suggested reducing small and useless daily expenses.

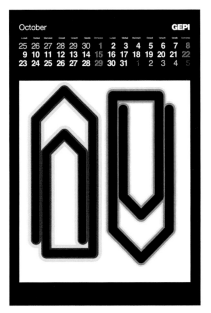

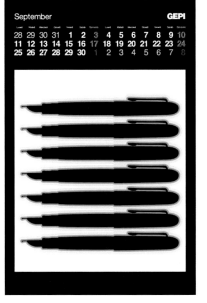

2016 Calendar

A Collection of the Best Magazine Covers from the Previous Year

302

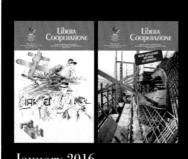

January 2016

L	M	M	G	V	S	D
				1	2	3
4	5	6	7	8	9	10
11	12	13	14	15	16	17
18	19	20	21	22	23	24
25	26	27	28	29	30	31

AGCI
ASSOCIAZIONE
GENERALE
COOPERATIVE
ITALIANE

June 2016

L	M	M	G	V	S	D
		1	2	3	4	5
6	7	8	9	10	11	12
13	14	15	16	17	18	19
20	21	22	23	24	25	26
27	28	29	30			

AGCI
ASSOCIAZIONE
GENERALE
COOPERATIVE
ITALIANE

Notes
The theme for the calendar for this new year is to construct a collection of your best work from the past year.
Use the 140x210 mm format.
12 pages + a cover.
Black metal spiral binding.

Unify
Your best works can be freely selected but they must be coordinated. The alternative is to insert 12 elements from one single project.

March 2016

L	M	M	G	V	S	D
	1	2	3	4	5	6
7	8	9	10	11	12	13
14	15	16	17	18	19	20
21	22	23	24	25	26	27
28	29	30	31			

AGCI
ASSOCIAZIONE
GENERALE
COOPERATIVE
ITALIANE

November 2016

L	M	M	G	V	S	D
	1	2	3	4	5	6
7	8	9	10	11	12	13
14	15	16	17	18	19	20
21	22	23	24	25	26	27
28	29	30				

AGCI
ASSOCIAZIONE
GENERALE
COOPERATIVE
ITALIANE

20.
Laying Out
This Book

A Methodology
On Every Page

1. 4. The format of this book is 160x240 mm. The grid is based on the use of the golden section.
It begins with the principle that the golden rectangle can be created by drawing a square, dividing it into two parts and tracing a diagonal of one of these parts, then raising the diagonal along the vertical axis to obtain the height of the golden rectangle.

Or, beginning with a base of 136 mm, multiplied by 1.618 to obtain a height of 220.048, which we can round down to 220.

The inner grid on each page measures 136x220 mm, with a margin of 12 mm at the binding and outer edges and footer, while the upper margin is 8 mm because the golden section includes the header.
Having identified the need for a separation between the space reserved for images and that for text, captions and titles, a space was set aside at the top of the page to allow for a 12 mm margin on four sides of the page.

The entire book is laid out in Frutiger. This typeface was selected not only because it was considered most coherent with the graphic design of the book, but also to allow other typeface families to serve as examples. It is used in bold (main titles); in its light version (secondary titles and subtitled); and in its regular version (for the main bodies of text).

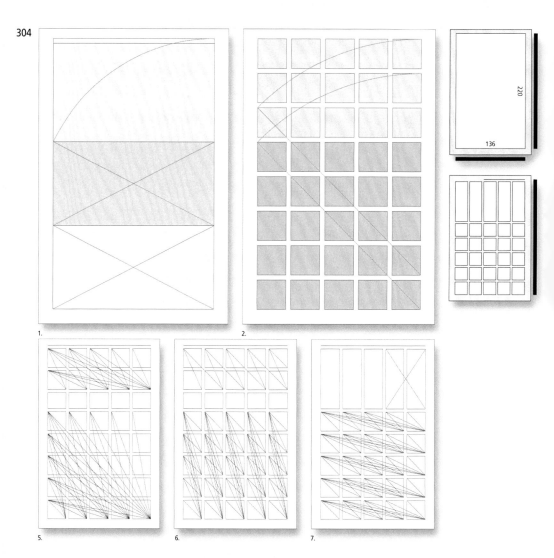

1.

2.

220

136

5.

6.

7.

5. 7. The illustrations show only a few of the many possible ways to fill the grid and ensure a rigid though animated layout.
8. 10. The position of texts within the grid: in one, two, three, four and five columns.

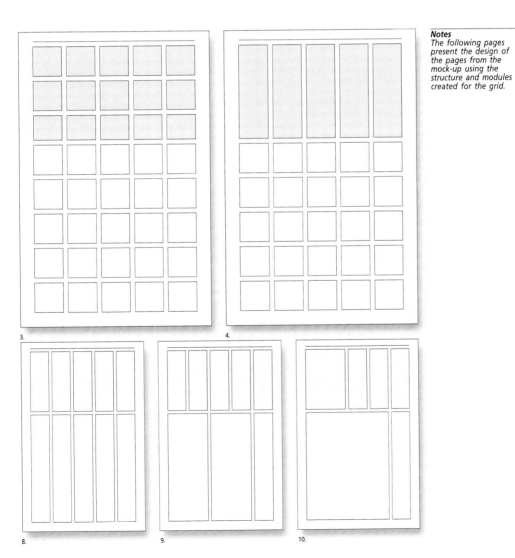

3.

4.

8.

9.

10.

Notes
The following pages present the design of the pages from the mock-up using the structure and modules created for the grid.

305

The book was laid out using a variety of solutions that, while rigorously respecting the grid, offer a reading of references and connections.
It is not a book to be read from front to back.
In fact, it offers three levels of reading:
a first level occupies the space of two horizontal modules with a total width of 52 mm;
this text, composed in Frutiger with a size and leading of 8.5, is the main text and almost always introduces the content of the chapter.

The second level is almost didascalic.
It develops in the upper part of the page in Frutiger 6.5 with a leading of 6.5, set in five columns, each 24 mm wide.
It is positioned at the top of the page because, other than captions for the images, as on this page, it develops the issues mentioned in the main text, offering an expansion that serves to better explain the notions presented.

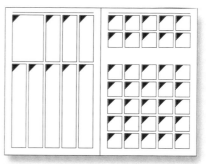

A third level consists of the "Notes", "Workbook" and "Bibliography".
These texts are always presented on the right side of the page.
They are composed in Frutiger Italic 6.5 in a 24 mm wide column.
The notes develops secondary themes, additional connotations, references and suggestions useful for applying the contents of the book.

The images in the book occupy the fixed space of the grid.

306

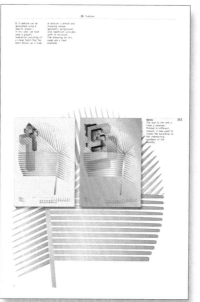

1.

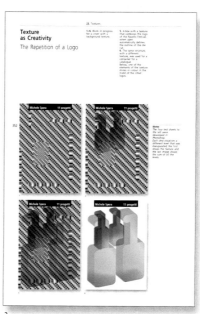

2.

Notes
The pages to the left are from the book you are reading.
They have been reproduced here in a reduced format based on percentages obtained using the indications found in the "Proportions" chapter.
Pages 1, 2, 6 and 7 were reduced by 32.5%; pages 3, 4, 5, 8, 9 and 10 by 20.8%.

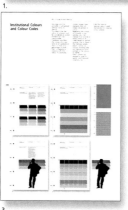

3.

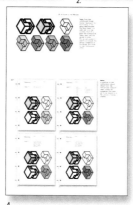

4.

5.

It is based on 25 modules (5x5) and defines a square at the bottom of the page. In many cases, the layout also uses the upper part of the page, identified as "service space", both for requirements of composition and to enrich the pages themselves.

In some cases three images have been laid out in the space of four modules, as in some examples on these pages, allowing us to recover the total height assigned to the space reserved for images.
A header at the top of the page contains the number and title of the chapter.
It is a constant presence on every page that serves to identify the topics explored.

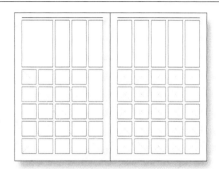

Notes
On the page shown here to the left, each of the logos occupy the space of one main module.
In other cases, as on the page in the lower right, the image occupies all of the available space, while still respecting, as much as possible, the upper and lower spaces.
These are specific cases when the image is of particular importance.

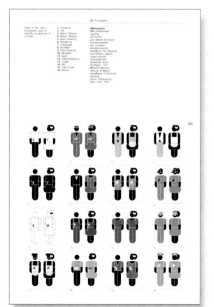

6.

7.

8.

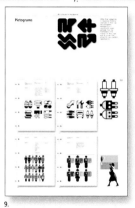

9.

10.

The layout is fully justified in the main text and flush left at all other levels.
This structure is evident not only in the layout of the text, but also in the height of the columns where we have tried, as much as possible and compatible with the needs of the text, to obtain the most harmonious columns.
All of the texts are condensed by 90% to obtain, often in the justification of a module, the least possible number of turns.

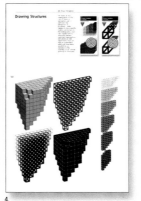

Notes
The pages shown to the left are from the book you are reading. They have been reproduced here in a reduced format based on percentages obtained using the indications found in the "Proportions" chapter. Pages 1, 2, 6 and 7 were reduced by 32.5%; pages 3, 4, 5, 8, 9 and 10 by 20.8%.

1.

2.

3.

4.

5.

The turns of flush left text were often corrected by seeking a ratio between the rows of text and their syntax.
In other words, an attempt was made to ensure a coincidence, as much as possible, between the flush left justification and the division of the rows of text.
This is "intelligent" flush left justification. It is less casual than the turns automatically created by word processing and publishing software.

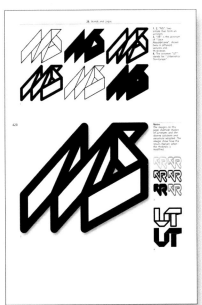

Notes
In the second edition of the book, printed in 4 colours, some of the pages were maintained in the original black. The chromatic alternation, beyond the needs of representation, also favours a variegated reading and a visual rhythm.

1.

2.

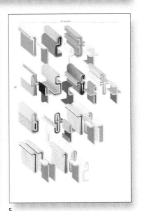

3.

4.

5.

The Grids

The Measurements of the Vertical and Horizontal Axes

1./4. In desktop publishing software, the grids for texts and illustrations are designed by providing not only the measurements of the base and height, but also their position with respect to the page margins. These values are expressed as the distance of each cage from the left margin (x) and the upper margin (y). A grid positioned 12 mm from the left margin and 12 mm from the upper margin will have the coordinates x=12, y=12.

When beginning a project, it is worthwhile reconstructing this type of grid using Cartesian coordinates and thus the values of the horizontal (x) and vertical (y) axes. Each variation on this theme will give us the positions of the cages ready for use, with the advantage of transferring precise mathematical information to anyone working on the project regarding any possible position.

310

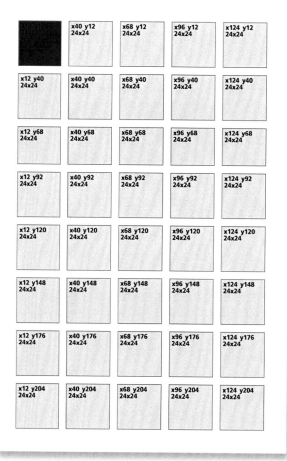

1.

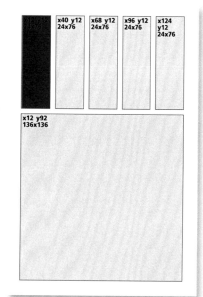

2.

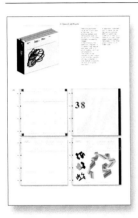
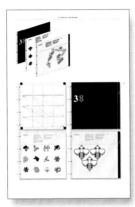

We can now insert the project in a mock-up structure designed using mathematical coordinates at a ratio of 1/1. The science inherent to the study of the grid offers both a useful service and the formal coordinates of an analytically well studied layout.

311

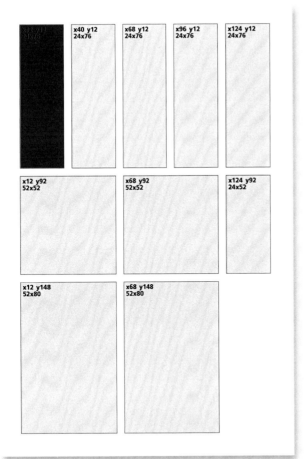

3.

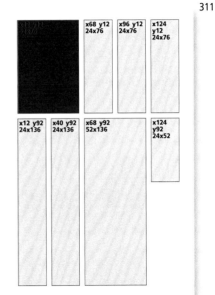

4.

21.
Stationery

Formats
and Templates

1. Letterhead paper is generally UNI A4, 210x297 mm. Considering that UNI formats are obtained by constructing a square whose height is equivalent to the diagonal raised in the vertical with respect to the base of the square, we can draw a first module of 210x97 mm, and a second module of 210x200 mm. The line of separation once again gives us the ratio of 5/7, which is the fractional relationship between the two areas.

The ratios of margins is 1, 2, 3 and 4. In our case they are 10 mm at the top, 20 at the outer edge, 30 and the binding edge and 40 at the bottom. Obviously, they can vary based on different requirements. We have now identified the useful grid. The line of separation identifies the point where the paper can be folded and inserted in an envelope.

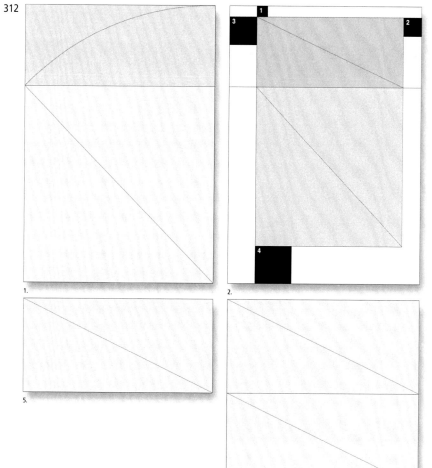

1.

2.

5.

6.

Notes
In the example shown here, the margins are 10, 20, 30 and 40 mm. Obviously, they can be modified, so long as the proportions are maintained, and the binding edge margin is not less than 25 mm.

A horizontal line placed 97 mm from the top of the page facilitates this operation.
3. On this page of letterhead we obtained a first module of 210x97 mm and a second module of 210x200.
The first module can ideally be divided by two to obtain two spaces: the first of these spaces contains the company name, brand or logo, address, etc.; the second can be used for various commercial references, if necessary, and the address of the recipient.

4. We consider the lines of separation between the spaces as ideal lines.
They can also be printed.
These horizontal lines can be assigned different thicknesses: 0.3 points to the line that divides the first two zones; 0.6 to that which separates the institutional space from that designed to contain the text of the letter.

5. 6. The first module of the letter is equal to 210x97 mm;
the second measures 210x200 mm.

7. 8. A half page generally serves for short notes.
It measures 210 mm in width by 200 mm in height.
The construction of the grid of the second sheet repeats th same structure found on the letterhead.

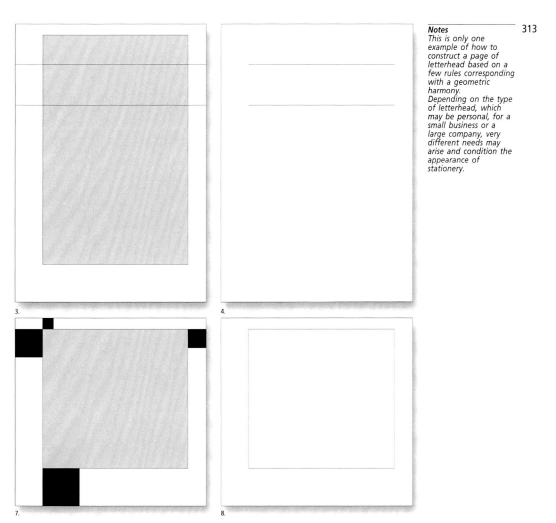

3.

4.

7.

8.

Notes   313
This is only one example of how to construct a page of letterhead based on a few rules corresponding with a geometric harmony.
Depending on the type of letterhead, which may be personal, for a small business or a large company, very different needs may arise and condition the appearance of stationery.

1. Standard letterhead is generally laid out on UNI A4 paper, measuring 210x297 mm. The second line, at 0.6 points, is 97 mm from the upper margin and delimits the space reserved for the brand, company name, addresses, departments and other information. It also helps when the time comes to fold the paper for insertion in an envelope.

The space between the two lines, in standard letterhead, contains the company name to the left, while to the right the point marks the start of the recipient's address line.
This space coincides with the window in a mailing envelope.
A logo printed on this stationery has a base of 48 mm.
It is printed in black, plus the company colour. The company typeface is Helvetica in its regular and bold versions.
The logo is printed in 20/20 size.
The company name and other texts are in 8/8 text.
The text and lines are printed in black.

2. A half sheet is used for short notes.
It measures 210 mm in width by 200 mm in height, which maintains the layout of a UNI A4 page and the folding marks.
The second line divides the page into two perfectly equal parts.

Some letterhead uses an image of the company logo at a large scale, printed lightly and positioned at the beginning of a text area as a background to the text; this offers protection against attempts at counterfeiting.
The colour of the image in the background must be printed at a maximum of 20%, while if it is black this value should be no more than 7%.

2. The folding of the sheet coincides with the thickest line, located 97 millimetres from the upper margin.

314

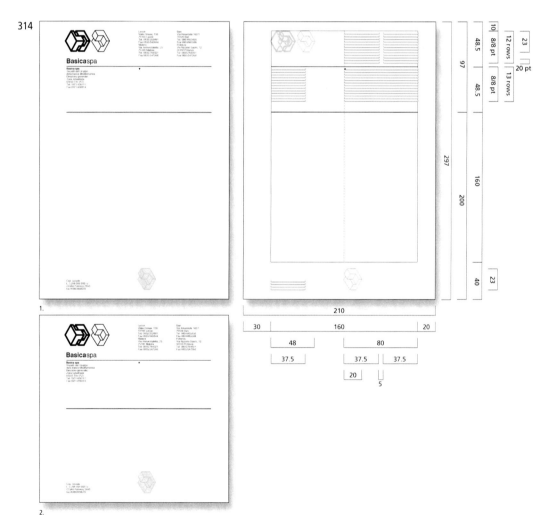

1.

2.

Folding this part of the page gives us the second fold line, brining the bottom margin up to the first fold line.

This automatically divides the page into three parts, with a respective height, from the top, of 97 mm, 100 mm and 100 mm. The uppermost part, shorter than the other two, avoids any problems during folding.

The division of a sheet of letterhead into three modules also facilitates the subdivision of the letter itself into rigorous areas. Each with its own specific role.

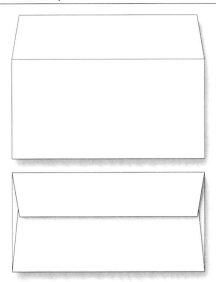

315

Notes
The type of paper used for letterhead varies based on its use and intended recipient.
It is any case important to use the same type of paper for the letterhead and the envelopes.
General stationery can be created using 80 g/m2 paper.
More representative versions can be realised using 90 g Conqueror.

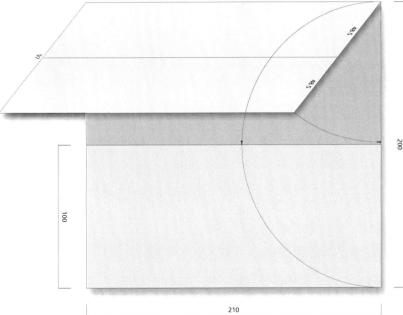

3.

316

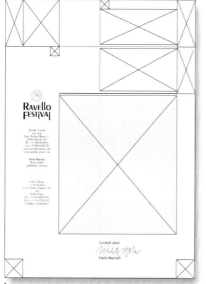

1.

2.

3.

4.

Letterhead and Writing Paper

For Personal Use

1./8. When letterhead is designed for personal rather than corporate use, it is not necessary to design a particular structure that contemplates spaces to be filled using mechanographic processes, nor is it tied to a pre-established use corresponding with windows in mailing envelopes, nor are we forced to provide lines corresponding with the leading of a typewriter.

In this case, it is sufficient to design a proper piece of letterhead using basic rules, correct margins and appropriate measurements.
It is possible to be more creative, and there are less restriction.
The following pages offer a few examples of letterhead that may contain only a logo, a name and an address.

Notes   317
These examples almost always feature a horizontal line corresponding with the folding points of the page: it facilitates the fold and also offers an elegant way to separate the different parts of a letter.

1.

2.

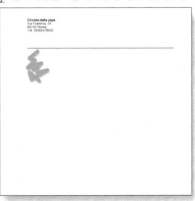

4.

3.

Letterhead
and Writing Paper

For Personal Use

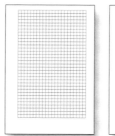 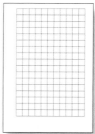

9. Examples of personal letterhead.
The internal grid is modified based on the number of columns inscribed in each module.

318

1.

2.

3.

4.

1. Levin & Schneider's letterhead is an integral part of their corporate identity. It features areas of colour typical of their logo.

1.

Notes
To heighten the quality of a page of letterhead you have designed, use a carefully selected support: the market offers a vast range of top quality papers. Don't use so-called "American embossing", a technique that consists in covering paper with a fine dust that is fixed by heat during printing: while economic, it is of poor quality.
When raised lettering is absolutely necessary, ask that it be realised with a punch. This is much more costly, but undoubtedly of greater effect and elegance. Raised logos are timeless: however, beware of the line weights used in the design of the logo itself.

Letterhead and Writing Paper

Typed Pages

1./3. When designing a page of letterhead, in addition to the company name, address, etc., to be printed in a print shop, it is also necessary to design the space for texts added using a typewriter.

Typed text, like mechanographic text, uses systems of measurement that do not correspond with either typographic measurements (Didot and Pica), or metric decimal measurements. However, all four systems must coexist on a page of letterhead. In fact, the dimensions of the UNI formats are expressed in millimetres, typographic texts in points and Didot or Pica rows, a typewriter uses its own systems, depending upon the type of machine.

The dimensions, based on the space of a letter (the pass), can be of one of the following systems: **Micron**, **Eletto** (Elite), **Pica** (not to be confused with the typographic system of the same name), **Gigante**. The examples on this page use a pass of 1/10 of an inch and a leading of 5 mm.

320

1.

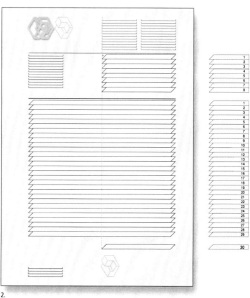

2.

3.

4. Typed text.
Pass of 1/10 of an inch, leading of 5 mm. This measurement has to do with the spaces in which it will be necessary to intervene later (recipient's address, various references, subject of the letter, etc.).

Dear
Prof. Mario Rossi
Via Magenta, 25
0165 Rome, Italy

Notes
In proportional typing, the width of each character is based on multiples of elementary units and corresponds with 0.705 mm (1/36 of an inch).
Wide characters measure 4 elementary units, or 2.82 mm (1/9"); intermediate characters measures 3 units, or 2.117 mm (1/12"); narrow characters 2 units, or 1.41 mm (1/18").

The letterhead is laid out on UNI A4 paper, which measures 210 x 297 mm. It features an upper margin of 10 mm, a left margin of 30 mm, a right margin of 20 mm and a lower margin of 40 mm. The page is ideally divided into three parts: the first, from the top, is 97 mm high; the second and third are both 100 mm. The fold line for the page coincides with a 0.6 point horizontal line located 97 mm from the top of the page.

The first zone is further divided in half by a 0.3 point horizontal line; the first space, for institutional references, contains the company logo and company name and address; the left area of the second space contains and numeric references and the date, while the name of the addressee is to the right. The address is typed by aligning the typewriter with the reference point. There is a reference line that divides the area for text on the letterhead, which coincides with the alignment of the first line of the addressee's name above, and with the space for a signature, below.

The text of the letter is contained in a cage measuring 160x160 mm, which can host 32 rows of typed text at 1/10" and with a leading of 5 mm. Each row contains approximately 64 keystrokes, and the cage can contain a total of 2,000 keystrokes.

For texts longer than 2,000 keystrokes, use a second page.

For very shorttexts it is also possible to use a second page: it contains 10 rows for a total of 600 keystrokes.

The leading of dates and reference codes is the same as that used for the typed text, in order to ensure a constant alignment and uniform spaces for the typewriter.

Yours sincerely,

4.

Business Cards

Formats
and Templates

1. The format of business cards, for ease of use, has been linked to that commonly used for credit and bank cards.
They measure 80 mm in width and 50 mm in height.
The grid is designed with a margin of 5 mm, inside which are various spaces for a logo, company name, the person's name, their title, etc.

A business card is generally printed on 250/300 g/m2 Bristol card. Other types of paper can also be used, for example opaline or Conqueror, Rusticus or Murillo by Fabriano.

322

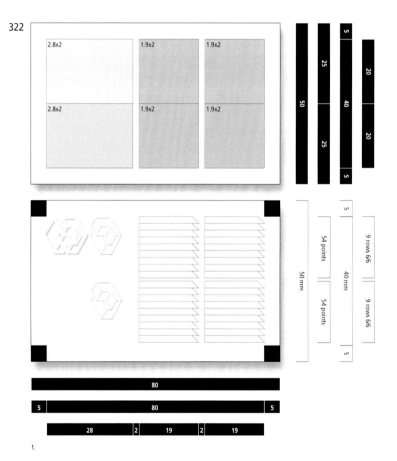

1.

Notes
The grid of a business card is divided into specific zones.
This assists with the positioning of various texts, logos, etc., facilitating the uniform appearance of all business cards.
It will happen that someone will ask to use italics or English only for the president's card: do not give in. Even this business card must be aligned with the general approach of your design, with small changes that may only involve the type of printing, the colour and type of paper.

2./7. As an example, we have chosen to illustrate a complex business card: designing a simple one would be just that, simple.
In this case, the company has various offices, there is a lot of text, the logo is repeated below for each company that is part of the Group, with its own institutional colours.
The typeface is Helvetica 8 with a leading of 8. This is rigorously the same for every text, with the sole variations offered by rounded, italics, regular and bold.

The difference between the business card of someone like the president of a company, and that which serves merely to provide an address, consists solely in the printing of the logo. In the first case it is raised, while in the second case it is printed in black, plus the institutional colour of the different companies of the Group.

One way to differentiate business cards is to print them on different paper: a more representative card can be printed on the same paper used for other company stationery, though with a heavier weight. It is possible to use so-called "American" embossing or punchcutting.

323

Basica spa
Direzione generale:
Zona industriale
65050 Tito (PZ)
Tel. 0971/438111
Fax 0971/438314

Mario Rossi
Presidente

Viale Grassi, 136
73100 Lecce
Tel. 0832/252691
Fax 0835/345844
Via Annunziata, 25
75100 Matera
Tel. 0835/784321
Fax 0835/547266

Via Amendola 162/1
70126 Bari
Tel. 080/4855456
Fax 080/4865588
Via Nazario Sauro, 2
00100 Potenza
Tel. 0835/784321
Fax 0835/547266

2.

Viale Grassi, 136
73100 Lecce
Tel. 0832/252691
Fax 0835/345844
Via Annunziata, 25
75100 Matera
Tel. 0835/784321
Fax 0835/547266

Via Amendola 162/1
70126 Bari
Tel. 080/4855456
Fax 080/4865588
Via Nazario Sauro, 2
00100 Potenza
Tel. 0835/784321
Fax 0835/547266

Basica spa
Direzione generale:
Zona industriale
65050 Tito (PZ)
Tel. 0971/438111
Fax 0971/438314

Il Presidente

3.

Basica spa
Direzione generale:
Zona industriale
65050 Tito (PZ)
Tel. 0971/438111
Fax 0971/438314

Mario Rossi

Viale Grassi, 136
73100 Lecce
Tel. 0832/252691
Fax 0835/345844
Via Annunziata, 25
75100 Matera
Tel. 0835/784321
Fax 0835/547266

Via Amendola 162/1
70126 Bari
Tel. 080/4855456
Fax 080/4865588
Via Nazario Sauro, 2
00100 Potenza
Tel. 0835/784321
Fax 0835/547266

4.

Viale Grassi, 136
73100 Lecce
Tel. 0832/252691
Fax 0835/345844
Via Annunziata, 25
75100 Matera
Tel. 0835/784321
Fax 0835/547266

Via Amendola 162/1
70126 Bari
Tel. 080/4855456
Fax 080/4865588
Via Nazario Sauro, 2
00100 Potenza
Tel. 0835/784321
Fax 0835/547266

Basica spa
Direzione generale:
Zona industriale
65050 Tito (PZ)
Tel. 0971/438111
Fax 0971/438314

Mario Rossi

5.

Basica spa
Direzione generale:
Zona industriale
65050 Tito (PZ)
Tel. 0971/438111
Fax 0971/438314

Viale Grassi, 136
73100 Lecce
Tel. 0832/252691
Fax 0835/345844
Via Annunziata, 25
75100 Matera
Tel. 0835/784321
Fax 0835/547266

Via Amendola 162/1
70126 Bari
Tel. 080/4855456
Fax 080/4865588
Via Nazario Sauro, 2
00100 Potenza
Tel. 0835/784321
Fax 0835/547266

6.

Viale Grassi, 136
73100 Lecce
Tel. 0832/252691
Fax 0835/345844
Via Annunziata, 25
75100 Matera
Tel. 0835/784321
Fax 0835/547266

Via Amendola 162/1
70126 Bari
Tel. 080/4855456
Fax 080/4865588
Via Nazario Sauro, 2
00100 Potenza
Tel. 0835/784321
Fax 0835/547266

Basica spa
Direzione generale:
Zona industriale
65050 Tito (PZ)
Tel. 0971/438111
Fax 0971/438314

7.

Envelopes

Formats and Templates

1. 2. This envelope has a window and a format of 230 mm in width by 110 mm in height.

The envelope can be printed with the company logo using the same criteria and dimensions used for a page of letterhead. The position of the image takes into account the centring with respect to the paper and thus adopts wider margins.

324

Lecce
Viale Grassi, 136
73100 Lecce
Matera
Via Annunziatella, 25
75100 Matera

Bari
Via Amendola 162/1
70126 Bari
Potenza
Via Nazario Sauro, 12
00100 Potenza

Basicaspa

Basica spa
Società del Gruppo
della banca Mediterranea
Direzione generale:
Zona industriale
65050 Tito (PZ)

Notes
The dimensions of the window in the envelope respect UNI regulations.
In fact, while the height is the maximum allowed, equal to 50 mm, the width is only slightly smaller to the maximum size suggested.
The reference sign indicates the starting point for the text containing the recipient's information with a sufficient tolerances tied to the smaller format of the page inside the envelope.

1.

2.

40

50

16,5

3. 4. This envelope has a window and a format of 230 mm in width by 110 mm in height. The height and width of the window and the distance of the window from the right and lower margins are shown in the drawing.

They are the maximum and minimum dimensions of the window based on UNI regulations. The values of 1.5 indicate the maximum allowable tolerances.

Notes
When we design a letter envelope, it is necessary to plan the space that will be occupied by the text containing information about the recipient; it is also necessary to ensure that this space coincides with the window in standard commercially available envelopes.

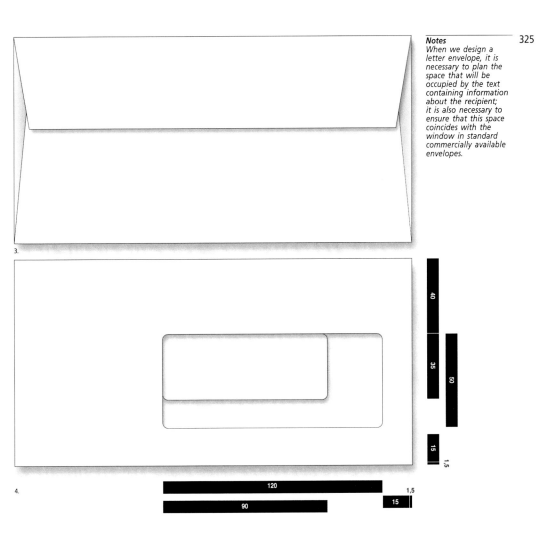

3.

4.

1. 2. Cards are designed using a format equal to 1/3 of the width of a UNI A4 page, or 210x99 mm. This format fits perfectly inside an "American" envelope. The structure is once again equal to that used for the letterhead. The margins are the same as that used for the letterhead: this ensures the centring of the image with that on the envelope.

As card is commonly used for more representative material, it will most likely be used for more important business cards. These latter may use the same type of paper, embossed printing for logos, etc.

3. 4. As an exception, cards can be given a different format. In this case we have adopted a horizontal A6 format, which measures 148x105 mm, while the envelope will be format C6, or 114x162 mm. Card may feature an opaline finish, with a weight of 250 grams. The interior of the envelope can be internally printed or be provided with a glued bluish trace paper.

Notes
This envelope designed for note cards is also printed with a raised logo.
The same envelope is used for the important note cards, such as those from the president, the director-general, etc.

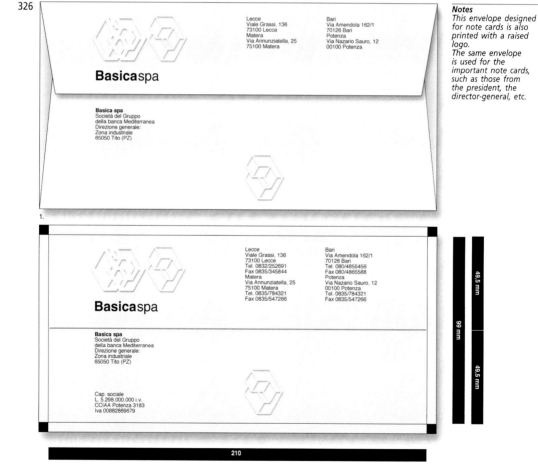

1.

2.

Notes
*The type of card
illustrated to the left
can be considered
"unique" to the
material designed
so far.
It has its own use,
and is less "corporate"
and more "personal".*

105 mm

114 mm

162

148

3.

Larger Envelopes

Structure and Formats

1. 2. Larger envelopes are based on a division of a format into four equal parts.
This structure is to be maintained for all large envelope formats.
The fourth model in the lower left contains the recipient's address. It is to be positioned at the point of reference marking the start point for text.
A horizontal line separates it into two modules above and two below.

The most common commercially available large envelopes are:
230x160 mm
260x190 mm
330x230 mm
360x260 mm
400x300 mm.
For large quantities, large envelopes can be made to order.
They are commonly made of 120 g/m2 "Siling" type white or Havana Kraft paper.

3. Large envelopes in UNI formats.
C6, 162x114 mm
B6, 176x125 mm
C5, 229x162 mm
B5, 176x250 mm
C4, 324x229 mm
B4, 353x250 mm

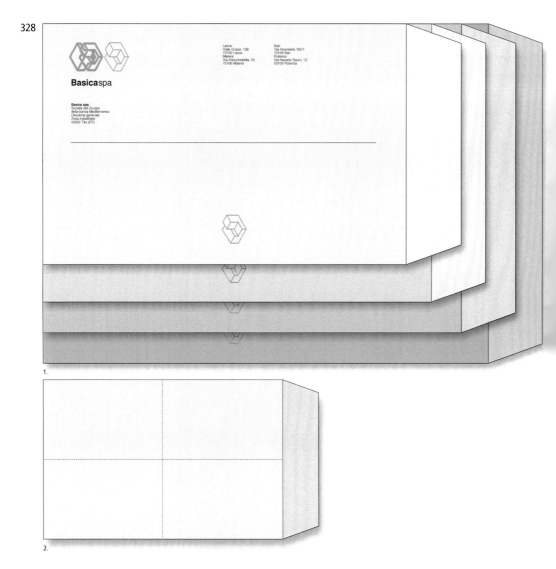

1.

2.

4. 5. Printing large envelopes, especially when they are required in different sizes, is undoubtedly a significant cost.
In this case, it is worth considering the printing of an adhesive label on Fasson paper: it can be applied other than to envelopes, regardless of their size, also to packages.
Printed in multiple versions on standard sheets of paper, they can also be inserted in a printer.

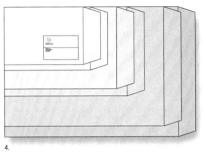

4.

5.

329

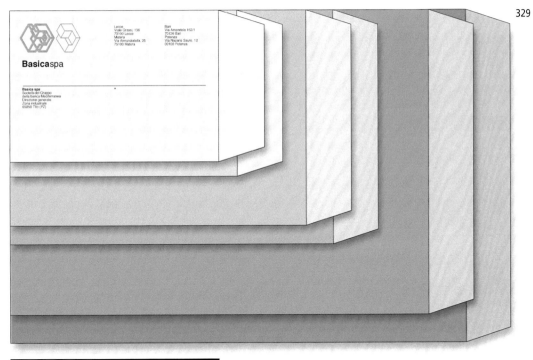

162x114 C6

176x125 B6

229x162 C5

250x176 B5

324x229 C4

353x250 B4

3.

22.
Forms

The Coexistence Between Different Systems of Measurement

1./7. In forms, as in letterhead, other than texts including company names, titles, etc., to be printed in a print shop, it is also necessary to provide space for texts that can be printed with mechanographic systems.

It is necessary to consider the space these texts will occupy and leave enough room and ensure the harmony between these texts and pre-printed texts.

1.

2.

3.

Mechanographic writing uses systems of measurement that do not correspond with either systems of typographic measurement or the metric decimal system. Yet all three systems must coexist in the same module.
In fact, the dimensions of UNI formats are all expressed in millimetres, typographic texts in points and Didot or Pica rows, while mechanographic systems have their own characteristics, which vary from machine to machine.

The most common pass is the Pica, equal to 1/10 of an inch, or 2.54 mm; the most common leading is 5 mm, or 1/6 of an inch, equivalent to 4.23 mm;
the possible combinations between pass and leading are:
a) pass=1/10",
leading 5 mm;
b) pass=1/10",
leading 4.23 mm.
The examples on this page use combination a).

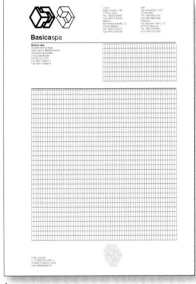

4.

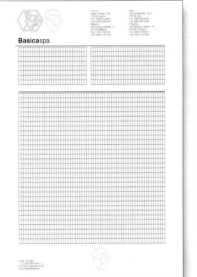

a5.2.

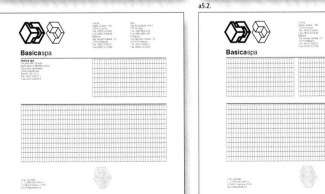

6.

7.

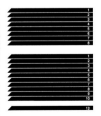

1. 2. The raster, that is, the grid designed using dimensions based on a pass of 1/10 of an inch and a leading of 5 mm, proves indispensable to the design of forms.

As the forms are designed to be printed on mechanographic systems, the entire structure needs to be based on this scale of values.

It is worth creating a transparency of the raster to lay out the texts of the forms or, for those who use a computer, it is enough to print a trace version of this grid to ensure that the typographic rows correspond with the rows to be printed using other systems.

The use of horizontal lines or columns becomes particularly important when designing forms. Used in different weights and thicknesses, they help identify preordered spaces and separate different zones with precise functions.

332

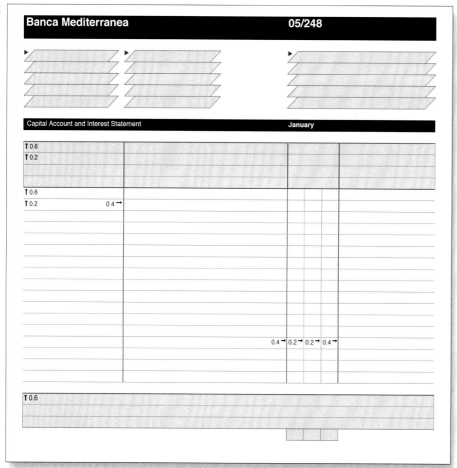

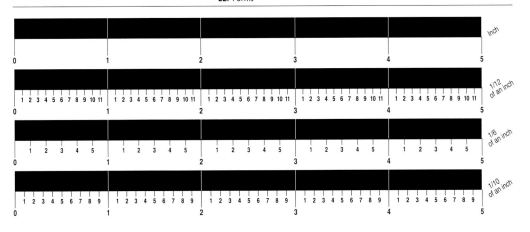

Inch

1/12 of an inch

1/6 of an inch

1/10 of an inch

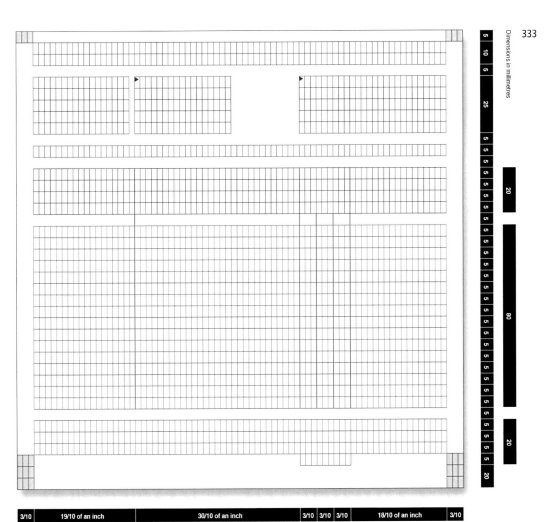

333

Dimensions in millimetres

| 3/10 | 19/10 of an inch | 30/10 of an inch | 3/10 | 3/10 | 3/10 | 18/10 of an inch | 3/10 |

Dimensions in inches   1: 0.2 pt horizontal line   2: 0.4 pt horizontal line   3: 0.6 pt horizontal line   9/10

2.

The Raster

A Guide
for Eliminating Mistakes

Below and following
are a set of grids
(raster in German) with
the passes and leading
used most commonly in
the 1/1 format for the
exact layout of texts to
be printed using
mechanographic
systems.
The grids respond to
the criteria of a graphic
scheme that makes it
possible to define all of
the alignments within
the modules.

1. Vertical grid.
Spacing 1/10 of an inch.
Leading of 5 mm.

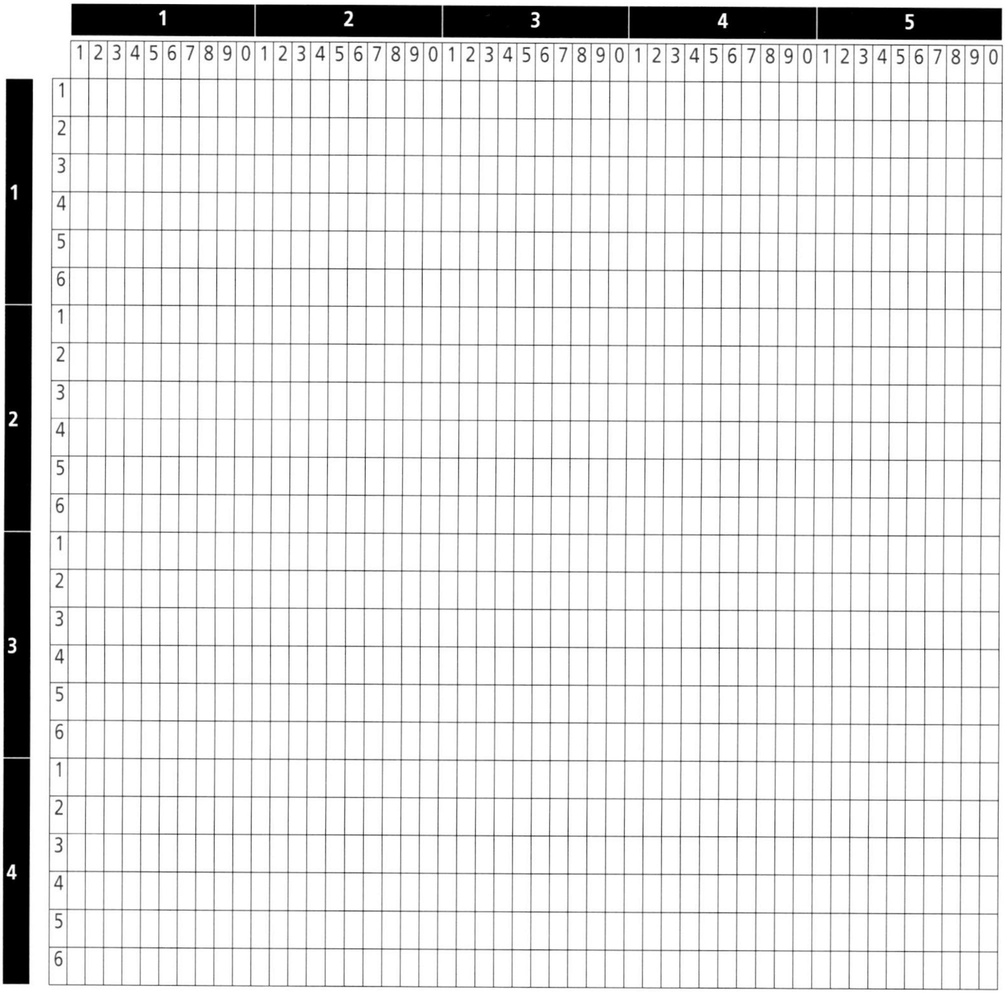

334

2. Vertical grid.
Spacing 1/10 of an inch.
Leading of 1/6",
or 4.23 mm.

1. Vertical grid.
Spacing 1/10 of an inch.
Leading of 5 mm.

For pre-printed forms, which to be successively printed on using mechanographic systems, in general the system of measurement is one of those described here.

Before designing a page of letterhead for your client, ask what kind of equipment they use in the company; avoid discovering too late that your typographic rows and measurements do not correspond.

2. Horizontal grid.
Spacing 1/10 of an inch.
Leading mm 5.

336

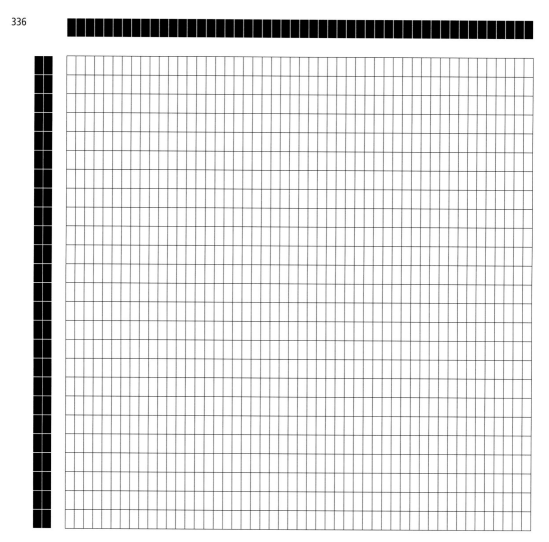

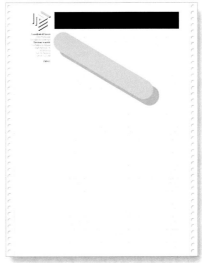

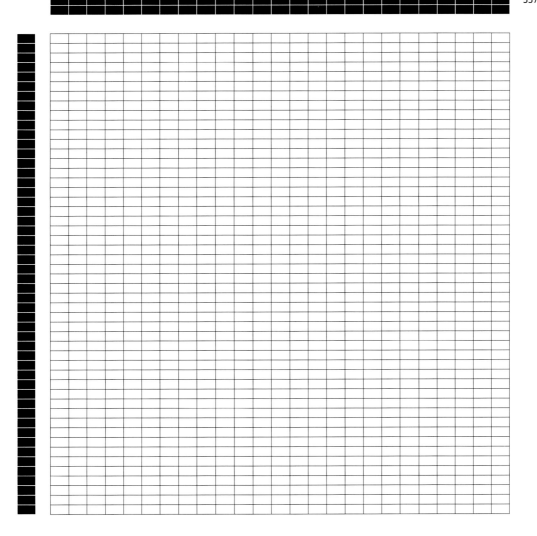

1. Vertical grid.
Spacing 1/10 of an inch.
Leading 1/6", equal to
4.23 mm.

2. Horizontal grid.
Spacing 1/10 of an inch.
Leading 1/6",
equal to 4.23 mm.

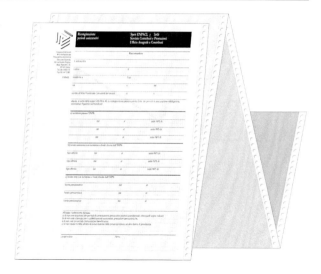

338

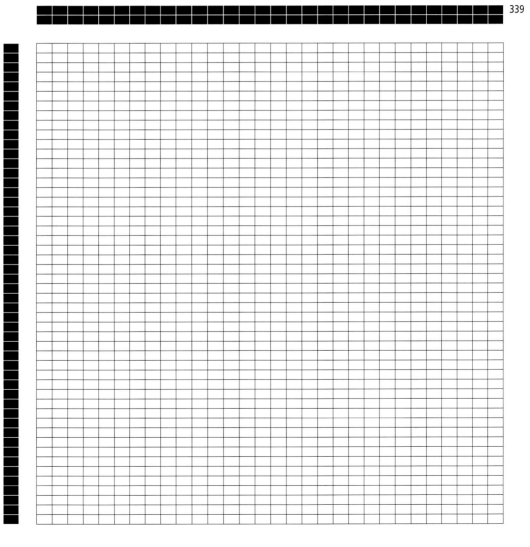

Spaces
to be Highlighted

A Light
Texture

1. 2. As part of a global image designed for a company, forms have particular, and sometimes highly complex characteristics and functions.
As mentioned, other than containing no less than three systems of measurement, which significantly complicates the work of a graphic designer who needs to collaborate with and carry out controls in the mechanographic centre of the company where he or she works, they must also be functional and simple to use, as they are used not only by trained professionals, but also by a vaster public.

More and more companies now use computers and laser printers.
In this case it is worth providing a file of the standard invoices, forms and pre-printed material you design: this facilitates the work of employees responsible for filling them out and guarantees a perfect reproduction during the phase of printing.

340

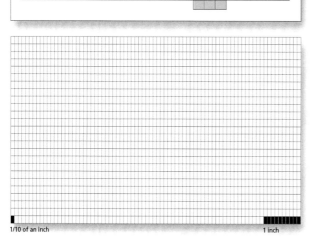

1/10 of an inch   1 inch

3.

3. Forms can feature a textured background using a very light hatch positioned at the start of the text area; this solution, adopted for example in a chequebook, protects against eventual falsifications of any writing.
The colour of the background image must be printed at no more than 20% of the colour, while black images should be printed at a maximum of 7%.

4./7. A chequebook, or block of shares, bonds, deposit certificates, registered securities, certified warranties and securities in general that must offer protection against counterfeiting are printed using lithographic or chalcographic processes up to seven colours from a single original to which a mechanographic print is added when filling out the name of the issuee.

The application of a texture in general produces a decent effect, however it is rare to see compositions that are not derived from an overlap of rather banal volutes and graphic decorations.

341

Banca Mediterranea

li   19   Lire

S332.2/04200 2 Filiale di Potenza Sede

A vista pagate per questo assegno bancario n.

Lire

a

Firma

NUMERO ASSEGNO
0007015

NUMERO ASSEGNO
0007015

CODICE BANCA
000809

CAB
015

NUMERO CONTO
02458

23.
Textures

A Rhythmic Modularity

1. A composition guided by a logical and controlled repetition of individual elements generates a texture. Aggregation can be obtained using a modular grid whose ratios correspond to logical criteria and where the repetition of individual elements is dictated by a rhythmic rather than a casual geometric order. There are infinite ways to create a texture.

Normally it is the result of a design created specifically so that its parts, when assembled, coincide and overlap to create a unique graphic form.
As Amedeo Grütter stated, this often generates forms whose result transcends the idea behind the original element. The following pages provide only a few examples of a myriad of possible textures.

Notes
When you design a texture, remember the scale at which it is to be printed.
A 0.3 point thick line reduced by 50% will be 0.15 points and difficult to print.

Bibliography
Textures
La caratterizzazione visiva e tattile delle superfici, *edited by Corrado Gavinelli* Quaderni di design *Series directed by Bruno Munari*

342

LUCIDITRASTEVERE
Show / Ristorante / Pianobar / Cantina
Via Enrico De Nicola
Aperto dalle 20 alle 2

Inaugurazione
20 dicembre 1970 alle ore 20,00

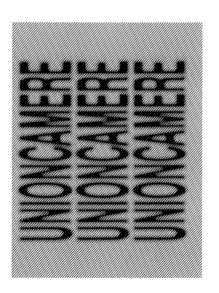

3. A texture can be generated using a specific graphic. In this case, we have used a graphic mediation consisting of a linear hatch that has been blown up in scale.

A texture is almost any drawing whose geometric progression and repetition coincides with its structure. The drawings on this page are a clear example.

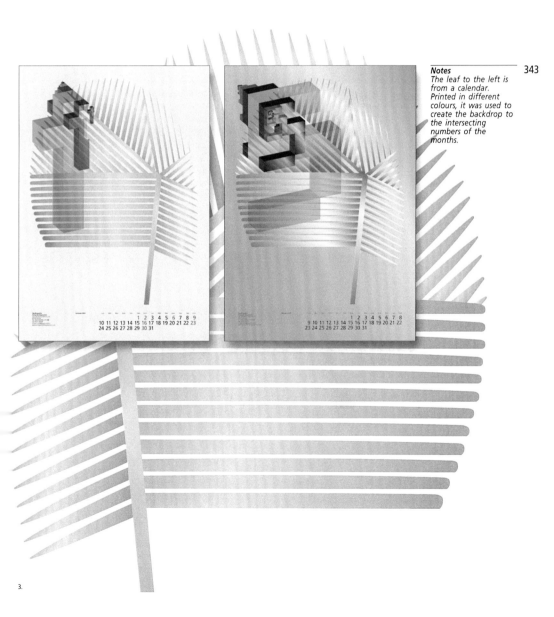

Notes
The leaf to the left is from a calendar. Printed in different colours, it was used to create the backdrop to the intersecting numbers of the months.

3.

1. This texture was
used as a backdrop for
shares issued by a
credit institution.
It was printed once in
cyan at 20%; a second
time with an increase
in the percentage of
cyan.
Designed with a logo
in six different weights,
gradually heavier, the
texture creates a
sequence.
The assembly of these
elements requires an
oblique direction that
was partially corrected
by aligning a each new
series at the top.

2. The six different
versions of the logo
with gradually heavier
line weights constitute
the base for the
construction of the
texture.

3. Textures designed
for Verona Villafranca
Airport.
The repetition of the
logo generated a very
dynamic texture.

4. This texture in the
negative was used for
the internal finish of a
yearly accounting
statement.
In this case, the
background was
printed in a tenuous
colour, while the
texture is in white.

3.

344

1.

2.

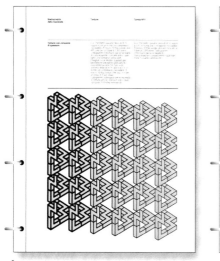
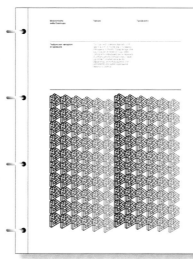

5. The texture for Mediocredito della Basilicata illustrated on two pages of the Bank's corporate identity manual.

5.

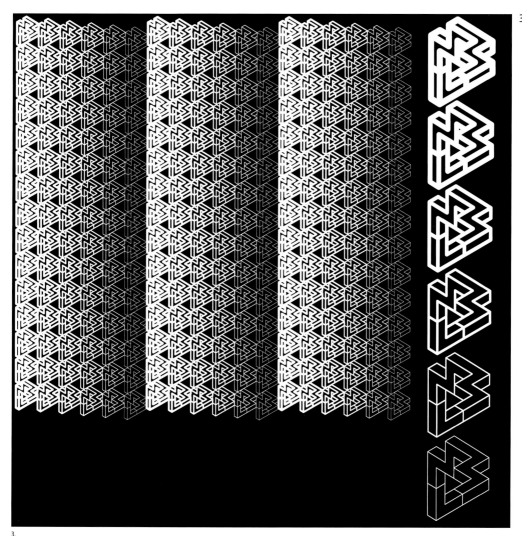

3.

1. The consistent repetition of a sign generates a texture. Through its interaction, the sign is modified, and the resulting image acquires other meanings and different readings. A variability of forms can be obtained using different weights of colour, even within a constant element that is rhythmically repeated; a similar result can also be obtained by varying the line weights of elements that maintain a constant dimension.

2. 3. The base element of the construction of a texture.
The upper profile coincides with the lower one, but not perfectly: this offset generates a visual vibration in the observation of the modules.

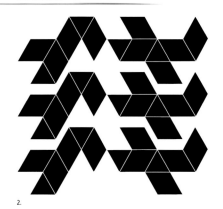

2.

346

Notes
When the elements of a texture are differentiated in their weight, colour or only in the saturation of the same colour, this determines a reading of only one of the elements or a group of elements.

3.

1.

4.

4. 5. The effects of a texture obtained from the overlapping of lines often produces unexpected and unpredictable results. The image reproduced below, designed in the 1960s without a computer, was obtained by projecting the same element (PRI) 19 times on an orthochromatic film fixed to a *tratteggigrafo* drawing instrument to obtain the first series. The texture is the result of the combination of 50 different series. The same element can be repeated with opportune variations in line weights.

6. The repetition of a curved line produced this texture. It belongs to a series of drawings from 1972 created by hand using coloured ballpoint pens, using a guide whose movements were programmed based on a specific code of offsets.

6.

347

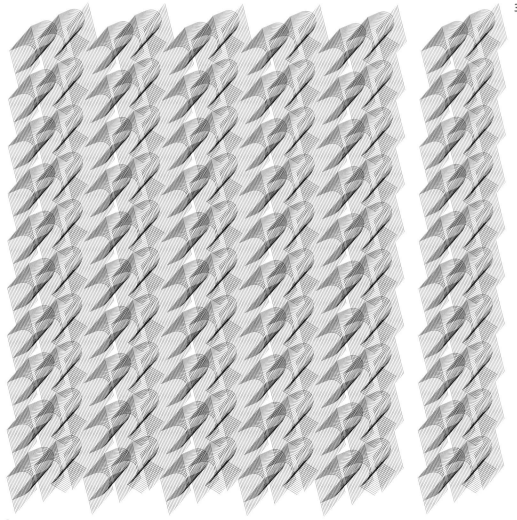

5.

1. A texture can be obtained through the rhythmic repetition of a text.
In the example in figure 1, the text used for a folder created for Unioncamere was repeated with alternating rhythms of combination, each with its own line weight.

2. The criteria of combination, and that used for the line weights, is visible in the drawing presented beside the texture.

3.

3. The creation of a texture can give rise to very curious phenomena of perception.
The combination of two texts, one of which is inverted, can lead to what Gaetano Kanizsa, in his book *Grammatica del vedere*, defines the "masking" effect.
He writes "known forms are masked when the addition of other lines creates the condition for the coercive constitution of new units based on non empirical factors, such as closure, symmetry and proper continuation".

348

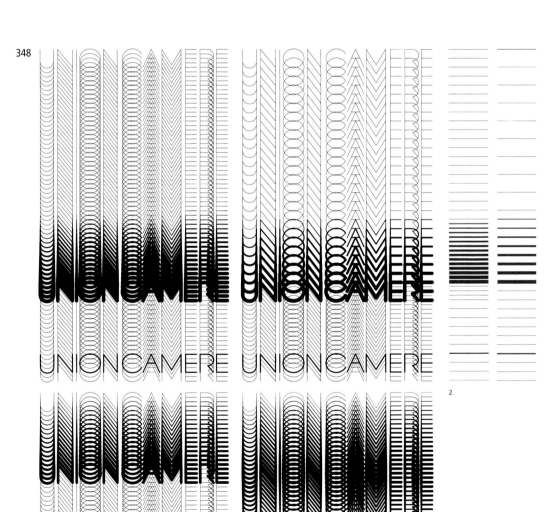

2.

1.

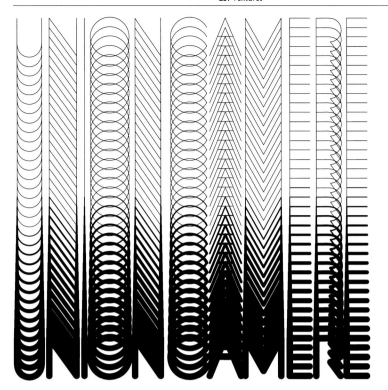

Workbook
Develop a logotype and
assemble its different
thicknesses to produce
a texture.
Positive, negative and
colour tests.

The Repetition of a Logo

To Design a Texture

1. 2. This extremely simple texture was constructed using a grid of constant modules.
The elements of which it is composed are aligned at the intersection of the modules, at an equal distance, though with different visual results owing to the different weights.

1.

350

2.

1. 2. A logo, repeated
in different weights,
generates a texture in
which some elements
assume a colour.
The drawings show
studies and projects for
different versions in the
negative and positive.

Texture
as Creativity

The Repetition of a Logo

1./4. Work in progress for a cover with a background texture.

5. A box with a texture that combines the logo of the Ravello Festival, when open automatically defines the outline of the die cut.
6. The same structure, with a different texture, was used for a container for a catalogue.
Below, one of the elements of the texture shines in colour in the midst of the other logos.

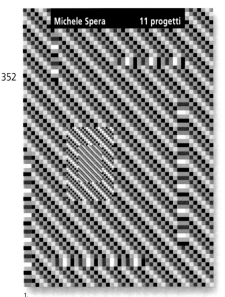

1.

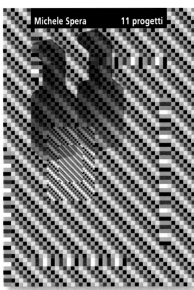

2.

Notes
The four test sheets to the left were developed in Photoshop.
Each step visualises a different level that was manipulated; the first shows the texture and the last image shows the sum of all the levels.

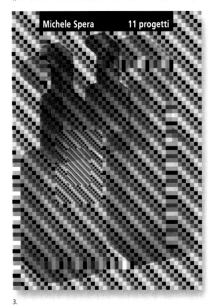

3.

4.

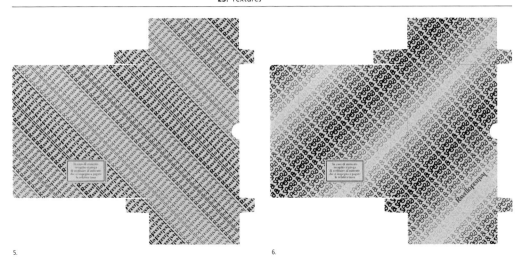

5.

6.

353

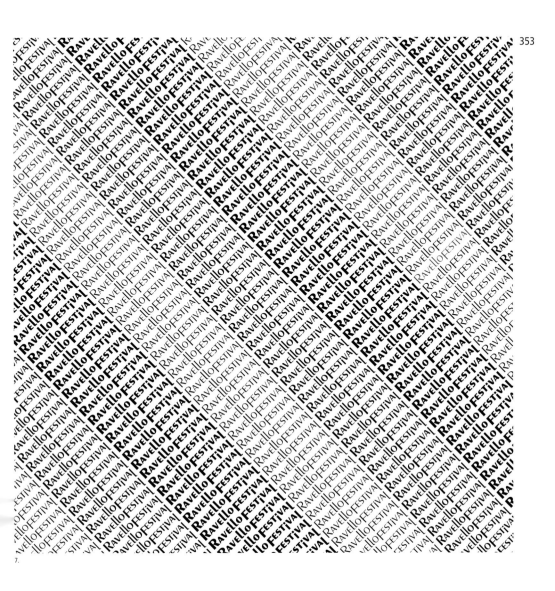

7.

24.
Signage
and Display Panels

Information Systems

Signage must be designed taking into account a range of factors that require specific studies: their position (site plans, current and proposed layouts); the industrial or custom design of supports and structures; dimensions and modularity (technical drawings and feasibility, materials, anchors, etc.); colour palettes (colour selection, colour studies, etc.); typeface selection (differentiated spacing code, type sizes and dimensions, reading distance); graphic design of pictograms and directional indications.

There are many companies specialised in the industrial production of signage, whose characteristics respond to the various needs of different clients.
Here is a list of just a few:
Cicrespi spa (20060 Liscate Milan, Via Trieste) active for many years, the company offers a manual that explains the methodology behind the production of its signs;
Cartel srl (20146 Milan, Via Antonio Cecchi 8).

Students can contact these or other companies to request catalogues and other material.

354 When we enter a multi-storey car park, well designed signage guides us and immediately indicates the levels of the parking structure, the availability of stalls, the exits and the directions of travel; without these references we would be unable even to remember where we left our automobile. Signage helps us, using a universal language of standardised signs and short words. It guides us through a hospital, a supermarket and through the departments of a vast store. In modern airports it helps us to orient ourselves, to find the right departure "gate", information desk and the exit.
When it is part of the design of exhibition spaces, signage helps us find our way, it identifies different zones and sectors, it indicates the route to be followed. Of course there is also street signage, or that for a subway system or a tram network and other means of public transport. Logos, pictograms, maps and plans are married with clear, concise and legible lettering to create a "system" of information.
When a signage project embraces "the graphics of an environment", it becomes evident that a graphic designer, who must confront an information system that contemplates the integration between architecture and design, between graphics and furnishings, must work side by side with an industrial designer and an architect to arrive at a coherent result.
Signage is generally included in the study of coordinated image packages that contemplate the use of a company's image in a wayfinding and information package; but it also exists on its own in the world of architecture, in the furnishing of spaces and public areas, where this discipline requires particular and complex studies. When developing a signage system, we must consider a range of aspects that ensure a correct design:

1) In relation to general planning we must explore how people move through a building and how a chain of information should be constructed. We must examine the need for the interchangeability and flexibility of information, the correct positioning of signs in relation to different routes, whether or not they must be illuminated, what type of illumination is present, etc.
2) In relation to load-bearing structures, we must design external signage with simple and clean lines, easy to install and maintain. We should consider the possibility to install it on its own supports, attached to the wall, perpendicular to the wall or suspended, with the correct dimensions as part of a modular system that allows for the combined realisation of panels and plaques, whose technical characteristics are resistant to the elements, etc.
3) In relation to reading distances, we must select a certain typeface and its dimensions, codifying a differentiated spacing system, establish a "zone of respect" that permits the coexistence between texts, pictograms, directional indications, etc.
4) In relation to colour we must design a colour code that identifies a determinant category of information, areas, divisions and sectors, and which determines paths, directions, etc.
5) In relation to layouts, we must select formats and establish grids that contemplate the positioning of directional indications, text and pictograms.

Notes
The typical characteristics of a signage system are its modularity, soft and rounded edges, opaque finishes, materials resistant to the elements that guarantee it will last. Panels, posts and connectors for assembly and installation are generally industrially produced systems. Panels may be in baked enamel finished 5/10 aluminium, with an aluchrome rust treatment. Connectors are made of extruded aluminium. Support posts are generally 38 mm in diameter, with heights up to 1500 mm, or 76 mm with heights up to 3500 mm. They are completed by protective end caps.

Be careful when evaluating the zone of respect inside which you plan to place indications: a text that occupies an entire panel risks becoming confused with the information on an adjacent panel.

Visual
and Anthropometric
Factors

The Characteristics of Display Panels

1. The dimensions of characters on information panels in relation to reading distance.
Typeface used: Frutiger Roman and Bold.
At a distance of 3 metres it is possible to read a letter that is 8 mm tall;
at a distance of 40 metres it is possible to read a letter that is 100 mm tall.

The wider the spacing, the easier the text is to read, even up to an angle of 30 degrees.

Point dimensions are in Pica.
Attention: the dimensions indicated in the table are the minimums consented and presuppose optimum lighting conditions.
In an anomalous condition with scarce lighting, type sizes must be increased by 30 to 50 percent.
It is also important that the text/background relationship is dictated by the maximum possible contrast.
For example:
black text on a white or light grey background; white text on a black background; black text on a yellow background, etc. A few examples of colour combinations are shown to the right.

355

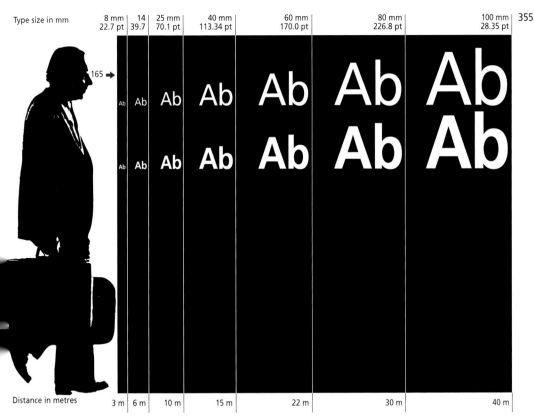

Type size in mm	8 mm 22.7 pt	14 39.7	25 mm 70.1 pt	40 mm 113.34 pt	60 mm 170.0 pt	80 mm 226.8 pt	100 mm 28.35 pt
Distance in metres	3 m	6 m	10 m	15 m	22 m	30 m	40 m

165 →

4.

Visual and Anthropometric Factors

The Characteristics of Indoor Signage

1. Type size for captions on information panels in relation to reading distance. Typeface used: Frutiger Roman.
Ratio 1:1

A visit to a museum is enjoyable when the objects, paintings and materials on display are accompanied by explanatory captions that are aesthetically pleasing and, above all, legible.
Attention when choosing a typeface, the colour of the background, the mandatory reading distance (we must remember protective ropes in front of precious artworks) and, as a result, the type size.
Remember that texts should be within an angle of 60 degrees with respect to a vertical axis of 165 cm, the average height of the human eye.

2. The values listed here are of assistance when choosing these ratios, though the conditions in which they are applied can vary greatly and it is necessary to be able to offer solutions to a very wide range of needs.
Texts can be realised using various different techniques:
die cut using a plotter (rendering 100); digitally printed (rendering 80); silkscreened (rendering 90); laser printed (rendering 60).

356

Visual and Anthropometric Factors Reading distance in relation to type size Ratio 1:1	Text size in a well lit environment	Text size in an environment with average lighting	Text size in an environment with poor lighting
Reading distance = 35 cm	Type Size 6 — Ab	Type Size 7.8 — Ab	Type Size 10.14 — Ab
Reading distance = 70 cm	Type Size 10.14 — Ab	Type Size 13.18 — Ab	Type Size 17.14 — Ab
Reading distance = 105 cm	Type Size 17.14 — Ab	Type Size 22.27 — Ab	Type Size 28.96 — Ab
Reading distance = 300 cm	Type Size 36 — Ab	Type Size 44 — Ab	

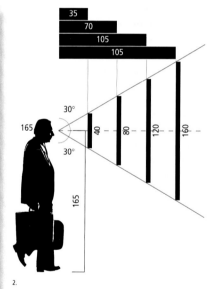

35
70
105
105

30°
165
30°

40 80 120 160

165

2.

4.

Here we offer as an example only a description borrowed from the Cicrespi catalogue of panels for external use, mounted on legs or suspended:
Realised in treated heavy extruded aluminium profiles with a baked enamel finish and two coats of black paint.
Texts in molten vinyl, with a dimensional stability at temperatures between -60°C and +107°C.
Posts for in-ground applications are realised in 70 mm diameter black anodised heavy extruded aluminim.
Panels are mounted in a dedicated channel in the face of the posts.

All panel groups can be illuminated from a sealed fluorescent light housing to be fixed, using special connectors, to the top of the assembled panel. Supports for suspended panels, 50 mm in diameter, are provided with accessories in black anodised aluminium that allow for the removal and replacement of panels without the need to remove installed supports.

3. Examples of signs using a grid that defines the exact position of all text. Handmade signage in treated wood. Directional indicators placed in a square grid. Be careful of thier direction: they occupy different amounts of space depending on which way they point.

4. An eye test card, similar to that found in any optometrist's office. Optometry is the part of opthalmology that deals with the examination of the functioning of the eye and, above all, considers movements, vision and refraction. An eye test chart is to be read at a distance of 3 to 4 metres. To calculate the reading distance for the table shown here, measure the height of the red line (here = 7.266 mm) and multiply it by 0.069. Ex.: 7.266 mm x 0.069 = 0.5 metres, the ideal distance for reading this chart.

4.

357

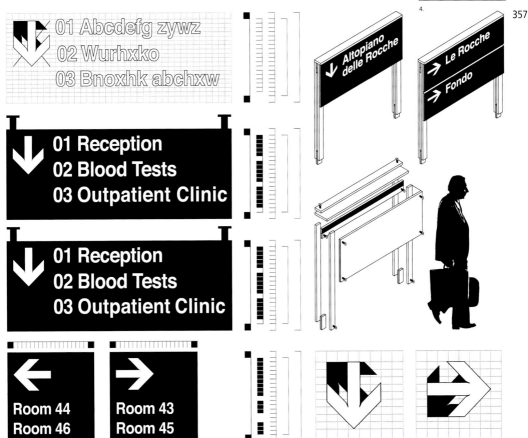

3.

Drawing an Arrow

A Clear Path

The arrow is one of those graphic symbols that exists in the intermediate zone between a visual image and a written sign. This transition from image to symbol reminds us that writing itself developed from pictograms.
Like a letter, this particular sign is one of the myriad elements that, assembled in a rational manner, produces a proper piece of signage.

In phototypesetting and desktop editing, we divide one EM into 18 parts, each of which is a submultiple.
This criteria can be adopted as the base for a system that can be used to identify the units of measurement that create the ratios between the various parts of a signage project.

1. 2. The arrow studied here (from a project by the author) is constructed on a grid of 324 modules (18x18), with a base and height of equal dimensions. The grid constitutes the zone of respect inside which the arrow 'lives', positioned with a margin of 1 module above and to the left.
In the drawing below, the arrow has a different ratio, where the height is equal to the base plus one module.

358

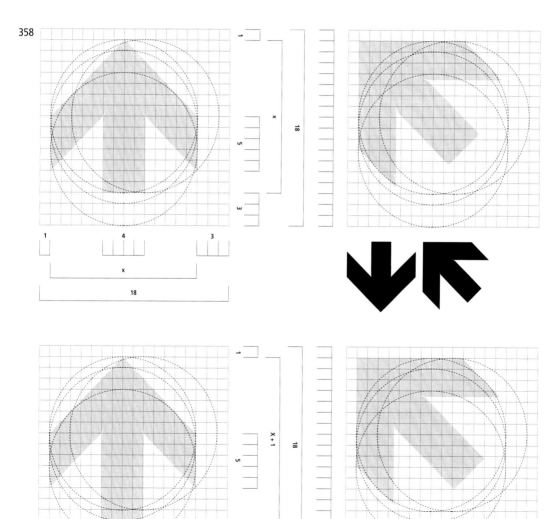

3. The choice of whether to adopt the first or second criteria derives from the opportunity of leaving a larger or smaller zone of respect around this symbol.
The two solutions are compared in the image to the right.

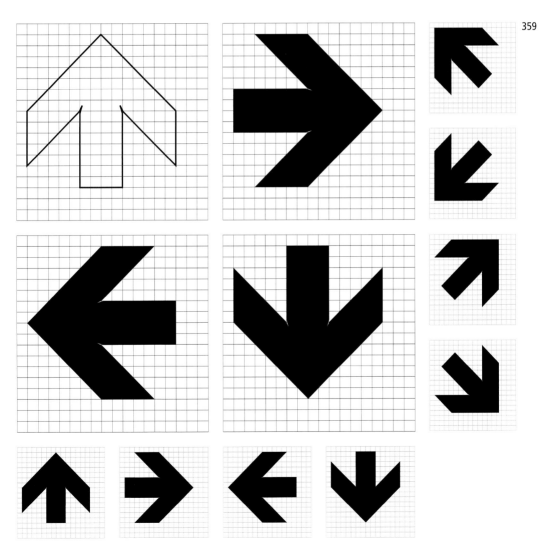

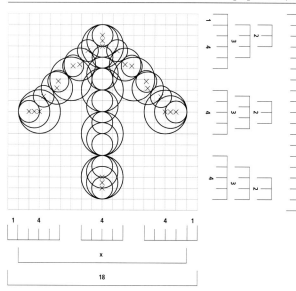

Constructed once again on a grid of 324 modules (18x18), with a base and height of equal dimensions, this arrow is designed with rounded ends.

360

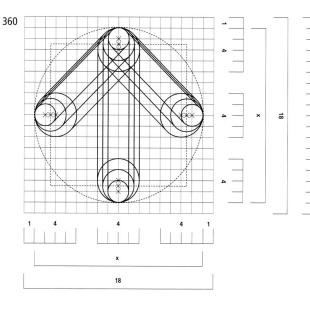

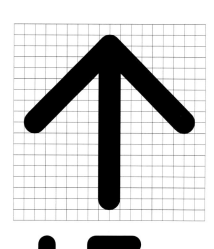

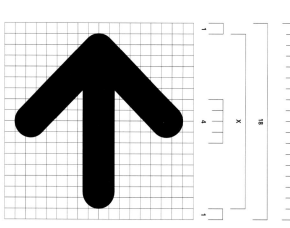

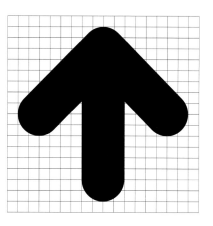

The image below shows five series of arrows, set in a grid of one hundred square modules. The ratio between the "point" and the "tail" varies according to a geometric progression. The first series begins with a tail of 5 modules and the thickness of the point is measured along the grid at 45° with variations from 1 to 5 modules. The second series narrows the tail to 4 modules, the third to 3 and so on.

The arrow symbol is as old as mankind itself. The weapons of prehistoric man were pointed like an arrow, and ancient graffiti shows that the arrow symbol was used to indicate a direction, applied to tree trunks or rocks to indicate a route. During the Middle Ages, lances and arrows were used as indicators; other indicators include the hands of a clock and the zodiac sign for Sagittarius is another arrow.

At the end of the nineteenth century, in London, a proposal was made to eliminate writings that indicated a direction and to substitute them with a symbol with a universal value. These proposals were later ratified in Paris in the early twentieth century. The first street signs in Italy, in which a curved arrow indicated a dangerous bend in the road and a horizontal arrow the direction of travel, appeared in 1905. Naturally, the arrows featured a more realistic form, with a hooked point and feather-like stylised tail similar to royal stems.

From this moment onward, there has been an infinite number of proposals, regulations and variations tied to different types of arrows with different meanings. One curious experiment was made in 1962 (Gwyneth de la Marc & Walker) to test the legibility and recognisability of various forms of arrows by different subjects under different conditions of observation. The test demonstrated that the most recognisable form of an arrow was that with a thick and full inverted V-shaped point and a thinner tail. The results of this experiment were incorporated in the international road signage system.

361

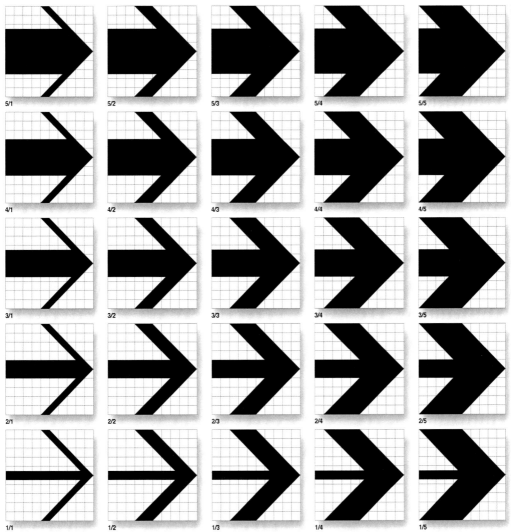

From Typeface Design to the Tools for Making Corrections

The criteria to be adopted when designing an arrows is the same applied by designers to particular letters with the same identical phenomenology of perception.

1. Those who use a computer are unlikely to notice in a glyph the small adjustments to the design of the glyphs of a typeface, present in the original design of an alphabet. These subtle adjustments and almost invisible optical corrections are often ignored by programmers, with serious effects on the harmony of written texts.

The example on this page shows an upper case letter A. At the intersection between the oblique lines we can read an excess of black.
This is an optical effect that should be corrected through the construction of a glyph with a small adjustment, a subtle 'excavation' that lightens the black produced by the intersection of lines and compensates this excess.
The same correction has been transferred to the design of our arrow.

362

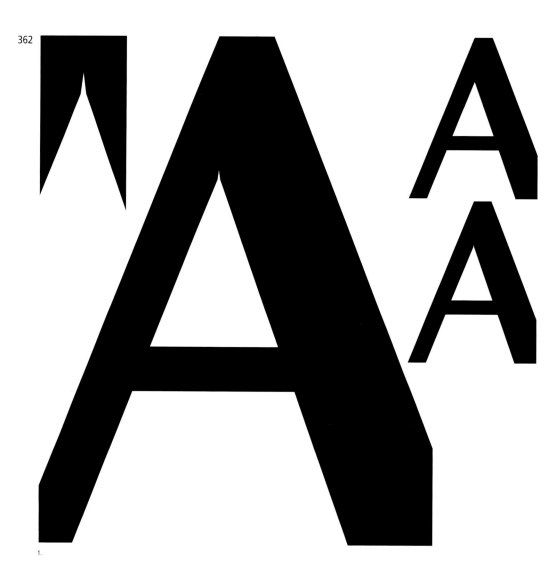

1.

2. An optical correction was made at the point of intersection between the oblique lines, creating a wedge at their interstices.
To make this correction, we created a second module equal to 1/18 of the first, within which we designed a wedge. Naturally, it is possible to use other dimensions and other geometric forms.
It must be remembered that the examples shown to students are merely indicative of a methodology of design.

3. 4. Enlarged detail of the optical correction. It can be noted how the intervention in the smaller version harmonises the reading of the sign without interfering with it.

5. The arrows before and after optical correction. In the first, the black area is summed at the point of intersection between the lines. To measure the effect of the optical correction, close your eyes slightly: as with the shutter of a camera, you will acquire a depth of field and truer overall vision of what you are looking at.

5.

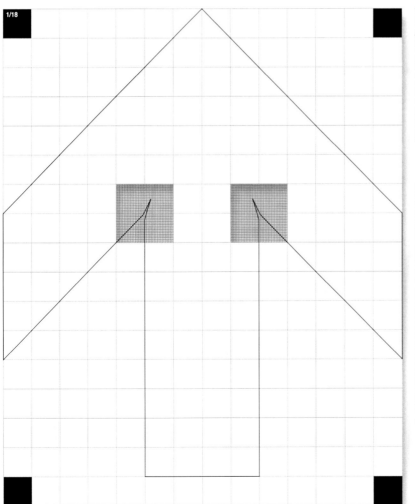

2.

Workbook
Design an arrow on a pre-established grid and, where the intersection of lines generates an excess of black, make the necessary optical correction.
The design of the correction should also correspond with a geometric criteria that is related to the total grid.

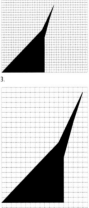

3.

4.

Signage
for a Convention

Information Symbols and Pictograms

1. 2. Signage for a convention, Genoa 1975.
Direction signs and pictograms.

A signage system can be divided into three principal categories:
a) identification signs, which identify a site or presence of a service;
b) direction signs: indicating the direction to be followed to reach a certain location;
b) information: all other signs offering information about services.

364

PARTITO REPUBBLICANO ITALIANO STAMPA **ANSA**

PARTITO REPUBBLICANO ITALIANO SETTORE D **DELEGATI**

PARTITO REPUBBLICANO ITALIANO STAMPA **ADN KRONOS**

PARTITO REPUBBLICANO ITALIANO SETTORE S STAMPA

PARTITO REPUBBLICANO ITALIANO STAMPA **ITALIA**

PARTITO REPUBBLICANO ITALIANO SETTORE I INVITATI

PARTITO REPUBBLICANO ITALIANO STAMPA **ASCA**

PARTITO REPUBBLICANO ITALIANO SETTORE A DELEGAZIONI

1.

A pictogram is a graphic symbol designed to be immediately and internationally understood.
Its graphic form must visualise the meaning it expresses without the need for any prior knowledge.

A pictogram is a response in visual esperanto to planetary globalisation and the need to communicate using a language free of linguistic and cultural references.

2.

Notes
Some students used particular colours for their signage projects. In the world of signage, where legibility is paramount, the evaluation of colour, its intensity (the maximum is that offered by the pure colours of the spectrum), contrast (created through the combination of colours) is an important moment in any design process.
Below is a scientifically accredited scale of values of contrasts that offer the highest legibility, in the following order:
1. Black on yellow
2. Green on white
3 Red on white
4. Blue on white
5. White on blue
6. Black on white
7. Yellow on black
8. White on red
9. White on green
10. White on black.

Signage
for an Exhibition

Signposts and Totems
In Versilia

1. The examples on this page present a signage project for the first Marble Exhibition held in Carrara in 1968. The entire layout of the exhibition was marked by totems constructed from slate quarried in Liguria. They were 240 centimetres in height, with a triangular base, each 26 cm in length. The height of 240 cm was divided into four modular parts; information was always aligned at 160 cm from the top and silkscreen printed.

The prismatic form made it possible to "stand" the totems with one face along the edge of the exhibition routes, leaving the other two faces, bearing the same information, visible. The typeface used was Helvetica bold, with a height of 9.6 cm, or 256 points. They were legible at more than 30 metres.

Information was always printed in white; in some cases, when the totems were to be read from a very close distance, such as indications about types of marble, the opaque black surface of the slate was printed with text in glossy black enamel.

366

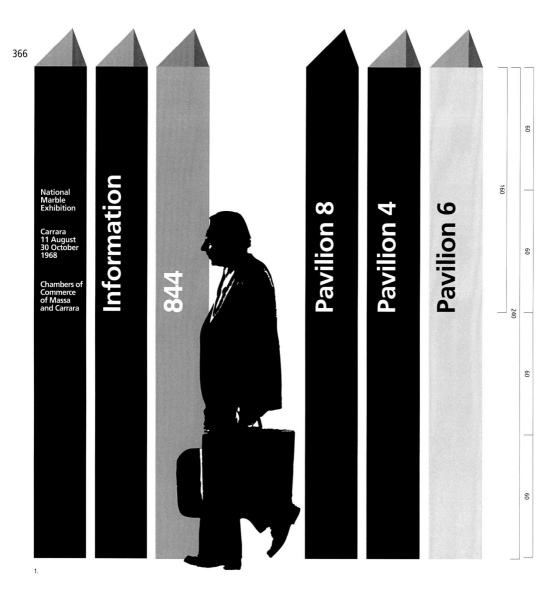

National
Marble
Exhibition

Carrara
11 August
30 October
1968

Chambers of
Commerce
of Massa
and Carrara

Information

844

Pavilion 8

Pavilion 4

Pavilion 6

60
160
60
240
60
60

1.

2. The same triangular form, with the same height but sides measuring 120 cm, was used to promote the event.
These totems were positioned along the boardwalks of Versilia, Viareggio and Carrara, along the streets and sidewalks, with one side facing the sea, and the other two visible to anyone travelling in either direction.
One side of the totem was sectioned into three parts, with a plant, located inside

the totem itself, protruding from one of them. The base supporting the plant also served to stabilise the totem.

3. Using the same criteria, and different measurements, other structures were created to indicate materials on display, to contain business cards, and so on.

4. Another design, realised in a limited number of prototypes, was a proposal for new street numbers presented to towns in the area of Versilia.

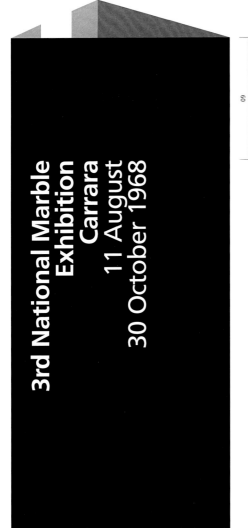

2.

3.

4.

The Layout of a Historic Exhibition

An Alphabet to Define the Image of the Exhibition

This historic exhibition was held in 1966 to celebrate the twentieth anniversary of the Italian Republic (1946/1966). It was presented inside the offices of *La Voce Repubblicana* and various sections of the Italian Republican Party (Pri).
Simple self-supporting hinged black painted panels made for easy transport to other locations, while the graphics were developed around the use of large numbers referring to different years.

1. 2. Each number was designed in two different versions, the second of which was studied to allow for a more harmonious combination with other numbers. This produced numbers with their own, exclusive identity. Below are a few examples of combinations of numbers and tests using different solutions.

368

1.

2.

Notes
Numbers, together with the tool of language, are one man's fundamental acquisitions.
The universally adopted number is based on ten so-called Arab positional numerals (the value of 0, 1, 2, 3, 4, 5, 6, 7, 8, 9 is given by their position).
Another type of numbering is additive (for example Roman numerals) whereby the 7 glyphs I, V, X, L, C, D and M assume a different value depending upon whether it precedes or follows another, and thus to which it is added or from which it is subtracted.

Numbers

The *Fil Rouge* of the Exhibition

Numbers play the leading role in this exhibition.
In the image, the figures and numbers (6 is a figure and 66 is a number) have the same function as the letters of the alphabet in the writing of words. They have their own lexicon, their own language and their own graphic. Below is the visualisation of the title of the exhibition: "1946/1966, la Repubblica".

369

Each section is introduced by a panel marked by a year. The panels show various documents, newspapers and photographs in a chronological itinerary through history and politics.
To the right, the logo for the exhibition was cut out in styrofoam and painted.

370

Notes
The year 1878 (the year of the death of Giuseppe Mazzini) was translated into images using a lettering system studied for the exhibition.
Below are some of the panels with the logo.

Totems
for a Convention

Information Panels

The review of the craft
industry, promoted by
the Ministry of Industry
in 1988, consisted of
four sessions.
The project was created
for the entire cycle of
this event with a colour
variation for each
session.
The totems were made
from die-cast
aluminium posts with
rubber feet.
Laminate panels were
fitted into grooves in
the supports.
Each face hosted a
70x100 cm format.

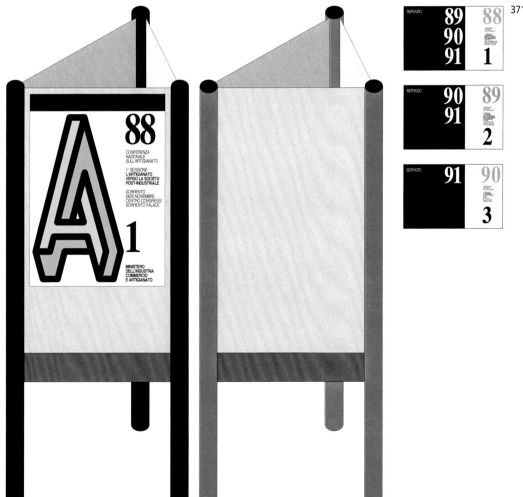

1.

A Backdrop
for a Convention

Telecom TiMedia

1. Early studies of the application of the logo to printed material.
The final version is that in reflex blue, the institutional colour used by Telecom.
To the right are the name cards, and below the notepad and folder.

2. The logo is shown at the top of the page to the right.
At the centre is the backdrop.
Made from two panels, respectively 6 and 4 metres, it was assembled with a space between the two panels that allowed access to the room.
As the drawing shows, the logo also overlaps in plan and is partially repeated on the two screens to create a uniform reading of the general image when viewed from a distance.

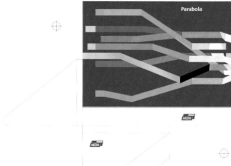

1.

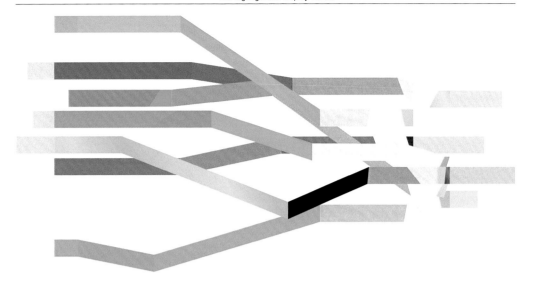

373

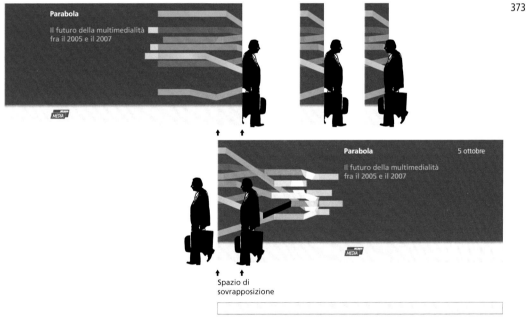

Spazio di
sovrapposizione

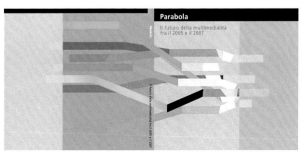

2.

Numbers

Finding
Information

Studied for one of the conventions organised by Federnotesi, this alphanumeric code, developed using a grid of 54 modules (6x9), uses figures to connote the image of the event in every element of communication, from the poster to the backdrop, from information panels to wayfinding signage, from stands to badges. Below are the variations of the lettering systems.

374

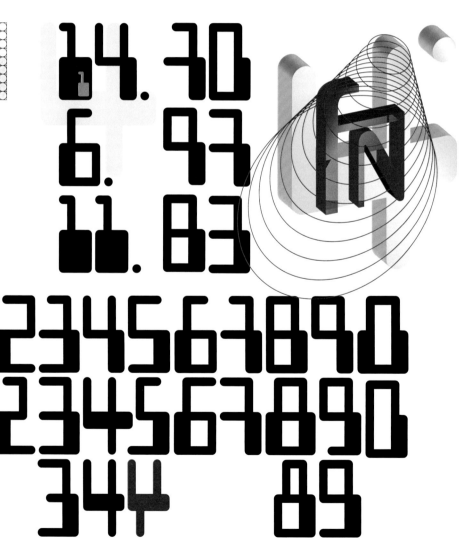

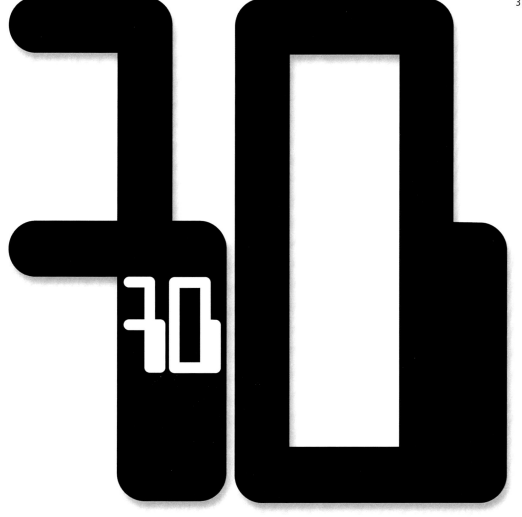

A 180-Metre Long Tunnel

Signage for the Ravello Festival

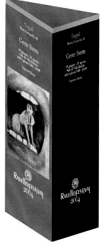  

376

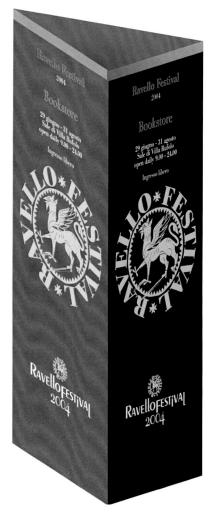

Notes
What could be more fascinating for a graphic designer than to be asked to cover two walls in a 180-metre long tunnel? Performances, concerts, conventions and events all find a place on these panels, each of which measures 100x140 centimetres. They were installed, uninterrupted, along the walls of the tunnel, reproducing a photograph, a drawing or an image, each accompanied by the event program. Everything was rigorously highlighted by a large number marking the date. The lettering, in Bodoni, justified left and right along a central axis. The images are the same used in all of the material, from the program to invitations, from postcards to posters.
The installation, by Raffaele Cioffi, used wood supports on aluminium rails, with neon lighting in a continuous protective housing.

To illustrate the vastness of the program, the following section presents a look at the panels used to decorate the tunnel, a summary list of events from the 2004 Ravello Festival.

1.

2.

3.

377

27/30 June
Education
XIX Summer Seminar
I sogni dell'impresa.
Visioni, progetti,
decisioni

27 June
Symphonic Music
Orchestre
Philharmonique
de Nice

28/31 June
Visual Arts
Dreams
Photography Exhibition
by **Grete Stern**

28 June
Musical Walks
String Quartet
"Manuel Canales"

29 June
Visual Arts
La vita è segno
Lo Studio Spera
& Spera

29 June
Trends
Escola do Teatro
Bolshoi no Brasil

2 July
Symphonic Music
Hungarian Radio
Symphonic Orchestra of
Budapest
Conductor: **László**
Kovács

4 July
Musical Walks
Musica non stop
Orizzonti Ensemble

6 July
Musical Walks
Sleep, and peraphs
dream...

7 July
Preview - Trends
Meeting with
Maurice Béjart

8 July
Trends
Béjart Ballet Lausanne

4.

5.

378

6.

7.

8.

9 July
Preview – Symphonic
Music
Meeting with
Yurij Temirkanov

9/10 July
Symphonic Music
**Philharmonic Orchestra
of Saint Petersburg**
Conductor: **Yurij
Temirkanov**

11 July
Musical Walks
**Musica non stop
Coro Polifonico
"Laeti Cantores".
Neapolitan Clarinet
Quartet**
*Lucy in the Sky
with Diamonds*

13 July
Trends
Philip Glass in concert

14 July
Musical Walks
I have a dream...
Ensemble Dissonanzen

15 July
Preview – Education
Meeting with
Mariano Rigillo

15 July
Education
Genius loci
Neruda's Dream

15 July
Musical Walks
Graffiando Vento

16/17 July
Symphonic Music
**Philharmonisches
Orchester Detmold**
Conductor: **Erich
Wächter**

18 July
Special Events
*Matinée di musica
per banda*
Banda "Città di Minori"
Preview
Musical Walks
Meeting with
Frederic Rzewski
Musical Walks
Un sueño de revolución

20 July
Trends
**Herbie Hancock, Wayne
Shorter, Dave Holland
and Brian Blade
in concert**

21 July
Musical Walks
*Violin solo:
homage to Luciano
Berio*
**Francesco D'Orazio
Ensemble**

22 July
Education
Tea with the author
A petit tour:
from the Ravello
Festival to Anacapri
*Give us today our daily
horror*

9.

10.

11.

23 July
Education
Conference: *Dream
and networks. Betting
on Italian Quality*

24 July
Education
Conference: *Dream
and networks. Betting
on Italian Quality*

24 July
Special Events
*A Deluge is Good for
the Geraniums*
Performance
by **Enrico Bertolino**
and **Fabio Bonifacci**

25 July
Musical Walks
**Music non stop
Duo Terracciano
Ensemble of the
Benevento State
Conservatory**
Smile!

27 July
Feast of San Pantaleone
Concert Band
Fireworks

28 July
Musical Walks
Street Virtuosi

29 July
Education
Tea with the author
A petit tour:
from the Ravello
Festival
to Anacapri
*Reading in Dreams,
Reading Dreams*

1 August
CineMusic
**A Midsummer Night's
Dream** (1935)
CineMusic Young
people
Les Choristes (2004)
Film-concerto
Nosferatu (1922)

31 August
Visual Arts
**Mindscapes
Paesaggi mentali**
Photography Exhibition

2 August
"Cinema and Dreams"
Retrospective
Il posto delle fragole
(1958)
Film-concert
Rapsodia satanica
(1915)
**"Ravello CineMusic
2004" Prize
Primo amore** (2004)
CineMusic Young
People
**Scooby Doo 2
Monster Unleashed**
(2004)

3 August
CineMusic
One from the Heart
(1982)
Totò Jazz
La Banda degli onesti
"Ravello CineMusic
2004" Prize
**What Will Happen
to Us** (2004)
CineMusic Young
People
**Sinbad: The Legend of
the Seven Seas** (2003)

379

12.

13.

4 August
"Cinema and Dreams"
Retrospective
Dreams (1990)
Film-concert
Secret of a Soul (1926)
"Ravello CineMusic
2004" Prize
L'amore ritorna (2004)
CineMusic Young
people
**Looney Tunes
Back in Action** (2003)

5 August
**Homage to Federico
Fellini, creator of
dreams**
Fellini Jazz
8 e 1/2 (1963)
Director: Federico Fellini
CineMusic Young
people
Peter Pan (2003)

380

14.

6 August
CineMusic
"Cinema and Dreams"
Retrospective
Open your Eyes (1997)
Showstoppers
Chrissy Caine
CineMusic Young
people
in collaboration with
the Giffoni Film Festival
national preview

7 August
CineMusic
"Cinema and Dreams"
Retrospective"
Eyes Wide Shut (1999)
**Music in your Eyes
The Ennio Morricone
Soloists**
Film: national preview
CineMusic Young
people
Brother Bear (2003)

15.

8 August
Special Events
Music matinée
Special music from films
"Città di Minori" Band
Preview – CineMusic
**Meeting with
Dino Risi**
CineMusic
"Cinema and Dreams"
Retrospective
The Dreamers (2003)
Awarding of the
"Ravello CineMusic
2004" Prize
The Italian dream of
the 1960s
Il sorpasso (1962)
CineMusic Young
People
**Pirates of the
Caribbean: The Curse
of the Black Pearl**
(2003)

16.

10 August
Special Events
Treasure Hunt Musical
Created by Lina
Wertmuller

11 August
Special Events
**Sunrise Concert
Krakow Opera
Orchestra**

11 August
Musical Walks
As it were...

12/14 August
Education

17.

A petit tour:
from the Ravello
Festival
to Anacapri
Life is a Dream
The past and the future
in literary visions

13 August
Trends
Peppe Barra
Concerto variato

19 August
Education
Tea with the author
A petit tour:
from the Ravello
Festival
to Anacapri
We grow only if we
dream
Are infancy and
adolescence still the
age of dreams?

18.

20 August
Preview
Trends
Meeting with
Salvatore Sciarrino

21 August
Trends
Lohengrin 2
Drawings for a garden
of sound

381

22 August
Musical Walks
Music non stop
Percussion Time

24 August
Musical Walks
Th "boom": when Italy
dreamed in musicals...
Mameli Ensemble
Voices

19.

26 August
Education - Tea with
the author
A petit tour:
from the Ravello
Festival to Anacapri
The Enigma of Dreams
The line between art
and folly

27 August
Conference:
Ethics and Finance
In collaboration with
the Fondazione Monte
dei Paschi di Siena
and S3.Studium

27 August
Trends
The Fairy Queen
Semi-Opera in a
prologue and five acts
by Henry Purcell

28 August
Musical Walks
Awake my Love!
Dreams and torments
of love
The Madrigalisti
della Pietrasanta

20.

29 August
Special Events
Musical matinée
"Città di Minori" Band

29 August
Trends
Concert by
Körnerscher Sing-Verein
Dresden

21.

382

22.

23.

24.

31 August
Musical Walks
Triplo sogno
Variations on a theme
by Wagner

1 September
Musical Walks
**Full Cycle of the
Sonatas for Violin and
Piano**
by Ludwig van
Beethoven

2 September
Musical Walks
**Full Cycle of the
Sonatas for Violin and
Piano**
by Ludwig van
Beethoven

3 September
Musical Walks
**Full Cycle of the
Sonatas for Violin and
Piano**
by Ludwig van
Beethoven

Training Course by
Salvatore Accardo

5 September
Chamber Music

8 September
Chamber Music
Violinist:
Salvatore Accardo
Pianist:
Giorgia Tomassi

11 September
Chamber Music
Piano duo:
**Aglika Genova
Liuben Dimitrov**

13 September
Chamber Music
Trio Matisse

15 September
Chamber Music
Pianist:
Michele Campanella

18 September
Chamber Music
Pianist: **Carlo Grante**

19 September
Torello Festival
Fireworks

20 September
Chamber Music
Savinio Quartet

22 September
Chamber Music
Borciani Quartet

25.

26.

27.

28.

25.
Pictograms

Abbreviated Communication

The number of graphic symbols is infinite. Letters, numbers, mathematical symbols and codes used by special disciplines are all graphic symbols. Graphic symbols are also pictograms. They summarise an object whose image offers a recognisable correlation with the object represented; or they can be abstract, with no visible relationship with the object or concept they represent.

1. The "Olympic Village" pictogram from the 1964 Tokyo Olympics.

2. 3. Pictograms from the Mexico City (1968) and Munich (1972) Olympics identifying the same destination, with a different design.

384 The first phase of the industrial revolution took place in Great Britain in the mid eighteenth century. The world of manufacturing began to make use of steam engines, new sources of fuel such as coal, new means of transportation like the railway, and a new organisation of factories. This produced a concentration of workers in cities and a substantial capitalist transformation of agriculture.

The grand World's Fairs of London and Paris drew masses of visitors from different nations and with different languages. They needed to be guided through the exhibitions and pavilions displaying the wonders of technology. This gave birth to the first archaic information and road signs, which sought to overcome the problem of language.

For the majority of illiterates in the pre-modern world, pictograms offered the best visual guide. Even today a traveller unfamiliar with the language of a country being visited or unable to decipher its alphabet, needs to be able to find the closest telephone or a lift.

Hence the importance of pictograms, intended as the universal and recognisable representation of services.

One of the first systems of road signs and directions was studied by the Italian Touring Club in 1895. In 1900 a congress of International Leagues of Touring Clubs from different countries considered a proposal to standardise road signage. In 1909 nine European governments adopted a selection of symbols for level crossings, speed bumps, etc. However, the most important unification of these pictograms was completed in 1926 and, in 1949 "The European Road Signs" program was adopted.

The Austrian Otto Neurath can be considered the father of modern pictograms. He was responsible for creating the indications used at the Museum of Vienna in 1924, the publication *Geselleschaft und Wirtschaft* from 1930 and the creation of the Isotype system.

Another precursor of modern symbols is the Japanese Katzumie, director of the 1964 Tokyo Olympics. He presented the first version of the Olympic pictograms that would be reused, in different derivations, at successive events.

When designing a pictogram, a graphic designer must consider two basic aspects: the first has to do with the necessity that the symbol designed is as comprehensible as possible; the second aspect is relative to how this design is expressed. It must be extremely synthetic, clear and basic; it must guarantee immediate legibility.

In his book *Il disegno applicato alle arti grafiche*, Amedeo Grütter suggests a method for arriving at the maximum possible stylization by verifying the links that exist in a symbol between its meaning and the graphic used to express it. He writes: "Once you have identified and selected the graphic form, it is enough to eliminate the elements in the drawing that do not appear indispensable to the completeness of what is depicted. Be careful not to surpass the point at which the message would no longer be comprehensible, or comprehensible only with difficulty, or only in part. At this point we will have reached the maximum stylization for its perception".

Notes
The industrial revolution was a consequence of technological innovations. The use of steam for power (J. Watt), inventions in the textile industry between 1733 and 1790 (Kay, Hargreaves, Arkwright, Crompton) and new procedures in the steel industry created by Darby, led to the rise of the capitalist factory, occupied by salaried workers, or the proletariat.

1.

2.

3.

Some of the many pictograms used to identify occupations in a hotel.

1. Template
2. Lift
3. Maid / Waiter
4. Maid / Waiter
5. Base Drawing
6. Reception
7. Lifeguard
8. Builders
9. Base Drawing
10. Workers
11. Gym
12. Administration
13. Cooks
14. WC
15. Care Giver
16. Nurse

Bibliography
▼Recommended reading:
Otl Aicher and Martin Krampen
Zeichensysteme der visuellen kommunikation
Handbuch fur designer, architekten, planer, organisatoren
Verlagsanstalt Alexander Koch
Stuttgart, 1977.
▼Rudolf Modley, William R. Myers,
Handbook of Pictorial Symbols,
Dover Publications, New York, 1976.

385

1.

2.

3.

4.

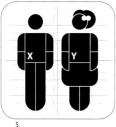

5.

6.

7.

8.

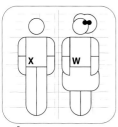

9.

10.

11.

12.

13.

14.

15.

16.

Pictograms that indicate a service in an airport or a taxi stand in Los Angeles are different from those in London, Paris or Rome.
We can find different symbols indicating the same service, or identical symbols indicating different services.
The task for tomorrow's graphic designers is to standardise the most important graphic symbols as part of a new universally recognised language, based on past experience.

Below:
some of the 30 pictograms designed for ENFAP, the UIL Labour Union's professional training organism.
They identify the thirty divisions of the various training courses.
Designed based on a square module to ensure flexible use, while technically responding to any variation in dimensions.

1. Social Services
2. Industry
3. Electrical
4. Livestock-Fishing
5. Transportation
6. Electro-Mechanical
7. Social Assistance
8. Industrial Management
9. Maritime
10. Ship Building
11. Business Restructuring
12. Food Services

386

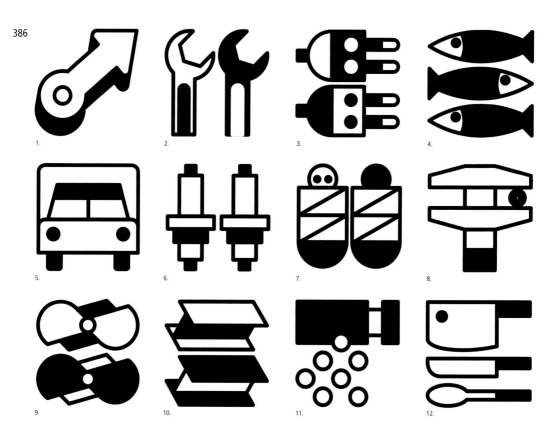

1.
2.
3.
4.
5.
6.
7.
8.
9.
10.
11.
12.

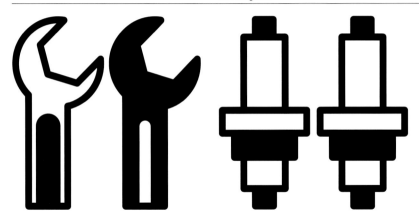

1. Pages from the dedicated chapter of the ENFAP manual illustrating the pictograms for training courses.

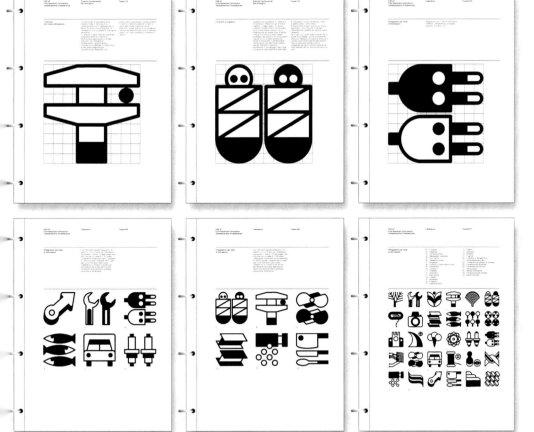

1.

This pictogram was "loaned" to the AIMA in Rome, the Italian Association of Alzheimer Patients. It was used, in 1987, for an advertising campaign consisting of 100x140 cm billboards posted in Rome. The addition of strings supporting the limbs signifies the support offered by AIMA.

The variations produced by the movements of the limbs through the rotation of individual elements belongs to the studies of symbols for sport (see the previous pages). The pictogram is articulated by assembling 16 different elements and making opportune rotations based on circles used to construct the geometry of the graphic.

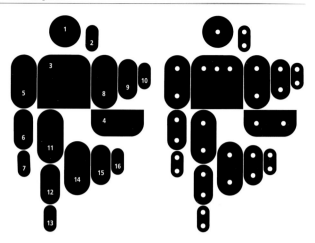

388

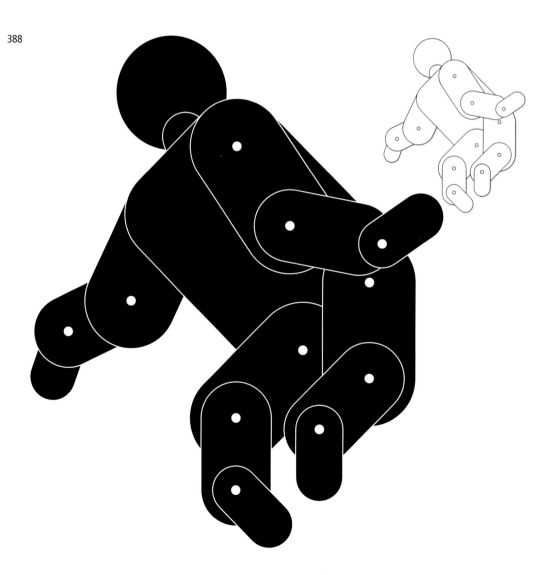

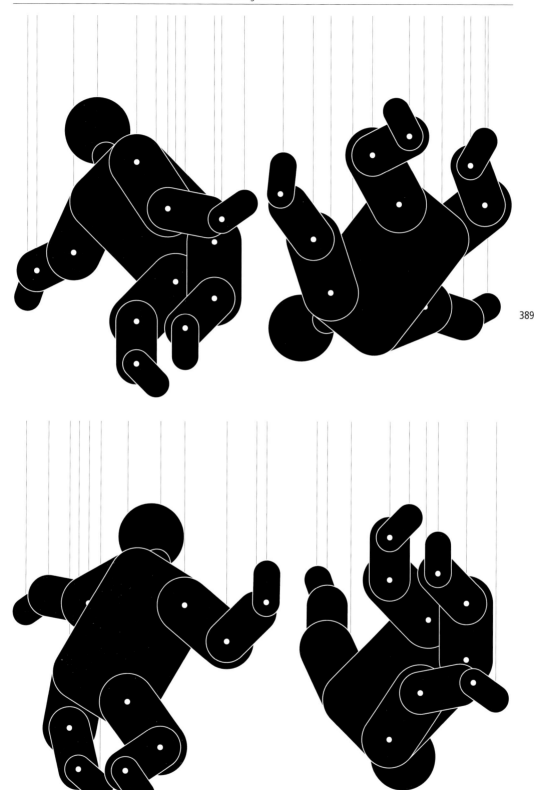

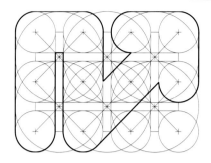

PALLUCCO

| ARIETE LEONE SCORPIONE | TORO VERGINE CAPRICORNO | GEMELLI BILANCIA ACQUARIO | CANCRO SAGITTARIO PESCI |

Left: a poster designed for the 1979 Milan Furniture Fair and illustrated by the signs of the Zodiac.
Those at the top were printed in white on Fasson adhesive paper; the ones at the bottom were printed in black (like the background), and die-cut to half thickness: when removed, they became visible and created a host of different new designs.

390

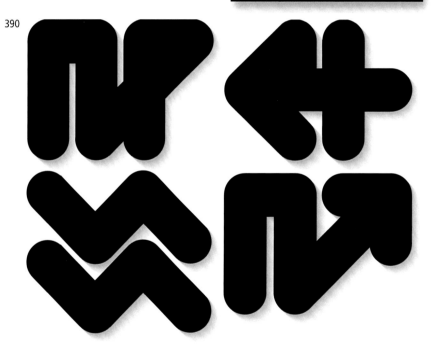

Bibliography
▼*1,000 pictograms,*
Corporation Pictograph,
New York, 1942.
Symbols designed under
the direction of Rudolf
Modley by Karl
Koehler, Henry Adams
Grant, John Carnes, etc.
▼*Graphische*
Voorstellingen,
Graphic symbols,
The Netherlands
Foundation for
Statistics.
Among other things, it
collects a representative
selection of symbols
from the Museum for
Social and Economic
Affairs in Vienna.
▼*Symbol Signs,*
American Institute of
Graphic Arts, for the
United States
Department of
Transportation, 1974.
A systematic collection
of symbols classified by
service or use.
▼*Shepherd's Glossary*
of Graphic Signs and
Symbols, Dover 1971.
A collection of
particular symbols used
by the International
Organization for
Standardization in
Geneva (ISO).
▼*Henry Dreyfuss,*
Symbol Sourcebook,
McGraw-Hill, 1972.
A collection of
pictograms and
professional symbols.

Pictograms

Trades, Professions, Sport,
Buildings, Vehicles,
Equipment, etc.

The many pictograms printed on these pages belong to a vast study by the author, presented here only in part for obvious reasons of space. They are designed on a general grid of 15x15 modules (in cyan) corresponding with an inner container of 13x13 modules (in red). The choice was made not to provide a legend for each pictogram, as each automatically communicates its meaning.

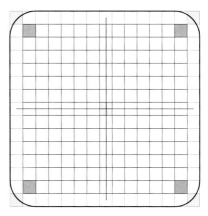

391

392

393

394

Notes

Identify a content and visual path that requires pictograms. Study a grid that serves as a guide for the various designs. Try to make the designs as synthetic as possible, without losing their meaning. Reduce them to their smallest dimensions and ensure they maintain their legibility.

26.
Brands and Logotypes

Signs of Synthesis

1. 130. Young graphic designers must show an interest in the scientific aspects of their profession. They need to learn the codes, ratios, proportions and methods that may initially be triggered by a methodology rather than by subjective analysis.
The many brands and logos printed here were the object of in-depth study with students. We examined the design process behind each one, from the initial brief to intermediate steps to the prudent and shared arrival at a decision.
A brand is the most difficult project for a graphic designer: it requires the greatest need for synthesis and the greatest amount of knowledge from which to distil it.

Using a sign as "brief" as possible, its symbolism must express and identify contents, in some cases very difficult.
A brand must be imagined in black and white; colour is a successive identity that must not interfere with the initial design.
The duration of a brand is theoretically unlimited in time.
It must survive all possible requirements and evolutions of a company.
If an advertising campaign is short-lived, the brand must outlive any trends and stand the test of time.
A brand is a signature.

A *brand* represents a company. As such, it is always present in advertising and corporate literature and accompanies every communication.

The following pages are illustrated by many of the brands designed by the author and by Gerardo Spera.

1.

2.

3.

4.

5.

6.

7.

8.

9. AGCI ASSOCIAZIONE GENERALE COOPERATIVE ITALIANE

10.

11.

12.

13.

14.

15.

16.

17.

18.

19.

20.

21.

22.

23. FIERA INTERNAZIONALE MARMI MACCHINE

24.

25.

26.

27.

28.

29.

30. COMUNE DI PISTOIA

31.

32.

33.

34.

35. UNIONE DEI COMUNI DELL'ALTOPIANO DELLE ROCCHE

36.

37. FEDERATION INTERNATIONAL DES DROITS DE L'HOMME

38.

39.

40.

397

41.

42.

43.

44.

45.

46. POTENZA CAMERA DI COMMERCIO INDUSTRIA ARTIGIANATO E AGRICOLTURA

47.

48.

49.

50.

51. AIMA

52.

53.

54.

55. ISERNIA CAMERA DI COMMERCIO INDUSTRIA ARTIGIANATO E AGRICOLTURA

56.

57.

58.

59.

60. PESARO E URBINO CAMERA DI COMMERCIO INDUSTRIA ARTIGIANATO E AGRICOLTURA

61.

62.

63.

64.

65.

66.

67.

68.

69.

70.

398

71.

72.

73.

74.

75.

76.

77.

78.

79.

80.

81.

82.

83.

84.

85.

86.

87.

88.

89.

90.

91.

92.

93.

94.

95.

96.

97.

98.

99.

100.

101.

102.

103.

104.

105.

106.

107.

108.

109.

110.

399

111.

112.

113.

114.

115.

116.

117.

118.

119.

120.

121.

122.

123.

124.

125.

126.

127.

128.

129.

130.

400

131.

132.

133.

134.

135.

136.

137.

138.

139.

140.

141.

142.

143.

144.

145.

146.

147.

148.

149.

150.

151.

152.

153.

154.

155.

156.

157.

158.

159.

160.

161

162

163

164

165

166.

167.

168.

169.

170.

171.

172.

173.

174.

175.

176.

177.

178.

179.

180.

401

181.

182.

183.

184.

185.

186.

187.

188.

189.

190.

191.

192.

193.

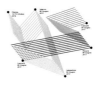

194.

195.

196.

197.

198.

199.

200.

201.

202.

203.

204.

205.

206.

207.

208.

209.

210.

402

211.

212.

213.

214.

215.

216.

217.

218.

219.

220.

221.

222.

223.

224.

225.

226.

227.

228.

229.

230.

231.

232.

233.

234.

235.

Symbols, logos and iconography from the Grande Oriente d'Italia.

The Symbol

A Sign
that Can be Born
of Other Signs

1./20. The symbol for the "Sinistra repubblicana" (Republican Left) political party is born from a sign. Designed for an electoral pamphlet in 1970, showing the "R", the first letter of "Repubblicani".
This new political group, which brings together the republican left, uses the same sign, inverted, to speak of the other origin of this political movement.

1. Colour version
2. BW version
3. Grey version
4. Outline version
5. Postage version
6. Background version
7. Background version
8. Background version
9. With corolla + colour
10. With corolla in black
11. With corolla in grey
12. Postage stamp

Originals
13. Original design
14. Original in 3D
15. Inverted original
16. Inverted original in 3D
17./20. Original sequence

404

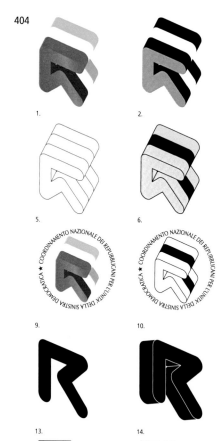

1.

2.

3.

4.

5.

6.

7.

8.

9.

10.

11.

12.

13.

14.

15.

16.

17.

18.

19.

20.

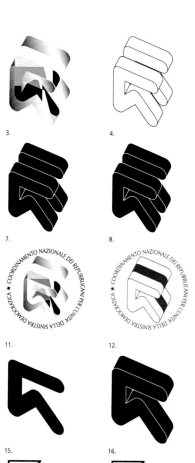

Notes
Variations of the symbol designed in different versions for different printed materials.

Bibliography
▼*Albe Steiner
Comunicazione visiva
Fratelli Alinari Idea
Milano 1977*
▼*Hampel, Grulich
Politische plakate der welt
Verlag Bruckmann KG
München 1971*
▼*Michele Spera
Materiali grafici per il partito repubblicano
Edizioni La Ragione
Roma 1987*
▼*Michele Spera
194 storie di un segno
Edizioni Socrates
Roma 1996*
▼*AA.VV.
La nuova immagine socialista
Il compagno
Quaderno di propaganda*
▼*AA.VV.
Images of an Era:
the American Poster
1945/75
Smithsonian Institution
Cambridge*

1./20. Studies for the design of a brand for Federnotai.
The design of a brand can give rise to many variations: all of the solutions tested constitute a body of research that serves not only to determine the most correct elements of the sign, but also to use it, in any possible application and illustrated form on company letterhead.

21./22. The Endas brand is a texture constructed by assembling five brands so that they coincide along one edge.
During the studies, the assembly of a brand can give rise to curious and unpredictable forms.
This exercise, other than stimulating experimentation with a sign in all of its possible expressions, may also produce textures, images and solutions that can be used as part of a company's global communications strategy.

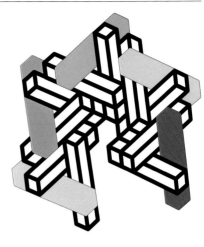

Bibliography
Federnotai
Corporate image manual,
Rome 1994

405

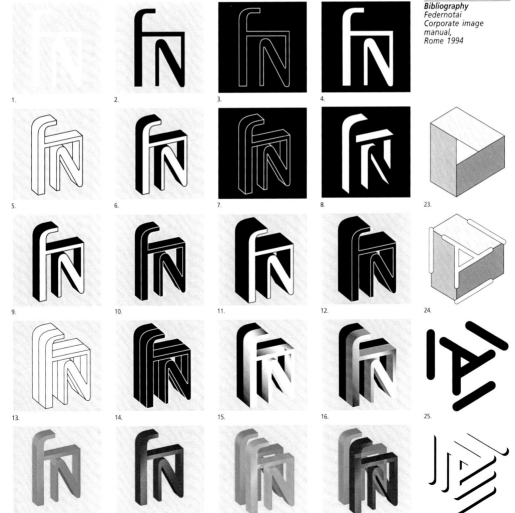

1. 2. 3. 4.

5. 6. 7. 8. 23.

9. 10. 11. 12. 24.

13. 14. 15. 16. 25.

17. 18. 19. a20. 26.

23./26. The sequence behind the construction of the brand for the Order of Labour Consultants: from the triangular form of the brief to the final product.

27./40. The Innocenti brand is represented by a letter "i".
It originates not only from the initial letter of the name of this car company, but also from the fact that the company took the name "Nuova Innocenti".
This inspired the connotation used for the corporate identity package, using a symbol rotated 45° to represent the change in management.
Also shown here are some of the studies and variations developed prior to arriving at the final version.

41. Four versions of the ENDAS logo (see the chapter dedicated to the Manual).

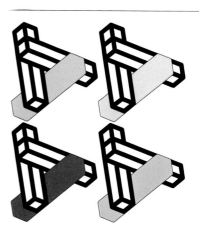

41.

406

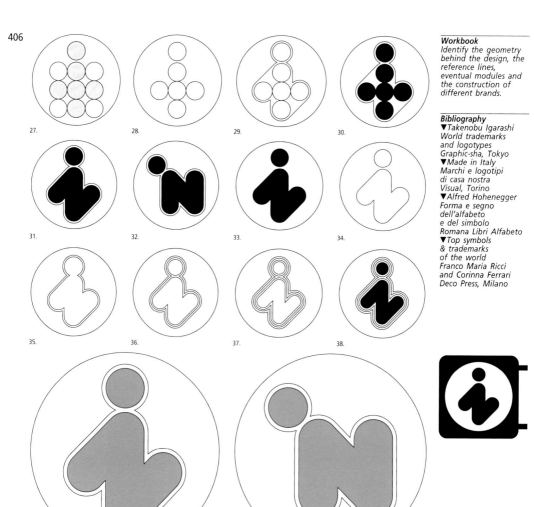

27.

28.

29.

30.

31.

32.

33.

34.

35.

36.

37.

38.

39.

40.

Workbook
Identify the geometry behind the design, the reference lines, eventual modules and the construction of different brands.

Bibliography
▼*Takenobu Igarashi World trademarks and logotypes Graphic-sha, Tokyo*
▼*Made in Italy Marchi e logotipi di casa nostra Visual, Torino*
▼*Alfred Hohenegger Forma e segno dell'alfabeto e del simbolo Romana Libri Alfabeto*
▼*Top symbols & trademarks of the world Franco Maria Ricci and Corinna Ferrari Deco Press, Milano*

1. The design of a brand can also return to ancient traditions of engraving and copper plates.
The origin of the brand shown here is explained in the text to the right, taken from the book by the author *194 storie di un segno*, Edizioni Socrates, 1996.

"Perhaps it was a reconsideration of so many years, or because one dark winter morning I headed back to my native city, which got me thinking about my origins.
The Speras are an ancient family from Lucania.
In his book L'eredità della priora, Carlo Alianello speaks of the Speras, of embraces in the dark, without being able to look into each others' eyes, of the conspirators who opposed the Piedmontese in 1860, of those who were executed.
They called us "the Casarsa", a reference to an old house that caught fire, though no one knows how. Perhaps as revenge, I don't know. Yet since this time, for generations, we were known as "the Casarsa". At the time I didn't know, I knew nothing of my roots.
But that winter curiosity led me to look through old papers. I found the letters written by Francesco Saverio Nitti to my father, evidence of fascist persecutions in my grandparents' home, historic photographs, certificates of excellence for a certain type of stud bull, and the photograph of an ancient house.
I redrew that house, as faithfully as possible. I added the flames pouring from the windows. I created a symbol that I use on certain pieces of letterhead or for the reconstruction of my family tree.
Now I know why, as a child, my father's oldest friends referred to me as 'the little Casarsa', as they pinched my cheeks".

Notes
This brand was used on the letterhead and business cards as the symbol of a small publishing house.

407

1.

Logotypes

When Text
Becomes Image

What name should be given to a brand that identifies a company: companies that deal in copyright (®, "TM" in the USA) tend to define the two principal graphic connotations of a sign or text respectively as a *figurative logo* and a *denominative logo*.

Logo, from the Greek suffix "logos", which has the same root as "logic", has the value of a discourse, a word, or language.
A logo is a group of two or more letters united into a single character or graphic form to identify a product, a company or an entity.
The word "logo" is derived from the English logotype, composed of "logo" and "type", letter.
The header of a journal can be considered a logotype.

1. 5. Some applications of the "Federnotai" logotype; the "Alexander" logo for a shop in Pescara, the "Vides Cinematografica" logo for Franco Cristaldi, the "Texing.e" logo and, below, the logo for the Agricolae.eu Press Agency.

408

Notes
Some software makes it possible to convert any glyph into a drawing by retracing its construction. It is evident how a letter can be manipulated to create a logo.

1.

2.

3.

4.

5.

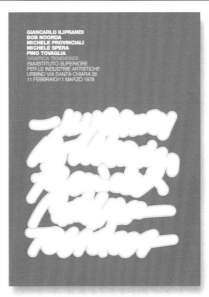

6.

6. Posters for two graphic design exhibitions in Rome and Urbino. A signature is a logotype. The figure illustrates the signatures of the give graphic artists who participated in the exhibition.
While each signature has its own semantic value, the graphic design gives each a unique visual language.

409

102ª ASSEMBLEA DEGLI AMMINISTRATORI DELLE CAMERE DI COMMERCIO

1.

1. 2. Two different interpretations of the "Unioncamere" logotype. Re-designed for various occasions for assemblies, meetings, conventions, etc., it is used on all graphic material accompanying these events. The logos assume the "relative" meaning of an image within the overall image of Unioncamere.

410

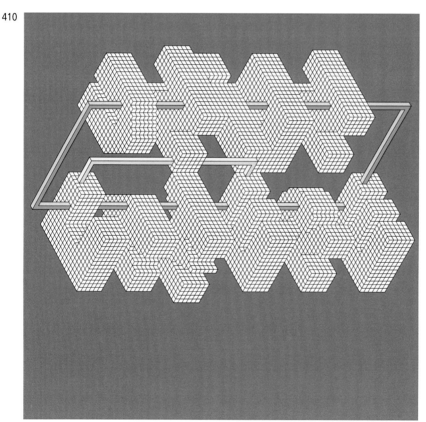

2.

RavelloFestival
2004

411

Notes
The logo for the 2004 edition of the "Ravello Festival", designed in different versions: above is the horizontal version; below the vertical one.
The latter is shown in two colour options, in this case dark red, used for particular events. Beside it is the application of the logo to the covers of Italian and English programs. The year of reference in Bodoni, the institutional typeface of the Ravello Festival, shown here in grey, is already an updated appendix tested to promote the 2005 edition.

1. This reworking of Ugo La Malfa's signature, from the early 1960s, became the logo for a series of communications with the headline "A signature that's a guarantee".

1.

412

2.

2. The "Spoletini" logo in a three-dimensional study that verifies the results of the assembly of its two different components.

3. Pages from the manual.

413

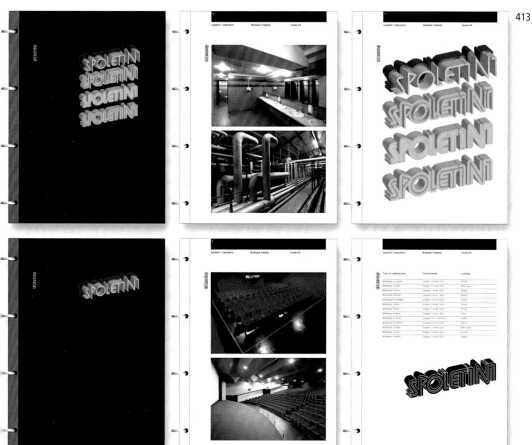

3.

Designing an Alphabet
And Creating a Logotype

414

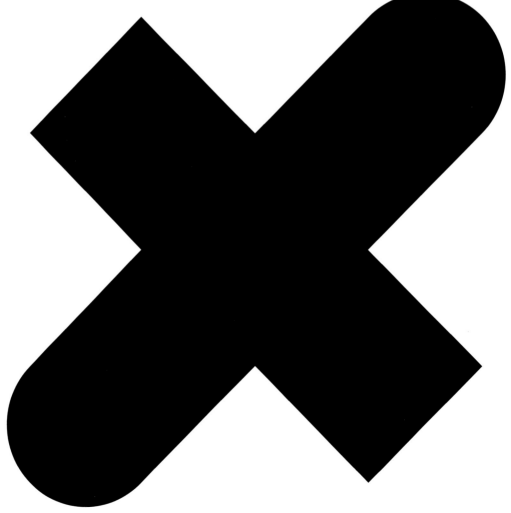

Studying a logotype may involve the design of an alphabet or at least part of one. This experiment can become a tool of design that is also useful, when not indispensable, for a graphic artist. Designing the glyphs of an alphabet required to compose the logotype we stimulate an interest in the traditions of typography, for the techniques of lettering and the study of ancient writings.

In traditional typography, a glyph of a certain size was designed with ratios that differed from smaller versions. There was a greater attention to detail, a minor width, a smaller proportional space in combinations. The study of glyphs helps students hone their perceptive skills, and learn to intelligently use their eyes and hands.

The Acronym

Initial Letters That Become a Brand and a Figurative Logo

1. An acronym is a collection of letters, initials of other words, that create a sort of "signature". Translated into a graphic form, an acronym becomes a brand. The acronym "CNA" stands for "Confederazione Nazionale dell'Artigianato", the National Confederation of Crafstmen.

2. The design of this acronym begins with a unique matrix that is then doubled and offset by 45°. The final design is obtained by stitching together the two masters and closing the figure. The distance between the two matrixes is a results of a series of tests to reduce the sign.

3. Studies of the reading of the CNA acronym and the relations between variations in line weights, legibility and reduction in the search for the best visualisation. Line weights are indicated in millimetres in the margin.

416

1.

0.14

0.33

0.52

0.71

0.90

1.10

3.

2.

4. 5. The acronym Enfap stands for "Ente di Formazione e Assistenza Professionale" (Organism for Possessional Education and Training).
The acronyms Spin 2, Spin 81 and Spin 83 designed for the IBI, Intergovernmental Bureau for Informatics, updated on various occasions with the date of events.

4.

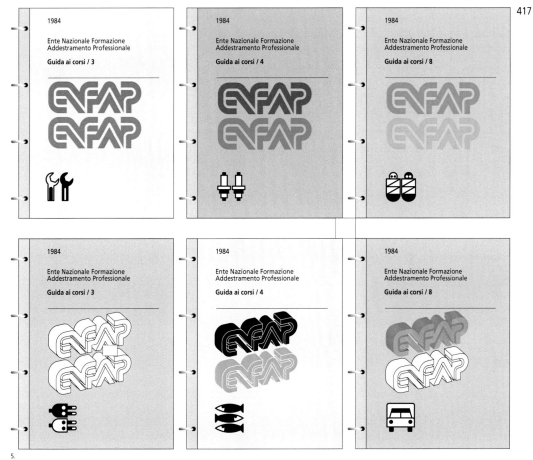

5.

Notes
The Istituto Tagliacarne brand illustrated on some of the pages from the coordinated identity manual.
Above, the construction of the symbol, inspired by the origins of the modules of the Unioncamere brand, of which it is an integral part; below, versions in colour, in black, etc.

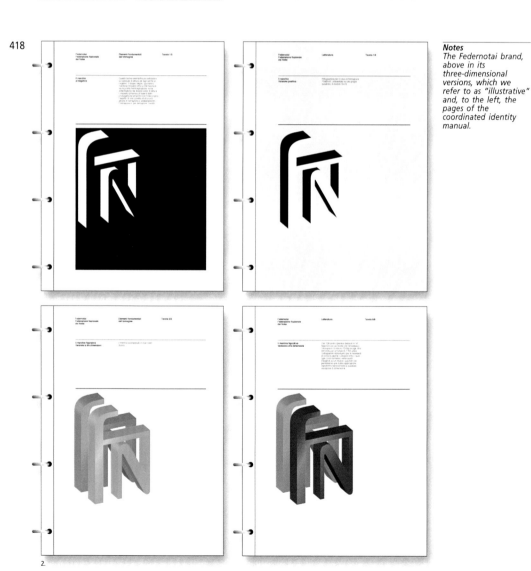

Notes
The Federnotai brand, above in its three-dimensional versions, which we refer to as "illustrative" and, to the left, the pages of the coordinated identity manual.

2.

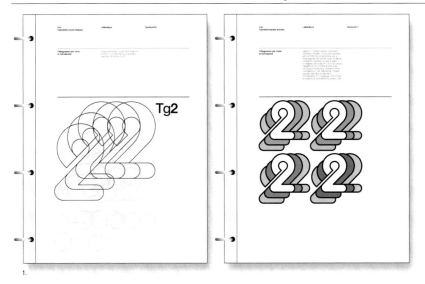

1.

419

Notes
The Tg2 logo for the RAI, Radiotelevisione italiana, in the pages of the manual illustrating how it is to be used. Above, the construction of the logo and a hypothetical colour code; below, versions in colour, in negative, in black, etc.

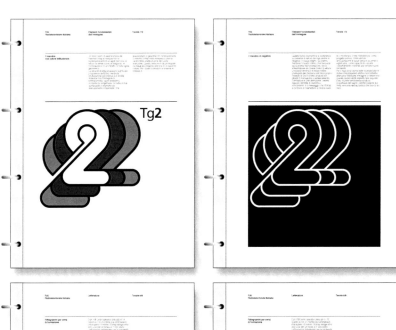

2.

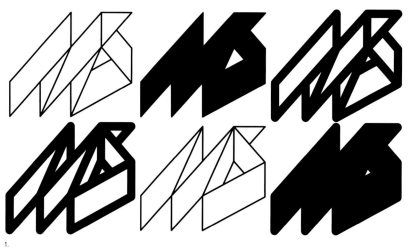

1.

2.

1. 2. "MS", two initials that form an acronym.
3. "VR" is the acronym of "*Voce Repubblicana*", shown here in different versions and thicknesses.
4. The acronym "UT" stands for "*Urbanistica Territoriale*".

Notes
The designs on this page illustrate studies of acronyms and the diverse solutions and variations adopted. The images show how the result changes when the thickness is modified.

3.

4.

1.

1. The logo of Aitr, the Italian Association of Rehabilitation Therapists.
It is composed of a denominative and a transparent figurative logo.
2. 3. Two covers of the magazine published by the Association where the logo is used as a header for this specialised fortnightly review.
4. The denominative logo in a three-dimensional outline version.
5. This postage stamp encloses the logo in a corolla containing the Association's full name.

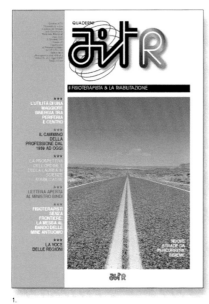

1.

2.

5.

421

Notes
A denominative and a figurative logo are fused into a single image, though with different appearances developed to meet different needs and adapt to different communications.

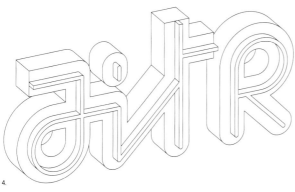

4.

27.
Newspapers and Journals

Modularity
for Complex Graphic
Situations

1. 2. 3. 4. The newspaper reprinted here, the studies of the grids, spaces, page layout and everything else required to design a newspaper or journal refer to a periodical printed in the early 1980s, and which lasted for 10 years.
Issue number 56 (with a particular graphic design to reinforce the periodical's long life), was the first to adopt a new look.
One characteristic of this project was the choice to eliminate any hierarchy in the titles. The small scale of the publisher (the

Federation of Young Republicans), the fact that those in charge were all young and thus projected toward new horizons, the trust they placed in their graphic artist, all made it possible to create an innovative project, above all with an exceptionally rational structure that refutes any temptation that may generate confusion, dictated by improvised choices. Reading some of the history of the design of newspapers may offer a better understanding of how these contingencies have proven fundamental.

This project, like all others presented in this book, is intended solely as one example, and a stimulus for further study.

1.

2.

Notes
Pages 1, 2, 3 and 4 are reprinted with an 18.6% reduction. Pages 5 to 10 are reprinted with a reduction of 11.9%

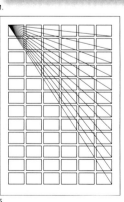

5.

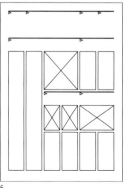

6.

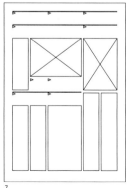

7.

All newspapers and journals of a certain importance have an original design with their own page layout. The grid consists of a modular system in which each module is based on a specific number of columns and the height of a page. The daily newspaper is the most complex graphic product because it requires constantly changing solutions to the organisation of a page.

5./10. The grid for a newspaper with the structure of the pages beside it.

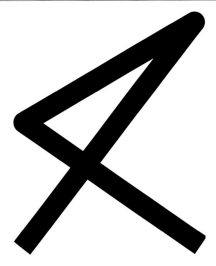

11. 12. A page of advertising from *Per*, the fortnightly publication for young republicans (the sign on the page in the form of a symbol reproduces the design of the grid) and the layout of the header.

423

3.

4.

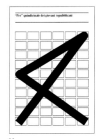

11.

12.

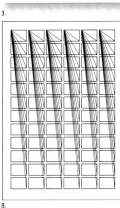

8.

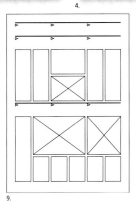

9.

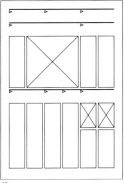

10.

1./10. The format of this fortnightly journal is 280 mm (w) by 400 mm (h).
This format suits both rolled paper, necessary for the rotary and offset rotary printing of an elevated number of copies, as well as a 64x88 format, to be stamped using the offset process.
The top, left and right margins are all 19.5 mm, and the bottom margin 25.5 mm.

The layout module is equal to 36 mm in width by 25 mm in height. The space between modules, in height and width, is 5 mm.
The layout grid, which consists of 6 modules in width and 12 in height, has a total of 72 modules and occupies a space that measures 241 mm in width by 355 mm in height.

424

1.

2.

Notes
Pages 1, 2, 3 and 4 are reprinted with an 18.6% reduction.
Pages 5 to 10 are reprinted with a reduction of 11.9%

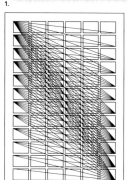

3.

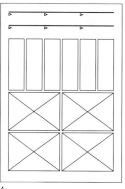

4.

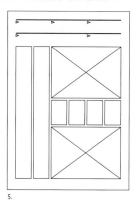

5.

Workbook

425

Purchase copies of Italian dailies (for example, *La Repubblica, Il Sole 24 Ore*, etc.) and foreign dailies (for example, *The Times, The New York Times, The Herald, Examiner*, etc).
Purchase copies of Italian and foreign periodicals.
Compare their layouts.

6.

7.

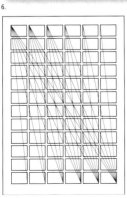

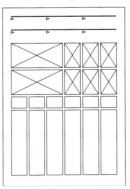

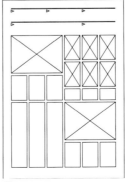

8.

9.

10.

1. 2. Layouts created using XPress feature a grid with the measurements of the x and y axes for each module.
These dimensions are calculated considering the zero value as coinciding with the paper format and not with the layout grid.

3. The facing page shows a grid that summarises the various indications relative to the construction of a page layout grid.
To assist with the reconstruction of the design process, all measurements are shown in centimetres, in rows and in Didot points, the number of rows that can be contained in a column at 9/9 and 10/10 type and, finally, the measurements in inches.

4./6. The use of horizontal lines is fundamental for creating a division between articles or groups of articles.
In the original they are of three weights:
0.5 points for the division between columns;
1 point for the division between articles;
3 points for the horizontal division between articles.

1.

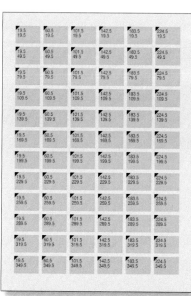

2.

Notes
Take a look at the chapter on page layout: you will find a host of useful technical information for the design of a newspaper or magazine.

Workbook
Analyse the layout of the pages and grids of various newspapers and magazine and reconstruct their modules.
If possible, work backwards to establish the original design.

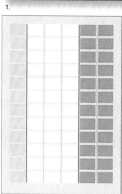

4.

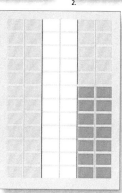

5.

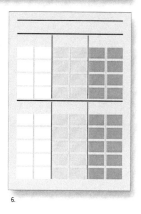

6.

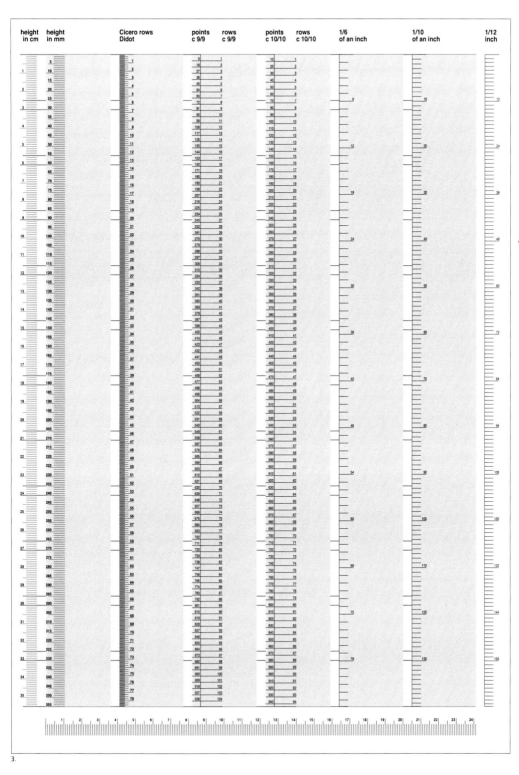

427

3.

Designing to a Grid

Visual Spaces and Rigorous Geometry

The denser a grid is with modules, the greater the possibilities offered during layout. However, the legibility of an order within the page decreases, because the alignments are less recognisable. Reconciling this dense network of requirements, often in a large journal with highly complex requirements in terms of communication, is an undertaking visible in very few of these publications.

It is enough to look at the projects by Peter Palazzo for the *New York Herald Tribune* from 1960, one of the first to apply a grid and a modular system to a daily newspaper; or the project by Louis Silverstein for the *New York Times*; or that by Paul Back for *Newsday*; or Massimo Vignelli for the *Herald*; or by Frank Ariss for the San Francisco *Examiner* from 1973; or Alan Fletcher's design for *Il Sole 24 Ore*. All examples of extraordinary projects that have little to do with their effective and real application.

1. 2. 3. The grid of a journal highlighting the vertical spaces in ascending order, and the horizontals with measurements of heights and widths.

428

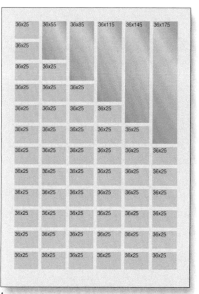

1.

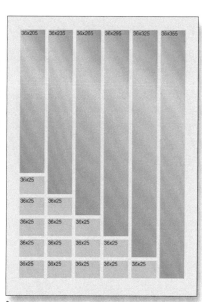

2.

Notes
The *Times* of London offers a unique example in the history of daily newspapers. In 1931 Stanley Morrison designed a special typeface: Times Roman.

5.

6.

7.

4. 11. Identification of the visual spaces of a journal.
The grid is constructed from two main areas, each consisting of 36 modules.
The diagonals geometrically identify the modules and margins.
The diagonal of the entire grid identifies all of the 72 modules and crosses them two by two in the vertical (modules marked in black) dividing the page into 6 uniform spaces, marking the ideal alignment for articles.

5./10. Studies of the various possible page layouts inside the grid.
Other than the grid of the journal, these images also show the position inside it of the spaces that divide the page into zones with precise functions.
The first six modules are dedicated to the recognisability of the page and the theme explored on each page.

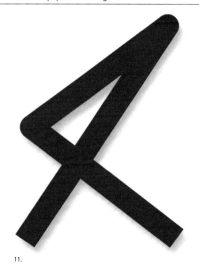

11.

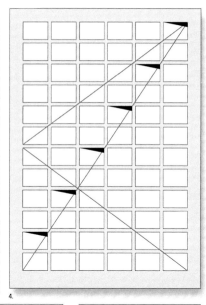

3.

4.

Workbook   429
Design a newspaper.
Typical grid and modules.
Design a grid with measurements in Cicero, points and millimetres.
Refer to the chapter on typing and the layout grid for typed documents.

8.

9.

10.

The Evolution of Newspapers and Magazines

A Long History of Compromises

How has the graphic design of daily newspapers evolved? What role was played by graphic designers in the construction of journals that must guarantee a coexistence between the needs of graphics and the urgency to communicate, as rapidly as possible, endlessly long titles beside short ones, monographic pages facing pages dense with a variety of information, and graceful italics forced to compete with advertising inserts?

This is a task that requires an intelligent collaboration between a graphic designer and an editor, the desire to be innovative and, above all, a great many compromises.
The newspapers we can buy today at a newsstand are not those that were laid out with such care and accuracy, some by famous designers.
In the best case, they are an ugly copy of those designs, which remained prototypes.

This section offers a summary look at the history of important newspapers and a few considerations by Allen Hurlburt, read and commented on in the classroom.
In his book *The grid: A modular system for the design and production of newspapers, magazines and books* he retraces the complex evolution of the graphic design of various publications. Stories of victories are accompanied by those of defeats suffered by graphic designers in this field.

430

The first journals in Italy were created during the 1500s. The most famous was *L'Avviso*, published in Venice, capital of the nascent publishing industry, by Manuzio. It contained news about arriving shipments, price lists, exchange rates, news and events from the world. More than news, the information was a set of notices - *avvisi* in Italian or gazette. It contained only commercial information and notices.

The first real newspapers, as we know them today, a tool not only of information but also of opinions and commentary, appeared in the 1600s in the most advanced nations.
However, also in these countries their impact was such that they often faced censorship and obstacles. In Great Britain Defoe's *Review*, Swift's *Examiner* and articles by Addison, Steele and Johnson offered readers a hand in identifying a national conscience and contesting those in power.
In Italy, the *Gazzetta di Parma* was published after many trials and tribulations in 1725, making it the country's oldest newspaper. The first true newspaper was the *Gazzetta veneta* by Gaspare Gozzi printed in 1760. It consisted of eight small pages, published twice a week. Gozzi later edited the *Osservatore veneto*, inspired by the English *Spectator*, an example for all European journalism, for both its layout and content. It contained the first commentaries, journalistic "pieces", current events and descriptions of happenings in Venice. Gozzi's legacy was taken up by Baretti with *La Frusta* and later by Verri's *Il Caffè*.

It is impossible to trace the entirety of the complex evolution of the design of newspapers.
Initially dailies used narrow columns of text, set between lines in an exclusively vertical direction. After 1930 they began to seek a layout that privileged the horizontality of the page. The trend not to emphasise the vertical gradually led to the elimination of the lines of text between columns and this was considered for some time the latest novelty in newspaper design, though in many cases the result was a hodgepodge of styles. Until 1960, the majority of newspapers used eight columns per page. Later, almost all of them adopted a division in six columns. At the same time, this new structure led to the adoption of a basic 9 point text, rather than the traditional 8 and 7 points.
This change was undoubtedly brought about by a problem of legibility. In fact, the typeface that consents the greatest ease of legibility occupies a space of approximately 15 pica rows and the optimum type size is 9 points with a total of 45 keystrokes per row (see the chapter "Legibility").
Prior to the 1930s, titles were arranged in narrow columns and, almost always, printed in upper case, often in very narrow typefaces and rather small point sizes. After the 1930s, even the way of producing a title was profoundly modified: upper and lower case letters, spanning multiple columns horizontally.
An exploration of newspaper graphics would require a great deal more space. We will limit ourselves here to retracing some of the most important events

in their history.
In 1932 Stanley Morison designed a typeface for the *Times* of London: Times Roman and laid out its new graphic design.
Replacing the gothic (old English) type with the clear letters of Times created a newspaper that, while derived from classical forms, looked extraordinarily modern. His work revolutionised the design of newspapers and the way of conceiving of thier format. Division lines separated zones inside the grid, reinforcing the harmony of structure, with photographs that were no longer set between them.
An important contribution was made by Peter Palazzo for the study of the *Sunday Herald Tribune* and the identification of the newspaper page as a modular organisation of cages and grids.
After 1960 many other graphic designers introduced a modular grid. This system produced two different approaches: seeking assistance from an external consultant, true specialists in graphic design, though who have little familiarity with the problems of running a newspaper; turning to internal graphic designers who certainly operate in close symbiosis with the editor, have a better understanding of the reality and needs of a newspaper but, at the same time, can be hindered by internal pressures. Important newspapers have generally opted for the creation of an internal group.
Until 1966 the *London Times* maintained its tradition of filling the first page with classified ads. Yet, from this moment onward, it moved toward a format that was well proportioned and well organ-

ised, under the editorial direction of Jeannette Collins.
Morrison's Times Roman typeface remained, and the headlines (leading titles) were uniform in weight and left justified with occasional contrasting symmetrical arrangements. Rows in bold were used to increase the horizontal emphasis of the page.
From its beginnings, the *London Sunday Times* has been completely separate from the daily. It was not involved in Morrison's restyling, however, in recent years it was redesigned in an interesting format by its editor Harold Evans and its art director Edwin Taylor.
The *New York Times* has maintained forms with ties to tradition with greater tenacity than its counterpart in London. Until only recently, its first page was one of the last bastions of decorated titles.
In 1960, the director of the *Times*, Louis Silverstein, decided to restructure the design of the pages of the daily editions and the Sunday edition. His layout (6 asymmetrical columns) for the Op ed Pages, with strong graphic illustrations became an example of structural changes at the *Times*, and influenced the treatment of this type of content in many other papers. Louis Silverstein gradually worked his way through the other special sections and the appearance of the news pages. In 1976 the *Times* underwent another change, passing from 8 to 6 columns. Tabloid formats, which accounted for the majority, concentrated on black headlines and the boldness of their presentation rather than the quality of an overall design.

Bibliography
▼*Allen Hurlburt*
The grid:
A modular system for the design and production of newspapers, magazines and books.
Van Nostrand Reinhold Company, New York.

1.

1. 2. Two pages from *Sinistra Oggi*, the fortnightly publication of the Left Wing Republicans.

2.

There have been exceptions, and one of the most recognisable is *Newsday*, a highly successful journal in provincial America. Redesigned by its art director Paul Back, the layout adopted the serious, almost repressed tone of a new magazine and diversified itself from the confusion shouted from the pages of other major tabloids. The cage is based on a grid of 304 modules that occasionally makes use of ad hoc boxes. One characteristic of the layout is the way in which advertising content is organised. Small ads are grouped together in single pages or rectangular units that do not invade the editorial space.

In 1971 Massimo Vignelli designed a new Sunday journal for New York City, called the *Herald*. He created a format with a number of interesting characteristics. The creative key to the new journal was a modular grid that divided the space horizontally. This led to a complete control of the space of the page, without limiting the possible coexistence between all types of material, from text to images.

The page, which measures 431x570 mm, consisted of 6 columns with 6 vertical divisions and 17 horizontal divisions. One of the unusual characteristics of this grid is the return to the rule of airiness in the division of the columns. This format was designed also to take advantage of the use of the computer to lay out the pages, lightening the work of composition and page layout.

While the *Herald* had a short-lived run, its design was close to a perfect application of the grid studied specifically for a newspaper.

The same year that Massimo Vignelli designed the format for the *Herald* in New York, Frank Ariss, who had studied design at London's Royal College of Art, embarked on an interesting program to redesign the *Minneapolis Tribune*.

This project was the product of two studies. It was based on a grid with precise vertical and horizontal measurements that produced the space necessary for titles in Helvetica and columns with 9 point text and a leading of 1/2 point of space between the rows. Frank Ariss called his approach "graphic engineering" and his program was studied to amalgamate with new techniques made possible by the computer, at the time being adopted by the *Minneapolis Tribune*.

The redesign resulted in a notable cleanliness and a significant savings in the time required to compose the texts, lay them out and go to print.

An interesting innovation introduced by this project was the adoption of the English tradition of positioning the most important article on the first page to the left, rather than to the right, now adopted by almost all newspapers.

The paper contains a host of other typographic innovations: instead of the indent at the start of a paragraph, an empty line separates the paragraphs; articles that run over by only a few lines are contained on the same page; titles use upper case letters only when the structure of the phrase allows, when they begin a new line.

One year after the introduction of this format by the *Minneapolis Tribune*,

Frank Ariss dedicated himself to another program to redesign the *San Francisco Examiner*. Based on the same format and using an identical grid, this project introduced Sans Serif typefaces for both the text and titles. The first prototype of the *Examiner* was issued in July 1973.

Another interesting example of a newspaper redesign is offered by the Italian economic daily newspaper *Sole 24 Ore* designed by Alan Fletcher. The grid of 9 units designed by Fletcher is unusual, though it brings together a large number of different column widths, that introduce a variety to this format and permit the editor to manipulate the varied content typical of this paper.

Speaking of the new project for the *Sole 24 Ore*, Alan Fletcher, evidently disappointed, confessed: "The design of the *Sole 24 Ore* is a difficult undertaking. The compromise with the sophistication of typography is inevitable, the control of the page layout is minimum and perfection unattainable.

The graphic style must be energetic, violent and distinguishable in order to be visible".

28.
Advertising Formats

The Modules of
La Repubblica

Advertisements (or "advertising spaces" for the space they occupy) are generally found in daily newspapers and periodicals.
Normally, these spaces are sold by an advertising sales company hired by the editor of a newspaper. Purchasers are almost always advertising agencies who arrange the formats, frequency and rhythm of publication, above all in the case of an advertising campaign. Graphic designers who do not own their own agency can directly acquire advertising space.

It is important to know the dimensions of the spaces available in various newspapers, their position on a page, how the original designs are to be laid out and what formats they are to be provided in to obtain the best results.
Leading advertising sales companies offer brochures for various publications indicating the dimensions, costs, techniques of printing and reproduction and the formats and supports for submissions: on paper, film, positive or negative, selection, etc., or whether a chromalin proof or original is to be provided.

To learn more, other than speaking with a sales company, there are also specialised books and magazines that collect this information.
Dati e tariffe pubblicitarie is one of these publications: it offers up-to-date information on tarrifs, technical information and the distribution of over 2,000 publications in Italy.
Facing page, top right: manchettes for *La Repubblica*. They are found at both sides of the header and measure 42 mm in width by 37 mm in height.

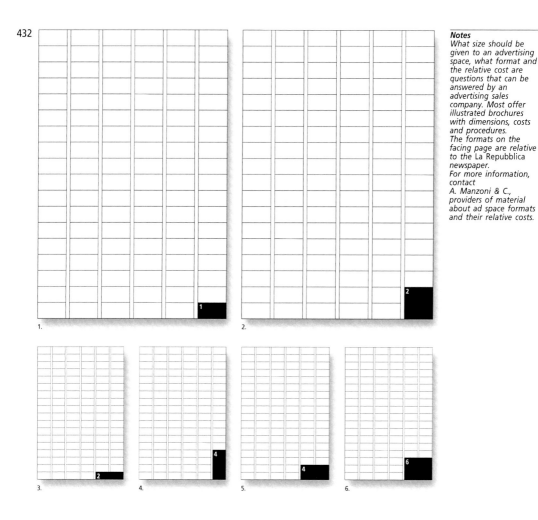

1.

2.

3.

4.

5.

6.

Notes
What size should be given to an advertising space, what format and the relative cost are questions that can be answered by an advertising sales company. Most offer illustrated brochures with dimensions, costs and procedures.
The formats on the facing page are relative to the La Repubblica newspaper.
For more information, contact A. Manzoni & C., providers of material about ad space formats and their relative costs.

1.
1 module, 42x23
2.
2 modules, 42x46
3.
2 modules, 90x23
4.
4 modules, 42x92
5.
4 modules, 90x46
6.
6 modules, 90x69
7.
8 modules, 90x92
8.
9 modules, 137x69
9.
10 modules, 90x117
10.
12 modules, 90x140

11.
12 modules, 137x92
12.
14 modules, 90x165
13.
15 modules, 137x117
14.
16 modules, 90x188
15.
16 modules, 185x92
16.
18 modules, 90x212
17.
20 modules, 185x117
18.
21 modules, 137x165
19.
22 modules, 90x260
20.
24 modules, 137x188
21.
27 modules, 137x212

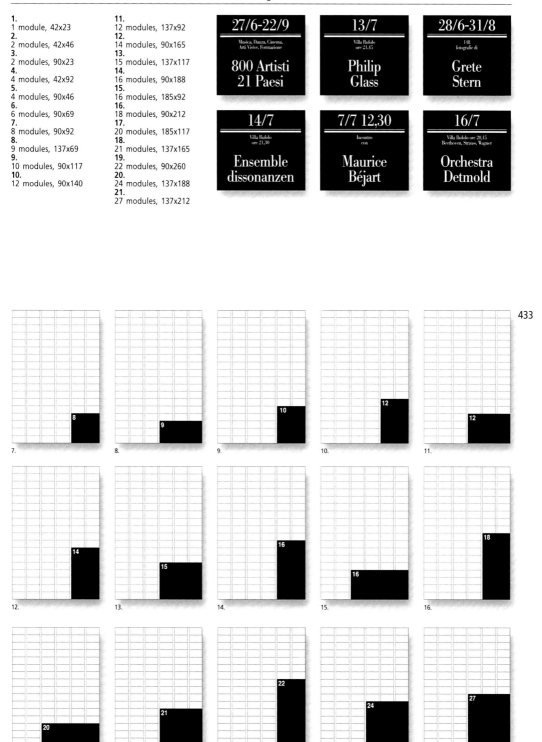

433

1.
12 modules
280x46 mm
Format allowed only
for "sponsorships".

2.
18 modules
42x433 mm
Format allowed only
for "book" advertising.

3.
108 modules
280x433 mm
Full page.

4.
234 modules
578x433
Two page.

5.
28 modules
185x165
Special format
inserted without other
advertising

6.
32 modules
185x188
Special format
inserted without other
advertising

7.
33 modules
137x260
Special format
inserted without other
advertising

8.
36 modules
90x433
Special format
inserted without other
advertising

9.
36 modules
185x212
Special format
inserted without other
advertising

10.
42 modules
280x165
Special format
inserted without other
advertising

11.
44 modules
185x260
Special format
inserted without other
advertising

12.
48 modules
280x188
Special format
inserted without other
advertising

13.
54 modules
280x212
Special format
inserted without other
advertising

14.
54 modules
137x433
Special format
inserted without other
advertising

434

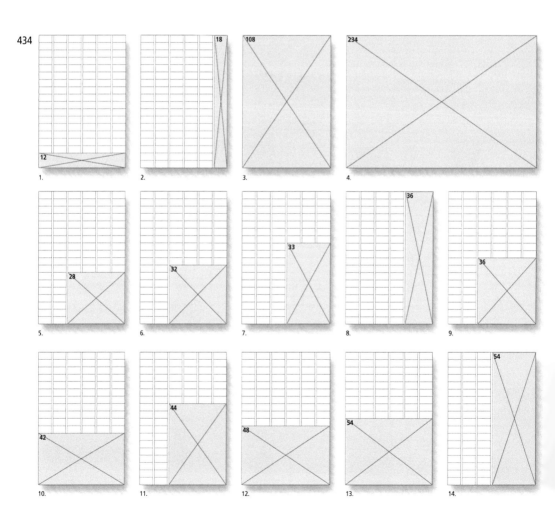

Characteristic
techniques of the daily
newspaper
La Repubblica
and the inserts *Affari*
& Finanza and *Salute*;
the periodicals *Musica!*
Rock & altro,
Il Venerdì
and *L'Espresso*.

	La Repubblica	Affari & Finanza	Salute
Periodicity	Every day	Weekly Monday	Weekly Saturday
Printing Procedure	Flexo/Napp and Roto offset	idem	idem
Number of modules/page	108	108	108
Sub. of b&w material	from 3 to 5 days prior to publishing date	from 3 to 5 days idem	from 3 to 5 days idem
Sub. colour material	18 days prior to publishing date	18 days idem	18 days idem
Material requested	1 copy positive photo paper	1 copy idem	1 copy idem
Dither	24/26 lines	24/26 lines	24/26 lines
Halftone Screen	Round point	Round point	Round point
Reading Point	minimum 5% Maximum 90%	minimum 5% Maximum 90%	minimum 5% Maximum 90%
Colour	Full tone digital file, with treated images in CT, EPS or TIFF; texts in Macintosh format using Quark XPress 3.3.1 complete with the registration of all upper and lower case fonts, print and screen. Supports adapted to the transfer of digital information: Sy Quest 44.88 or 270 MB, CD ROM + 2 proof sheets (digital proofs) + 1 copy on positive photographic paper.		
Recommendations	Avoid positioning texts smaller than 12 point on coloured backgrounds. Small serifed texts, lines, frames comprised of more than one colour with even the slightest offset will appear thick, blurred and in any case unpleasing to the eye.		

	Musica! Rock & altro	Il Venerdì	L'Espresso
Periodicity	Weekly Wednesday	Weekly Friday	Weekly Saturday
Cover Date	Wednesday	Friday	following Friday
Printing Process	Rotogravure	Rotogravure	Rotogravure
Dither	54 lines	60 lines	48 lines
Binding	Metal Staple	Metal Staple	Metal Staple
Submission of Material	4 weeks prior to publishing date	4 weeks prior to publishing date	4 weeks prior to publishing date

Notes
*The information to the
left is taken from the
brochure provided by
A. Manzoni & C., the
concessionaire of
advertising for these
papers to advertising
agencies and
advertisers.*
*You can ask for
information about
advertising space in
other newspapers by
asking their relative
concessionaires.*

435

Advertising Spaces

Insertion Dimensions of Various Local Newspapers

These pages provide a few indications relative to local newspapers and periodicals, as found in the brochure published by A. Manzoni & C.
They refer to the newspapers listed below, in tabloid, traditional and other formats.
All measurements are expressed in millimetres.

436

Tabloid Format modules	Module	8 modules	12 modules	18 modules	24 modules	24 modules	27 modules	36
	wxh	2x4	2x6	3x6	3x8	6x4	3x9	6x6
Luna Nuova	42x21	89x93	89x141	135x141	135x189	276x93	135x213	276x141
Corr. Rivoli/Collegno	42x21	89x93	89x141	135x141	135x189	276x93	135x213	276x141
Il Canavese	38x18	80x78	80x118	122x118	122x158	248x78	122x178	248x118
La Nuova Settimo Torinese	38x18	80x78	80x118	122x118	122x158	248x78	122x178	248x118
Nuova Periferia Chivasso	38x18	80x78	80x118	122x118	122x158	248x78	122x178	248x118
La Sentinella del Canavese	43x23	90x93	90x141	137x141	137x189	280x93	137x213	280x141
L'Occasione	43x23	90x93	90x141	137x141	137x189	280x93	137x213	280x141
La Sesia	43x21	90x93	90x141	137x141	137x189	280x93	137x213	280x141
La Piazza Grande	43x21	90x93	90x141	137x141	137x189	280x93	137x213	280x141
Il Corriere di Alba e Bra	43x21	90x93	90x141	137x141	137x189	280x93	137x213	280x141
Corriere di Novara	38x19	83x80	83x121	128x121	128x161	262x80	128x182	262x121
Corriere Valsesiano	42x21	90x84	90x126	136x126	136x168	279x84	136x189	279x126
Il Resegone	40x21	86x84	86x126	129x126	129x168	258x84	129x189	258x126
Notes	43x43	86x172	86x258	129x258	129x344	258x172	129x387	258x258

Traditional Format	Module wxh	8 modules 2x4	12 modules 3x4	18 modules 3x6	18 modules 9x2	24 modules 6x4	24 modules 4x6	27 modules 9x3
Corriere di Chieri	36x33	77x155	118x155	118x236	364x74	241x155	159x236	364x114
Corriere di Moncalieri	36x33	77x155	118x155	118x236	364x74	241x155	159x236	364x114
La Guida	40x42	84x170	129x170	129x256	395x85	260x170	172x256	395x127
La Nuova Provincia	37x40	78x164	118x164	118x247	365x81	242x164	160x247	365x123
Il Monferrato	37x40	78x164	118x164	118x247	365x81	242x164	160x247	365x123
Il Piccolo	36x41	76x174	116x174	116x263	356x85	236x174	156x263	356x129
Giornale di Merate	38x40	80x175	122x175	122x265	375x85	249x175	164x265	375x130

Other Formats	Module wxh	8 modules 2x4	12 modules 2x6	18 modules 3x6	24 modules 3x8	24 modules 6x4	24 modules 3x8	27 modules 3x9
La Voce Alessandrina	43x43	88x172	88x258	131x258	131x344	263x172		131x387

	Module wxh	8 modules 2x4	12 modules 3x4	14 modules 7x2	18 modules 3x6	21 modules 7x3	24 modules 4x6	27 modules 3x9
La Provincia Granda	43x39	90x162	137x162	324x80	137x243	324x121	184x243	137x365

	Module wxh	8 modules 2x4	12 modules 3x4	16 modules 8x2	18 modules 3x6	24 modules 6x4	24 modules 4x6	32 modules 8x4
Giornale di Lecco	41x35	86x151	130x151	357x74	130x229	265x151	175x229	357x151

	Module wxh	8 modules 2x4	12 modules 3x4	18 modules 3x6	14 modules 7x2	24 modules 6x4	24 modules 4x6	21 modules 7x3
Il Biellese	45x28	95x118	145x118	145x178	344x58	294x118	195x178	344x88
Eco di Biella	45x28	95x118	145x118	145x178	344x58	294x118	195x178	344x88

	Module wxh	2 modules 1x2	4 modules 2x2	10 modules 2x5	20 modules 4x5	40 modules 4x10
Anteprima Torino	40x22	40x48	85x48	85x122	175x122	175x250

Layout	N. columns	N. modules per column	Modules per page
Tabloid Format	6	18	108
Traditional Format	9	12	108
La Voce Alessandrina	6	9	54
La Provincia Granda	7	11	77
Giornale di Lecco	8	13	104
Eco di Biella	7	16	112
Il Biellese	7	16	112
Anteprima Torino	4	10	40

437

Tabloid Format	36 modules 4x9	44 modules 4x11	48 modules 6x8	54 modules 6x9	108 modules 6x18	Manchettes wxh	Window wxh
Luna Nuova	182x213	182x261	276x189	276x213	276x432	37x47	88x93
Corr. Rivoli/Collegno	182x213	182x261	276x189	276x213	276x432	37x47	88x93
Il Canavese	164x178	164x218	248x158	248x178	248x358	50x30	80x78
La Nuova Settimo Torinese	164x178	164x218	248x158	248x178	248x358	45x60	80x78
Nuova Periferia Chivasso	164x178	164x218	248x158	248x178	248x358	50x30	80x78
La Sentinella del Canavese	185x213	185x263	280x189	280x213	280x430	45x45	90x93
L'Occasione	185x213	185x263	280x189	280x213	280x430	45x45	90x93
La Sesia	185x213	185x263	280x189	280x213	280x430	47x41	90x97
La Piazza Grande	185x213	185x263	280x189	280x213	280x430	45x45	90x90
Il Corriere di Alba e Bra	185x213	185x263	280x189	280x213	280x430	43x43	
Corriere di Novara	173x182	173x223	262x161	262x182	262x365	83x65	
Corriere Valsesiano	184x189	184x231	279x168	279x189	279x378		
Il Resegone	172x189	172x231	258x168	258x189	258x390	40x75	86x126
Notes	172x387			258x387		43x43	

Traditional Format	30 modules 5x6	36 modules 9x4	45 modules 9x5	54 modules 9x6	108 modules 9x12	Manchettes wxh	Window wxh
Corriere di Chieri	200x236	364x155	364x195	364x236	364x497	62x55	77x74
Corriere di Moncalieri	200x236	364x155	364x195	364x236	364x497	62x55	77x74
La Guida	215x256	395x170	395x213	395x256	395x520	49x61	84x130
La Nuova Provincia	201x247	365x164	365x206	365x247	365x496	60x54	84x129
Il Monferrato	201x247	365x164	365x206	365x247	365x496	60x54	84x129
Il Piccolo	196x263	356x174	356x218	356x263	356x510	55x38	
Giornale di Merate	206x265	375x175	375x220	375x265	375x517	57x45	80x130

Other Formats	32 modules 4x8	36 modules 4x9	48 modules 6x8	54 modules 6x9		Manchettes wxh
La Voce Alessandrina		175x387		263x387		47x47

	28 modules 7x4	33 modules 3x11	35 modules 7x5	36 modules 4x9	77 modules 7x11	
La Provincia Granda	324x162	137x445	324x203	184x365	324x445	

	36 modules 6x6	40 modules 8x5	48 modules 8x6	52 modules 4x13	104 modules 8x13	Manchettes wxh	Window wxh
Giornale di Lecco	265x229	357x190	357x229	175x520	357x520	35x50	86x112

	28 modules 7x4	33 modules 3x11	35 modules 7x5	36 modules 4x9	77 modules 7x11	
Il Biellese	344x118	145x328	344x148	195x268	344x328	
Eco di Biella	344x118	145x328	344x148	195x268	344x328	

Advertising Inserts

Technical Requisites for Insertions in Periodicals

The technical requisites for insertions in periodicals are taken from the brochure published by A. Manzoni & C., the ad sales company for these newspapers. The company provides information to ad agencies. They refer, among other publications, to the periodicals *L'Espresso* and *Il Venerdì*.

1. 4. Various advertising inserts.
The use of black, above all in small formats, draws more attention to the ad.
However, beware of line weights: despite the use of new technologies, newspapers do not permit high levels of refinement primarily owing to the type of paper they use.

438

Final Designs for Print
They generally consist of a rigid card with a graphic sign or photograph indicating the space of the illustrations, accompanied by a trace overlay with various graphic instructions.
When approving a final layout, it is worth remembering the following rules: the format, either full bleed or with margins, must be marked by four crosshairs defining the full size dimensions with respect to the format of the magazine, or in proportion to it; in full bleed ads, leave a space of 5 mm around the edge and distance texts at least 6 mm from the bleed edge for soft cover publications and at least 8 mm for magazines assembled with metal staples; where possible avoid positioning full colour positive or negative texts on coloured backgrounds, with a type size of less than 12 points. In fact, with even the smallest offset during printing, small serifed texts and lines and multiple colour frames will look thick, blurred and unpleasing; for the colours of texts, brands and backgrounds it is worth attaching colour samples, but make sure they can be obtained using normal inks and remembering that the simplest and strongest colours offer the best guarantees of the highest quality result.
The final submission is to be accompanied by all originals, glossy images, black & white and photocolour images.

Colour Originals
Photocolour images must be well balanced, perfectly in focus, rich in colour and tonal changes; they must be clean, free of holes and scratches.
Non-transparent colour originals such as dye transfers, photographic copies, mock-ups should possess all of the above characteristics and should not be fixed to rigid supports.
Avoid manual touch-ups. When they are necessary, highlight the area that has been retouched.
Avoid asking to block out images when the subjects have blurred or imprecise edges. As much as possible, avoid excessive enlargements as images will lose saturation and may become "grainy".
It is opportune to use duplicates when: the original requires particular corrections, the ad space uses more than two photocolours, when requesting overlaps. Duplication at full size offers the best guarantee of a quality result.
The following are not suitable to regular reproduction: negative colours; display folders; posters; printed material of any type; progressives and selections. It is appreciated when you provide recommendations about quality, that help understand the spirit of the advertising message and thus the main part of the ad, in order to "channel" inevitable tolerances during printing.

1.

2.

Notes
The text on these pages offers a valid example of technical annotations and recommendations that may be transferred by an advertising sales company to operators preparing inserts for periodicals.
The specificity of questions, the indication of methods and procedures assists the graphic artist and helps guarantee a result free of surprises.

Special Advertising Spaces

The request for an advertising space is validated only after examining and approving a complete ad (indications about margins, paper weight, the blueprints for images and texts). This model must be sent to Manzoni's Special Advertising Office at least 45 days prior to the publication of the ad.

Technical characteristics: maximum format (closed ad) 20x27 cm for *L'Espresso* and *Le Scienze*, 21x27 cm for *Il Venerdì*. Ads must have a 5 mm trimming margin (only for "stapled" types).

Beginning with the quartino format, an insert must have a 1 cm space at the side. Ottavi and their multiples must be closed at the top. Inserts must be submitted folded. Each copy must bear the initials "I.P.". Cost estimates for special ads (special papers, sample containers, die-cuts, etc.), will be prepared after technical tests of samples provided (at min. 50 pieces).

Cultura repubblicana per una grande forza democratica a sinistra

Roma
12 ottobre 1996
Centro Congressi
Parco dei Principi
Ore 10/18

Relazioni di
Giorgio Bogi
Massimo Scioscioli
Giuliano Amato
Enzo Bianco
Massimo D'Alema
Gino Giugni
Tullio Gregory
Antonio Maccanico
Andrea Manzella
Adriano Musi
Orazio Petracca
Giorgio Ruffolo
Gustavo Visentini

3.

Special conditions:
Reservations must be made at least 5 weeks prior to the publishing date.
Inserts must be received at least 10 days prior to the publishing date, forwarded to the addresses indicated in the contract.
For technical reasons, inserts requiring cellophane wrapping must be agreed upon beforehand.
To the right: 9 modules in *La Repubblica*.

Originals in Black&White

Black and white photographs must be in the correct position and perfectly in focus. They should be flexible and not fixed to rigid supports or materials.
Manual touch-ups should be avoided, and when necessary, touch-up areas should be highlighted.
Where possible, do not use 30x40 cm formats, also in order to avoid damaging undulations to the original.
Avoid asking to block out images when the subjects have blurred or imprecise edges.
The following are not suitable to regular black&white reproduction: photocolour/negative colour; colour and black&white prints; continuos and halftone films.

Colour Selections and Black&White Positives

When deciding to directly manage the layout of these materials, consider the following:
any films provided must be suitable to the successive printing process adopted by the printer; colour samples submitted as a reference for final results must show a valid correspondence with tests made in our print shop; in the presence or absence of these conditions, the responsibility of the printer will be strongly limited to the correctness of the remaining work entrusted to the printer (die-cutting and printing); preventative technical collaborations designed to avoid possible dissatisfaction with the results obtained, may be requested by our technical department in a timely manner prior to submission; material may be submitted in digital format, on 44.88 or 270 MB Sy Quest, or CD ROM; texts are to be in XPress version 3.3.1.

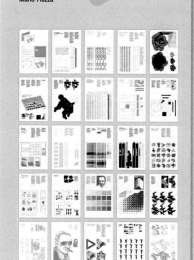

Corso di laurea in Disegno industriale
Prima facoltà di Architettura
Università di Roma La Sapienza

Michele Spera
La progettazione grafica
tra creatività e scienza
Gangemi Editore

Palazzo delle Esposizioni
Sala multimediale
Roma, 13 aprile 2002, ore 18

Parleranno del libro
Giovanni Anceschi, Domenico De Masi,
Mario Lunetta, Tonino Paris,
Mario Piazza

4.

Notes   **439**
At the top of this page we have provided technical indications for advertising inserts. Advertising inserts generally straddle a signature and are fixed with a metal staple (bind in), which serves to fix it to the periodical. Inserts that are not fixed are known as "buck slips".

Advertising Spaces

The Technical Characteristics of Various Newspapers

The technical requisites for insertions in periodicals are taken from the brochure published by A. Manzoni & C., the ad sales company for these newspapers. The company provides information to ad agencies. They refer to a selection of local papers and local editions of *La Repubblica*.

440

Local Newspaper	Area of distribution	Number of days published	Format wxh	Module in mm	Column height in mm	Number of columns
Alto Adige	Trentino Alto Adige	7 days	Tabloid	42x18	433	6
Dolomiten	Alto Adige	7 days (excl. Sunday)	Tabloid	43x21	429	6
Magazin	Alto Adige	Friday	Magazine	45x22	286	4
Wirtschaftskurier	Alto Adige	Wednesday	Magazine	45x22	286	4
L'Arena	Verona	7 days	Traditional	37x42	510	9
Il Giornale di Vicenza	Vicenza	7 days	Traditional	37x42	510	9
Il Mattino di Padova	Padua	7 days	Tabloid	42x23	433	9
La Tribuna di Treviso	Treviso	7 days	Tabloid	42x23	433	6
La Nuova Venezia	Venice	7 days	Tabloid	42x23	433	6
Corriere delle Alpi	Belluno	7 days	Tabloid	42x18	433	6
Gazzetta di Mantova	Mantua	7 days	Tabloid	42x18	433	6
La Provincia Pavese	Pavia	7 days (excl. Monday)	Tabloid	43x23	433	6
La Provincia (Cremona)	Cremona	7 days (excl. Monday)	Tabloid	42x18	433	6
La Prealpina	Varese	7 days	Traditional	39x31	513	9
Brescia Oggi	Brescia	7 days	Traditional	37x42	510	9
Gazzetta di Regio	Reggio Emilia	7 days	Tabloid	42x18	433	6
Gazzetta di Modena	Modena	7 days	Tabloid	42x18	433	6
La Nuova Ferrara	Ferrara	7 days	Tabloid	42x18	433	6
Il Tirreno	Tuscany	7 days	Tabloid	42x23	433	6
Il Centro	Abruzzo	7 days	Tabloid	42x23	433	6
Il Centro Marche	The Marche	7 days	Tabloid	42x23	433	6
Quotidiano	Apulia	7 days (excl. Monday)	Tabloid	42x23	433	6
La Nuova Sardegna	Sardinia	7 days	Tabloid	42x23	433	6

Local editions of *La Repubblica*	Area di distribution	Number of days published	Format wxh	Module in mm	Column height in mm	Number of columns
La Repubblica Torino	Piedmont	7 days	Tabloid	42x23	433	6
La Repubblica Genova	Liguria	7 days	Tabloid	42x23	433	6
La Repubblica Milano	Lombardy	7 days	Tabloid	42x23	433	6
TuttoMilano	City and Prov. of Milan	Thursday	Pocket	58x45	187	2
La Repubblica Ann. Ec.	City of Milan	Tuesday	Tabloid	42x23	433	6
La Repubblica Bologna	Emilia Romagna	7 days	Tabloid	42x23	433	6
La Repubblica Firenze	Tuscany	7 days	Tabloid	42x23	433	6
La Repubblica Ann. Ec.	City of Florence	Thursday	Tabloid	42x23	433	6
La Repubblica Roma	Lazio	7 days	Tabloid	42x23	433	6
TrovaRoma	City and Prov. of Rome	Thursday	Pocket	58x45	187	2
La Repubblica Ann. Ec.	City of Rome	Tuesday	Tabloid	42x23	433	6
La Repubblica Napoli	Campania	7 days	Tabloid	42x23	433	6

Timing for the submission of material:
black&white: 5 days prior to the date of publication
colour: 7 days prior to the date of publication.

Density as a percentage of point size.
Min. 10/Max. 90.

The following section briefly described the type of printing used by the papers listed on this page:

Offset
A printing technique in which the inked image is transferred ("offset") from a plate to a rubber blanket, then to the printing surface.

Rotary Offset
Offset printing using paper rolls.
It can be considered a modern version of rotary printing and, like this latter, features terminals for folding, stapling and cutting. It can print up to 30,000 copies per hour.

Flexography
Similar to typical rotary printing.
It uses a flexible matrix in a synthetic material that is curved around a cylinder, similar to a "flong".

Rotary Printing
A printing system that utilises the principle of transforming a flat printing matrix into a round matrix by applying it to a cylinder.
Rotary printers use rolled paper.
It is possible to print up to 80,000 copies per hour.

Rotogravure
Printing machine based on the principle of chalcography.
The engraved cylindrical matrix transfers the print directly to the surface of the paper.
It is possible to print up to 80,000 copies per hour.

441

Local Newspaper	Dither lines black&white	Dither lines colour	Type of printing	Material black&white	Material colour
Alto Adige	25/30	40	Offset	Pos. film or coated	Sel. pos. film + progress.
Dolomiten	34	54	Roto Offset	Paper copy or FLP	Sel. pos. film + progress.
Magazin	34	54/70	Offset	Paper copy or FLP	Sel. pos. film + progress.
Wirtschaftskurier	34	54	Roto Offset	Paper copy or FLP	Sel. pos. film + progress.
L'Arena	27/30	40	Offset	Pos. film or coated	Sel. pos. film + chromalin
Il Giornale di Vicenza	27/30	40	Offset	Pos. film or coated	Sel. pos. film + chromalin
Il Mattino di Padova	24/28		Flexo	Pos. film or coated	
La Tribuna di Treviso	24/28		Flexo	Pos. film or coated	
La Nuova Venezia	24/28		Flexo	Pos. film or coated	
Corriere delle Alpi	25/30		Offset	Pos. film or coated	
Gazzetta di Mantova	24		Flexo	Pos. film or coated	
La Provincia Pavese	28/32		Offset	Neg. film full page Coated other formats	
La Provincia (Cremona)	34	40	Offset	Positive film	Sel. pos. film + progress.
La Prealpina	30	40	Roto Offset	Positive film	Sel. pos. film + progress.
Brescia Oggi	27/30	40	Offset	Pos. film or coated	Sel. pos. film + chromalin
Gazzetta di Regio	24		Flexo	Pos. film or coated	
Gazzetta di Modena	24		Flexo	Pos. film or coated	
La Nuova Ferrara	24		Flexo	Pos. film or coated	
Il Tirreno	25/28		Offset	Pos. film or coated	
Il Centro	40		Offset	Pos. film or coated	
Il Centro Marche	40		Offset	Pos. film or coated	
Quotidiano	25	25	Offset	Positive film Double pos. film (r+n)	
La Nuova Sardegna	25		Flexo	Neg. film top emuls. only form. picc. "paper"	

Local editions of La Repubblica	Dither lines black&white	Dither lines colour	Type of printing	Material black&white	Material colour
La Repubblica Torino	24/26		Flexo	Positive paper print	
La Repubblica Genova	24/26		Flexo	Positive paper print	
La Repubblica Milano	24/26		Flexo	Positive paper print	
TuttoMilano	48		Roto Offset	Positive film	
La Repubblica Ann. Ec.	24/26		Flexo	Positive paper print	
La Repubblica Bologna	24/26		Flexo	Positive paper print	
La Repubblica Firenze	24/26		Flexo	Positive paper print	
La Repubblica Ann. Ec.	24/26		Flexo	Positive paper print	
La Repubblica Roma	24/26		Flexo/Offset	Positive paper print	
TrovaRoma	48		Roto Offset	Positive film	
La Repubblica Ann. Ec.	24/26		Offset	Positive paper print	
La Repubblica Napoli	24/26		Flexo/Offset	Positive paper print	

Advertising Spaces

The Formats of
Il Tempo
Il Messaggero
Il Sole 24 Ore

1. The grid used by the newspaper *Il Tempo*. Constructed from 7 columns it measures 520 mm in height, with a 45 mm (w) x 32 mm (h) for a total of 105 modules.

2. The grid used by the newspaper *Il Messaggero*. Constructed from 8 columns it measures 500 mm in height, with a 42 mm (w) x 33 mm (h) for a total of 122 modules.

As examples only, the table below lists the costs of a type of insertion known as "legal advertising" offered by *Il Tempo*. These costs may be subject to change. Exact costs can be requested from the Area Nord Pubblicità advertising sales company, that provided the information shown here.

442

The formats of *Il Sole 24 Ore*

modules	Format
1 module	41x43
2 modules	41x88
3 modules	41x133
4 modules	41x178
6 modules	41x268
2 modules	84x43
4 modules	84x88
6 modules	84x133
8 modules	84x178
12 modules	84x268
3 modules	128x43
6 modules	128x88
9 modules	128x133
12 modules	128x178
15 modules	128x223
18 modules	128x268
8 modules	172x88
12 modules	172x133
16 modules	172x178
20 modules	172x223
24 modules	172x268
15 modules	215x133
30 modules	215x268
42 modules	260x315
56 modules	301x360
63 modules	301x400
12 modules	41x535
24 modules	84x535
36 modules	128x535
48 modules	172x535
60 modules	215x535
20 modules	390x100
45 modules	390x223
108 modules	390x268
95 modules	765x210
228 modules	765x505
54 modules	390x268
10 modules	84x223
114 modules	765x250

Format	Columns	Base	Height	Cost (Italian Lira)
1 module	1	45 mm	32 mm	720,000
2 modules	1	45	67	1,440,000
3 modules	1	45	102	2,160,000
4 modules	1	45	137	2,880,000
5 modules	1	45	172	3,600,000
6 modules	1	45	207	4,320,000
7 modules	1	45	242	5,040,000
8 modules	1	45	277	5,760,000
9 modules	1	45	312	6,480,000
10 modules	1	45	347	7,200,000
11 modules	1	45	382	7,920,000
12 modules	1	45	417	8,640,000
13 modules	1	45	452	9,360,000
14 modules	1	45	487	10,080,000
15 modules	1	45	520	10,800,000

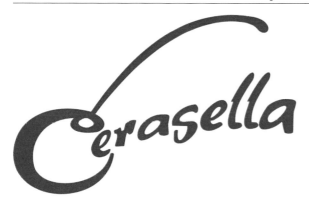

1. 4. Various ads, printed with a full bleed on 115x165 mm format, for a ceramics manufacturer, *Next* magazine, Monte dei Paschi di Siena, Sanseverino Ties.

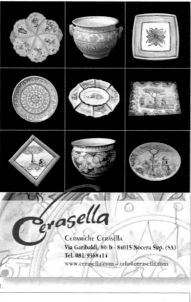

1.

2.

Notes
For full bleed images (see fig.5) whose position is not known, consider a margin of at least 3 mm on all four sides to allow for trimming.
For odd numbered pages, no margin should be added to the binding edge.

3.

4.

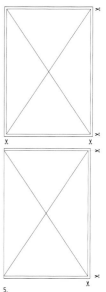

5.

la Carta dei Valori

Il Messaggero
Technical Info:
Column height
500 mm.
Column width
42 mm.
Layout
8 columns.
Offset printed

Material:
Coated, contact
emulsion positive film.
Mock-ups and
finals with deduction of
all costs for printed
material.
For colour prints:
selection, colour test
and b&w films.
For continuos printing
positive film.

Dither:
30 lines per cm2 for
b&w material; 32 lines
per cm2 for colour
material.

The Spaces of
Il Messaggero
1.
1 module, mm 42x33
2 modules, mm 42x70
3 modules, mm 42x105
4 modules, mm 42x140
5 modules, mm 42x176
6 modules, mm 42x210
7 modules, mm 42x248
14 modules, mm
42x500
2.
2 modules, 89x33
4 modules, 89x70
6 modules, 89x105
8 modules, 89x140
3.
10 modules, 89x176
12 modules, 89x210
14 modules, 89x248
28 modules, 89x500
4.
3 modules, 135x33
6 modules, 135x70
5.
9 modules, 135x105
12 modules, 135x140

6.
15 modules, 135x176
18 modules, 135x210
7.
21 modules, 135x248
42 modules, 135x500
8.
4 modules, 182x33
8 modules, 182x70
9.
12 modules, 182x105
16 modules, 182x140
10.
20 modules, 182x176
24 modules, 182x210
11.
28 modules, 182x248
32 modules, 182x280
12.
56 modules, 368x248

444

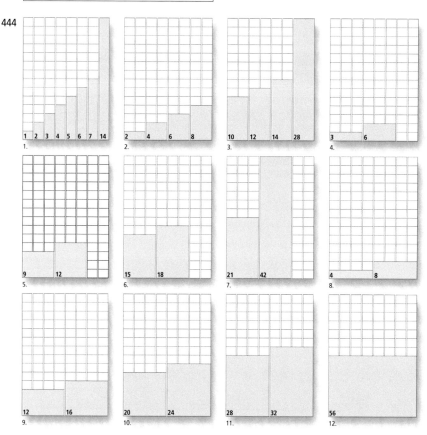

Notes
*The newspaper Il
Messaggero specifies
that module formats
are calculated at 1/14
of a column. This
means that the formats
in the price list are
indicative and subject
to small variations,
without changes to
pricing.
Deadline for reservation
of space and
submission of material:
4 days prior to the
date of publication for
b&w; 10 days for
colour.*

1. Drawing for an ad campaign for ACI, the Italian Automobile Club.
Design by Gerardo Spera, drawing by Fabiano Spera.
2. 4. Advertising for *Smoking* magazine. Format 230x300 mm. The uniform graphic, adjusted to the needs of the text, can provide continuity to what is communicated and helps create an "image".

2.

3.

4.

5.

445

Notes
Designed by Gerardo Spera, the advertising for Smoking emphasises the number of the corresponding issue with a sort of halo. There are two visual themes: a pipe and a cigar, both wrapped by the magazine's header.

Workbook
*Design a series of messages for the same client.
Ensure the uniformity of the graphic layout and the continuity of the image.
Coordinate typefaces, sizes and grids.*

Advertising Pages
by Spera&Spera

Uniform Graphic Messages
That Create an "Image"

446

Spera&Spera, la grafica come altro. Michele e Gerardo Spera operano con le maggiori aziende italiane progettando, nel campo della comunicazione visiva, corporate identity, progetti integrati ed editoria, con un forte accento sulla sperimentazione e la creatività. Impostato come laboratorio interdisciplinare in cui operano più persone, lo studio di design consultancy interviene in tutta la gamma della comunicazione, dal marchio all'allestimento di una mostra, dalla pagina pubblicitaria al manuale di corporate identity, dal coordinamento editoriale al depliant, dalla brochure all'illustrazione, fino agli impianti di un periodico. Offrono servizi di comunicazione "chiavi in mano" e forniscono ai loro clienti l'attuazione del progetto. www.speradesign.eu

Spera&Spera, la grafica come altro. Michele e Gerardo Spera operano con le maggiori aziende italiane progettando, nel campo della comunicazione visiva, corporate identity, progetti integrati ed editoria, con un forte accento sulla sperimentazione e la creatività. Impostato come laboratorio interdisciplinare in cui operano più persone, lo studio di design consultancy interviene in tutta la gamma della comunicazione, dal marchio all'allestimento di una mostra, dalla pagina pubblicitaria al manuale di corporate identity, dal coordinamento editoriale al depliant, dalla brochure all'illustrazione, fino agli impianti di un periodico. Offrono servizi di comunicazione "chiavi in mano" e forniscono ai loro clienti l'attuazione del progetto. www.speradesign.eu

Spera&Spera, la grafica come altro. Michele e Gerardo Spera operano con le maggiori aziende italiane progettando, nel campo della comunicazione visiva, corporate identity, progetti integrati ed editoria, con un forte accento sulla sperimentazione e la creatività. Impostato come laboratorio interdisciplinare in cui operano più persone, lo studio di design consultancy interviene in tutta la gamma della comunicazione, dal marchio all'allestimento di una mostra, dalla pagina pubblicitaria al manuale di corporate identity, dal coordinamento editoriale al depliant, dalla brochure all'illustrazione, fino agli impianti di un periodico. Offrono servizi di comunicazione "chiavi in mano" e forniscono ai loro clienti l'attuazione del progetto. www.speradesign.eu

Spera&Spera, la grafica come altro. Michele e Gerardo Spera operano con le maggiori aziende italiane progettando, nel campo della comunicazione visiva, corporate identity, progetti integrati ed editoria, con un forte accento sulla sperimentazione e la creatività. Impostato come laboratorio interdisciplinare in cui operano più persone, lo studio di design consultancy interviene in tutta la gamma della comunicazione, dal marchio all'allestimento di una mostra, dalla pagina pubblicitaria al manuale di corporate identity, dal coordinamento editoriale al depliant, dalla brochure all'illustrazione, fino agli impianti di un periodico. Offrono servizi di comunicazione "chiavi in mano" e forniscono ai loro clienti l'attuazione del progetto. www.speradesign.eus

Spera&Spera, la grafica come altro. Michele e Gerardo Spera operano con le maggiori aziende italiane progettando, nel campo della comunicazione visiva, corporate identity, progetti integrati ed editoria, con un forte accento sulla sperimentazione e la creatività. Impostato come laboratorio interdisciplinare in cui operano più persone, lo studio di design consultancy interviene in tutta la gamma della comunicazione, dal marchio all'allestimento di una mostra, dalla pagina pubblicitaria al manuale di corporate identity, dal coordinamento editoriale al depliant, dalla brochure all'illustrazione, fino agli impianti di un periodico. Offrono servizi di comunicazione "chiavi in mano" e forniscono ai loro clienti l'attuazione del progetto. www.speradesign.eus

Spera&Spera, la grafica come altro. Michele e Gerardo Spera operano con le maggiori aziende italiane progettando, nel campo della comunicazione visiva, corporate identity, progetti integrati ed editoria, con un forte accento sulla sperimentazione e la creatività. Impostato come laboratorio interdisciplinare in cui operano più persone, lo studio di design consultancy interviene in tutta la gamma della comunicazione, dal marchio all'allestimento di una mostra, dalla pagina pubblicitaria al manuale di corporate identity, dal coordinamento editoriale al depliant, dalla brochure all'illustrazione, fino agli impianti di un periodico. Offrono servizi di comunicazione "chiavi in mano" e forniscono ai loro clienti l'attuazione del progetto. www.speradesign.eu

Spera&Spera, la grafica come altro. Michele e Gerardo Spera operano con le maggiori aziende italiane progettando, nel campo della comunicazione visiva, corporate identity, progetti integrati ed editoria, con un forte accento sulla sperimentazione e la creatività. Impostato come laboratorio interdisciplinare in cui operano più persone, lo studio di design consultancy interviene in tutta la gamma della comunicazione, dal marchio all'allestimento di una mostra, dalla pagina pubblicitaria al manuale di corporate identity, dal coordinamento editoriale al depliant, dalla brochure all'illustrazione, fino agli impianti di un periodico. Offrono servizi di comunicazione "chiavi in mano" e forniscono ai loro clienti l'attuazione del progetto. www.speradesign.eu

Spera&Spera, la grafica come altro. Michele e Gerardo Spera operano con le maggiori aziende italiane progettando, nel campo della comunicazione visiva, corporate identity, progetti integrati ed editoria, con un forte accento sulla sperimentazione e la creatività. Impostato come laboratorio interdisciplinare in cui operano più persone, lo studio di design consultancy interviene in tutta la gamma della comunicazione, dal marchio all'allestimento di una mostra, dalla pagina pubblicitaria al manuale di corporate identity, dal coordinamento editoriale al depliant, dalla brochure all'illustrazione, fino agli impianti di un periodico. Offrono servizi di comunicazione "chiavi in mano" e forniscono ai loro clienti l'attuazione del progetto. www.speradesign.eu

Spera&Spera, la grafica come altro. Michele e Gerardo Spera operano con le maggiori aziende italiane progettando, nel campo della comunicazione visiva, corporate identity, progetti integrati ed editoria, con un forte accento sulla sperimentazione e la creatività. Impostato come laboratorio interdisciplinare in cui operano più persone, lo studio di design consultancy interviene in tutta la gamma della comunicazione, dal marchio all'allestimento di una mostra, dalla pagina pubblicitaria al manuale di corporate identity, dal coordinamento editoriale al depliant, dalla brochure all'illustrazione, fino agli impianti di un periodico. Offrono servizi di comunicazione "chiavi in mano" e forniscono ai loro clienti l'attuazione del progetto. www.speradesign.eu

447

Spera&Spera, la grafica come altro. Michele e Gerardo Spera operano con le maggiori aziende italiane progettando, nel campo della comunicazione visiva, corporate identity, progetti integrati ed editoria, con un forte accento sulla sperimentazione e la creatività. Impostato come laboratorio interdisciplinare in cui operano più persone, lo studio di design consultancy interviene in tutta la gamma della comunicazione, dal marchio all'allestimento di una mostra, dalla pagina pubblicitaria al manuale di corporate identity, dal coordinamento editoriale al depliant, dalla brochure all'illustrazione, fino agli impianti di un periodico. Offrono servizi di comunicazione "chiavi in mano" e forniscono ai loro clienti l'attuazione del progetto. www.speradesign.eu

Spera&Spera, la grafica come altro. Michele e Gerardo Spera operano con le maggiori aziende italiane progettando, nel campo della comunicazione visiva, corporate identity, progetti integrati ed editoria, con un forte accento sulla sperimentazione e la creatività. Impostato come laboratorio interdisciplinare in cui operano più persone, lo studio di design consultancy interviene in tutta la gamma della comunicazione, dal marchio all'allestimento di una mostra, dalla pagina pubblicitaria al manuale di corporate identity, dal coordinamento editoriale al depliant, dalla brochure all'illustrazione, fino agli impianti di un periodico. Offrono servizi di comunicazione "chiavi in mano" e forniscono ai loro clienti l'attuazione del progetto. www.speradesign.eu

Spera&Spera, la grafica come altro. Michele e Gerardo Spera operano con le maggiori aziende italiane progettando, nel campo della comunicazione visiva, corporate identity, progetti integrati ed editoria, con un forte accento sulla sperimentazione e la creatività. Impostato come laboratorio interdisciplinare in cui operano più persone, lo studio di design consultancy interviene in tutta la gamma della comunicazione, dal marchio all'allestimento di una mostra, dalla pagina pubblicitaria al manuale di corporate identity, dal coordinamento editoriale al depliant, dalla brochure all'illustrazione, fino agli impianti di un periodico. Offrono servizi di comunicazione "chiavi in mano" e forniscono ai loro clienti l'attuazione del progetto. www.speradesign.eu

Spera&Spera, la grafica come altro. Michele e Gerardo Spera operano con le maggiori aziende italiane progettando, nel campo della comunicazione visiva, corporate identity, progetti integrati ed editoria, con un forte accento sulla sperimentazione e la creatività. Impostato come laboratorio interdisciplinare in cui operano più persone, lo studio di design consultancy interviene in tutta la gamma della comunicazione, dal marchio all'allestimento di una mostra, dalla pagina pubblicitaria al manuale di corporate identity, dal coordinamento editoriale al depliant, dalla brochure all'illustrazione, fino agli impianti di un periodico. Offrono servizi di comunicazione "chiavi in mano" e forniscono ai loro clienti l'attuazione del progetto. www.speradesign.eu

Spera&Spera, la grafica come altro. Michele e Gerardo Spera operano con le maggiori aziende italiane progettando, nel campo della comunicazione visiva, corporate identity, progetti integrati ed editoria, con un forte accento sulla sperimentazione e la creatività. Impostato come laboratorio interdisciplinare in cui operano più persone, lo studio di design consultancy interviene in tutta la gamma della comunicazione, dal marchio all'allestimento di una mostra, dalla pagina pubblicitaria al manuale di corporate identity, dal coordinamento editoriale al depliant, dalla brochure all'illustrazione, fino agli impianti di un periodico. Offrono servizi di comunicazione "chiavi in mano" e forniscono ai loro clienti l'attuazione del progetto. www.speradesign.eu

Spera&Spera, la grafica come altro. Michele e Gerardo Spera operano con le maggiori aziende italiane progettando, nel campo della comunicazione visiva, corporate identity, progetti integrati ed editoria, con un forte accento sulla sperimentazione e la creatività. Impostato come laboratorio interdisciplinare in cui operano più persone, lo studio di design consultancy interviene in tutta la gamma della comunicazione, dal marchio all'allestimento di una mostra, dalla pagina pubblicitaria al manuale di corporate identity, dal coordinamento editoriale al depliant, dalla brochure all'illustrazione, fino agli impianti di un periodico. Offrono servizi di comunicazione "chiavi in mano" e forniscono ai loro clienti l'attuazione del progetto. www.speradesign.eu

29.
Packaging

Three-Dimensionality

1. To create a piece of packaging we must first design what it looks like, unfolded.
The package shown in figure 1 has only two "glue points".
By folding the flaps of the cover, and forcing the folds, the flaps overlap and automatically close the box.

Once we have designed the unfolded structure, it can be cut along its edges and marked with a round tipped punch along the fold lines.
To obtain a more precise result, the paper can be scored (without cutting it) along the fold lines: this is known as "half cutting" and is realised along the external part of the fold.

2. During packing and stacking, when the boxes are placed one atop the other, they should occupy the least amount of space possible.
The space between one box and another is known as "negative" space.
We must pay attention to the form of packaging.
It is important that a cardboard box can be folded along its crease lines to save precious space during transportation and shipping.

448 Once again we borrow terminology from the Anglo-Saxon world to identify the work of a graphic designer: "packaging" is a broader term than the Italian "imballaggio", and better explains the vast range of graphic and paper-related interventions indicated by this word.
The design of a box, a container for products, a label, the appearance of a soda can, a wrapper or countertop display case, a platic bag or box for ties is packaging.
It is often entrusted with conveying the image of a product itself; its more or less attractive appearance can determine the success of a product.
In this case, the designer becomes a true beauty consultant. In "dressing" the product he must seek out its identity and target, or adopt a common and recognisable criteria for the various products in a particular range.
Other than designing the graphics, the graphic designer must also design the form, in this case three-dimensional. The volume must be suitable to the product, more or less faithfully replicating it and considering eventual additional items that serve as protection. The primary material of our work here is cardboard. We will invent our box and design a precise structure, including prototypes and tests of their functionality.
The structure will indicate cuts and fold lines for die cutting. Cut lines will be cut by sharp steel blades to create the profile of the box, while the fold lines will be half cut by dull steel blades to mark the creases.

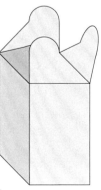

1.

Notes
*When designing a container, we must consider the image, likely consolidated, of the product it contains and the company that makes it.
A brand, lettering, institutional colours and other elements that are part of a "corporate image" must be respected and clearly represented.
The form you will give to the package must consider the product, the material you decide to use, the ease of stacking, the type of closure and, finally, the graphic design of the different faces.*

Bibliography
▼*F.A. Paine, M. Fusi, Manuale dell'imballaggio Etas Kompass Milano 1964*

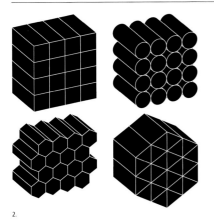

2.

3. A bookmark in brush finished steel, produced by Bristol-Myers Squibb as a gadget for physicians is housed in a specially designed container.
To the right, the die for a folder.

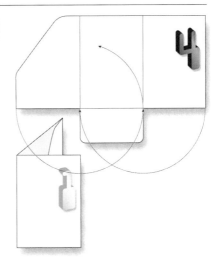

Notes
In the field of graphic design, we are accustomed to working in two dimensions; the envelope of a package offers us a third dimension, and more faces to be designed to express the image of a product.
Thus, as Hohenegger tells us, we must adopt the stance of a sculptor, who reads his work from all possible points of view.

3.

The Die

A Plywood Base and Steel Profiles

1. 3. A die consists of a plywood base marked by a cut that traces the design of the package. This cut is then filled by steel profiles that project just enough to reach the depth required during the passage of the machine.
The profiles may be sharp and cutting or dull and rounded, when they only need to mark a fold.
Rubber spacers at the sides of the profiles help push the paper out of the die.

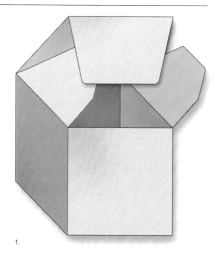

1.

450

Notes
A die cut box, with cuts and pressure marks, both carried out simultaneously by the "die cutter".
The die cutter cuts out the external the profile of the package, and simply impresses deep lines where it is to be folded for construction.

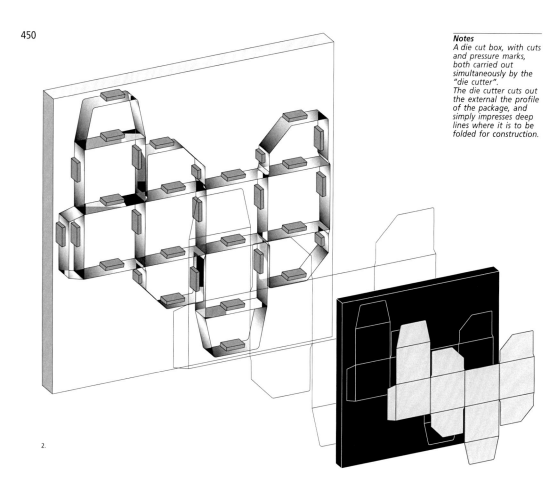

2.

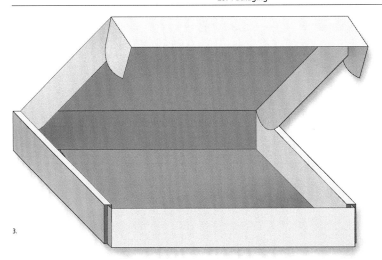

3.

3. 4. This box in microwave safe double sided cardboard can be assembled without any glue, simply by following the proper sequence of folds.

5. Two steel profiles set into a wood base. The first projects enough to cut, while the second, with a rounded edge, projects only enough to mark the create a "crease" that marks the support where it is to be folded.

451

Notes
When the flaps of a box coincide, it is necessary to carve out the point of intersection.
This will allow for precise folds without overlaps.
The closing flaps would have problems if the other parts were not just a touch smaller so that they can be folded and overlapped without interference.

4.

5.

Packaging

Dressing a Product

1. 2. A box of antibiotics produced by Bristol-Myers Squibb. Below is the final design of the box with the outlines for the die cutter and the general layout.
3. Box for a frozen fish company.

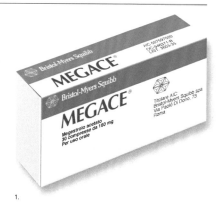

1.

452

Notes
In the world of pharmaceutical products, packaging plays a very important role. In general, the boxes of life-saving medication or antibiotics offer only information, and the image is more scientific and obliges one to read it.
On the contrary, over the counter products (which can be purchased without a prescription) are generally brightly coloured, more attractive and more similar to commercial products.

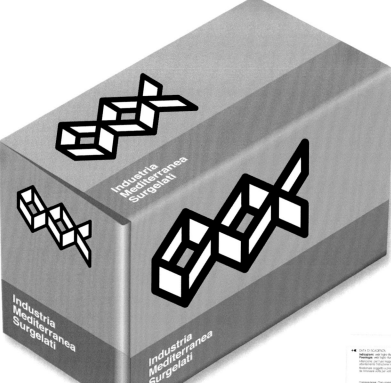

3.

2.

L'ESCALIER   VIA BOCCA DI LEONE 84   ROMA

4.

5.

6.

4. 8. Shopping bags and sacks: some examples of the fun that can be had dressing a products. The bag by Levin & Schneider, toy distributors in California, features a pocket, similar to a kangaroo's pouch, that contains a die cut bear that children can play with.

LEVIN & SCHNEIDER

LS INC. 2266 DAVIE AVENUE SUITE 110 LOS ANGELES CALIFORNIA 90040 PH 213/727.7232

7.

LEVIN & SCHNEIDER

8.

453

Notes
The fortune of a product can be largely attributed to how it is packaged, and to the added value of its appearance.
Figure 3 shows a package for frozen fish that uses the company's brand as a seal of quality.

Packaging and Paper

Creativity Waiting to be Developed

Similar to origami, where the invention of folding paper has yet to cease offering new ideas, packaging also offers constantly new forms of expression and solutions.
Thus it is no accident that packaging is almost always the work of specialists in this particular field of graphic design.
The joy of creating forms by folding paper becomes a tool of design that is separate from the aims of packaging and a method of research.

1. The figure below shows a study for a line of packaging for perfumes, creams, emollients and other cosmetics by Gepi.
It is evident that for this type of product the aesthetic form of the perfume bottles (first and second row) and the boxes in which they are housed (second and third rows) dominates the functionality of the packaging.

The analysis of this type of study of forms, completed by hand as the first step in their production, intends to stimulate young designers to learn to use paper as a raw material for projects, where experiments in three dimensions can stimulate creativity.

454

Notes
Packaging is an art that requires a great deal of manuality and passion: we must be craftsmen to invent, cut and curve, to carefully fold unusual and curious forms, to create fantasies that come to life in three dimensions.
The love for paper and its expressive possibilities are charged with invention.

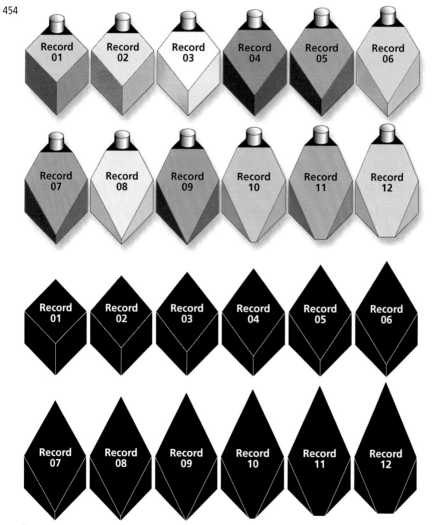

1.

2. 3. The design of the perfume boxes responds to a progressive geometric criteria.
Each number corresponds with a cut and a crease.
To the right is form number 8 and below the layout of the die cuts.

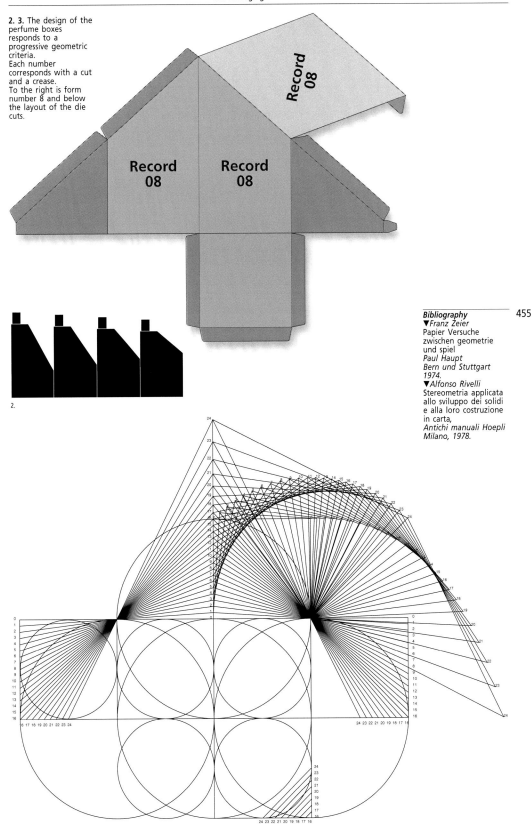

Record
08

Record
08

Record
08

2.

Bibliography
▼*Franz Zeier*
Papier Versuche zwischen geometrie und spiel
Paul Haupt
Bern und Stuttgart
1974.
▼*Alfonso Rivelli*
Stereometria applicata allo sviluppo dei solidi e alla loro costruzione in carta,
Antichi manuali Hoepli
Milano, 1978.

455

3.

CD Containers

Creativity Waiting to be Developed

1. 2. Studies and projects for CD cases produced by the Ravello Festival.
3. The bag.
4. 5. Studies and projects for the cover of a multimedia DVD produced by the Ravello Festival offering commentary on an exhibition held in Ravello.

456

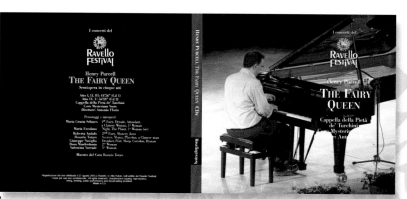

1.

2.

Workbook
Design a series of CD covers based on a unique theme.
Uniform their graphic appearance and ensure the continuity of their image.
Coordinate typefaces, sizes and grids.

4.

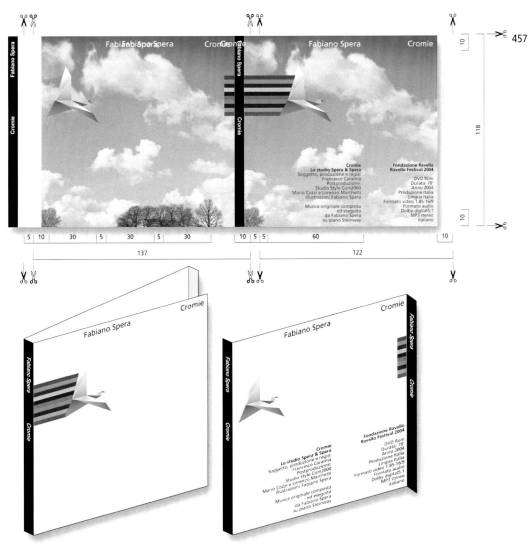

457

5.

A Box for 90 Postcards

Events at the Ravello Festival

The 2004 Ravello Festival featured a rich program of events, ranging from symphonic to chamber music, from opera to ballet, from cinema to the visual arts, from cultural discussions to entertainment.
Leading orchestras and performing groups were invited, together with prestigious artists and important personalities.
The *fil rouge* that holds the pearls of this program together, in an attractive though non-constrictive manner, and which evokes a Wagnerian *Leitmotiv*, is the theme of the "dream", seen from multiple points of view:
music art, science, ecology, philosophy, sociology, literature, economics.

The Ravello Festival wishes to permit a full immersion in an atmosphere of a pleasing spiritual caress. This is made possible by the serenity of the landscape, the gentle climate, the evocative strength of ancient monuments, the quality of the events, the courtesy of encounters. A perfect combination of Latin classicism and Oriental grace, in the heart of the Mediterranean, ensures an elegant pause, a creative reflection, and a tasteful comparison.

The Festival's cultural offering accompanies guests throughout the summer without affecting their privacy; it presents opportunities for enjoyment without imposition; it satisfies a vast scale of subtle desires without hindering an intention to seek out solitude, a love for silence, free thinking.
The Ravello Festival is presented as a possibility to think and experiment with a model of life founded on introspection, on creative otium, on supportive emulation, ethics and aesthetics.
A model of life free of the destructive and competitive delirium and senseless activism.

458

459

460

461

462

463

30.
A Coordinated Image Manual

Format

There are many possible formats for a manual. The pages shown here are just one example, based on the following dimensions: 255 mm in width x 297 mm in height.
They have been designed to be collated in a ring binder.
Each of the pages has four 5 mm diameter holes, at 80 mm on centre.
The centre of the holes is 10 mm from the binding edge; and 28.5 mm from the top and bottom edges of the page.

The useful space that remains is 210x297 mm, a classical UNI A4 page. The most commonly used paper is 250/300 gram coated paper.
It guarantees the correct reproduction of the images found on each page.
It can be printed from 70x100 paper, in general white, which can contain nine leafs per folio.

The system of holes makes it possible to insert various elements, such as an envelope for discs that can be used to provide printers with fundamental elements, colour samples, material samples (for example, vinyl), ready to use films (for example rasters for forms), paper samples for stationery, etc.

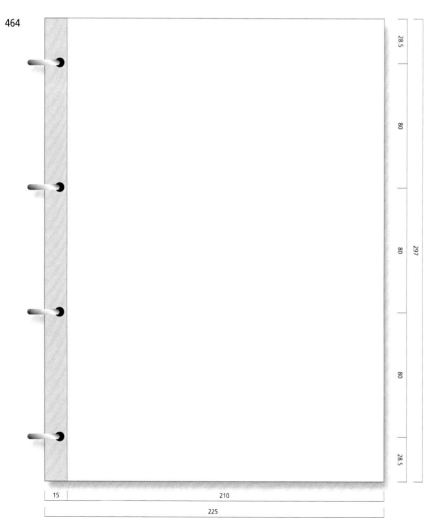

Notes
Graphic design is the result of two indissoluble components: creativity and science.
The first permits us to create an image inspired by the aesthetic and formal taste possessed by a graphic designer by vocation; the second component is that of science, in other words the rational application of codes, proportions, ratios and mathematics, in a word, rationality and logic.
While the first component is natural and inherent to the very choice of this profession, the second must be cultivated and pursued with tenacity.
The first is always debatable and subjective; the second is incontestable and objective.
The correct equilibrium between these two components permits a graphic designer to rationalise the project he or she is working on, to lay down lines, even instinctively, though codified by the science of geometry.
The manual is the correct tool for applying these two components:
it must rationally and geometrically explain every aesthetic choice you have made, and every proposal related to content and form.
This is why a manual can be considered a true distillation of this profession.

The Construction
of the Grid

Format

We pursue the logic that teaches us to ensure there is a reason behind every part of our project.
For the construction of the pages of a manual we turn once again to the golden ratio.
After establishing a 15 mm margin at top, right and bottom of the page, based on a dimension of AB of 267 mm, we can create the golden section of AB. This value is equal to 165 mm (165.01854). B will be equal to 101.97775, which we can round up to 102.

This gives us two distinct zones, A and B, where A is equal to 165x102 mm and B to 165x165 mm. We can further subdivide A into four parts. We will use this space for the necessities described on the following pages.

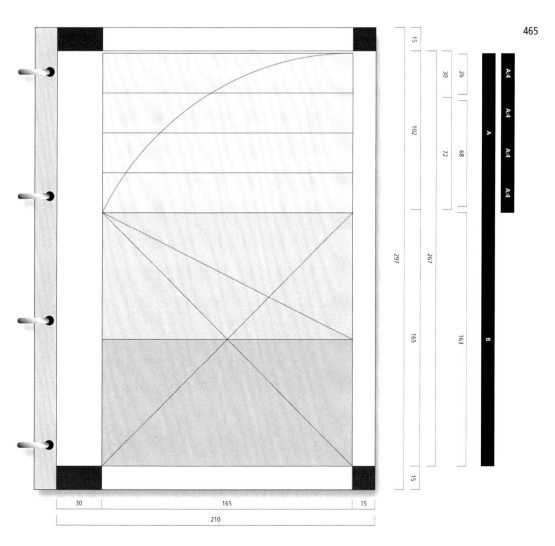

The Template and the Grid

The design of grids obtained using the golden section.
The base format of 165 mm is subdivided into three columns, with a 5 mm space between columns.
This gives us a dimension of 51.666 mm.

This is the width of each column of text.
The three large zones identified in this manner are used as follows:
zone A is dedicated to explanatory texts accompanying the drawings. In particular, zone A1 contains, in the order of the three columns into which it is subdivided, the name of the company for which the manual has been prepared;
the title of the chapter; the number of the chapter and that of the drawing.

Zone B is dedicated to the images present on the page.
The use of bold and regular typefaces identifies the importance of the texts in relation to the general context.
The first two horizontal lines from the top of the page are 0.3 points; the third, which separates the text area from the image area, is 0.6 points.

466

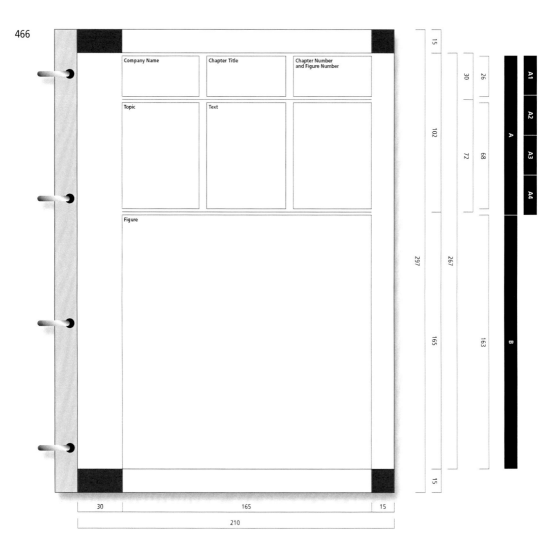

Laying Out the Page

Texts are placed inside the grid that has been constructed as described.
In this case, only one of many almost infinite possibilities, the texts are composed in Helvetica regular and bold, 10 point with a 10 point leading, left justified.
Consider two possible examples:
the texts can be composed using the same institutional typeface used by the company for which you are designing the manual; the texts use a completely different typeface.

The width of the columns of text is 51.666 mm; the quantity of rows available in this structure is 7 for the upper part, 19 for the lower part and 46 rows for the space dedicated to images. However, in some cases, for example drawings that serve to provide the codes for printing letterhead, it can be used for text.

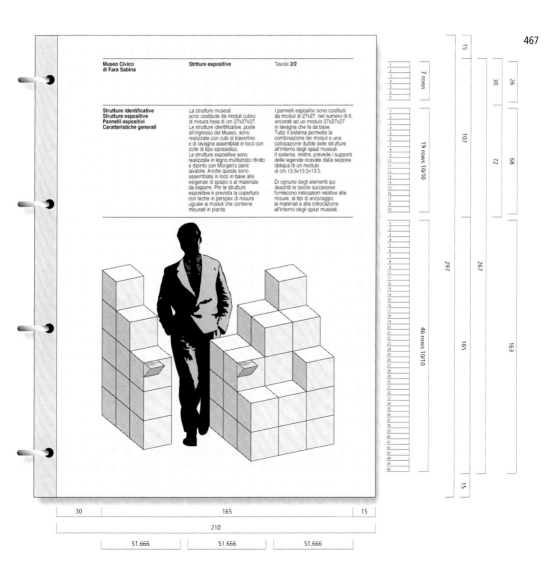

The Print Layout

9 Pages On a 70x100 Folio

1. The pages of the manual, when the pre-established format is 22.5x29.7 cm, can be printed on 70x100 cm folio.
Unlike a classical book, which has to be assembled in octavos, sextodecimos, etc., and which requires the folding of a folio printed in verso e recto, for the pages of the manual, printed only on one side, all that is required is to trim and collate the pages.
This means they can be laid out one beside the other and without the need for two cuts.

2./4. The useful space on each page is 21x29.7 cm.
If one page illustrates a piece of letterhead that measures exactly 21x29.7 cm, the page has to be doubled: in this case the left page, 22.5x29.7 cm and hole punched, will contain the texts describing the letterhead and eventually the logo to be reproduced; the right page will have exactly the same dimensions as the letterhead and thus can be reprinted at 1:1 scale.

The letterhead can be positioned on a facing page or on the back of the page: in this case it is necessary to print the 70x100 sheet on both sides.
If the design to be reproduced requires more space, the page can be composed of three pages that, in this case, can be folded into the manual.
The fold lines are marked by a crease.

468

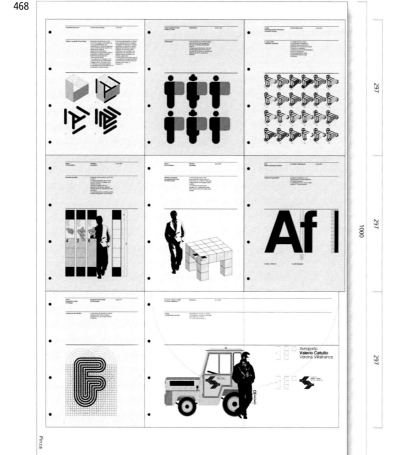

1.

2.

3.

4.

Separators

For a Rapid Identification of Sections and Topics

A separator immediately identifies chapters and topics. It can be created using Murillo black card, with white silkscreened text. Or using coloured plastic coated card, and so on.
To create a thumb index it is necessary to use a die cutter.
Your own creativity, and the budget can guide you through the development of this indispensable element of any manual.

5./6. The tab with the chapter numbers protrudes by 15 mm, and thus the format of the separators measure 24x29.7 cm.
When using a projecting tab, the pages will have to be die cut.
The design of the container for the manual must take into account the projection of the separators.

7./10. The separator can contain various types of information. The chapter number, which is always found on the tab, can be shown in a larger size on the page, together with the title of the chapter.
Remember that the manual is a practical tool for using a company's image and it should be simple to use, functional and allow for rapid consultation.

469

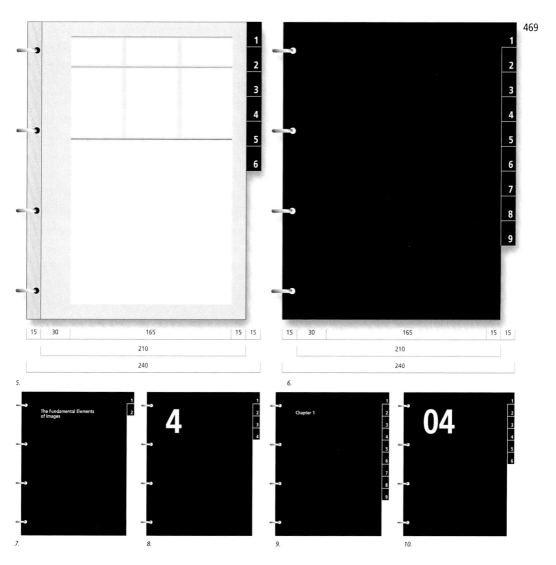

5. 6. 7. 8. 9. 10.

31.
A Guide to the Manual

Corporate Identity

What is "corporate identity" and why we need to design a coordinated image manual, in other words a vast architecture of communication: the text presented on this page, borrowed from the introduction to the Dreher Beer manual, designed by Unimark, offers a clear and unmistakable explanation.

The text was part of the research. It was read and discussed during a lesson that was part of the Industrial Design course, based on the conviction that this study would prove very useful to students who consider a manual to be the maximum objective in the profession of a graphic designer.

Students are reminded that even a project of modest dimensions can assume the form of a manual.
This tool, other than obliging a designer to observe codes, proportions and anything else imposed by a rationally planned image, also obliges the proper presentation of the project itself.

470 "Every company, large or small, whether it is aware or not, has a "corporate image", to borrow an Anglo-Saxon term. It is impressed in peoples' minds and recalled the moment they decide to choose you, through one of your products or services. This "image" is created by all of the visual expressions of a company, whether products, packaging, brands, letterhead, advertising, vehicles, staff uniforms, etc. These are the heterogeneous elements that over time inform the public about the nature, quality and efficiency of a company. Thus it is clear that the more a company wishes to stand out, and in the most positive manner, the more it must construct a "personal image" that separates and differentiates it from other companies operating in the same sector. A clear, strong and unmistakable "corporate identity" works in a company's favour, while a confused, uncertain and antiquated "corporate identity" works against it [...].
The first step toward achieving this result is the programming of the "image". This means that each element is studied with a final objective in mind. This programming must take into account the characteristics of the elements that make up this "image", dynamic elements owing to the fact that their intrinsic nature is subject to continuous evolution and transformation.
The tools of this programming must permit this evolution, while ensuring the general "image" remains unaltered. Coordination is the most suitable tool. Coordination that affects all aspects of this "image". Every visible manifestation of a company becomes part of its unified "image", which can be divided and dilated over time, without ever becoming fractured and remaining present in its entirety through the consistent reuse of a series of fundamental elements. These are the fundamental elements of the brand and the logotype. The diverse combination at different dimensions of these elements gives birth to everything else.
This book establishes these elements and presents them in all of their principal applications. The result is the new "image" of Dreher beer: an image we consider unified, even if it is divided and dilated in various dimension and a host of different materials. However this book, in addition to illustrating a current situation, also wishes to be a tool. This is precisely why it was created. Anyone who has to create anything, even the smallest part of this "image", will find what they need here. As a manual, it is deigned to be followed rigorously, to the letter, without admitting any adaptations or interpretations. Only in this way can the "Dreher image" conserve its validity and ensure that every piece is a perfect part of a larger design. A design composed of a vast number of coordinated parts".

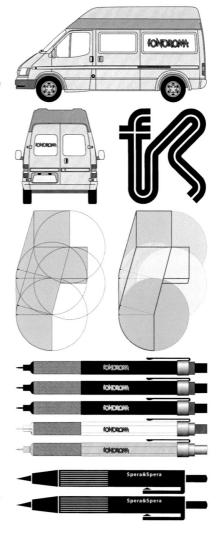

The Table of Contents

A Guide to the Construction of a Manual

The table of contents presented here is only an example.
Each company has its own specific activities and needs, and these needs must serve as the basis for the construction of each specific manual.
The brief, the acquisition of all information about the activities and objectives of the company for which an image is being prepared, is indispensable not only to the design of the proper brand, but also to the production of the proper manual.
The correct starting point in the construction of a coordinated image can be suggested by a list of topics containing the primary items to be considered during the design process.
Many of the items can be eliminated, others will have to be added. In any case, this list is certainly a good place to start.

471

Bibliography
This bibliography presents only a few examples, as this type of manual is generally confidential and difficult to acquire.

By Bob Noorda and Unimark I mention the manuals for Agip, Dreher, the New York Subway, Coop, etc.; by Massimo Vignelli for Lancia; by Mimmo Castellano the Ice manual; by Borislav Ljubicic for the 8th Mediterranean Games in 1979.

By the author, the manuals for Innocenti, Maserati, Rai (Tg2, Tribune), Endas, the Banca Mediterranea, Enfap, Unioncamere, Consulenti del lavoro, the Chambers of Commerce of Potenza, Pesaro and Urbino, Confindustria, Gepi, Verona Villafranca Airport, Mediocredito della Basilicata, the Lanificio Gatti, Farmacap, etc.

By Walter Landor I mention the manual for Alitalia, one of the first produced for an Italian company, and that for Montedison.

Workbook
Acquire copies of manuals for different companies. Compare and analyse them.

The Table of Contents

A Guide to the Construction of a Manual

In this chapter we look at one example of how to construct a coordinated image manual without entering into the specific theme of page content.
The pages do not illustrate how to develop a differentiated spacing, but are only intended to suggest the importance of considering this issue in a manual.

For specific topics, please refer to the dedicated chapters.

1./4. An example of a table of contents containing the various items and two pages, one dedicated to the motivations behind the design of an image, and the second dedicated to how to use the manual.

5. A disk pocket with two holes that allow it to be inserted in the manual.

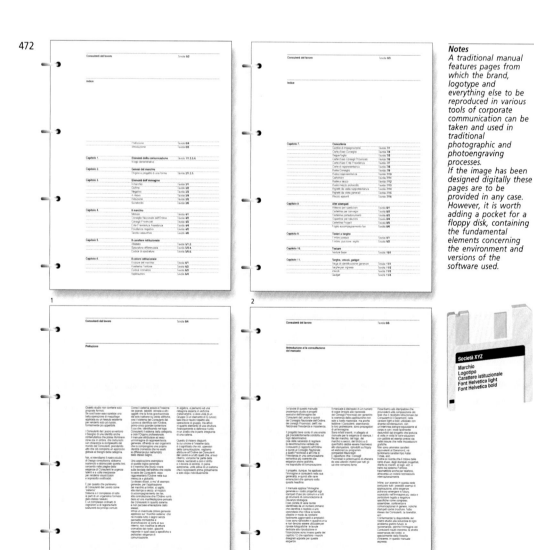

Notes
A traditional manual features pages from which the brand, logotype and everything else to be reproduced in various tools of corporate communication can be taken and used in traditional photographic and photoengraving processes.
If the image has been designed digitally these pages are to be provided in any case. However, it is worth adding a pocket for a floppy disk, containing the fundamental elements concerning the environment and versions of the software used.

6. A hole punch. This device can punch through a certain number of sheets of paper, generally creating 4 holes at 80 mm on centre.
Below are two of the most common binding rings used to collate punched pages.
The second type of ring guarantees the alignment of the pages along the binding edge.

The manual, as a tool for applying an image designed by a graphic designer, becomes a testing ground in which every part of a project can be verified and expanded.
By applying this methodology to any project, no matter how modest, students can find a very useful and ordered key to the presentation of any drawing.
Once again, creativity finds a rational space of expression, based on a logic that requires the skills of a graphic designer.

7.

7. The hole punch shown to the left, available at a very modest cost, makes it possible to easily collate the pages of an early project.

Workbook
Design the format and relative grid for a manual used as a portfolio and workbook.
Insert drawings and research material related to the themes explored during the course.
Allow for space on the pages for images as well as an explanation of the methodology behind them.

473

6.

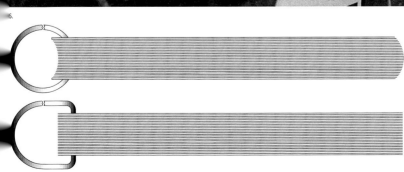

Explaining a Brand

A manual provides methods and codes, in a word, the instructions for the correct and rigorous application of a coordinated image to all instruments of communication used by a company.
The first chapter of a classical manual features clear and reproducible versions of the fundamental elements of the image: the brand and logotype.

The initial chapter also gives an added value to this instrument.
It explains how the brand was born, the roots of its design, the approach pursued to arrive at its definitive form using dedicated drawings.
Other than offering a design method, these drawings also help to better understand the brand and its role within a vaster communications plan.

1. 2. The steps in the construction of the brand for the *Ordine dei Consulenti del lavoro*.
It is derived from three main components that emerged from the brief.

3. 4. The steps in the construction of the brand for the Istituto Tagliacarne.
It is derived from the base module of the Unioncamere brand (see the following pages), of which the Institute is a part.

474

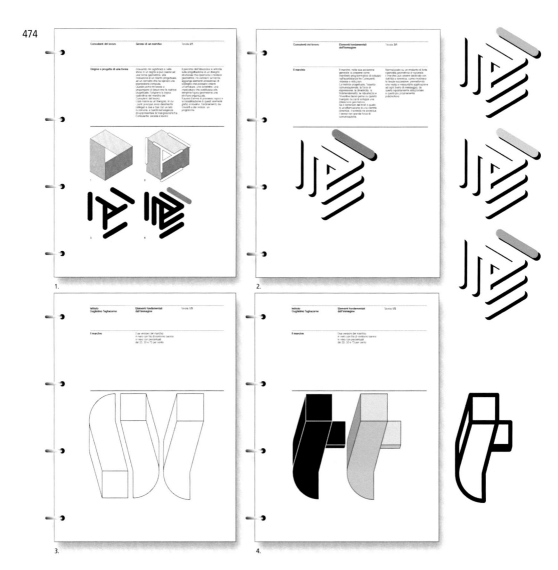

1.

2.

3.

4.

475

Notes
The Innocenti brand was created by rotating a letter "n", the first letter of Nuova Innocenti, the name of the new production wing of the Milanese company following its acquisition by Alessandro de Tomaso.

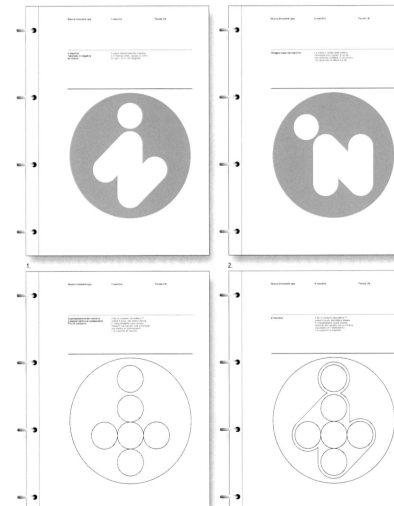

1.

2.

3.

4.

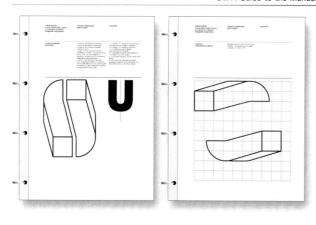

The Unioncamere brand, the Italian Union of Chambers of Commerce, is a visualisation of the union between two elements that are strongly integrated to create a compact and synthetic image.
The strength of this sign is the meaning of the word "union", in other words the coming together of many Chambers of Commerce, with the prerogatives, requirements and instances institutionally represented by Unioncamere.
The brand is born from a simple design input.

The meaning, deciphered here, is the secret part of the symbol, the part that is destined to be memorised unconsciously.
1) The letter "U", the first letter of Unioncamere marks the origin of its construction;
2) The letter "U" is split into two parts;
3) One of the two parts is flipped 180°;
4) The two parts are assembled to create a unique sign;
5) The two parts are then rotated 90°;
6) The resulting form is then assigned a third and purely virtual dimension.

476

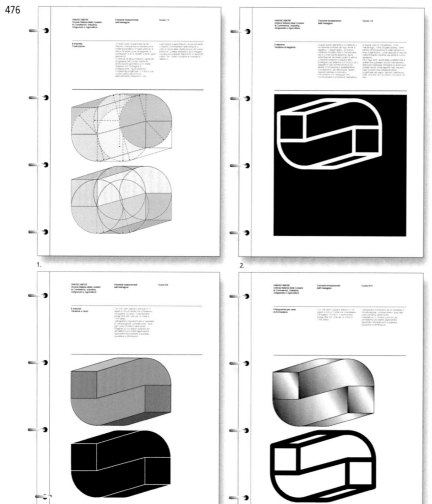

1.

2.

3.

4.

Notes
*The wood model shown below is the three-dimensional construction of the Unioncamere brand.
It proved very useful in arriving at the final graphic and studying it "in reality".
It was later adopted as the form of a sculpture-prize.*

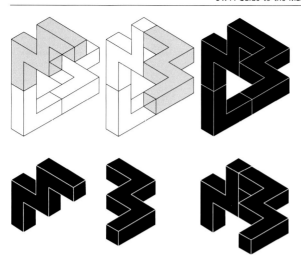

The brand developed for Mediocredito della Basilicata, shown here to the left, is based on the reconstruction of a letter "M" and a letter "B", the first letters of Mediocredito and Basilicata.
The decomposition of the elements shows how the final design was developed.

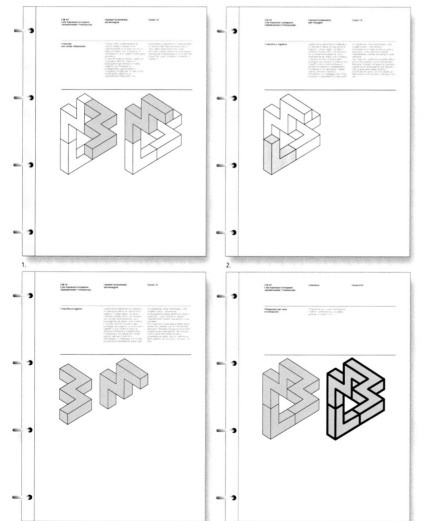

1.

2.

3.

4.

Notes   477
The manual designed for Mediocredito della Basilicata consists of approximately 200 pages, gradually updated to respond to the changing needs of communication over the years.
This was possible thanks to the relationship maintained with the bank over many years.

Celebratory Logos

Small Manuals
for Special Events

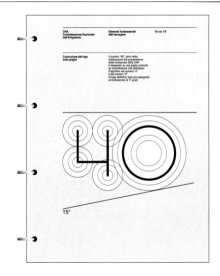

A project with the objective of creating a symbol, and applying it to printed material accompanying events marking an anniversary can assume the form of a small manual.
On this page we show the image for the fortieth anniversary of the foundations of the CNA, the National Confederation for the Craft Sector, and some of the explanatory drawings.

478

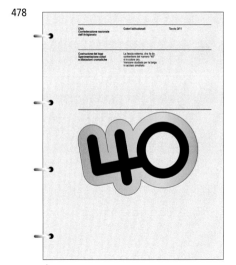

1.

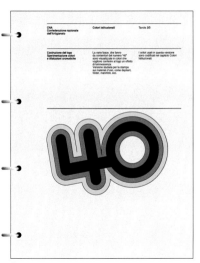

2.

3.

4.

CNA
NATIONAL CONFEDERATION
OF CRAFTSMANSHIP

1945/1985
FORTY YEAR
ANNIVERSARY

The poster celebrating the 40th anniversary of the foundation of the CNA, the National Confederation of Craftsmanship, explodes in all of its grandeur in this 100x140 cm format.

479

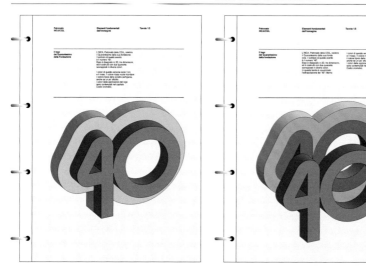

Below is a symbol created for the one hundredth anniversary and the thirty-third anniversary of Bristol Meyers and a symbol for the seventy-fifth anniversary of INA.

480

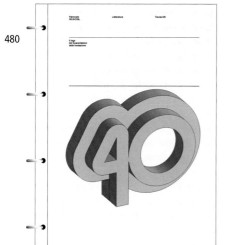

INCA/CGIL
1945/1985

FORTY YEARS OF WORK
AT THE SERVICE
OF THE WORKING CLASS

The post celebrating the 40th anniversary of the INCA foundation, supported by the CGIL, the Italian General Confederation of Labour, explodes in all of its grandeur in this 100x140 cm format.

Note

In the poster, the number "40" rises like the sun behind a black cloud representing the dark years of fascism.

481

The Negative Version of a Logo

When designing a brand, it is important to verify its appearance in a negative version. In fact, owing to an optical effect that dilates white space, a brand can undergo even relevant distortions in its legibility.
This is why it must be verified and, eventually, corrected.

1./4. The drawings show a few examples of brands in their negative versions.

482

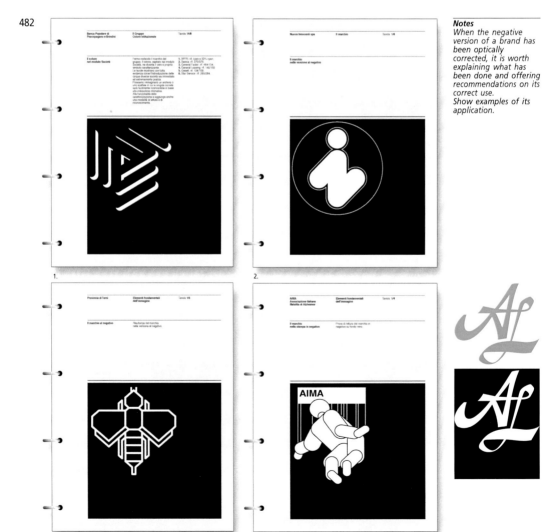

1.

2.

3.

4.

Notes
When the negative version of a brand has been optically corrected, it is worth explaining what has been done and offering recommendations on its correct use.
Show examples of its application.

A Logo and a Corolla

Stamps, Punches, Seals

The corolla around a brand gives it an aulic appearance, and an elevated level of importance when applied to official documents.
Shown here is a text from one of the manuals printed below, which accompanies the version of the brand ringed by a corolla.
A punch is created with negative-positive cliché mounted on a special device for dry stamping.
It can be used in lieu of a rubber stamp when a document requires a certain level of prestige, for example official acts and notarised documents.

A seal is made from a negative cliché mounted on a support. No longer used for legal purposes and authorisations as it was in the Middle Ages, and despite having been substituted by the humble rubber stamp, a seal can still be used for acts that, in addition to purely economic information, terms of social and civil solidarity, especially at the international level, or for documents of particular importance in promotional terms. This without excluding the use of a seal for issues of corporate representativity and the sponsorship of cultural and philanthropic activities.

483

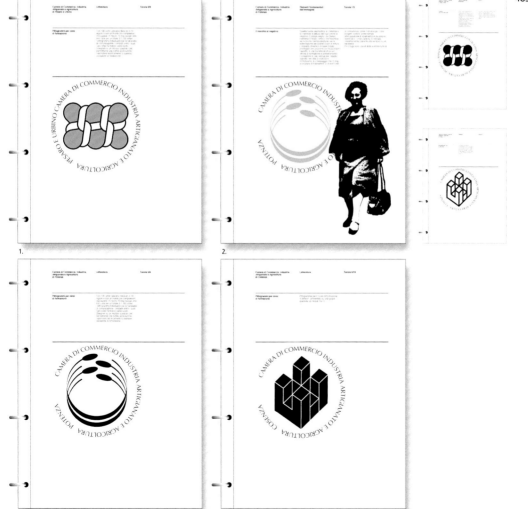

1.

2.

3.

4.

The Logotype

The Constant and Repeated Use of a Sign

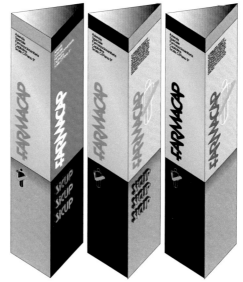

484

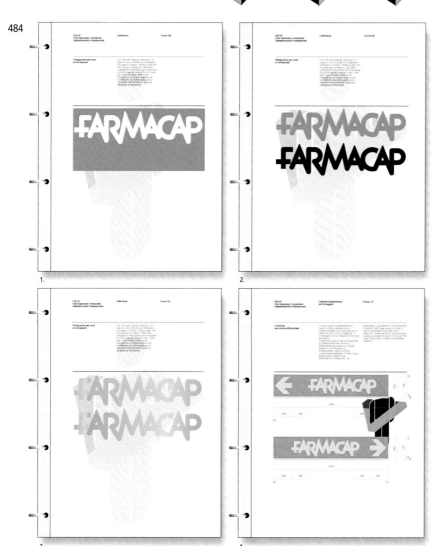

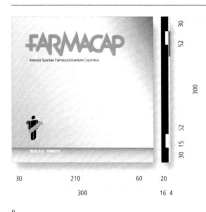

30   210   60   20
300   16 4

9.

1./8. The image of Farmacap, the company that manages the City of Rome's municipal pharmacies, from the dedicated pages of the manual.
From the sign for pharmacies, to the symbol of the "cross" that identifies a pharmacy and must respond to pre-established codes, to signage totems and street signs, the logotype is always present and serves to communicate information.

9. Situated at the entrance to the Farmacap offices, this nameplate measures 300x300 mm.
It consists of a 20 mm wood support fixed to the wall with 4 special screws.
An anodised aluminium or brush finished stainless steel plate is fixed to this support.
The denominative and figurative logos are etched into the metal and filled with enamel paint using Farmacap's institutional colours.
The four flat head screws are set flush and concealed.

Farmacap logo colours:
Green, Pantone 363, equal to Cyan 76% + Yellow 100% + Black 23,5%;
figurative logo colours:
Orange, Pantone Orange 021 = Magenta 51% + Yellow 87%;
Red, Pantone 187 = Magenta 91% + Yellow 72% + Black 23,5%.

Notes
The logotype is shown in its base form and various versions.
These latter, opportunely illustrated, can be very useful when applying the image to special items of corporate literature, such as covers, folders, etc.

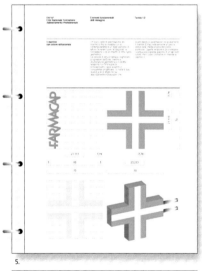

5.

6.

7.

8.

The Construction of a Logo

1./4. The drawing illustrating the construction of a logo permits its rigorous reconstruction as necessary. Accompany it with measurements, imagining that someone may have to create an immense rooftop version.

The many signs required to normalise a brand have a very impressive visual impact.
The design of a logo comes forth in all of its complex harmony. When it is well designed, this construction can be used in a concealed manner on the cover of a year end accounting statement, for example, a drawing of this type can transmit strong values of communication.

486

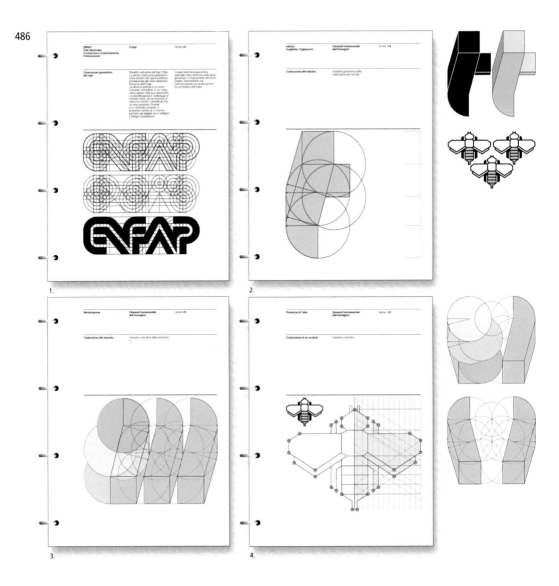

1.

2.

3.

4.

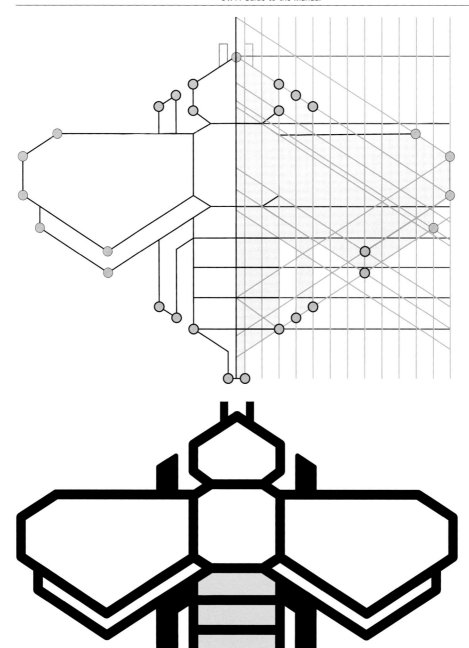

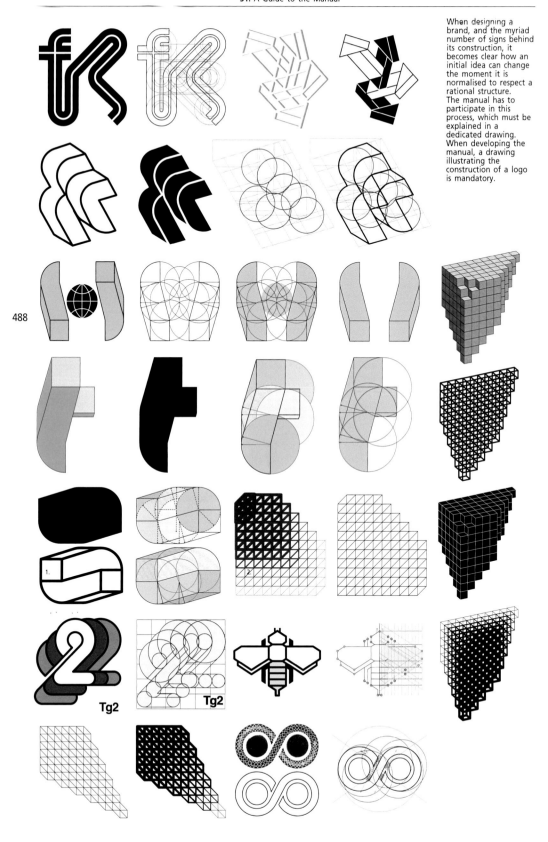

When designing a brand, and the myriad number of signs behind its construction, it becomes clear how an initial idea can change the moment it is normalised to respect a rational structure. The manual has to participate in this process, which must be explained in a dedicated drawing. When developing the manual, a drawing illustrating the construction of a logo is mandatory.

488

The many signs required to normalise a brand have a very impressive visual impact.
The design of a logo comes forth in all of its complex harmony. When it is well designed, this construction can be used in a concealed manner on the cover of a year end accounting statement, for example, a drawing of this type can transmit strong values of communication.

489

Institutional Colours and Colour Codes

Any logo must be printable in white/black without losing its identity.
This means that the colour of a brand must be considered an added element, and not indispensable.
Translated into b&w, the colours of a logo take on an appearance that is a result of a percentage of black that corresponds in intensity with the colour it substitutes.

Certain images have elements that will always be printed in colour.
Regarding the colours of a brand, a logo, vehicles, etc., the manual must provide a broad selection of codes based on unified systems. One of these is the Pantone system, which codifies ink colours, ensuring they are reproduced when printed in flat colours or CMYK.
Other systems are related to types of paints, solid coloured materials, etc.

1./4. The manual features colour coded illustrations for creating colour samples.

490

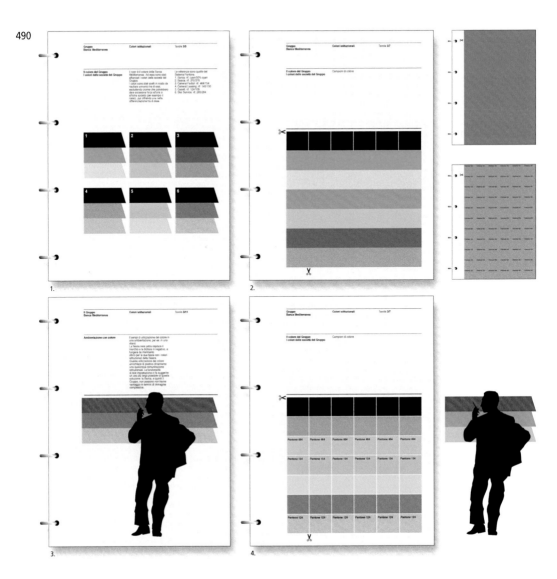

1.

2.

3.

4.

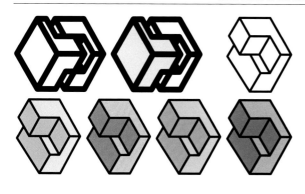

Pages from the coordinated image manual developed for the holding of the Banca Mediterranea. The Bank brand is a solid split into two volumes; the first is given the institutional colour cyan, and the second is white. The second volume is used to distinguish the various companies of the Group, each with its own institutional colour.

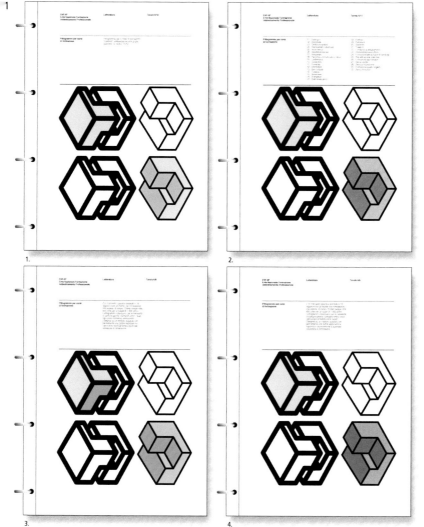

Notes
In addition to the institutional colours shown here, the manual also imagines other colours for companies that have yet to be created or in the process of being created.

This page from the Endas manual shows the colour code assigned to Regional Offices.

While the colour of Endas Nazionale is silver, each of the Regional offices has its own specific colour. This colour is present inside the brand, in the "free time" module, and in those cases when colour serves as a tool of recognition within the national structure.
The colour code was developed for those regions home to Regional Offices and the two autonomous provinces of Trento and Bolzano.

The colour code table shown below assigns specific colours to the 19 Regional offices and those in the two autonomous provinces. Colours are referred to the internationally recognised Pantone system, now widely used by printers.

The table provides colour references for every colour, whether it is to be printed autonomously or in CMYK (see the percentages; in any case, the Pantone number is to be communicated to the printer.

Legend:
The symbol ➜ indicates the Pantone colour number used;
the symbol ★ indicates the percentages for obtaining the same colour in CMYK printing:
C = cyan
M = magenta
Y = yellow
K = black

Region	City	Address	Pantone Number ➜	Percentages	4
A. Endas nazionale	00184 Rome	Via Cavour, 238	➜ Silver	none	
B. Endas nazionale	00184 Rome	Via Cavour, 238	➜ Black	none	
1. Valle d'Aosta	00100 Aosta	St. Pont Suaz, 14	➜ Pantone n. 203	M 34	
2. Piedmont	00123 Turin	Via Giolitti, 19	➜ Pantone n. 245	C 15+M 60	
3. Lombardy	20121 Milan	Via Ugo Foscolo, 3	➜ Pantone n. 247	C 38+M 94	
4. Trentino Alto Adige	39100 Bolzano	Via Piave, 3	➜ Pantone n. 266	C 94+M 94	
5. Trentino Alto Adige	38100 Trento	Via Os Mazzurana, 54	➜ Pantone n. 265	C 56+M 56	
6. Friuli Venezia Giulia	31133 Trieste	Via del Coroneo, 13	➜ Pantone n. 264	C 27,5+M 30,5	
7. Liguria	16151 Genoa	Via CDondero, 8	➜ Pantone n. 297	C 50	
8. Veneto	30173 Venice Mestre	Piazza del Lavoro, 3	➜ Pantone n. 312	C 100+G 15	
9. Emilia Romagna	40121 Bologna	Via Gallera, 11	➜ Pantone n. 300	C 100+G 15	
10. Tuscany	56100 Pisa	Lungarno Pacinotti, 8	➜ Pantone n. 348	C 100+G 79+N 27,5	
11. The Marche	60121 Ancona	Corso Mazzini, 25	➜ Pantone n. 355	C 100+G 91+N 6	
12. Umbria	06100 Perugia	Via Dante Alighieri, 6	➜ Pantone n. 376	C 56+G 100	
13. Lazio	00184 Rome	Via Cavour, 238	➜ Pantone n. 397	C 11,5+G 100+N 11	
14. Abruzzo	67100 L'Aquila	Via della Genca, 16	➜ Pantone n. 109	M 8,5+G 94	
15. Molise	86100 Campobasso	Via Pirandello, 37	➜ Pantone n. 123	M 30,5+G 94	
16. Campania	80134 Naples	Via Maddaloni, 6	➜ Pantone n. 137	M 34+G 91	
17. Apulia	70121 Bari	Via Cardassi, 36	➜ Pantone n. 151	M 43+G 87	
18. Basilicata	75100 Matera	Via Ascanio Persio, 4	➜ Pantone n. 165	M 60+G 100	
19. Calabria	88100 Catanzaro	Via Pianogrande, 14	➜ Pantone warm red	M 79+G 91	
20. Sardinia	09100 Cagliari	Via Tempio, 10b	➜ Pantone n. 185	M 91+G 76	
21. Sicily	90138 Palermo	Piazza Verdi, 6	➜ Pantone n. 186	M 91+G 76+N 6	

Drawings from the coordinated image manual developed for Endas.

Right: The 24 versions of the brand with the modules bearing the institutional colour of the national body and the colours of the regional offices.

1. This drawing highlights only the modules of the brand and the institutional colour assigned to them.

Notes
The colours of Endas. They were assigned based on a general criteria and the use of colours to group together offices in the North, Centre, South and Islands of Italy.

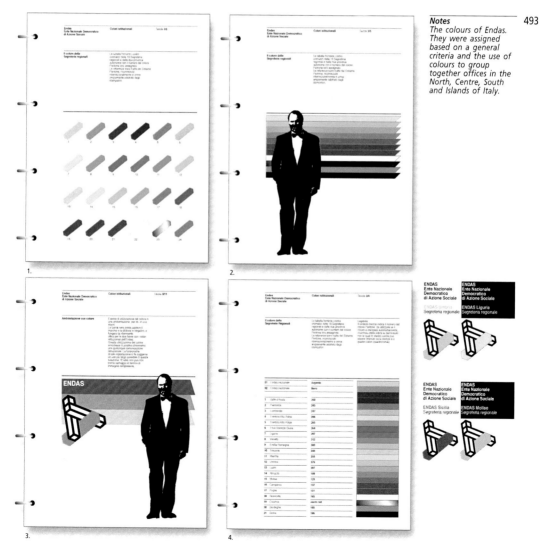

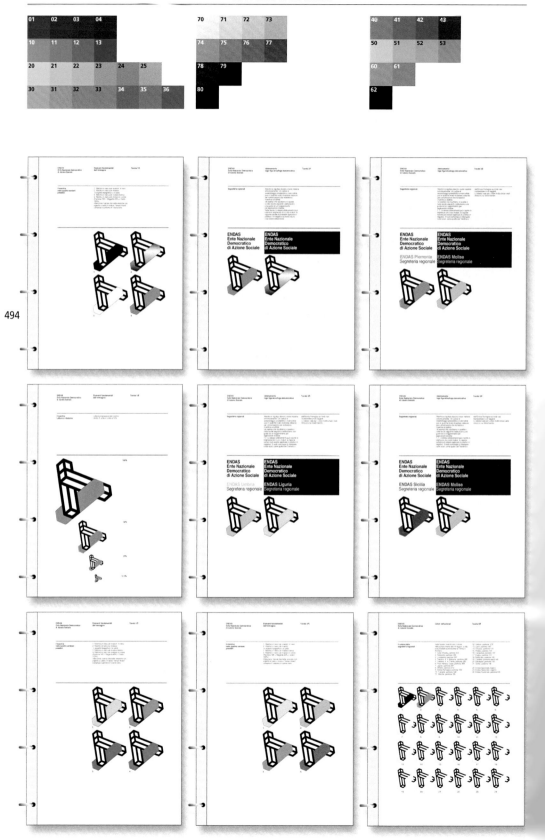

494

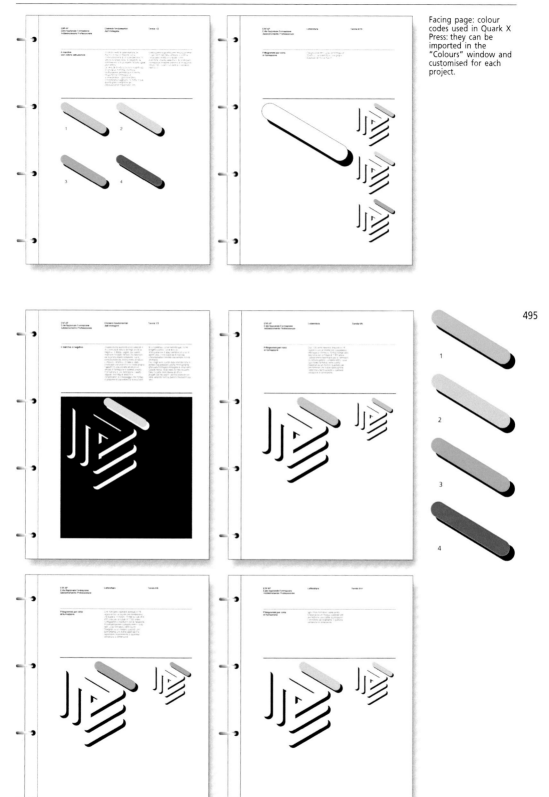

Facing page: colour codes used in Quark X Press: they can be imported in the "Colours" window and customised for each project.

495

Corporate Identity
Manual.

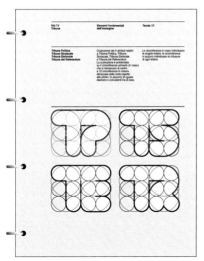

496

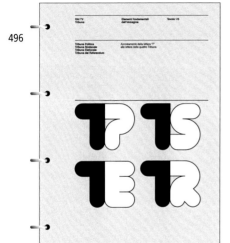

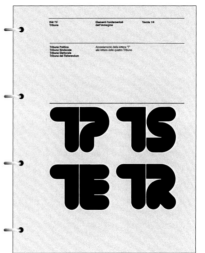

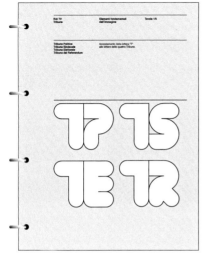

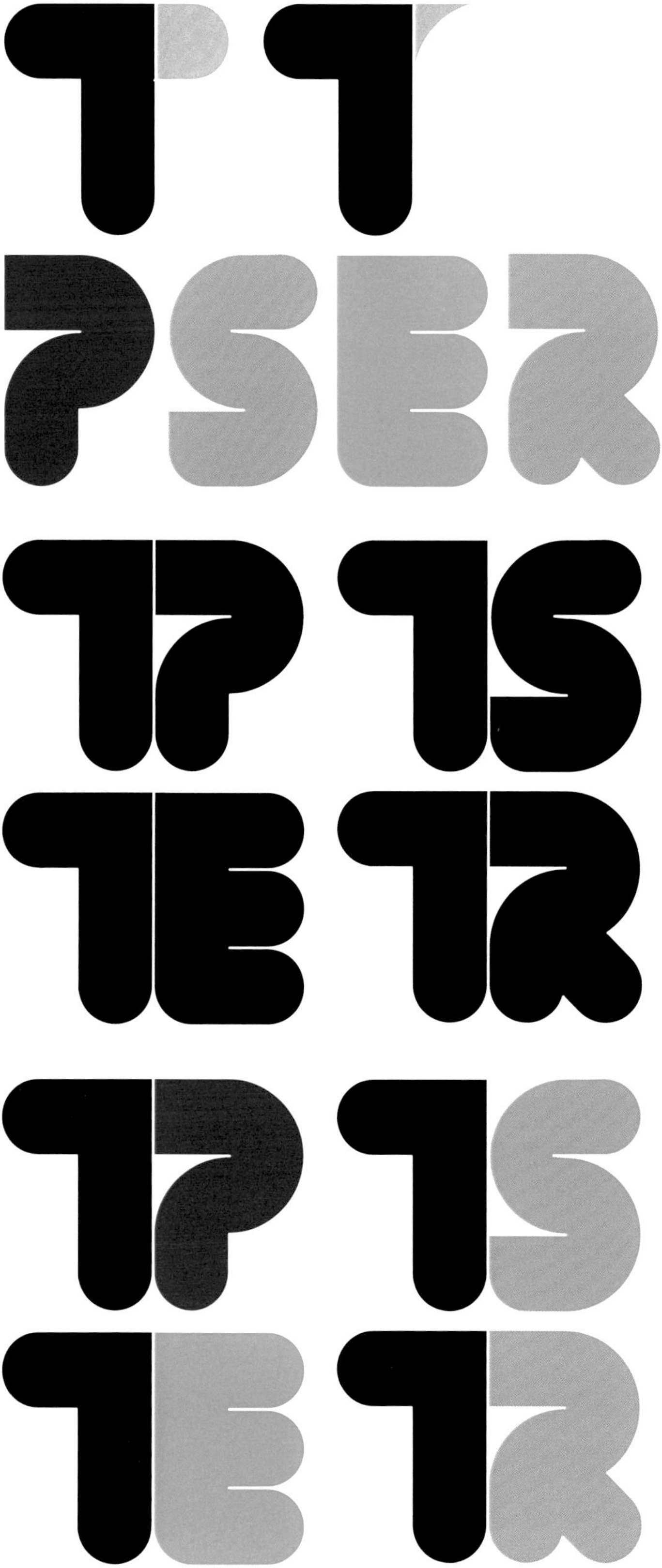

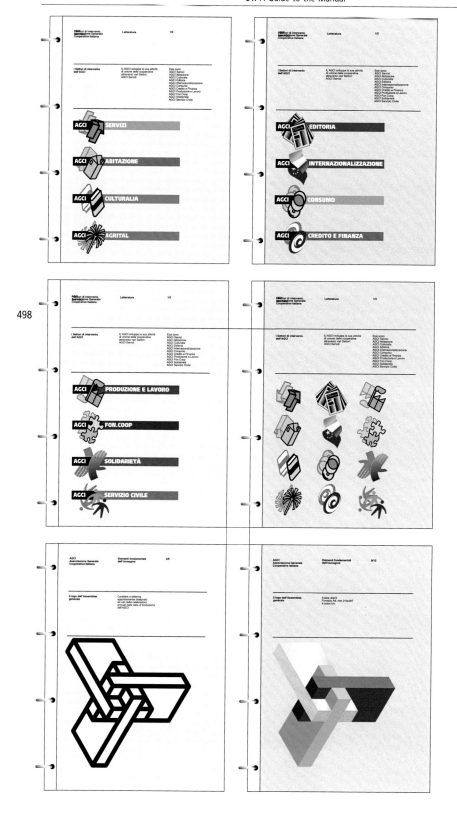

498

499

The RAL Colour Standard
RAL is a system used to indicate colours of paints, finishes and plastic materials using a correspondence with typographic colours. RAL Classic is the most famous and common system. The RAL Design and RAL Effect collections offer more colour variations. The RAL colour standard is managed by *RAL Deutsches Institut für Gütesicherung und Kennzeichnung.* RAL, originally the acronym for the German *Reichs-Ausschuß für Lieferbedingungen und Gütesicherung*

(Imperial Commission for Delivery Terms and Quality Assurance, instituted in 1925 by the Weimar Republic), is now used to define a scale of standardised colours used primarily for paints and finishes.

There are two RAL Classic scales: RAL 840-HR comprising a total of 213 opaque colours and RAL 841-GL comprising a total of 196 bright colours.

To the left is a selection of RAL sample charts and, below, a few conversions from RGB, CMYK and Pantone to RAL.

Notes
Attention:
The samples shown here as references are unable to properly show the exact RAL colours.
To be sure they are selecting the right colours, I suggest students acquire an official RAL colour fan, though it must be remembered that it is sold in two versions: one with a semi-opaque and another with a glossy finish. Finally, I remind readers to apply the correct colour conversions.

RAL	Pantone (best match)	CMYK %	RGB (hex)
ral 1000 Beige vert	4525	0 6/38/18	ccc188
ral 1001 Beige	728	0/18/43/11	ceb487
ral 1002 Jaune Sable	465	18/31/56/0	d0b173
ral 1003 Jaune signalisation	137	0/34/91/0	f2ad00
ral 1004 Jaune d'Or	124	0/27/100/6	e4a700
ral 1005 Jaune miel	131	0/27/100/9	c79600
ral 1006 Jaune maïs	144	0/47/100/0	d99300
ral 1007 Jaune de chrome	144	0/47/100/0	e69400

Institutional Typefaces and Spacing Codes

This chapter can become very rich with information and illustrations. From that showing the institutional typeface in all of its versions to the drawing codifying combinations of letters based on the differentiated spacing code; from the code table to that which applies it to the various needs of the company.

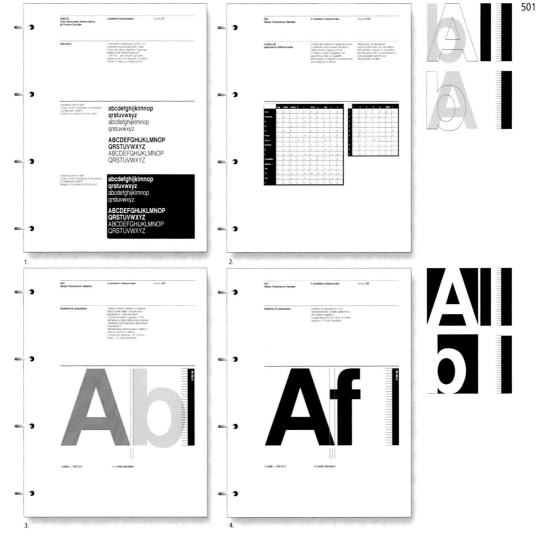

1.

2.

3.

4.

501

Stationery

The chapter on stationery is perhaps that which requires more pages than any other.
The vast quantity of printed material, the diverse uses of letterhead, the dozens of annexes to this topic oblige us to produce dozens of illustrations. This process affects the normalisation of printed material because, as you will discover, as you move forward, all of the layouts must be tied back to a single format to ensure a uniform overall result.

1./4. A page from the manual explains how letterhead is laid out, the spaces dedicated to company information, those for the recipient's information, the subject of the letter, the date, and so on.
Everything should be accompanied by precise and easy to understand dimensions.

502

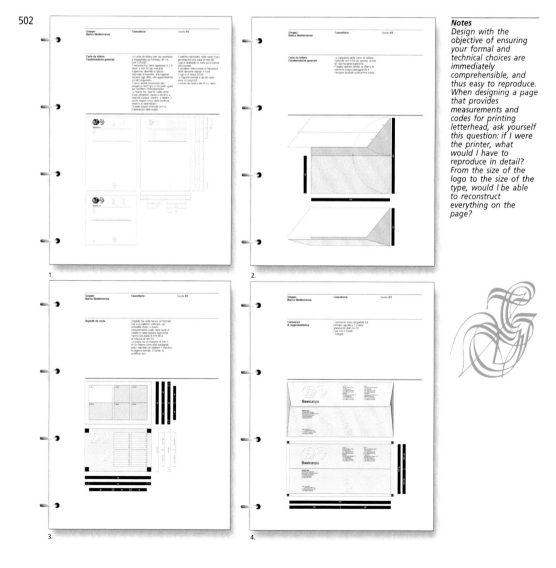

1.

2.

3.

4.

Notes
Design with the objective of ensuring your formal and technical choices are immediately comprehensible, and thus easy to reproduce. When designing a page that provides measurements and codes for printing letterhead, ask yourself this question: if I were the printer, what would I have to reproduce in detail? From the size of the logo to the size of the type, would I be able to reconstruct everything on the page?

Other drawings will explain how letterhead paper is to be folded, the layout of more representative paper and that for everyday use, for minutes or notepads.
In relation to each type of letter paper, indicate the type of paper to be used, for example Diamant for general paper, Conqueror for more representative versions; kraft for large envelopes, Bristol card for business cards, etc. A window envelope makes it possible to use the recipient's address printed on the letter it contains: it will show through the window.

This means it is necessary to design letterhead with a correspondence between the window in the envelope and the address on the letter.

UNI regulations codify these measurements and offer a certain tolerance regarding the size and position of the window.

503

Notes
Window envelopes can be used for commercial correspondence, but never for personal or more representative letters.

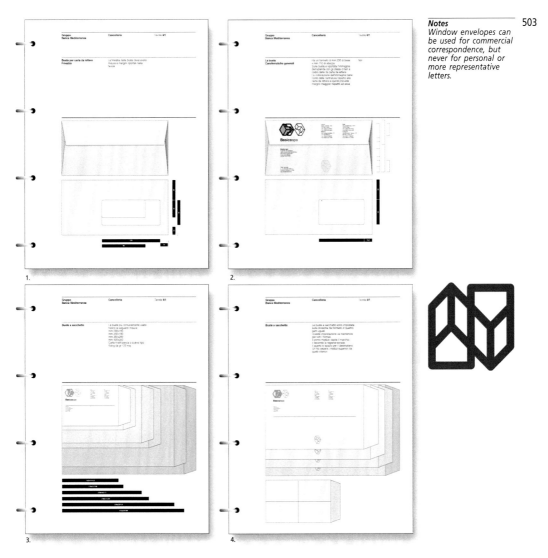

1.

2.

3.

4.

Vehicles
and Means of
Transportation

An Image in Movement

The application of an image to vehicles offers a very fascinating challenge for a graphic designer.
This image lives in large spaces, what is more in movement. It can be the crowning jewel of a vast project. It will be important to understand what use the company intends to make of this image and what vehicles it uses.

Acquire a set of brochures provided by car and truck manufacturers illustrating the characteristics of different vehicles. Above all, try to get your hands on documents with dimensions.
These drawings will serve as the base for the reconstructions to which you can apply the company's image, complete with dimensions, colour codes and any other technical elements, such as paints, vinyls, etc.

Your designs will be printed on a plotter, ensuring the faithful reproduction of brands, logos and any other information. The vinyl letters will be applied to two protective layers that allow the graphics to be fixed to the side of the vehicle in a single operation.

504

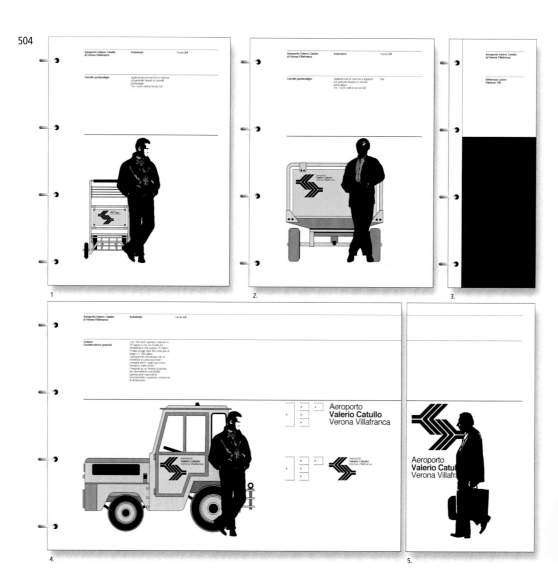

1.

2.

3.

4.

5.

3. 8. The manual can contain colour samples for paints.
The format is equal to 1/3 of 210 mm plus 15 mm for the holes, for a total base of 85 mm.

4. 7. In the case of particularly large drawings, the page will be based on the base format of 225 mm plus two 210 mm pages, for a total of 645 mm.
The page can be folded into the manual.

505

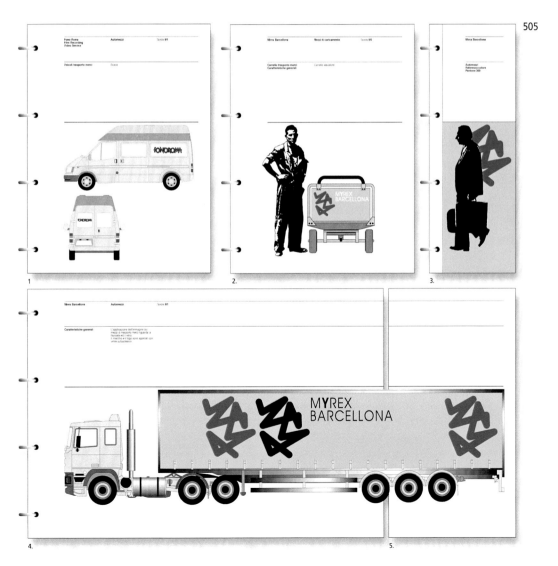

1.

2.

3.

4.

5.

Displays

In addition to the general characteristics of a design or layout, the manual will also contain dimensions for individual elements of structures, modules, legends, paint types and methods of assembly.
Indicate the typeface to be used, the relative type sizes, colour codes, etc.
Indicate the printing techniques and those for the reproduction of texts, graphics and drawings.
A complete project at full scale.

Musaeum (from the Greek *Mousêion*, "sacred space of the Muses") was the name given to the building in Alexandria, Egypt, built by Ptolemy II Philadelphus and containing the famous library; this is the origin of the name given to collections of art housed in dedicated buildings.
This was the starting point for a museum that not only can be recognised by a brand, a sign, a colour code, but above all as a space of knowledge and the clear and transparent transmission of fragments of history.

506

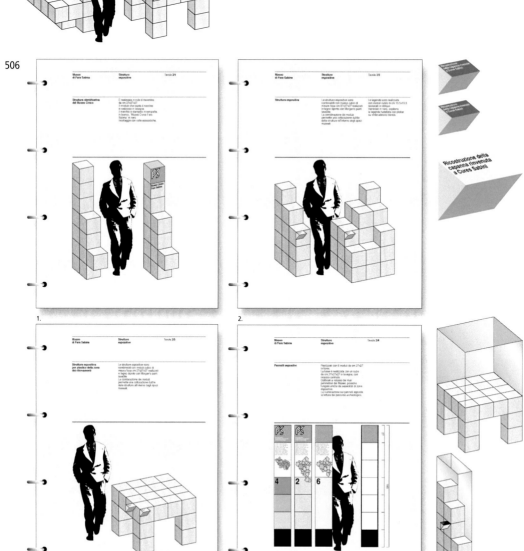

1.

2.

3.

4.

Pictograms

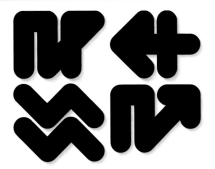

Other than appearing in drawings showing examples of their use, the pictograms belonging to a coordinated image package must be illustrated in the manual on their own and at a scale that allows for their perfect reproduction.

507

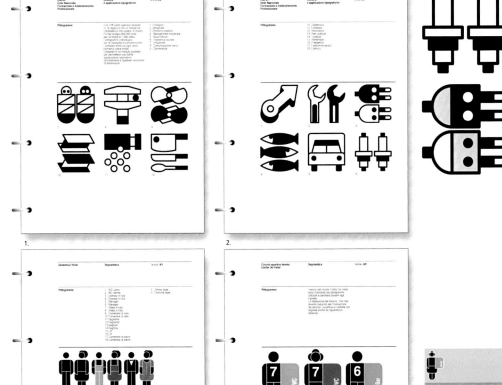

1.

2.

3.

4.

An Optical Texture
for a Heraldic Brand

The symbol of the Town of Pistoia in Tuscany features a bear, an image with an ancient tradition.
The image of the bear was redesigned with a linear halftone that was successively adjusted to create a texture.

It is important to submit your work in the most dignified manner.
The front, back and spines of a CD case can be laid out using a computer and printed with customised colour labels.
The standard dimensions of a cover are 122 mm (w) x 118 mm (h).

509

32.
A Manual Designed by Students

Stefania Tuzi
Premise
What is the
Ponte della memoria
and Why It Was Created

Students involved in the project:
Andrea Bennati
Fabiana Conti
Marta Costantini
Lorenza De Agostini
Cecilia Fabretti
Giuseppe Galati
Alessio Oriani
Chiara Santarelli
Massimo Scacco

510

The *Ponte della Memoria* cultural association was created in August 2000 to support the trial for Italian *desaparecidos* in Argentina. The primary objective, other than offering concrete support to witnesses and families, was that of using culture (debates, exhibitions, theatre, press conferences, etc.) to draw as much attention as possible to this crime against humanity, for too long ignored by mass media and almost unknown to the general Italian public.

To support this trial, the *Ponte della Memoria* organised a series of events designed to offer evidence and stimulate a reflection on the theme of the *desaparecidos*, emphasising the importance of the role of memory. The past thus become an emblematic space for understanding the present. Memory is the foundation of our history, it creates a continuity between what we were and what we are; it creates a sense of common belonging. For this reason it is important not to lose memory, considering that it is one of the most fragile things we posses, and becomes even more fragile every time we forget a piece of our past. There are no boundaries to cruelty and for this reason we believe that the *desaparecidos* are not only Argentinian, but belong to the entire world. We cannot remain indifferent in the face of the crimes that continue to be committed each day against thousands of people around the world Culture and human rights are concepts that cannot be considered separately. Theatre, art, music, in a word culture, in all of its expressions, able to speak of reality using a symbolic language, can become indispensable tools for describing and transmitting the history of those nations that have suffered the horrors of a dictatorship to a vast public.

Culture is also the most effective tool for spreading a sense of solidarity and creating a relationship founded on integration between different peoples and different cultures. Within this dialogue, memory, recollections and the valorisation of different identities represent a heritage for creating a better society.

For this reason, the *Ponte della Memoria*, intends to use culture to expose and denounce the violation of human rights and crimes against humanity, and to promote a culture of peace and solidarity.

Perhaps one cannot, what is more one must not, understand what happened, because to understand [...] is almost to justify.
Quizàs lo que ha sucedido no se deba comprender, si, no se debe comprender, porque comprender es casi Justificar.
Forse, quanto è avvenuto non si può comprendere, anzi, non si deve comprendere, perché comprendere è quasi giustificare.
Primo Levi

Project Philosophy

Considerations and Notes on the Development of the Project

In the image, above: some of the students who participated in the project.
Below:
Marta Costantini presents the Association's manual and the various studies of the logo to Marcello Gentile, one of the lawyers of the victims' families.
For Marta this was almost a pre-exam.

The Association brings together people who dedicate themselves generously and selflessly to the humanitarian cause. In this complex structure, dedicated to improving human life, managers, architects, sociologists, cultural operators, legal pathologists work to legally, sociologically and even economically aid and assist those people, not only in Argentina, but around the world, who have suffered violence at the hands of a dictatorship. The Association also works to ensure that those in difficulty are assisted during every step of legal proceedings.
The Ponte della Memoria non-profit association felt the need to construct a visual identity that would respond to the needs of communicating the complexity and variety of its work, with a clarity that was also formal.
The first operation proposed was the modification of the name of the Association, from "Associazione culturale Ponte della memoria" to "Ponte della memoria, Associazione culturale per i diritti umani".
In terms of communication, this proposal appeared more incisive and immediate.
A paradigmatic application of this general logic is the logo that appears on every communication: it will represent the entirety and global qualities of the Association.

The same can be said, as a general example, of the application of the logo to stamps and seals, fax transmission forms, etc., of the connotation we wish to give to an association that was designed as a system and not a partial emanation.

The logo was designed by Alessio Oriani and selected from approximately twenty different proposals that were analysed and discussed; the project philosophy was developed by Fabiana Conti, Marta Costantini, Lorenza De Agostini and Chiara Santarelli; the documentation, images and advertising materials, posters, etc., were designed and laid out by Andrea Bennati, Giuseppe Galati and Massimo Scacco; the Internet website was designed by Cecilia Fabretti.

Thanks to the architect Stefania Tuzi for her precious collaboration and her dedication in providing students with material and research and a vast collection of iconographic material.

511

Old loves that are no longer here / the hope of those who lost / all the promises that go away / and those who fell in any war. / All is kept in memory / dream of life and history.

The deception and complicity / the freedom of those responsible for genocide / the pardon and the Punto Finale / to the beasts of that hell. / All is kept in memory / dream of life and history.

Memory awakes to injure / the sleeping people / that don't let it live / free like the wind.

The disappeared that we look for / with the colour of their births / hunger and abundance that come together / mistreatment with its bad memories. / All is nailed into memory / thorn of life and history.

Two thousand would eat for a year / with what a military minute costs. / How many would stop being slaves / for the price of a bomb thrown to the sea. / All is kept in memory / dream of life and history.

Memory stabs until it bleeds / the peoples that tie it / and don't let it go / free like the wind. / All the dead of the AMIA

/ and those of the Israeli Embassy / the secret power of weapons / a justice system which looks and doesn't see. / It's all hidden in memory / refuge of life and history.

It was when churches went silent / it was when soccer ate everything / that the Palottine fathers and Angelelli / left their blood in the mud. / It's all hidden in memory / refuge of life and history.

Memory blows up until it defeats / the peoples that trample on it / and that don't let it be / free like the wind.

The bullet to Chico Mendez in Brazil / 150 thousand Guatemalans / The miners that face guns / Student repression in Mexico. / It's all loaded in memory / weapon of life and of history.

America with destroyed souls / The children killed by the death squad. / Mugica's ordeal for the slums / The Dignity of Rodolfo Walsh. / It's all loaded in memory / weapon of life and of history.

Memory aims until it kills / the people who try to silence it / and don't let it fly / free like the wind.

512

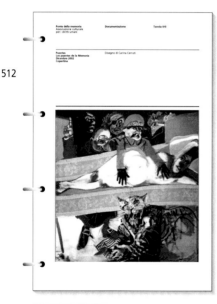

Notes
In this highly suggestive song León Gieco confronts the theme of memory recording the victims in Argentina, but also of more recent attacks by Amia and the Israeli Embassy, without forgetting the pain and repressions of other Latin American countries (Brazil, Guatemala, Mexico) and the famines that plague these populations.
In particular, verse n. 11 was played on RAI 1 during Edoardo Spera's interview of Stefania Tuzi.
During the interview they also spoke of the work by students of the Industrial Design course during the second semester of 2003.

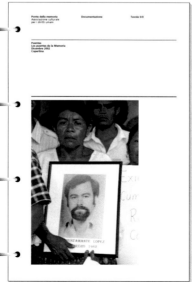

Above: the cover of the catalogue from the exhibition Buena memoria, un racconto fotografico di Marcelo Brodsky. *Rome, Palazzo delle Esposizioni, October-November 2000. Italian Ministry of Cultural Heritage and Activities, Ministry of Foreign Affairs. City of Rome, Department of Cultural Policies.*

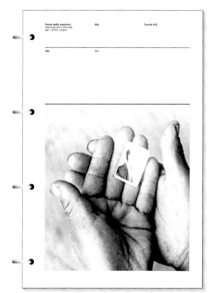

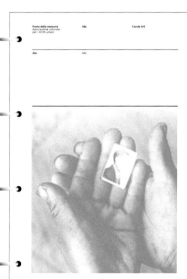

Notes
The symbol designed on the street is that adopted in Argentina by the Mothers of Plaza de Mayo. It represents the classical head scarf worn by mothers searching for their missing children, in memory of their childrens' pañuelo.

513

Carlos died in a clash with the Army in December 1975.
Carlos is a graphic designer.
He is closed, private. He is a special designer, capable of resolving problems and creating things in his own way. He says that drawing causes him a great deal of suffering, but that it also fills him with joy and internal emotions.

He is solitary, and wants to live in the South.
Something impossible to define keeps him tied to the city, perhaps his friends.
From the exhibition catalogue.

514

From the chapter dedicated to the design of the posters, in 70x100 format and its submultiples.
In some cases, existing material was redesigned, borrowing images, texts and suggestions;
in others entirely new situations were drawn, though based on a matrix inspired by research.
Other posters were inspired by the reworking of brands that, while not selected, were emotionally important to the illustration of an event.

Pinochet, represents the prototype of the dictator.
His cloak, his posture and attitude almost express an automatic perception of the tragedy his regime produced.
Inside the "O" of the word "NO" it is clearly possible to read the image of a suffering face, the face of a child and a violated infancy.
This gestural image was graphically reinterpreted with a strong accent on violence.

Giorgio Bucciarelli and
Stefania Tuzi discussing
a possible layout of the
panels for an exhibition
at the Casa della
Cultura in Rome with
students.

Ponte della memoria

Por la vida
y la libertad
Juicio y castigo
a los culpables

**Ponte
della memoria**
Associazione
culturale
per i diritti umani

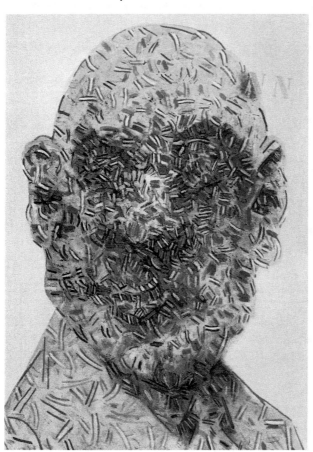

Notes
80 gram, 70x100
gr 80 tissue paper
printed in 4 colours.
Drawing by
Hermenegildo Sábat
"Desaparecido",
published in Puentes,
Los puentes
de la Memoria,
August 2000.

515

33.
Visual Perception

Optical Illusions

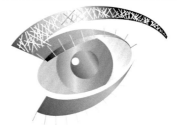

Left:
Michelangelo Merisi
da Caravaggio,
Medusa, painting
realised in c. 1597.
Below: a drawing
of an eye.

516   We live in an era when images play a determinant role in our everyday lives: newspapers show us photographs of the latest events and the kitchen table is animated by the splashy images adorning biscuit boxes; upon leaving the house we discover that the mailbox is filled with advertising flyers featuring photographs of exotic countries or postcards proposing evocative images; travelling to work we are overwhelmed by roadside posters, gigantic billboards and road signage; the street itself id adorned with arrows, indications, stops and visual information; upon arrival at work, diagrams, tables and charts offer us up-to-date information; our desk is covered with illustrated books and photographs decorate the walls.

When we finally return home, to relax we turn on the television, a window on the world, and we observe a succession of more or less pleasing or dramatic images. We can also head to the cinema, to experience a story told in images.

Then, if our profession is that of being a graphic designer, we are faced with images flashing before our eyes all day long, without pause.

The evocative power of visual images is unsurpassable. It can affect our emotions, substitute the written word, and supplant lengthy verbal explanations.

The use of images can entirely substitute verbal communication and, as with pictograms, establish a universal form of communication between people who speak different languages, creating what is almost a visual Esperanto.

Yet, to what point are the images we design "real", and what is the dividing line between subjective and objective fact?

Extensive and complex studies teach us that visual perception does not always faithfully reflect the world around us and, in particular, not all representations correspond with what is commonly perceived. The intention of this short chapter is not to investigate philosophical or psychological studies of perception. Over the past century, this highly complex theme has been explored by scholars, by ancient and new investigators and experimental figures from various schools.

A vast bibliography speaks volumes about the breadth of these studies.

Here instead, I propose an overview of selected visual phenomena, above all to help students understand a problem whose importance should be familiar, above all to a manipulator of images. I also indicate how research can aid those seeking more information about these issues and their relationship to graphic design.

The principal source of this investigation is an issue of the Italian edition of *Scientific American*, "L'immagine visiva, Illusione e realtà, Problemi della percezione visiva", (The Visual Image, Illusion and Reality, Problems of Visual Perception), Editore Le Scienze.

From this material based on difficult studies, which I leave to experts in these fields, I have culled a selection of topics that, at least in indicative terms, explore the most representative phenomena of perception and those of most use to us. I am fully aware that many other examples and research can foster more in-depth explorations.

The chapter is accompanied by some of my images and studies that, once again rooted in very personal reasons and experiences, are intended solely as one approach to exploring and learning about the theme of perception. I hope this initial approach will trigger a broader interest in such a complex theme.

Bibliography
▼*E.H. Gombrich
L'immagine visiva
Illusione e realtà
Problemi della
percezione visiva
Italian edition of
Scientific American
Le Scienze spa Editore
Milano 1978*
▼*E.H. Gombrich,
Arte e illusione,
Edizioni Einaudi*
▼*R. Amheim
Arte e percezione
visiva,
Edizioni Feltrinelli*
▼*Gaetano Kanizsa,
Grammatica del vedere
Saggi su percezione
e gestalt,
Società editrice
Il Mulino, 1980*

1. The square has equal sides, however, the eye perceives it as if the base were larger than the height. The optical square should be designed with a slightly larger height.

2. It is easy to observe in this figure that the two parts of the square divided in two by a horizontal line are different: the lower part looks smaller than the upper part. The optical dividing line of a square is thus higher than its geometric dividing line.

3. A black band drawn at the centre of this square clearly overpowers the lower part. When positioning this graphic element it is necessary to consider an optical correction.

4. The same band in figure 3, this time vertical at the centre of the square, appears thinner than the same horizontal band.

5. A perfect circle positioned at the centre of the square looks wider than it is high. Once again, it is necessary to make an optical correction to re-establish the correct visual reading.

6./7. A white square on a black background looks larger than a corresponding black square on a white background. Unlike black, white generates a visual expansion.

8./9. Horizontal lines drawn on a square look thicker; vertical lines tend to look longer.

10. The Müller-Leyr arrows appear to have different dimensions, but they are all exactly the same.

11./12. At the intersection of white we see black spots; at the intersection of black lines we see a confusion of black that pollutes the reading of the arrow. This requires a small excavation at the point of intersection.

13./14. A square is widened by horizontal lines, and elongated by vertical lines.

15. Segments AC and BC both have the same length.

16/17. In both figures, the diagonals are made from a continuous line, even though they appear offset and interrupted.

18. The reading of the perfect parallelism of vertical lines is polluted by oblique lines.

19. The Necker cube can be read in all of its ambiguity.

20. In this illusion studied by Hering the two horizontal lines are perfectly parallel.

21./23 The drawings published in 1858 by H. Schröder emphasise how shading can suggest diverse readings and invert the reading of planes.

24. In this Ponzo image converging straight lines imply a reading in perspective.

25. The eye reads two horizontal straight lines not as equal but in relation to what seems to be a perspective.

517

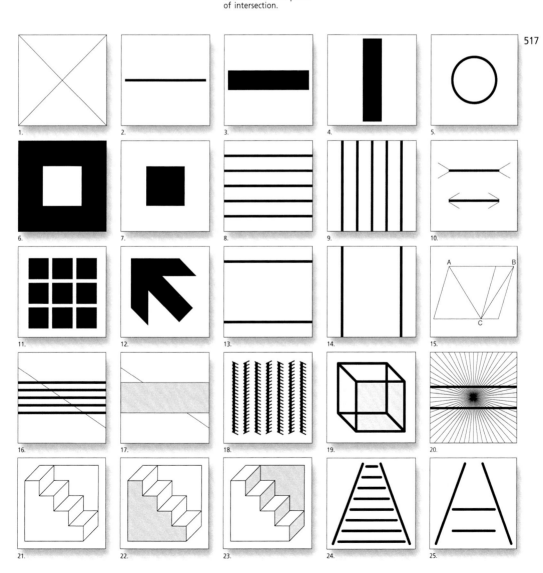

1. 2. 3. 4. 5. 6. 7. 8. 9. 10. 11. 12. 13. 14. 15. 16. 17. 18. 19. 20. 21. 22. 23. 24. 25.

Spatial Frequency

Frequency and Contrast

These two pages show squares filled with halftones made from lines of the same weight, with an increase in the frequency of the lines of two units for each successive pass.
The modules are all of the same size and with the same succession: on the left page with black lines on a white background; on the right page with white lines on a black background.
It is possible to note how the modules marked by numbers 25 and 50 have the same intensity as in both cases the black and white produce a 50% halftone.

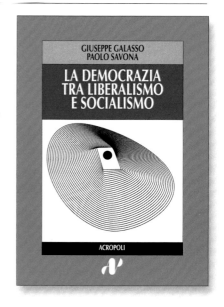

GIUSEPPE GALASSO
PAOLO SAVONA

LA DEMOCRAZIA
TRA LIBERALISMO
E SOCIALISMO

ACROPOLI

518

1. 2. 3. 4. 5.

6. 7. 8. 9. 10.

11. 12. 13. 14. 15.

16. 17. 18. 19. 20.

21. 22. 23. 24. 25.

Spatial frequency studies can explain a certain number of consecutive effects. For example, Colin Blakemore and Peter Sutton, from the University of Cambridge discovered that if we stare for a few minutes at a model of stripes, and then at another similar model, with narrower bars, the latter will appear even narrower and closer together than they are in reality.

When areas of chiaroscuro succeed one another in a regular sequence, it is said that the resulting figure presents a certain spatial frequency. If we look at the drawings on these pages, moving them away from our eyes, or observing those where the lines gradually grow thicker, the details with a low contrast become difficult to perceive. This diminution in the perception of contrast is explained by the fact that the system of vision is less sensitive to contrast when the interval between spaces of chiaroscuro diminishes.

Fergus Campbell and Lamberto Maffei, in an in-depth study of "Contrast and Spatial Frequency" also observed that "the noteworthy fact is that the visual system is much more sensitive to contrast at certain spatial frequencies than at others, exactly like the ear is more sensitive to certain acoustic frequencies than others".

The image to the right was used for a convention organised by the Ministry of the Interior entitled "Traffico di esseri umani" (Human Trafficking). The photograph is sectioned into four parts, and each is treated with a different level of focus. The image gradually degrades, the frequencies are spatial and consist in variations of density and obscurity.

As Leon D. Harmon tells us, "as a musical note is formed from a fundamental frequency and its harmonics, an optical image consists of combinations of single frequencies that form a spatial spectrum".

519

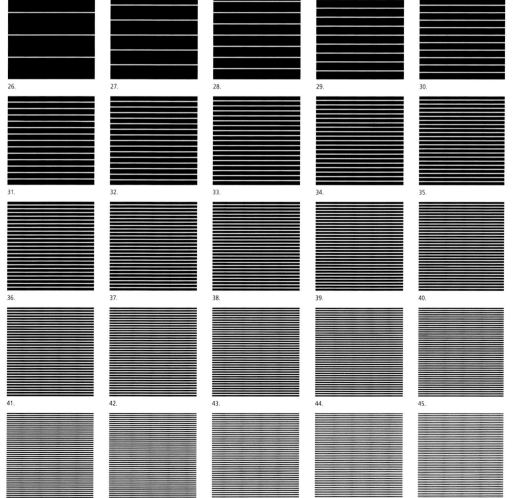

26.   27.   28.   29.   30.

31.   32.   33.   34.   35.

36.   37.   38.   39.   40.

41.   42.   43.   44.   45.

46.   47.   48.   49.   50.

The Discrimination of Structures

The frequency of the lines that make up a brand can give it different aspects, unusual solutions and even totally unexpected results.
Endless study and experimentation with the expressive possibilities of a sign, investigated in every possible detail, stripping it down the bare bones, will lead us toward the definitive version.

1. From an original idea we can generate the definitive version of a brand, the result of a progressive thinning of lines and the combination of others. This is a work of synthesis that benefits from the study of language.
In the brand illustrated here there is an evident application of the principle of similarity that uncovers homogenous groupings (so-called "marks") and foresees the combination of the elements that determine, by creating units with a more powerful visual strength, sufficient to produce the stability of the image.

The manipulation of an image is one method for arriving at the definition of a complete sign. The approach is influenced by two factors: an orientation toward an aesthetic balance and a rigorous criteria of ratios between visual perception and information, in other words, between this latter and its correct graphic transcription.

520

LA TUA CASA
NELLA TUA CITTÀ
NELLA TUA REGIONE

I REPUBBLICANI
UNA SICUREZZA

Elezioni amministrative 1970

1.

2. The brand illustrated here was initially conceived using a "systematic" graphic construction; this involves the gradual "normalisation" of a sign, adopting a process of simplification, eliminating information, and seeking the maximum visual efficiency, in other words, those conditions that make it possible to extract useful and easily perceived information.

3. The "construction" of the image of the rooftops of a village, using lines with different angles (from a 1970 poster for the PRI). The respect for some of the principles of visual perception (figure/ground, proximity/similarity, regularity, etc.) and the appropriate use of the variables of an image (scale, value) as well as other so-called visuals of separation (colour, orientation, form) make it possible to correctly transcribe information, and to elaborate until it exalts the principal internal relations between the parts.

2.

521

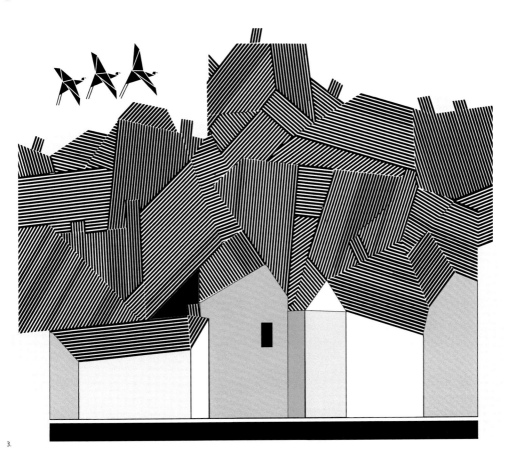

3.

Halftone Screens

A Rhythmic and Orthogonal Frequency

1. The points of a halftone are organised by a very dense pattern of equidistant and orthogonal lines. The dots assume a gradually larger or smaller dimension, depending on whether we begin with the lighter or darker parts.

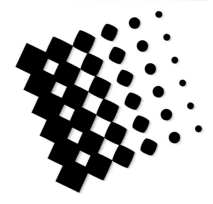

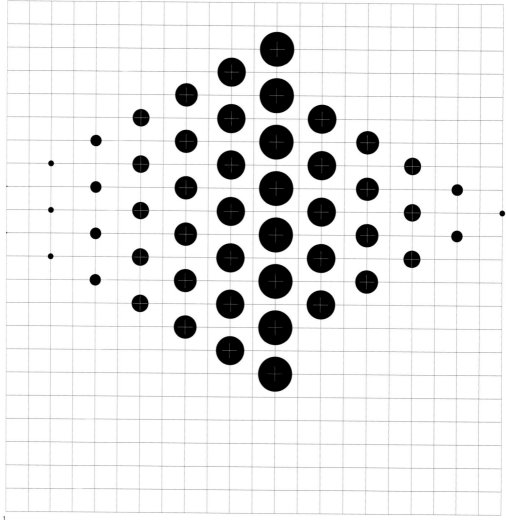

1.

2. When printing, the grey parts of a photograph are impossible to reproduce without the use of halftones, which break down the tonality of black into miniscule black dots.
The halftone placed between a photograph and the film onto which the image is halftoned, reads the various tones and renders them reproducible through the expansion or contraction of the dots of the raster.

The frequency of dots in a halftone is more or less dense and measured in lines per square centimetre.
In general, the frequency ranges from a minimum of 20 lines to a maximum of 120 lines per square centimetre.
In the illustration, the second series of dots has a frequency of lines that corresponds with half that of the first, though the percentage of black remains unchanged.

3.

3. The elements that make up the drawing shown here can be compared to a halftone.
During printing, the designer must imagine the format in which the drawing will be reproduced, to ensure that the signs of which it is comprised do not meld with the background and compromise the reading of the image.

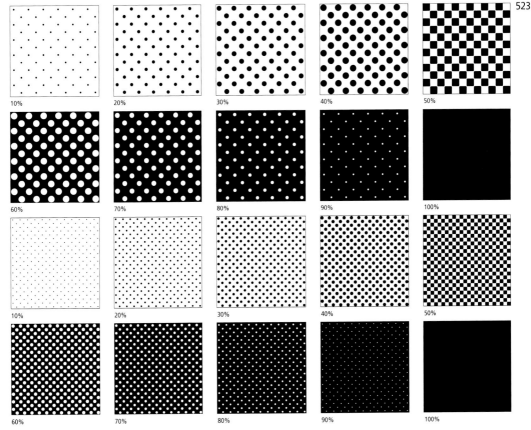

2.

Halftone Screens

A Sequence of Dots to Reproduce an Image

The frequency of dots in an image can be more or less dense, depending on how many dots are printed per square centimetre. A halftone of 60 lines reproduces a photograph with a density of 60 dots per square centimetre; a halftone of 24 lines creates an image with 24 dots per square centimetre.

Obviously, the lower the number of dots, the less detailed the image.
The density of the halftone must be selected based on the type of paper used during printing: the smoother the paper (coated), the more the halftone can be dense. The most common halftone used for printing on coated paper is 80 lines; daily newspapers print with a halftone of 28 lines.

In a good print it should be possible to read the dots of the halftone; a properly printed photograph should never have a totally white area, but only a very light dot, known as a paper point.
The halftone should never reach a value of 100%, in either black or white: a best practice is never to exceed the value of 94%.

524

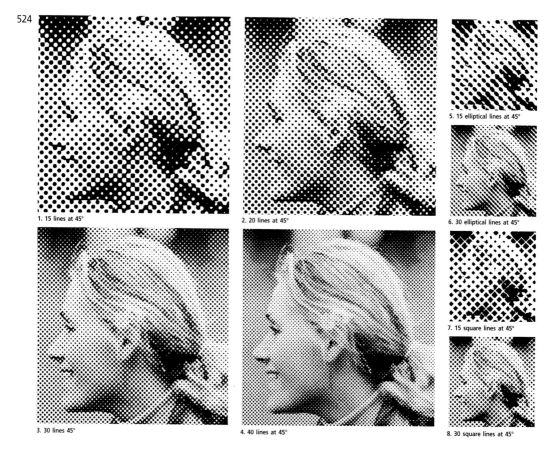

1. 15 lines at 45°

2. 20 lines at 45°

5. 15 elliptical lines at 45°

6. 30 elliptical lines at 45°

7. 15 square lines at 45°

3. 30 lines 45°

4. 40 lines at 45°

8. 30 square lines at 45°

9. 15 lines at 45°

10. 20 lines at 45°

11. 30 lines at 45°

12. 40 lines at 45°

13. 15 lines at 0°

14. 40 lines at 0°

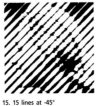

15. 15 lines at -45°

16. 40 lines at -45°

Notes   525
*Prior to the use of the
computer, manipulating
an image to reproduce
a photograph and
arrange it for printing
required the use of a
photographic halftone
system.
The enlarger, with its
scales in percentage
values, was used for
this purpose.
Resting on a well
illuminated original, a
new film sheet was laid
on a frame, with the
desired halftone; a
vacuum sucked out any
air to ensure the
perfect adherence
between the two films;
exposure time was
based on the
percentage of
reduction.
These systems are now
impossible to find,
though they offered
graphic designers the
possibility for creative
interpretations or
particular manipulations
of an image.*

Halftone Screens

Linear Halftones

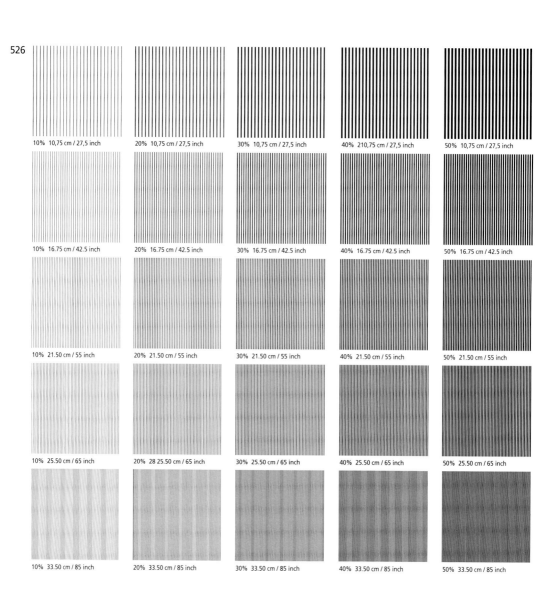

10% 10,75 cm / 27,5 inch	20% 10,75 cm / 27,5 inch	30% 10,75 cm / 27,5 inch	40% 210,75 cm / 27,5 inch	50% 10,75 cm / 27,5 inch
10% 16.75 cm / 42.5 inch	20% 16.75 cm / 42.5 inch	30% 16.75 cm / 42.5 inch	40% 16.75 cm / 42.5 inch	50% 16.75 cm / 42.5 inch
10% 21.50 cm / 55 inch	20% 21.50 cm / 55 inch	30% 21.50 cm / 55 inch	40% 21.50 cm / 55 inch	50% 21.50 cm / 55 inch
10% 25.50 cm / 65 inch	20% 28 25.50 cm / 65 inch	30% 25.50 cm / 65 inch	40% 25.50 cm / 65 inch	50% 25.50 cm / 65 inch
10% 33.50 cm / 85 inch	20% 33.50 cm / 85 inch	30% 33.50 cm / 85 inch	40% 33.50 cm / 85 inch	50% 33.50 cm / 85 inch

When enlarged, a linear halftone can produce very interesting effects. The examples show different images created using different values of linear halftones.

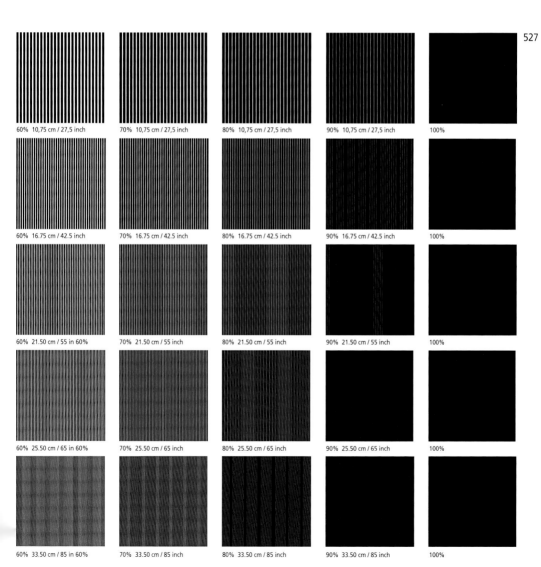

60% 10,75 cm / 27,5 inch   70% 10,75 cm / 27,5 inch   80% 10,75 cm / 27,5 inch   90% 10,75 cm / 27,5 inch   100%

60% 16.75 cm / 42.5 inch   70% 16.75 cm / 42.5 inch   80% 16.75 cm / 42.5 inch   90% 16.75 cm / 42.5 inch   100%

60% 21.50 cm / 55 in 60%   70% 21.50 cm / 55 inch   80% 21.50 cm / 55 inch   90% 21.50 cm / 55 inch   100%

60% 25.50 cm / 65 in 60%   70% 25.50 cm / 65 inch   80% 25.50 cm / 65 inch   90% 25.50 cm / 65 inch   100%

60% 33.50 cm / 85 in 60%   70% 33.50 cm / 85 inch   80% 33.50 cm / 85 inch   90% 33.50 cm / 85 inch   100%

Optical-Geometric Illusions

Graphic Surfaces

1. Anomalous surfaces are subject to and reproduce optical illusions. In the figure below, anomalous lines are affected by the entire surface, with an evident loss in parallel relations.

2. The vertical lines in figure 2 are perfectly parallel, however, the eye perceives them in perspective.

3. A derivation of the Möbius strip was used to construct this drawing for a poster for the Italian Republican Party.

3.

528

1.

2.

The Müller-Lyer and Ponzo Illusions

The Consistency of Dimensions

1. The most famous of all optical distortions is probably the arrow of Franz Müller-Lyer, presented in 15 versions in 1889.
The central line is of the same height in both examples, though it appears shorter or longer depending on whether the arrows face inward or outward.
This figure is so simple, and the distortion so evident, that it was used as the principle example in many hypotheses and experiments.

2. 3. In the Ponzo figure, converging straight lines imply a reading in perspective; as a consequence, the eye reads the two horizontal lines as being unequal and in relation to what once again appears as a perspective.

4. The brand for the "Sestans" company featured a rung ladder during a preliminary study.
The experimental intention was to characterise the brand by referring to the illusory reading of the ladder.

Notes
Two equal rectangles appear markedly unequal when overlapped on a perspective image of converging lines.
The upper rectangle, the more distant if it were a real object between the lines, appears larger than the lower (apparently closer) image.
This illusion is known as the "Ponzo illusion".

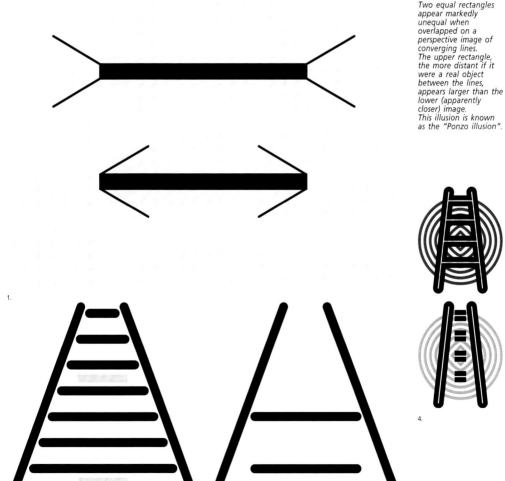

1.

2.

3.

4.

Mach Bands

Edges and Contrasts

1. Mach bands created from horizontal lines. The lines are all of the same thickness, from the left toward the centre; from the centre toward the right they gradually grow thicker. When observed from a certain distance, the figure appears to be crossed, at the centre, by a vertical white strip, known as the Mach band.

2. The lines all have the same thickness from the right toward the centre; from the centre toward the left they gradually grow thinner. Viewed from a certain distance, the figure appears to be crossed by a vertical bland strip.

3. The brands for the *Comitati per lo sviluppo dell'imprenditoria femminile*. The female face is obtained using horizontal lines tapered in relation to the grey tones of an original image. In the drawing it is possible to read the phenomenon of Mach bands.

3.

530 Edges play an important role in how we perceive objects.

In almost all cases, the first line we draw to represent an object is that which defines its edges.

However, our eye also reads edges in solid areas. Their visibility is proportionate to the contrast in luminosity or in the colours of adjacent areas.

If we observe the shadow projected by an object, at its edges we can read a lighter or darker line that defines its outline. These lines are known as Mach bands.

Ernst Mach studied them in 1865, and formulated a principle: "Whenever the light intensity curve of an illuminated surface has a concave or convex flection with respect to the axis of the abscissa, that particular place appears brighter or darker, respectively, than its surroundings".

Before these phenomena were studied and codified, the Impressionists and Divisionists, with notable intuition, represented these bands of light in their paintings: the works of Manet exalt the edges of figures with subtle bands of colour that emphasise this phenomenon.

A familiar effect of contrast can also be found in photocopies.

In these documents, black surfaces tend to exclude fields to the advantage of their margins.

Mach bands can also be considered the inspiration behind Optical Art.

1.

2.

Notes
If you hold a piece of black card underneath a lamp, it will produce a shadow.
Around the shadow it will be possible to read an area of penumbra that gradually grows darker until it merges with the shadow.
If you look carefully at the edges of the area of penumbra, you will be able to read a subtle band of light at the lightest edge and a darker band toward the darkest edge.
These are Mach's bands.

Bibliography
Floyd Ratliff,
"Contorno e contrasto
Illusione e realtà
Problemi della
percezione visiva",
Italian edition of
Scientific American

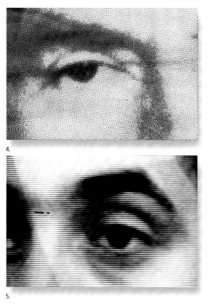

4.

Comune di Pistoia
Regione Toscana
**Progettazione del paesaggio
e dell'ambiente**
Convegno internazionale
Pistoia Palazzo comunale
10/11/12 giugno 1982

Seconda edizione
del Convegno biennale
Verde urbano, vivaismo,
forestazione

5.   6.

4. 5. 6. Photographs printed with a linear halftone produce the phenomenon of Mach bands.

7. The Pluralia brand, constructed from tapering lines produces phenomena that lead to aberrations in their reading and optical perception.

8. Three symbols and a photographic elaboration. The construction of these drawings create lines of different thicknesses and combinations, whose reading can be linked to the phenomenon of contrast.

531

7.

8.

The Necker Cube

Multistable Perception

1. While observing inversions in drawings of crystals, L. A. Necker noted how the perception of the depth of a transparent rhomboid was spontaneously inverted. The grey area can appear as both an external and an internal surface inside a transparent box. To the left: the depiction of a cube; to the right the depiction of the rhomboid used by Necker to illustrate his theory.

2. In the figure developed by Poggendorff, the two segments of the diagonal line appear not to belong to the same straight line. It was proposed by the scholar in 1860.

3. Ewald Hering studied this optical illusion. While the horizontal lines are two parallels, when they are placed atop the texture, they appear wider apart at the centre.

532 The observation of optical illusions dates back to Ancient Greece. However, it was only during the past century that interest in these illusions became more general, with the publication of figures with the ability to generate errors in the use of optical and photographic instruments. There was also a systematic experimentation by scholars intent on investigating one of the most curious aspects of a visual phenomenon that distorts form and mediates the reality of graphic representation.

The first scientific description of the phenomenon of ambiguity in the reading of a drawing represented in three dimensions can be found in a letter by Louis Albert Necker from 1832: he observed that the drawing of a transparent rhomboid inverts its depth; in other words, depending on how it is observed, in one case we read its front face, and in other cases another. This well known effect is now generally represented by an isometric cube.

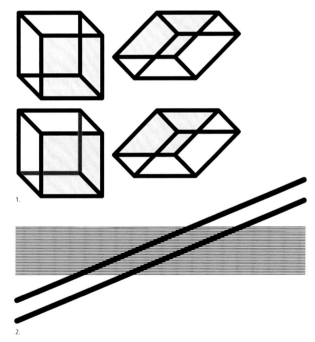

1.

2.

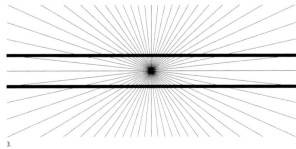

3.

Schröder Stairs
Reversible Figures

Vito Riviello   Potenza e la vita
Città fra paesi   la scala ci affatica
                  ci riposiamo
Schwarz   sulla piazza

Images that change in appearance and can be read with different degrees of depth are particularly fascinating. A reversible figure communicates a stimulus to the observer that corresponds with different readings of the same drawing.

1. 3. The drawings published in 1858 by H. Schröder show how shading can suggest different readings by inverting planes.
In figure 2, Schröder's stair to rest on the lower side; in figure 3 it appears to rest on the upper side.

4. The original drawing by Schröder.

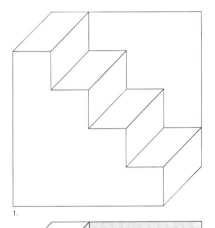

1.

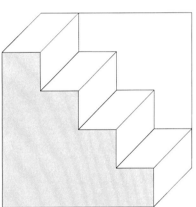

2.

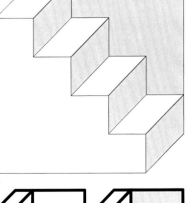

3.

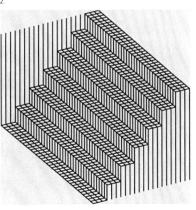

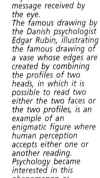

Notes
The human brain can perceive a reversible figure in different ways, in the absence of any alteration to the message received by the eye.
The famous drawing by the Danish psychologist Edgar Rubin, illustrating the famous drawing of a vase whose edges are created by combining the profiles of two heads, in which it is possible to read two either the two faces or the two profiles, is an example of an enigmatic figure where human perception accepts either one or another reading. Psychology became interested in this phenomenon as something that could teach us about the very nature of perception.

Communicating Information

Choosing a Language of Transcription and Visual Variables

The elaboration and interpretation of information is a field in which graphic design is widely applied.
When a group of numbers, data or statistics needs to be visualised as an image, be it a histogram, a network or a map, that summarises this information and renders it visually elementary, we must identify relations between the various parts.
This is both the role and function of graphic design. Using a system of signs and a visual language, graphic design deciphers the information contained in statistics.

The visibility of a graphic construction requires a clear separation between its constituent elements. That which is not "discriminant" must be suppressed, as it is of no value to the reading of information. The "objects" must not be divided and the graphic must not disturb their perception.
The graphic must suppress all that is common to the elements; it must make use of all of the "visual variables" (from black to white, and not from light grey to dark grey); it must eliminate "noise", in other words, perceptions that are not important and of no use, and which only create disturbances; in short, it must reduce information to similar elementary parts.

1./6. The elaboration of a graphic adopts one of two approaches: *value* (the tone of reproduction from light to dark) and *scale* (from small to large). The final result must not exceed 4 or 5 levels of value (figs. 1 and 2); for a greater quantity of information it is worthwhile using scale (figs. 6 and 7).
In figure 3 the zones are obtained using 10 halftones of different strengths, from 10% to 100%; figure 6 uses signs of different scales that support a much broader reading.

534

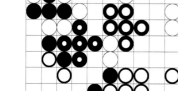

11.

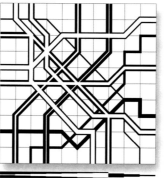

2.

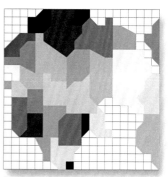

3.

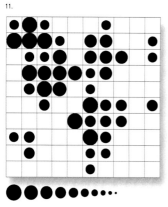

4.

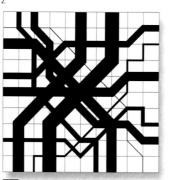

5.

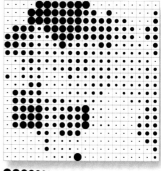

6.

ROME	MILAN	TURIN	GENOA	FLORENCE	ANCONA	PALERMO	PERUGIA	SPOLETO	CATANIA	POTENZA	RIETI	CESENA	PIETRASANTA	SALERNO	NAPLES	VENICE	VICENZA	MESTRE	TREVISO
50	6	8	5	15	20	12	11	7	28	30	35	29	16	18	48	23	32	27	16

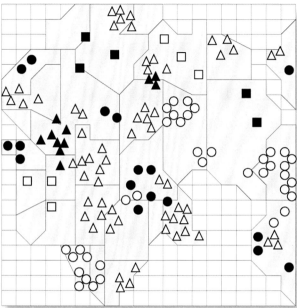

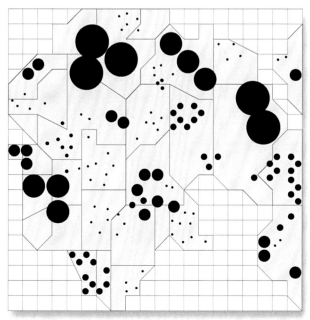

7.

7. The table to the left contains two types of information: x tells us the cost of a piece of land in a given location; y tells us where this location is, and where the most expensive land is. Figure 7a proposes a visualisation that transcribes land prices based on differences in form, in other words, it transcribes *quantities* using a *non-ordered* visual variation. It provides a response to a question in x (what is the cost of land in Rome?) under the condition that we memorise the legend, though it does not respond to the question in y (where are the most expensive pieces of land?).

Figure 7b permits an immediate understanding of the differences in price, responds to the question in y and shows groups defined by geographic and numerical proximity. It provides a grouping of information. The construction of figure 7b uses only visually ordered variables: *scale* and *value*. Students interested in learning more about this topic, merely hinted at here, can immerse themselves in the study of information graphics by Jacques Bertin, listed in the bibliography. This text scientifically explores the graphic treatment of information and its laws of visibility.

535

Notes
The use of halftones makes it possible to highlight different zones. The eye distinctly perceives up to 10 ranges of halftones, while a computer perceives 216.

Bibliography
Jacques Bertin
La grafica e il trattamento grafico dell'informazione
Eri, 1981

Workbook
Graphic elaboration of data provided by ISTAT. Visual variables. The scale should be logarithmic. This requires that we multiply the numbers by a constant quantity.

The Ambiguity of Forms

From Penrose to Escher

The ambiguity of representation is a recurring theme in the work of Escher.
He explores all of the possible representations of objects, beginning with the studies of scholars of perception, and dilating their results.
From an attentive study of Möbius strips he created his series of *Knots*; in another case he tripled the Penrose triangle in various study sketches for a series of lithographs.

1. 3. The tribar, an object that cannot be constructed, but only photographed from a single point of view. The construction of a typical grid of an Escher drawing.

5. 8. Posters for the PRI, the Italian Republican Party, for a series of training courses.
The Penrose triangle is reproduced in various ways.
The constructions are inspired by studies of visual perception.

536

1.

2.

4.

3.

6.

4. In February of 1958, the *British Journal of Psychology* published Penrose's "impossible triangle", also known as the tribar.
The characteristic of this triangle is that it is constructed from inexact connections between entirely regular elements. The three 90° corners are exact, but incorrectly connected to create an impossible three-dimensional figure. This drawing inspired Escher to develop an entire series of lithographs, including *Waterfall*, in which he dilates the absurdity of the Penrose triangle by proposing it three times in the same image.

7.

7. Graphic elaborations of the Penrose tribara, repeated three times, as in Escher's drawing.

9. The symbolism of knots appears in many images, almost all of which are metaphoric. *The Ashley Book of Knots* by Clifford Ashley (Doubleday, 1944) is illustrated by no less than 7,000 drawings. Also worthy of consultation is *Knots* by Alexei Sossinsky (Harvard University Press), which explores mathematical theories linked to this topic.

537

8.

9.

Bibliography
M.C. Escher
29 Master Prints
Harry N. Abrams
New York, 1981
Bruno Ernst
The Magic Mirror of
M.C. Escher
Benedikt Taschen
Verlag, Berlin, 1990.

The Penrose Triangle

Impossible Architecture

A broad understanding of phenomena of perception, specifically the Penrose triangle, can offer us the possibility to investigate methods and criteria for resolving an image. Beginning with the objectivity of a form, we can push our research toward a fascinating design that allows for an intentionally ambiguous reading.

1. So-called "impossible images" emphasise how our eye reads two-dimensional drawings with clearly incompatible information about distances.
The famous triangle developed by Lionel S. Penrose and R. Penrose offers a very clear example of the

difficulty of observing a third dimension in the two dimensions of an image.
Of all optical illusions, the Penrose triangle is that which most certainly had the greatest influence on the research of graphic designers.
Its fictitious third dimension, the fulsome provocation of an impossible architecture present in this famous triangle, has inspired some of the most curious logos, drawings and graphic explorations.

2. 4. The Endas logo is clearly derived from the Penrose triangle.
The figure illustrates the dynamic and evolution of this sign that gradually grows more complex.

5. 6. Logos that use the virtual third dimension. All of the figures designed with a depth are paradoxes: we see them as flat (as they were effectively drawn), and as having a virtual depth.

7. A compass designed for CNA combines various Penrose triangles.
The information about distance is even more of a paradox.
The "Italia, Italia!" logo, created for a series of posters for the PRI, the Italian Republican Party. They continue to test the "tribara", here with the addition of a photographic distortion obtained using an enlarger.

Bibliography
Richard L. Gregory
"Le illusioni ottiche
Illusione e realtà
Problemi della
percezione visiva"
Italian edition of
Scientific American

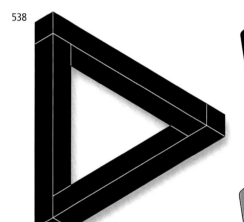

1.

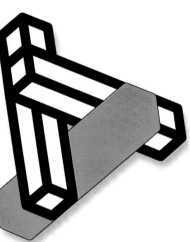

2.

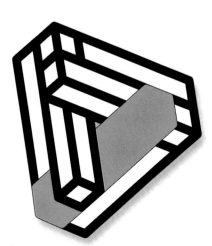

3.

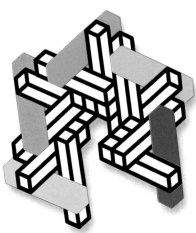

4.

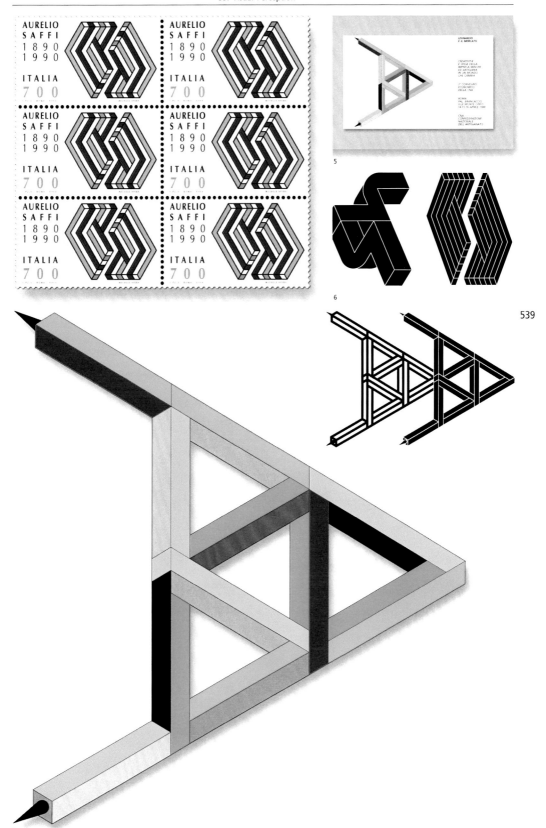

539

Drawing Stars

It is evident how these structures, developed at various times, make recourse, through their impossible architecture, to explorations of virtual depth.
Below, six different ways of graphically interpreting the same drawing.

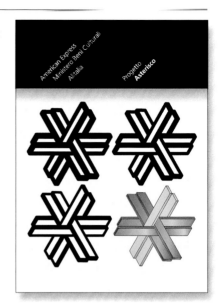

540

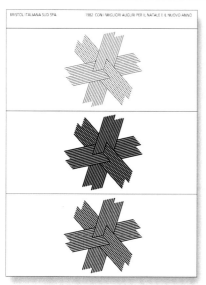

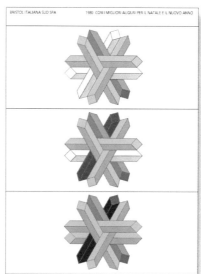

Notes
Cf. "Novum
gebrauchsgraphik",
2/1980.
The image of Bristol-
Meyers Squibb.

541

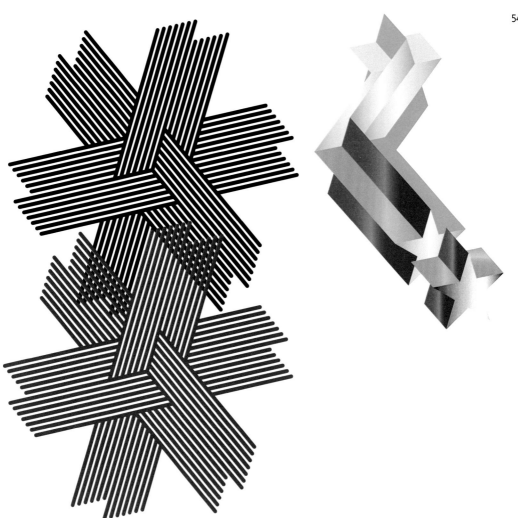

Drawing Structures

For more on the investigation of the role of vision in perception and in particular the perception of structures, I refer readers to the scientific studies summarised in the bibliography; I will limit myself here to proposing themes, cognitive investigations and above all real experiments that can help us understand what and how many possibilities are available in the assembly of an infinite quantity of structures.

542

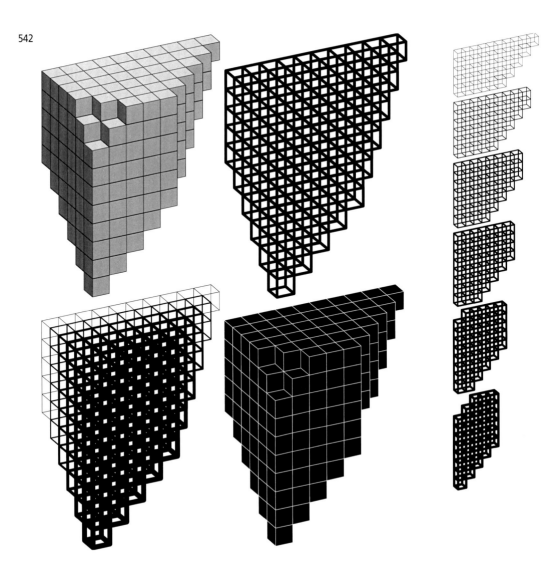

The complex structures on these pages, whose construction will be explained on the following pages, were developed from 1967 onward.
Used for posters and various communications, they originate from a base drawing comprised of different recognisable cells. They are used to generate, based on a calculated frequency, in some cases logarithmic, other cells without a recognisable content and in some cases overlapping.
That which can be perceived and recognised becomes impossible to distinguish, despite the fact that the basic elements of their construction remain unchanged.

The composition of co-penetrating solids illustrated below has a precise hierarchical order.
An indefinable obscurity gives way to the perception of the final cell that reveals its three-dimensionality.
The identification of precise mathematical laws for a drawing, offers an immediate understanding and legibility of its structure.

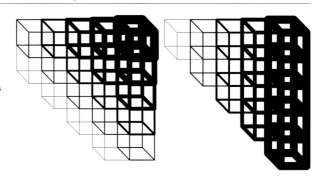

543

A poster for an Umbrian newspaper and, below, a structure whose modules increase in thickness based on a predefined metric and a correlated mathematical equation.

In the drawing on the facing page, a primary cell is gradually doubled in quantity until it reaches a total of 128 units, merely a graphic and not a mathematical limit. At the same time, the thickness is reduced from a maximum of 34 points to a minimum of 0.265 points.

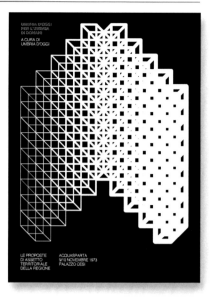

544

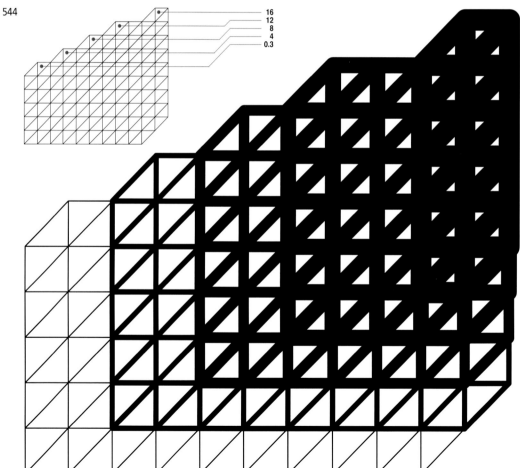

16
12
8
4
0.3

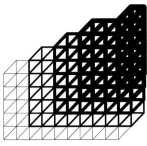
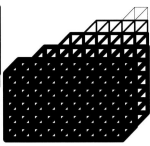

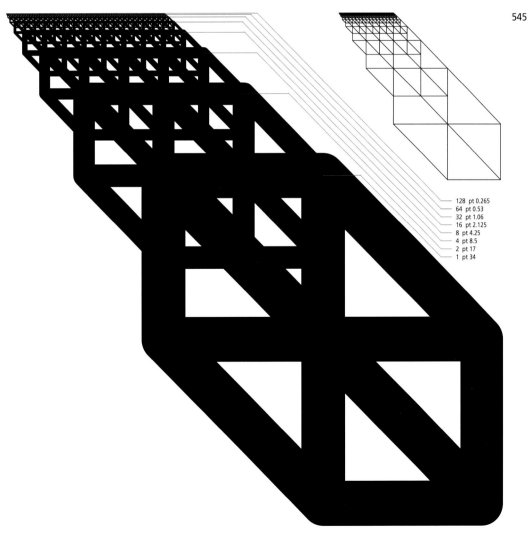

128	pt 0.265
64	pt 0.53
32	pt 1.06
16	pt 2.125
8	pt 4.25
4	pt 8.5
2	pt 17
1	pt 34

Drawing Ribbons

From Strips of Paper to Polygons

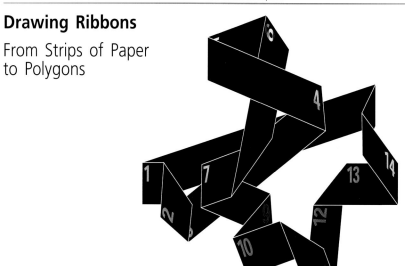

An initial strip of folded paper, and with the Möbius strip clearly in mind, lead to the studies and drawings illustrated here. Research becomes relevant to design when the strips are transformed into polygons.
See the following page.
Also see the chapters "Politics" and "Political Graphics".

546

Notes
A "polygonal" is a plane figure bounded by a finite chain of straight line segments closing in a loop.

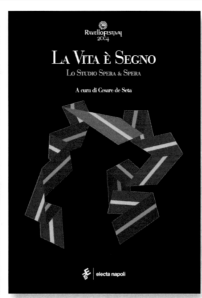

How a Ribbon Becomes a Sign

From Strips of Paper to Polygons

In this series of posters for piano concerts, the images originated from ribbons of paper folded into polygonals.

1. A ribbon for a poster; beside it is the de-codification of the sign.

2. The sequence of the translation in which the movement of the ribbon is traced by nine points, then five, three and two, until a unique segment is identified. The sign gradually grows thicker until it becomes almost impossible to trace the path of the ribbon.

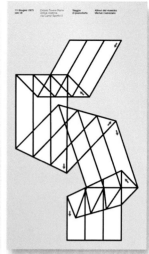

1.

548

2.

3. The evolution of a ribbon that becomes a sign.

4. The original sign drawn with a single thickness; as it evolves it develops into different thicknesses based on a progressive mathematical formula.

5. The program-invitation for a convention on Local Autonomies held in Milan in 1979.
The drawing shows a ribbon in different versions, including one in the three colours of the Italian flag (the *tricolore*).
It is possible to observe how the original version developed into all of the others used in the brochure.

549

3.

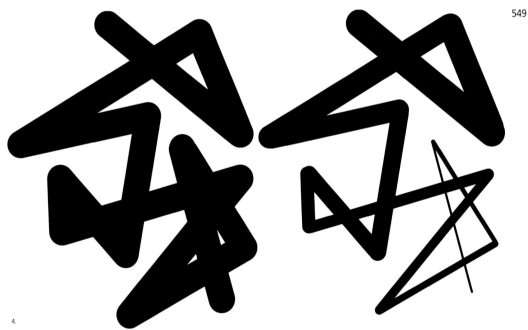

4.

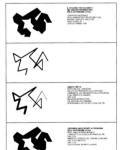
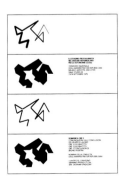

5.

Illustrations

The Relationship between Sign and Weight; The Factor of Enlargement

1. On this page: a drawing printed from an Illustrator file with 0.3 point lines; the same drawing with 0.6 point lines; the third version is a b&w outline with 0.4 point thick lines; the fourth is in .tiff format.

A graphic designer can also be an artist, but must first be aware of the rules of representation.

He or she must be able to reduce an element to its essential information, to give it clarity and memory, to provide it with the synthesis that exalts its essentiality and facilitates its reproduction.

The rapid analysis of reduction tests shown here, as an example, helps us understand how the reading of these images requires a priori knowledge not only of expressive possibilities but also of the decisive techniques used to develop a drawing.

The difficulties in interpreting the dense network of a line drawing is instructive because it can be traced back to the theory of communication.

The drawings illustrated here, depending on how an original was enlarged or reduced, and based on the frequency of the lines of which it is composed, are subject to casual interferences we refer to as "noise".

The density of the lines of which the drawing is comprised, comparable to the density of the tone that produces halftones.

Similarly, the information transmitted by the illustrative process is parcelised, gradients are tranformed into repetitive steps that can be very few, and thus almost illegible, or so few as to be completely invisible to the naked eye, or so far apart that it is not possible to read them as a whole or so close together that they merge into an indistinct black surface.

550

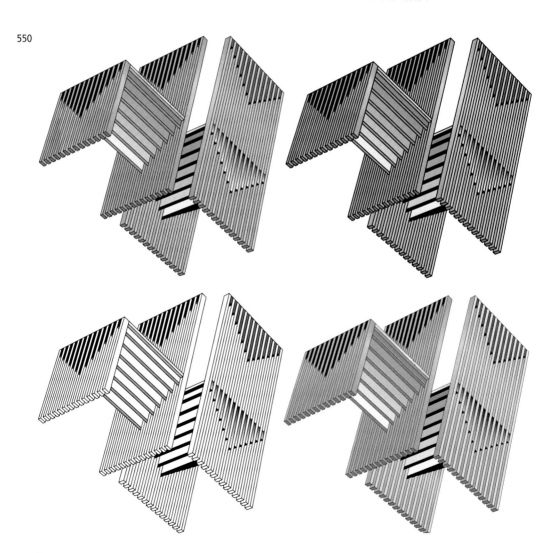

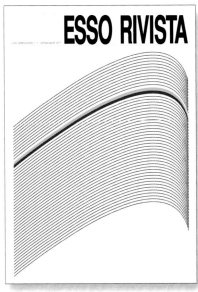

3. 4. The two drawings are identical and printed from a single matrix; the second is a proportional reduction. We can verify how in the smaller drawing the lines are closer together, giving the portrait a realistic dimension that, however, is not of benefit to the drawing as it was originally conceived.

We must be aware of the vast diversity between the two images. The larger image rewards the "artistic" qualities of the drawing, while the reduction makes it "simpler", and almost photographic.

551

4.

3.

1. 2. A study of drawings and evaluation of line weights.
In figure 1 the drawings are printed with a line weight of 0.2 points and 0.4 points respectively. There is a visible loss in the details of small elements where the line weight is greater.

2. The weight of the signs in figure 2 varies automatically in its reduction, which appears more "photographic".

1.

552

2.

6.

7.   8.

9.   10.

7. 10. The logo of the Socrates publishing house is based on the only known image of the Greek philosopher. When applying the logo, the line weights are not proportionate to automatic reductions, but instead modified to ensure it remains legible.
6. Original drawing
7. Proportional reduction
8. Drawing with 0.27 point line weights.
9. Drawing with 0.35 point line weights.
11. Drawing with 0.45 point line weights.

11. 13. An original drawing and print tests based on a progressive increase in line weights in the search for the correct level of definition.
Variations in line weights automatically varies the reproduction of the image, which gradually appears more "photographic".

553

11.   13.

34.
Political Graphics

Four Artefacts: Structures, Signs, Ribbons and Dilations

What has become of political communication? In dark times such as these, it is impossible to avoid an excursus, albeit rapid, through the world of political graphics, from the period between 1962 and 1994. These pages present a few examples of communications that made the Italian Republican Party, specifically that under the guidance of Ugo La Malfa, so categorically recognisable in any apparition.

It is not like me to discuss this issue; though I am obliged to show young students, who certainly did not experience those years, the level of political communication at this time. This exploration is accompanied, at the bottom of the page, by one of the many texts written on this topic, in this case by Massimo Bucchi, and published in *La Repubblica* on 4 November 1996.

554 "The dream of communication creates monsters. They are the monsters of the everyday, of the obvious, of conformism. In graphic design, as elsewhere, these monsters are affable, friendly and pleasing to look at. It is pleasant and easy to spend time with them; they offer easy stimuli and ask only to be left alone, not to be asked to transmit a message that is anything more than tautology. They are viruses that once they have penetrated slowly consume taste and intelligence. It is a curtain that thickens, like some rising fog. Removing the identity of a personal evolution, which can be historicised; it appears that graphic communication today cultivates the tendency to choose this or that fragment from a universe of icons in which everything is equivalent, in only one possible world.

This autobiographic book[1] by one of Italy's leading "historic" graphic artists, offers us a lost interpretation.

It is a story of more than thirty years of activity, from 1962 to 1995, as a subtle *fil rouge* that co-penetrates politics, industry, labour, economic choices and the frontiers of civilisation.

Everything is viewed through graphic design, in which geometry becomes image, the detail refers to a general structure that is already a vision of the world, as part of a sort of visionary *finalissimo* in which aesthetics becomes vital commitment.

There can be no wonder in learning that Spera, a passionate man from Southern Italy, offered us the most rational forms of graphic design during these decades. He is the representative of the grand tradition of a South that has consistently produced, not in opposition to itself, but simply to its stereotypes, lucid and abstract ideas that have always anticipated historic and social reality.

Forever faithful to his language, Spera has worked for important clients and, at the same time, for a renewal in the world of political graphics. His posters for the Republican Party remain an example of a style that has generated followers, though very few successors in his attempt at a global approach, a redefinition of the relationship of communication, long before its content. His works were computerised prior to the advent of the computer. They are post-industrial at the dawn of the industrial era. But above all, they are strictly personal, and dense with an emotional identity.

In the book, their fullest reading is highlighted by the history of relationships that created them and either gave birth to, or in some cases (given that the book is not a catalogue of successes, but also of difficulties) impeded, their "public" appearance [...].

Yet few graphic designers are as bound to the past and tradition as Spera, a Lucan from Potenza, whose most rarefied forms are not a play of lines, but actual objects. X-rays of objects, abstractions of objects, structures of reality. If something is striking, it is the concreteness of the symbol, the emphasis on a function, the isolation in the movement of a form of the point at which maximum meaning is obtained.

Unwilling to be guided, as much in his early years as when he had achieved international recognition, in his recounting of a lifetime and not of a career, Spera confirms that monsters begin precisely where our memory of ourselves ends."

Massimo Bucchi,
Michele Spera, "La vita è segno",
La Repubblica, 1 November 1996

Notes
1) Michele Spera, *Centonovantaquattro storie di un segno*, preface by *Domenico De Masi*, *500 pages*, *Edizioni Socrates*, *Roma 1996.*

Structures

The Repetition of Modules and the Geometric Iteration of Line Weights

This chapter begins with a presentation of graphic material created almost exclusively for the Italian Republican Party from the 1960s onward. It presents the sequence of three distinct graphic typologies that for years defined the image of the political party headed by Ugo La Malfa:
1) structures;
2) the sign;
3) ribbons and their derivations.

Refer also the chapter "Perception".

I structured these aggregate drawings, whose construction was triggered more by technical invention and less by a creative process, for the first time in 1967.
This involved days on end spent in a dark room.
My pupils focused on the light of an enlarger that creates signs.
That dilates them.
That exalts them as part of some mysterious chemical process.
I learned everything in print shops.
To use lenses better than a computer, which did not exist at the time.

This was the early 1960s, when we spent nights in the print shop, preparing brochures and propagandistic material for the Italian Republican Party.
Marcello was not a graphic designer, but worked in the print shop run by the brothers Gino and Angelo De Rossi;
I didn't know it at the time, but he taught me the magic of dilating a sign in a dark room.
That was my school.
I used this technique an infinite number of times in diverse projects, since 1966.

Young Southern Italians

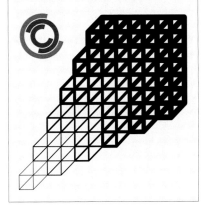

Convention promoted
by the Federation of
Young Republicans
Messina,
13 May 1968
Filarmonica Laudamo
Corso Cavour

It is increasingly clearer to everyone that Southern Italy is the first problem to be faced by a "new" left. However, before being a problem of economic restructuring and new industrial settlements, the South is a problem of men. In fact, only if young people in all fields, from culture to politics, from industry to administration, are able to create a new managing class that differs radically from that which preceded it, can Southern Italy become the California of Italy.

A poster for regional election results from 1970; the PRI rose to 3% and earned a million votes.

...Così io vedo Michele Spera e le sue opere. He offers mysterious messages, which originate as games, arising in the imagination and immediately intelligently measured, ordered in wonder. His works are infinite geometries that amaze their observers, signs offered to the masses, hung in the streets, on the covers of journals, of books, in other cases closed inside massive tomes, often surmounted by warnings, overlying calls to attention. I step aside and enter into the ellipses, squares, polygons and lines that run, encircle, and depart for an infinite voyage. It is similar to advancing through labyrinths with no exit, filled with joyfulness and mystery, where desire consists of research. Every destination is here, in the maps of ink, in the strips of coloured paper. Participating in a similar harmony means abandoning oneself to vision...

Elio Pecora, *Città e Campagna*, 1970

These pages present a series of political posters and communications that use similar and coordinated graphic representations.

556

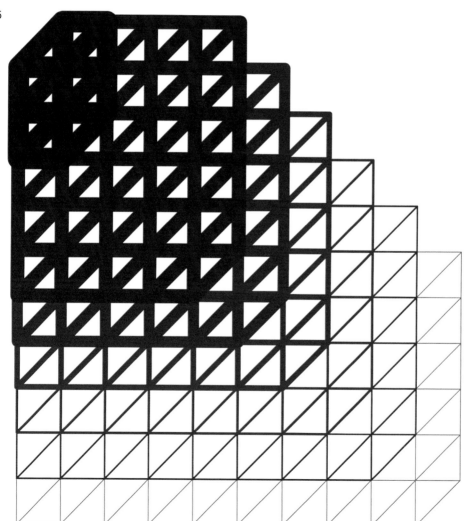

IL PRI
UNA FORZA
NUOVA
UNA FORZA
CHE CRESCE

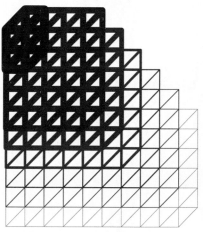

ADMINISTRATIVE ELECTIONS 1970
ONE MILLION VOTES FOR THE PRI

**UMBRIA TODAY
FOR THE UMBRIA
OF TOMORROW**

CURATED BY
UMBRIA D'OGGI
REPUBLICAN
PERIODICAL
OF INFORMATION

CONVENTION
OF PROPOSALS
OF TERRITORIAL
PLANNING
FOR THE REGION
ACQUASPARTA
9/10 NOVEMBER 1973
PALAZZO CESI

557

**EIN MAXIMUM
AN LEBENSQUALITAT
BEI GROSSTMOGLICHEM
FREIHEITSRAUM
FUR ALLE**

REPUBLIKANISCHE PARTEI ITALIENS

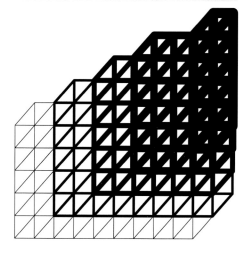

**XXII CONGRESS
OF THE ROMAN UNION OF THE PRI
PROJECTING THE CITY**

ROME EUR
PALAZZO DEI CONGRESSI
22/24 OCTOBER

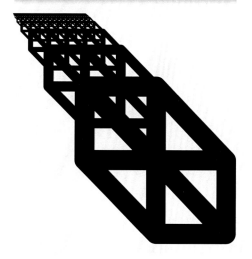

**IX NATIONAL CONGRESS
OF THE REPUBLICANS
OF FRIULI VENEZIA GIULIA**

GORIZIA, 29 JANUARY 1978
COM AUDITORIUM

**TODAY, LOOKING
TOWARD THE FUTURE**

CONGRESS OF REPUBLICANS
OF THE PROVINCE OF ROME
ARICCIA, 8/10 JANUARY 1983

558

**SICILY
TODAY'S CONSENSUS
FOR A PROJECT FOR THE FUTURE**

11TH REGIONAL CONVENTION
OF THE REPUBLICAN PARTY
PALERMO 6/7 FEBRUARY
FIERA DEL MEDITERRANEO

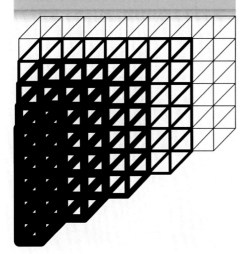

**LET'S TAKE BACK THE PROJECT
FOR METROPOLITAN PLANNING
AND OPEN IT UP TOWARD THE REGION**

OPEN SEMINAR OF THE ROMAN UNION
OF THE ITALIAN REPUBLICAN PARTY
ROME 8 MAY 10:00 A.M.
HOTEL LEONARDO DA VINCI

**POLITICAL UNION TRAINING
SEMINAR
FOR REPUBLICAN MANANGERS**

MILAN, 28/29 NOVEMBER 1981
FEDERATION OF THE ITALIAN
REPUBLICAN PARTY

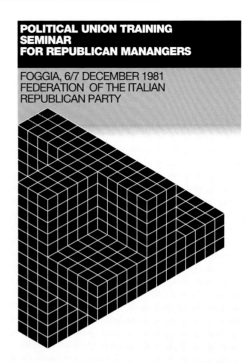

**POLITICAL UNION TRAINING
SEMINAR
FOR REPUBLICAN MANANGERS**

FOGGIA, 6/7 DECEMBER 1981
FEDERATION OF THE ITALIAN
REPUBLICAN PARTY

559

**POLITICAL UNION TRAINING
SEMINAR
FOR REPUBLICAN MANANGERS**

NAPLES, 6/7 DECEMBER 1981
HOTEL ORIENTE
VIA ARMANDO DIAZ

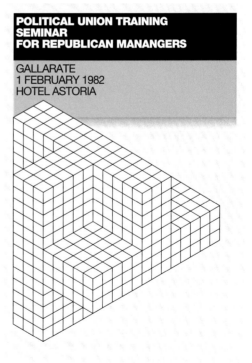

**POLITICAL UNION TRAINING
SEMINAR
FOR REPUBLICAN MANANGERS**

GALLARATE
1 FEBRUARY 1982
HOTEL ASTORIA

The Sign

From a Primitive Gestural
Sign to a Codified Sign

When experience is united with the ardor of invention we navigate under a clear and boundless sky. It was the early Sixties, and I spent hours in the print shop preparing pamphlets and propaganda for the [Italian Republican] party.
I spent entire days in the dark room. Staring into the light of the enlarger that created different signs. It dilated them. It exalted them as part of some mysterious chemical process.

I learned so much inside the print shop. I learned to use lenses better than a computer, which didn't exist at the time. When overlapping one colour atop another inside the dark room, I noticed this caused a slight blurring of my drawings, which were dilated just enough to ensure they were precisely aligned. This is how I discovered that I could lay out a drawing with a technical pen, create a negative and project it, out of focus, onto a sheet of orthochromatic film.

The more out of focus it was, the fatter the sign became, and the rounder the corners. This discovery led to the future production of all of my signs, logos and images. They acquired a magic and unusual quality: this was the dilation of a sign, long before the advent of the computer.

Interview with Michele Spera in Design Culture edited by Matteo-Nicola Munari 2018 http:// www.designculture.it/

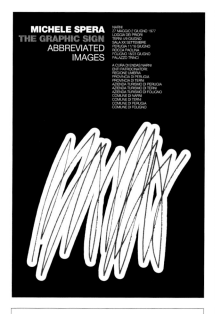

561

HOW TO OVERCOME THE CRISIS ECONOMICS AND INSTITUTIONS

NATIONAL CONFERENCE OF THE PRI ELISEO THEATRE VIA NAZIONALE 28/29 MAY ROME

AT A TIME OF CRISIS SUCH AS THE PRESENT THE ALTERNATIVE OFFERED BY THE LEFT IS AN ADVENTURE. VOTING FOR THE CHRISTIAN DEMOCRATS IS NOT THE WAY OUT

ANOTHER FORCE FOR GOVERNING

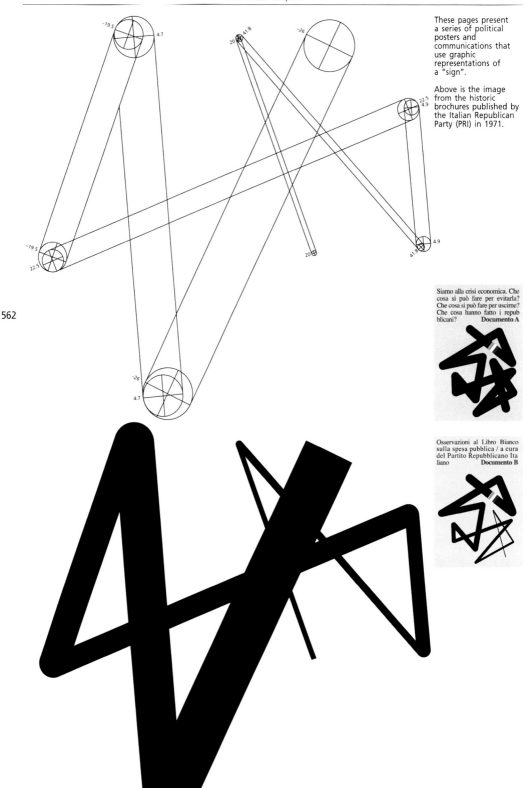

These pages present a series of political posters and communications that use graphic representations of a "sign".

Above is the image from the historic brochures published by the Italian Republican Party (PRI) in 1971.

Siamo alla crisi economica. Che cosa si può fare per evitarla? Che cosa si può fare per uscirne? Che cosa hanno fatto i repub blicani? **Documento A**

Osservazioni al Libro Bianco sulla spesa pubblica / a cura del Partito Repubblicano Ita liano **Documento B**

1929/1979
90 YEARS OF CLERICAL PRIVILEGES
**YOUNG REPUBLICANS
AGAINST THE CONCORDATO**

**DISINTEREST
IS ISOLATION**

FEDERATION OF YOUNG REPUBLICANS
MEMBERSHIP DRIVE 1979

563

**CATHOLICS IN POLITICS: A STORY
VIEWED FROM THE LAIC DIMENSION**

CONVENTION OF THE FEDERATION
OF YOUNG REPUBLICANS
BOLOGNA 16/18 APRIL
HALL OF MIRRORS

BEYOND THE HEDGE

III CONGRESS OF THE FEDERATION
OF YOUNG REPUBLICANS OF LAZIO
FIUGGI, 26 APRIL 1981
MUNICIPAL LIBRARY

LET'S BUILD THE SCHOOL TOGETHER
REGIONAL CONVENTION
OF THE ITALIAN REPUBLICAN PARTY

ITALIAN REPUBLICAN PARTY
BROLETTO ROOM
NOVARA, PIAZZA DEL DUOMO
18 OCTOBER 1977

LET'S BUILD THE SCHOOL TOGETHER
IV NATIONAL ASSEMBLY
OF REPUBLICAN STUDENTS

FEDERATION OF YOUNG REPUBLICANS
MONTESILVANO, PESCARA
28/30 OCTOBER 1975

564

**THE REPUBLICAN PRESENCE
GOVERNING AND DECIDING**

ITALIAN REPUBLICAN PARTY
MEMBERSHIP DRIVE 1982

**SICILY
AFTER SCHOOL
PROFESSION AND RESEARCH**

TWO REPUBLICAN LAWS FOR THOSE
ENTERING THE WORLD OF WORK
BARI HOTEL JOLLY 2/3 MAY

565

**REPUBLICAN PARTY
MEMBERSHIP DRIVE 1979**

IN EUROPE
WITH EUROPE

**REPUBLICANS
IN THE EUROPE OF THE NINE**

CONGRESS OF THE ELD
DEMOCRATIC LIBERAL EUROPEANS
VENEZIA LIDO 7/9 MAGGIO 1979
EXCELSIOR HOTEL

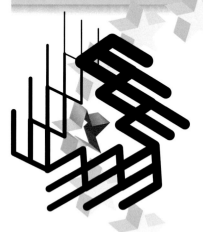

Ribbons

Using Folded Strips of Paper to Communicate

These pages present a series of political posters and communications that use similar and coordinated graphics.

Examining,
critically discussing events,
problems, situations. Offering the essential.
This is our work, each day.
Creating a free newspaper,
whose prestige is founded on precision
and objective judgment.

LA VOCE REPUBBLICANA
00186 Roma, via Tomacelli 146

Publishing the essential,
framing events and situations.
Discussing, commenting.
Politics, economics, culture, society.
A free and different newspaper,
founded on precision
and objective judgment.

LA VOCE REPUBBLICANA
00186 Roma, via Tomacelli 146

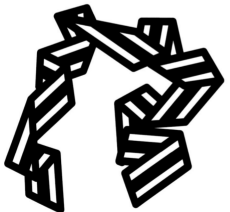

Michele Spera
Graphics and Politics

Naples
Circolo Cattaneo
Via dei Mille, 25
Opening 22 June
Ridotto del
Teatro Sannazzaro
Via Chiaia

Michele Spera
Graphics and Politics

Naples
Circolo Cattaneo
Via dei Mille, 25
Opening 22 June
Ridotto del
Teatro Sannazzaro
Via Chiaia

567

YOUNG PEOPLE
FROM THE OTHER ITALY

XXXIII CONGRESS
OF THE FEDERATION
OF YOUNG REPUBLICANS
CASTROCARO, 18/21 NOVEMBER

LOCAL AUTONOMIES
CITIZENS AT THE HEART
OF A REPUBLICAN PROJECT

NATIONAL CONVENTION
OF REPUBLICAN
ADMINISTRATORS
SATURDAY 15 SEPTEMBER
VIALE STURZO 45, MILAN
AERHOTEL EXECUTIVE

Thin strips of folded paper

...This is how I rediscovered the practical and lyrical functionality of paper. I filled my studio with "offcuts", leftovers and trimmings of white paper. I remembered the construction of paper hats for bricklayers or paper airplanes launched by students in a a mixture of war and evasion and other games and combinations for offices and storage spaces.

Was all this necessary, of was it an accident that I began searching for the most concealed movements and meanings?

In the autumn of 1969, in a scientific manner, I visualised the first pieces of folded paper. I sought to give them meaning and sense, to assign political content to a fold.

Besides simply folding paper, to my torment I discovered I could wrap and unwrap it to create a range of "models".

It was like discovering a simple fact tied to the magic of three-dimensional volume. All that was needed was a fold to transform paper into a fantastic sculpture. I then searched for volumes, axes and suddenly the facets unfolded into the required meanings, breaking free of the prismatic magma, the mystery of an apparent immobility. This is how the hand of a craftsman finds poetry, finds harmony in content and form. Paper responds as a living material, which can be composed and sublimated. It is strong like other more important and tested materials.

Wrapped, unfolded or cut, it offers an unexpected possibility to seek out unique forms, original themes, new names. It also presents itself as an alternative to materials forced to live in a dimension codified for many years in their expression and language.

With paper it is possible to create a spring or a sailboat or a city.

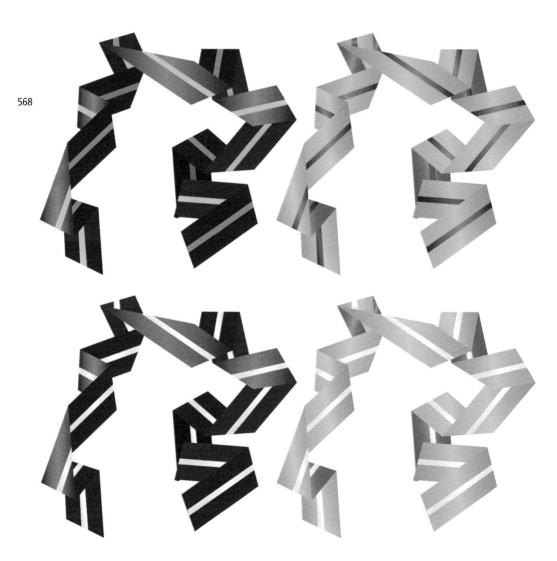

There is a need for the talent of diamond cutters, to give light to the many obscure facets that have only just become visible, as if they have just sprouted, images that are still dirty and through some imagined rhythm or plausible modulation find not only poetic light, but also intrinsic meaning in their effective position. This discourse appears to begin in a workshop filled with who knows what instruments and which instead comes from the old school "airport" of paper airplanes, with the difference that at the time they were used for some innocent game; today, for a persuasion of incredible value. I continue to invent by metaphor.

Michele Spera, Sottili strisce di carta piegate, Territorio, D'Elia editore, 1975

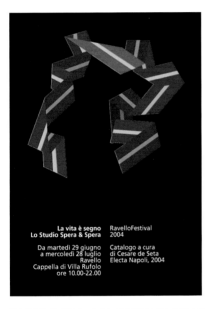

569

570

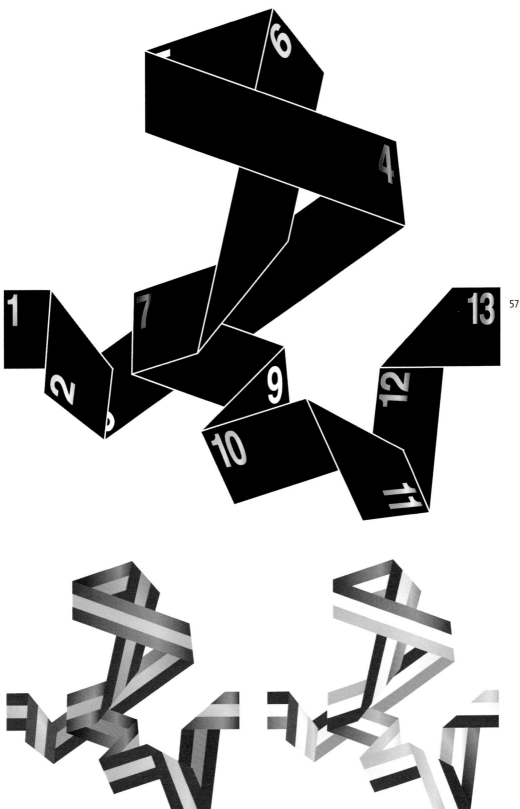

Optical Dilations

From a Signature to a
Fascinating Logotype

572

GIANCARLO ILIPRANDI
BOB NOORDA
MICHELE PROVINCIALI
MICHELE SPERA
PINO TOVAGLIA

GRAFICA TENDENZE
GALLERIA ARTIVISIVE
VIA BRUNETTI 60 / ROMA
9/30 DICEMBRE 1977

GIANCARLO ILIPRANDI
BOB NOORDA
MICHELE PROVINCIALI
MICHELE SPERA
PINO TOVAGLIA

GRAFICA TENDENZE
ISIA / ISTITUTO SUPERIORE
PER LE INDUSTRIE ARTISTICHE
URBINO / VIA SANTA CHIARA 36
11 FEBBRAIO / 11 MARZO 1978

A Neighbourhood, A Number

The Districts of the City

This graphic was invented for the 1976 elections in the fourteen districts of Florence. The campaign was later extended to Perugia, Rome and gradually to other Italian cities.
A postcard was sent to all inhabitants of the city, with a list of ten important themes (housing, health, education, parks, etc.) in need of a solution. Citizens of each district were asked to mark a maximum of four themes whose resolution was continued most urgent with an X.
The postcards that returned were used to create the posters: this

involved nothing other that the attribution of each with the different colours indicated by each district.
This meant that each district had its own personalised poster, with its preferences, candidates, location in the city, plus a general poster, with all fourteen numbers, posted throughout the city as a sort of summary.
The numbers were prefabricated using a modular system so that they always occupied the same space.
Inside each number, the four circumferences identify a colour that changed to meet the needs of

communicating by colours, based on a pre-established colour code and the priorities of the interventions to be carried out.
The fixed theme, the number that appears on each poster, becomes a recognisable graphic sign that is always different, with a unique colour, but also with different colours, with a unique alphabet expressing different messages. This structure made it possible to construct a general image that could be used in a unique environment, mapped and measured in a succession of different moments; it also determined a visual

Health Services

Sports Facility

Landscaped Area

Landscaped Area

School

Cultural Facilities

Nursery Schools

Water/River Regimentation

Neighbourhood Markets

Nursery Schools

persistence created by the constant presence of always different modular signs, in a condition of continuous decomposition and reorganisation, legible throughout the city.

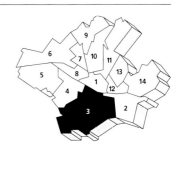

575

Coordination

The Same Image for Different Communications

The design of this star, following a large number of studies in October 1983, was used to re-propose the strategy from a 1981 convention: repeating an image over a political theme and exploding it at the culminating moment of the congress that was being prepared. An occasion was offered with the book by Spadolini, published as part of the "I quaderni del Pri" series. I worked on the cover and the drawing of the star, as if it were an episode, a detail, a prelude to the grand exploit at Milanofiori.

1. The posters on the facing page feature an inscribed gird obtained using the golden section to permit the insertion of a particular text.
In this case the useful base of 65 cm was multiplied by 1.618 to obtain a grid of 58.7 x 95 cm, and a second grid of 6.29 x 95 cm.

The drawing is a proportionate reproduction of the base format of a 70x100 cm poster. With a constant margin of 2.5 cm on all four sides, the inscribed grid measures 65 cm in width by 95 cm in height.
The further subdivision of the grid is based on a 65x65 cm square and a 30 cm high upper zone.
This latter space was further subdivided by the number of rows of text, plus an area of respect at the bottom, equal to the height of the typeface.

576

THE REPUBLICANS
THE PARTY OF DEMOCRACY

35th NATIONAL CONGRESS
OF THE ITALIAN REPUBLICAN PARTY
MILANOFIORI CONGRESS CENTRE
27/30 APRIL 1984

THE REPUBLICANS
THE PARTY OF DEMOCRACY

MEMBERSHIP DRIVE 1984

THE REPUBLICANS
THE PARTY OF DEMOCRACY

by Giovanni Spadolini
With essays by Paolo Bagnoli, Luciano Cafagna,
Orazio M. Petracca, Alfredo Pieroni, Rosario Romeo,
Alberto Ronchey, Piero Scoppola, Leo Valiani

THE REPUBLICANS
THE PARTY OF DEMOCRACY

For the moral, institutional and economic
renewal of the Republic 1981/1984
Report by Giovanni Spadolini
from the 35th National Congress of the Pri

Coherence Over Time
The Conventions

**TAKING BACK THE PROJECT FOR
METROPOLITAN URBAN PLANNING
OPENING UP TOWARD THE REGION**

OPEN SEMINAR
OF THE ROMAN UNION OF THE PRI
ROME 8 MAY 1982, 10 A.M.
LEONARDO DA VINCI HOTEL

**THE PROPOSAL OF THE PRI
FOR RECOVERING THE ROLE
OF REGIONAL GOVERNMENT**

REPUBLICAN PARTY CONVENTION
VENICE 11/13 JUNE 1982
CHAMBER OF COMMERCE

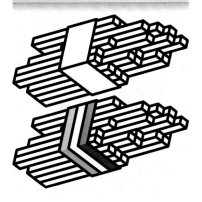

**ORGANISING
THE FUTURE**

CONVENTION OF REPUBLICAN MANAGEMENT
AND ADMINISTRATORS FROM LAZIO
ROME, 14/15 DECEMBER 1984
LEONARDO DA VINCI HOTEL

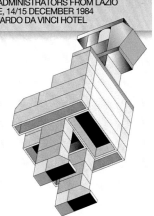

**MEETING OF
REPUBLICAN MANAGERS
FROM SOUTHERN ITALY**

FOR A POLICY
FOR SOUTHERN ITALY
NAPLES, 31 MARCH 194
EXCELSIOR HOTEL

Notes

*I must confess, looking
back on these drawings
after many years, I have
no problems or regrets.
On the contrary, I
believe now more than
ever, that they express
the intrinsic contents
of each theme
explored at the time
with highly graphic
though equally precise
methods.
A sort of concatenation
whose rhythm is
marked by elements of
varying strengths and
the image of the 1982
seminar at the
Leonardo Da Vinci
Hotel.
The convention was
based on the idea of
considering the Italian
capital as indissolubly
linked to the towns
and villages
surrounding it.
The drawing clearly
expresses the concept
of a territory composed
of various realities, of
diverse dimensions, that
together develop a
unique metropolitan
area.
To the same degree,
the convention on
education featured a
liberating image that
expressed the sense of
flight experienced by
those who confront the
world upon graduation.
There is also the idea
of the twenty regions
held together by a
concept of what it
means to belong to a
nation.*

577

These posters were selected at random, from among the last and few designed at great pains during the period when Ugo La Malfa was party secretary.

It was a time that privileged grand strategies of communication dictated by agencies, with a reckless focus on a party for the masses. We no longer knew where we were headed, we were no longer participants.

Above all, with so many "new" words, it was impossible to link party strategy to a criteria of interpretation that responded to this question.

We emigrate and, like survivors, we stop to consider an experience lived for so many years that grows more and more distant from our ideals.

A RAILWAY FOR THE MARCHES

SITUATIONS AND PROSPECTS FOR AN INLAND RAIL LINE SASSOFERRATO, AVIS ROOM 2 APRIL 1978, 10 A.M.

IMPROVING THE BILL ON HEALTH REFORM BEING DISCUSSED IN THE SENATE

ROME, HOTEL LEONARDO DA VINCI 30 SEPTEMBER/1 OCTOBER 1978

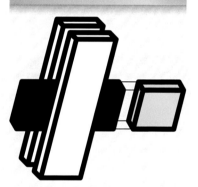

Notes
Two men who fight, controlled by strings; a game found in a fair stall, an idea for illustrating the right to labour strikes.

AGAINST DRUGS A LAW THAT PROTECTS AND CONTROLS COMMUNITIES

FEDERATION OF YOUNG REPUBLICANS RIMINI, 12 NOVEMBER 1984 TEATRO ITALIA ROOM, VIA TEIROLI, 42

THE FUTURE OF THE CHEMICAL INDUSTRY STUDY CONVENTION

ECONOMIC STUDIES CENTRE PIEDMONT FEDERATION OF THE PRI TURIN, 7/8 NOVEMBER 1972, S. PAOLO INST.

This imaged from November 1982 could be titled *Difficult navigation. A ship without a helmsman.* At this time, Spadolini asked for a design for the covers of books that recounted the wear caused by the endemic conflict between political parties during his presidency, *The Difficult Government.* A period that was both hindered and blocked. He liked the idea a lot; he considered it the correct visual representation of his experience.

GIOVANNI SPADOLINI
DIFFICULT GOVERNMENT

10 JUNE 1981/30 NOVEMBER 1982
PARLIAMENTARY BATTLES
PREFACE BY ANDREA MANZELLA
VOLUME 1

GIOVANNI SPADOLINI
DIFFICULT GOVERNMENT

10 JUNE 1981/30 NOVEMBER 1982
PARLIAMENTARY BATTLES
PREFACE BY ANDREA MANZELLA
VOLUME 2

579

Notes
Il governo difficile.
The image created for two books by Giovanni Spadolini.
To the left, a poster supporting the Republican initiative for the legal recognition of junior executives and a provincial congress in Ariccia; below elections in Trieste.

TO THE VOTERS
OF SICILY

We Republicans are asking for the votes of Sicilians to resolve the problems faced by Sicily, respecting the autonomy of the Region and the unity of the Republic, and not in order to reinforce in Rome the pretexts and ambitions of power of the one or the other.
Giovanni Spadolini

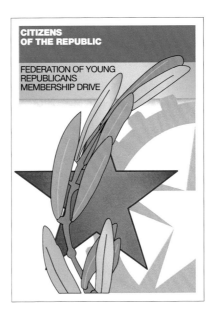

CITIZENS
OF THE REPUBLIC

FEDERATION OF YOUNG
REPUBLICANS
MEMBERSHIP DRIVE

Cancelling, forgetting. I used graphic signs to cancel so much ugliness from so many years; even this is a sign of cancellation, natural, spontaneous, a warning against the danger of drugs.
The second poster, on the same theme, uses another photograph from the series; in this case the same image visualises an absence, a non-presence.

The slogans were the work of a group and all of the publications realised successively on this theme referred to the same photographs.

580

**AN ABSENCE
A CONVENTION ON DRUGS**

FEDERATION OF THE YOUNG
REPUBLICANS OF LAZIO
ROME HOTEL FLEMING
SATURDAY 26 4:30 P.M.

**A HOLE
IN THE INSTITUTIONS**

NATIONAL CONVENTION PRI/FGR
VERONA 4 OCTOBER 10:30 A.M.
MUNICIPAL LIBRARY
NERVI ROOM

Notes
To the right, drawings for the campaign for the first European elections in 1984.

**CATHOLICS IN POLITICS: A STORY
VIEWED FROM THE LAIC DIMENSION**

CONVENTION OF THE FEDERATION
OF YOUNG REPUBLICANS
BOLOGNA 16/18 APRIL
HALL OF MIRRORS

**TERRORISM
DESERTERS OF REASON**

STUDY SEMINAR
FEDERATION OF YOUNG REPUBLICANS
PALAZZO BRASCHI
ROME 27/28 JUNE

A Serene "No"

The Referendums

In 1974 we were involved in the campaign for the referendum on divorce. In opposition to other political powers who opted for dramatic tones, we chose a serene approach to communication.
In that boiling political climate, we coined the slogans "A serene NO from the nation's social conscience", "Reflect, NO to indifference".
The Party was on the barricades, but we won the battle.

The poster was a window onto a blue sky; for the Republican Women's poster I used a photograph of my beautiful wife embracing our first son Gerardo.
It was a victory not only for the Party, but for the entire Nation and for us.
It was on this occasion that Livio Zanetti, at the time director of *L'Espresso*, and Gregoretti, asked me to design the first cover dedicated to the "NO" victory: a tongue wagged in the face of the "YES" supporters.

Meanwhile, young people paraded through the streets shouting: "Fanfani, you imp, you have lost the championship!".

582

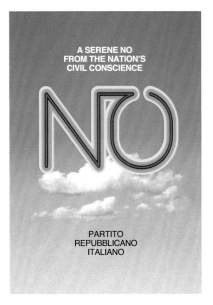

Notes
The word "NO" was used in bright colours for successive referendums.

MATERA, LA PROVINCIA,
IL MEZZOGIORNO

5Y CONGRESSO PROVINCIALE
DEI REPUBBLICANI
MATERA PRESIDENT HOTEL
2 DICEMBRE ORE 9.30

CALABRIA
SENZA ILLUSIONI
CONCRETAMENTE

9Y CONGRESSO REGIONALE
DEI REPUBBLICANI DELLA CALABRIA
CATANZARO 12/13 GENNAIO
HOTEL GUGLIELMO

BENI CULTURALI
E ASSETTO DEL TERRITORIO

CONVEGNO DEL PRI
PERUGIA 2/3 FEBBRAIO
SALA BRUGNOLI
PALAZZO CESARONI

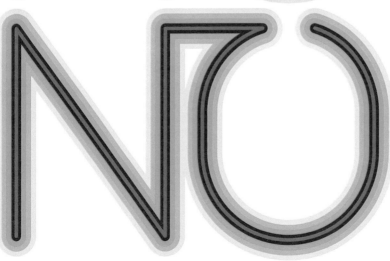

583

Notes
In 1981 there were
other referendums:
one proposing an
abrogation, another a
reductive modification
to abortion laws;
others involved
legislation on measures
of public order. The
"NO" design from the
1974 divorce
referendum and the
1978 abrogation of
Royal Laws was used
for a third time,
though with
completely different
colours.

Spadolini and Visentini

An Appointment on the Train

"An Appointment on the Train": a series of posters for the administrative elections campaigns in the Veneto region. Italy changes, and election campaigns change.
The Republicans, "a small party of the masses" in historic areas, though primarily an opinion party in newly settled areas, understood this new reality in time.

The end has come to the era of political rallies in public squares, of propaganda as it is intended by traditional formulas.
We must also be able to speak another language: a harsh language, when necessary, but without renouncing a smile, a less dark and grey image of political commitment.

This led to the very original idea of the electoral train "with Spadolini and Visentini", travelling by rail from Verona to Treviso, passing through Vicenza, Padua, Venice and Mestre.
At each stop, they would meet with citizens and voters, under the aegis of friendliness and cordiality.
Few speeches, a lot of handshaking. Just one more example of the "Republican style".

584

Notes
I like to show the continuity of the image of a political party over the course of years of collaboration with a graphic artist.
On this page are 4 posters from 1985.
Below is a poster from 2017 and on the facing page are a series of communications from 1965.

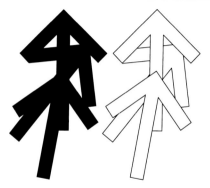

Image for membership recruitment by the *Federazione giovanile repubblicana,* Federation of Young Republicans, 1965. I was national secretary of the FGR Iperide Ippoliti.

The arrows designed for membership in the Federation would later inspire the image for the debate between La Malfa and Amendola in 1966 at the Palazzo dei Congressi in Rome and for a 1968 brochure printed by the FGR entitled "Ideology in the New Society".

Federation of Young Republicans
Membership Drive 1965

A democratic, reformist, libertarian commitment.

La Malfa / Amendola
Debate

What Left for the West?
EUR, Palazzo dei Congressi
27 April 1966

585

NATIONAL CONVENTION OF REPUBLICAN LABOUR
TURIN, VIA GIOLITTI 26
HALL OF THE
CHAMBER OF COMMERCE
7/9 DECEMBER 1976

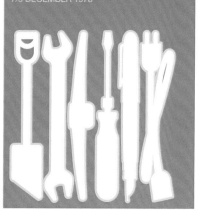

NATIONAL CONVENTION OF REPUBLICAN LABOUR
LAZIO FEDERATION OF THE PRI
ROME, 22 APRIL 1976
TEATRO CENTRALE
9:30 A.M.

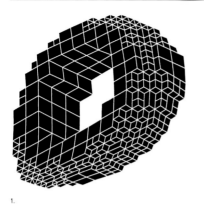

1.

2.

1. The symbol of the
"Ugo La Malfa" clubs.
2. Ugo La Malfa's
signature in a 4x3
metre poster from the
Expo in Bari.
3. The 1979 poster
commemorating the
death of Ugo La Malfa
features the dates of
his birth and death.
4. The 1999 poster,
used twenty years later
in occasion of the
twentieth anniversary
of Ugo La Malfa's
death, returns to the
same theme, this time
in colour and with the
two dates.

586

Notes
There is a clear matrix
in the studies of the
legibility of the text
that, divided in half, in
positive and negative,
is highly suggestive and
an inspiration for the
sketch.

Ugo La Malfa

Ugo La Malfa
16.5.1903
15.4.1979

3.

Ugo La Malfa

Ugo La Malfa
15.4.1979
15.4.1999

4.

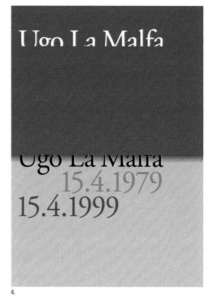

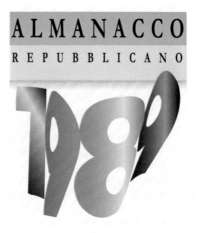

Posters for the Women's Movement

It has ancient roots. It was the first women's movement in Italy; it was born, even if not in an organised fashion, under Mazzini, and has always pursued the primary objective of achieving real equality between men and women, at home, at work, in society and in politics.
Beside the posters is the symbol I designed in 1969, when Fernanda Missiroli was secretary.

It is a brand, and like all good brands, it is invasive and impossible to cancel. It has its own contagious strength capable of indelibly characterising an event, a date, years of work and facts that have remained integral throughout the history of the movement. This butterfly-bird played a part in the lives of Republican women.

WOMEN COMMITMENT, NOT PROXY

NATIONAL ASSEMBLY OF THE GROUPS OF THE REPUBLICAN WOMEN'S MOVEMENT RIMINI, 13/15 JANUARY 1984 AZIENDA DI SOGGIORNO

FAMILY PLANNING

FAMILY AND PROCREATION INSTITUTION OPEN DEBATE IN ROME PIAZZA CAPRETTARI, 6 JUNE 1972

MOVIMENTO FEMMINILE REPUBBLICANO

587

A HOUSE OF CARDS AND WORDS WOMEN SPEAK OUT

NATIONAL ASSEMBLY OF THE GROUPS OF THE REPUBLICAN WOMEN'S MOVEMENT ROME, PIAZZA CAPRETTARI, MARCH 1981

A HOUSE OF CARDS AND WORDS WOMEN SPEAK OUT

NATIONAL CONVENTION OF THE FMR ROME, 17/18 APRIL 1981 RESIDENCE RIPETTA

35.
UNI Regulations

DIN, ISO, UNI, CEN, EN, ENV
What They Mean

Offices of the Ente Nazionale di Unificazione

▾ Bari
c/o Tecnopolis Csata
Novus Ortus
Strada provinciale
Casamassima
70010 Valenzano (BA)
▾ Bologna
c/o CERMET
Via Aldo Moro, 22
40068 San Lazzaro
di Savena (BO)

▾ Brescia
c/o AQM srl
Via Lithos, 53
25086 Rezzato (BS)
▾ Catania
c/o CFT Sicilia
Piazza Buonarroti, 22
95126 Catania
▾ Florence
c/o Associazione
Industriali Provincia
di Firenze
Via Valfonda, 9
50123 Firenze
▾ Naples
c/o Consorzio Napoli
Ricerche
Corso Meridionale, 58
80143 Naples
▾ Milan
Via Battistotti Sassi, 11b
20133 Milan

▾ Rome
Piazza Capranica, 95
00187 Rome
▾ Turin
c/o Centro Estero
Camere di Commercio
Piemontesi
Via Ventimiglia, 165
10127 Turin
▾ Vicenza
c/o Associazione
Industriali Provincia
di Vicenza
Piazza Castello, 3
36100 Vicenza

The need to normalise and standardise industrial production by providing rules and regulations, to develop common tables of contents, internationally standardised formats, standard measures and a unique yardstick for reading documents led to the birth, in the early twentieth century, of the first organisations to deal with standardisation.

The first regulatory body was created in Great Britain in 1901; in 1921 an association of Italian mechanical industries created the UNIM, *Associazione nazionale fra gli industriali meccanici* (National Association of Mechanical Industries), transformed in 1946 into the *Ente Nazionale Italiano di Unificazione* (Italian National Unification Body).

The year 1946 was also the year of the constitution in Geneva of the International Organization for Standardization (ISO), which substituted its predecessor, the International Federation of National Standardizing Associations (ISA).

All of the world's leading industrialised nations have their own regulatory body. Some are government run, while others are open associations between industrial groups. Almost all of these bodies are members of ISO.

The standards developed by regulatory bodies serve as recommendations: they become binding only when they are transformed or incorporated into laws issued by the State.

It is possible to purchase copies of these regulations, but also to simply consult them by visiting the various offices listed at the top of the page.

The Regulations

From the beginning of the last century to the present day, the concept of regulation has evolved significantly. From the primitive sense of setting out *règle fixant les conditions d'exécution d'un objet ou d'élaboration d'un produit dont on veut unifier l'emploi ou assurer l'interchangeabilité* we have moved toward increasingly broader intentions.

In 1986, ISO, the International Organization for Standardization, defined standardization as an *activity of establishing, with regard to actual or potential problems, provisions for common and repeated use, aimed at the achievement of the optimum degree of order in a given context.* This means that the activity of standardization is extended from the unification of dimensions to the definition of product performance and processes.

Regulatory bodies are recognised organisms, in general associations involved in on-going process of standardization. Their role is to involve all interested parties in the development of regulations and to curate their publication in the most technically and formally correct manner.

Standardization takes place on various levels: from the most general to the most specific. This means that standardization ranges from basic unifications (alphabets, symbols, codes, units of measurement, terminologies) to general and specific methods, materials, parts, products and equipment.

Notes
European regulations are voluntary and private. Unlike public regulations which are binding. Regulations are issued by the ISO, incorporated by the CEN and adopted by UNI.
The development of an ISO regulation can take up to 8 years.

For these notes on standards reference was made to publications by the Ente Nazionale di Unificazione, the 1996 UNI Catalogue and specific bulletins.

There are also specific publications about particular regulations which may also prove useful. If, for example, you find yourself working on a theme such as workplace safety, you can purchase a book dedicated to mandatory signage for construction sites.

UNI regulations on graphic design can be consulted by visiting one of the offices of the *Ente Nazionale Unificazione* (Italian National Unification Body).
In Rome, at Piazza Paganica number 95, you will be shown into a room where you can leaf through a selection of catalogues, differentiated by topic and containing all of the regulations that have been issued, each with its own specific code.

For further information, you can purchase the various brochures you are interested in; while they can be costly, they contain all of the results of studies and instructions issued by the different commissions issuing these regulations.
You will find answers to questions about the technical and chromatic characteristics of paint used for road signage, official dimensions of road signs, terminology relative to type, and so on.

Standardization occurs through the emanation of technical regulations (ISO 1978), whose application is not mandatory, but only recommended.
Regulations must be: accessible to the public, in order to guarantee the possibility to learn about their existence and benefit from their content;
developed through the cooperation with and consensus or general approval from all parties involved;
founded on combined results in the sciences, technology and experience, such that they are representative of the "state of the art", in term defined as the "state of development reached at a certain moment in the technical capacities of products, processes or services, based on proven scientific, technological or experimental results"; with the objective of offering optimum advantages for the community in its entirety, to offer a tool of civil progress;
approved by a qualified and recognised national, regional or international body to have objective validity.
Standardization takes place primarily at the national level, though many international bodies have been operating for decades.

These are the bases of the work developed by: ISO, International Organization for Standardization, founded in London in 1947, a reference for regulatory bodies in 76 countries (UNI in Italy); ISO pursues the objective of promoting standardization around the globe.
The work of ISO is realised by more than 20,000 technicians around the world, organised in 182 technical committees and 1,838 work groups; to

date, ISO has published just under 8,850 regulations.
The CEN, *Comité Européen de Normalisation*, founded in 1961 is a reference for regulatory bodies in the 18 members of the EEC and EFTA (European Free Trade Association); it works to promote the use of international standards (ISO) and to harmonise regulations across Europe. The CEN publishes the EN European regulations, the ENV experimental regulations and the HD harmonisation documents. This work is developed by approximately 300 technical committees consisting of more than 2,000 work groups.
UNI is a legally recognised association representing Italy in Europe. Its activities consist in elaborating, publishing and promoting regulations and building archives of national and foreign regulations. The preparation of UNI regulations, by more than 20,000 technicians, is divided into 56 committees.
The Assembly consists of members, generally companies, scientific or scholastic institutions, and professionals. Naturally, there is a commission for graphic design.
It is possible to ask to become a member.

589

Notes
An example of the development of regulation UNI 9874 which defines the constituent elements of a typical glyph of the alphabet: stems and serifs.

Field of application: The regulation is applied to all type obtained using any system of composition, printing and multimedia communication.

Graphic Technology Typical Letter of the Alphabet (UNI 9874) Design Study: UNI "Graphic Design", meetings held during 1989 and 1990. Examination and approval: Letter from the president of the UNI "Graphic Design" committee, delegated by the committee, and dated 10 July 1989. Final examination and approval: UNI Central Technical Committee, meeting held on 29 May 1990. Ratification: UNI President, deliberation issued on 11 July 1991.

36.
The AIAP
The Italian Design Association for Visual Communication

The AIAP Standard Contract

The Standard Contract for Communication Services, Consulting and Design presented in this section, courtesy of the AIAP and its president Mario Piazza, was drawn up by the Association and published in its 2000 Rate Table.
The introduction to the contract states: "The climate of trust and reciprocal participation that often develops between a graphic designer and the client, is one of the conditions that makes it possible to achieve the levels of excellence and lasting results that any collaboration should strive to reach.

On the other hand, we known it is impossible to consolidate any professional relationship without a clear and shared understanding of the responsibilities of the graphic designer and the client, the methods of providing the services and the restrictions placed on them, which naturally include purely economic aspects.
With this in mind, the standard contract is intended as a point of reference for professional commissions, with the spirit of contributing to the improvement and reinforcement of relations between a graphic designer and the client.

[...] "The standard contract must be accurately reviewed, modified and incorporated with any additional or simplified clauses, in order to guarantee its sutaibility and precision in relation to the characteristics of a specific project and the relations the graphic designer and client intend to establish."

Standard Contract for Graphic Design Services

This agreement was stipulated on (...) between the Client (name and surname) of (company name) headquartered in (address) and the Graphic Designer (name and surname) of the (studio or agency) headquartered in (address) for the Project (project name).

1. The Project
Project Description

1.1 Schedule and Deadlines
The Graphic Designer and the Client agree that the Project is to be developed in accordance with the following schedule:

The Graphic Designer reserves the right to modify the schedule and deadlines, in the event the Client does not respect agreed upon deadlines for the provision of material or concession of the necessary authorisations. The Graphic Designer also reserves the right to accept eventual changes to the scope or complexity of the services, under the terms established herein.

2. Services
The Graphic Designer will provide the basic and additional services described herein.

2.1 Basic Services
The basic services the Graphic Designer agrees to provide for the Project consist of consultancy, research, design, quality control, coordination and implementation of the Project.
As part of the basic services, the Graphic Designer will prepare and present to the Client all material necessary to demonstrate or describe his/her intentions, and prepare all that is required to print, manufacture, install or implement the Project in another form.

2.2 Additional Services
In addition to the basic services described above, the design fee may also include additional services, though only to the extent defined herein. Additional services may include: the preparation of texts, photographs or illustrations; special originals such as symbols, logotypes, non-standard typefaces, maps, diagrams and schematics; the preparation of existing material for reproduction, for example: partial or total redesign, illustration touch-ups, diagrams or maps; production services, such as the setting and correction of drafts; the preparation of special material for presentations, including detailed perspective drawings, scale models, prototypes and presentation slides.
When one or more of these services is requested by the Client, though not provided by the Graphic Designer as an additional service, they may be provided by a third party coordinated by the Graphic Designer and billed as reimbursable expenses.
The following additional services will be provided by the Graphic Designer for the Project:

2.3 Realisation of the Project
The services provided by the Graphic Designer under this agreement do not include operations related to the reproduction, printing, fabrication or installation of the Project.
The Client and the Graphic Designer agree that these operations may be provided by third parties and that the services of the Graphic Designer relative to these operations will be limited to technical specifications, coordination and quality control. Unless otherwise agreed in writing herein, the Graphic Designer will have no responsibility toward third party suppliers of these services, and their costs will be paid directly by the Client.
While not responsible for the realisation of the Project, the Graphic Designer may, in a supervisory role, pay for these services; in this case, the Graphic Designer will have the right to request reimbursement for these costs plus a coordination fee of ...%.

3. Professional Fees

3.1 Fees
For the services described herein, the Client agrees to pay the Graphic Designer the following fees, net of all taxes:

3.2 Standard Fees
When specified in this agreement, the Client will pay the Graphic Designer based on the standard rates established by the AIAP in its national rate table. The standard fees for the Graphic Designer will remain unchanged up to a limit of:

3.3. Payment Conditions
The Graphic Designer will issue invoices in accordance with the following schedule and deadlines. Fees will be paid as follows:

The Client will pay the Graphic Designer's invoices within (...) days of receipt.

3.4 Revisions and Additions
The fixed or estimated fees, up to a maximum sum, will be based on the time estimated to complete the services as specified herein and during normal working hours. Eventual other services, or services different from those described herein will be invoiced as additional services, and will not be considered as part of the aforementioned fixed or estimated fees.
Additional services include, as examples only, changes to the scope of the services, variations in the complexity of one or more elements of the Project and any other change made following the approval of a specific phase of the Project, and the documentation or preparation of original material.
The Graphic Designer will inform the Client of any necessary additional services and request approval when they may increase the total cost of the Project with respect to the fixed or estimated fees, as per item 3.1.

Notes

Notes
Students entering the profession can request admission to the AIAP, Italian Association for the Development of Visual Communication (Via Amilcare Ponchielli 3, 20129 Milano, +39 02 29520590, aiap@aiap.it). Each year, the AIAP issues a Guide with a rate table of professional fees based on the AIAP system, reference fees, designer's fees and royalties, the standard contract for graphic design services and consultancy, laws governing relations between graphic designers and clients, copyright and intellectual property, the registration of brands and logotypes in foreign markets, the procedures for registering brands, patents for models and patents for inventions. The AIAP also publishes a Code of Ethics and Professional Conduct; Notizie Aiap, a periodical of information on the Association's activities; Quaderni Aiap, a series of publications dedicated to the history, theory and methodology of graphic design.

To calculate the cost of a project, an issue of great interest to students about to enter the profession, the AIAP provides a system for calculating professional fees. The system is also available on CD-ROM compatible with Microsoft Excel® (Windows® and Mac). The software illustrates the different phases and procedures for the correct use of the calculation. Each screen is accompanied by explanations of the various items shown and provides hints on how to complete the tables. The cells highlighted in grey are those to be modified (not protected); the other protected cells use pre-established formulas to calculate

the resulting values following the insertion of the requested data. The basic element for calculating professional fees is the hourly rate obtained by dividing the annual operating costs and salary costs by a total annual number of hours. The hourly rate is then multiplied by the hours necessary to complete the project to obtain a reasonable estimate of costs. A simple and rapid evaluation of the costs of a project is provided by the AIAP in a series of Reference Rate Tables. The Tables were recently updated for a few categories and to be aligned with the

increasing use of digital instruments that take into account increasingly more specific requirements and a global role in the management of communication. Three main items can be noted:
1. Design.
2. Design with particularly creative aspects.
3. Production (realisation of a project, finish layout, final material on digital support, applications). Fees can be quantified

as "period-specific", "flat rate" or "rate calculated". Period-specific means that fees are based on hours or days; flat rate refers to an omni-comprehensive fee that includes design fees and all expenses; rate calculated means that the fees are based on the adoption of the prices suggested in the AIAP Rate Tables. The cost of developing a project also depends on other factors: the importance of the client, the inherent complexity of the project, the commitment required to complete the project, the frequency and continuity of relations with the client and, last but not least, the designer's fame.

3.5 Urgent Services
The Client will pay a supplementary fee for services rendered outside of normal working hours to respect special deadlines or when the Client does not respect a deadline for the provision of information, material or approvals.
Urgent services will be calculated at …% of the basic fee.
Normal working hours for the Project are:

3.6 Reimbursable Expenses
The Client will reimburse the Graphic Designer for all expenses sustained during the performance of the services, including costs of typesetting, taking or reproducing photographs, filming, computer graphics, hardware or software, proofs, photocopies, presentation material, montages, long-distance fax and telephone costs, postage and local couriers, shipping, travel and lodging. Mileage will be charged at a fixed rate of (…) per km.
Reimbursable expenses will be invoiced at cost plus …%.

3.7 Estimates of Reimbursable Expenses and Implementation Services
Estimates of reimbursable expenses and the cost of implementation services, such as the printing, fabrication or installation of the Project, will be indicated purely for programming purposes. The Graphic Designer will do his/her best to respect the estimates provided, but

will not be responsible for eventual additional costs that, in any case, will be provided to the Client in a timely manner.

3.8 Documentation
The Graphic Designer will record all hours of work and reimbursable expenses and present them to the Client, upon request, for eventual verifications.

3.9 Delay in Payment
The Client will be charged ….% for delayed payments.

4. Client Obligations

4.1 Client Representative
The Client will nominate a single representative with full authority to provide and obtain all information and authorisation necessary or eventually requested by the Graphic Designer.
The Client's representative will manage the coordination of all briefings, changes and decisions relative to any persons or parties involved in the Project, with the exception of the Graphic Designer and his/her subcontractors. The Client's representative is:

If, following approval of the Project or part thereof, the Client or other authorised parties should request changes that require the Graphic Designer to provide additional services, the Client agrees to pay all costs for these additional services.

4.2 Material Provided by the Client
The Client will provide ac-

curate and complete information and material and be responsible for the quality and completeness of all information and material supplied.
The Client guarantees ownership of all material provided, or the right to use the material and permit its use by the Graphic Designer for the Project. The Client agrees to guarantee, defend and hold the Graphic Designer harmless in the event of any claim, legal action, damages or expenses, including legal expenses, deriving from or related to legal action undertaken by third parties for violation or infraction, past or present, of third party rights to material provided by the Client.
All texts provided must be written in a suitable manner for typesetting. Photographs, illustrations or other visual material provided by the Client must be of a professional quality and in a format suitable for reproduction, without the need for further preparations or modifications.
The Client agrees to pay any costs related to material supplied that does not respect these standards.
The Graphic Designer agrees to return all material to the Client within 30 days of payment of all fees.
The Client will provide the following materials and services for the Project:

4.3 Final Approval
The Client will approve all texts, graphics and definitive material prior

to production. The signature of the Client's representative will be considered decisive for the approval of all final material, prior to going to print, fabrication or installation. All material submitted will be considered approved after 30 days in the absence of any specific communication from the Client.

5. Responsibilities of the Graphic Designer

5.1 Protection of Material
The Graphic Designer will take all reasonable precautions to protect original documents and material provided by the Client.

5.2 Instructions to Third Parties
The Client expressly empowers the Graphic Designer with the right to act on its behalf in providing instructions to others or organisations involved in the Project, for example, photographers, illustrators, editors, printers, manufacturers or other suppliers.
The Client may provide these instructions or authorisations solely via the Graphic Designer. The Client will be bound by all instructions issued by the Graphic Designer, under this agreement.

5.3 Changes to the Project
If, following the approval of the Project, or during the course of its realisation, the Client should choose to make changes, the Graphic Designer agrees from this moment,

Notes
Graphic designers will generally provide a colour layout of typical pages; the designer will then assume responsibility for applying this information to the other parts of the project, providing its final version on a digital support. The cost of films (even when supplied by the graphic designer) and equipment is paid by the client. A project will include low resolution scans (72 DPI). The cost of high resolution scans is to be paid by the client and regulated by specific agreements. The term production control refers to the coordination of the entire project and quality control.

In the image, from the left: Alberto Lecaldano, Giovanni Lussu, Michele Spera and Gerardo Spera at the "Ludovico Quaroni" First Faculty of Architecture in Rome.

592 under the condition that any corrective measures are made in collaboration, or agreement, with the Graphic Designer.

5.4 Imitations
The Graphic Designer agrees not to create Projects for other Clients that may be construed as imitations of the Project developed under this agreement.

6. Rights and Ownership
Rights and ownership are pursuant to the Italian "Copyright Law" (in particular Law 633 from 22/04/41 and Decree Law 1485 from 14/12/42), and various international conventions regulating patents, drawings, models, brands, creative works and protection against unfair competition.
6.1 Rights
All services provided by the Graphic Designer under this agreement will be for the exclusive use of the Client, excepting only their use for promotional purposes by the Graphic Designer. Upon payment of all fees and expenses the Client will acquire commercial rights to all approved material created by the Graphic Designer for the Project.
Having acquired these rights, the Client assumes all business risk and civil and penal responsibility for the distribution and use of the Project.

6.2 Ownership
All drawings, originals, specifications and other visual presentation material remain the property of the Graphic De-

signer.
The Client will have the right to the temporary possession of this material solely for its reproduction: all material must be returned, unaltered, to the Graphic Designer. All preliminary projects and visual presentations by the Graphic Designer will remain the property of the Graphic Designer and may not be used by the Client without written authorisation from the Graphic Designer.
The Project remains the property of the Graphic Designer when the Client does not intend to acquire the rights to its use.
The Graphic Designer must conserve all originals, drawings and specifications for which rights to reproduction have been granted for a specific period after the date of stipulation of this agreement. At the end of this period, all of the aforementioned material may be destroyed, except when the Client has requested in writing that it be conserved and agreed upon the costs of storage.
The Client may access to all material, under reasonable conditions, for purposes of revision.
The period specified for the conservation of material by the Graphic Designer is:

6.3 Contracts With Other Parties.
The Graphic Designer, after informing the Client, may enter into contracts with third parties for the provision of services, including the writing of texts, photographs and il-

lustrations, or elaborations of any other nature.
The Client agrees to respect the terms and conditions agreed upon between the Graphic Designer and third parties, including eventual requests to be credited.
For this material, the Graphic Designer will seek to obtain for the Client reproduction rights analogous to those provided by the Graphic Designer to the Client under this agreement.

7. Various

7.1 Code of Ethics
The Graphic Designer will provide the services in accordance with the AIAP's "Code of Ethics and Professional Conduct" and regulations governing "Self-Discipline" in manners of communication.

7.2 Graphic Designer's Credit
The Graphic Designer has the right to be credited on all completed or visual material, such as drawings, models or photographs. The same credit line will be included in all publications of the Project by the Client.
Unless otherwise stipulated herein, the Client may proceed, without specific authorisation, to use the Graphic Designer's name for promotional purposes or other objectives related to this material. The Graphic Designer is to be credited as follows:

7.3 Client's Credit
Unless otherwise stipulated in this agreement, the Graphic Designer may proceed, without specific

authorisation, to use the Client's name for the promotion, publication, etc. of the Project and its material. The Client is to be credited as follows:
7.4 Samples and Photographs
The Client will provide the Graphic Designer with copies of all printed material or realisations. Copies must be of the highest quality. The Graphic Designer may use these copies for publication, exhibition or promotional purposes. The Client will provide the Graphic Designer with (...) copies.

7.5 Confidentiality
The Client will inform the Graphic Designer in writing of the eventual confidentiality of any part of the material or information provided or any part of the Project.

7.6 Taxes and Levies
The Client agrees to pay any taxes for the use, or other costs of transfer, applicable to the services provided under this agreement.

7.7 Assignment
Neither party is permitted to assign or transfer their interests under this agreement without written authorisation from the other party.

7.8 Withdrawal
Either party may withdraw from this agreement by providing written notice to the other party.
In the event of withdrawal by either party for just cause, the Graphic Designer will retain initial payments received and

Notes
When asked to calculate the costs of designing and printing a book, when it is the first in a series, it is necessary to agree separately on the cost of studies for the entire series, based on the complexity and type of the specific project.

In the image:
Giorgio Bucciarelli and
Michele Spera during a
lesson from the
Graduate Course in
Industrial Design.
Below: a visit to
Leonardo da Vinci-
Fiumicino Airport in
Rome.
Giorgio Bucciarelli
introduces students to
the problems of
signage.

the Client will pay the Graphic Designer, based on the standard rate table, for all hours spent on the Project until the moment of withdrawal, pay all sums owing under this agreement.

For services interrupted during the preliminary phase, the Graphic Designer will have the right to 1/3 of the total fees and the reimbursement of all costs. Payments received will be put toward the compensation of all sums owing.

7.9 Applicable Law
This agreement is governed by the laws of the nation in which the Graphic Designer provides the services.

7.10 Court of Law
In the event of disputes between the parties over the interpretation of this agreement, or any issue inherent to the object of the commission, or in the event of legal action over payment for services rendered by the Graphic Designer, the Court of Law will be that having jurisdiction where the Graphic Designer resides.

7.11 Disputes
This agreement represents all understandings between the Client and the Graphic Designer, and modifications are accepted only in writing.

7.12 Declarations
The Client declares to possess all powers and authority required to enter into this agreement and that the agreement will be binding for the Client and applicable based on all terms foreseen.

8. Extensions and Other Conditions

9. Signatures
This agreement was stipulated between the Graphic Designer and the Client on the date specified on page (...).

The Graphic Designer

The Client

593

Notes
In addition to providing indications about the costs of a project, the AIAP Guide also provides useful news about other professional associations. There is also an appendix with a summary of laws on copyright, intellectual property, procedures for registering brands, patents for models and for inventions and the rights deriving from them.

3.
We see graphic design as an activity positioned within the general system of design oriented toward the needs of man. Alongside urban planning, architecture, industrial design and environmental design. Graphic design not only accompanies, but also interacts with them. Graphic design and urban planning in techniques of prefiguration, in systems of visualisation and methods of representation. Graphic design and architecture not only as tools for presenting a project, but also directly present in the text of a completed building.
Graphic design is found in the environment in urban signage for the city, for transportation, etc. [...]

4.
To the same degree that architecture was seen during the 1930s as a guide for the world of design, during the 1960s, with the transition from production to consumption, industrial design assumed the role of a conceptual coordinator, during the 1990s graphic design came to occupy a strategic position within the culture of design.

5.
In the wake of developments in numerous sectors, and despite very different appearances [...] we recognise our profession as a unified activity. [...] In practical terms, as we observe the transition from trades to specialisations, we also note that, when forced to confront a complex project, the problem shifts to the governance of processes and the key role becomes that of directing and coordinating. Furthermore, in theoretical terms, in the many and diverse methodological procedures of individual fields, it is not difficult to find a common ground in the approach to the structuring of problems and their resolution. To both of these aspects, to practice and theory, we link the problem of education, which must be reconsidered and organised based on this renewed identity. [...]

6.
Faced with the pollution produced by a plethora of communication and a complementary indifference toward the culture of images [...] we emphasise the new responsibilities of the graphic designer. We defend quality design in the field of visual communication. We lay claim to our responsibilities toward users. A skill that, what is more, is requested of us by the best clients. [...]

7.
We commit to using all of the initiatives designed to promote the recognition of our professional identity, in relation to the general public and our vast range of clients. With this Charter we commit to working, as in other countries and in harmony with the intentions of international organisations and national associations, toward a constituent of design. We also commit to constructing a programme of events to publicise the various aspects of our profession and the discipline of graphic design.

---

document the eventual participation or contributions of colleagues when speaking with their clients.

3.5 Members may not intentionally work at the same time for a client or employer in direct competition with one another, or without informing them of this situation.

3.6 Members agree not to accept eventual instructions from a client when these instructions comport the violation of rights of intellectual property or copyright, governed by applicable laws, nor are they to knowingly act in such a manner that may arrive at a similar violation.

3.7 When searching for professional opportunities, members must adopt the principles of open and fair competition, avoiding any superficial or reckless denigration of the work and reputation of their colleagues.

3.8 Members are reminded that the activities of graphic design belong to a system of serial production. Taken in its entirety, this activity tends to multiply the products of design services into infinite examples that contribute to saturating the system of communication and leading to phenomena defined by experts as "visual pollution".
The design choices inherent to a designer's activities cannot then be considered "neutral" even with respect to the progressive degradation of the environment and the waste of resources. There-fore, members must encourage the maximum possible conservation of energy, recycling of products and semifinished products and the use of biodegradable materials for packaging and wrapping. Members must consciously consider the consequences of their work and do their utmost to ensure that their work is not cause for direct or indirect damages to the health of people, animals or other living beings, the ecological system or the environment in general.

4. Professional Fees
4.1 Members must not enter into activities of a speculative nature, either individually or in competition with other colleagues, when, for example, compensation is foreseen by the client solely in the case of the acceptance of one of the proposals submitted to the client. This rule applies equally to solutions developed for complex projects, to simple proposals and preliminary suggestions.

4.2 Members agree to work only for a fee, copyright, salary or other form of retribution agreed upon with the client, and foreseen and regulated by a regular commission, contract or estimate, in accordance with the indications provided in the "Guide to Professional Fees for Graphic Design" published by the AIAP. The only exception admitted to this rule is related to works commissioned by charitable institutions or institutions of mutual assistance or not for profit associations.

4.3 Members are invited not to hold back percentages, hidden discounts, retributions of dubious nature for commission rights, gratuities or payments from contractors or suppliers, without informing the client, in those cases when professional services have been rendered. At the same time, members are invited to charge a reasonable fee for management and administration services, informing and receiving approval from the client, as a percentage applied to all articles or services charged as reimbursable expenses and invoiced to the client as part of the accounting system adopted by the professional or service provider.

4.4 Members are asked not to subcontract the principal works of an assignment or design project commissioned by a client or employer, unless the client or employer has been fully informed and agrees to proceed with the subcontract.

4.5 In all professional situations in which they find themselves, members must demonstrate fair judgment and correct behaviour toward colleagues and rectitude toward clients.
Members agree to discourage any actions that would harm the reputation of anyone working in the field of graphic design and visual communication. Members are asked to dissuade anyone with an interest in behaving in ways contrary to the content of the present Code and to communicate the discovery of eventual infractions.

595

The Code of Ethics and the Graphic Design Charter

The AIAP Italian Association for the Development of Visual Communication

The Graphic Design Charter

1.
It is our goal to ensure that the system of communication and information has a generalised presence, a capillary distribution and a powerful appearance. The industry of communication and information must be an attractive part of the contemporary scenario. It is possible to observe unsettling parallel phenomena of visual pollution and a saturation of communication. These are symptoms of a system in which technologies and devices, far from being self-sufficient, require guidance, choices and orientations. Graphic design has become a transversal presence. Where there is communication there is graphic design. Like communication, graphic design is everywhere. It exists where culture meets publishing. Graphic design is found where systems of transportation become information. Graphic design intervenes in the multimedia structure of politics. Graphic design is present not only in the divulgation, but also in the modelling of science. Graphic design is in action whereby industrial products interact with users. Graphic design exists in the world of commerce where consumers encounter products. Graphic design is also in the world of sport, in the image of large events and their communication via mass media.

2.
We confirm a new centrality of graphic design. In the hyperindustrial culture of the masses, quantity, fragmentation, lack of homogeneity, the dislocation of what is required for people's lives, produce a demand for new syntheses and orientations. Without a doubt, entities, institutions, businesses confronting the problem of communication are taking a first step toward the qualification of the goods and services they produce [...]

594

You are invited to read this Code carefully and to adopt its principles in all of your professional activities. You are also invited to distribute it among your colleagues, collaborators, students, clients and the general public.
This Code is intended as an announcement of what the public and clients can expect from graphic design professionals and the rules of behaviour that should govern relations between professionals. It is an affirmation of our staunch resolution to maintain the highest levels of professional responsibility.
This document is inspired by the Model Code of Professional Conduct for Communication Designers published by the International Council of Graphic Design Associations (ICOGRADA).

0. Premise
0.1 The AIAP is an association of professionals in the fields of graphic design and visual communications.
Its principal functions are:
• promoting and safeguarding elevated standards of quality, promoting specific initiatives to protect the development of its technical and disciplinary fields and the correctness of the professional services offered by its members;
• increasing, at all levels of society, the recognition of the importance of graphic design to the development of human activities and the improvement of civil cohabitation;
• using a program of integrated activities (publications, exhibitions, educational activities, lectures, debates, exchanges and projects of interest to the public) to promote excellence in graphic design in all of its applications;
• favouring the expansion of relations among professionals, educators, scholars and critics, clients and the world of industry and research;
• spreading a culture of the daily practice of the principles of professional ethics, with a particular focus on the need to reinforce a clear understanding of criticism, design, ecology and society.

1. Introduction
1.1 This code of ethics and professional conduct is published and made available by the AIAP, such that each of its members adopts its principles in the performance of their services. All members of the Association agree to respect the rules of this Code together with the regulations and Statute of the Association.

1.2. This document was created to provide all members of the Association with a set of rules, accepted as a condition of membership with the AIAP. The document proposes indications and guidelines for ethical conduct during the performance of all professional services.
This document also serves to expand the respect for these rules to the entire professional body of technicians, operators, clients and anyone working in the field of education, tied in any way to the sectors of graphic design and visual communications.

2. Respect for the Regulations
2.1 AIAP members agree to respect the content of this Code, its laws, regulations and the content of other codes of professional conduct for those working in the fields of design and graphic design, including the rules of self-regulation applied in correlated fields. AIAP members also commit to respecting the laws and codes of professional conduct applicable in the countries where they provide services. Should these laws be in contrast with the content of this Code, members agree to bring eventual discrepancies to the attention of the President of the Association to receive clarifications and instructions.

2.2 Members who, in the opinion of the AIAP's Governing Council and Board of Arbitrators, have failed, more or less seriously, to respect the spirit and structure of the present Code may be reprimanded, suspended or expelled from the Association, as deliberated by the Council. These actions may be publicly announced. Similar actions may be implemented only after the member has been offered a suitable opportunity to justify the irregularities observed in his/her professional conduct, as raised by the AIAP's Governing Council or Board of Arbitrators, and only after this Board has referred and recommended actions to the Council that have been accepted by the Council.

3. Professional Responsibilities
3.1 Members of the Association must provide professional services in a competent manner and always with rectitude and honesty; they must act in the interests of their clients, though always within the limits of their professional responsibility, avoiding any actions that may damage their status as professional consultants. Members agree to work toward elevated standards of quality in the content of their graphic work and communications, supporting the objectives of the AIAP. These actions involve both the expansion of new horizons for the profession and the realisation of exemplary products, developed as part of a relationship with clients marked by the highest levels of correctness and collaboration.

3.2 Members must consider as private and confidential any and all material relative to the dealings of their clients or employers. This information may not be provided to third parties without the express consent of clients or employers.

3.3 Members may adopt specific initiatives of self-promotion to publicise the particular nature of their services, though always in an objective and dignified manner. Members are not to knowingly accept a commission being developed or developed in the past by another professional, without first informing the other professional, or ascertaining that any previous commissions have been correctly resolved between that professional and the client. It must be remembered here that the codes of language are used to transcribe within the "space" of a work of graphic design the message that a client intends to communicate to potential interpreters and/or users of this message. The interpreter is the market, by which we intend not only the source of demand and offer, but primarily the scenario of transit of information, desires, expectations and opinions. The fact that any graphic design project is always developed with specific intentions (those of the client, the designer and the interpreter) does not signify that any one of these three "intentional variables" prevails over the others, but instead emphasises the multifaceted aspect of any graphic product designed to communicate a message.
Thus, in considering the entire process of producing a "communicative product" it is not possible to ignore a more general evaluation of the contribution made by all of the professionals who partake in its creation, without forgetting that the figures mentioned above are also accompanied by the figure entrusted with translating a project into an "object" of communication, whose indispensable skills and capacities are often fundamental to the quality of the final result.

3.4 Members may not intentionally copy the work of their colleagues and are invited to clarify and

37.
Interview
to Michele Spera
on Designculture

edited by
Nicola-Matteo Munari
www.designculture.it

Introduction

Michele Spera is an acclaimed Italian graphic designer.
He was born in 1937 in Potenza, Basilicata. After studying architecture in Rome, he started to design the corporate communications of the Italian Republican Party, dedicating himself to this task from 1962 to 1995. For the Party, he developed an identity system that was truly original thanks to both its unifying consistency, rigorous style, and characteristic iconography (e.g. He never used portraits of politicians's faces, as usually happens).
During his career, Spera designed many trademarks including that of Innocenti and Maserati cars, and worked for major corporations including Confindustria and RAI, the Italian national public broadcasting company.
From 1974 to 1995, he also worked as an art director at Treccani, the Institute of the Italian Encyclopaedia.
Member of the scientific committee of the Industrial Design Centre in Montevideo in 1990, Spera taught packaging at the ISIA of Rome (the High School for Artistic Industries) from 1969-72 and coordinated image at the ISIA of Urbino in 1976-78. Since 1997, he teaches industrial design for visual communication at Sapienza Università di Roma.
A true promoter of graphic design culture, Spera published many books about this discipline, his work dealing with socio-political issues and his teachings.
With his geometric style, made of modules and lines with rounded edges — the result of a technical intuition that demonstrates the originality and the strong experimental nature of his work — Spera managed to anticipate the characteristic language of graphics drawn with the computer, which would only be revealed a few decades later.

Enjoy your reading,

Nicola-Matteo Munari _____

Interview published
on 20 February 2018
and recorded
on 22 January 2018

  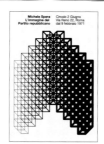 

01
**What is your definition
of design?**
Design improves the human
spirit by educating
it to beauty and by
promoting cultural models
that add quality to life.

02
**Is graphic design part
of your general definition
of design?**
Yes, I think so. But in graphic
design, beauty should be
combined with both
emotional contents and
the rationality that we have
inherited from the great
masters of the past, who
cultivated it with discipline
and passed it to the rest
of humanity on to future
generations.

03
**Do you think that there
is a methodic difference
between architecture, graphic
design and product design?
Or do you think that
the methodology of design
is always the same,
independent from the field of
its application?**
The purpose of design
is always the same, but
methodology should respond
to the specific needs
of each discipline.

04
**What is the purpose
of design?
And what is its utility?**
Design produces enjoyable
shapes, images,
and objects without
imposing them.
It satisfies a wide range of
wishes, without preventing
free thinking.
Design should be conceived
as the possibility
to think and to experiment
a way of life based
on introspection, culture,
ethics, and aesthetics –
a way of life free
from delirious competitiveness
and free from bad taste.

05
**You have studied
architecture. Do you think
that studying architecture
has been important,
or fundamental
for your activity as a graphic
designer?**
When I studied architecture
at the Sapienza Università di
Roma, design wasn't part
of the study program.[1]
I consider myself
a self-taught designer.

1.
The first design
school to be
founded in Italy,
the Scuola
Politecnica di
Design, was
founded in 1954
but it was only in
1993 that industrial
design became a
degree course at
the Faculty of
Architecture of
Milan Politecnico.
And it was only in
2000 that the first
academic Faculty of
Design in Italy was
established with
subsequent courses
in communication
design.
While only in 2008-
10, design degrees
by private schools
such as SPD, NABA,
and IED received a
legal recognition
in Italy.

Somehow, I studied
with those people who were
my great masters: Leonardo
Sinisgalli, Libero De Libero,
Alfonso Gatto, Carlo Levi,
and many others, also
friends of mine.
They taught me beauty.

06
**What are the essential
qualities that a project of
good design should possess?**
Form and content, emotion
and reason, fantasy and
rigour. But quoting Umberto
Eco about social networks,
I think that the computer
ruined collective taste
by giving rights to
non-professionals.

07
**And what are the constant
features of your graphic
design?**
To render every element
of the communication as
a symbol. In fact, it is not
by chance that there are only
a few photographs in my
posters.
I always try to reinterpret
photographs by using a pure
graphic connotation.
(The most essential shapes are
objects, abstractions of
objects, structures of the real.)

08
Can design be art?
Maybe. Indeed, some
of my screen printed drawings
can be found in the
collections of national
museums.[2]

09
**For many years, you have
designed the communication
of the Italian
Republican Party. In this case,
what was your aim as a
designer? What did you want
to produce?**
In 1962, I was appointed
corporate designer of the
Party by Ugo La Malfa, the
Party secretary.
My goal was to produce
a coordinated global image
that could be distinguished
by voters in all of its
applications.
I proposed that all the Party's
communications –
independent of their content
– should be
expressed with an identical
graphic, to let
it become the image
of the Party itself.
Even before reading their
verbal content, you can
recognise that they are
the posters of the Republican
Party.[3]

2.
Actually, we should
distinguish between
drawings with a
more
aesthetic value and
works of graphic
design with a more
practical value.

3.
Also before reading
the name of the
party itself.]

600 This communicational imprint was ideal to the enlightened men who represented the Party, who all embraced my proposals and never criticised my work.

10
Do you think is it possibile, or inevitable to have a personal style in design?
To Fabrizio Cicchitto, then coordinator of the Socialist Party, who asked me to design their corporate identity, I answered that I couldn't design something good for the Socialists as well because their communications would have inevitably been interpreted like those of the Republican Party, that I before designed.

11
Do you think that the popular circulation of many graphic design artefacts implies a civic responsibility by designers?
In an article published by the newspaper *La Repubblica*, Massimo Bucchi wrote that in my graphic work, geometry becomes an image, thus suggesting a vision of the world where aesthetics represents a social commitment.[4]

12
Why did you choose to become a graphic designer? What job did you want to do in the future as a child?
My first encounter with graphic design was at Quinto Orazio Flacco High School in Rome. I redesigned all the ugly covers of my school books. At that time, I wasn't aware of the graphic design profession. It was my dear friend and classmate Nino Calice – the best in the class, and later senator of the Italian Communist Party – who told me that I would have to be a graphic designer.

13
Is there anyone whose work or thoughts you particularly admire? Or someone who influenced your activity as a designer?
Once, I frequented one bookshop only: Vito Riviello's bookshop in Potenza. In the shop, there was a basement where I met with other intellectuals from Potenza and guests like Manlio Rossi Doria, Ignazio Gardella, Pannunzio, Compagna, Ciranna, and many others. Then, I finally went to Rome! I lived

4.
The quote has been changed to make it more omprehensible. The literary translation of the original Italian phrase is the following:
"A graphic work in which geometry becomes image, the detail refers to a general structure that is already a vision of the world, in a sort of final visionary in which aesthetics becomes a vital commitment."

with the poet Vito Riviello in a tiny apartment in Piazza dell'Orologio, right under Borromini's tower. At that time, I had guests such as Libero De Libero, Leonardo Sinisgalli, Alfonso Gatto, Giacomo Porzano, Bruno Caruso, Carmelo Bene, Dacia Maraini, Carlo Levi, Licisco Magagnato, and Domenico De Masi who once wrote: "I came in touch with Michele Spera's graphics when I was working at *Nord e Sud*, the magazine of Francesca Compagna (...) The perfect images of Michele Spera, and those of Olivetti and Italsider, were completely different from the graphics of all the other groups, parties, and entrepreneurs." These were the people who taught me to live.

14
What do you consider your strongest skill as a designer?
Consistency, perseverance and humility.

15
What is the importance of experience? How can it contribute to design?
When experience is united with the ardor of invention we navigate under a clear and boundless sky.
It was the early Sixties, and I spent hours in the print shop preparing pamphlets and propaganda for the [Italian Republican] party.
I spent entire days in the dark room.
Staring into the light of the enlarger that created different signs. It dilated them. It exalted them as part of some mysterious chemical process. I learned so much inside the print shop.
I learned to use lenses better than a computer, which didn't exist at the time.
When overlapping one colour atop another inside the dark room, I noticed this caused a slight blurring of my drawings, which were dilated just enough to ensure they were precisely aligned. This is how I discovered that I could lay out a drawing with a technical pen, create a negative and project it, out of focus, onto a sheet of orthochromatic film.
The more out of focus it was, the fatter the sign became, and the rounder the corners.
This discovery led to the future production of all of my signs, logos and images. They

602 acquired a magic and unusual quality: this was the dilation of a sign, long before the advent of the computer.

16
What is the role of graphic design in contemporary society?
The role is quite unclear. Clients lack culture more than ever, and dialogue becomes difficult.
I pushed my students to cultivate an innovative approach to institutions, the State and ministries, that should all feel the need for clarity in their corporate communications to improve their relationship with citizens.
This is the real challenge for the new generations of graphic designers – to bring clarity to bureaucratic communication.

17
You have dedicated a lot of yourself to teaching. What is the most important thing for a student of graphic design to learn?
My teaching was driven by one single approach: that aesthetic emotion should be produced by logic.

Consequently, I didn't train graphic artists but graphic designers, who have to learn technique, methodology, history and culture – the science of the craft.[5]
Actually, I think it is of paramount importance to learn the basics before you can break the rules. But when that finally happens, it means that the teacher has completed his role.

18
How many books did you write and why did you write them?
There is a moment when you need to stop and to think about your life, your work and your experiences.
Then, you understand that you need to explain — also to yourself — why and how you have created those images. Basically, you need to search for the reasons behind your signs and your geometry, to decode your entire career.
This is why, over the years, I have written several books about myself, graphic design and my lessons at the university.

Thank you very much.
Thanks.

5.
The Italian word for craft, "mestiere", doesn't necessarily imply manual labour.

Michele Spera

Emigranti di poppa,
emigranti di prua

Firenze, Piazza Santa Croce
Dal 13 Ottobre 2016

GIANCARLO ILIPRANDI
BOB NOORDA
MICHELE PROVINCIALI
MICHELE SPERA
PINO TOVAGLIA

GRAFICA TENDENZE
GALLERIA ARTIVISIVE
VIA BRUNETTI 60 / ROMA
9/30 DICEMBRE 1977

Francesco Borromini (1599-1667) was a Baroque architect.

Leonardo Sinisgalli (1908-1981) was a renowned poet, writer and art critic.

Libero De Libero (1903-1981) was a poet and art critic.

Alfonso Gatto (1909-1976) was a poet and writer.

Carlo Levi (1902-1975) was a renowned writer, painter and anti-Fascist politician.

Manlio Rossi Doria (1905-1988) was an economist, politician, and educator.

Ignazio Gardella (1905-199) was an acclaimed architect, engineer and industrial designer.

Mario Pannunzio (1910-1968) was a journalist and politician.

Francesco Compagna (1921-1982) was an Italian Minister, politician and educator.

Giuseppe Ciranna was a publisher. Giacomo Porzano (1922-2007) is a painter.

Bruno Caruso (1927) is a painter, engraver, and writer. Carmelo Bene (1937-2002) was an acclaimed actor, director, playwright and poet.

Dacia Maraini (1936) is a renowned writer, poet, playwright, and screenwriter.

Licisco Magagnato (1921-1987) was an art critic.

Domenico De Masi (1938) is a sociologist.

Regione Siciliana	Franco Balan	**Museo Civico**
Comune di Caltagirone	Antonio Barrese	Caltagirone
Assessorato Beni Culturali	Giulio Cittato	al Carcere Borbonico
Museo Civico	AG Fronzoni	15 Marzo/15 Aprile 1987
	Giancarlo Iliprandi	
Comune di Roma	Italo Lupi	**Artivisive**
Assessorato alla Cultura	Enzo Mari	di Sylvia Franchi
	Armando e Maurizio	Roma, Via Sistina 121
Rassegna di graphic design	Milani	30 ottobre/10 dicembre
La progettazione sistematica	Bob Noorda	1990
nella grafica italiana	Michele Provinciali	
	Michele Spera	
	Heinz Waibl	

38.
The pubblications of Michele Spera

1.

6.

11.

1.
Michele Spera
Grafica e politica
Catalogue from the exhibition at the Sannazzaro Theatre, Naples
With an essay by Roberto Mango,
Circolo Cattaneo, Naples, 1973

2,
Michele Spera
Grafica e comunicazione
Siena Town Hall
With an essay by Elio Mercuri
Preface by Enzo Carli
Town of Siena, 1974

3.
Michele Spera
Segno grafico, l'immagine abbreviata
Perugia, Foligno, Terni, Narni
With an essay by Licisco Magagnato
Town of Narni, 1977

4.
Michele Spera
Bianco, rosso, il verde, alla ricerca degli italiani
With an essay by Licisco Magagnato
Preface by Mauro Dutto
Studio Artivisive, Rome, 1983

5.
Michele Spera
L'immagine del verde
With an essay by Carlo Ludovico Ragghianti
Preface by Giovanni Spadolini
Studio Artivisive Rome, 1984

6.
Michele Spera
Giulio Picciotti
Una politica, un'immagine.
Graphic material by Michele Spera for the Italian Republican Party
With an essay by Giulio Carlo Argan
Preface by Giovanni Spadolini
Editrice La Ragione, Rome, 1987
280 Pages

7.
Michele Spera
194 storie di un segno
With an essay by Domenico De Masi
Edizioni Socrates, Rome, 1996
500 Pages

8.
Michele Spera
La progettazione grafica tra creatività e scienza.
The Lessons of Michele Spera at the First Faculty

of Architecture
Sapienza Università di Roma
With an essay by Tonino Paris,
Gangemi Editore, 2001
Pgg 400

9.
Michele Spera
Abecedario del grafico
The Lessons of Michele Spera at the First Faculty of Architecture
Sapienza Università di Roma
With an essay by Tonino Paris
Seconda edizione
Gangemi Editore, 2005
600 Pages

10.
Michele Spera
Gerardo Spera
La vita è segno
Edited by Cesare de Seta
Catalogue from the exhibition in Ravello
Electa Naples, 2004.
192 Pages

11.
Michele Spera
L'immagine del Partito Repubblicano Una rilettura, 1962/2008
With an essay by Francesco Nucara
e Domenico De Masi
Gangemi Editore, 2008
448 Pages

12.
Michele Spera
I luoghi del perduto
With an essay by Alessandro Cecchi Paone
Edizioni Cisl Fnp, 2012
80 Pages

13.
Michele Spera,
Raffaella Spera
Emigranti di poppa, emigranti di prua
With an essay by Domenico De Masi
Gangemi Editore, 2016
144 Pages

14.
Michele Spera
Graphic Design between creativity and science
Lessons from the Graduate Course in Industrial Design at the "Ludovico Quaroni" Faculty of Architecture, Sapienza Università di Roma
Gangemi Editore, 2018
608 Pages

2.

3.

4.

5.

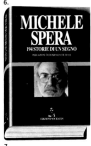

7.

8.

9.

10.

12.

13.

14.

605

39.
An Essential Bibliography

606

Otl Aicher,
Martin Krampen
**Zeichensysteme
der visuellen
kommunikation**
Handbuch fur designer,
architekten, planer,
organisatoren
Verlagsanstalt
Alexander Koch
Stuttgart 1977

Walter Amstutz
**Who's who
in graphic art**
Graphis Press
Dübendorf 1962

Walter Amstutz
**Who's who
in graphic art**
De Clivo Press
Dübendorf 1982

Luigi Astori
**Disegno geometrico
dei caratteri**
Enciclopedia
della stampa
Aggiornamento n. 6
Politecnico di Torino

A. Bandinelli,
G. Lussu, R. Iacobelli
Farsi un libro
Biblioteca del Vascello
Stampa Alternativa
Roma 1990

Jacques Bertin
**La grafica e il
trattamento grafico
dell'informazione**
Eri, 1981

Bruno Blasselle
**Il libro dal papiro
a Gutenberg**
Universale Electa/Gallimard
1997

Giovanni Brunazzi
Immagine coordinata
Gruppo Editoriale Forma
Torino 1984

Ronald G.Carraher,
Jacqueline B.Thurston
**Optical illusions
and the visual arts**
Reinhold Publishing
Corporation
New York
Studio Vista London
1966

Rob Carter,
Ben Day, Philip Meggs
**Typographic design:
form and
communication**
Seconda edizione
Van Nostrand Reinhold
New York 1993

Pierre Duplan,
Roger Jauneau
**Progetto grafico
e impaginazione**
Tecniche nuove,
Milano 1987

James Craig
**Production for the
graphic designer**
Watson-Guptill
Publications
New York 1974

Denis Guedj
L'impero dei numeri
Universale
Electa/ Gallimard
1997

The Diagram Group
Rules of the game
Diagram Visual
Information Ltd
Londra 1974
Arnoldo Mondadori
Editore
Milano 1976

Marina Di Bernardo
Il carattere in tipografia
Omaggio a G.B. Bodoni
Sintesi grafica srl
Roma 1989

Walter Diethelm,
Form+communication
Abc Verlag
Zürich

Edoardo Fazzioli
Caratteri cinesi
*Dal disegno all'idea,
214 caratteri per
comprendere la Cina*
Arnoldo Mondadori
Editore
Milano 1986

Giorgio Fioravanti
Il manuale del grafico
Zanichelli
Bologna 1987

Giorgio Fioravanti
Il dizionario del grafico
Zanichelli
Bologna 1993

Adrian Frutiger
**Segni & simboli.
Disegno, progetto**
Stampa Alternativa &
Graffiti 1996

Adrian Frutiger
**Il mondo dei simboli.
Passeggiate tra i segni**
Stampa Alternativa &
Graffiti 1997

Denis Guedj
L'impero dei numeri
Universale Electa/Gallimard
1997

Amedeo Grütter
**Il disegno applicato alle
arti grafiche**
Romana Libri Alfabeto
Roma 1979

Hampel, Grulich
**Politische plakate
der welt**
Verlag Bruckmann KG
München 1971

Steven Heller
Paul Rand
Phaidon Press Limited
London 1999

Walter Herdeg
Diagrams
The graphic visualization
of abstract data
The Graphis Press
Zürich 1974

Walter Herdeg
Archigraphia
Architectural and
environmental graphics
The Graphis Press
Zürich 1978

Alfred Hohenegger
**Forma e segno
dell'alfabeto
e del simbolo**
Romana Libri Alfabeto
Roma

Alfred Hohenegger
Graphic Design
Romana Libri Alfabeto
Roma 1973

Allen Hurlburt
The grid
Van Nostrand Reinhold
Company
New York 1978

Giancarlo Iliprandi
**Storia della
comunicazione visiva**
Isia Urbino
Urbino 1977

Takenobu Igarashi,
**World trademarks
and logotypes**
Graphic-sha
Tokyo

Gaetano Kanizsa
Grammatica del vedere
Saggi su percezione
e gestalt
Il Mulino Biblioteca

Giovanni Lussu
La lettera uccide
Storie di grafica
Stampa Alternativa
& Graffiti
Roma 1999

Carlo Mezzetti,
Giorgio Bucciarelli,
Luciano Lunazzi
**Il disegno, analisi
di un linguaggio**
La Goliardica Editrice
Roma 1975

Notes
*An important part of
this bibliography
consists of Corporate
Identity Manuals,
considered an objective
and synthesis of
graphic design.
Difficult to obtain,
owing to the very
nature of the material
they contain, tied to
corporate
communication
strategies, the manuals
the students were able
to consult and discuss
in the classroom were
primarily those
designed by the author
of this book. They were
made available to
students and are
mentioned separately
here, together with
those by other authors
that were also studied
and analysed.*

Rudolf Modley
**Handbook
of pictorial symbols**
Dover Publications, Inc.
New York 1976

Per Mollerup
Marks of excellence
The history and
taxonomy of
trademarks
Phaidon Press Limited
London, 1999

Bruno Munari
**Design e comunicazione
visiva**
Laterza, 1993

Bruno Munari
(a cura di)
**La scoperta
del quadrato**
Zanichelli
Bologna 1978

Italo Mussa
Il Gruppo Enne
Bulzoni Editore
Roma 1976

Ernst Neufert
**Enciclopedia pratica
per progettare
e costruire**
Editore Ulrico Hoepli
Milano 1958

F.A. Paine, M. Fusi
**Manuale
dell'imballaggio**
Etas Kompass
Milano 1964

Peter and Susan Pearce
Polyhedra primer
Van Nostrand Reinhold
New York 1978

Giuseppe Pellettieri,
Guido Stefanelli
(a cura di)
Il Carattere
Editrice Raggio
Roma 1947

Tom Porter,
Sue Goodman
**Manuale
di tecniche grafiche**
Clup 1985

Alfonso Rivelli
**Stereometria applicata
allo sviluppo dei solidi
e alla loro costruzione
in carta**
Antichi manuali Hoepli
Milano, 1978

Ben Rosen
Type and Typography
The designer's
type book
Reinhold publishing
corporation
New York 1963

Michele Spera
Bianco, rosso, il verde
Studio Artivisive
Roma 1984

Michele Spera
L'immagine del verde
Studio Artivisive
Roma 1983

Michele Spera
**Materiali grafici per il
partito repubblicano**
Edizioni La Ragione
Roma 1987

Michele Spera
194 storie di un segno
Edizioni Socrates
Roma 1996

Michele Spera
**La progettazione
grafica tra creatività
e scienza**
Gangemi Editore
Roma 2001

Albe Steiner
Comunicazione visiva
Fratelli Alinari
Milano 1977

I.Schwarz-Winklhofer,
H.Biedermann
**Il Libro dei segni
e dei simboli**
Casa Editrice Bietti
Milano 1974

Antonio e Ivana Tubaro
**Lettering,
studi e ricerche**
Istituto Europeo
di Design, Idea Books
Milano 1992

Hermann Zapf
**Dalla calligrafia alla
fotocomposizione**
Edizioni Valdonega
Verona 1991

Heinz Waibl
**Alle radici della
comunicazione visiva
italiana**
Centro di Cultura Grafica
Como 1988

Franz Zeier
Papier
Versuche zwischen
geometrie und spiel
Paul Haupt
Bern und Stuttgart 1974

AA.VV.
**Images of an Era:
the American Poster
1945/75**
Smithsonian Institution
Cambridge

AA. VV.
**Illusione e realtà
Problemi della
percezione visiva**
Le scienze
Edizione italiana di
Scientific american
Le Scienze spa editore
Milano 1978

AA.VV.
**L'arte della carta
a Fabriano**
Cartiere Miliani 1991

AA.VV.
**Le modificazioni
di un mestiere**
(a cura di Cecilia Cecchini,
Massimo D'Alessandro
I Quaderni di Itaca
Gangemi Editore
Roma 1999

AA.VV.
L'Italia grafica
Associazione italiana
industrie grafiche e
trasformatrici
Milano 1967

AA.VV.
**Made in Italy,
Marchi e logotipi
di casa nostra**
Visual
Torino 1982

AA.VV.
**M.C. Escher
29 master prints**
Harry N.Abrams,
New York 1971

AA.VV.
**Rassegna della
istruzione artistica**
Corso superiore di
disegno industriale e
comunicazione visiva
Roma 1972

AA.VV.
Texture
La caratterizzazione
visiva e tattile
delle superfici
a cura di Corrado
Gavinelli
Quaderni di design
Collana diretta
da Bruno Munari

AA.VV.
**Top symbols
& trademarks
of the world**
Franco Maria Ricci
e Corinna Ferrari
Deco Press
Milano

**Corporate Identity
Manuals**

By Walter Landor we
mention the manual
for Alitalia, one of the
first produced for an
Italian company, and
that for Montedison;
by Unimark, we
mention the manuals
designed for Agip,
Dreher, the New York
Subway, Coop;
by Massimo Vignelli
for Lancia
and the Termini
Railway Station in
Rome;
by Mimmo Castellano
the manual for the Ice;
by Borislav Ljubicic
that for the 6th
Mediteranean Games
in 1979.

Manuals by the author
of this book include
those for Innocenti,
Maserati, Rai (Tg2, e
Tribune elettorali),
Endas, the Banca
Mediterranea,
Ithe Banca di
Pescopagano and
Brindisi, Enfap,
Unioncamere,
Consulenti del lavoro,
the Chambers of
Commerce of Potenza,
Pesaro and Urbino,
Confindustria,
Gepi, Verona
Villafranca Airport,
Mediocredito della
Basilicata, the Lanificio
Gatti, Federnotai,
the Associazione
generale delle
cooperative italiane,
Onaosi, Romeo Group,
etc.

GANGEMI EDITORE®
SpA
INTERNATIONAL

FINITO DI STAMPARE NEL MESE DI LUGLIO 2018

www.gangemieditore.it